TREATING COMPLEX CASES

The Wiley Series in

CLINICAL PSYCHOLOGY

J. Mark G. Williams
(Series Editor)

*School of Psychology, University
of Wales, Bangor, UK*

Further titles in preparation. *A list of earlier
titles in the series follows the index.*

TREATING COMPLEX CASES

The Cognitive Behavioural Therapy Approach

Edited by
Nicholas Tarrier
Adrian Wells
and Gillian Haddock
University of Manchester, UK

JOHN WILEY & SONS
Chichester · New York · Weinheim · Brisbane · Singapore · Toronto

Copyright © 1998 by John Wiley & Sons Ltd,
Baffins Lane, Chichester,
West Sussex PO19 1UD, England

National 01243 779777
International (+44) 1243 77977
e-mail (for orders and customer service enquiries):
cs-books@wiley.co.uk
Visit our Home Page on http://www.wiley.co.uk
or http://www.wiley.com

Published in paperback December 1999

Other Wiley Editorial Offices

John Wiley & Sons, Inc., 605 Third Avenue,
New York NY 10158-0012, USA

WILEY-VCH Verlag GmbH, Pappelallee 3, D-69469 Weinheim, Germany

Jacaranda Wiley Ltd, 33 Park Road, Milton,
Queensland 4064, Australia

John Wiley & Sons (Asia) Pte Ltd, 2 Clementi Loop #02-01,
Jin Xing Distripark, Singapore 129809

John Wiley & Sons (Canada) Ltd, 22 Worcester Road,
Rexdale, Ontario M9W 1L1, Canada

British Library Cataloguing in Publication Data

A catalogue record for this book is available from the British Library

ISBN 0-471-97840-X (Hardback)
0-471-97839-6 (Paperback)

Typeset in 10/12pt Palatino by Saxon Graphics Limited, Derby
Printed and bound in Great Britain by Bookcraft (Bath) Ltd, Midsomer Norton, Somerset
This book is printed on acid-free paper responsibly manufactured from sustainable forestry, in which at least two trees are planted for each one used for paper production.

616.8914

CONTENTS

ABOUT THE EDITORS

Nicholas Tarrier is Professor of Clinical Psychology in the Department of Clinical Psychology, School of Psychiatry and Behavioural Sciences, University of Manchester. He graduated with a first class Honours degree from the University of Nottingham, an MSc in Experimental Psychology from the University of Sussex, an MSc in Clinical Psychology from the University of Manchester and a PhD from the Institute of Psychiatry, London University. His main research interest has been in the psychological and psychosocial aspects of psychosis, including the development of non-drug treatments. Other interests include PTSD and the evaluation of cognitive-behavioural treatments in general. He has published seven books and 112 journal publications and he is Past-President of the British Association for Behavioural and Cognitive Psychotherapy.

Adrian Wells is Senior Lecturer in Clinical Psychology in the Department of Clinical Psychology, School of Psychiatry and Behavioural Sciences, University of Manchester. He graduated from Aston University with an Honours degree in Behavioural Science, a PhD, and an MSc in Clinical Psychology from Leeds University. He completed a post-doctoral Diploma in Cognitive Therapy at the Center for Cognitive Therapy, University of Pennsylvania, and has worked with Aaron T. Beck and the Oxford Cognitive Therapy group in the development and evaluation of Cognitive Therapy of Anxiety Disorders. His main research interests are Cognitive Theory and Therapy of Anxiety Disorders, including Social Phobia, and Generalised Anxiety Disorder. Other interests include attentional processes in emotional disorder, intrusive thoughts and metacognition. He is an award-winning author, having published two books, and publishes extensively in peer review journals.

Gillian Haddock is Senior Lecturer in Clinical Psychology in the Department of Clinical Psychology, School of Psychiatry and Behavioural Sciences, University of Manchester. She also holds an Honorary Consultant Clinical Psychologist appointment in the mental health unit of Tameside and Glossop Community and Priority Services NHS trust. She graduated with a BSc (hons) from the University of York, and a Masters and PhD in Clinical Psychology from the University of Liverpool. Her main research interests have been in assessment, treatment and psychopathology of psychosis, with particular emphasis on the application of cognitive-behavioural treatments to psychosis. She has published two books and a number of journal articles in this area. She holds the British Psychological Society May Davidson award for contribution to clinical psychology in the first 10 years since qualifying and is currently Chair-Elect of the British Association for Behavioural and Cognitive Psychotherapies.

LIST OF CONTRIBUTORS

W.T. Behary	*Cognitive Therapy Centers of New Jersey, USA*
R. Bouma	*Faculty of Health & Beh. Sc., School of Applied Psychology, Griffith University, Natham Campus, Queensland 4111, Australia*
R. Calam	*Dept. of Clinical Psychology, University of Manchester, Withington Hospital, W. Didsbury, Manchester M20 8LR, UK*
K.M. Chard	*Dept. of Education/Counselling, University of Kentucky, USA*
M.J.V. Fennell	*Dept. of Psychiatry, University of Oxford, Warneford Hospital, Oxford OX3 7SX, UK*
E. Forrester	*University of Oxford, Department of Psychiatry, Warneford Hospital, Oxford OX3 7SX, UK*
A. Freeman	*Philadelphia College of Osteopathic Med., Dept. of Psychiatry, Univ. of Pennsylvania Med. Ctr, 4190 City Ave., Philadelphia, PA 19131, USA*
P. Gilbert	*Dept. of Clinical Psychology, Kingsway Hospital, Derby DE22 3LZ, UK*
A. Hackmann	*University of Oxford, Department of Psychiatry, Warneford Hospital, Oxford OX3 7JX, UK*
G. Haddock	*Dept. of Clinical Psychology, University of Manchester, Sch. of Psychiatry & Beh. Sc., Withington Hospital, W. Didsbury, Manchester M20 8LR, UK*
W.K. Halford	*Faculty of Health & Beh. Sc., School of Applied Psychology, Griffith University, Natham Campus, Queensland 4111, Australia*

K. Howells — *Dept. of Psychology, University of South Australia, GPO Box 2471, Adelaide, Southern Australia 5001*

J.T. Jackson — *Philadelphia College of Osteopathic Med., Dept. of Psychiatry, Univ. of Pennsylvania Med. Ctr, 4190 City Ave., Philadelphia, PA 19131, USA*

T.M. Keane — *NCPTSD, Department of Veterans Affairs, 150 South Huntington Avenue, Boston, MA 02130, USA*

M.O. Kimble — *NCPTSD, Department of Veterans Affairs, 150 South Huntington Avenue, Boston, MA 02130, USA*

D. Kingdon — *Mental Health Group, Southampton University, Royal South Hants, Brinton's Terrace, Southampton SO14 0YG, UK*

A.P. Morrison — *Clinical Psychologist, Dept. of Psychological Services Mental Hlth Ser. of Salford, Prestwich Hospital, Bury New Road, Manchester M25 3BL, UK*

N. Morrison — *University of Oxford, Department of Clinical Psychology, Warneford Hospital, Oxford OX3 7SX, UK*

P.A. Resick — *Center for Trauma Recovery, Univ. of Missouri–St. Louis, 8001 Natural Bridge Road, St. Louis, Missouri 63121-4499, USA*

H.C. Richards — *University of Oxford, Department of Psychiatry, Warneford Hospital, Oxford OX3 7SX, UK*

D.S. Riggs — *NCPTSD, Department of Veterans Affairs, 150 South Huntington Avenue, Boston, MA 02130, USA*

P.M. Salkovskis — *University of Oxford, Department of Psychiatry, Warneford Hospital, Oxford OX3 7SX, UK*

J. Scott — *Department of Psychological Medicine, University of Glasgow, Gartnavel Royal Hospital, Glasgow, G12 0XH, UK*

G.L. Sidley — *Psychology Services Mental Health Services of Salford, NHS Trust, Bury New Road, Prestwich, Manchester M25 3BL, UK*

N. Tarrier — *Dept. of Clinical Psychology, University of Manchester, Sch. of Psychiatry & Beh. Sc., Withington Hospital, W. Didsbury, Manchester M20 8LR, UK*

T.L. Weaver   *Center for Trauma Recovery, Univ. of Missouri–*
                       St. Louis, 8001 Natural Bridge Road, St. Louis,
                       Missouri 63121-4499, USA

A. Wells   *Dept. of Clinical Psychology, Sch. of Psychiatry &*
                       Beh. Sc., University of Manchester, Rawnsley
                       Building, Manchester Royal Infirmary, Manchester
                       M13 9WL, UK

J. Young   *Cognitive Therapy Centers, 40 Scribner Hill Road,*
                       Wilton CT 06897 USA

SERIES PREFACE

The Wiley Series in Clinical Psychology aims to provide a comprehensive set of texts covering the application of psychological science to the problems of mental health and disability. Of all the developments in the field over the last two decades, the growth of cognitive behaviour therapy (CBT) in the treatment of a wide range of psychological problems must be ranked the most prominent.

But for all its popularity, a concern has grown that the rush to demonstrate its efficacy has failed to take account of the exclusion criteria employed in the outcome trials, or the long-term maintenance of the gains made during the acute phase of the treatment. Not that this problem is unique to CBT; most outcome trials exclude just those participants (for example, chronically suicidal patients) who are likely to be the most difficult to help in day-to-day clinical practice. So we know that CBT ought to be effective, but we feel that there may exist an uneasy gap between the research literature and the sort of cases we see in the clinic.

It is this issue that is taken head-on in this book. Specialists who have worked with the most difficult and complex cases tell us how they use their skills to tackle the most intractable problems. The book examines these issues in social phobia, obsessional problems, chronic depression, PTSD, eating disorders, parasuicide, violence, victims of rape and sexual assault, and personality disorders. It tackles the issues of shame and guilt, and low self-esteem. The editors' own expertise and interest in the psychological treatment of psychosis is shown in three chapters on this topic.

This text is comprehensive, written by clinicians of international standing who have both rich clinical experience and an extensive academic knowledge. It will be an invaluable guide for both students and practitioners across the full range of mental health disciplines.

PREFACE

INTRODUCTION TO COMPLEX CASES

The practice and application of cognitive therapy has expanded enormously in the past ten years from the early days of behaviour therapy successfully being used to treat situational anxiety, and the subsequent development of cognitive therapy in the treatment of depression. An increasing number of disorders and clinical problems have gone under the cognitive behavioural microscope in the challenge to find more effective and systematic treatments. Cognitive behaviour therapy has advanced both in its explanatory power and in its therapeutic practice, as can be witnessed by this volume. It is probably true to say that the expansion has been most usefully influenced by a developing interface between clinical research and clinical practice. Research, including clinical trials, has traditionally addressed 'pure' disorders but the challenges of clinical practice are often the more *complex cases* which do not fit comfortably into simple case conceptualisations or diagnostic categories.

Patients with extensive co-morbidity, chronic unremitting conditions, enduring vulnerabilities, psychotic conditions, persistent difficulties with social relationships, and de-stabilising social problems are increasingly becoming the reality of the cognitive behaviour therapist's caseload. Patients with complex problems are not necessarily those who enter into research trials, so that the validation of cognitive behavioural treatments has been carried out on a select and carefully recruited population. Nevertheless, just as case formulation based on an improved understanding of specific disorders has enhanced treatment, we believe that case formulation is central to the clinical challenge of successfully treating complex cases. The case formulation approach addresses the idiosyncratic and complicated interplay between multifaceted causative and maintaining factors. This is accomplished in a hypothesis-driven empirical manner that is particularly suited to the systematic treatment of complex cases.

In this volume we have asked some of the most experienced cognitive behaviour therapists who are experts in their field to address clinical problems and disorders that are likely to be encountered by the more experienced clinician who is treating patients with complex problems in their clinic. Thus, we have attempted to produce a book that will be helpful to clinicians as a clinical guidebook based on empirical foundations. The chapters in this book cover a diverse range of problems and disorders; we have not restricted the content to disorder categories but have included chapters on problems such as anger, low self-esteem, abuse, and shame. These constructs cut across disorders and may be particularly useful in formulating complex cases. The disorder-based chapters focus on the areas of psychosis, personality disorders, and the more complex emotional disorders such as chronic depression, post-traumatic stress, obsessive-compulsive disorder, and social phobia. Many of the chapters highlight difficulties and complexities that exist for the clinician in conceptualising these cases and in implementing treatment. However, they go beyond raising awareness of issues and provide, where appropriate, specific guidance on dealing with problems of engagement, socialisation, and the implementation of treatment in complex cases.

Nicholas Tarrier
Adrian Wells
Gillian Haddock

Chapter 1

COGNITIVE THERAPY OF SOCIAL PHOBIA

*Adrian Wells**

Interpersonal difficulties are symptomatic of a wide range of psychological disorders. For example, depressed or socially anxious individuals avoid social interactions or may act withdrawn. Personality disorders are particularly likely to be associated with interpersonal problems and anxieties. Someone who is paranoid is prone to mistrust others and show suspiciousness in a way that can interfere with relationships. A person with borderline or avoidant personality is likely to act in a way to avoid abandonment or criticism. Such avoidance may be associated with a tendency to form intense and unstable relationships, or lead to postponement of forming relationships in order to avoid rejection. In all of these cases a person's behaviour perpetuates interpersonal difficulties and potentially contributes to the main fears of rejection, failure, criticism, and abandonment. Feedback loops or vicious cycles of this type are central to conceptualising the maintenance of negative appraisals and beliefs in psychological disorder.

This chapter describes the feedback cycles that maintain interpersonal anxiety in the form of social phobia. Social phobia, which in its most severe form shares features with avoidant personality disorder (Holt, Heimberg & Hope, 1992), is a complex problem to conceptualise and treat. Its complexity arises from the fact that the problem is maintained by multiple feedback loops, and some of the central cognitive factors involved in maintenance are often obscured at the surface level by negative automatic thoughts concerning fear of attracting attention and being negatively evaluated. A complexity in treatment emerges from the fact that the therapeutic situation is itself a social encounter that is likely to be contaminated by

* Department of Clinical Psychology, University of Manchester, UK

Treating Complex Cases: The Cognitive Behavioural Therapy Approach.
Edited by Nicholas Tarrier, Adrian Wells and Gillian Haddock.
© 1998 John Wiley & Sons Ltd.

the patient's social phobia. The person with social phobia may thus censor information, engage in subtle avoidance in the therapy situation, or act in a manner that is distracting for the therapist. These variables combine to render assessment, engagement, and implementation of strategies in treatment more demanding. This situation has been compounded because, until recently, a comprehensive and specific cognitive model of the disorder was not available. The cognitive therapist has depended on more generic theoretical approaches such as the general schema theory of anxiety of Beck, Emery and Greenberg (1985). However, conceptualisation of a disorder and treatment effectiveness is typically improved when more specific models of disorder maintenance are developed and used. This chapter focuses on a model of social phobia advanced by Clark and Wells (1995), which was derived from clinical analysis informed by a cognitive-attentional model of emotional disorder (Wells & Matthews, 1994). This model offers specific guidance in the development of individual case formulations and in the design and implementation of treatment strategies. In this chapter I present the model and describe the treatment derived from it. However, before this the next two sections offer an overview of the nature of social phobia, and a synopsis of findings from cognitive behavioural treatment evaluations.

CHARACTERISTICS OF SOCIAL PHOBIA

The primary feature of social phobia is 'a marked and persistent fear of one or more social or performance situations in which the person is exposed to unfamiliar people or to possible scrutiny by others. The individual fears that he or she will act in a way (or show anxiety symptoms) that will be humiliating or embarrassing' (DSM-IV: APA, 1994, p. 416). A 'generalised' subtype of social phobia is specified if the fears include most social situations; under such circumstances the additional diagnosis of avoidant personality disorder should also be explored. Anxiety in social situations in social phobics may take the form of situational panic attacks, and the feared social situation is avoided or endured with intense anxiety or distress. 'Performance anxiety, stage-fright, and shyness in social situations are common and should not be diagnosed as social phobia unless the anxiety or avoidance leads to clinically significant impairment or marked distress' (DSM-IV, p.416).

Avoidant Personality Disorder

Social phobia and avoidant personality disorder (APD) show marked overlapping features to the extent that these constructs may be alternate operationalisations of the same disorder. The overlap is particularly evident with generalised subtypes of social phobia. Holt, Heimberg and Hope (1992) have suggested that avoidant personality disorder is severe generalised social phobia. Individuals with avoidant personality disorder are preoccupied with being criticised or rejected in social situations. Situations such as a promotion at work are avoided because the new responsibilities may result in criticism from co-workers. These individuals avoid making friends unless they are certain of being liked and accepted without criticism. However, a feature of the disorder that is somewhat different from social phobia is the tendency to exaggerate the potential dangers of ordinary situations. The person with APD tends to have low self-esteem and hypersensitivity to criticism. The disorder is marked by a chronicity of symptoms that often begin in early childhood as shyness, isolation, and fear of strangers and new situations. Whilst shyness in childhood is common, individuals who go on to develop avoidant personality disorder may become increasingly shy and avoidant during adolescence and early adulthood.

To the extent that generalised social phobia and avoidant personality disorder are describing the same or overlapping problems, the cognitive model of social phobia presented in this chapter could be used to guide the treatment of APD. However, the chronicity and rigidity of the problem modifies the goals of treatment that are realistically attainable over a brief intervention period. In particular, extended time is often required in more severe cases of APD to develop an effective collaborative working relationship. Fear of criticism and fear of implementing new behaviours are more likely to impede therapeutic progress. The therapist may have to pay particular attention to keeping the therapeutic relationship collaborative. A lifetime of avoidance as a predominant strategy for dealing with fear of criticism and of new activities influences the rate of progress in treatment. Individuals with APD are more likely to show reluctance to attempt behavioural experiments, and a graduated slower approach to exposure experiments is often essential.

COGNITIVE BEHAVIOURAL TREATMENT

Evaluations of cognitive behavioural treatments for social phobia have used interventions which have varied in their emphasis. However, all of the approaches help patients to modify negative beliefs about their performance in social situations, and fears of negative evaluation. The more cognitive-oriented approaches have used variations of Rational-Emotive therapy (e.g. Emmelkamp et al., 1985), cognitive therapy based on Beck's general schema theory (e.g. DiGiuseppe et al., 1990), and anxiety-management techniques (Butler et al., 1984). Taken together, these studies provide support for the effectiveness of cognitive behavioural interventions. However, these treatments have not been based on a specific model of social phobia. Heimberg et al. (1990) have developed a group cognitive therapy of social phobia based on a more specific analysis and disputation of problematic cognitions. In a comparison of this approach with an equally credible educational-supportive psychotherapy, 75% of cognitive therapy patients were improved compared to 40% of supportive psychotherapy patients. Lucas and Telch (1993) replicated this comparison and added an individual treatment based on the group approach. The individual and group treatments did not differ in outcome, but both cognitive treatments were superior to educational-supportive treatment.

Overall, treatment evaluations show that exposure and cognitive behavioural treatments are effective. There is mixed evidence that adding a cognitive therapy component to exposure improves outcome. Both cognitive therapy alone and exposure produce similar results (Heimberg & Juster, 1995: for review). However, the cognitive component of treatments has normally consisted of a heterogeneous range of strategies both within and across studies, and it is possible that a specific theory-based and more systematic treatment may produce better results. In particular, the use of a specific theory-based treatment may enhance cognitive change. The degree of improvement in cognitive measures such as irrational beliefs (Emmelkamp et al., 1985), and Fear of Negative Evaluation (e.g. Mattick, Peters & Clark, 1989) is small in studies of exposure, and in studies of cognitive restructuring.

A COGNITIVE MODEL OF SOCIAL PHOBIA

In this section the cognitive model of social phobia advanced by Clark and Wells (1995) and subsequently elaborated by Wells and Clark (1997) is presented. In this model social phobics are thought to engage in-situation processing and behaviour that maintains a negative impression of the social self and anxiety in feared social situations. The model draws on theoretical work by Beck, Emery and Greenberg (1985), Heimberg and Barlow (1988) and Hartman (1983), and a significant contribution is drawn from the self-regulatory executive function (S-REF) model of emotional disorder advanced by Wells and Matthews (1994, 1996).

The social phobia model identifies three phases of processing involved in the maintenance of social phobia: anticipatory processing, in-situation processing, and post-event processing also known as the 'post-mortem'. All three phases contribute to the distress experienced by socially anxious individuals before, during or after exposure to feared social situations.

In-situation Processing

The central aspect of the cognitive model deals with the processing that occurs during exposure to feared social situations. The main features of this model are presented in Figure 1.1. On encountering feared social situations

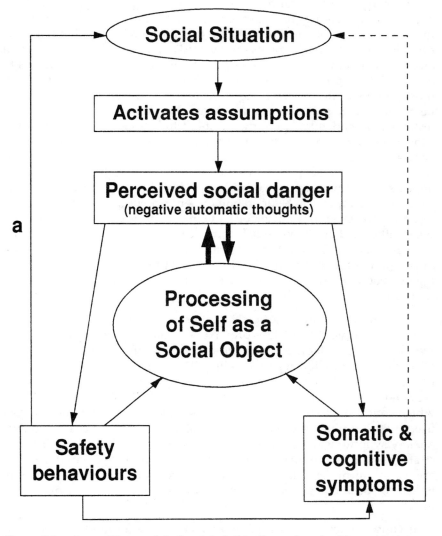

Figure 1.1. A cognitive model of social phobia. Reproduced with permission from Wells, A. (1997). *Cognitive Therapy of Anxiety Disorders: A Practice Manual and Conceptual Guide* (p. 169). Chichester, UK: Wiley.

the social phobic becomes concerned about his/her ability to present a favourable impression of the self. This is manifested as negative automatic thoughts focusing on possible failure to present a desired impression. The individual with social phobia fears 'failed performance'. In particular, the social phobic is concerned about showing signs of anxiety (e.g. blushing, shaking, babbling, sweating, etc.), and is worried about acting in a way that is embarrassing or will cause others to form a negative impression of the self (e.g being boring, or appearing 'weird'). These negative automatic thoughts are accompanied by a shift in the direction of attention. The person with social phobia becomes self-focused and begins to process internal anxious symptoms, and an impression of how s/he thinks s/he appears to others. This impression often occurs in the form of an image from an observer perspective in which the individual sees the self as if from another person's vantage point. In this image anxiety symptoms and other manifestations of inadequate performance tend to be exaggerated and highly conspicuous. In some instances this processing of the self as a social object occurs as a feeling rather than an image. However, a key feature of this felt-sense is that it implicitly conveys the information that the observable self appears conspicuous in a negative and undesirable way. For example, the social phobic appears to be operating under an assumption: 'If my anxiety symptoms feel bad they must look bad'. In summary, the impression of the self is influenced predominantly by interoceptive information, in which the felt sense of anxious symptoms contributes to a construction of a distorted impression of the observable self. Examples of the content of self-processing in anxiety-provoking social situations in social phobia are presented in Table 1.1.

In an attempt to reduce the social dangers of humiliation, loss of status, or loss of self-worth, anxiety-provoking social situations are avoided. Avoidance is problematic since the individual fails to encounter situations that can modify negative beliefs. If avoidance is not possible the social phobic will engage in safety behaviours (Salkovskis, 1991) which are intended to avert feared social catastrophes (Wells et al., 1995), but which contribute to the maintenance of social anxiety. Safety behaviours used by social phobics typically consist of attempts to conceal or control anxiety symptoms (shaking, sweating, babbling, blushing), or consist of strategies for 'stage managing' one's social performance (trying to appear interesting, intelligent, or relaxed). Examples of safety behaviours linked to specific negative thoughts of five social phobics are presented in Table 1.1.

Four consequences of using safety behaviours contribute to the maintenance of social phobia. First, safety behaviours maintain self-focused processing as the individual constantly monitors performance and attempts

Table 1.1 Examples of negative automatic thoughts, self-processing, and safety behaviours across five social phobics

Negative automatic thoughts	Self-processing	Safety behaviours
1. I don't know what to say. People will think I'm stupid.	Self-conscious: Image of self as a plain, unintelligent, 'bimbo'.	Avoid eye contact, don't draw attention to self, say little, let partner do the talking, plan what to say, pretend to be interested in something.
2. I'll shake and lose control. Everyone will notice me.	Self-conscious: 'The shaking feels so bad so it must look bad'. Image of self losing control.	Avoid cups and saucers, grip objects tightly, move slowly, tense arm muscles, take deep breaths, try to relax, avoid looking at people, hold cups with both hands, rest elbows on table.
3. What if I get anxious? People will notice and not take me seriously.	Self-conscious: Image of self as a bright red jibbering wreck with hands and arms 'jingling' about.	Grip hands together, stiffen arms and legs, look away, ask questions, cover face with hair, wear extra make-up.
4. What if I sweat? They will think I'm abnormal.	Self-conscious: Image of beads of sweat on forehead and top lip and hair looking soaked.	Wear T-shirt under shirt, keep jacket on, use extra deodorant, wear light colours, hold handkerchief, keep arms next to body, wear cool clothes.
5. I'll babble and get my words wrong. People will think I'm stupid.	Self-conscious: Is aware of own voice and hears self as timid, weak and pathetic.	Monitor speech, try to pronounce words properly, rehearse sentences mentally before saying them, speak quickly, ask questions, say little about self.

social self-regulation. The problem with continued self-processing is that it interferes with the processing of external social cues. Such cues are more likely to provide data concerning other people's reaction to the self, and thus contribute to the correction of maladaptive self-appraisals and beliefs. Second, some safety behaviours exacerbate unwanted symptoms. This is problematic because some symptoms are interpreted as further evidence of 'failed performance' and personal inadequacy. Intensified interoception emerging from escalating symptoms contributes to dysfunctional processing of the self as a social object. For example, the social phobic who attempts to avoid babbling and getting words wrong may mentally rehearse and censor sentences before saying them, may attempt to pronounce words carefully, and mentally check what they have just said in order to confirm that it was acceptable. The mental load imparted by these strategies is likely to interfere with verbal fluency and the individual's ability to perform spontaneously in the social situation. The person who is worried about losing control of hand tremor and who attempts to control this by gripping objects tightly, using both hands, and moving slowly is likely to amplify the subjective sense of loss of control and impair fluent movement. Third, the non-occurrence of feared social catastrophes can be attributed to use of safety behaviours thus preserving maladaptive beliefs concerning the likelihood and consequences of 'failed performance'. Fourth, a problem with safety behaviours as outlined in the present model relates to the effect that these responses have on the social situation itself. Clark and Wells (1995) propose that some safety behaviours 'contaminate' the social situation. More specifically, social phobics appear less friendly and less interested because of the use of certain safety behaviours such as reduced eye contact, lack of self-disclosure, and trying to be relaxed. This influence is depicted by the feedback arrow marked 'a' in Figure 1.1.

Anticipatory processing and the post-mortem

Before entering anxiety-provoking social situations, social phobics are prone to ruminate about what will happen in the situation and how they will cope. This can take the form of mental planning of behaviours in an attempt to anticipate difficulties and generate ways of dealing with problems. A problem with anticipatory processing is that it is invariably negative, and it primes the individual for dysfunctional self-focused processing prior to entering the social situation. Thus, unhelpful processing configurations (cf. Wells & Matthews, 1994; 1996) are in a state of chronic readiness prior to entering the feared situation.

After leaving the social situation, biased processing of the social self does not end. Individuals with social phobia tend to recall and dwell on aspects of the situation and analyse their own behaviour. Because attention was predominantly self-focused during the situation the contents of this 'post-mortem' are skewed in the direction of negative self-relevant information such as feelings, symptoms, and an impression of how one must have appeared to others. Little information is recalled concerning the actual reaction of other people to the self. Thus, the post-mortem acts in strengthening a negative impression of the social self, and does not provide information capable of disconfirming distorted negative self-appraisals and beliefs. Even when a social situation has gone well it is likely to be discounted and attributed to luck or to the attributes of other people rather than attributed to the self. The social phobic's preoccupation is with how they felt in the situation, which influences appraisals of how other people may have reacted to them.

BELIEFS, ASSUMPTIONS AND RULES

Three types of knowledge or beliefs are thought to predispose individuals to the cyclic self-focused processing that maintains and intensifies social anxiety in the model: unconditional beliefs about the social self; conditional assumptions, expressed as 'if-then' propositions; and rigid rules for social self-regulation. Examples of these types of schematic knowledge are presented in Table 1.2.

Table 1.2 Examples of schema content in social phobia

Unconditional beliefs
    I'm weird
    I'm unlikeable
    I'm a failure/inadequate
    I'm stupid
    It's abnormal to be anxious

Conditional assumptions
    If people see I'm anxious they will think I'm weak and pathetic
    If I appear nervous I am less competent
    If I get my words wrong people will think I'm stupid
    If people see I'm anxious I'll be a soft target
    If I attract attention people will judge me negatively

Rigid rules
    I should always be able to cope
    I must always be articulate
    I must always be sociable
    I need to be liked by everyone
    I must create a good impression

Negative self-beliefs and assumptions may develop from repeated negative socialisation experiences and can be shaped throughout life. The nature of these beliefs may partially explain different patterns in the onset and course of social phobia. Shyness early in life may be associated with negative beliefs about the self and the sensitivity of innate interpersonal-anxiety programmes. However, there may be a range of pathways in the development of social phobia. Another possibility is that individuals acquire inflexible and unrealistic rules concerning social self-regulation. The individual may function without undue anxiety for much of his/her life until these rules become violated and the resulting self-discrepancy activates the cycle of dysfunctional social self-evaluation. In such cases social phobia may be more closely associated with critical incidents that focus the individual's appraisals on the failure to meet important goals for maintenance of a positive social self-image. In some instances rules represent commands that are intended to compensate for negative aspects of self. For example, a recent patient held the belief, 'I'm a soft target', and had the compensatory rules: 'I must never show signs of anxiety; I should always keep my distance'.

Aside from conceptualising beliefs in social phobia in terms of their content, it may prove clinically useful to consider the stability of negative self-beliefs. Negative self-beliefs in social phobia are not necessarily in a chronic state of activation, and the triggering conditions for activation are often highly specific. Treatment may focus on ways of stabilising a favourable self-image rather than only challenging the content of negative self-beliefs. In summary it is clear that studies are required to explore the nature of beliefs in social phobia. Such research efforts should focus on the dynamic aspects of belief (Wells & Matthews, 1994, 1996) rather than viewing beliefs in purely static content terms.

EMPIRICAL SUPPORT FOR THE MODEL

Self-attention and the Distorted Impression of the Self as a Social Object

A central feature of the model is the idea that social phobics use interoceptive information to construct an impression of themselves, which they assume reflects what other people observe. A range of studies have reported findings that are consistent with this assertion. The idea that self-focus is associated with social anxiety has a long tradition in the self-consciousness literature (Buss, 1980; Fenigstein, Scheier & Buss, 1975). Fenigstein, Scheier and Buss (1975) report significant positive correlations between public self-consciousness (the tendency to focus attention on observable aspects of self) and social anxiety. Further evidence of self-focused processing in social situations is evident in a study by Stopa and Clark (1993). They found that social phobics reported more negative self-evaluative thoughts (e.g. 'I'm boring') than did controls during conversation with a stooge but did not report more negative thoughts about evaluation by the stooge (e.g. 'She thinks I'm boring'). Johansson and Öst (1982) showed that social phobics were more accurate than control subjects in estimating their heart rate changes in social situations, suggesting an enhanced awareness of interoceptive information. The effect of emotional/interoceptive information on social self-processing is evident in a study by Arntz, Rauner and van den Hout (1994), in which social phobics and control subjects were presented with scripts describing hypothetical social situations in which they were participants. The scripts varied along two dimensions: the presence of objective danger or safety information and whether the subject felt anxious or non-anxious. After imagining being in the scripted situation, subjects were asked to rate how dangerous they thought the situation was. The estimates of control subjects were only influenced by the presence of objective danger information, whilst social phobics' estimates were also influenced by anxiety response information.

In a recent direct test of the hypothesis that socially anxious subjects use interoceptive information to construct a distorted impression of the self in social situations, Papageorgiou and Wells (1997) used a heart-rate feedback paradigm. Two groups of high socially anxious subjects (high Fear of Negative Evaluation, FNE: Watson & Friend, 1969) and two groups of low FNE subjects were given either feedback of an increase in heart rate or no feedback prior to a social interaction task consisting of holding a conversation with a stooge. Consistent with the social phobia model, FNE interacted with feedback. The high FNE subjects who received feedback reported significantly greater anxiety, more negative self-ratings of performance, and a greater observer perspective in imaginal recall of the situation compared with high FNE subjects not receiving feedback. Subjects low in FNE were not affected by the feedback. Thus, the effects of feedback appear to be specific to those subjects high in FNE, a result consistent with predictions based on the model.

There are several sources of data supporting the idea that social phobics construct a distorted impression of themselves as a social object. Direct support for this assertion was found in a study by Wells, Clark and Ahmad (1998). In this study social phobic and non-anxious control subjects were asked to recall and image two recent situations in which they felt anxious: a social situation, and a non-social situation. With the image in mind subjects were asked if their predominant impression was one of being outside of the self, seeing the self from another person's vantage point (the observer perspective), or one of being inside one's body looking out at the situation (the field perspective). Social phobics reported an observer perspective for the social image but not for the non-social image, whilst non-anxious subjects reported a field perspective for both images. In a different study the observer perspective was demonstrated following exposure of social phobics to a feared social situation. Moreover, an experimental manipulation consisting of exposure to the feared social situation plus external-focused attention produced significantly greater shifts from an observer to a field perspective in imaginal recall than exposure alone (Wells & Papageorgiou, 1998).

Further evidence of distorted self-processing may be found in the studies of McEwan and Devins (1983), and Bruch et al. (1989). These investigators compared self-ratings with observer ratings of visible signs of anxiety in patients high and low in social anxiety or subjects high and low in shyness. Socially anxious and shy subjects overestimated the visibility of their anxiety.

If social phobics are self-focused in social situations they should show diminished attention to, and diminished memory of, aspects of social situations/stimuli. Winton, Clark and Edelmann (1995) investigated accuracy in detecting negative emotion in briefly presented (60 millisecond) slides of different emotional expressions. Each slide was followed by a pattern mask intended to prevent continued controlled processing of the facial stimuli. Students scoring high in FNE correctly identified more negative facial expressions than did low FNE subjects, but a signal detection analysis revealed that this was because high FNE subjects tended to rate a briefly presented face as more negative irrespective of the facial expression. A different pattern of attention is observed in studies which have used social stimuli presented as words. In particular, social phobics show slower colour-naming times for social threat words but not for physical threat words in the modified Stroop test (Hope et al., 1990; Mattia, Heimberg & Hope, 1993). Using dot-probe methodology (Macleod, Mathews & Tata, 1986), Asmundson and Stein (1994) found that, compared to non-patient controls, social phobics were quicker at locating dots that followed social threat words (e.g. 'foolish') than dots following either neutral words or physical threat words. This suggested that social phobics had shifted attention towards social threat stimuli but not to physical threat or neutral word stimuli. At first sight these results may appear to conflict with predictions of reduced attention to social stimuli derived from the present model. However, attentional bias towards social threat stimuli in the form of words is not a problem for the model since word stimuli are unlikely to resemble the actual stimuli that elicit social anxiety and the processing configuration typified by self focus. In order to observe reduced attention to social cues the model predicts that it is necessary to use test materials that represent naturally occurring social stimuli, and perhaps to test patients under conditions of social anxiety.

Effects of Manipulating Safety Behaviours, and Self-attention

Two studies have directly tested the effect of manipulations of safety behaviours and of attention on beliefs and social anxiety in feared social situations. The model predicts that use of within-situation safety behaviours impedes belief and anxiety change, and therefore abandoning safety behaviours should enhance exposure effects. Wells et al. (1995) exposed patients with social phobia to a feared social situation for a brief time period (usually 5 minutes) under two conditions: abandonment of safety behaviours (exposure plus dropping safety behaviours), and behaviour as usual (exposure alone condition). Participants in the study received both interventions in a randomised order. Exposure plus abandonment of safety behaviours produced significantly greater reductions in anxiety and negative beliefs than exposure alone. The model also predicts that reducing self-focused attention and shifting to external focus in social situations should facilitate reductions in negative beliefs and anxiety in feared social situations. Wells and Papageorgiou (1998) tested this prediction in eight social phobics during exposure to a feared idiosyncratic social situation. The participants engaged in external focused attention, and behaved as usual. All subjects received both conditions in a random sequence. The rationales for each exposure condition were equally credible. Exposure plus external attention led to significantly greater improvements in measures of in-situation anxiety and negative beliefs, and shifted patients from an observer to a field perspective in their post-exposure images of the situation. These results support the hypothesis that safety behaviours and self-focused attention impede anxiety and belief change in feared social situations, and support the view that it is important to modify safety behaviours and attentional processes in treatment in order to maximise disconfirmatory experiences and reduce anxiety.

COGNITIVE THERAPY: A PRACTICE OUTLINE

In previous work I have presented a detailed account of cognitive therapy based on the social phobia model (Wells, 1997). In the remainder of this chapter the main components of this treatment will be described. Space does not permit a review of assessment and so the interested reader is referred to Wells (1997).

Treatment should be designed to follow a particular sequence, the reasons for such a sequence being as follows: first, it is necessary to configure the patient's attention and behavioural responses in a way that potentiates therapeutic gains made in subsequent behavioural experiments. We have seen, for example, how it is necessary to modify attention and safety behaviours to improve the effects of exposure experiments. Second, strategies such as reducing safety behaviours and shifting to external attention can have an immediate effect of reducing the intensity of anxiety symptoms whilst not compromising disconfirmation. Third, the model is somewhat complex and it is better to deal with individual components in a systematic fashion to enhance patient comprehension. The sequence of treatment is as follows:

1. Construct an idiosyncratic formulation based on the model and socialise in the model.
2. Implement increased and decreased safety behaviours' manipulations, and shift to external attention.
3. Use video feedback to correct the distorted self-image.
4. Focus on interrogating the environment and challenging specific predictions by behavioural experiment.
5. Work on assumptions and beliefs.
6. Relapse prevention work.

Each of these phases will now be considered in turn.

Formulation and Socialisation

The construction of an idiosyncratic formulation based on the model requires eliciting the relevant information from recent social anxiety episodes. If avoidance is marked recent episodes may be unavailable and then the therapist and patient should concentrate on using the therapeutic encounter itself as a situation, or an analogue social phobic situation may be created in the clinic. The case conceptualisation can be constructed by entering the vicious cycles depicted in Figure 1.1 at any point. Typically, discussion begins by asking patients about the content of thoughts experienced just prior to, or on entering the feared social situation. When determining the nature of emotional responses the therapist should ask how the patient felt (emotionally) and elicit physiological and cognitive symptoms associated with anxiety. Negative automatic thoughts should be elicited by asking about negative thoughts that occur just before or on entering the situation. Once these have been elicited the next step is to access the patient's safety behaviours. This can be accomplished by asking if the patient engaged in any behaviours to try and prevent an idiosyncratic feared social catastrophe or to conceal symptoms. The central component of the model, comprised of self-processing, is elicited by asking the patient if they felt self-conscious in the social situation, and if so, asking what they were most self-conscious of? In this domain specific questions should be directed at determining how the patient thought s/he appeared to others in the situation, and should determine if this is represented as an image or a 'felt-sense'. The following dialogue illustrates the usage of a series of questions to elicit information used in constructing the formulation depicted in Figure 1.2.

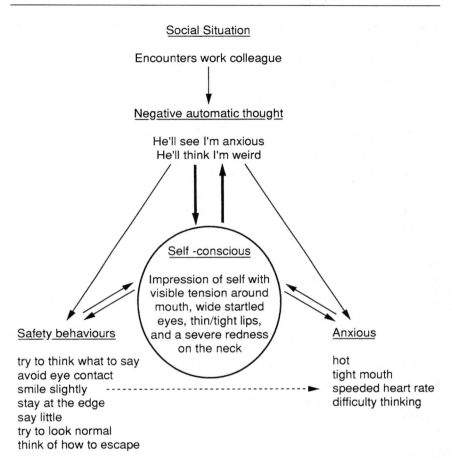

Figure 1.2   An idiosyncratic case formulation of social phobia based on the model.

T: Can you think of the last time you felt socially anxious in a social situation?

P: Yes. I was talking to an old work colleague last week, and I just felt really anxious

T: OK. I'm going to ask you some questions about that episode. What was the first thought that went through your mind when you saw your colleague?

P: I thought, God, I hope he doesn't notice me.

T: What's the worst that could happen if he did notice you?

P: Well he did notice me, and I had to talk to him.

T: It sounds like you didn't want to talk to him. What was bad about talking to him?

P: I thought he would see I'm anxious and think I'm weird.

T: So the negative thought you had was he'll see I'm anxious and think I'm weird?

P: Yes.

T: When you thought that how did it make you feel?

P: More anxious, I just wanted to avoid him.

T: When you felt anxious what symptoms did you notice?

P: I felt hot, my mouth was tight, and I could feel my heart speeding up.

T: Did you notice any other symptoms such as your mind racing or your mind going blank?

P: Yes, I couldn't think of what to say. I was trying to work out what to say, but I was finding it hard to think.

T: You said you were trying to think of what to say. That sounds like a coping strategy that you have developed. Did you use any other strategies to conceal your anxiety or stop him thinking you were weird?

P: I avoided looking at him, tried not to talk about myself, and kept a slight smile on my face.

T: How did keeping a slight smile on your face help?

P: It makes him think I'm interested and paying attention to what he's saying. Also it makes it less likely that he'll notice the tension around my mouth.

T: So it sounds as if you have a number of tricks or safety behaviours that prevent bad things from happening. Do you do anything else to stop people thinking you're weird or anxious?

P: I sometimes stay at the edge of the group and say little.

T: When you were talking to your colleague did you feel self-conscious?

P: Yes, very.

T: What were you most conscious of?

P: Trying to look normal, and thinking of how I could escape as quickly as possible.

T: They sound like additional safety behaviours. Do you have an impression of how you looked whilst talking?

P: I probably looked anxious.

T: Did you have an impression of what that looked like?

P: Yes. With visible tension around my mouth, and wide eyes, like a startled look.

T: What would I be able to see if I saw the tension round your mouth?

P: My lips would be thin and tight.

T: Would I see anything else?

P: Yes, you would see redness on my neck.

T: All over your neck?

P: Yes, the whole thing would look like a severe rash or something.

It is often necessary to sample more than one social-anxiety episode in order to build up a full conceptualisation of the problem.

Once the formulation is constructed the therapist proceeds with socialisa-tion. Initially this consists of sharing the model with the patient and dis-cussion of the role of feedback cycles linking safety behaviours to symptoms and self-consciousness, and discussing evidence for the nega-tive self-impression. In particular, the therapist should ask where the patient's evidence supporting the belief that anxiety symptoms look con-spicuous comes from. The point which is emphasised here is that the patient has been unable to check-out other people's true reaction because the patient has been predominantly self-focused rather than focused on others in the feared situation. (Note: when there is a co-morbid occurrence of paranoid ideas this pattern is likely to be different. In this instance the patient may report selective scanning of the social environment for signs of people paying attention to him/her.)

Socialisation continues with manipulations of safety behaviours, and self-focused attention. These strategies also provide early symptom relief, and will later serve as a catalyst for disconfirmatory processing.

Increased and Decreased Safety Behaviour Manipulations

Early in treatment (typically, the first or second session), the case concep-tualisation is illustrated with behavioural experiments that manipulate safety behaviours and the patient's direction of attention. These manipu-lations also configure the individual to process disconfirmatory informa-tion, by establishing a cognitive set, modulating symptom intensity, and introducing disconfirmatory experiences. The steps involved in this manoeuvre are as follows:

1. The role of safety behaviours in exacerbating symptoms and preventing disconfirmation is discussed. Specific belief-linked safety behaviours are identified. Some behaviours are covert and others more overt, therefore detailed analysis of the full range of behaviours is required. In most cases

a review of recent anxiety-provoking social situations is sufficient for identifying safety behaviours. However, a behaviour test should be used when discussion alone fails to elicit behaviours. Behaviour tests usually consist of entering an actual or analogue feared situation followed by a detailed review of negative automatic thoughts, feelings, self-processing, and behaviours.

2. The patient is exposed to a feared social situation whilst increasing safety behaviours. The behaviours that are increased should be discussed in detail so that the patient knows exactly what is required. Feared social situations may be reproduced in the therapist's office using colleagues, but if this is not possible *in vivo* work is necessary. Following exposure under increased safety behaviour conditions, the next step is exposure under conditions of decreased or abandoned safety behaviours, and external-focused attention. Here, the patient is given detailed instruction in dropping specific safety behaviours before exposure. When safety behaviours are habitual this may be difficult at first, and the therapist may assist by modelling the abandonment of safety behaviours or by allowing an initial practice period. Exposure then proceeds under this new condition. Following each manipulation the therapist should ask for patient ratings of anxiety, self-consciousness, and belief in specific social catastrophes. These dimensions can be rated on 0–100 rating scales administered verbally. The aim of this procedure is to demonstrate that when safety behaviours are decreased social catastrophes do not occur, and to show that self-consciousness and symptom intensity decrease.

3. Exposure plus abandonment of safety behaviours and external focusing are assigned as homework tasks. Patients are asked to shift to external (other-focused) attention in social situations in order to check-out the extent to which others pay attention to them.

Video Feedback Experiments

Since a central component of the cognitive model is the notion that patients hold a distorted impression of how they think they look to others, treatment aims to correct the distorted self-image. Video feedback of the true observable self, when anxious in social situations, is a principal technique used for this purpose.

There are several complexities, if this is to be a corrective experience, in showing socially anxious patients videos of themselves in social situations. First, a social situation that activates anxiety and feared observable responses must be used. Failure to do this leads the patient to discounting the exercise as inappropriate or inaccurate. Second, seeing oneself on video is likely to induce anxiety and embarrassment, and will activate negative self-processing. Such negative self-processing by the patient whilst viewing feedback interferes with the objective processing of the patient's appearance. Third, socially phobic individuals most often have not objectified in *concrete observable terms* how they think they appear when anxious. Responses such as 'I feel bad therefore I must look bad' require *objectification* so that the presence or absence of 'looking bad' can be evaluated. These difficulties can be minimised by:

1. Ensuring that patients are anxious whilst being videotaped. This is achieved by selecting a situation high on the anxiety hierarchy, and by using videotape techniques early on in therapy. In order to confirm that anxiety is present the therapist should ask for ratings of anxiety (0–100) during the videotaped task.

2. Once the patient has been successfully videotaped whilst anxious in a social situation, the patient should be asked to run a 'mental video' of the social encounter focusing on how s/he thinks s/he looked in the situation. At this stage the conspicuousness of symptoms should be objectified. For example, if the patient believes that tension around the mouth and shaking would be apparent, the observable intensity of these responses is determined. This can be done by asking the patient to demonstrate the intensity of the symptom, and capturing this on video as well, or by the patient instructing the therapist to model the intensity of the symptom. With symptoms such as blushing, the patient can be asked to illustrate the intensity of blushing by choosing one of a series of coloured cards of varying shades of redness. When sweating is a problem the patient can instruct the therapist to splash varying amounts of water on his/her face to resemble the observability of symptoms. Video feedback of social performance is then presented and compared with the objectified content of the patient's mental video. Several viewings of the video may be required in order to fully process the implications of the exercise.

Subsequent experiments of this kind may be practised using deliberate exaggerations of symptoms so that the patient can begin to form a more accurate impression of the observable self.

Interrogating the Environment and Testing Specific Predictions

After the first three to four sessions, treatment should increasingly focus on de-catastrophising the implication and meaning of showing symptoms, or of 'failed' social performance. In this context patient and therapist work together in eliciting specific predictions concerning the reaction of other people in social situations.

Behavioural experiments provide a powerful means of decatastrophising. Mini-surveys can be used to determine what people think when they observe particular symptoms. However, a powerful strategy involves experimenting with deliberately showing particular symptoms or engaging in instances of 'failed performance'. For example, a patient fearful of shaking and spilling a drink can be asked to deliberately tremble and spill some of a drink in a public place. In order to maximise the potential for such procedures to change negative appraisals and beliefs concerning other people's reactions, the consequences of the target behaviour should be carefully operationalised. The following dialogue illustrates this operationalisation process:

T: What's the worst that could happen if you tremble and spill your drink?

P: People will notice and think I'm an alcoholic or something.

T: How many people do you think will notice?

P: Probably not that many.

T: How many would that be?

P: Probably three or four people.

T: So you think that four people will notice, and they will think you are an alcoholic. If they did think you were an alcoholic how might they look at you?

P: They'd have a look of disgust or an angry expression.

T: Can you give me a detailed description of what that would look like?

P: They'd stare at me and look disapproving.

T: What would disapproving look like?

P: They'd probably frown and say something about me to someone they were with.

T: How much do you believe that they will look that way?

P: Sixty per cent.

Operationalisation phases like this should be followed by behavioural experiments in which the patient enters the feared social situation and deliberately trembles and spills some drink whilst focusing attention on the reaction of other people. Typically, very few people in the situation actually look at the patient, and if they do the nature of their attention is fleeting and does not appear negative as operationalised. These discrepancies are used to challenge the patient's prediction.

Socially phobic patients worry about what other people might think of them. A key to success in behavioural experiments with social phobia rests on the ability to operationalise and objectify the thoughts of others. One way to test-out what other people think of you is to ask direct questions. This strategy can be constructed around the use of probe questions. This requires patients to deliberately introduce feared responses in social interactions, and then discretely ask for feedback from a particular participant. For example, a socially anxious patient may be asked to deliberately say less in a group interaction, or to deliberately pause or stammer in conversation. Following the interaction the patient should then ask questions about how noticeable his/her response was, and how other people interpreted it. One patient treated recently was a stammerer with social phobia; he worried about stammering and believed that others would think he was 'inadequate, weak, scatty, and confused'. He was asked to deliberately stammer during a couple of interactions with friends and housemates, and then ask if they had any thoughts about his stammering and if so what they were. At first he was hesitant about doing this but after a partial attempt he became more confident and discovered that no one thought he was inadequate, weak, scatty, and confused. Most people stated that they had not thought much about the stammering since they were accustomed to it. Therefore, the experiment was repeated with people who were less familiar. Their response to the question was that they admired how well the patient coped with stammering, and they thought of stammering as a sign of intelligence. After practising deliberately stammering the patient began to find the exercise fun, since the deliberate commission of stammering became his private joke.

Bandwidth manoeuvres

It is common for people with social phobia to restrict their social behaviour in social situations. Some socially anxious individuals have led restricted social lives for many years, and operate within the confines of restricted behavioural repertoires. For example, a patient may refrain from making complaints in public, or from asking for directions, or on visiting a waiting room may sit very still, remain quiet, and try to blend into the background. The tendency to blend into the background is a safety behaviour that prevents the individual discovering that a wide range of behaviours are acceptable and do not lead to intense negative attention from others. The patient therefore leads a narrow existence, constantly aware of the possibility that at any moment they will attract undesirable forms of attention. Bandwidth manoeuvres involve acting in ways that the patient has considered socially 'dangerous' so that s/he may discover that a wide range of behaviours are acceptable. Moreover, the deliberate commission of 'unacceptable' behaviours allows the practice of strategies for re-evaluating the significance of behaviours, and for maintaining control over the situation.

Modifying Assumptions and Beliefs

The strategies already reviewed for challenging predictions and negative thoughts should also be used to challenge assumptions and beliefs. Many of the negative self-appraisals challenged early in treatment will be direct reflections of belief. Nevertheless, some schemata are more resistant to change. Unrealistic rules for, and conditional assumptions about, social performance should be modified with specific behavioural experiments and with the bandwidth manoeuvres discussed previously. Negative self-beliefs such as 'I'm weird; I'm boring; I'm inadequate' may change in response to modifying negative self-image, and challenging negative appraisals of symptoms. However, these beliefs persist in some cases and contribute to residual social anxiety. They should be conceptualised as vulnerability markers for the development of subsequent problems. More stable negative self-beliefs are often viewed as a hallmark of complex cases. These beliefs may arise from a negative social-learning history such as maltreatment in the home or amongst the peer group, or as a response to particular attitudes of others. Typically, these beliefs are held as unquestioned and over-simplified constructions of the self and others in a social domain. Because they are simplified and unquestioned, a preliminary strategy for weakening these schemata consists of defining the constructs represented in the beliefs and questioning the evidence for the belief. I have suggested a sequence of strategies for schematic modification (Wells, 1997):

1. Begin by defining the central dysfunctional concept. For example: what does the patient who believes they are 'weird' mean by the term 'weird'? The construction of a detailed definition is often the first time a patient has analysed the construct in detail. This renders the belief more tangible and facilitates a logical reanalysis.
2. Generate a full range of characteristics that define/constitute weirdness. Then systematically evaluate the number of characteristics that the patient actually has. The aim is to establish that the patient has few of the defining characteristics of weirdness.
3. The distorted nature of the belief should be emphasised, and then evidence for the belief examined. Armed with the concept that the belief is distorted, reinterpretations of the evidence are elicited. For example, a patient believed he was 'boring', and support for this belief was located in the present and the past. His present day evidence was that his work colleagues interacted little with him, and he felt excluded. On careful examination of a range of possible reasons for this he decided the most likely explanation was that he showed little interest in them. A follow-up experiment to test this out involved him actively greeting his colleagues upon his arrival at work. It also emerged that he normally refrained from self-

disclosure as he believed that this would highlight how boring he was. In further experiments he was asked to increase his level of self-disclosure. When he did this he discovered that his colleagues were more likely to speak to him, and not less likely to do so as he had predicted. The evidence from his past seemed particularly salient in supporting his belief. He reported that his parents had given most of their attention to his younger brother who was considered to 'have all the brains'. This situation was reframed by reviewing the abilities that the patient had, and by de-coupling the concepts of intelligence and being boring (e.g. If you are intelligent does that automatically mean you are not boring?)

4. A replacement self-belief should be specified which can be used as a self-statement whenever the negative belief becomes activated.

5. The patient is encouraged to behave in new ways that are capable of sustaining the replacement self-belief. A useful strategy here is the development of a new 'script' for social behaviour that increases the propensity of positive social feedback from others.

Other strategies for dealing with maladaptive schemata include positive data logs, continua work, and use of flashcards. The positive data log requires that the patient keeps a note of positive daily experiences that are supportive of replacement positive self-beliefs. The aim of this strategy is to counteract selective attention to negative experiences, and to strengthen a data base supportive of more realistic self-beliefs. Continua should be used when patients show high levels of dichotomous reasoning. This technique is aimed at introducing shades of grey and more sophisticated judgements in the cognitive repertoire, that can stabilise affective and self-image instability. Flashcards can be used to summarise replacement self-beliefs and to carry supporting evidence. These may be viewed as metaphorical replacement schemata that the patient should attempt to internalise over time.

Relapse Prevention

The final sessions of treatment should focus increasingly on relapse prevention. Residual belief at the negative automatic thought and schema levels is elicited and modified before termination of therapy. Continual avoidance of social situations or use of safety behaviours are often a marker for unresolved fears. It is important that avoidance is eliminated or reduced to the minimum level possible before the end of treatment. This will invariably involve repeated exposure experiments like those advocated earlier in this chapter. During the final session the therapist and patient should work on a 'Therapy blueprint'. This consists of a summary of material learned about social phobia during the course of treatment. It usually contains an example of an idiosyncratic case conceptualisation, examples of negative automatic thoughts, safety behaviours, and avoidance. It also contains a summary of strategies for dealing with social anxiety plus a summary of results from behavioural experiments. The blueprint summarises a number of continuing targets that will be pursued as ongoing homework tasks. Progress towards meeting these goals can be reviewed at subsequent booster sessions scheduled at intervals of several months following treatment.

SUMMARY AND CONCLUSIONS

Until recently social phobia was a complex problem to formulate and to treat. In this chapter I have described the Clark and Wells (1995) model of social phobia and illustrated how treatment based on the model (e.g. Wells, 1997) is implemented. This model is derived in part from the Self-Regulatory Executive Function Model (S-REF; Wells & Matthews, 1994) of emotional disorder, which imparts an important role to dysfunctional processing configurations in emotional disorder. We have seen how aspects of this configuration—self-focused attention, attentional bias, rumination, performance deficits and behavioural strategies—can be specifically operationalised in modelling the maintenance processes in social phobia. Unlike general schema theory, which has tended to emphasise the content of thought in a rather static way in emotional disorder, the present model assigns a pivotal role to attentional processes, and in particular the interplay between self-processing and behaviour in the maintenance of dysfunctional beliefs and anxiety.

Preliminary data from clinical evaluations of this treatment suggest that the treatment is effective, and controlled clinical evaluation is in progress.

REFERENCES

American Psychiatric Association, APA (1994). *Diagnostic and Statistical Manual of Mental Disorders* – Revised, 4th edn. Washington, DC: APA.

Arntz, A., Rauner, M. & van den Hout, M.A. (1994). 'If I feel anxious, there must be danger': The fallacy of ex-consequentia reasoning in inferring danger in anxiety disorders. Manuscript submitted for publication.

Asmundson, G.J.G. & Stein, M.B. (1994). Selective attention for social threat in patients with generalized social phobia: Evaluation using a dot-probe paradigm. *Journal of Anxiety Disorders*, **8**, 107–117.

Beck, A.T., Emery, G. & Greenberg, R.L. (1985). *Anxiety Disorders and Phobias: A Cognitive Perspective*. New York: Basic Books.

Bruch, B.A., Gorsky, J.M., Collins, T.M. & Berger, P.A. (1989). Shyness and sociability reexamined: A multicomponent analysis. *Journal of Personality and Social Psychology*, **57**, 904–915.

Buss, A.H. (1980). *Self-consciousness and Social Anxiety*. San Francisco, CA: Freeman.

Butler, G., Cullington, A., Munby, M., Ames, P. & Gelder, M. (1984). Exposure and anxiety management in the treatment of social phobia. *Journal of Consulting and Clinical Psychology*, **2**, 642–650.

Clark, D.M. & Wells, A. (1995). A cognitive model of social phobia. In: R. Heimberg, M. Liebowitz, D.A. Hope & F.R. Schneier (Eds), *Social Phobia: Diagnosis, Assessment and Treatment* (pp. 69–93). New York: Guilford Press.

DiGiuseppe, R., McGowan, L., Sutton-Simon, K. & Gardner, F. (1990). A comparative outcome study of your cognitive therapies in the treatment of social anxiety. *Journal of Rational-Emotive and Cognitive-Behaviour Therapy*, **8**, 129–146.

Emmelkamp, P.M.G., Mersch, P.P.A., Vissia, E. & Van der Helm, M. (1985). Social Phobia: A comparative evaluation of cognitive and behavioural interventions. *Behaviour Research and Therapy*, **23**, 365–369.

Fenigstein, A., Scheier, M.F. & Buss, A.H. (1975). Public and private self-consciousness: Assessment and theory. *Journal of Consulting and Clinical Psychology*, **43**, 522–527.

Hartman, L.M. (1983). A meta-cognitive model of social anxiety: Implications for treatment. *Clinical Psychology Review*, **3**, 435–456.

Heimberg, R.G. & Barlow, D.H. (1988). Psychosocial treatments for social phobia. *Psychosomatics*, **29**, 27–37.

Heimberg, R.G., Dodge, C.S., Hope, D.A., Kennedy, C.R., Zollo, L. & Becker, R.E. (1990). Cognitive behavioral group treatment of social phobia: Comparison to a credible placebo control. *Cognitive Therapy and Research*, **14**, 1–23.

Heimberg, R.G. & Juster, H.R. (1995). Cognitive-behavioral treatments: Literature review. In: R.G. Heimberg, M.R. Liebowitz, D.A. Hope & F.R. Schneier (Eds), *Social Phobia: Diagnosis, Assessment and Treatment* (pp.261–309). New York: Guilford Press.

Holt, C.S., Heimberg, R.G. & Hope, D.A. (1992). Avoidant personality disorder and the generalised sub-type of social phobia. *Journal of Abnormal Psychology*, **101**, 318–325.

Hope, D.A., Rapee, R.M., Heimberg, R.G. & Dombeck, M.J. (1990). Representations of the self in social phobia: Vulnerability to social threat. *Cognitive Therapy and Research*, **14**, 177–189.

Johansson, J. & Öst, L.G. (1982). Perception of automatic reactions and actual heart rate in phobic patients. *Journal of Behavioral Assessment*, **4**, 133–143.

Lucas, R.A. & Telch, M.J. (1993). *Group versus individual treatment of social phobia*. Paper presented at the annual meeting of the Association for Advancement of Behavior Therapy, Atlanta, GA (November).

MacLeod, C., Mathews, A. & Tata, P. (1986). Attentional bias in emotional disorders. *Journal of Abnormal Psychology*, **95**, 15–20.

Mattia, J.I., Heimberg, R.G. & Hope, D.A. (1993). The revised Stroop color-naming task in social phobics. *Behaviour Research and Therapy*, **31**, 305–313.

Mattick, P.P., Peters, L. & Clark, J.C. (1989). Exposure and cognitive restructuring for social phobia: A controlled study. *Behavior Therapy*, **20**, 3–23.

McEwan, K.L. & Devins, G.M. (1983). Is increased arousal in social anxiety noticed by others? *Journal of Abnormal Psychology*, **92**, 417–421.

Papageorgiou, C. & Wells, A. (1997). *Social self-perception: Effects of false heart-rate feedback in socially anxious subjects.* Paper presented at BABCP 25th Annual Conference, Canterbury, UK (July).

Salkovskis, P.M. (1991). The importance of behaviour in the maintenance of anxiety and panic: A cognitive account. *Behavioural Psychotherapy*, **19**, 6–19.

Stopa, L. & Clark, D.M. (1993). Cognitive processes in social phobia. *Behaviour Research and Therapy*, **31**, 255–267.

Watson, D. & Friend, R. (1969). Measurement of social-evaluative anxiety. *Journal of Consulting and Clinical Psychology*, **33**, 448–457.

Wells, A. (1997). *Cognitive Therapy of Anxiety Disorders: A Practice Manual and Conceptual Guide.* Chichester, UK: Wiley.

Wells, A. & Clark, D.M. (1997). Social Phobia: A cognitive approach. In: G.C.L. Davey (Ed.), *Phobias: A Handbook of Description, Treatment and Theory.* Chichester, UK: John Wiley.

Wells, A., Clark, D.M. & Ahmad, S. (1998). How do I look with my mind's eye? Perspective taking in social phobic imagery. *Behaviour Research and Therapy*, **36**, 631–634.

Wells, A., Clark, D.M., Salkovskis, P., Ludgate, J., Hackmann, A. & Gelder, M. (1995). The role of in-situational safety behaviours in maintaining anxiety and negative automatic thoughts. *Behavior Therapy*, **26**, 153–161.

Wells, A. & Matthews, G. (1994). *Attention and Emotion: A Clinical Perspective.* Hove, UK: Erlbaum.

Wells, A. & Matthews, G. (1996). Modelling cognition in emotional disorder: The S-REF Model. *Behaviour Research Therapy*, **34**, 881–888.

Wells, A. & Papageorgiou, C. (1998). Social Phobia: Effects of external attention on anxiety, negative beliefs, and perspective taking. *Behaviour Therapy*, in press.

Winton, E.C., Clark, D.M. & Edelmann, R.J. (1995). Social anxiety, fear of negative evaluation and detection of emotion in others. *Behaviour Research and Therapy*, **33**, 193–196.

Chapter 2

COGNITIVE THERAPY PANIC AND AGORAPHOBIA: WORKING WITH COMPLEX CASES

*Ann Hackmann**

INTRODUCTION

A panic attack is defined (American Psychiatric Association – APA, 1980) as a sudden onset, an intense feeling of apprehension or impending doom that is associated with at least four of a list of symptoms which includes palpitations, breathlessness, dizziness, trembling, blurred vision, nausea, chest pain and parasthesias. Occasional panic attacks are common, but the diagnosis of panic disorder is reserved for individuals who experience recurrent panic attacks, at least some of which come on out of the blue. The current version of the American Psychiatric Association's Diagnostic and Statistical Manual of Mental Disorders (DSM-IV – APA, 1995) divides panic disorder sufferers into those who can identify certain situations as particularly likely to trigger panic, and who therefore tend to avoid these situations, and those who cannot identify such situations and show no gross situational avoidance (panic disorder with or without agoraphobia). There is a final category of agoraphobia without a history of panic disorder. Agoraphobia as such is not a codable disorder, although it is defined as anxiety about being in places or situations from which escape might be difficult or embarrassing in the event of an unexpected or situationally predisposed panic attack or panic-like symptoms (such as dizziness or diarrhoea). In this chapter patients with panic disorder and mild or no agoraphobia will be described as panic patients, whilst those with moderate or severe agoraphobia with or (far less commonly) without a history of

* University of Oxford Department of Psychiatry, Warneford Hospital, Oxford, UK

Treating Complex Cases: The Cognitive Behavioural Therapy Approach.
Edited by Nicholas Tarrier, Adrian Wells and Gillian Haddock.

panic disorder will be referred to as agoraphobics. This classification will be used, as it reflects more closely the criteria used by clinicians prior to DSM-IV, and thus utilised by them in describing the patients in most of the studies referred to in this paper.

The cognitive model of panic disorder (Clark, 1996) suggests that people who suffer from panic attacks do so because they have a relatively enduring tendency to misinterpret bodily sensations (particularly those of anxiety) as being indicative of an impending physical or mental catastrophe. Cognitive therapy aims to remove this tendency (Clark, 1996), and overcome avoidance, which is secondary to panic. Theoretically it would seem likely that cognitive therapy for panic, combined with a degree of exposure to any feared or avoided situations, should be a good treatment for agoraphobia with or without a history of panic disorder, as well as for panic disorder itself. Instead of a having a habituation rationale the purpose of this exposure element would be to provide an opportunity for the patient to test and correct any catastrophic predictions he or she might be making about possible causes or consequences of the bodily sensations accompanying panic (or more limited attacks of panic-like symptoms).

In recent years the treatment of panic disorder has been improved to the point where it has been possible to produce high end-state functioning in about 80% of patients, with good follow-up results, after only four and a half hours of cognitive therapy (Clark et al., 1995). A previous trial had secured similar results after 12 sessions (Clark et al., 1994), and there are a number of other trials which have also demonstrated a very high success rate (Beck et al., 1992; Margraf & Schneider, 1991; Arntz & van den Hout, 1996; and Öst & Westling,1995). In these studies patients were almost all diagnosed as meeting criteria for panic disorder with no, mild or moderate avoidance on the SCID (Structured Clinical Interview for DSM-IIIR: First et al., 1995).

There have been few studies of the effects of cognitive therapy on more severely agoraphobic patients. Exposure therapy has been shown to be at least moderately effective in the treatment of the majority of a group of agoraphobics of mixed severity, although one third were not significantly improved (Mathews, Gelder & Johnston, 1981). Michelson and Marchione (1989) studied a group of agoraphobics of varying levels of avoidance, in a large study of 72 patients meeting DSM-III criteria for agoraphobia with panic, who were randomly allocated to cognitive therapy plus graded exposure, relaxation training with graded exposure, or exposure alone. All three treatments were associated with significant reductions in panic, anxiety and phobic avoidance, but where there were significant between-group differences these favoured cognitive therapy plus graded exposure.

An Oxford study of seven patients with panic disorder with moderate or severe avoidance results suggested that it was possible to produce a drop in the frequency of panic attacks with purely cognitive interventions, not involving any exposure or breathing retraining (Salkovskis, Clark & Hackmann, 1991). More recent studies of a group of 18 agoraphobics with moderate or severe avoidance have shown that presenting them with the cognitive model and then encouraging them to drop their safety behaviours (i.e. behaviours designed to avert feared catastrophes such as fainting) and thus test their predictions about possible catastrophic outcomes greatly enhances the benefits of exposure to feared situations, both during a single, brief experimental session (Salkovskis et al., 1997, submitted), and during a short course of therapy (Salkovskis et al., 1997, in preparation). During therapy patients in each group received the same number of hours of individual treatment (one hour of planning, plus two one and a half hour sessions of treatment), including the same duration of actual exposure. At the end of the period of 10 days during which the treatment took place there were highly significant differences between the groups on measures of panic, general anxiety and avoidance, in favour of the cognitive treatment. Despite these encouraging findings our clinical experience suggests that some of the most severe agoraphobics may still prove quite difficult to treat.

In this chapter an outline will be given of the basic ingredients required to treat panic disorder and agoraphobia. There is a large overlap in the techniques required to treat these two groups of patients, and most of the difference lies in the emphasis which may need to be given to the different components in the treatment of particular individuals. However, it has been our impression that some problems are more frequently encountered with more avoidant patients, and where this is the case it will be indicated. Details of where difficulties may crop up with each aspect of treatment will be given, together with suggestions as to how these may be overcome. In each section case examples will be provided to show how difficulties encountered were tackled.

The components required in cognitive therapy for panic and agoraphobia include the following:

1. Establishing a suitable setting for therapy.
2. Detailed examination of recent experiences of panic, in order to be able to study the links in the vicious circle of panic.
3. Changing the catastrophic misinterpretations of bodily sensations, by examining the true causes and consequences of the symptoms of panic attacks, or panic-like symptoms, using verbal discussion and behavioural experiments.
4. Working with images, where verbal techniques appear inadequate on their own.

5. Identification of the triggers for panic attacks.
6. Overcoming avoidance (of places, activities, etc.).
7. Dealing with underlying core beliefs about the self, the world and other people.
8. Removing any other blocks to progress.

DIFFICULTIES IN EXECUTING COGNITIVE THERAPY FOR PANIC AND AGORAPHOBIA.

The components of treatment will now be described and discussed, with particular reference to difficulties which may be encountered.

Establishing a Suitable Environment for Therapy

Most people suffering from neurotic disorders can be relied upon to attend therapy sessions in a clinical setting, on a regular basis. Agoraphobia presents a practical problem, as it makes attendance anxiety provoking or even impossible. Extra time therefore may have to be allocated by the therapist to travel to the patient's home, set up a tape-recorder to record the session for the patient, or meet the patient in a suitable place, such as a nearby shopping centre. Patients also need to be socialised as to the purpose of the visit, so that the situation does not become a 'coffee morning', the television is switched off, and visitors and phone calls are discouraged. The more anxious and avoidant the client, the more tempted they will be to postpone the business part of the session, or even the session itself. Such tendencies may have to be openly discussed in therapy, and the contract may need to be renegotiated from time to time.

Mary came for treatment of severe agoraphobia with a history of panic disorder. Sessions were scheduled for twice a week at her own home. Mary often rang to cancel appointments, or was not at home when the therapist arrived. When therapist and patient did manage to meet, Mary's friend Doris was present, and did most of the talking, explaining just how bad Mary felt. The therapist tackled this situation by pointing out what was happening, and asking Mary to explain what was going on, so that they could decide what to do. Mary explained that whilst she longed for a cure she was very afraid of the therapy itself. A previous therapist had attempted exposure therapy with her, taking her to a shopping centre, and leaving her to find her own way home. The therapist explained that they were going to collaborate, and Mary would never have anything sprung on her unexpectedly. She also said that it would be nice to have Doris present in the sessions, as she might help Mary to remember what she learned in therapy, and encourage her to put it into practice. However, in the actual sessions it would be best for her to keep a low profile, so that Mary could provide accurate information about her own thoughts and feelings.

Part of establishing a suitable environment for therapy is to ensure that relatives or friends are not expressing unhelpful or undermining beliefs between the sessions.

Betty, a moderately avoidant agoraphobic with a history of panic disorder, was responding moderately well to therapy, and had been asked to go out more during the week with her husband. On one occasion she had had a severe panic attack and had to go home. On discussion it was revealed that when she got anxious her husband had insisted that they set off for home, as he was sure it was only a matter of time before she would go mad like her maternal grandmother, and consequently he did not think it was a good idea for her to really push herself. When he mentioned this she had (understandably) become much more anxious, and had a panic attack. Subsequently the therapist involved the husband more in therapy, and challenged his unhelpful beliefs, using cognitive therapy techniques.

Detailed Examination of Recent Experiences of Panic

During each session of cognitive therapy for panic the therapist will almost always ask the patient to describe a recent experience of panic. This is gone through meticulously, frame by frame, with the patient describing exactly what they were doing, thinking, feeling and experiencing in their body, as the panic attack unfolded. In this way it is hoped that the vicious circle model of panic may be repeatedly generated, using the patient's own material, in a way that will help them understand what is happening, and how to break into it. Most patients take to this quite readily, and find it helpful. However, if the patient tends to use cognitive avoidance because they are afraid to think directly about their frightening experiences this can prove a frustrating situation for the therapist, unless skilful questioning is used.

Dawn was describing a recent panic attack. She described coming home from the vet, putting her key in the door, and 'coming over all funny'. The therapist asked what was going through her mind, to which she replied she just wanted to get the cat indoors before something happened. The therapist asked what she thought might happen and she replied 'I dread to think'. After a little encouragement she revealed that she might pass out and 'that would be it'. Asked what would happen if that was it she answered, 'God knows what might happen'. Finally the therapist remarked that it appeared that she might be having some ideas about what might happen which were a bit too frightening to think or talk about, and she agreed. She said that in fact she always thought that she might die during a panic attack, and the way in which she pictured it happening depended on the exact mixture of sensations which she was experiencing at that time. Once the whole topic was opened up in this way the therapist could begin to help her challenge the actual catastrophic thoughts.

In this example the therapist was able to overcome the patient's tendency to speak in a vague way, using euphemisms, rather than face her frightening thoughts. The therapist summarised frequently, using the patient's own words, worked very slowly, and suggested to the patient that she seemed to have fears that she had not voiced. It is also important to investigate links between particular thoughts, and specific bodily sensations, and to enquire about images, since these can help to disambiguate meanings.

Accompanying the patient in a situation which activates panic-related beliefs is also helpful in accessing frightening ideas, particularly in avoidant clients who may say that they do not know what they fear will happen in a particular situation like a crowded shop, and they do not want to stay long enough to find out. Patients often wish to leave once they begin to have catastrophic thoughts, but can often be persuaded to come back into the feared situation after withdrawing briefly and discussing exactly what they were thinking whilst they were panicking. Having identified the actual feared catastrophe in this way it is easier to devise ways of testing how realistic their fears are then and there, through discussion and small behavioural experiments.

Changing Catastrophic Misinterpretations of Bodily Sensations, Using Discussion Techniques and Behavioural Experiments

Here one of the main difficulties encountered may be that the patient is too afraid to attempt the behavioural experiments that might be helpful in elucidating the true causes and consequences of their bodily sensations in panic. A common example is that many patients are afraid to hyperventilate for more than a few seconds, because they are so afraid that it could damage them (the very belief which the behavioural experiment would be designed to disconfirm). In such cases it may possible to do the hyperventilation a number of times, gradually increasing the length of time, and of course it may be helpful if the therapist and/or a relative is happy to model the experiment, and emerge unharmed at the end of a lengthy period of hyperventilation. It is also possible to reassure them in advance that subjects in experiments in the Netherlands have hyperventilated for up to 45 minutes without harm. Nevertheless the most avoidant patients may still refuse to do any experiments involving changing their breathing. Sometimes it helps if the therapist can make use of other incidental observations to underline the point without having set out to do so.

Sophia was afraid that hyperventilation could immediately cause her to pass out. For this reason she was unwilling to experiment with changing her breathing for more than a few seconds at a time. Repeated attempts resulted in her always stopping almost at once, and putting her head between her knees. During one of these attempts the therapist's boss burst into the room, and reminded the therapist that they should be at a meeting. Sophia sat up at once, immediately apologised for being slow, and began to hyperventilate in a vigorous way for several minutes, without fainting. The therapist was then able to capitalise on this accidental behavioural experiment, so that the patient realised that the findings suggested that whilst hyperventilation might make her dizzy it would not make her lose consciousness.

Thus the therapist's openness and creativity will be taxed with more avoidant clients. The therapist will also need to be very aware of any patterns in the symptoms of which the patient is unaware, and will need to plan experiments to test their hunches.

Sophia also had a lot of difficulty accepting that her symptoms were not those of a brain tumour. Her work in an office involved proofreading, and she often saw the page shimmer in front of her. She also reported strange shimmering sensations when looking at a male colleague wearing a striped shirt, when the venetian blind was down in the office, and when she drove through an avenue of trees. The therapist realised that all of these situations involved striped patterns, and was able to show her a striped diagram, designed to induce an illusion of movement. The patient was able to try this out on her husband, and discover that this also gave him a shimmering sensation. The patient was reassured by this piece of detective work, and less worried about a brain tumour.

In the cognitive treatment of panic, emphasis has been placed on identifying and dropping safety behaviours, that is pieces of behaviour expressly designed to avert a feared catastrophe. These would include things like tensing one's legs or holding on to someone to prevent falling over, or taking deep breaths to prevent suffocation or fainting. These need to be dropped in order to discover that panic symptoms are not in fact harmful. Leaving safety behaviours intact tends instead to reinforce the idea that one has done something to save oneself from the feared catastrophe, which might still occur on a future occasion (Salkovskis, 1991; Salkovskis, Clark & Gelder, 1996; Salkovskis et al., submitted). This would appear to be particularly important in the treatment of agoraphobia, where it helps speed up any progress which might be made with exposure treatment, by enabling patients to test their frightening predictions about what might happen to them as a result of their bodily sensations (Salkovskis et al., in preparation). Safety behaviours can be very subtle, and there can be many of them. It is important for the patient to be encouraged to drop all of them, in order fully to overcome all the fears they have. Meaningful links exist between within-situation safety behaviours and specific catastrophic beliefs activated at that time (Salkovskis, Clark & Gelder, 1996). For example, someone afraid of going mad might attempt distraction to control their thoughts, whilst someone who feared a heart attack might sit down quietly and try to calm down.

Maureen was severely agoraphobic. In her bag she carried a bottle of water, which she sipped whilst out, and a packet of mints. Without these she was afraid that her throat might close over if she got anxious. She would not go out without a shopping trolley on which she could lean if she felt faint, and she was also inclined to tense up her legs in case they gave way. She constantly used distraction, counting lamp-posts and reading number-plates, because she was afraid that if she let herself think anxious thoughts she might lose control and go mad. All these safety behaviours were dropped at different times in therapy, so that she could discover for herself that these predictions were not valid.

Working with Images

Sometimes anxious patients report having images of catastrophic outcomes of panic. Often the contents of these images can be dealt with using the usual range of discussion and behavioural experiments, but sometimes it is more economical of time, and more effective, to use an imagery technique instead, to change the meaning of the image. Often the images in anxiety disorders depict a possible future catastrophe, and are further-more frozen in time, so that they stop at the very worst moment. Here it can be extremely useful to *finish out* the image, and hence to decata-strophise the catastrophe.

Owen suffered from moderate agoraphobia, centring round the fear that he would be sick in public. This problem had begun following a wedding, at which he had been suffering from food poisoning. He had recurrent images of him-self vomiting in places like big department stores. He was asked to imagine that he did vomit, in Marks and Spencer. He was then asked to stay with the image, and picture what would happen next. The anxiety soon dropped, and he began to smile as he pictured several staff members arriving. He visualised one clean-ing up, whilst the other led him to a rest room, gave him some water, phoned for a taxi, and gave him some of the store's gift vouchers.

Sometimes finishing out the image leads to even more frightening images of what might happen next. In such cases more complex transformations can be helpful (Hackmann, 1997).

Emma suffered from panic disorder. She was afraid that she would go mad in a panic attack, and visualised men in white coats coming to take her to a men-tal hospital. This appeared to be partly a memory, since this is what had hap-pened to her mother in the 1930s, when she became psychotic. In the image Emma felt very small, and saw the men as huge. She was able to get some con-trol over this image by imagining herself growing to the point that she could put her hands on their shoulders. The men then shrank in the image, and their frightening shouting also got quieter, until they turned into yapping poodles, which made her laugh. Here the transformation appeared to be related to the meaning she was giving to having the image when anxious. Initially it seemed to her to predict her future, but on discussion, and by playing around with the content, she was able to reframe it as a product of memory and her own anxi-ety, rather than a reflection of present reality.

Identifying the Triggers for Panic Attacks

At some point in therapy the therapist begins to try to help the patient identify the triggers in panic attacks. This can be quite difficult, as it often feels to the patient in retrospect that the attack just came on out of the blue. Triggers can in fact often be other emotional states, which the client has not recognised. This ties in quite well with the observations of Goldstein and Chambless (see e.g. Goldstein & Chambless, 1978; Chambless & Gracely, 1989; Goldstein & Stainbeck, 1991), which indicate that some agoraphobics have an interpersonal style characterised by fear of accepting and expressing negative feelings, which can lead to them failing to recognise emotions such as anger. They speculate that this results from the lack of a secure base in childhood, which leads to a tendency to suppress, deny or avoid painful feelings, since problems which arise tend to seem insoluble. This can lead to chronic anxiety, coupled with a lack of self-sufficiency, non-assertiveness, trouble functioning independently, a great fear of being alone, and an exaggerated fear of the possible destructive effect of their own angry feelings. The arousal associated with their unrecognised emotions can lead to misinterpretation of these autonomic symptoms as being due to an unexpected physical catastrophe. Part of therapy is therefore to learn to recognise, accept and express difficult feelings in an appropriate way.

Gemma (severely agoraphobic) had a panic attack one night after typing a huge pile of letters for her husband's business. He approached her with a final long letter he hoped she might type, just as she was clearing up and feeling pleased that she had finished. She noticed that her heart began to pound, and feared that she might be having a heart attack. Conversation with the therapist revealed that she felt so beholden to her family for helping her cope with being agoraphobic that she felt that any expression of her anger would be unacceptable to them. Role-plays of appropriate assertion were conducted, and in fact her family did not find her new behaviour unacceptable at all.

Sometimes panic attacks can be triggered in the session, and it is important for the therapist to realise if this is happening, and feed it back in a helpful way to the client. This can transform what seems to be a very frightening and confusing experience for the patient into a useful one.

Paulette was having her second session of cognitive therapy for panic. She and her therapist were going over a recent panic attack together and trying to make sense of it. Suddenly Paulette announced that the therapist was obviously a very clever man. It all made sense to him, but she was feeling utterly confused, and it did not make sense to her, so she thought that she would leave the session, and she probably would not return. Luckily the therapist had a hunch about what might be going on. He asked her if she was feeling confused, and when she had started to feel like that. It transpired that she had begun to feel dizzy and confused whilst remembering how she had felt during a panic attack in London. She had felt perfectly alright until they started to dwell on how she felt. The therapist then helped her reframe the frightening confusion she experienced as a symptom of anxiety, rather than evidence that she was stupid, and she then settled down again.

Overcoming Avoidance

Many patients with panic disorder with agoraphobia avoid places where they fear they may panic, and disconfirming their beliefs involves returning to such places. It is interesting to wonder why some people with panic disorders become avoidant (Clum & Knowles, 1991), and why certain places are characteristically avoided, particularly since many of them are public places, where one might expect there to be more help available in the event of a panic attack or panic-like symptoms than there would be at home. Of course a number of studies (Pollard & Cox, 1988; de Ruiter & Garssen, 1989; Telch et al., 1989) suggest that agoraphobics (in contrast to panic disorder patients with little or no avoidance) share some of the same concerns as social phobics (i.e. fears that they may say or do something that would embarrass them, whilst under the scrutiny of others) which could mean that they fear the embarrassment of having a panic attack or being ill in a public place. However, this seems to be only part of the story. The cognitive model is sometimes viewed as specifying that anxiety results from the overestimation of the probability of danger. However, Salkovsis (1996) has pointed out that Beck, Emery and Greenberg (1985) have drawn out a much broader conceptualisation, which can be described by the following anxiety equation:

$$\text{Anxiety} = \frac{\text{perceived probability of threat} \times \text{perceived cost/awfulness of danger}}{\text{perceived ability to cope with danger} + \text{perceived rescue factors}}$$

A recent study of the images of agoraphobics suggests that in their case it is not only the perceived probability of a physical or mental catastrophe which is distorted, but also the imagined interpersonal cost, together with doubts about their ability to cope or be rescued, if this should happen in a public place (Hackmann & Surawy, 1997, in preparation). For example, many agoraphobics fear fainting, relative to the number of less avoidant panic disorder patients who fear it (Salkovskis, 1990; Telch et al., 1989), and for them it appears to be particularly terrible, partly because of the way in which they imagine others would react. For some the fear is that a huge, embarrassing crowd would gather, whilst others fear that everyone would ignore them, and in both cases they may fear that they might never reach the safety of home.

Paul suffered severely from agoraphobia, and was afraid of a large number of physical and mental catastrophes. The therapist worked away patiently with him for some time, and attempted to show that he was not about to faint, have a stroke or a heart attack, develop a brain tumour, go mad, become confused, be sick, or anything else, when he experienced the bodily sensations of anxiety. Eventually the therapist asked the patient whether he ever had an image or mental picture of these things happening. It transpired that he did, and that he always pictured similar things. He saw himself fall to the ground, and then a large crowd gathered. An ambulance was called, and he was unable to explain that he was only suffering from a panic attack. He was taken to hospital, and kept there against his will. The therapist and patient then did behavioural experiments, in which first the therapist and then the patient pretended to collapse in a busy shopping centre. They were able to discover that, contrary to his predictions, only a few people offered help, and when he said he was alright no-one called an ambulance or took him to hospital. Such experiments produced an immediate and marked improvement in his symptoms, very much in contrast with the previous work on the probability of the feared catastrophes.

Some agoraphobics also appear to have a poor perception of their ability to cope with difficult situations. Hoffart (1995) has shown that low scores on a measure of perceived self-efficacy predict situational avoidance more strongly than other measures, such as a measure of the strength of catastrophic beliefs about the symptoms of panic. Chambless and Goldstein (1982) report that agoraphobic patients show low scores on the Bernruiter Inventory of self-sufficiency. Reich, Noyes and Troughton (1987) found that patients with panic disorder who had high levels of situational avoidance were more likely to meet criteria for dependent personality disorder, and Kleiner and Marshall (1987) reported a high degree of dependent behaviour in agoraphobics, prior to the onset of the agoraphobia. It is also reported that a history of school phobia is more common in agoraphobics than in panic disorder patients without agoraphobia, and the relatives of agoraphobics are also more likely to suffer from school phobia or agoraphobia (Deltito et al., 1986; Gittelman-Klein & Klein,1984). These findings all indicate that agoraphobics may have had early lives which have fostered ideas about how difficult it is to cope in the world when one is alone, although one must bear in mind that in some instances there may be criterion contamination, since some of the fears of doing things alone may in fact be truly secondary to the presence of panic, and may not reflect pre-existing doubts about the self. Nevertheless an important aspect of therapy is the exploration of how realistic fears about being able to cope alone actually are. Therapists and patients can do behavioural experiments to test such predictions.

In therapy Linette had largely overcome her fears of catastrophic outcomes from panic symptoms. However, she was still fearful that if she felt unwell whilst away from home she might lose her way, or not manage to get back to safety. She carried a piece of paper in her bag, with her name and address on it, in case she could not remember it, or could not ask for help. Essentially she felt as if she was a lost child, as soon as she left her habitual, familiar environment. She was encouraged to leave the piece of paper at home, and to deliberately try to lose herself in unfamiliar surroundings, and ask for help in finding her way home. This proved useful in building her confidence.

Thus, two features of agoraphobia which appear in the SCID definition may require more therapeutic attention than they do in the treatment of panic disorder. These are that agoraphobics fear that escape may be embarrassing, or help unavailable in the event of a panic attack, or panic-like symptoms. This seems paradoxical at first, since in reality help probably would be available speedily in a public place. However, there are beliefs which might make one less optimistic in such a situation. One would be that one doubted one's own ability to cope or get help, and another would be a lack of trust that others would be at all willing to help. Behavioural experiments such as those described above are helpful in getting patients to test their interpersonal predictions about the consequences of panicking in various situations. However, it may also be necessary to use schema change techniques to work on longstanding core beliefs, as described below.

It is interesting to note that as in a previous study of the images of patients with hypochondriasis (Wells & Hackmann, 1993) recurrent images accompanying anxiety have proved extremely useful clinically in understanding the full complexity of people's fears. In both disorders images illuminate the interpersonal cost aspect of the feared catastrophe, including fears about the lack of coping strategies and rescue factors.

Dealing with Anything Else which still Motivates Avoidance when the Catastrophic Interpretations have been Removed or Greatly Reduced

In some cases, such as the two described above, there has been a long-standing pattern of interpersonal problems, which was the background on which the panic disorder and/or agoraphobia developed. Working in the here and now on the probability, cost, coping and rescue aspects of the feared catastrophes may not be enough in itself to overcome the pattern of avoidance and fear. In chronic, severe agoraphobia the Axis I disorder can have its roots in avoidant or dependent personality disorder, with long-standing beliefs about the self, the world and other people. In addition to Axis I work the Axis II work may also need to be done, as outlined by Beck, Freeman et al. (1990), and Young (1990). It should be stressed that cases like these are the small minority, and most cases can be speedily improved or cured with the use of skilfully applied Axis I techniques, such as those described above.

Paul felt rather better after doing some of the experiments described in the last section, but was still inclined to have phases of having panic attacks, followed by resumed avoidance. One day whilst dwelling on the image described above he suddenly exclaimed that he knew where it came from. When he was 3 years old he had been taken to hospital because he was sick, and left there without explanation by his parents, who promised to come back, but did not do so for three days. At first he concluded he must be lost, and told the nurses his address, hoping they would take him home. When they ignored this he decide that his parents must have found a way to get rid of him. He knew he was an unwanted child, in a family with four children, a sick mother and a poor father. The idea that he was unwanted and unloved had persisted from that time, and he imagined that if he was admitted to hospital he would be kept there for ever, and would not be visited or rescued by anyone. This memory was 'repaired' using imagery techniques like those described by Edwards (1990), as part of the work on his avoidant personality disorder. The memory was reframed as meaning that although his parents left him without explanation they did so because this was hospital in the 1950s, and they did in fact love him very much. The change in meaning was brought about by him imagining the scene in his parents' home, at the point at which they were considering whether to send him to hospital. Into this he inserted an image of his adult self bursting in through the door in a blaze of light, and warning his parents not to do it, or (if they must send him to hospital) at least to explain to him that they did love him, and would soon be coming to take him home. This work produced more dramatic and lasting improvement than any other intervention. He felt more secure in his present day relationships, and therefore less anxious about being separated temporarily from people like his wife and children. This appeared to be because his basic belief that he was unlovable appeared to have been modified by the 'repair' of this early memory.

Linette (who was severely agoraphobic) overcame her panic attacks and agoraphobia to a marked extent, but remained afraid of getting lost, and never being able to rejoin those she loved. She said she just hated the feeling of being alone. She had a memory which frequently came to her when she was afraid of being separated from home. She saw herself alone in her child-minder's kitchen, with a little cat. She was staring at the wall and feeling very afraid that no-one would ever arrive to collect her. The child-minder had left her thinking that her aunt would soon come to pick her up, but this had not happened for several hours. As well as being haunted by this memory she pictured getting better as being like going through a wall, and leaving her family behind. For her getting better threatened her attachment to others. In therapy she drew herself and the wall, and in a later session she drew her family going through the wall with her, and all the nice places they would then be able to visit. She also drew herself moving freely through a gap in the wall, and moving back whenever she wanted to. These sessions helped her understand which childhood experiences had made her vulnerable to developing agoraphobia, and gave her the courage to begin to explore the world more widely, either accompanied by her family, or on her own.

Removing any other Remaining Blocks to Progress

Sometimes, despite all the best efforts of therapist and patient, there remain blocks which make progress extremely difficult. Examples would be: superstitious fears of trying to get better, in case this tempts providence (a belief also sometimes encountered in hypochondriasis, Wells & Hackmann, 1993); or a fear that if the person were to get better after long illness this would mean that they had been to blame for their illness, and could have got better before. Once again the therapist has to use ingenuity to devise appropriate experiments, and somewhat unorthodox methods may have to be used.

Gemma (also mentioned above) felt afraid to work at therapy and risk improving. She had a firmly held belief that there was no point in being positive, as it invariably led to being struck down by fate. She therefore took care to hold on to a pessimistic, avoidant way of life. In therapy she and the therapist both tried acting in a negative way for a week, and then acting in a positive way in the following week. She was reassured to find that nothing untoward occurred during the second week. Nevertheless therapy got stuck, because she was also worried that if she got better others would blame her for her years of illness. In the end this was resolved by putting her on a high dose of imipramine for some months. She was then able to put all that she had learned about agoraphobia, panic and her avoidant personality into practice, and she was also able to cure a friend of panic attacks. The imipramine gave her extra courage to test out new ways of reacting, and also made her feel better about what other people might think of her recovery. She was weaned off the medication seven years ago, and has never looked back.

SUMMARY

Cognitive therapy has a great deal to offer in the treatment of panic disorder and agoraphobia. However, therapists will need plenty of practice at thinking on their feet and making use of their observations before feeling competent in this area. Some clients pose tougher problems for the therapist, who will need to be aware of cognitive and emotional avoidance, multiple subtle safety behaviours, and the interpersonal cost issues of feared catastrophes. In some cases there may be unusual beliefs supporting reluctance to change, and long-standing issues which make being independent seem threatening. Such issues will need to be tackled in therapy.

A fully comprehensive model of panic disorder and agoraphobia needs to encompass observations such as the fact that agoraphobics are more likely to have social evaluative concerns than panic patients without agoraphobia, they have a lower levels of perceived self-efficacy, and less hope that others will be willing to help them if they are in distress. It also appears that in line with Bowlby's work (1969, 1973) some agoraphobics may also have problems with separation anxiety, and may have childhoods characterised by insecure attachment. It is interesting that Deltito et al. (1986) found that whilst there was a 60% incidence of school phobia in agoraphobics there was not a single case in the patients with panic disorder without a history of agoraphobia. Also some agoraphobics have a tendency to find it difficult to recognise, accept and express negative feelings. They may also be motivated to try to avoid thinking about unpleasant things. All these tendencies can present obstacles to the smooth application of cognitive therapy for panic, and so therapeutic strategies will have to be devised to deal with them.

The major areas of difficulty when working with panic disorder and agoraphobia have been outlined in this chapter, together with some ideas about how to work with them. Despite the complexities, the results can be extremely rewarding, when after weeks of avoidance and evasion something finally falls into place and large areas of life are finally reclaimed.

Dawn had been housebound with severe agoraphobia since the birth of her second child, five years previously. She had not been able to leave the house alone with any of her children during this time, even to play in the garden. Her therapy sessions were often cancelled at the last moment, with excuses, and many weeks of therapy went by before she could be persuaded to step outside her front gate. However, when she finally tried some simple behavioural experiments in the street she was delighted to find that she did not faint or fall down. Encouraged by this she walked with the therapist and her youngest child to a park at the end of the road. The child was full of joy as he played on the slide and swings in the lovely spring sunshine. Following this experience Dawn was able to take the children to school each day, and to help in the classroom for a couple of days each week, as well as taking them on outings with her husband or sister. Although the cure was not complete the quality of life for the family was greatly enhanced.

REFERENCES

Amercian Psychiatric Association (1980). *Diagnostic and Statistical Manual of Mental Disorders*. Washington, DC: American Psychiatric Association.

American Psychiatric Association (1995) *Diagnostic and Statistical Manual of Mental Disorders*. (4th edn). Washington, DC: American Psychiatric Association.

Arntz, A. & van den Hout, M. (1996). Psychological treatments of panic disorder without agoraphobia: Cognitive therapy versus applied relaxation. *Behaviour Research and Therapy*, **34**, 113–121.

Beck, A. T., Emery, G. & Greenberg, R. L. (1985). *Anxiety Disorders and Phobias*. New York: Basic Books.

Beck, A. T., Freeman, A. & associates. (1990). *Cognitive Therapy of Personality Disorders*. New York: Guilford.

Beck, A. T., Sokol, L., Clark, D. A., Berchick, B. & Wright, F. (1992). Focused cognitive therapy of panic disorder: A crossover design and one year follow-up. *American Journal of Psychiatry*, **147**, 778–783.

Bowlby, J. (1969). Attachment and loss. In *Attachment*. New York: Basic Books.

Bowlby, J. (1973). Attachment and loss: Separation anxiety and anger. In *Attachment*. New York: Basic Books.

Chambless, D. L. & Goldstein, A. J. (1982). *Agoraphobia: Multiple Perspectives on Theory and Treatment*. New York: Wiley.

Chambless, D. L. & Gracely, E. (1989). Fear of fear and the anxiety disorders. *Cognitive Therapy and Research*, **13**, 9–20.

Clark, D. M. (1986). A cognitive approach to panic. *Behaviour Research and Therapy*, **24**, 461–470.

Clark, D. M. (1996). Panic disorder: From theory to therapy. In P. M. Salkovskis (Ed.), *Frontiers of Cognitive Therapy*. New York: Guilford.

Clark, D. M., Salkovskis, P. M., Hackmann, A., Middleton, H., Anastasiades, P. & Gelder, M. G. (1994). A comparison of cognitive theory, applied relaxation imipramine in the treatment of panic disorder. *British Journal of Psychiatry*, **164**, 759–769.

Clark, D. M., Salkovskis, P. M., Hackmann, A., Wells, A. & Gelder, M. G. (1995). *A comparison of standard and brief cognitive therapy for panic disorder*. Paper presented at the World Congress of Behavioural and Cognitive Therapies, 10–15 July.

Clum, G. & Knowles. (1991). Why do some people with panic disorders become avoidant? A review. *Clinical Psychology Review*, **11**, 295–313.

de Ruiter, C. & Garssen, B. (1989). Social anxiety and fear of bodily sensations in panic disorder and agoraphobia: a matched comparison. *Journal of Psychopathology and Behavioural Assessment*, **11**, 175–184.

Deltito, J. A., Perugi, G., Maremmani, I., Mignani, V. & Cassano, G. B. (1986). The importance of separation anxiety in the differentiation of panic disorder from agoraphobia. *Psychiatric Developments*, **3**, 227–236.

Edwards, D. J. (1990). Cognitive therapy and the restructuring of early memories through guided imagery. *Journal of Cognitive Psychotherapy*, **4**, 33–50.

First, M. B., Spitzer, R. L., Gibbon, M. & Williams, J. B. W. (1995). The structured clinical interview for DSM-III-R personality disorders (SCID-II): I. Description. *Journal of Personality Disorders*, **9**, 83–91.

Gittelman-Klein, R. & Klein, D. (1984). Relationship between separation anxiety and panic agoraphobic disorders. *Psychopathology*, **17**, 56–65.

Goldstein, A. J. & Chambless, D. L. (1978). A re-analysis of agoraphobia. *Behavior Therapy*, **9**, 47–59.

Goldstein, A. J. & Stainback, B. (1991). *Overcoming Agoraphobia: Conquering Fear of the Outside World*. New York: Viking Penguin.

Hackmann, A. (1997). The transformation of meaning in cognitive therapy. In M. Power & C. R. Brewin (Eds.), *The Transformation of Meaning in Psychological Therapies*. Chichester: Wiley.

Hackmann, A. & Surawy, C. (1997). Recurrent images and memories in agoraphobia. *In preparation*.

Hoffart, A. (1995). Cognitive mediators of situational fear in agoraphobia. *Journal of Behaviour Therapy and Experimental Psychiatry*, **26**, 313–320.

Kleiner, L. & Marshall, W. (1987). The role of interpersonal problems in the development of agoraphobia with panic attacks. *Journal of Anxiety Disorders*, **1**, 313–324.

Margraf, J. & Schneider, S. (1991). *Outcome and active ingredients of cognitive behavioural treatments for panic disorder*. Paper presented at Annual Conference of Association for Advancement of Behaviour Therapy, New York, 26 November.

Mathews, A. M., Gelder, M. G. & Johnston, D. W. (1981). *Agoraphobia: Nature and Treatment*. London: Tavistock.

Michelson, L. & Marchione, K. (1989). *Cognitive behavioural, and physiologically-based treatments of agoraphobia: a comparative outcome study.* Patper presented at the AABT, November, Washington D.C.

Öst, L. G. & Westling, B. (1995). Applied relaxation vs. cognitive therapy in the treatment of panic disorder. *Behaviour Research and Therapy,* **33**, 145–158.

Pollard, C. A. & Cox, G. L. (1988). Social-evaluative anxiety in panic disorder and agoraphobia. *Psychological Reports,* **6**, 323–326.

Reich, J., Noyes, R. & Troughton, E. (1987). Dependent personality disorder associated with phobic avoidance in patients with panic disorder. *American Journal of Psychiatry,* **144**, 323–326.

Salkovskis, P. M. (1990). *The nature of and interaction between cognitive and physiological factors in panic attacks and their treatment.* University of Reading: upublished PhD Thesis.

Salkovskis, P. M. (1991). The importance of behaviour in the maintenance of anxiety and panic: A cognitive account. *Behavioural Psychotherapy,* **19**, 6–19.

Salkovskis, P. M. (1996). The cognitive approach to anxiety: Threat beliefs, safety-seeking behaviour and the special case of health anxiety and obsessions. In P. M. Salkovskis (Ed.), *Frontiers of Cognitive Therapy.* New York: Guilford.

Salkovskis, P. M., Clark, D. M. & Gelder, M. G. (1996). Cognition behaviour links in the persistence of panic. *Behaviour Research and Therapy,* **34**, 453–458.

Salkovskis, P. M., Clark, D. M. & Hackmann, A. (1991). Treatment of panic attacks using cognitive therapy without exposure to feared situations or bodily sensations. *Behaviour Research and Therapy,* **29**, 161–166.

Salkovskis, P. M., Clark, D. M., Hackmann, A., Wells, A. & Gelder, M. G. (1997). Cognitive behavioural treatment of agoraphobia: safety behaviours and disconfirmation in therapy. *In preparation.*

Salkovskis, P. M., Clark, D. M., Hackmann, A., Wells, A. & Gelder, M. G. (1997). An experimental investigation of the role of safety behaviours in the maintenance of panic disorder with agoraphobia. *Journal of Abnormal Psychology* (submitted).

Telch, M. J., Brouillard, M., Telch, C. F., Agras, W. S. & Taylor, C. B. (1989). Role of cognitive appraisal in panic-related avoidance. *Behaviour Research and Therapy,* **27**, 373–383.

Wells, A. & Hackmann, A. (1993). Imagery and core beliefs in health anxiety: Content and origins. *Behavioural and Cognitive Psychotherapy,* **21**, 265–273.

Young, J. (1990). *Cognitive Therapy for Personality Disorders: A Schema-focused Approach.* USA: Professional Resource Exchange.

Chapter 3

THE DEVIL IS IN THE DETAIL: CONCEPTUALISING AND TREATING OBSESSIONAL PROBLEMS

Paul M. Salkovskis*, Elizabeth Forrester*, H. Candida Richards* and Norma Morrison†

INTRODUCTION

Cognitive theory allows a clear understanding of both the origin and the maintenance of obsessive-compulsive disorder. The purpose of this chapter is to consider working with complex OCD cases within a cognitive behavioural framework. Some cases may be more complex than others because of largely independent problems pre-dating or coincident with their obsessional problems. We also suggest that, by the very nature of the problem, most OCD cases become more complex with the passing of time as a consequence of the sufferer's often counter-productive continuing efforts to control his or her mind and behaviour. The ways in which sufferers try to do this become more complex (and therefore more difficult to make sense of) as the problem becomes more chronic. Unfortunately, most obsessional patients are referred specifically for CBT some considerable time after the development of their problem. Obsessional concerns frequently change over a period of time, and an individual may evolve from being a checker to a washer to a ruminator, with occasional remissions in OCD symptoms. Additional psychological difficulties (such as depression) may interact with the psychological factors involved in the OCD, resulting

* University of Oxford Department of Psychiatry, and † Department of Clinical Psychology, Warneford Hospital, Oxford, OX3 7JX,UK

Treating Complex Cases: The Cognitive Behavioural Therapy Approach.
Edited by Nicholas Tarrier, Adrian Wells and Gillian Haddock.
© 1998 John Wiley & Sons Ltd.

in a more deeply entrenched set of difficulties. Self-esteem, in particular, is likely to be adversely affected by having chronic OCD. When obsessional thinking has been the guiding principle in a person's life over many years, the development of alternative ways of relating to the world can present a substantial challenge for both patient and therapist.

FUNDAMENTALS OF THE COGNITIVE APPROACH TO OCD

Elevated Responsibility Appraisal

Examination of clinical and research data suggests that a cognitive behavioural theory may provide the best supported and most comprehensive current account of obsessional problems. The theory proposes that people suffering from obsessions do so because they make particularly negative appraisals of intrusive thoughts, images, doubts and/or impulses. In particular, they interpret the occurrence and/or content of such intrusions as indicating that they are in some danger of bringing about harm to themselves or other people; that is, they believe that they are in danger of being responsible for such harm. A crucial aspect of this theory is that it is hypothesised that it is this *perception* of responsibility which results in obsessionals making efforts to 'neutralise' intrusions and seeking to prevent the harm which is the focus of their concerns. Responsibility appraisal thus generates both the attempts to neutralise intrusions and doubts, and the discomfort experienced following intrusions. (See Rachman, 1993; Salkovskis, 1985, 1989a, 1996a,b; Salkovskis & Kirk, 1997; Salkovskis, Richards & Forrester, 1995, for more detailed accounts of this theory.)

Responsibility is used in a specific way in the context of the cognitive behavioural theory. The responsibility appraisal which is hypothesised as characterising obsessional problems is operationally defined as *'The belief that one has power which is pivotal to bring about or prevent subjectively crucial negative outcomes. These outcomes are perceived as essential to prevent. They may be actual, that is, having consequences in the real world, and/or at a moral level'* (Salkovskis et al., 1996).

The general structure of this conceptualisation closely parallels the cognitive approach to other types of anxiety disorder in that a particular non-threatening situation becomes the focus of concern as a result of negative misinterpretations of apparently innocuous stimuli; these interpretations are said to arise from particular beliefs concerning danger or threat. The way in which anxiety manifests therefore depends on the focus of threat perceptions and the emotional, behavioural and attentional consequences.

The cognitive behavioural theory regards intrusive thoughts, impulses, images and doubts as an integral part of normal everyday experience. However, when people develop a tendency to misinterpret their own mental activity as indicating personal 'responsibility' it is predicted they will experience the pattern of discomfort and neutralising characteristic of obsessional problems. In those people where this tendency becomes relatively enduring, a full blown obsessional disorder will develop.

Maintenance Mechanisms

The *interpretation* of obsessional intrusions and doubts as indicating increased responsibility has a number of important and interlinked effects: (i) increased discomfort, anxiety and depression; (ii) increased focused attention on these intrusions; (iii) greater accessibility of the original thought and other related ideas; (iv) active and usually counter-productive attempts to reduce the thoughts and decrease or discharge the responsibility which is perceived to be associated with them, including behavioural and cognitive 'neutralising' responses. These may include compulsive behaviour, avoidance of situations related to the obsessional thought, seeking reassurance (having the effect of diluting or sharing responsibility) and attempts to get rid of or exclude the thought from the mind.

Each of these effects contributes not only to the prevention of anxiety reduction but also to increased preoccupation and a worsening spiral of intrusive thoughts (Salkovskis, 1989c) leading to maladaptive affective, cognitive and behavioural reactions. Intrusions interpreted as relevant to responsibility will therefore tend to persist and become the focus of further thought and action; irrelevant ideas can be considered but no further thought or action will ensue. In some instances, where a feared consequence is seen as *imminent*, behavioural responses can have the additional effect of preventing disconfirmation of the person's negative beliefs (Salkovskis, 1996a; c). For example, a patient may believe that failing to wash his hands vigorously for 15 minutes could lead to severe illness in his family. After his having washed in this way, none of his family become ill, providing him with evidence consistent with his initial belief, and leaving the belief intact (or even strengthening it) for subsequent occasions when the thought of contamination occurs again. Unlike other anxiety disorders (with the important exception of hypochondriasis), the feared catastrophes are more often seen as likely to occur at some distant time (e.g. family developing cancer, the patient going to hell after they die), and this makes disconfirmation difficult. Even in the washing example given above, the fear might be that infection in family members may be present but undetected for some months or even years before causing harm.

Appraisal of responsibility arising from the *occurrence* and *content* of intrusions can be at least partially independent, although often linked. A patient who was unable to get rid of bizarre and unpleasant thoughts and images interpreted this apparent resistance to his efforts at control as a sign that he was in danger of losing control and behaving in some unpredictable and violent way. He became preoccupied with efforts intended to prevent unwanted thoughts from coming in to his mind, and attempted to regiment his thinking. In this instance, it was primarily the *occurrence* of intrusions which was misinterpreted. In another example, a patient experienced repeated and vivid images of herself lying dead in front of her local shop, and of her family assembled round a coffin in which she lay. She interpreted the occurrence of *these particular images* as a prediction of the future, and was especially disturbed by the fact that the images represented real places and people, and by their vividness and detail. Here, the *content* of the intrusions was of relatively greater importance.

Although these two facets of appraisal are most commonly linked in obsessional problems ('Having *these* thoughts means that I am a danger to my family'), this is not necessarily obvious in every instance. For example, a positive thought might be negatively appraised if it occurs incongruously on a sad occasion (e.g. an erotic thought at a funeral). When the *meaning* of the particular thought occurring is taken into account, however, the link between occurrence and content is usually evident.

In order to prevent the occurrence of intrusions and/or be aware of and limit the implications for responsibility, the obsessional patient often feels that it is necessary to pay close attention to his or her mental processes. The deployment of effortful strategies and attention towards the *control of mental activity* involves a variety of phenomena which may all contribute to the experience of obsessional symptoms and their maintenance. These may include, for example, attempts to be sure of the accuracy of one's memory, to take account of all factors in one's decisions, to prevent the occurrence of unacceptable material, to ensure that an outcome has been achieved when the difference between achieving it and not achieving it is imperceptible (for example, deciding that one's hands are 'properly' clean after washing in order to remove 'contamination'). The choice of strategies is best understood from a safety-seeking perspective; the patient will react in ways which he or she believes are most likely to be effective in reducing the threat of being responsible for avoidable harm. Safety behaviours can thus be directed at either *preventing harm* or *preventing responsibility for harm*. However, behaving in this way is likely to inflate the perception of responsibility further. This process seems to be like the common inference that 'I'm running so there must be something very scary about this situation'. The key belief may be that if one accepts that one can influence an event then one assumes responsibility for the possible outcomes. That is, by acting to *reduce* one's responsibility, one implicitly accepts the implication of *being* responsible in the first place. The short term 'evasion' or transfer of responsibility therefore has the additional unwanted effect of strengthening more enduring beliefs concerning the extent to which one is responsible overall.

A further complication presented by a number of safety strategies is that, by their nature, they appear to produce directly counter-productive effects. The person who 'stares harder and harder at the switch' to make themselves 'totally believe that it is off', for instance, usually experiences a degree of dissociation due to their fixed concentration on one unmoving point whilst at the same time closely monitoring mental processes (being sure that it is off), and this feeling of *un*reality is the precise opposite of the sureness which they explicitly seek. Research by Richards (Richards, 1995; 1997), suggests that OCD clients who engage in prolonged rituals often operate different termination criteria for finishing a neutralising action from those used by normals executing similar (but not prolonged) neutralising. Generally speaking, these OCD sufferers place more emphasis on internally referenced criteria, such as 'feeling sure', 'remembering clearly' and 'it feeling just right' relative to externally referenced criteria like 'the dirt had gone', than did the non-obsessional neutralisers. Conscious and deliberate efforts to feel extra sure or remember extra clearly, however, tend to generate doubt as opposed to yielding certainty, as well as creating the implicit expectation for future occasions that substantial effort may be required before a satisfactory endstate is reached. Clinical experience suggests that many obsessionals who use these internal criteria either never achieve the feeling they seek or find that, at the end of a long period of trying, they feel further from the desired state than at the start. For example, a patient who bathed for eight hours each day in an attempt to 'feel clean' would invariably leave the bath feeling dirtier than when he had begun.

Dysfunctional Assumptions and Thinking Errors

The cognitive theory proposes that people are predisposed to making particular appraisals because of assumptions which are learned from childhood onwards or as a result of unusual or extreme events and circumstances. Some assumptions which characterise OCD patients are described in Salkovskis (1985) and include:

'Having a thought about an action is like performing the action'.

'Failing to prevent (or failing to try to prevent) harm to self or others is the same as having caused the harm in the first place.'

'Responsibility is not reduced by other factors such as something being improbable.'

'Not neutralising when an intrusion has occurred is similar or equivalent to seeking or wanting the harm involved in the intrusion to happen.'

'One should (and can) exercise control over one's thoughts.'

If someone holds these attitudes very strongly, then the overt and covert behaviours characteristic of people suffering from obsessional problems tend to follow naturally.

The effects of these type of assumptions are often described in terms of 'thinking errors' (Beck, 1976); thinking errors are characteristic distortions which influence whole classes of reactions. Thinking errors are not of themselves pathological; in fact, most people make judgements by employing a range of 'heuristics', many of which can be fallacious (Nisbett, 1980). The cognitive hypothesis suggests that OCD patients show a number of characteristic thinking errors which link to their obsessional difficulties; probably the most typical and important is the idea that.

'any influence over outcome = responsibility for outcome'

Another important type of thinking error related to responsibility perceptions has been identified by Shafran and her colleagues (Shafran, Thordarson & Rachman, 1996). 'Thought–action fusion' refers to three broad classes of belief: (i) that thinking something makes it more likely to happen (thought as cause); (ii) that thinking something is morally equivalent to doing it (sin by thought); or (iii) that because a thought has occurred this reflects the person's true wishes (thought as a reflection of true feelings and wishes).

STANDARD COGNITIVE BEHAVIOURAL TREATMENT

Although it is structured and focused, cognitive behaviour therapy should not, of course, be practised prescriptively. The broad aim of therapy is to allow the obsessional patient to identify their present beliefs about the problem (e.g. 'I am a danger to myself or others if I fail to act to prevent harm') and to help them consider a less threatening alternative (e.g. 'I am worried about the possibility of being a danger to myself or others and therefore I attempt to cope by using counter-productive strategies'). It is, however, possible to identify a number of steps or stages in CBT for obsessional problems. These are:

1. Assessment, in which the therapist and patient work together to develop and agree a comprehensive cognitive behavioural account of the

maintenance of their obsessional problems. Reaching this shared understanding involves the identification of key distorted beliefs, and the collaborative construction of a non-threatening *alternative account* of their obsessional experience and preoccupations to allow the patient to explicitly test beliefs about the nature of their problem, including their inflated sense of responsibility for harm to themselves and/or others.

2. Detailed identification and self-monitoring of obsessional thoughts and the patients' appraisal of these thoughts, combined with exercises designed to help the patient to modify their responsibility beliefs (for example, by using behavioural experiments intended to illustrate the effects of particular obsessional coping strategies and through the use of the modified daily record of dysfunctional thoughts; for an example of such a record, see Figure 3.1).

3. Discussion techniques for challenging appraisals and basic assumptions upon which these are based. Normalising the person's experience is often emphasised. Frequently, the aim is modification of the patient's negative beliefs about the extent of their own personal responsibility (for example, by having the patient describe all contributing factors for a feared outcome and then dividing the relative contributions in a pie chart in order to help the person deal with the tendency to see responsibility in all-or-nothing terms).

4. Behavioural experiments to illustrate the counter-productive effects of supposed safety strategies such as thought suppression or internally referenced criteria for terminating action. A particularly effective technique is to ask the client to alternate their current strategy with a more adaptive one and observe the results of each. A client who was instructed to use only his 'feeling sure' strategy for determining whether his alarm was set, on some days of the week, and only his 'intellectual recognition that the switch was up' on the remainder, for instance, swiftly discovered that *trying* to feel sure actually made him more uncomfortable and decreased his perceived certainty. Such 'alternating treatments' experiments require careful setting up and the client has to record the outcomes. They are used to illustrate how these apparently helpful strategies are actually maintaining the problem.

5. Identification of the way in which neutralising increases preoccupation and anxiety in the longer term. Behavioural experiments evaluate the effects of not neutralising as opposed to immediate neutralising. This is usually done in the context of having the patient make specific predictions about what will happen to factors such as their negative beliefs, degree of preoccupation and doubt, discomfort and urge to neutralise if they do and do not neutralise (Salkovskis et al., 1997).

6. Helping patients to identify and modify underlying general assumptions (such as 'not trying to prevent harm is as bad as making it happen

IDENTIFYING MISINTERPRETATIONS

Situation in which the intrusion occurred and any trigger which set it off	Intrusive thought image or impulse	What the intrusion meant to you (the negative significance you attached to it)	Belief rating for significance (0-100)	Discomfort when intrusion occurred (0-100)	What neutralizing response (e.g. checking, putting right, pushing idea out of your mind) you wanted to make and in what way this seemed as if it would help	Strength of urge to neutralize (0-100)
Seeing a paper / tv story about a missing child	Thought that I am the type of person who is attracted to children.	That I could be attracted to children and therefore I am sick, abnormal + evil	40	90	Thinking of an attractive woman	90
Hearing people talk about young sons / daughters	Again the sense that I am attracted to children	That I am sick, abnormal and evil	40	90	Thinking of an attractive woman	90
Driving to work and seeing children going to school	That I am attracted to these children.	Sick, abnormal, different	45	90	Thinking of an attractive woman	90
Seeing stories of child abuse	That I have the same feelings if not intent as these people	That I am sick, abnormal and could be an evil person	40	90	Thinking of an attractive woman	90

Figure 3.1   Dysfunctional thought record adapted for use in obsessional problems to identify appraisals and linked neutralising with a clinical example.

deliberately') which give rise to their misinterpretation of their own mental activity.

The general style of therapy is that of guided discovery. Through questioning and discussion, patient and therapist reach a shared understanding of the nature of the problem which the patient is suffering from (see Salkovskis & Warwick, 1988; Salkovskis, 1989b; Salkovskis & Kirk, 1997 for a description of treatment strategies).

WHERE THINGS CAN GO WRONG: PREVENTING, PREDICTING AND SOLVING PROBLEMS IN THE TREATMENT OF OCD

The Importance of Assessment and Formulation

Proper assessment and formulation are crucial to dealing with complex cases. The therapist needs to resist the temptation to begin treatment before a good working understanding is achieved, as this will almost invariably lead to misdirected treatment strategies. The temptation to 'do something, no matter what' is often strongest in the most severe, complex and chronic of cases, where the patient tends to be particularly distressed and the assessment and formulation particularly difficult. Assessments may prove problematic for a number of reasons; for example, the patient may be so accustomed to their difficulties that they unwittingly minimise the extent to which their OCD interferes with their lives, and may have lost sight of how their own behaviours deviate from the norm. Often, patients may be extremely embarrassed about what they actually do, or the kinds of intrusive thoughts that they experience (however, as we shall go on to see, it is not only embarrassment that prevents disclosure of the exact content of these thoughts). The focus of the problem ('diagnosis') is not always clear, and it can be especially difficult to differentiate obsessional ruminations from worries associated with GAD as many of the concerns are often quite similar. Since obsessional problems tend to be highly idiosyncratic it means that the formulation must take into account the various facets of the patient's experience.

It is fundamental to the practice of cognitive therapy that the therapist and patient work together to reach a shared understanding (conceptualisation) of the way the patient's problem works, and in OCD reaching this understanding is itself a crucial component of treatment. The most effective way of changing a misinterpretation (whether it be of a symptom, a situation or a thought) is to help the person come up with an alternative less threatening interpretation of their experience. At the beginning of therapy patients usually believe that, to a greater or lesser extent, their problem is that they are in danger of some terrible catastrophe. If this belief is held very strongly, the patient is unlikely to engage properly in psychologically (or psychiatrically) based treatment. For example, the obsessional patient believes that his thoughts mean that he is a child molester, a potential murderer, a blasphemer and so on. Given such beliefs it is not surprising that he seeks to deal with the situation by fighting his thoughts and neutralising any consequences of their occurrence in attempts to ensure that he cannot be responsible for any harm or be otherwise blamed. It is therefore necessary that in the early stages of treatment the patient is helped to see that there may be an alternative explanation of the difficulties they are experiencing. The patient is introduced to an idiosyncratically based cognitive model which offers a quite different and less threatening account of their problems. The therapist and patient work together to draw a diagram summarising the formulation agreed, using the specific beliefs and reactions discussed during the session. Figure 3.2 shows the general form this will usually take. Components are added or removed according to the specific pattern of problems experienced by the patient, and their own words are used throughout.

This idiosyncratic version of the diagram is used in the discussion as the key alternative explanation of the patient's problems.

In the example used above, it is not that he is a child molester but rather that he is *worried about and believes* that he might be a child molester and is therefore plagued more and more by the very intrusive thoughts which he seeks to exclude as a result of his fear and failed (and counter-productive) coping attempts. For treatment to be effective, it is vital that the patient agrees that therapeutic strategies should be aimed at reducing such worries rather than the fruitless attempts to reduce risk (which are also likely to result in a worsening of the worries). The formulation should help him understand why this is so.

Throughout treatment the two possible explanations for the patient's problems are considered alongside each other. The patient is invited to consider how the two alternative views match up to their experience, and which, at any given time, they are using to understand their situation.

Home Visits

For OCDs with compulsive rituals, it is important to include home visits. At the assessment stage, the reason for this is that the patient's description of their rituals may not reflect the extent to which their activities deviate from the norm. An example of this is a woman who, amongst a wealth of

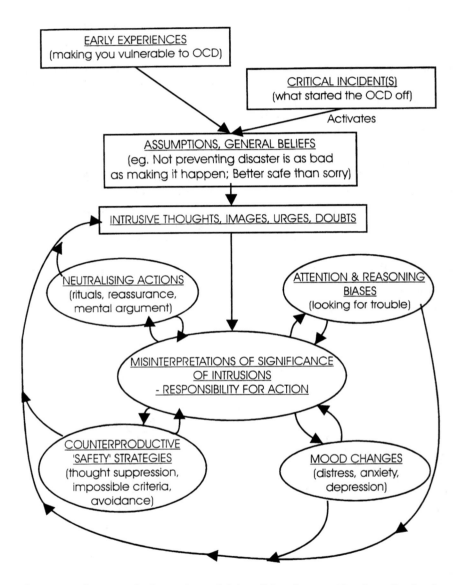

Figure 3.2   Integrated schematic model describing the cognitive hypothesis of the origins and maintenance of obsessional problems.

other obsessional concerns, explained how she was compelled to vacuum the house daily and that this would take up the whole day. One might assume that the reason for this being so time-consuming is that she did an extremely thorough job, moving furniture and vacuuming in every corner. However, when observed in action the picture was quite different: she would commence with getting the vacuum cleaner from the cupboard, washing her hands thoroughly, and then soaking some kitchen paper with disinfectant which was used to wipe the soles of the special slippers reserved for household chores. After this, the vacuum cleaner would be thoroughly wiped with disinfectant before a small area (approx. 1 sq ft) would be vacuumed. Slipper soles would again be wiped before she was able to step on to the 'clean' area. The vacuum hose would have to be disinfected again, as she could not be sure that it had not inadvertently touched an 'unclean' area of the floor and become contaminated. Progress with the actual vacuuming was naturally extremely slow, and extreme care would be taken not to come into contact with any of the furniture or other items in a room that might be 'unclean', such as the waste paper bin. She was unable even to contemplate vacuuming into the corners or behind any pieces of furniture as it posed too great a threat, and also would potentially prolong the already lengthy period of time that vacuuming normally took her.

During the treatment phase, home visits are necessary when compulsive activities cannot be easily replicated in the therapist's office, or when the necessary triggers would not occur outside the home. This may include compulsions and rituals involving bathing or handling pets, for example, where facilities to work with these difficulties may not be available in the clinical setting.

Specifying Goals

As with any problem, it is necessary to set out some mutually agreed goals for therapy which are realistic and achievable within the course of therapy. Although OCD patients do not have a monopoly on unrealistic expectations, many appear to have the goal that they would like to be free of unwanted thoughts. Without dismissing this outright, the therapist needs to explore how realistic this is, and how life would be if we never experienced intrusive thoughts, and were instead obliged to choose what we were going to think about next. Socratic questioning here usually swiftly leads to the realisation that deliberately deciding what to think at all times would present an intolerable burden and prevent any novel and creative insights and ideas.

It is also important to explain that obsessional concerns reflect a kind of sensitivity which is unlikely to disappear completely. However, it would be desirable to be able to disregard unwanted intrusive thoughts and not be bound by the compulsions and rituals that currently limit functioning and cause considerable distress.

Normalising the Obsessional Experience

It is reported that 90% of the population experience intrusive thoughts indistinguishable from obsessional thoughts (Rachman & de Silva, 1978; Salkovskis & Harrison, 1984), so they are not an abnormal phenomenon *per se*. This means that a major goal of therapy is to help the patient accept that intrusive thoughts are likely to occur and should not be controlled, suppressed or neutralised. This involves helping the patient understand the creative and problem-solving function of intrusions (Salkovskis, 1989c), and the way in which attempts to control intrusions are counter-productive.

As already described, it is the way the obsessional patient interprets the occurrence and content of their intrusive thoughts which results in discomfort and neutralising reactions. Many patients (and clinicians) consider the obsessional beliefs to be so strange as to amount to insanity (see, for example, Enright, 1996). An example of this is thought–action fusion, in which people are afraid that thinking about something unpleasant may make it happen.

In the course of discussions, the patient should be encouraged to consider his or her own intrusive thoughts—both obsessional and non-obsessional—in order to see for himself that discrimination is exercised. It is also valuable to use examples of situations in which intrusive thoughts may gain salience for non-clinicals such as a sudden thought concerning the whereabouts of one's passport—no action is generally taken if lying in the bath at home, but if the same thought occurred on the way to the airport …

Part of the problem with successful normalising is that many therapists believe obsessional patients' beliefs to be particularly bizarre. In workshops training mental health professionals to treat obsessional problems, the first author conducts the following exercise, which the reader may wish to try. First, think of the person for whom you care most in the world. Now take a pen and write:

'I wish that _____ would die violently this afternoon',
completing the phrase with your loved one's name.

Our experience is that the majority of professionals taking part in training will not comply. Those who do tend to experience some discomfort, and many of these then score out the words or tear the paper up (thanks to Roz Shafran and Jack Rachman for this idea). When working with people suffering from obsessional problems, explaining this exercise and its results in people not suffering from obsessions can be helpful in the normalising process. Discussion can usefully focus on why this is problematic, how people can overcome these problems, and why someone who is particularly sensitive to feeling responsible for harm coming to others might find it particularly worrying (and common) to think such things.

Disconfirmation

It is easy to fall into the trap of attempting to disconfirm worrisome thoughts. This is particularly likely when the logic of each of the patient's concerns appears to be easily refuted; this leads to a chain of reassurance, emergence of a new doubt, further reassurance and so on. For example, the person who is afraid that they may have said something obscene in a social situation can be helped by the therapist to examine the reaction of other people at the time. However, some concern is likely to recur in subsequent social situations, requiring further discussion and, in effect, reassurance, and so on. The therapist also needs to bear in mind that obsessional concerns usually include negative consequences in the longer term, such as foreseeing harm that may happen at any time in the future. For example, a patient believed that a failure to ritualise in response to specific situations could lead to a family member having an accident at *any* future time. Obsessional patients sometimes ask the therapist to help them be certain that the things they fear will not happen if they no longer neutralise. In discussion or role-play, the patient considers the advice they would offer a friend seeking such certainty. Having established that it is not possible, the focus is turned to the likely consequences of continuing their current pattern of neutralising, avoidance and other safety strategies. The therapist aims for the conclusion that what *can* be guaranteed is that continuing in such a way will ensure the persistence of the problem.

Again, it is important to stress that the fundamental basis of obsessional problems lies in the way that the patient interprets or appraises intrusive thoughts and related mental phenomena. It is particularly important to note that, although in many anxiety disorders it is possible to help the patient change their beliefs through the process of the disconfirmation of the feared consequences (Salkovskis, 1991), this is seldom true in obsessional problems (Salkovskis, 1996a). The patient needs to be reminded that there are really two possible explanations for the problems they are experiencing: it could be that they really are in danger of causing harm or failing to prevent harm and that they therefore have to do everything they possibly can to avert such harm; or it could be that they are someone who is worried about harm and that their problems are coming from this particular anxiety and concern rather than from any actual reality of harm. It is emphasised at every opportunity that these two different views make contradictory predictions about what would be helpful. In particular, it is stressed that constant effort to prevent something which one is concerned about is inevitably going to have the effect of increasing preoccupation.

As well as the difficulties of attempting to disconfirm some potential future event, a further problem is presented by the fact that a number of obsessional concerns regard the kinds of risks that we all face—a car accident or developing cancer, for instance. This leads us to one of the key issues in therapy—how we all manage to live with these risks. Patients often seek a recipe for resolving this problem ('How often should I wash my hands ?'; 'When should I check?'). The idea is that they should be helped to arrive at their own general formula rather than being given a specific one by the therapist. Specific answers such as 'Twice should always be enough' are unlikely to produce more than a brief respite, if any. The discussion focuses on factors such as the pros and cons of taking or eliminating risks and ways of bringing about behavioural change to increase subjective comfort at risk taking (e.g. changing the style with which life is approached). For example, someone troubled by obsessional checking asked the first author whether it was possible to offer them a guarantee that, if they only checked their door once, they would not be burgled. The response was that he could not. However, it was possible to guarantee that, if he continued to check at his present level, he would continue to be tortured by obsessional problems. The patient was then asked to imagine that it was possible to be free of his obsessional problem. If this could be guaranteed, would he be prepared to give up all the valuables in his house to make it happen? Would it be worth it ? It was pointed out that in fact he didn't have to give up his valuables, just to 'risk' them. Another useful analogy is with insurance; sometimes the cost of insuring is greater than the risk justifies. Discussion may lead some sufferers to conclude that the obsessional problem is more unpleasant than the consequences which it is intended to avert. It is helpful to focus this discussion on the way in which the obsessional often weighs the short-term consequences of compulsive behaviour against the long-term consequences of making a mistake. For example, going back to check his door only takes a patient 15 minutes, and this seems trivial against being burgled. However, the more appropriate comparison is between the consistently repetitive, distressing and time-consuming pattern of checking typical of the obsessional problem on the one hand and the *possibility* of being burgled on the other. To this can be added some consideration of the likelihood of the obsessional behaviour preventing the feared consequence.

Sometimes, discussion of risk taking reveals highly idiosyncratic cost issues; there are some things which the person is not prepared to risk being responsible for, however remote that risk may seem. In such instances, it is helpful to work with the patient to identify the way in which elevated 'awfulness' estimates are increasing anxiety and neutralising. Frequently, this is the awfulness of being responsible for harm, and therapy needs to involve modification of general assumptions concerning the implications of responsibility for harm. Helping the patient to identify the origins of inflated cost estimates can suggest ways of challenging such estimates.

In some cases, however, it *is* possible to help the patient disconfirm their feared catastrophes, although this is seldom a first line approach in therapy and experience suggests that it can be a risky strategy in that it can lead to checking/reassurance spirals. Disconfirmation-based strategies are most likely to be effective in those whose assessment and formulation indicates that they hold general assumptions concerning thought–action fusion ('thinking/imagining something bad can make it happen'). Initial discussion can focus on the person's evidence for such a belief and the possible mechanism by which such a link might work. A contrast might be drawn with positive thoughts (e.g. 'I will win a prize in the lottery'; 'I will be promoted at work'). The link with anxiety/worry is highlighted as part of the discussion. The therapist might then demonstrate a behavioural experiment on this (e.g. repeatedly saying 'I wish I would have a heart attack right now; I wish my mother would die violently in the next few minutes'). The patient is invited to do something similar, and their reactions to (i) the idea of this and (ii) the reality of doing it are discussed from a cognitive perspective. The exercise is integrated with the formulation, and homework set with the emphasis on the patient taking responsibility for saying and thinking.

Linking the Individual's History to the Formulation

People with a history of obsessive-compulsive disorder are likely to maintain a heightened sense of responsibility for events which may not be completely within their control. Sometimes there are very obvious links between the patient's early experience and their heightened sensitivity to responsibility. A more detailed assessment of the origins of such beliefs can be helpful as a way of challenging these ideas in the present, especially in cases where dysfunctional assumptions about responsibility are extremely difficult to change. For example, the patient can respond to a strongly held unconditional belief by reminding him/herself that this is a product of 'brainwashing'. That is, beliefs which they learned from important authority figures as a child are returning and that they are responding to these as if they were still a child. An alternative is to challenge the idea from an adult perspective and consider whether these beliefs (i) were true then and (ii) are still true now.

It has been suggested that there are at least five characteristic patterns of experience involved in the development of an inflated sense of responsibility (Salkovskis, Shafran, Rachman & Freeston in press). These are: (i) patients who have, from an early age, believed themselves to be crucially responsible, usually as a result of excessive responsibility being placed upon them due to the absence, actions or incompetence of others, for example, the eldest child of a depressed mother and alcoholic father who assumes responsibility for siblings; (ii) patients who have been overprotected to the point of seldom having felt responsible for even minor actions; (iii) people who have had an experience which they erroneously believe indicates that they have caused harm, for example wishing someone dead, followed by their actual death a short time later; (iv) people who have had an experience which has indeed contributed to harm (e.g. the person who left their television on by mistake and whose house subsequently burned down); (v) patients exposed to rigid and extreme codes of conduct and duty.

Sarah was referred with obsessive ruminations about strangling her baby son. Two events from her childhood gave her a strong conviction that she was a potential source of harm to others. When Sarah was 2 years old, her parents fostered a baby girl. Sarah was told by her mother that she came into the room and found Sarah trying to smother the baby with a pillow. Although Sarah has no memory of the actual incident, she remembers being told this frequently by her mother and having the tale repeated many times to others, both within the family and out. She has no idea whether she had been actually trying to do this or whether that was the way her mother chose to interpret the situation. Later, when she was almost 5 years old (just before she started school), she remembers playing with a neighbour's dog and throwing a stick into a lake for it to fetch. The dog went in and drowned. She recalls standing with the neighbour, both of them in tears. These events appear to have fuelled her belief that she could be a potential source of harm to others.

Sarah was helped to challenge her beliefs about being a potential source of harm, ('What sort of mother is likely to be distressed about the possibility of harming her child?'), and helped, through guided discovery, to realise that having a thought is not the same as wanting to carry it out. An intervention that she seemed to find useful was actively producing the thought in an anxiety-provoking situation to test out whether it caused the feared outcome to happen. She would sit for approximately 15 minutes every evening in a darkened room beside the baby's cot and think 'I'm going to strangle Jamie'. (A loop-tape could have been used at this point, but Sarah did not possess a personal stereo.) She rated the level of her anxiety at the beginning of the session and at the end which demonstrated to her that she was not likely to do it because she was thinking it and that the more often she did this, the more her anxiety diminished. She also used imagery techniques, such as turning the image into an amusing scenario, to help her realise that an image is just an image and has no importance. Her belief ratings (that she was a potential source of harm to others) dropped off quite rapidly from 80% to 1% by the end of eight sessions.

Another example is that of Xiaohong, a young Chinese woman with a compulsive checking problem. Xiaohong was brought up in a middle-class intellectual family where honesty, integrity and intellectual achievement were highly valued. As this was during the era of the Cultural Revolution and the Red Guards, this was not a safe time for such families. As a result, from an early age, Xiaohong had been taught to exercise extreme caution about what she was going to say or write. In fact, she can remember being told often by her father, 'Think it three times before you say it'. She also remembers members of her family and friends of the family being arrested and questioned. On one occasion, when she was about 12, her parents were taken away to be questioned and were away for a day and a half. Meanwhile, she was responsible for her younger sister and did not know if her parents would be allowed to return or not. Her early experience was that the world was a dangerous place, that she was responsible for the safety of others, and that it was necessary at all times to exercise a great deal of caution. It is easy to see how assumptions arose such as, 'If I do not take every precaution, bad things will happen', and, 'If there is any possibility that I can influence a negative outcome, then it is my duty to do it'.

The first thing that made a difference for Xiaohong was normalisation of intrusive thoughts as her interpretation of her problem was that she might be going mad. Her beliefs about responsibility were tackled and she was encouraged to take on an increasing amount of responsibility. Her criterion of checking 'till it feels right' was challenged and ERP was introduced as a behavioural experiment. Overestimation of danger was challenged by showing her how to calculate the probability of any catastrophic outcome and her feeling of responsibility was challenged by the use of responsibility pie charts. By the end of 15 sessions, she regarded her problem as 70% improved and was continuing to work on it.

Dealing with Therapist Issues and Problems Which May Threaten the Therapeutic Relationship

Although we have paid quite a lot of attention to the need to develop a collaborative relationship in the therapeutic situation, the actual dynamics of the relationship are often overlooked. In carrying out therapy with obsessional patients, one is no more or less likely than elsewhere to find therapist issues interfering with the course of therapy. Indeed, many of the issues would be identical to those found working with other groups, such as a belief that a lack of progress must signify a lack of effectiveness on the part of the therapist. Therapists may believe that OCD patients are difficult to work with, and that there is seldom much improvement in their condition so that therapy starts with an expectation of failure. At times, the experience of the patient and therapist may be so far apart that it is well nigh impossible for the therapist to empathise in any way with the patient. As the therapist does not share the patient's basic beliefs about the influence of thoughts and about responsibility, the fact that their patient feels compelled to walk backwards round the plum tree 12 times in order to avert any possible danger to himself or his family may appear plain crazy. The opposite situation also occurs, where the therapist indeed shares some of the patient's beliefs, for example that one must do everything one can to protect oneself against germs, or that it is 'tempting fate' to think bad thoughts about a member of the family. This would obviously operate against effective therapy, and therapist-oriented supervision may be crucial here.

Therapists may be particularly likely to encounter problems if they have difficulties with clients who place inordinate emphasis on detail (such that sessions overrun and there is a sense of not being able to see the wood for the trees) as this is a common characteristic in OCD. Sometimes the emphasis on detail masks continued efforts to seek reassurance, and the therapist needs to identify this by asking what the client fears will happen if a particular detail is *not* discussed in therapy, before moving on to conceptualise the role of this reassurance in preventing the client taking the risk of being in a position of full responsibility for themselves. It can also happen that a client will consider it his or her responsibility to communicate *all* details to the therapist in order for the 'cure' to be effective. This can be challenged, using an analogy with a picture postcard. Is the essence of the picture best appreciated by making sure all minute details are painstakingly itemised, or by standing back to gain an overall impression? Understanding and tackling such problems is obviously likely to improve the therapist's disposition toward the client. In many cases, however, certain therapists will specifically need to overcome their own reluctance to interrupt the client's desired agenda (usually such therapists fear they will hurt or 'damage' the client or the bond with the client), whilst others will have to address their own impatience or irritability (usually associated with the perception either that the client is being deliberately obstructive, or with fears that therapy is progressing too slowly so that personal or institutional standards cannot be met).

Many OCD clients have tried throughout their lives to restrict their experience of affect, and this can both frustrate the course of therapy (especially where there is habitual cognitive avoidance that makes the relevant cognitive material difficult to access) and mean that the therapist is blocked from empathising because there is no evident emotion with which to 'connect'. Since identifying 'hot' cognitions is essential for effective cognitive therapy, therapists here need to resist the (often strong) temptation to collude with the client in avoiding 'hot' material for fear that any experience of emotion will be too, or even unbearably, upsetting. Sometimes it is possible to bring beliefs about the dangerousness or undesirability of emotion into the open, make them explicit, and collaboratively set up behavioural experiments to test them. Discussion of the pros and cons of blocking off one's emotions may also be useful. For certain clients, avoidance of emotion may, however, by now be so habitual that more directive encouragement to focus on affect may be required. This is often best done by the therapist working hard to imagine what emotions they themselves would feel in the situations described by the client, and then incorporating suggestions as to possible affect into a summary of what the client has just reported, leaving a pause afterwards to let any affect emerge. For instance, a client who persistently answered questions as to how he *felt*, by instead reiterating lengthy excerpts of his (neutralising) 'rational self-talk', only finally demonstrated emotion when the therapist deliberately prompted him with 'That sounds really *upsetting*' (pause) following a description of boyhood experiences of bullying, academic failure, and harsh criticism from parents. Gentle guiding and collaborative exploration of the client's feelings, and any subsequent reactions to experiencing them, can thus be linked to specific cognitive material of crucial importance in the overall formulation.

Setting up Behavioural Experiments

Salkovskis (1996a) suggested that interactions between cognitive and behavioural elements are involved in the maintenance of all anxiety problems, and discusses the close coordination of both cognitive and behavioural techniques. In a similar way to the cognitive approach to agoraphobia and panic, behavioural experiments are an essential component of therapy for OCD, although they are unlikely to lead to the same 'aha' experience that panic patients get when they drop their safety behaviours, owing to the difference in time spans for the feared disastrous consequence.

Caution should be exercised with the focus of behavioural experiments. Where a patient has concerns regarding contamination with HIV the focus of exposure is not to the HIV virus *per se*, but to toilet door handles, for instance, since avoidance of such a situation is one of the key components fuelling the concern. The therapist is not attempting to disprove the likelihood of contracting HIV but is reinforcing the alternative (psychological) view of their presenting problem as one of worry. Thus, behavioural experiments directly test appraisals, assumptions and processes hypothesised to be involved in the patient's obsessional problems (e.g. demonstrating that attempts to suppress a thought lead to an increase in the frequency with which it occurs, or showing that beliefs such as 'If I think it I therefore want it to happen' are incorrect). Each behavioural experiment is idiosyncratically devised in order to help the patient test their previous (threatening) explanation of their experience against the new (non-threatening) explanation worked out with their therapist. In brief, behavioural experiments may involve a range of strategies including the following broad categories:

1. Behavioural experiments designed to assess the extent to which a particular process may be playing a role in maintaining the patient's fears.
2. Other experiments designed to elicit processes which may be increasing symptoms themselves (such as intrusive thoughts) or the fear and distress associated with these symptoms.
3. Exposure exercises (in ruminations, particularly commonly using loop-tape) where the patient is given the opportunity to discover that repetition of their intrusive thoughts or eliciting stimuli (hopefully, with reduced levels of negative appraisal of responsibility) results in a decrease in the discomfort experience.

Although a great deal of emphasis in the treatment of ruminations is placed upon the usefulness of the loop-tape as an eliciting strategy this particular technique has to be embedded in the overall framework of the cognitive behavioural approach.

CO-MORBIDITY

Often, OCD patients meet criteria for more than one Axis I disorder at once (Rasmussen & Eisen, 1992), which can make conceptualisation and treatment more difficult. The key to dealing with multiple problems is the formulation. This will help identify those cognitive factors which:

- are common to, or underlie, all of the client's problems (see Persons, 1989)
- characterise one disorder but interfere with successful treatment of another
- are specific to just one disorder

On the basis of such a formulation, the therapist can plan how to proceed, and can adjust treatment appropriately when setbacks occur. Generally it tends to be profitable to make (and be able to demonstrate) progress on a specific discrete problem at first, as this builds-up hope, motivation and the credibility of the cognitive behavioural approach. Sometimes, however, any progress will appear to be frustrated by the client's other difficulties, and then it may be important to tackle more common or underlying factors such as pervasive reasoning or attentional biases, or even assumptions and core beliefs. Sharing a simple model of the whole formulation, especially indicating how the different problems fit together in terms of maintenance and origins in early learning experiences, is often immensely encouraging to the client, as it shows that their situation is both comprehensible and alterable, as opposed to being overwhelming or in some sense their 'fault'.

Depression

The most common co-morbid disorder with OCD is depression (Goodwin, Guze & Robins, 1969; Rasmussen & Eisen, 1992; Rosenberg, 1967; Swedo & Rapoport, 1989). It has been suggested that where depression is clearly secondary and of moderate severity, OCD symptoms should be targeted. Secondary depression frequently occurs when OCD has been a chronic problem (a considerable number of patients have been sufferers for many years before they present in therapy, or have had previously unsuccessful treatment), when it occurs as a result of a 'Learned Helplessness' scenario (Abramson, Seligman & Teasdale, 1978). Depression here often has the character of 'demoralisation' and clients can find it empowering to have it thus construed, rather than as an additional 'illness' which compounds their troubles. This formulation can enhance motivation to work on the OCD and its successful treatment should then result in the remission of the depressive symptoms (Yaryura-Tobias & Neziroglu, 1983). If, however, the depression is severe, there is evidence that there will be poor compliance with regard to behavioural interventions such as eliminating neutralising (Foa, 1979; Rachman & Hodgson, 1980) and then it would be more appropriate to target the depression first.

In cognitive terms, depression tends to impede treatment of OCD because it means that the frequency of thoughts concerning defectiveness, incompetence and responsibility for bad things, is likely to be high anyway, and because helplessness, hopelessness, and negative interpretations undermine cognitive and behavioural change. Depressed OCD clients are particularly vulnerable when setbacks occur, and the therapist needs to communicate empathy for the client's position, as the *client* sees it, whilst transmitting a confidence (which the therapist himself or herself may not always feel!) that change *is* both achievable, and, importantly, worth achieving. Considerable reserves of patience and fortitude may be required to deliver this combination over a lengthy time period.

Generalised Anxiety

A less common, but possibly even more troublesome co-morbid condition is generalised anxiety disorder (GAD). The most obvious immediate problem is what to focus on first. In this type of case, careful conceptualisation is even more important than usual as it can prevent the therapist from pursuing fruitless directions.

An example of this was Henry, a businessman in his mid- forties. Henry was referred for treatment for OCD, specifically checking rituals. A history was taken, focusing mainly on this aspect although it was apparent that he had other anxieties. A formulation was worked out, again focusing on the OCD symptoms, and the patient was socialised into the cognitive model. However, it quickly became apparent that this was not appropriate as, every week, Henry arrived with a different set of problems for the agenda, ranging from generalised anxiety to social phobia and low self-esteem, with his checking problem being almost an incidental addition. No sooner had one worry been tackled in therapy before a new set popped up. It became obvious that a new and more all-encompassing formulation was needed to regain some sort of focus. When this was done, with the fundamental focus becoming his low self-esteem and feeling of vulnerability, it was possible to deal with his problems in a way that made both him and the therapist feel more focused, and that made it possible for each intervention to be related back to the formulation.

The previous case illustrates the way in which GAD can be masked by OCD symptoms, the latter often being easier for the patient to articulate because they may be more obvious if they involve an extensive overt compulsive component. However, it is also the case that obsessive ruminators may be either overlooked or misdiagnosed as the symptoms they present with can strongly resemble GAD, especially where worry or mental debate is a prominent neutralising method. The crucial distinction diagnostically, relates to the ego-dystonicity, or otherwise, of the intrusive thought which prompts neutralising. DSM-IV (American Psychiatric Association, 1994) describes ego-dystonicity as referring 'to the individual's sense that the content ... is alien, not within his or her own control, and not the kind of thought that he or she would expect to have'. An obsessional intrusion is, by definition, not experienced (as in GAD) as excessive concern with real-life problems, but is regarded by the sufferer, at least at some point during the disorder, as *in*appropriate in its topic.

Cognitively conceptualised, the combination of GAD and OCD is problematic because the GAD results in a cognitive milieu where high frequencies of thoughts concerning potential catastrophes are generated, and reasoning and attentional biases cause inflated perception of risk; these then propel the individual towards neutralising actions. The temptation for the therapist is often to challenge specific overestimations of risk, but this may offer little benefit, or even prove counterproductive, since:

1. The client's drive to eliminate all uncertainties (Dugas, Freeston & Ladouceur, 1997) may result in him or her assiduously producing flaws in the counter-evidence he or she has just adduced, or else switching to a new source of possible uncertainty or risk. The therapist then usually slips unwittingly into the trap of becoming a semi-permanent reassurance figure!
2. The client may adopt lengthy self-challenge attempts into his or her own neutralising repertoire. This is seldom helpful, since reasoning biases distort the process, and the function served, self-reassurance, prevents the client increasing their tolerance of risk and uncertainty, as is necessary for lasting improvement.

Panic

A somewhat rarer combination is panic and OCD. Most commonly in these cases, the catastrophic misinterpretations which maintain the panic concern ideas of going crazy or losing control over one's mind or behaviour, and are at least partially based on misinterpretations of the occurrence of intrusive thoughts (e.g. 'such weird thoughts must mean I'm going mad') or of the occurrence of compulsive behaviour (e.g. 'if I feel so driven to do this, what other ghastly things might I feel compelled to do?'). It is usually beneficial to begin by cognitive formulation of the panic, then incorporating appropriate normalisation material where needed.

Psychosis

OCD is not infrequently diagnosed in individuals with psychotic disorders such as schizophrenia. To date, there has been no systematic evidence that psychological treatment is helpful with OCD in these circumstances, although general developments in the use of cognitive behavioural approaches with psychosis (Chadwick & Birchwood, 1994; Chadwick & Lowe, 1994; Chadwick et al., 1994; Morrison, Haddock & Tarrier, 1995) clearly hold out promise. Morrison indeed argues that many hallucinatory phenomena themselves represent extreme misinterpretations of intrusive thoughts, and there is some encouraging pilot therapeutic work (Morrison, 1994), focused on remediating such misinterpretations.

Within a pure OCD, phenomena can occur which, to the untrained ear, may sound quasi-psychotic. Very high levels of dissociation may at times be experienced, leading to symptoms being reported unusually. Extreme hypervigilance may provoke occasional perception of trigger stimuli where none are present, as in the case of a client who 'saw' brown marks on towels which were clean. The remainder of the presentation, however, generally clarifies the diagnosis, since the unusual symptoms are limited to areas where the person is obsessional.

Sometimes an OC problem does form on the basis of a psychotic delusion. For example, William was referred for help with an obsessional problem with number-plates. He would stand at the corner of a street waiting to cross the road, but unable to do so until a car with the 'right' year letter on the number-plate passed. If there had been four 'bad' letters passing him, he had to wait for four 'good' letters before he could cross. As there were many more 'bad' letters, William was often immobilised for up to two hours or more, becoming increasingly agitated. William had been hospitalised on two previous occasions, distressed by paranoid delusions, and on several more had been maintained on anti-psychotic medication. His obsessional problem was driven by the belief that a previous female manager of his was 'out to get him' and that towards that end, she had taken control of all cars whose year letter was the same as hers. Then, as he associated a year with personal troubles for himself, he came to the conclusion that she had also taken control of those, until he was in the position where more rather than less of the cars on the road were intent on causing him some harm. Harm included harm to his family such as illness, death, or loss of job. Anything bad which happened to him or his family was taken as further proof of his beliefs. Although medication reduced the belief that his ex-manager was controlling the cars, the obsessional behaviour did not go away. It appeared to have become autonomous

due to the fact that the maintenance cycles were still in place, and unfortunately he could not be persuaded to change these as he still felt the risk was
too great.

Overvalued Ideation (OVI)

There has long been debate as to whether OCD itself shades into psychosis
at some extreme end of a continuum and an articulate argument has been
put forward (Kozak & Foa, 1994) that overvalued ideas (OVI) may constitute a midpoint along such a continuum. Whilst Marks and his colleagues
(Ito et al., 1995) found no relationship between the outcome of ERP and
the strength with which obsessional beliefs were held, Foa (1979) has suggested that marked overvalued ideation is associated with poor outcome.
Cognitive therapy offers particular hope for the treatment of OVI
(Salkovskis & Warwick, 1985). However, clinical experience suggests that,
except in cases of simple misinformation, pronounced OVI (in which the
client is wholly convinced that *others'* views are unequivocally mistaken)
may sometimes reflect somewhat unusual factors, such as a history of
depressive psychosis (Salkovskis & Warwick, 1986). In general, the cognitive approach to OVI resembles that for any other difficulty; the therapist
works collaboratively with the client to ascertain the evidential or historical basis for their beliefs, and then to evaluate the evidence for these beliefs
against more realistic alternatives.

Obsessive Compulsive Personality Disorder (OCPD)

Beck, Freeman, et al. (1990) describe the many ways in which the presence
of a personality disorder can hamper the therapeutic alliance and process.

It has been proposed that 55% of OCD patients also have pre-existing
OCPD (Rasmussen & Tsuang, 1986), although estimates vary widely.
OCD certainly commonly arises against a background of more ego-syn-
tonic but counter-productive traits, such as perfectionism, scrupulosity or
preoccupation with detail. These can pose difficulties in the treatment of
OCD because the patient may be seeking some kind of compromise: they
wish to be rid of the troublesome thoughts whilst continuing to behave in
a way that may be viewed as obsessional such as writing the 'perfect'
essay, or keeping their home in immaculate order at all times.
Maintaining compulsive behaviours in *any* form means that there is
always scope for a newer version of their OCD to attach itself to these

residual behaviours. The therapist and client may need to collaborate on a relapse prevention plan that enables the client to spot early warning signs as well as to experiment with more flexible ways of thinking and responding in their life as a whole.

Self-esteem

OCD is frequently associated with low self-esteem. It is often difficult to assess whether this has arisen due to the nature of the disorder (i.e. because the sufferer perceives himself to be different from other people and prey to a particularly 'senseless' problem so they feel bad about themselves) or whether this has been a problem for the person all along and in fact may have made them more vulnerable to developing OCD in the first place. Whichever of those may be the case, it results in increasing the patient's problems as it makes them more vulnerable to feeling that they have to get things right. They are more likely to feel devastated by their mistakes and therefore feel that they have to try even harder (OCD partly develops because sufferers try too hard). Low self-esteem thus feeds into a vicious circle which can both keep the problem going and be a potential cause of relapse.

In a general way, low self-esteem causes people to overestimate their faults and weaknesses, and to underestimate their qualities and strengths, thus increasing their tendency to make predictions in a negative way about how they will cope with situations (Fennell, 1997). If the person feels sufficiently anxious at the prospect, he will avoid the situation completely and therefore deny himself the opportunity to find out that he could have coped with it after all. The more situations are avoided, the more self-esteem is eroded and the more the belief in the necessity to avoid triggering intrusive thoughts or rituals grows.

Nicky exemplified the problem just described. Her mother was disabled but very determined not to let it interfere with her life, from which Nicky formed the belief that one had to be strong. Her father had a 'nervous breakdown' and the marriage split up for one year when Nicky was 10 years old. Nicky formed the idea at the time that any form of mental illness was a sign of weakness. She also reports having wondered if her father left because she was a fat and ugly child. (Nicky is a normally attractive young woman but does not see herself in that way.) Throughout her childhood, Nicky did not feel good about herself. One way she found of compensating for her lack of self-esteem was academic achievement. At the time of treatment, she expressed beliefs such as 'The only way I can feel good about myself is if people like me', 'I'm weak', and 'I'm a nasty person'. These beliefs about herself fed into her obsessional problem for, when she had thoughts of causing harm to others, she believed that being a 'flawed' person, she might do it. Tackling her low self-esteem began with the prejudice model (Padesky, 1990). She immediately saw the relevance to her beliefs about herself. When she looked at evidence for her beliefs she was able to see that her 'evidence' derived from her view of herself rather than from having any basis in reality. She also said it gave her a glimmer of hope that her beliefs about herself were not based on fact. She began keeping a positive data log, made a list of good things about herself to keep referring to and was encouraged to keep challenging negative thoughts about herself. The evidence from childhood was also challenged—that her father had left because of her, that her father had never cared much for her and that her friendships always crumbled because she was lacking in some way. Also challenged was the belief that she was weak. Her evidence for that was that she had a 'mental problem', could not manage her money (as if any student on a grant can!), and was not going to perform well enough to pass her MPhil. As her self-esteem improved, this seemed to facilitate her ability to see the intrusive thoughts as just thoughts and not as a sign that she was mad or bad.

FURTHER DIFFICULTIES IN WORKING WITH THE OBSESSIONAL PATIENT

So far, discussion has concentrated on aspects of therapeutic technique that facilitate working with obsessive-compulsive disorder. From experience, all therapists know that there is no such thing as a 'text-book patient' and there are frequently additional factors which pose difficulties in therapy. Some of the most frequently encountered difficulties with obsessional patients are outlined below.

Engagement Issues Revisited

As stressed throughout this chapter, engagement in therapy is crucial to the success of CBT regardless of the presenting problem. However, it is not unusual to encounter clinical attempts to impose psychological treatment on obsessionals. For example, a severe obsessional washer was admitted for intensive inpatient treatment. The principles of exposure and response prevention were explained to her (although it was later clear that she neither fully understood nor agreed with the account she was given). When she continued to wash excessively, she was reprimanded, and then the tops were removed from the taps in her room in order to make water unavailable. Not surprisingly, she rapidly found alternative places to wash. Staff and patient became locked into an adversarial position; as the situation progressed, the staff began to label the patient as poorly motivated and personality disordered. Such damaging situations need to be avoided, and are best prevented by being collaborative and focusing on mutually agreed goals.

The commonest cause of failure in forming collaborative relationships is the failure to reach a *shared* understanding of the problem, as outlined earlier. This usually occurs because the therapist fails to use the patient's own experience in building-up and exploring the formulation. Often, therapists disregard objections raised by the patient rather than seeing these as indications of beliefs which seem to the person to be inconsistent with the model as applied to them.

Signs that engagement is beginning to fail or has failed include sulkiness in therapy sessions, withdrawal, arguments, resistance to suggestions, not attempting homework or doing it in selective or counter-productive ways. Interestingly, many of the same phenomena occur in the therapist. Once these signs develop, the therapist needs to redouble attempts to empathise with the patient's situation, and provide the patient with a safe environment in which they can acknowledge the difficulties they are experiencing, including those with the therapist. Burns (Burns & Auerbach, 1996) suggests that there are two main reasons for failure of empathy with patients who may be behaving in an angry or hostile manner. These are that the patient: (i) thinks that the therapist has not listened or understood just how bad they feel; or (ii) may be angry because of something the therapist has done or said during the session (e.g. answered the phone, or been late for the appointment).

A general strategy for increasing empathy is to encourage both positive and negative feedback at the end of each session. Whilst this is usually basic practice in good cognitive therapy, it is frequently overlooked. However, the patient may deny that anything is wrong. In such instances, Burns suggests that the therapist discloses that they felt that the patient seemed a little uncomfortable, and goes on to ask whether, if they *were* annoyed or dissatisfied, they would find it easy or difficult to say so. It is often helpful for the therapist to admit to not having provided the best help initially, and acknowledge that it can be difficult to express dissatisfaction (or other negative feelings) but that it can also make therapy more rewarding and effective. This openness can provide a useful foundation for re-establishing a shared understanding, and often results in a better therapeutic relationship as the patient modifies a confrontational style that may have been intended to protect their fragile self-esteem. The therapist must remember that, for the patient to change the way in which they deal with their problem, they have to 'admit' to having previously dealt with it in a 'wrong' and damaging way. When the therapist admits their own fallibility and demonstrates a willingness to change their approach in a collaborative way, this increases the likelihood that the patient will be inclined to make stronger attempts to change and to take a more active part in therapy.

More frequently, it is the case that the patient is at least partly engaged but there are areas in which he or she may demonstrate some reluctance or hesitation. This may take the form of only selectively completing previously agreed homework assignments, or reverting to former models that have provided them with a different understanding of their problem (even if these are incompatible with the approach the therapist is currently trying to engender). A useful way to deal with this is to have the patient systematically review the pros and cons of different ways of conceptualising their problem. This should enable differences between models to be highlighted and explored and, if helpful, put to the test. Having the patient devise a flash card reminding them of the cognitive behavioural formulation (and the evidence for it) can be beneficial in such situations.

A further illustration of a partially engaged OCD patient is the person who is obviously unhappy with their current level of functioning, but fears that there may be negative consequences of treatment. For instance, the overly neat and tidy person will be transformed to a slob, or the religious fanatic will perceive a decline in his relationship with God. This is one of the few times when reassurance is appropriate. The therapist can contract that, if at the end of therapy this feared consequence occurs, they will assist the patient to resume his former obsessionality!

The 'Empty Life' Problem

For some people, particularly those who have been OCD sufferers for some years, or whose rituals have expanded to such an extent that they take up practically all their waking hours, a further complication is that of an 'empty life'. The sufferer cannot envisage a life free from OCD, or what they could do with all the extra time that they will have at their disposal. Rituals and compulsions may give order and purpose to the day. From the point of view of therapy, one has to be careful that successful elimination of one ritual does not leave a void which is subsequently filled by another one (either new or pre-existing).

If the therapist believes this may be a problem, it is best to discuss this with the patient by asking what their life would be like without the obsessional problem; what would fill the time now if the problem had never developed;

how the person would like to fill it. Once realistic ideas are agreed, the steps toward achieving such goals are discussed, and the patient encouraged to work on building-up such activities in parallel with the work on dealing with their obsessions. In the most extreme early onset cases, we have suggested to the patient that, as a consequence of their OCD, they have missed out on important aspects of their adolescent development. It would therefore follow that they may need to work on developing all that they missed (e.g. education, learning to socialise), so that they have to cram the development they missed into a couple of years.

For some patients, it is not so much that OCD has inadvertently precluded all other activities, but that compulsions and rituals may have evolved as a means of avoiding these activities. In this way, removing the OCD may reveal further problems such as social phobia, agoraphobia, interpersonal skill deficits or difficulties with life goals, which the OCD has previously masked.

Supernatural and Religious Beliefs

Therapists working with patients whose obsessions focus on religious areas may believe that, in order to challenge obsessional beliefs, they have to challenge the person's fundamental religious ideas. This is seldom a good idea as well as being ethically dubious. Instead, the therapist should rely on helping the patient find the basis of their excessive worries in their religious beliefs, then try to deal with these within the person's religious framework. For example, a patient was afraid that they were in danger of not being a good Christian if they didn't attempt to neutralise blasphemous intrusions. The therapist asked them to list the criteria for being a good Christian; the patient noted that 'neutralising blasphemous thoughts' did not appear on the list. Another patient was afraid that treatment of his blasphemous obsessions was 'learning a trick to deaden his conscience' and would make him less religious. In this instance, the patient agreed to stop neutralising for three months in return for a promise from the therapist that he would help him become more obsessional again if he found that his religious fervour had been diminished. In fact, the patient was surprised to find that his religious feelings deepened as he spent more time in 'positive communication with God as opposed to continual neutralising'.

Extreme Avoidance

In some cases, avoidance may be engaged in to the extent that the client seems minimally troubled by their OCD. This can sometimes be difficult to detect as it can be extremely subtle and may have been the pattern for quite some time. The patient's family might also be heavily involved without even realising. Asking the question, 'Is there anything that you *don't* do because of your obsessional problem?' may fail to reveal the full extent of the avoidance. It can pose difficulties in trying to devise a behavioural experiment if the patient's obsessional concerns relate solely to an activity they do not currently engage in. An example of this was a nurse on long-term sick leave whose main worry was that she might administer some routine procedure and make a mistake, such as in inserting a Hickmann line, and not realising until too late. She claimed that there was no analogue situation which would activate her intrusive thoughts.

CONCLUSION: THE DEVIL IS IN THE DETAIL

Cognitive behavioural strategies for helping people suffering from obsessional problems are still in a relatively early stage of development. Obsessional problems present a particular challenge for the therapist because of the temptation to deal with the patients' fears through reassurance directed towards obviously senseless thoughts. Obsessional patients have almost invariably tried such logic, and doubts and further intrusions have overwhelmed their logical answers. It is not possible to deal with an obsessional problem by helping the person to obsess in greater detail, although many will welcome the attempt for the temporary relief it might offer. Dwelling on the detail of particular dangers in order to convince someone suffering from obsessional problems that their fears will not come true will invariably fail to help, and will often have the effect of increasing distress in the longer term. We describe this to our patients as 'putting out a fire with gasoline' and 'digging your way out of a hole'. The key to successful behavioural or cognitive behavioural treatment is to consider and evaluate the possibility that it may be most sensible to view the problem as one of distressing but otherwise harmless preoccupation and worry. It is, of course, normal to worry about one's worst fears. The strategies used to deal with preoccupation and worry are usually quite different to those used to deal with imminent disaster and blame.

NOTE

Paul Salkovskis is Wellcome Trust Senior Research Fellow in Basic Biomedical Science.

Candida Richards and Elizabeth Forrester are supported by Wellcome Trust Grants.

REFERENCES

Abramson, L. Y., Seligman, M. E. P. & Teasdale, J. D. (1978). Learned helplessness in humans: critique and reformulation. *Journal of Abnormal Psychology*, **87**, 49–74.

American Psychiatric Association. (1994). *Diagnostic and Statistical Manual of Mental Disorders*. (4th edn). Washington DC.: American Psychiatric Association.

Beck, A. T. (1976). *Cognitive Therapy and the Emotional Disorders*. New York: International Universities Press.

Beck, A. T., Freeman, A. & Associates. (1990). *Cognitive Therapy for Personality Disorders*. New York: Guilford.

Burns, D. D. & Auerbach, A. (1996). Therapeutic empathy in cognitive-behavioral therapy: Does it really make a difference? In P. M. Salkovskis (Ed.), *Frontiers of Cognitive Therapy*. New York: Guilford.

Chadwick, P. & Birchwood, M. (1994). The omnipotence of voices: A cognitive approach to auditory hallucinations. *British Journal of Psychiatry*, **164**, 190–201.

Chadwick, P. D. J. & Lowe, C. F. (1994). A cognitive approach to measuring and modifying delusions. *Behaviour Research and Therapy*, **32**, 355–367.

Chadwick, P. D. J., Lowe, C. F., Horne, P. J., Higson, P. J. et al. (1994). Modifying delusions: The role of empirical testing. *Behavior Therapy*, **25**, 35–49.

Dugas, M. J., Freeston, M. H. & Ladouceur, R. (1997). Intolerance of uncertainty and problem orientation in worry. *Cognitive Therapy and Research*, **21**, 593–606.

Enright, S. (1996). Obsessive compulsive disorder as a schizotype. In R. Rapee (Ed.), *Controversies in the Anxiety Disorders* . New York: Guilford.

Fennell, M. J. V. (1997). Low self-esteem: a cognitive perspective. *Behavioural and Cognitive Psychotherapy*, **25**, 1–26.

Foa, E. B. (1979). Failure in treating obsessive-compulsives. *Behaviour Research and Therapy*, **17**, 169–176.

Goodwin, D. W., Guze, S. B. & Robins, E. (1969). Follow-up studies in obsessional neurosis. *Arch Gen Psychiatry*, **20**, 182–7.

Ito, L. M., De Araujo, L. A., Hemsley, D. R. & Marks, I. M. (1995). Beliefs and resistance in obsessive-compulsive disorder: Observations from a controlled study. *Journal of Anxiety Disorders*, **9**, 269–281.

Kozak, M. J. & Foa, E. B. (1994). Obsessions, overvalued ideas, and delusions in obsessive-compulsive disorder. *Behaviour Research and Therapy*, **32**, 343–53.

Morrison, A. P. (1994). Cognitive behaviour therapy for auditory hallucinations without concurrent medication: A single case. *Behavioural and Cognitive Psychotherapy*, **22**, 259–264.

Morrison, A. P., Haddock, G. & Tarrier, N. (1995). Intrusive thoughts and auditory hallucinations: A cognitive approach. *Behavioural and Cognitive Psychotherapy*, **23**, 265–280.

Nisbett, R. E. (1980). *Strategies and Shortcomings of Social Judgement*. Englewood Cliffs, NJ.: Prentice-Hall.

Padesky, C. A. (1990). Schema as self-prejudice. *International Cognitive Therapy Newsletter*, **6**, 7–8.

Persons, J. B. (1989). *Cognitive Therapy in Practice: a Case Formulation Approach*. New York: W.W. Norton.

Rachman, S. J. (1993). Obsessions, responsibility and guilt. *Behaviour Research and Therapy*, **31**, 149–154.

Rachman, S. J. & de Silva, P. (1978). Abnormal and normal obsessions. *Behaviour Research and Therapy*, **16**, 233–248.

Rachman, S. J. & Hodgson, R. J. (1980). *Obsessions and Compulsions*. Englewood Cliffs, NJ.: Prentice-Hall.

Rasmussen, S. A. & Eisen, J. L. (1992). The epidemiology and clinical features of obsessive compulsive disorder. *Psychiatr. Clin. North Am.*, **15**, 743–58.

Rasmussen, S. A. & Tsuang, M. T. (1986). Clinical characteristics and family history in DSM-III obsessive-compulsive disorder. *Am. J. Psychiatry*, **143**, 317–22.

Richards, H. C. (1995). The cognitive phenomenology of OCD repeated rituals . Poster Presented at World Congress of Behavioural and Cognitive Therapies, Copenhagen, July.

Richards, H. C. (1997). *Why isn't once enough?* Paper presented at 25th Anniversary conference of the BABCP, Canterbury.

Rosenberg, C. M. (1967). Familial aspects of obsessional neurosis. *Br. J. Psychiatry*, **113**, 405–413.

Salkovskis, P. M. (1985). Obsessional-compulsive problems: a cognitive behavioural analysis. *Behaviour Research and Therapy*, **23**, 571–583.

Salkovskis, P. M. (1989a). Cognitive behavioural factors and the persistence of intrusive thoughts in obsessional problems. *Behaviour Research and Therapy*, **27**, 677–682.

Salkovskis, P. M. (1989b). Obsessions and compulsions. In J. Scott, J. M. G. Williams & A. T. Beck (Eds), *Cognitive Therapy: a Clinical Casebook*. London: Croom Helm.

Salkovskis, P. M. (1989c). Obsessive and intrusive thoughts: Clinical and non-clinical aspects. In P. M. G. Emmelkamp, W. T. A. M. Everaerd & M. J. M. van Son (Eds), *Fresh Perspectives on Anxiety Disorders*. Amsterdam: Swets & Zeitlinger.

Salkovskis, P. M. (1991). The importance of behaviour in the maintenance of anxiety and panic: A cognitive account. *Behavioural Psychotherapy*, **19**, 6–19.

Salkovskis, P. M. (1996a). The cognitive approach to anxiety: Threat beliefs, safety seeking behaviour, and the special case of health anxiety and obsessions. In P. M. Salkovskis (Ed.), *Frontiers of Cognitive Therapy* (pp. 48–74). New York: Guilford.

Salkovskis, P. M. (1996b). Cognitive behavioural approaches to the understanding of obsessional problems. In R. Rapee (Ed.), *Current Controversies in the Anxiety Disorders*. New York: Guilford.

Salkovskis, P. M. (1996c). Resolving the cognition behaviour debate. In P. M. Salkovskis (Ed.), *Trends in Cognitive behaviour Therapy*. Chichester: Wiley.

Salkovskis, P. M. & Harrison, J. (1984). Abnormal and normal obsessions: A replication. *Behaviour Research and Therapy*, **22**, 549–552.

Salkovskis, P. M. & Kirk, J. (1997). Obsessive-compulsive disorder. In D. M. Clark & C. G. Fairburn (Eds), *The Science and Practice of Cognitive Behaviour Therapy*. Oxford: Oxford University Press.

Salkovskis, P. M., Rachman, S. J., Ladouceur, R., Freeston, M., Taylor, S., Kyrios, M. & Sica, C. (1996). *Defining responsibility in obsessional problems*. Proceedings of the Smith College Women's Room—after the Toronto Cafeteria.

Salkovskis, P. M., Richards, C. & Forrester, E. (1995). The relationship between obsessional problems and intrusive thoughts. *Behavioural and Cognitive Psychotherapy*, **23**, 281–299.

Salkovskis, P. M., Shafran, R., Rachman, S. & Freeston, M.H. Multiple pathways to inflated responsibility beliefs in obsessional problems: possible origins and implications for therapy and research. *Behaviour Research and Therapy* (in press).

Salkovskis, P. M. & Warwick, H. M. (1985). Cognitive therapy of obsessive-compulsive disorder: Treating treatment failures. *Behavioural Psychotherapy*, **13**(3), 243–255.

Salkovskis, P. M. & Warwick, H. M. (1986). 'Cognitive therapy of obsessive-compulsive disorder: Treating treatment failures': Reply. *Behavioural Psychotherapy*, **14**(1), 91–93.

Salkovskis, P. M. & Warwick, H. M. (1988). Morbid preoccupation, health anxiety and reassurance: a cognitive behavioural approach to hypochondriasis. *Behaviour Research and Therapy* **22**, 549–552.

Salkovskis, P. M., Westbrook, D., Davis, J., Jeavons, A. & Gledhill, A. (1997). Effects of neutralizing on intrusive thoughts: An experiment investigating the etiology of obsessive-compulsive disorder. *Behaviour Research and Therapy* **35**(3), 211–219.

Shafran, R., Thordarson, D. S. & Rachman, S. (1996). Thought–action fusion in obsessive compulsive disorder. *Journal of Anxiety Disorders*, **10**(5), 379–391.

Swedo, S. E. & Rapoport, J. L. (1989). Phenomenology and differential diagnosis of obsessive-compulsive disorder in children and adolescents. In J. L. Rapoport (Ed.), *Obsessive Compulsive Disorder in Children and Adolescents*. Washington DC: American Psychiatric Press.

Yaryura-Tobias, J. & Neziroglu, F. (1983). *Obsessive Compulsive Disorders: Pathogenesis–Diagnosis-Treatment*. New York: Marcel Dekker.

Chapter 4

WHERE THERE'S A WILL ... COGNITIVE THERAPY FOR PEOPLE WITH CHRONIC DEPRESSIVE DISORDERS

*Jan Scott**

INTRODUCTION

For many clinicians, people with chronic depression represent their image of 'heart sink' clients. However, with appropriate supervision and support, it may be possible to convince these clinicians that there is evidence that cognitive therapy (CT) can be beneficial to many of these clients. This chapter tries to raise awareness of why we need to offer psychological interventions to this client population, identifies some advantages to using CT in particular and then briefly outlines modifications to CT. A case study is included followed by an overview of outcome data. It is hoped that clinicians will be encouraged to try CT with a group of clients who are often relegated to long-term follow-up clinics waiting for the opportunity to try the next 'wonder' drug.

THE ROLE OF PSYCHOLOGICAL INTERVENTIONS

All professionals working with people experiencing chronic depressive disorders are psychologically important to those clients. Individuals suffering from persistent symptoms have usually experienced significant disappointments and demoralisation following the failure of several previous

* Dept. of Psychological Medicine, University of Glasgow, UK.

Treating Complex Cases: The Cognitive Behavioural Therapy Approach.
Edited by Nicholas Tarrier, Adrian Wells and Gillian Haddock.

treatment regimes and they often describe perceived or actual rejection by the clinicians offering those treatments. The client and their 'significant others' may become increasingly sceptical or lose hope entirely about the possibility of remission. A clinician will rarely help the client to achieve a good outcome unless they are able to offer the client information, education, advice, realistic hope and psychological support as an integral part of the treatment package.

A number of individual symptoms of chronic or refractory mood disorders may be amenable to psychological interventions. For example, hopelessness, suicidal ideation, low self-esteem, poor problem-solving strategies or avoidant coping style are highly prevalent in clients with chronic or partially remitted mood disorders (Krantz & Moos, 1988; Scott & Wright, 1996; Cornwall & Scott, 1997). All of these symptoms can be tackled through the use of cognitive and behavioural techniques either alone or in combination with pharmacotherapy. In addition, non-adherence to medication, which occurs in about 20–50% of this client population (Klerman, 1990), has been successfully treated through cognitive behavioural approaches (Cochran, 1984; Rush, 1988).

There are a number of psychosocial difficulties that may be causes or consequences of chronicity or treatment refractoriness. Reviews of unipolar mood disorders suggest that lack of social support, poor marital or family relationships, and high levels of expressed emotion (EE) or a preponderance of negative life events after the onset of the index illness episode, may all be associated with chronicity (Akiskal, 1982; Thase & Kupfer, 1987; Scott, 1988, 1995; Paykel, 1994; Thase, 1994). In some instances, successful treatment with pharmacotherapy allows the client to draw on their own coping skills and resolve these difficulties. However, depressed clients with characteristics such as high levels of pre-morbid neuroticism and high scores on measures of dysfunctional attitudes are likely to show a poor response to antidepressant monotherapy (Scott, 1988; Paykel, 1994; Thase, 1994). Bothwell and Scott (1997) have similarly shown that in a sample of severely depressed inpatients who received adequate pharmacotherapy, high levels of dysfunctional attitudes (particularly related to approval) and low self-esteem at admission were the most robust predictors of non-recovery at two-year follow-up. As these 'drug-refractory' psychological symptoms are often associated with partial remission or increased risk of relapse there is a strong argument for the simultaneous or sequential use of psychotherapy as an adjunct to pharmacotherapy (Cornwall & Scott, 1997).

There are some instances where the use of a specific psychological therapy is indicated. For example, only about 50% of clients with chronic minor affective symptoms or dysthymic disorder respond to pharmacotherapy (Markowitz, 1994). These individuals may be candidates for specific approaches such as cognitive therapy (CT). Furthermore, clients with chronic depressive disorders may have co-morbid physical or mental disorders that compound the difficulty in obtaining a satisfactory treatment response. Even if the individual adheres to medication, physical disorders may limit the options for pharmacotherapy, whilst Axis II disorders may show a poor response to medication alone. As personality disorders and substance misuse disorders each occur in at least 30% of this client population (Shea et al., 1990; Thase, 1994), there is often a need to use a combination of pharmacotherapy and psychological interventions. There is also a small literature on the successful use of CT, either alone or in combination with medication, for clients with psychotic depression (for a review see Scott & Wright, 1996).

Finally, many individuals with a chronic depressive disorder who show a full or partial symptomatic response to pharmacotherapy still exhibit considerable impairment in their social, family and work role functioning. Psychosocial interventions can play a crucial role in rehabilitating these individuals, supporting them through the process of reintegration with their family and community and preventing future relapse.

THE ADVANTAGES OF COGNITIVE THERAPY

Clients with chronic depression do not do well with unstructured approaches as these tend to increase rather than decrease their sense of hopelessness and helplessness (Scott, Cole & Eccleston, 1991). There is anecdotal evidence that a basic package of medication plus structured clinical management similar to the approach used in the NIMH study (Fawcett, Epstein & Feister, 1987) is beneficial to a significant minority of clients with chronic major depressive disorders. However, the majority will benefit more from a course of time-limited, 'manualised' (or 'guide-line-driven') therapy, such as CT, that is of proven efficacy in acute mood disorders (Beck et al.,1979; US Department of Health & Human Sciences [US DHHS], 1993; Scott, 1995). The CT approach shares a number of characteristics with other brief effective models of psychotherapy (Zeiss, Lewinsohn & Munoz, 1979; Teasdale, 1985; Scott, 1995). The therapy provides the individual with an understandable model of their experience. Plans for producing change are made in logical sequences and the therapy encourages the independent use of skills by the client. Importantly, the individual begins to develop a sense of self-efficacy and belief in their ability to cope with current and future adversity.

Cognitive therapy has also been adapted for use with personality and psychotic disorders in both the inpatient and outpatient setting and with couples and families. Given the importance of interpersonal factors in chronic depression, it is always pertinent to consider whether the client's needs would be better met if their partner or family were also involved in the therapy. (Group CT approaches are also tried at some centres.) Specific recommendations for including significant others in CT with this client population will be similar to those outlined for other individuals, and will largely depend on the case conceptualisation and the individual's preferences. Even if formal couples or family CT is not undertaken, there is evidence that enhancing the interpersonal focus of individual CT may be beneficial in chronic affective disorders (Markowitz, 1994; Scott & Wright, 1996). In Newcastle, we have described a model where individual CT with chronically depressed inpatients is supplemented by 3–4 family sessions targeted at improving understanding about the disorder and its treatment and dealing with negative family cognitions (Scott, 1992). When appropriate, partners or members of the family may be engaged as 'co-therapists' outside the regular therapy sessions to help the client undertake homework assignments or to provide observer reports of the client's activities.

It is possible and often beneficial to combine CT with pharmacotherapy (Scott, 1992; Wright et al., 1993). This may be particularly important as few, if any, clients with chronic depression will be referred for CT without having been offered at least one course of antidepressant medication. The client may also be committed to a biological explanation of their depression and it may be easier to engage them in a treatment approach that argues for the role of psychological and biological interventions, rather than offering them a competing model of their disorder. In many instances the client will be seeing a doctor to monitor their mental state and review their use of medication whilst meeting with another professional for CT sessions. The involvement of two therapists complicates the therapeutic relationship, but problems can largely be averted if the two individuals work together regularly in this way and they agree on the theoretical rationale for the combined treatment. The two therapists must also ensure that the messages given to the client about the combined treatment are consistent and that all three individuals communicate frequently about progress and try to make decisions about changes in strategy in a collaborative way.

This flexibility in the practice of CT allows a consistent cognitive framework to be applied to the whole spectrum of individual and interpersonal problems presented by most of the clients with chronic depression who seek psychotherapy as an adjunct, or sometimes as an alternative, to medication.

OVERVIEW OF CT FOR CHRONIC DEPRESSIVE DISORDERS

The CT interventions used in the treatment of chronic depressive disorders are based on the approach described by Beck and coworkers (Beck et al., 1979) for less severe conditions. It is apparent that, with few exceptions, the standard CT package of about 12–18 individual sessions is less beneficial to individuals with chronic depressive disorders and that 25–40 sessions may be a more realistic course of therapy. Most of the studies demonstrating significant reductions in levels of severity of depression, or higher recovery rates, report modifications to the CT approach to tackle the more pronounced, complex or enduring problems encountered by this client group (see Table 4.1). These modifications are highlighted in a number of CT manuals produced by clinicians working with clients with severe and chronic depressive disorders (Scott, 1992; Wright et al., 1993; Scott & Wright, 1996). The approaches all retain the essential elements of CT with a collaborative-empirical therapeutic relationship at the core of the treatment intervention. The cognitive model of emotional disorders proposed by Padesky and Greenberger (1996) is particularly useful in engaging this client population in CT (see later). The therapy is structured and problem-oriented and an agenda is set for each session. Clients are socialised to the cognitive model and are then taught how to use cognitive restructuring and behavioural techniques to reduce symptoms. The therapist is active, but the client is encouraged to play a significant role in designing and monitoring any agreed homework assignments. The therapist must be sensitive to the pace of therapy and a great deal of time and patience is required whilst experiments that potentially bring about small changes are negotiated with the client.

With cases of severe depression, both cognitive and behavioural techniques are used for acute symptom relief, but treatment techniques may be adjusted to help deal with high levels of agitation, insomnia, difficulties with concentration, or profound hopelessness. For example, sessions may be reduced in length but held more frequently, the overall course of treatment is usually extended (Thase, Reynolds & Frank, 1993; Scott, 1992).

Table 4.1   Modifications to CT for clients with chronic and refractory mood disorders

1. Increase frequency and reduce length of session (e.g. 3 x 20 minutes per week)
2. Extend course of therapy (e.g. 30 sessions)
3. Increase interpersonal focus of individual sessions
4. Offer a rationale for combination treatment (i.e. psychobiosocial causal model)
5. Prolong behavioural focus
6. Take symptom-oriented approach whilst working on the development of a more coherent conceptualisation
7. Introduce conjoint family sessions
8. If client is hospitalised, consider:
    milieu therapy
    pre-discharge planning and relapse prevention sessions

Scott (1992) recommended an extended behavioural emphasis often accompanied by 'overlearning' (repetition of behavioural assignments in different situations) during the initial stages of CT with inpatients. More complex cognitive interventions (such as identifying and challenging dysfunctional underlying beliefs) may be delayed until the client is better able to concentrate on and address psychological issues. It should be emphasised, however, that severely depressed people can often do at least some cognitive restructuring early in treatment. For example, a client with marked sleep problems not fully responsive to pharmacotherapy might be taught relaxation and imagery procedures in addition to methods of reducing intrusive negative thoughts. This early use of methods to tackle negative cognitive bias is very important as two of the most significant features of severe or chronic depressive disorders are hopelessness and suicidal ideation, as such cognitive interventions to curb hopelessness and reduce the risk of self-harm are often needed at the outset of treatment.

More intensive inpatient CT approaches have been advocated for severe or chronic depressive disorders. These include the use of a 'cognitive milieu' where staff members are trained in CT techniques so that the client can be exposed to multiple opportunities to learn cognitive and behavioural procedures. Staff members may be assigned to assist with homework assignments, behavioural interventions, or other components of treatment. Before discharge, clients often participate in relapse prevention exercises such as cognitive behavioural rehearsal. Most cognitive milieu units adopt a cognitive biological model in which CT and psychopharmacology are the predominant therapies.

Although CT has been described as a 'manualised' approach, most cognitive therapists employ considerable flexibility in developing a customised case conceptualisation and treatment plan for each client. In the treatment of dysthymia or mild depressions superimposed on a pre-existing personality disorder, the therapist may introduce intensive work on restructuring underlying dysfunctional attitudes at an early stage of the therapy process. However, in severe disorders, CT addresses the need for rapid symptom relief from the first session and only later tackle issues such as improving interpersonal functioning, developing social skills, and modification of dysfunctional underlying beliefs. Most importantly, because clients with chronic depression often present with complex difficulties, it may not be possible to arrive at a clear conceptualisation until much later in therapy. Early sessions may focus on teaching the client cognitive and behavioural strategies for tackling specific symptoms and building up their skill level, whilst constantly revising and revisiting the formulation, hoping that the 'noise in the system' is gradually being reduced. Lastly, it should be borne in mind that clients with chronic depression are certain that their negative predictions will come true; as therapy proceeds, this certainty is gradually undermined and clients with chronic depression invariably go through an extended period of anxiety on the road to recovery. A case history and some of the interventions employed are demonstrated in the following case study.

A Case Example: Edith

Edith was a 36-year-old married woman who lived with her husband and two children. She had been suffering from chronic primary major depression which had remained unresponsive to a range of appropriate antidepressant treatments for four years. Edith had a previous history of two episodes of major depression successfully treated with antidepressants, including a postnatal episode 12 years ago after the birth of her first child. Edith had always felt insecure in her relationship with her first child and felt increasingly threatened as (during the course of her illness) her daughter took over domestic and mothering roles within the home.

The current episode of depression was partly responsive to antidepressant treatment, but about two years after the episode began, Edith's mother had a cerebro-vascular stroke. Edith persuaded her husband and children that they should move house to be nearer to her mother, but shortly after moving her mother died. Her husband was angry at 'being made to move' and at losing his social network and changing jobs. The marriage, already under strain, deteriorated further. Edith's depression became worse and her family found it difficult to cope with her distress. A local physician prescribed her diazepam which she took frequently and excessively, eventually culminating in a non-fatal overdose. Admission was arranged to her local mental hospital where a wide variety of medications were prescribed to little effect over a period of six months. Edith had become self-focused and talked at length about every aspect of her depression. She refused to take part in bereavement work or other 'counselling' seeing these as 'too painful', but if staff stopped talking to her she expressed the view that they were rejecting her. Relationships with the staff on the unit became increasingly fraught and Edith was perceived as 'a difficult client who was not trying'. Weekend leave home was distressing to all the family. Edith did not wish to meet her new neighbours or the parishioners from the local church 'because of my current state', but the resulting social isolation reinforced her views of not being liked and she also developed mild paranoid ideas that her husband would leave her and go and live with 'one of the other women he meets day to day'. Problems came to a head when, as a last resort, the hospital suggested ECT. Edith refused and the unit felt they 'had nothing left to offer'. An impasse had been reached between Edith and the staff and so Edith's husband negotiated a transfer to Newcastle to a specialist affective disorders unit which offered in- and outpatient CT.

Sessions 1–3

The initial assessment was far from easy. Edith felt angry with the previous unit and saw transfer to Newcastle in terms of a punishment. Thoughts such as 'the other unit gave up on me' and 'my family just want to get rid of me' were very near to the surface, but provided excellent material to allow the therapist to socialise Edith into the CT model. Despite her reticence about talking to the cognitive therapist, she was able to generate other possible alternatives such as 'perhaps my family want me to come here for specialist help because they care about me and want me to recover', although she freely acknowledged she did not believe these alternatives with much conviction. The interview made slow progress, but it was agreed to continue the assessment over two more (daily) sessions until all the appropriate information had been explored. Unit staff were asked to have brief, gentle interactions in the interim to help Edith settle into the unit and to encourage her to consider a trial of CT

After three meetings the following symptoms were identified:

1. Behavioural: poor self-care; reduced activity levels; social withdrawal; escapism (particularly retiring to bed or using higher than prescribed doses of benzodiazepines).
2. Motivational: lack of interest or pleasure; everything too much effort; indecision
3. Affective: depressed; hopeless; anxious; irritable.
4. Cognitive: poor concentration; self-obsession; low self-esteem; negative self-image; transient ideas of self-harm (related to thoughts such as: 'My family would be better off without me'; 'This will never change, nothing will save me'; I'm a failure as a mother').
5. Physiological: anergia, early morning wakening, loss of appetite.

In order to understand chronic depressive disorder and its impact on the individual, a conceptualisation that encompasses cognitive (thoughts, images and beliefs), behavioural, affective, biological and environmental aspects of the individual's life is required. The approach described by Padesky and Greenberger (1996), with its clear acknowledgement of biology, is particularly useful as a stress-diathesis model can be emphasised that may incorporate neuroendocrine or other biological factors as precipitants of symptom shift.

To use this approach in chronic depression, the therapist asked Edith to describe her own views about the causes of her chronic depressive disorder and the problems this produced. Edith's aetiological theory was then incorporated within the framework of the model. Links between four aspects of the individual (cognitions, behaviour, mood and biology), and the interaction between these and the environment (past and present events or experiences) were stressed. The therapist then explained that small changes in one of these five

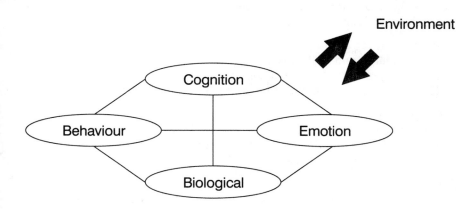

Figure 4.1   Padesky and Greenberger's cognitive model of emotional disorders.

areas may lead to small changes in another area. This rationale was used to engage Edith in CT through monitoring and linking changes in thoughts, behaviours, feelings and the biological symptoms.

Like many individuals, Edith had been given a 'biological' explanation of her symptoms and problems prior to coming to CT sessions. When the connections between the biological and other aspects of her experience were exposed, she was more able to understand the rationale for the use of CT (alone or in combination with medication) without having to totally reject other causal models. It became plausible that both medication and CT may start to bring about change, but the initial target symptoms or problems for these approaches may differ. In addition, this approach allowed an inroad into exploring Edith's attitudes toward her previous treatment, and her use of, and adherence with, medication.

The above approach allowed Edith's view (that her early childhood experiences lay at the root of her current depression) to be incorporated in the model outlined and she at least gained some confidence that the therapist was listening to her views. Furthermore, the Padesky and Greenberger model also allowed some discussion of the links between current symptoms and problems and Edith again began to view the therapist as trying to work with her to help her make sense of the problems she described. The initial prduction of a problem list and the interventions proposed then seemed to possess an inherent logic and the therapist was not perceived as telling Edith what she was experiencing, nor as dictating what they should do about it.

To try and create some sense of order from what Edith regarded as chaos and to make the issues seem more tangible, the problems were categorised into three groups: intrapersonal, interpersonal and day-to-day functioning.

A. *Intrapersonal problems:*
1. Feeling inferior and unlikeable.
2. Getting depressed about being depressed.
3. Ruminating about current situation and the loss of my mother.

B. *Interpersonal problems:*
1. Difficulties in marital relationship: husband's resentment about moving house and leaving his friends; the burden of my depression; my fear he will leave me and I will not cope.

C. *Problems in day-to-day functioning:*
1. Overwhelmed by basic tasks: poor self-care; difficulty occupying her time.
2. Loss of pleasure in any activities.
3. Tiredness, lack of energy, poor sleep.
4. Wanting to escape: avoiding people; retiring to bed; taking diazepam.

The therapist had also noted two other key interpersonal issues :

1. Difficulties in coping with the children: tension about daughter taking on a surrogate mother role with youngest; fears about being a 'bad mother'.
2. Social isolation: failure to keep in touch with old contacts; fear of trying to make new contacts in the neighbourhood (fearing she would introduce her husband to a potential new partner).

These were not included on the problem list at this stage, as gentle questions on these topics by the therapist were rejected. As the therapist had already discussed with Edith the need to revise the problem list after about 12 sessions or prior to discharge, the therapist decided to simply reinforce that it was highly likely that they would both identify other issues at a later date.

Finally, the introductory sessions and the use of Padesky and Greenberger's model revealed other crucial background information which allowed the therapist to develop hypotheses about underlying beliefs and Edith's potential acceptance or rejection of treatment. There was a family history of affective disorder in her grandfather and her own mother. Edith had vivid memories of feeling rejected by both individuals. This was particularly painful with regard to her mother as Edith felt that her mother preferred her older brother (possibly leading to underlying beliefs of inferiority). When her mother was unwell Edith was expected to remain at home and look after the family. A rather shy child, her frequent absences from school left her rather isolated from her peers (possibly enhancing her sense of inferiority and compounding it with beliefs about being unlikeable) . Her mother frequently took to her bed and Edith and her siblings were expected to be quiet so as not cause their mother any 'distress'. Edith was frequently punished for being noisy or 'badly behaved' (on exploration in later therapy sessions these were found to be minor misdemeanours) and was told that her mothers' continued ill-health was caused by the childrens' misbehaviour. (The therapist hypothesised that these and other experiences might have led to dysfunctional assumptions such as 'Unless I am perfect I will be harmful to others' and 'My personal worth depends on the opinions of others'. These ideas were noted to be used in discussions with Edith at a much later stage.) When she was a child, Edith's family were highly critical and suspicious of the doctors looking after her mother (furthermore, Edith mentioned in passing that on the night her mother died there was a delay in the arrival of the local doctor). Given these circumstances and her own recent experiences, the therapist also noted that Edith might not have much faith in the medical profession and might reject any treatment programme offered. On questioning, she admitted to a 'lack of faith in therapy' and so with her agreement this item was added to the problem list previously described.

Sessions 4–5

The first phase of therapy focused on Edith's ambivalence about the treatment programme and the identified problems in day-to-day functioning. The choice of this subgroup of problems was made in a more directive way than in outpatient CT. For Edith, one of the most distressing current problems was the marital difficulties she was experiencing; however, the therapist felt it would be inappropriate to start with this issue because of Edith's lack of skills to tackle such a complex problem and her low level of ability to cope on a daily basis. An early failure with such a major problem would be disastrous to a person with a chronic depressive disorder and the client would probably reject the therapy outright. Instead, two simpler tasks were set up in parallel, aimed primarily at improving functioning and developing skills which could later be applied to other problem situations:

1. In the session, Edith and the cognitive therapist would look in detail at her thoughts relating to CT.
2. Outside the session, Edith was introduced to her 'key worker' (a nurse on the unit). It was agreed that for the next three days the key worker would liaise with Edith and that they would jointly complete an activity schedule that monitored what Edith had done during the day.

The rationale for this approach was that in the first instance we aimed to promote fundamental behavioural changes and so we initially needed to monitor baseline activity. The other advantage of this approach was that although we monitored Edith's behaviour we did not explore complicated explanations of that behaviour. This can actually be quite liberating for both staff and clients when working with chronic depression (Williams, 1991). In the same way that writing down automatic thoughts on a piece of paper helps the individual to differentiate the thought from themselves, monitoring behaviour in this way promotes distancing. This allows client and staff to see the behaviour objectively as an aspect of the depression that needs to be changed without indulging in crude 'mad or bad' judgemental debates.

The only automatic thoughts elicited at this stage related specifically to the client's views of CT. We established that Edith believed 100% that 'cognitive therapy won't work for me'. As well as acknowledging this and thanking Edith for her honesty, the therapist explored similarities and differences between CT and other treatments that had failed. It was then negotiated with Edith that outside the session she would examine the idea in more detail by speaking with the staff and current inpatients about the treatment programme and reviewing a handout on the therapy programme. This approach obviously differs from others and contrasted sharply with Edith's previous experience where new treatments had often been presented in a very positive light to enhance engagement and any initial placebo effect. This tactic is understandable but may be particularly detrimental when offering CT to people with chronic depression as the therapist is aiming to instil 'realistic hope' without promising blindly to succeed in resolving her problems.

At the next brief session the therapist again talked with Edith about her views on CT. It was established that she had not read the handout because 'there didn't seem much point and I can't really concentrate', but she had talked with other people. The session was taken up by reviewing what other people had said and then reading the handout together. At the end, Edith rated her automatic thought that 'CT would not work for her' 80%. The therapist regarded this as good news; it suggested room for doubt, and was the beginning of engaging Edith in CT. Furthermore (given an actual non-response rate of 30–60%), it could be argued that Edith was moving toward 'healthy scepticism' about CT, regular monitoring of the idea that 'CT would not work for me' now needed to be challenged by experiences of the therapy.

Sessions 6–9

The first attempts at behavioural change focused on basic tasks, particularly self-care. The key worker agreed a daily schedule with Edith that allocated a specified *period of time* to self-care tasks and other staff acted as 'motivators' and 'reinforcers' to help her engage in these. A period of time was selected rather than completion of a particular task because setting tasks with someone who is indecisive and unmotivated often means half of the day would be wasted and there would be little time spent on other more positive or pleasurable activities. The rationale put to the client was to get as far as she could in the time with a list of self-care tasks in the allocated time, then to move on to the other unrelated activities on the schedule. Automatic thoughts about the tasks were not discussed at this stage, no debate was held about 'the point' of changing behaviour. The idea was promoted that the baseline schedule had shown lack of self-care to be a deficit and that an attempt would be made to change it. This tactic seemed to work as Edith's self-care improved and also she began to complete more tasks within the time period allocated. Furthermore, she spontaneously commented on feeling 'a little better'.

The other focus of these sessions was on the 'desire to escape'. Retiring to bed was initially tackled through behavioural and cognitive strategies. Firstly, the number of times she withdrew was noted from the schedule. Edith agreed to try to reduce the number of times per day she retired to her room. We used the 'Premack principle' to try and aid collaboration. Edith liked the opportunity to talk in more detail about many of her problems, but within the CT sessions it was obviously important to retain the structure of CT and to try not to rush in to trying to solve complex difficulties at home that might be more appropriately tackled later or after discharge. The therapist was conscious of the possible tension in this approach and the possibility that Edith would feel she was not being listened to (as she had commented in her assessment). It was therefore suggested that we linked her withdrawal behaviours to her desire to ventilate about her problems. She would be allowed 10 minutes of night staff time for each reduction in 'escapes' to her bedroom. Over the first week she managed to reduce her time alone considerably. The opportunity to talk reinforced the idea that she was being 'heard' (and valued) by the staff and further helped her to engage in CT. Furthermore, the nominated member of night staff got the chance to meet with Edith and gradually to shape the 'ventilation sessions' such that at a later stage these became the 'evening therapy' component of the CT programme.

The occasions when Edith still withdrew to her room allowed an important piece of work to be carried out on her automatic thoughts. It became clear that she always withdrew from situations where she perceived she might be judged, rejected or something might be asked of her that she feared she could not achieve. The nursing staff now turned their attention to these situations in her daily activity schedule and acted as 'collaborators' in any related tasks and carried out immediate *in vivo* tests of her automatic thoughts.

Sessions 10–12

Edith's difficulties in occupying her time were to a certain extent overcome by the structuring of her daily timetable. The unit had a general routine for all clients combined with specific activities agreed by the key worker and the client.

The lack of pleasure in day-to-day activities was tackled in a 'standard' CT approach. Edith was asked to make mastery and pleasure ratings of her daily schedule. The key worker then negotiated with her about trying to incorporate potentially enjoyable activities into the timetable. In order to demonstrate the alliance between the key worker and the cognitive therapist (whom Edith was seeing for the brief sessions) a joint session was held. Edith suggested that she found no activities enjoyable, so she was asked to identify with her key worker over the next few days the three 'least unenjoyable' activities. The key worker then monitored the next few days' activities carefully to ensure that the plan was carried through and was available to reinforce engagement in the tasks as required. At the next session, Edith reported on which activities had been most enjoyable (although all scored very low) and was asked to include the two that she had rated highest into her next schedule and to choose other activities from the list to try, or to suggest alternatives to include.

Although the use of benzodiazepine was controlled through her being an inpatient, it was now felt appropriate to tackle this issue. This was an important secondary complication of Edith's chronic depression, but was a problem with less stability than some of the other listed difficulties. The session started with a discussion of the use of diazepam before coming to the unit. Edith described that she felt distressed in a way that neither she nor anyone else could control. The distress was particularly characterised by feelings of tension and the general practitioner had prescribed diazepam with instructions that it could be taken as required up to a maximum of four times per day. Although Edith then found a means of controlling her tension through self-medication with diazepam, her usage quickly escalated.

Initially, the therapist deliberately reframed the behaviour as a coping strategy. It was important not to suggest to Edith that she had no coping skills, but rather to identify the advantages and disadvantages of the approach employed. This engaged Edith in the discussion about how she understood the need to control tension in order to function, that she wanted to deal with the thoughts surrounding the loss of her mother (that led to tension) and that a different coping strategy might be more appropriate. Edith acknowledged that the use of benzodiazepine was counter-productive as she eventually adapted to it and needed to take more medication to achieve the same level of relief. Furthermore, it never allowed her to deal with the source of her tension. Edith was reluctant to explore her previous relationship with her mother, but agreed to engage in a benzodiazepine withdrawal programme, to review with her key worker the cue characteristics of an effective coping strategy and to begin to identify any automatic thoughts relating to the loss of her mother.

The therapy had now been in progress for four weeks. Edith reported some increase in her motivation to engage because she felt 'understood' by the people working with her. The collaboration and pacing seemed to reassure her that she would not be 'forced' into accepting a treatment plan, but that discussions would lead to jointly selected targets. Reviewing the problem list revealed that inroads had been made into the problem in day-to-day functioning. The relative success in dealing with these issues had been important in instilling belief in the client that some improvements could be made in her life. These problems were subtly linked to the intrapersonal problems that Edith had described: ruminating about herself had been linked with 'escapism'. Issues relating to the death of her mother were being tackled through linking this with her benzodiazepine abuse.

The relearning of simple behavioural coping strategies also allowed some impact to be made on 'getting depressed about being depressed'. Finally, the positive therapeutic relationship was important in beginning to undermine the notion that Edith was unlikeable. The sessions were now reduced to twice weekly and there was a shift towards more cognitive as opposed to behavioural interventions.

Sessions 13–16

The exploration of thoughts relating to her mother's death allowed Edith to establish that she was not responsible for this event, which led to some improvement in her mood. It also allowed access to some issues relating to Edith's family. The therapist and Edith agreed that the move of house had generated a number of marital tensions, and Edith herself noted that her negative self-image had been reinforced by this and by her eldest child taking over some of her 'mothering role'. The next four sessions focused particularly on these issues. It was felt important that further individual work was done before approaching any members of the family and looking in more detail at the interpersonal relationships. Unless Edith was feeling more positive and secure about herself, it would be difficult to prevent any negative family interactions from undermining the fragile improvement in her self-esteem.

Reattribution techniques were used to help Edith review her sense of responsibility for the house move. She came to the opinion that whilst she had instigated the move, her husband took at least a portion of the responsibility for the move and she recalled, indeed, initially he had been very positive about his new job and the new friends he had made. Her views about being a 'bad mother' were revised by exposing the differences between how she had been before she became depressed as opposed to afterwards. The cognitive techniques used for these intrapersonal problems have been well described previously (see Beck et al., 1979; Fennell, 1997) and were reasonably successful with this client. The next sessions began to look at the family situation more specifically.

Sessions 17–24

As well as continuing to deal with the problems on Edith's list and continuing to reinforce her changed behaviour patterns, these sessions also offered support for the forthcoming family sessions. Issues that would need to be put on the agenda with the family were discussed in detail with Edith. Her ideas regarding her relationships with her husband and children, and her lack of a social network, were analysed with tentative plans about how they would be addressed. The aim was not just to explore the problems but also to get Edith to cognitively rehearse the family sessions (thus allowing Edith and the therapist to identify and overcome 'roadblocks'). In the family sessions, Edith would then be encouraged to present information and deal with questions herself rather than the family talking directly with the therapist and excluding Edith. This arrangement was carried out and helped the client feel more in control. It provided her family with evidence of the improvement in her functioning through her enhanced assertiveness and they felt more confident about expressing their opinions about issues (as they did not feel they had to protect Edith from their true beliefs). This allowed the therapist to focus on identifying and challenging distorted family cognitions and to act as a negotiator between Edith and her family regarding her place within the family system.

The family sessions revealed the family's anxieties that Edith's improvement would be short-lived. Her husband and eldest daughter expressed resistance to relinquishing activities previously carried out by Edith. For the weekend leave, the family were encouraged to carry out graded reallocation of tasks, so that Edith could gradually increase her level of responsibility in the household. They were all encouraged to note the outcome of this experiment and report back. This exercise was repeated on a number of weekends so that Edith gradually built up her confidence (any negative thoughts being tackled back at the unit) and her level of activity. The family were also presented with concrete evidence of change.

The next family sessions focused on specific aspects of interpersonal functioning and associated cognitions. Edith's husband was able to give clear reassurance that he had no intention of leaving her, but the couple did look at good and bad aspects of their marriage and resolved to carry out a number of tasks related to trying to 'change the negatives'. Attention was given to her interaction with both children, particularly her eldest daughter. Again positives were reinforced, whilst negatives were tackled appropriately. An example was that Edith's children had felt unable to go to tell her about their problems with school or friends because she had seemed preoccupied or distant, or they feared making her worse. They had increasingly confided in their father. It was resolved that Edith would set aside particular times on her weekend leave to have the chance to talk with each child individually as well as scheduling some 'family' activities each day.

Edith then set about tackling her social isolation. The first exercise was to write a letter to her previous confidante who lived near her old house. The task of re-establishing contacts was again carried out in a graded way accompanied by exploration of automatic thoughts. After the letter, a contact was made in person. Recent experiences (her prolonged 'absence' from social networks through illness and then hospitalisation) were linked to the insecurity she felt in the past during her prolonged absences from school (because of her mother's ill-health). This allowed the first attempts at exploration of her underlying beliefs.

Sessions 25–28

By this stage Edith was having extended periods of leave at home. Therapy sessions were now held weekly with a brief scheduled telephone contact with the therapist during her absence from the unit. During the weekly sessions, Edith began to identify anxious automatic thoughts relating to discharge and fears about coping in the future. These were tackled systematically, and time was also set aside for careful planning of how Edith would work on maintaining her cognitive and behavioural coping skills through self-monitoring and through the development of a hierarchy of strategies to be used at times of crisis. The latter were listed on a card which Edith kept with her.

Edith enlisted into a 'personal effectiveness' group (held near her home) on her own initiative, as she identified her need to improve her interpersonal skills. Through the church she had made one or two contacts with neighbours and had mainly found their attitudes sympathetic and supportive. This had countered her fears of rejection 'because I'm mad'. She had a significant setback because one individual overtly rejected her, but this provided excellent material to reinforce therapy techniques and to demonstrate the effectiveness of the approaches documented on the crisis card. It also acted as a 'warning' to Edith that there were a number of potential hurdles to that would need to be confronted after discharge.

Post-discharge

Edith was discharged from the unit after an 11-week admission. Two 'crisis' calls were received in the first few days. The events, thoughts and feelings were analysed and tackled cognitively by telephone. Both contacts were precipitated by feelings of 'panic' associated with a fear of not coping with a forthcoming social event and the fantasy that this would lead to a catastrophic relapse. The events were rehearsed and Edith was encouraged to ring back afterwards to report how it had gone. This allowed reinforcement of the use of the techniques and Edith felt more confident that the 'back-up system' was effective. Therapy post-discharge took the form of the standard CT approach (Beck et al., 1979). Although much of the work focused on low self-esteem, dysfunctional assumptions and core beliefs, it was still important to pay attention to activity scheduling, and reinforcing the testing of automatic thoughts and so on.

Edith eventually took up part-time work near her new home. She continued to make steady progress, but travelled to Newcastle every two weeks for CT. She remained fragile but coping. There were setbacks around the time of the anniversary of her mother's death, when her youngest child had difficulties with the move to senior school, and intermittently when her husband again expressed resentments about the move of house. She remained in outpatient CT for a further six months, then attended four booster sessions per year after that. At three-year follow-up she reported she was functioning well in the community and her husband said he was beginning to dare to think that the worst was over.

OUTCOME RESEARCH

There is a great deal of evidence that CT is an effective treatment for depression (for reviews of outcome research see: Hollon et al., 1992; US DHHS, 1993; Scott, 1995). Although most studies have been conducted on outpatient samples that meet research criteria for the diagnosis of acute unipolar major depressive disorder without psychotic features, there are five published studies of the use of CT for dysthymia. In addition, Fava et al. (1994, 1996) have specifically explored the acute and four-year outcome of clients with residual depressive symptoms who were treated with CT after receiving medication. In addition, there are three studies of inpatient CT for clients with dysthymia or treatment resistant chronic major depressive disorders.

Outpatient CT for Dysthymia and Residual Depressive Symptoms

Fennell and Teasdale (1982) reported that when a standard course of outpatient CT was offered to individuals with 'treatment refractory' dysthymia, only one out of five clients met criteria for recovery and the reduction in symptom severity between baseline and follow-up assessment was modest (mean HRSD scores fell by 24%). Harpin et al. (1982) reported a statistically significant 37% reduction in mean HRSD scores in

12 clients who had previously failed to respond to medication; at the end of therapy the recovery rate was 33%. Gonzales, Lewinsohn and Clarke (1985) undertook the largest study of CT for dysthymia providing 12 sessions (each session = 2 hours) of either individual or group therapy. They reported that 19 subjects with dysthymia met recovery criteria (34%). Stravinski, Sahar and Verreault (1991) treated six clients with dysthymia with 15 weekly sessions of individual CT and reported a response rate of 66%. Mercier, Stewart and Quitkin (1992) offered a maximum of 16 weeks of individual CT followed by four booster sessions over the subsequent six months to 15 clients with dysthymic disorders of over seven years duration. At 16 weeks, six clients (40%) met recovery criteria with four subjects remaining well at 10-month follow-up.

Fava and colleagues (1994; 1996) explored the effectiveness of sequential CT or clinical management (CM) for 40 clients who were assessed as having responded to antidepressant medication but who had residual symptoms of major depression. Subjects were randomly assigned to CT or CM and the medication was gradually withdrawn. At 24 months, there was a significant reduction in the level of residual symptoms in the CT group but not in the CM group, and during this period only three CT as compared to seven CM clients experienced a relapse. At four-year follow-up, this difference in outcome was significant with twice as many clients who received CM (70%) as compared to CT (35%) experiencing a depressive relapse (see Table 4.2).

Inpatient CT for Dysthymia and Treatment Refractory Major Depressive Disorders

The only controlled study of CT without medication for inpatients with dysthymia was performed by De Jong, Trieber and Henrich (1986). This study had significant limitations including a small number of clients in each treatment condition ($n = 10$) and the use of an outpatient control group. Treatment response was higher in hospitalized clients who received a complete package of CT (60%) as compared to inpatient cognitive restructuring (30%) or supportive outpatient therapy (10%). Although it was reported that gains were maintained at six-month follow-up, only 50% of the sample took part in this re-assessment.

Scott and colleagues (Barker, Scott & Eccleston, 1987; Scott, 1992) reported two studies of the use of a combined medication plus CT package in chronic treatment refractory major depression. In the first study, Barker, Scott & Eccleston (1987) reported no significant differences in response rate in 20 inpatients randomly assigned to standard inpatient treatment with

Table 4.2   Outcome research of CT for chronic and refractory depressive disorders

Study	CT model	Sample size	Recovery rate *n*	%
Outpatient Studies				
Fennell & Teasdale (1982)	30 sessions over 12–15 weeks	5	1	20
Harpin et al. (1982)	20 sessions over 10 weeks	12	4	33
Gonzales, Lewinsohn & Clarke (1985)	12 x 2 hourly group or individual sessions over 8 weeks	54	19	34
Stravinski, Sahar & Verreault (1991)	15 weekly sessions	6	4	66
Mercier, Stewart & Quitkin (1992)	Maximum 16 weekly sessions plus 4 booster sessions over 6 months	15	6	40
Total		**92**	**34**	**37**
Inpatient Studies				
De Jong, Trieber & Henrich (1986)	3 months of inpatient CT alone	10	6	60
Scott (1992):				
Sample 1	15 sessions of individual CT plus medication over 3 months	8	4	50
Sample 2	Cognitive milieu therapy plus medication over 3 months (about 30–40 hours of CT)	16	11	72
Total		**34**	**21**	**62**
Total for inpatient & outpatient studies		**126**	**55**	**44**

optimal medication as compared to optimal medication plus CT. However, in a second study of 24 clients with treatment refractory depression of at least four years duration, Scott (1992) noted that inpatient CT plus medication was more effective if given as a 'cognitively oriented hospital milieu' treatment package followed by outpatient CT for six months ($n = 16$; recovery rate = 70%) than in a standard individual CT format ($n = 8$; recovery rate = 50%). Furthermore, the percentage change in mean HRSD scores was 57% for CT milieu treatment (mean HRSD fell from 25.5 to 10.6) as compared to 42% for the standard CT approach (mean HRSD fell from 22.5 to 13.1). Preliminary data from a four-year follow-up study of 50 consecutive referrals to this clinic who had chronic treatment refractory depressive disorders and who were treated with CT plus medication demonstrated that the median time to recovery was 13 months and that 42% of clients met recovery criteria at 48 months (Scott,1996).

CONCLUSIONS

Clients with chronic depressive disorders present a challenge for any form of therapy. However, there is tentative evidence to support the effectiveness of CT for both severe and mild chronic depressions. Most outcome research of CT for dysthymia comprises open studies with small sample sizes. However, it should be noted that these studies are comparable in size and design to many studies of pharmacotherapy for this client population, and the mean recovery rate (40%) is also similar (Price, Charney & Heninger, 1986). Given that clients with dysthymia are known to have a low placebo response rate of about 15% (Roth & Fonagy, 1996) and often refuse to take antidepressant medication (Markowitz, 1994), these results should perhaps instil hope rather than despair in clinicians working with clients with chronic depressions.

The decision about whether to offer CT to a client will be influenced by the nature of the problems identified, the evidence for the effectiveness of the therapy for those specific treatment targets and the availability of an experienced, willing therapist. The importance of the latter should not be underestimated and needs emphasising in any discussion of the use of CT for chronic depressive disorders. Cognitive therapy research has demonstrated a significant correlation ($r = 0.5$) between therapists' adherence to the CT model and client outcome (DeRubeis & Feeley, 1991) and that individuals treated by an expert CT therapist are less likely to drop out and are significantly more likely to report symptomatic improvement than those treated by novice therapists (Burns & Nolen-Hoeksema, 1992). Level of expertise in CT is particularly important when treating individuals with chronic and severe disorders (Roth & Fonagy, 1996; Scott, 1996). However, this is not simply because of the research data, but also because novice therapists quickly become de-skilled and demoralised when trying to help clients who have experienced multiple treatment failures and who have little faith or enthuasiam for the new approach being proposed.

Expert CT therapists often find working with clients with chronic depressive disorders difficult. It is important to limit the number of such cases on therapists' case load and to receive regular supervision and/or peer support. Therapists have to be able to retain some sense of optimism as well as being prepared to tolerate working with partial conceptualisations with gaps that may never be answered fully. In such circumstances, the therapist must set realistic targets with the clients, and in many instances a coping rather than a mastery model will be more appropriate. Lastly, identifying something that the therapist particularly likes about each client and retaining a sense of intrigue as to why this individual developed a chronic disorder will also help the therapist keep going during the inevitable periods when progress is slow or there seems no obvious way to help move the process forward. If therapists can strike a balance between expecting too much and expecting too little, they may be able to help promote a better quality of life for a group of clients who have rarely received the attention they deserve.

REFERENCES

Akiskal, H. (1982). Factors associated with incomplete recovery in primary depressive illness. *Journal of Clinical Psychiatry*, **43**, 266–271.

Barker, W., Scott, J. & Eccleston, D. (1987). The Newcastle chronic depression study: Results of a treatment regime. *International Clinical Psychopharmacology*, **2**, 261–272.

Beck, A., Rush, A., Shaw, B. & Emery, G. (1979). *Cognitive Therapy of Depression*. New York: Guilford.

Bothwell, R. & Scott, J. (1997). The influence of cognitive variables on recovery in depressed inpatients. *Journal of Affective Disorders*, **43**, 207–212.

Burns, D. & Nolen-Hoeksema, S. (1992). Therapeutic empathy and recovery from depression in cognitive behavioural therapy : A structural equation model. *Journal of Consulting & Clinical Psychology*, **60**, 441–449.

Cochran, S. (1984). Preventing medical non-compliance in the outpatient treatment of bipolar affective disorder. *Journal of Nervous & Mental Diseases*, **176**, 45–54.

Cornwall, P. & Scott, J. (1997). Partial remission in depressive disorders. *Acta Psychiatrica Scandinavica*, **95**, 265–271.

De Jong, R., Trieber, R. & Henrich, G. (1986). Effectiveness of two psychological treatments for inpatients with severe and chronic depressions. *Cognitive Therapy & Research*, **10**, 645–653.

DeRubeis, R. & Feeley, M. (1991). Determinants of change in cognitive therapy for depression. *Cognitive Therapy & Research*, **14**, 469–82.

Fava, G., Grandi, S., Zielezny, M., Canestrari, R. & Morphy, M. (1994). Cognitive behavioural treatment of residual symptoms in primary major depressive disorder. *American Journal of Psychiatry*, **151**, 1295–1299.

Fava, G., Grandi, S., Zielezny, M., Rafanelli, C. & Canestrari, R. (1996). Four year outcome of cognitive behavioural treatment of residual symptoms in major depression. *American Journal of Psychiatry*, **153**, 945–947.

Fawcett, J., Epstein, P. & Feister, S. (1987). Clinical management—Imipramine/placebo administration manual. *Psychopharmacology Bulletin*, **23**, 309–324.

Fennell, M. (1997). Low self-esteem: A cognitive perspective. *Behavioural & Cognitive Psychotherapy*, **25**, 1–26.

Fennell, M. & Teasdale, J. (1982). Cognitive therapy with chronic drug refractory depressed outpatients : A note of caution. *Cognitive Therapy & Research*, **6**, 455–460.

Gonzales, L., Lewinsohn, P. & Clarke, G. (1985). Longitudinal follow-up of unipolar depressives : An investigation of predictors of relapse. *Journal of Consulting & Clinical Psychology*, **53**, 461–469.

Harpin, R., Liberman, R., Marks, I., Stern, S. & Bohannon, W. (1982). Cognitive behaviour therapy for chronically depressed patients: A controlled pilot study. *Journal of Nervous & Mental Diseases*, **170**, 295–301.

Hollon, S., DeRubeis, R., Evans, M., Weimer, M., Garvey, M., Grove, W. et al. (1992). Cognitive therapy and pharmacotherapy for depression: Singly and in combination. *Archives of General Psychiatry*, **49**, 774–781.

Klerman, G. (1990). Treatment of recurrent unipolar major depressive disorder. *Archives of General Psychiatry*, **47**, 1158–1162.

Krantz, S. & Moos, R (1988). Risk factors at intake predict non-remission among depressed patients. *Journal of Consulting & Clinical Psychology*, **56**, 863–869.

Markowitz, J. (1994). Psychotherapy of dysthymia. *American Journal of Psychiatry*, **151**, 1114–1121.

Mercier, M., Stewart, J. & Quitkin, F. (1992). A pilot sequential study of cognitive therapy and pharmacotherapy of atypical depression. *Journal of Clinical Psychiatry*, **53**, 166–170.

Padesky, C. & Greenberger, D. (1996). *Mind over Mood*. London: Guilford.

Paykel, E. (1994). Epidemiology of refractory depression. In W. Nolen, J. Zohar, S. Roose & J. Amsterdam (Eds) *Treatment Refractory Depression* pp. 3–18. London: Wiley.

Price, L., Charney, D. & Heninger, G. (1986). Variability of response to lithium augmentation in refractory depression. *American Journal of Psychiatry*, **143**, 1387–1392

Roth, A. & Fonagy, R. (1996). *What Works for Whom?* New York: Guilford.

Rush, A. (1988). Cognitive approaches to adherence. In A. Frances & R. Hale (Eds) *Review of Psychiatry:* Vol. 8. Washington: APA Press.

Scott, J. (1988). Chronic depression. *British Journal of Psychiatry*, **153**, 287–297.

Scott, J. (1991). Chronic depression: Epidemiology, demography and definitions. *International Journal of Psychopharmacology*, **10**, 12–19.

Scott, J. (1992). Chronic depression: Can cognitive therapy succeed when other treatments fail? *Behavioural and Cognitive Psychotherapy*, **20**, 25–36.

Scott, J. (1995). Psychological treatments of depression : An update. *British Journal of Psychiatry*, **167**, 289–292.

Scott, J. (1996). *Immediate and four-year outcome of CT for chronic, treatment refractory major depression.* Paper presented at the World Congress of Cognitive and Behaviour Therapies, Copenhagen, Denmark.

Scott, J., Cole, A. & Eccleston, D. (1991). Dealing with persisting abnormalities of mood. *International Review of Psychiatry*, **3**, 19–33.

Scott, J. & Wright, J. (1996). Cognitive therapy for individuals with severe and chronic mental disorders. *American Psychiatric Association Review of Psychiatry.* Vol. 16, pp. 153–201. Washington: APA.

Shea, T., Pilkonis, P., Beckham, E., Collins, J., Sotsky, S., Elkin, I. et al. (1990). Personality disorders and treatment outcome in the NIMH treatment of depression collaborative outcome study. *American Journal of Psychiatry*, **147**, 711–718.

Stravinski, A., Sahar, A. & Verreault, R. (1991). A pilot study of cognitive treatment of dysthymic disorder. *Behavioural Psychotherapy*, **4**, 387–394.

Teasdale, J. (1985). Psychological treatments for depression—how do they work? *Behaviour Research & Therapy*, **23**, 157–165.

Thase, M. (1994). The roles of psychosocial factors and psychotherapy in refractory depression. In W. Nolen, J. Zohar, S. Roose & J. Amsterdam (Eds) *Treatment Refractory Depression* pp. 83–95. London: Wiley.

Thase, M. & Kupfer, D. (1987). Characteristics of treatment resistant depression. In J. Zohar & R. Belmaker (Eds) *Treating Resistant Depression* pp. 23–45. New York : PMA Publishing Corp.

Thase, M., Reynolds, C. & Frank, E. (1993). Response to cognitive therapy in chronic depression. *Journal of Psychotherapy Practice & Research*, **3**, 204–214.

US DHHS (1993). *Depression in Primary Care. Vol. 2: Treatment of Major Depression.* Rockville: AHCPR Publications.

Williams, J.M.G. (1991). *The Psychological Management of Depression* (2nd edn, pp. 178–200). London: Routledge.

Wright, J., Thase, M., Beck, A. & Ludgate, J. (1993). *Cognitive Therapy with Inpatients.* New York: Guilford.

Zeiss, A., Lewinsohn, P. & Munoz, R. (1987). Non-specific improvement effects in depression using interpersonal skills training, pleasant activity schedules, or cognitive training. *Journal of Consulting & Clinical Psychology*, **47**, 427–439.

Chapter 5

COGNITIVE BEHAVIOURAL TREATMENT FOR COMPLICATED CASES OF POST-TRAUMATIC STRESS DISORDER

Matthew O. Kimble*, David S. Riggs* and Terence M. Keane*

INTRODUCTION

Working with patients who have experienced traumatic events is inherently complicated. The predominant psychological effects of trauma exposure encompass a wide range of signs, symptoms, and behaviours that are subsumed under the diagnosis of Post-traumatic Stress Disorder (PTSD; American Psychiatric Association, 1994). However, in survivors of trauma, psychological problems are not limited to those captured in the PTSD diagnosis. A substantial number of individuals with PTSD experience coexisting psychological disturbances including mood and anxiety disorders, personality change, substance abuse, and problems with anger, rage, and aggression (Kulka et al., 1990; Keane & Kaloupek, 1997). Difficulties for survivors of trauma often extend beyond strictly psychological issues; the biological sequelae to trauma include biochemical and perhaps structural changes in the brain (Bremner et al., 1995; Yehuda & McFarlane, 1997); the social sequelae of trauma include isolation, increased interpersonal conflicts, feelings of detachment, and generally poor occupational and social functioning (Kulka et al., 1990; Hearst, Newman & Hulley, 1986; Resick et al., 1981). Ideally, sound treatment of trauma patients addresses problems in each area. Practically, implementation of such a comprehensive approach presents numerous therapeutic challenges.

* Boston University School of Medicine, Massachusetts, USA

Treating Complex Cases: The Cognitive Behavioural Therapy Approach.
Edited by Nicholas Tarrier, Adrian Wells and Gillian Haddock.

In our experience, it is the presentation of numerous concurrent clinical concerns that makes a particular PTSD treatment case 'complicated.' While there exist widely researched and experimentally validated psychosocial treatments for PTSD (e.g. Foa et al., 1991; Keane, 1997; Keane et al., 1985; Resick & Schnicke, 1992), in those cases of PTSD complicated by other problems, it can be difficult to implement these treatments. In such cases, treatments targeted towards PTSD symptoms should be augmented with other approaches so that a client's concerns are comprehensively addressed. In this chapter, we will present a behaviourally based approach to the assessment and treatment of complicated cases of PTSD. The chapter will review the relevant theory and research that support such an approach, discuss the methods for assessment in such cases, and outline how to utilise empirically validated treatments for PTSD and associated problems. Additionally, the chapter will place the proposed assessments and treatment strategies among the broader context of therapeutic and extra-therapeutic issues that add to the difficulty of treating many PTSD cases.

Case Study

To illustrate the challenges in working with complicated cases of PTSD and to provide a basis for discussion later in the chapter, we will describe the case of Mr Robert J. Mr J. is a 48-year-old Caucasian male Vietnam veteran who presented at our clinic with complaints of combat-related nightmares, sleep difficulties, elevated startle response, hypervigilance, social isolation, anger problems, and suicidal thoughts. Our initial evaluation identified a number of other problems including marital distress, unemployment, and chronic pain in his legs and lower back. Further assessment revealed the presence of alcohol abuse and depression with borderline and antisocial personality characteristics.

Mr J. served almost two full tours of duty (22 months) in Vietnam as a Marine infantryman. He was discharged from the military secondary to combat-related injuries to his legs. Upon his return from Vietnam, he did not work for a year while recovering from his injuries. At that time, he began to drink in order to quell the pain in his legs and to help him sleep. After a year, he obtained work with a family friend and thereafter worked odd jobs for the next 22 years. He often drank on the job and was involved in frequent altercations with coworkers. He married, had two children, was divorced after 3 years, and then remarried 10 years later. Five years prior to presenting at our clinic, Mr J. lost his job due to company restructuring; he had not worked since. His drinking and PTSD symptoms became worse subsequent to his job loss. Both Mr J. and his wife reported an increase in conflict within the family over the last few years with a dramatic increase in the past 6 months. Both reported violent altercations in the past although, none resulted in injuries that required medical attention. At the time of evaluation, Mr J.'s wife was threatening to end the relationship, but feared doing so because of Mr J.'s potential for suicide.

As in the case of Mr J., trauma survivors can present a range of simultaneous psychosocial concerns; however research suggests that systematic analysis and treatment can ameliorate even the most complex combinations of problems. The results of randomised, controlled clinical studies indicate that trauma victims can experience relief from treatments focused on the alleviation of core PTSD symptoms (Keane et al., 1989a; Foa et al., 1991; Resick & Schnicke, 1992; Davidson & van der Kolk, 1996). In addition, empirically validated treatments for many of the concurrent problems such as substance abuse, depression, social isolation, chronic pain, marital distress, and violence are available. However, in cases such as that of Mr J., the presence of multiple serious problems may compromise the effectiveness or even contraindicate specific treatments for any individual problem. However, the conceptual framework provided by cognitive behavioural theory provides the therapist with a therapeutic strategy for even these most difficult cases.

COGNITIVE BEHAVIOURAL THEORY AND RESEARCH IN PTSD TREATMENT

The central role of anxious arousal and avoidance in PTSD and the presence of identifiable conditioning events led several authors to propose learning theories of PTSD based on Mowrer's (1947, 1960) Two-Factor Theory (Kilpatrick, Veronen & Resick, 1982). According to this theory, anxiety is conditioned to previously neutral cues present at the time of the traumatic event. Through generalisation and higher order conditioning, this arousal becomes associated with a broad range of stimuli. Avoidance behaviours, including avoidance of reminders of the trauma and detachment from others, develop in response to the anxiety and are reinforced by the reduction in arousal associated with their use. The persistence and generalisation of these avoidance behaviours contribute to broader deficits in functioning and can maintain these debilitating symptoms.

Two-factor theory contributed substantially to our understanding of PTSD and importantly led directly to the development of interventions for the disorder (e.g., Foa et al., 1991; Keane et al., 1985), however it has a number of limitations. In particular, a theory of human psychopathology that does not give a central role to cognitive processes such as attention, memory, and intrusive thoughts will necessarily be limited in its conceptual understanding of PTSD patients. In part to address some of these issues, theories of trauma reactions based on cognitive and information-processing models have been proposed (e.g. Chemtob et al., 1988; Foa & Riggs, 1993; Litz & Keane, 1989; McCann & Pearlman, 1990). Generally, these models propose that PTSD influences how an individual appraises the world, themselves, and others and provides specific predictions regarding behavioural and cognitive changes that occur when that individual interacts with the environment. Although information processing theories are useful in understanding aspects of post-traumatic reactions, their relatively recent development has limited their contribution to interventions for PTSD. One notable exception is the Cognitive Processing Therapy developed by Resick and her colleagues (Resick & Schnicke, 1992; Calhoun & Resick, 1993; Weaver, Chard & Resick, Chapter 16, this volume).

As described earlier, cognitive behavioural treatments for PTSD have focused primarily on the central role of anxiety and other aversive emotional states. Although several specific forms of cognitive behavioural treatments for PTSD have been developed, most have evolved from, or incorporated aspects of, empirically tested treatments for other anxiety disorders. Examples include variations of direct therapeutic exposure (e.g. Foa, et al., 1991; Boudewyns, et al., 1990; Keane et al., 1989a), Anxiety Management Training (e.g. Foa, et al., 1991; Keane et al., 1989a; Kilpatrick, Veronen & Resick, 1982) and combinations of the two (e.g. Resick & Schnicke, 1992).

Direct therapeutic exposure (e.g. desensitisation, flooding, prolonged exposure) successfully reduced PTSD symptoms in studies of rape victims (Foa et al., 1991) and combat veterans (Boudewyns et al., 1990; Keane et al., 1989a). Descriptions of such treatments are available in the literature (Lyons & Keane, 1989; Foa et al., 1991; Keane et al., 1994) and the reader is directed to these sources for a fuller explanation of these techniques. In brief, therapeutic exposure requires the client to directly confront traumatic cues and/or memories within the supportive context of the therapeutic relationship. Typically, this involves the client repeatedly relating the events of the trauma imaginally and verbally to the therapist. It has been argued that for exposure therapy to be optimally effective, the client must experience the aversive emotions associated with the memories as well as stimulus response and meaning components of the memory (Foa & Kozak, 1986; Lang, 1977). Prolonged presentations of the memory repeated multiple times inexorably lead to anxiety reduction and can even change cognitive appraisals of the event.

Anxiety Management Training (AMT), a term that describes a number of interventions targeted at improving an individual's ability to cope with anxiety symptoms, is also effective in reducing PTSD symptoms when used alone (Kilpatrick, Veronen & Resick, 1979; Foa et al., 1991). The most well studied of these approaches is Stress Inoculation Training (SIT: Meichenbaum & Jaremko, 1983) which was adapted by Kilpatrick, Veronen and Resick (1982) to address the needs of rape victims. SIT teaches strategies to address difficulties in each of three 'channels' where anxiety may manifest itself: the physical and autonomic channel, the behavioural or motoric channel, and the cognitive channel. Typical skills include muscle relaxation and breathing re-education for the physical channel, covert modelling and role-playing for the behavioural channel, and guided self-dialogue for the cognitive channel. Skills training can also include problem-focused groups that educate and teach skills associated with particular problems common to individuals with PTSD such as anger, assertiveness, communication, relationship distress, parenting difficulties, and poor social skills.

Resick and Schnicke (1992) have developed an effective cognitive behavioural treatment for rape survivors termed Cognitive Processing Therapy (CPT) that includes elements of both direct therapeutic exposure and anxiety management. CPT is a structured 12-session approach that relies heavily on cognitive restructuring techniques to alter cognitive distortions common among rape trauma survivors. CPT also includes direct exposure to the traumatic cues via the client's written descriptions of the event. According to the theory underlying this treatment, CPT improves on exposure techniques by addressing not just fear but also other feelings such as guilt, anger, and hopelessness (Resick & Schnicke, 1992).

Another recent development in the cognitive behavioural treatment of PTSD is Eye Movement Desensitisation and Reprocessing (EMDR: Shapiro, 1989, 1995). This largely atheoretical therapy has shown some promise in reducing PTSD symptoms (Boudewyns & Hyer, 1996; Wilson, Becker & Tinker, 1995), although other researchers have found no difference between EMDR and no treatment (Renfrey & Spates, 1994; Jensen, 1994). EMDR shares a number of treatment elements with well established cognitive and exposure therapies. For example, clients are asked to recall the events of their trauma, monitor physiological responses to the memory, and identify alternative cognitive appraisals of that memory. The treatment also prompts the client to engage in repeated sets of lateral eye movements while focusing on initial reactions and the therapeutic alternative cognition in treatment. The extent to which any one of these elements contributes to recovery is the focus of much controversy and requires further investigation (Keane, 1997).

The development of effective cognitive behavioural treatments for the symptoms of PTSD has clearly helped trauma survivors; however, the utility of such techniques when they are employed with patients suffering from multiple co-morbid psychological conditions and psychosocial problems, as in the case of Mr J., remains uninvestigated. Clearly, the presence of problems other than PTSD complicates the provision of these therapies to many traumatised individuals. For example, it is possible that problems other than anxiety are central to a given patient's impairment. Thus, anxiety reduction/management techniques may not address the client's primary problems or, more seriously, may exacerbate the client's current problems. Under these circumstances, the patient's additional problems need to be identified, prioritised, and successfully treated with available techniques.

Dealing with the many clinical issues presented by PTSD patients with concurrent diagnoses and psychosocial problems can be daunting for even the most experienced therapist. The lack of a single clear point of intervention, coupled with the typical clinician's desire to alleviate all of the survivor's problems, may lead the clinician to errantly engage in a series of unsystematic attempts to deal with multiple problems simultaneously (or at least those that are most predominant on any given day). Alternatively, clinicians may experience a sense of therapeutic helplessness in which they intervene inadequately in one area out of concern for exacerbating other existing problems. In the balance of this chapter, we will present a cognitive behavioural framework for conceptualising the assessment and treatment of complicated cases of PTSD that will provide therapists with points for intervention in these complex cases.

A CBT APPROACH TO COMPLICATED PTSD CASES

Cognitive behavioural therapy encompasses a variety of techniques designed to address the varied psychological and behavioural problems presented by clients. These techniques share several common elements that define the approach and guide intervention (Rimm & Masters, 1979). Among these common elements are three that will serve as the basis for the approach to PTSD outlined in the present chapter. First, the therapist assumes that maladaptive behaviours are, to some extent, learned and that learning principles can be effective in modifying these behaviours. Second, the therapist places value on obtaining empirical support for the efficacy of his/her interventions. Third, the therapist adapts the method of treatment to the client's problems.

In addition to these elements, the approach that we outline reflects a basic problem-solving philosophy regarding clinical decision making and intervention (Barlow, Hayes & Nelson, 1984; Barlow & Hersen, 1984; Nezu & Nezu, 1989). Within this approach, the clinician develops hypotheses as to the stimuli, responses, contingencies, and cognitive processes that serve to maintain the maladaptive behaviour and cognitions. During treatment, these hypotheses guide the implementation of specific interventions and lead to predictions about the results of these interventions. Data are collected over the course of treatment to evaluate the effectiveness of interventions and provide feedback to the clinician to further shape hypotheses. When data are consistent with a clinician's hypothesis, interventions continue based on that hypothesis. If the effects of any intervention are not as predicted, then the clinician generates a new hypothesis to guide future interventions. Thus, cognitive behavioural interventions are seen as a series of single case experiments in which hypotheses are developed, variables are manipulated through specific interventions, data are collected, predictions evaluated, and results guide future interventions.

When faced with a trauma survivor presenting with multiple problems, the therapist develops simultaneous hypotheses to account for the complex interrelations of symptoms, other problems, and a variety of maintaining factors. At present, considerable emphasis in behavioural formulations of PTSD is placed upon the role of anxiety and avoidance. These formulations hypothesise that patients are at least partially successful in avoiding anxiety through the use of various behavioural and cognitive strategies (e.g. withdrawal, dissociation). However, these avoidance techniques also contribute to the patients' failure to engage in the emotional processing during treatment that is thought necessary to recover from a traumatic event (Foa & Riggs, 1993; Keane et al., 1989a). Thus, behaviourally based therapies have tended to focus on the reduction of avoidance and escape strategies using techniques such as exposure therapy and response prevention. However, this conceptualisation, with its emphasis on the role of anxiety and avoidance, minimises other potential aetiologic and maintaining factors for the concurrent problems.

Although we do not wish to downplay the meaningful role of anxiety in the development of PTSD, we encourage a broader perspective that carefully assesses the extent to which anxiety plays an aetiologic or maintaining role across all functional problems. Remaining aware of four logical possibilities in the relationship between trauma-related anxiety and other problems, clinicians might consider that:

1. The problems arose from and are maintained by the need to manage/ control anxiety.
2. The problems arose in response to the anxiety, but are currently maintained by other factors.

3. The problems arose from and are maintained by factors unrelated to anxiety.
4. The problems arose for some reason unrelated to anxiety, but are maintained because they help manage/control anxiety.

Anxiety, therefore, is only one of many aetiologic and maintaining factors that may contribute to current problems and should not automatically become the sole focus of treatment. Indeed, to plan effective interventions for patients with PTSD, therapists must evaluate the role of many factors that could potentially maintain problematic behaviours. In addition, the complexity of these cases requires therapists to recognise the potential for particular interventions to have multiple effects, some positive and some negative. However, by more completely addressing the interrelations of a patient's problems, this approach holds the promise of producing more meaningful and lasting changes.

The Phasic Model for PTSD Treatment

This problem-solving philosophy, when utilised with individuals with multiple problems, leaves a therapist with numerous potential areas of intervention. One way to manage these complexities is to outline a series of treatment priorities to limit the issues that must be addressed at any one point in time. Elsewhere, Keane and his colleagues have outlined a flexible, phase-oriented approach to therapy with traumatised individuals (Keane, 1995; Keane et al., 1994). This conceptualisation of treatment is useful in its recognition of the phasic nature of PTSD and the importance of matching specific interventions to the current needs of the patient.

The phase-oriented approach to PTSD treatment delineates six phases that describe the course of therapy with adult trauma survivors. The *emotional and behavioural stabilisation phase* focuses on the management of the crisis that typically initiates the patient entering therapy and assures that the patient has adequate resources and skills to meet basic needs and to remain safe. During *the trauma education phase*, the clinician provides the patient with information regarding the consequences of exposure to traumatic events and the development of PTSD symptoms. The *stress management* phase focuses on the teaching of skills to help patients cope with stress, anxiety and interpersonal problems. The *trauma focus phase* emphasises the use of specific techniques, usually exposure-based, to alleviate the anxiety-related symptoms of PTSD. In the *relapse* prevention phase the patient is taught skills and strategies for dealing with relapse and future stressors. Finally, during the follow-up phase, the clinician and patient work together to monitor the patient's functioning and provide the structure and support necessary for the patient to maintain the gains that have been made.

Previous descriptions of this approach, while recognising that the treatment of PTSD cannot be easily compartmentalised, have suggested that the phases represent a nominal hierarchy such that interventions during one phase are designed to prepare the patient to move on to other phases of treatment (Keane, 1995; Keane et al., 1994). However, we wish to emphasise that the phases identify intervention strategies that may be utilised to a greater or lesser extent at various times throughout therapy. One advantage of the phasic model of treatment is that it acknowledges that PTSD *itself* has a phasic quality (Horowitz, 1986; Keane, 1995). One often sees an exacerbation of symptoms and functional problems associated with current stressors and trauma-related cues. The specific intervention strategies used in any given session may depend on the issues most salient at the time, as well as the goals of treatment as previously determined. For example, although safety and stabilisation issues may require more attention at the early stages of therapy, when dealing with complicated cases, these issues will likely be revisited. Similarly, though relapse prevention strategies require treatment gains prior to their implementation, these techniques may be used extensively prior to exposure-based treatments in order to promote the continued use of safety and coping strategies. Thus, the phase model serves as a heuristic device rather than as a prescriptive order in which treatment should always progress.

THE IMPORTANCE OF ASSESSMENT

Initial Assessment

A comprehensive evaluation at the outset of therapy is invaluable in order to provide the information necessary to make informed clinical decisions and prioritise treatment goals. Within the present model of treatment, assessment and intervention processes are inherently intertwined; assessment does not stop when the clinician introduces an intervention. Indeed, assessment during and after a particular intervention is equally valuable for identifying new points of intervention and accounting for the client's resistance to change. Once the therapist has developed initial hypotheses regarding the patient's identified problems and has specified a point of intervention, specific cognitive behavioural techniques can be introduced. Depending on the therapist's hypotheses, traditional anxiety reduction and stress management techniques may be augmented or even supplanted with treatments aimed at addressing the broad range of issues that contribute to problems for these clients.

In complicated cases, even assessment can be problematic as the therapist is faced with the difficult task of identifying and evaluating problems at multiple levels (e.g. cognitive, emotional, behavioural), in numerous domains (e.g. social, occupational, self-care), and across varying periods of time (e.g. now, over the past week, since the trauma). For example, while engaging in exposure therapy a clinician may want to evaluate moment-to-moment fluctuations in anxiety levels, other emotions that might reduce the efficacy of exposure (Foa et al., 1995), session-to-session changes in the severity of PTSD symptoms, the level of general stressors in the patient's life, alterations in risky behaviour, and global shifts in marital or work functioning.

Keane and colleagues have detailed elsewhere the importance of a comprehensive multimodal assessment of PTSD (Keane, Wolfe & Taylor, 1987; Keane, Newman & Orsillo, 1997; Malloy, Fairbank & Keane, 1983). Assessment needs to extend beyond the evaluation of symptoms and should include the nature of the trauma, the patient's unique response to that trauma, the patient's adaptation to ongoing symptoms, multicultural issues, co-morbidity, and other factors that affect treatment (Litz et al., 1992). Clearly, this is a complex task. To illustrate the nature of such an assessment in a complicated case, let us briefly revisit the case of Mr J. In this instance, multimodal assessment might include but is not limited to:

1. A clinical interview that includes an assessment of current safety and self-care issues, an evaluation of medical, occupational, social, and legal problems, and a history of traumatic events.
2. Formal psychiatric diagnostic interviews for both PTSD (e.g. Clinician Administered PTSD Scale (CAPS): Blake et al., 1990) and general psychiatric diagnoses (e.g. Structured Clinical Interview for DSM: Spitzer & Williams, 1995).
3. A medical exam.
4. A review of relevant documents including Mr J's medical records and military history.
5. Self-report measures of psychopathology and trauma exposure such as the PTSD Checklist (Weathers et al., 1993); Symptom Checklist-90-R (SCL-90-R: Derogatis, 1983); Beck Depression Inventory (Beck et al., 1961); Beck Anxiety Inventory (Beck et al., 1988); Minnesota Multiphasic Personality Inventory (MMPI-2: Butcher et al., 1989); and the Combat Exposure Scale (Keane et al., 1989b). (For a thorough review of available measures see Solomon et al., 1996).
6. Psychophysiological assessment to evaluate Mr J.'s level of arousal in response to trauma cues (Orr & Kaloupek, 1997).
7. An interview with Mr J's wife to assess marital problems, her perception of his symptoms, and her observations of Mr J's difficulties in other areas of functioning.

Hypothesising Relationships among Problems

Based on the initial assessment, an early schematic of the interrelations among the identified problems can be developed to guide the therapist in developing hypotheses and identifying points of intervention. In the case of Mr J. the initial schematic might look something like that presented in Figure 5.1. Arrows with a solid line are drawn to illustrate that the component at the source of the arrows serves to reinforce or increase the component at its termination. Arrows with a dashed line are drawn in order to illustrate that the component at the source inhibits or reduces the component at its termination. As is readily apparent in this schematic, Mr J's case is multifaceted and has numerous interacting components. 'PTSD Symptoms,' 'Suicide,' and 'Alcohol Abuse' are placed centrally in this diagram because they are Mr J's primary presenting complaints. Their centrality is not intended to represent these psychological symptoms as the key elements on which all other problems hinge. In Mr J's case, these are only three of many issues that significantly contribute to the distress in his life.

At first glance, the diagram may look hopelessly complicated. However, careful inspection reveals that it analyses the case into its many

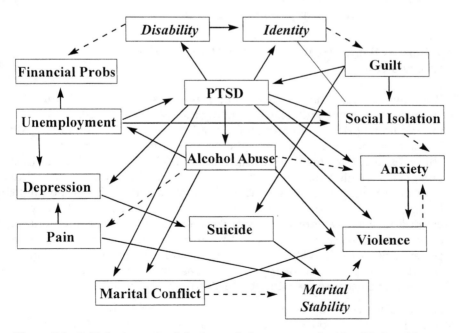

Figure 5.1   Initial schematic of the interrelations among the identified problems.

components and allows one to hypothesise how certain interventions might affect Mr J's life:

- The use of flooding or implosive therapy early in treatment, which can be associated with a period of exacerbation in PTSD symptoms, might serve to increase drinking, relationship conflict, violence, isolation, suicidal ideation, and feelings of guilt.
- Pushing for sobriety would likely cause in increase in Mr J's physical pain and PTSD symptoms while potentially decreasing violence, relationship difficulties, and financial problems.
- Decreasing marital conflict through couples or family work would likely decrease relationship conflict, alcohol intake, violence, depression and anxiety.
- The immediate initiation of anxiety management techniques may be problematic in that, in Mr J's case, trauma-related anxiety bolsters his veteran identity, gives validation for his service, and improves his finances via compensation.
- Psychopharmacological and cognitive behavioural treatments designed to decrease PTSD symptoms would ultimately lead to decreased alcohol intake, depression, violence, isolation, and guilt, but might result in the loss of veteran identity, increased financial problems at least for a time, and the eventual end to a marriage that is, in part, maintained by the wife's fear that Mr J. might kill himself.

Where to Begin: How Assessment Informs Points of Intervention

It should be clear that in such complicated cases, there are numerous avenues treatment could take. Evaluating the risks and benefits of possible interventions prior to initiating them is a key feature of treatment. In Mr J.'s case, we might consider detoxification and treatment of his substance abuse, exposure for his PTSD symptoms, marital therapy for him and his wife, skills training for anger, stress or pain management, and practical help in obtaining a job or government assistance. In addition, he might benefit from psychoeducation regarding his present condition, psychopharmacological intervention, and safety planning. Some intervention options, such as exposure, may not be appropriate given instability in a patient's life (see Litz, et al., 1990 for decision-making guidelines for direct therapeutic exposure), other options, such as inpatient detoxification, may not be viable because the patient refuses to comply with them.

A therapist needs to begin with those interventions that, based on the hypothesised relationships and informed from the initial assessment, present the greatest benefits with the least risks. In the case of Mr J., the analysis might lead to early interventions that would emphasise decreasing marital conflict and assure the safety of all involved. Such an initiative would carry little risk and considerable reward. Based on our hypothesised relationships, we would expect that assuring safety and decreasing conflict would decrease Mr J.'s anxiety, depression, and alcohol intake as well as overall violence in the household. However, a therapist cannot assume that any given intervention will have its desired effect. In order for a therapist to refine hypotheses and proceed systematically with treatment, careful and regular assessment throughout therapy is crucial.

Ongoing assessment

Although the need for assessment does not change throughout therapy, the nature of assessment shifts as therapy progresses. First, assessment needs to become economical. Clearly, clinicians can't allocate two hours to evaluate the current status of a case. Therefore strategies to gather the most information in the shortest amount of time are needed. Second, the assessment should be discrete; assessments that are intrusive or that distract from the therapeutic task may interfere with accomplishing treatment goals. Finally, assessment must be valid; that is assessment must answer the question one is asking as it relates to the established treatment goals. A level of flexibility and creativity is necessary on the part of the therapist in order to adapt or develop measures that accurately assess progress toward the goals of treatment.

How does one develop ongoing assessments that are economic, discrete, and valid? If a clinician is able to create a therapeutic environment in which assessment is integral and ongoing, the desired qualities of assessments will evolve naturally. By engaging in assessment often, both the clinician and the client become well practised. Along with the increasing practise comes a level of economy regarding the quality and quantity of information gathered. By assessing frequently, assessments also are likely to become less intrusive. If assessments are repeatedly part of treatment, they no longer interrupt treatment but rather become extensions of it. Finally, frequent assessments increase the likelihood that a therapist will be measuring what he or she intends to be measuring by providing numerous opportunities to either adjust one's measures or to look at a given question in multiple ways.

Providing Structure to Ongoing Assessment

In cases of complicated PTSD, we have found it helpful to conceptualise assessment as occurring within a 2 x 3 matrix (see Figure 5.2) which crosses

	SYMPTOMS	INTERVENTION	KEY EVENTS
WITHIN	**Moment to Moment** How do you feel right now?	**Change w/ Intervention** How do you feel after having tried X?	**Process Issues** How do you feel toward treatment?
BETWEEN	**Week to week** How did you feel this week?	**Change w/ Intervention** How did the homework go?	**Life Events** How did your week go?

Figure 5.2   Conceptualisation of assessment as occurring within a 2× 3 matrix.

the temporal frame of assessment (within and between sessions) with three content areas (symptoms, intervention, key events). We have found that this approach is comprehensive and ultimately enhances information retrieval by providing a framework to gather the data necessary for accurate clinical decision making. By obtaining information for all six cells in this matrix, the clinician can be assured that he or she has the data to implement successful interventions.

Assessment within a session focuses on relevant data that can be obtained while the clinician is sitting with the patient. Typically, assessment within session will incorporate patient self-reports and clinician observations to evaluate events occurring in the session. Between session assessment focuses on events that occurred during the week or changes that occur session-to-session. Between session assessment typically incorporates data from self-report instruments, self-monitoring, and observational information from significant others. Given that issues both between and within session can have a significant impact on treatment and the hypothesised associations among clinical issues, it's important that the clinician conducts assessments at both levels throughout therapy.

Each temporal level of assessment incorporates evaluations in each of three content areas: symptoms, interventions, and key events (illustrated as columns in Figure 5.2). Thus, within session, the clinician will evaluate:

(i) moment-to-moment fluctuations in symptoms and emotions as they may relate to events in session; (ii) the impact, within session, of interventions on emotions, cognitions, or behaviour; and (iii) cognitive and process issues that affect treatment. Between sessions assessments focus on: (i) session-to-session fluctuations in emotions or symptoms (ii) the impact of interventions occurring between sessions on symptoms and emotions; and (iii) key events outside of therapy that have an impact on symptoms or emotions. Ideally, after any given session, a therapist should have information about all six cells. We have found it helpful to have a corresponding question for each of the six cells as a prime to begin a discussion about any of the areas of assessment. These questions are also included in Figure 5.2.

Within Session Assessment

Cell 1: 'How do you feel right now?'

Within session moment-to-moment assessment utilises a variety of indicators including ratings of anxiety or distress by the patient or clinician, observations of facial affect, subjective and objective signs of physiological reaction and other indicators that the clinician identifies as meaningful in a particular case. Subjective ratings of the patient's overall anxiety or distress can be taken quickly (i.e. SUDS ratings) to get a sense of the patient's feeling state in the presence of particular cognitions, memories, or cues. The patient's facial expressions of fear, disgust, shame, anger, sadness and pain observed by the therapist during the session can be helpful measures of emotions the patient cannot or will not verbalise. Physiological markers such as heart rate, respiration, perspiration, muscle tension, and agitation can also be used as rough indicators of the patient's arousal. Attending to moment-to-moment fluctuations in affect or behaviour as well as events and stimuli associated with such changes can provide clinicians with important data pertaining to a patient's problems.

In a case such as that of Mr J., for example, a startle or a visible stiffening during the course of therapy might reflect an increase in tension associated with a dissociative flashback or an intrusive memory. In addition, the antecedents to such a reaction, such as muffled footsteps outside the office door or criticism, can provide valuable information regarding environmental cues that lead to distress for Mr J. Take, for example, a session in which Mr J. was seen with his wife during which the therapist observed that Mr J. winced in response to his wife's criticism. Following this observation by commenting on the event can provide the therapist and patient with additional useful clinical information. In this case, the therapist might start with a question such as 'I noticed you just winced. What just happened?' If Mr J. responds that he had a brief flash of a memory that often bothers him, the therapist now has a hypothesis to work with: criticism by Mr J.'s wife cues distressing memories. Based on this information, the therapist can plan interventions designed to break this pattern. Such interventions might include grounding techniques for Mr J., education for Mr J.'s wife, and perhaps instruction on how to improve communication and reduce criticism.

Cell 2: 'How do you feel after having tried the intervention?'

Once relevant measures for moment-to-moment assessment are established, these same indicators can be used to gauge the impact of various interventions within a session. Any number of measures can be taken prior, during, and after a specific intervention in order to evaluate changes that may have occurred as a result. In Mr J.'s case, during a flooding exercise, a therapist might want to assess his level of anxiety at different points during the session. Although it is reasonable to hypothesise that his anxiety will decrease with flooding, the therapist cannot be certain unless data are gathered. Therefore, the therapist would want to collect information about Mr J.'s level of anxiety prior to initiating the flooding exercise, during the exercise, and after flooding is completed. Reductions in reported anxiety and distress within and across flooding sessions have been suggested as evidence for the emotional processing thought necessary for recovery from PTSD (Foa & Kozak, 1986).

In contrast, if an early attempt to recount a memory was brief and associated with no change in Mr J.'s subjective anxiety, the therapist might hypothesise that Mr J. left out important elements of the memory. As in the case of moment-to-moment observations, the therapist would test this hypothesis by questioning Mr J. about the comprehensiveness of the flooding script. Additional intervention might include instructions to slow down the relating of the trauma, provide as much detail as possible, and fully experience the emotions associated with the memory. If Mr J. continues to report no feelings and provides little information during the flooding exercise, the therapist might begin to ask questions as the narrative progresses to encourage Mr J. to offer more detail. Questions such as 'Where are you now?', 'is anyone else around?,' 'What do you see/hear/smell/feel?' have proven useful in such circumstances.

Cell 3: 'How do you feel toward treatment?'

As one is evaluating the patient's response to various interventions within the course of a session, one must also be aware of process issues that may serve as barriers to such change. Any well meaning or well planned intervention will have little impact if the patient is unwilling or unmotivated to work with the therapist to achieve change. Assessment in this cell focuses on identifying thoughts and behaviours by the patient that interfere with accomplishing agreed upon treatment goals.

There are many issues that can serve as barriers to treatment that have been loosely characterised as forms of resistance. Among the complicated cases of PTSD treated in our clinic, commonly occurring issues that hinder therapy include mistrust, anger, betrayal, hopelessness, guilt, entitlement and the perceived benefits to remaining ill (e.g. value of 'victim' identity, compensation for disability). However, the number of issues that might interfere with therapeutic intervention is probably unlimited and therapists must remain aware of these potential pitfalls. Typically, the therapist will be alerted to problems in this area by a sense that the patient's verbally stated intention and his actual behaviour are inconsistent. In other words, the patient may say that he wants to learn strategies for controlling his anger, but be unwilling to practise these strategies in session.

For example, a therapist may note that during a particular session a patient like Mr J. was not fully engaged in a cognitive restructuring exercise. The patient might mumble his responses, offer only brief replies, and spend much of the session looking around the room and avoiding eye contact. The therapist might find it helpful to bring this to Mr J.'s attention immediately, perhaps even hypothesising out loud as to the cause of the patient's behaviour, for example, that there was something about the task that he was trying to avoid. If the behaviour persists despite the patient's verbal denials, the therapist should continue to monitor the behaviour so that the therapist and patient can work toward understanding the cause of the interfering behaviour. Typically, such prompting will lead to a discussion of process issues. At times, it will be necessary for the therapist to adjust the agenda of the session to address these issues even if it requires postponing or interrupting a planned intervention. In cases where resistance persists and is seen as avoidant, then the therapist should state the reason for altering plans and provide the patient with a timetable for beginning the next planned intervention.

Between Session Assessment

Between session assessment differs from assessment within session in its focus on events that occurred outside the therapist's office and its heavy reliance on self-monitoring. Part of the strategy of between session assessment is to provide a structure that fosters accurate reporting of events that occur during the week and encourages the patient to get into the habit of observing him or herself. It is not uncommon, particularly early in treatment, that patients will neglect to report significant events in their lives to their therapist, either because they are reluctant to discuss the event or they simply do not recognise them as important. It is for these reasons we have found it helpful to routinely ask the questions, 'How did you feel this week?', 'How did the homework go?', and 'How did your week go?' that respectively correspond with between session assessment of Cell 4 (symptoms), Cell 5 (interventions), and Cell 6 (key events).

Cell 4: 'How did you feel this week?'

Between session assessment of symptoms makes use of self-monitoring skills as well as more standardised and validated measures for PTSD or other targeted behaviours. While the more time-consuming measures will likely be used only periodically, self-monitoring typically occurs between all sessions. The identification and operationalisation of behaviours or events to be monitored may necessitate substantial education of the patient. Within session assessment of symptoms can often serve as a model for how to monitor behaviour at home and is particularly useful in identifying and discriminating when exactly a given behaviour occurs. Once a patient is able to recognise reliably the occurrence of a target event, he or she needs to systematically record them. Developing methods for self-monitoring that provide the therapist with valid information requires considerable investment on the part of the therapist.

For example, in a case such as that of Mr J., the therapist might be interested in recording baseline drinking behaviour. Therefore, accurate recording might require placing a tally sheet at any source that provides access to liquor: (i) in his wallet to count drinks at a bar; (ii) on his refrigerator; and (iii) on his liquor cabinet. In addition, recording sheets might provide room to record specific information such as date, time, type of drink (1 = beer, 2 = liquor), and number of ounces. This approach might require some further alteration if the patient does not record drinking that occurs in other situations such as at parties or over at a friend's house. Many of the in session indicators can be used as between session measures, but again one should not limit oneself to those used in session. Between session monitoring offers an opportunity to greatly expand the information base for developing hypotheses and designing interventions. We feel that it's important to reiterate that if it is meaningful and measurable it's important to monitor it.

Daily monitoring can be complemented by quick, valid, and relevant assessments of symptoms. Measures such as the PTSD Symptom Scale

(PSS-S: Foa et al., 1993) or the PTSD Checklist (PCL: Weathers et al., 1993) evaluate PTSD symptoms and can be given periodically throughout treatment in order to provide ongoing measures of symptom levels. There is no general prescription regarding when such instruments should be incorporated into the treatment but rather they should be utilised based on the current goals of treatment. For example, such instruments might be used on a weekly basis if a patient is engaged in a between session intervention at home such as relaxation exercises that might affect PTSD symptoms. These PTSD measures can be augmented with other measures that evaluate concurrent issues such as depression (BDI Beck et al., 1961) or anxiety (BAI: Beck et al., 1988). The use of such measures is important to the cognitive behavioural therapist as they accurately index gross changes in symptoms as they may relate to long-term involvement in therapy or major life events. Collaboration with the patient through plotting changes on a 'time-line' that includes significant life events that occur during the course of therapy can be an invaluable source of information to both the therapist and the patient and can provide a framework for further hypotheses and treatment.

Cell 5: 'How did the homework go?'

Asking this question each week allows the therapist and patient to monitor the patient's compliance with and response to suggested interventions. It keeps treatment focused on the interventions at hand and sets an expectation that new sets of skills need to be attempted at home as well as in the session. Plotting the accrued data in session and looking at behavioural or mood shifts associated with a given homework assignment can provide a sense of accomplishment and closure to a week's worth of self-monitoring and behavioural change. It also provides the essential information to determine the effectiveness of any given intervention as well as indicating potential adjustments that might improve treatment efficacy.

Patients who successfully complete a suggested intervention within session may have considerable difficulties when attempting to do it at home. For example, relaxation exercises that had gone smoothly during a treatment session might become problematic at home. The therapist might only become aware of this if the patient is asked directly, 'How did the relaxation exercises go?' or if the patient had monitored the relaxation intervention during the week. When describing problems with the homework, the patient may state that, 'I don't like to close my eyes when I am alone in a room' or 'I couldn't keep memories away when I tried to relax,' or ' There were just too many disruptions in my house.' At this point, the therapist would have a number of different possibilities to account for the patient's differential response at home versus in session and ideally the therapist would systematically manipulate each of these variables to investigate the individual contribution of each. However, in order to reduce intrusions, the therapist might instruct the patient to engage in relaxation in session with his eyes open versus closed and with or without the therapist verbally instructing him in order to reduce intrusions. Once a successful format for relaxation has been found (e.g. without therapist speech and with eyes open), the patient is instructed to follow this format at home. Patient self-monitoring during the ensuing week as well as follow-up questioning at the next session will advise the therapist as to the success of the adjustments made.

Cell 6: 'How did your week go?'

The numerous answers a clinician might get to this question from week to week in complicated PTSD cases is one of the aspects that makes such cases so difficult. The relationship between symptoms and life events is ongoing and dynamic and therapists' theories of how they are related in a particular case require constant modification. Any given treatment plan can and sometimes needs to be dramatically altered based on changes in the patient's life circumstances. The same intervention, for example exposure therapy, might have a very different effect depending upon the current circumstances in the patient's life. Although such an intervention might be extremely helpful when a patient is sober, is living in a stable household, and is successfully employed, it might have quite the opposite effect if the patient is drinking, is violent towards family members, or feels s/he is about to be terminated from a job.

As stated in the introduction, patients with chronic and complicated PTSD often have problems functioning in multiple arenas in their life. It is not unusual for a patient to present with substantive life issues such as homelessness, financial difficulties, relationship problems, custody issues, legal troubles, health problems, poor access to health care, and high-risk living arrangements. In such cases, it is common for crises to arise in one or more of these problem areas throughout treatment. When a crisis occurs, it is not unusual for the treatment to shift toward stabilisation issues while temporarily pushing aside planned treatment interventions. Such shifts are inherent to the treatment of complex cases and recognition that destabilising events will impinge on therapy at various times will minimise frustration for the therapist.

However, crises and subsequent moves toward stabilisation are not mutually exclusive with continuing planned interventions. Changes in life circumstances may require modifications in treatment plans but not necessarily so—it all depends on how likely the event is to affect the outcome of the intervention. If an event does not detrimentally affect a given plan, and all that can be done has been done to stabilise the situation (i.e. assessment, safety plan, appropriate referral), then the clinician should proceed as soon as possible to implement the intervention. Such an effort is important for a number of reasons: it keeps the treatment moving forward, it prevents the patient from feeling as if they are failing in some way, and it does not permit avoidance.

MULTIDISCIPLINARY TREATMENT

Clearly, the treatment of PTSD can be complicated. We have attempted to simplify the discussion by focusing primarily on the role of the psychotherapist in the treatment of these cases. However, complex patients typically present a range of problems that may require intervention by other professionals. For example, a psychiatrist may be required to prescribe and monitor psychopharmacological treatment and other physicians may be necessary to treat physical ailments that often accompany PTSD. Substance abuse specialists also may be involved in the case to address issues that fall within their areas of expertise. Social workers may be required to assist with access to essential social services. In addition to the participation of other professionals, treatment of PTSD may require interventions that fall within specialised areas of psychotherapy such as marital therapy or communication skills that might best be provided by therapists with particular training. Although there are obvious advantages to involving multiple professionals in the care of complicated cases, this approach also has some liabilities.

The involvement of multiple providers in the treatment of PTSD patients can exacerbate problems found in this population. In particular, the issues of vulnerability, shame, trust, and distress associated with repeated disclosure of trauma information can be problematic. For example, the fact that multiple professionals are aware of the details of the traumatic event may increase the patient's sense of vulnerability. Similarly, the sharing of information among the treatment providers that is so necessary for coordinated treatment may be perceived by the patient as a violation of trust. In our experience, poor compliance with multidisciplinary treatment stems from a failure of the professionals to address these issues and prepare patients for treatment. When such issues are not addressed, patients tend to comply only with those treatments that seem most palliative.

One possible solution to the problems associated with multidisciplinary treatment of complicated PTSD cases is an integrated clinic within which these patients can be treated by treatment teams. When a PTSD patient is admitted to this clinic, it is clear that the treatment will involve all appropriate members of the team and that information will be shared among the providers. Thus, from the beginning the patient is aware that information will be shared to improve treatment, not to violate their trust. Further, by openly sharing information among providers it is possible to reduce the number of times the patient is required to repeat information. The presence of medical, mental health, and social service providers within the clinic also allows for easy consultation within and across disciplines. Within this clinic, the therapist serves as one integral part of the total treatment team. In some cases, the therapist serves as the primary provider for a patient, conducting therapy and coordinating care with other providers. In other cases, the therapist provides short-term problem-focused treatment within their specialty (e.g. family therapy) for patients for whom they are not the primary clinician. In still other cases, the therapist may provide consultation to other primary providers. In complicated cases of PTSD, where numerous professionals are likely to be involved, an appropriate referral to a local clinic with comprehensive services is sometimes the most appropriate first step towards good treatment.

CONCLUSION

In this chapter, we have outlined a cognitive behavioural approach to complicated cases of PTSD. We have attempted to a provide a framework for treatment that is comprehensive and highly personalised and thus able to address the heterogeneous presentations of the disorder. Attempting to provide such a framework has led us to acknowledge the phasic nature of the disorder and its treatment, the role of ongoing assessment in determining points of intervention, and the advantages of treatment in the context of a multidisciplinary clinic. Good treatment of complicated cases of PTSD is never simple; rather, it requires a sensitive clinician, knowledgeable about the disorder, and systematic in his or her application of assessment and treatment regimens. As more randomised clinical trials are completed in the area of PTSD, the selective inclusion of effective treatment techniques into this larger treatment framework will yield improved outcomes even for the most complicated cases.

REFERENCES

American Psychiatric Association (1994). *Diagnostic and Statistical Manual of Mental Disorders* (4th edn). Washington, DC: American Psychiatric Association.
Barlow, D.H., Hayes, S.C. & Nelson, R.O. (1984). *The Scientist Practitioner: Research and Accountability in Clinical and Educational Settings*. New York: Pergamon.

Barlow, D.H. & Hersen, M. (1984). *Single Case Experimental Designs: Strategies for Studying Behavioral Change*. New York: Pergamon.

Beck, A.T., Epstein, N., Brown, G. & Steer, R.A. (1988). An inventory for measuring clinical anxiety: Psychometric properties. *Journal of Consulting and Clinical Psychology*, 893–897.

Beck, A.T., Ward, C.H., Mendelson, M., Mock J. & Erbaugh, J. (1961). An inventory for measuring depression. *Archives of General Psychiatry*, 4, 561–571.

Blake, D.D., Weathers, F.W., Nagy, L.M., Kaloupek, D.G., Klauminzer, G., Charney, D. & Keane, T.M. (1990). A clinician rating scale for assessing current and lifetime PTSD: The CAPS-1. *Behavior Therapist*, 18, 187–188.

Boudewyns, P.A. & Hyer, L. (1996). Eye movement desensitization and reprocessing (EMDR) as treatment for post-traumatic stress disorder (PTSD). *Clinical Psychology and Psychotherapy*, 3, 185–195.

Boudewyns, P.A., Hyer, L., Woods, M.G., Harrison, W.R. & McCranie, E. (1990). PTSD among Vietnam veterans: An early look at treatment outcome using direct therapeutic exposure. *Journal of Traumatic Stress*, 359–368.

Bremner, J.D., Randall, P., Scott, T. M., Bronen, R.A., Seibyl, J.P., Southwick, S.M., Delaney, R.C., McCarthy, G., Charney, D.S. & Innis, R.B. (1995). MRI-based measurement of hippocampal volume in patients with combat-related post-traumatic stress disorder. *American Journal of Psychiatry*, 152(7), 973–981.

Butcher, J.N., Dahlstrom, W.G., Graham, J.R., Tellegen, A. & Kaemmer, B. (1989). *Minnesota Multiphasic Personality Inventory MMPI-2. Manual for Administration and Scoring*. Minneapolis: University of Minnesota Press.

Calhoun, K.S. & Resick, P.A. (1993). Post-traumatic stress disorder. In D.H. Barlow (Ed.), *Clinical Handbook of Psychological Disorders: A Step by Step Treatment Manual*. New York: Guilford.

Chemtob, C., Roitblat, H.L., Hamada, R.S., Carson, J.G. & Twentyman, C.T. (1988). A cognitive action theory of post-traumatic stress disorder. *Journal of Anxiety Disorders*, 2, 253–275.

Davidson, J.R.T. & van der Kolk, B.A. (1996). The psychopharmacological treatment of post-traumatic stress disorder. In B. van der Kolk, S. McFariane & L. Weisaeth (Eds), *The Effects of Overwhelming Experience on the Mind, Body and Society*. New York: Guilford.

Derogatis, L. R. (1983). *SCL-90-R: Administration, Scoring and Procedures Manual-II for the Revised Version*. Towson, MD: Clinical Psychiatric Research.

Fairbank, J.A. & Keane, T.M. (1982). Flooding for combat-related stress disorders: Assessment of anxiety reduction across traumatic memories. *Behavior Therapy*, 13, 499–510.

Foa, E. B. & Kozak, M.J. (1986). Emotional processing of fear: Exposure to corrective information. *Psychological Bulletin*, 99, 20–35.

Foa, E.B. & Riggs, D.S. (1993). Post-traumatic stress disorder and rape. In J.M. Oldham, M.B. Riba & A. Tasman (Eds), *American Press Review of Psychiatry*, Vol. 12. Washington, DC: American Psychiatric Press.

Foa, E.B., Riggs, D.S., Dancu, C.V. & Rothbaum, B.O. (1993). Reliability and validity of a brief instrument for assessing post-traumatic stress disorder. *Journal of Traumatic Stress*, 6, 459–474.

Foa, E.B., Riggs, D.S., Massie, E.D. & Yarczower, M. (1995). The impact of fear activation and anger on the efficacy of exposure treatment for post-traumatic stress disorder. *Behavior Therapy*, **26**, 487–499.

Foa, E.B., Rothbaum, B.O., Riggs, D.S. & Murdock, T.B. (1991). Treatment of post-traumatic stress disorder in rape victims: A comparison between cognitive behavioral procedures and counseling. *Journal of Consulting and Clinical Psychology*, **59**, 715–723.

Hearst, N., Newman, T.B. & Hulley, S.D. (1986). Delayed effects of the military draft on mortality: A randomized natural experiment. *New England Journal of Medicine*, **314**, 620–624.

Horowitz, M.J. (1986). Stress response syndromes: A review of post traumatic and adjustment disorders. *Hospital and Community Psychiatry*, **137**, 241–249.

Jensen, J.A. (1994). An investigation of eye movement desensitization and reprocessing (EMD/R) as a treatment for post-traumatic stress disorder symptoms of Vietnam combat veterans. *Behavior Therapy*, **25**, 311–325.

Keane, T.M. (1989). Post-traumatic stress disorder: Current status and future directions. *Behavior Therapy* **20**, 149–153.

Keane, T. M. (1995). The role of exposure therapy in the psychological treatment of PTSD. *National Center for Post-traumatic Stress Disorder: Clinical Quarterly*, **5**, 1–6.

Keane, T.M. (1997). Psychological and behavioral treatment for PTSD. In P. Nathan and J. Gorman (Eds), *Treatments that Work*. Oxford: Oxford University Press.

Keane, T.M., Fairbank, J.A., Caddell, J.M., Zimering, R.T. & Bender, M.E. (1985). A behavioral approach to assessing post-traumatic stress disorder in Vietnam veterans. In C.R. Figley (Ed.), *Trauma and its Wake*. New York: Brunner/Mazel.

Keane, T.M., Fairbank, J.A., Caddell, J.M. & Zimering, R.T. (1989a). Implosive (flooding) therapy reduces symptoms of PTSD in Vietnam combat veterans. *Behavior Therapy*, **20**, 245–260.

Keane, T.M., Fairbank, J.A., Caddell, J.M., Zimering, R.T., Taylor, K.L. & Mora, C.A. (1989b). Clinical evaluation of a measure to assess combat exposure. *Psychological Assessment: A Journal of Consulting and Clinical Psychology*, **1**, 53–55.

Keane, T.M., Fisher, L.M., Krinsley, K.E. & Niles, B.L. (1994). Post-traumatic stress disorder. In M. Hersen and R.T. Ammerman (Eds), *Handbook of Prescriptive Treatments for Adults*. New York: Plenum.

Keane, T.M. & Kaloupek, D.G. (1997). Comorbid psychiatric disorders in PTSD: Implications for research. In R. Yehuda & A. McFarlane (Eds), *Psychobiology of Post-traumatic Stress Disorder*. New York: Annals of the New York Academy of Science.

Keane, T.M., Newman, E. & Orsillo, S.M. (1997). The assessment of military-related PTSD. In J. Wilson & T. Keane (Eds), *Assessing Psychological Trauma and PTSD: A Handbook for Practitioners*. New York: Guilford.

Keane, T.M., Wolfe, J. & Taylor, K.L. (1987). Post-traumatic stress disorder: Evidence for diagnostic validity and methods of psychological assessment. *Journal of Clinical Psychology*, **43**, 32–43.

Keane, T.M., Zimering, R.T. & Caddell, J.M. (1985). A behavioral formulation of post-traumatic stess disorder in Vietnam veterans. *Behavior Therapist*, **8**, 9–12.

Kilpatrick, D.G., Veronen, L.J. & Resick, P.A. (1979). The aftermath of rape: Recent empirical findings. *American Journal of Orthopsychiatry*, **49**, 658–669.

Kilpatrik, D.G., Veronen, L.J. & Resick, P.A. (1982). Psychological sequelae to rape: Assessment and treatment strategies. In D.M. Doleys & R.L. Meredith (Eds), *Behavioral Medicine: Assessment and Treatment Strategies*. New York: Plenum.

Kulka, R.A., Schlenger, W.E., Fairbank, J.A., Hough, R.L., Jordan, B.K., Marmar, C.R. & Weiss, D.S. (1990). *Trauma and the Vietnam War Generation: Report of Findings from the National Vietnam Veterans Readjustment Study*. NewYork: Brunner/Mazel.

Lang, P.J. (1977). Imagery in therapy: An information processing analysis of fear. *Behavior Therapist*, **8**, 862–886.

Litz, B.T., Blake, D.D., Gerardi, R.G. & Keane, T.M. (1990). Decision making guidelines for the use of direct therapeutic exposure in the treatment of post-traumatic stress disorder. *Behavior Therapist*, **13**, 91–93.

Litz, B.T. & Keane, T.M. (1989). Information processing in anxiety disorders: Application to the understanding of post-traumatic stress disorder. *Clinical Psychology Review*, **9**, 243–257.

Litz, B.T., Penk, W.E., Gerardi, R.J. & Keane, T.M. (1992). Assessment of post-traumatic stress disorder. In P. Saigh (Ed.), *Post-traumatic Stress Disorder: A Behavioral Approach to Assessment and Treatment*. New York: MacMillan.

Lyons, J.A. & Keane, T.M. (1989). Implosive therapy for the treatment of combat-related PTSD. *Journal of Traumatic Stress*, **2**(2), 137–152.

Malloy, P.F., Fairbank, J.A. & Keane, T.M. (1983). Validation of a multimethod assessment of post-traumatic stress disorders in Vietnam veterans. *Journal of Consulting and Clinical Psychology*, **51**, 488–494.

McCann, I.L. & Pearlman, L.A. (1990). *Psycological Trauma and the Adult Survivor: Theory, Therapy, and Transformation*. NewYork: Brunner/Mazel.

Meichenbaum, D. & Jaremko, M.E. (1983). *Stress Reduction and Prevention*. New York: Plenum.

Mowrer, O. H. (1947). On the dual nature of learning: A reinterpretation of 'conditioning' and 'problem-solving'. *Harvard Educational Review*, **17**, 102–148.

Mowrer, O.H. (1960). *Learing Theory and Behavior*. New York: Wiley.

Nezu, A.M. & Nezu, C.M. (1989). *Clinical Decision Making in Behavior Therapy: A Problem-solving Perspective*. Champaign, IL: Research Press.

Orr, S.P. & Kaloupek, D.G. (1997). Psychophysiological assessment of post-traumatic stress disorder. In J.P. Wilson & T.M. Keane (Eds), *Assessing Psychological Trauma and PTSD*. New York: Guilford.

Renfry, G. & Spates, R.C. (1994). Eye movement desensitization: A partial dismantling study. *Journal of Behavior Therapy and Experimental Psychiatry*, **25**, 231–239.

Resick, P.A., Calhoun, K., Atkeson, B. & Ellis, E. (1981). Social adjustment in victims of sexual assault. *Journal of Consulting and Clinical Psycholoqy*, **49**, 705–712.

Resick, P.A. & Schnicke, M. K. (1992). *Cognitive Processing Therapy for Sexual Assault Survivors: A Therapist's Manual*. Newbury Park, CA: Sage.

Rimm, D.C. & Masters, J.C. (1979). *Behavior Therapy Techniques and Empirical Findings*, 2nd edn. New York: Academic Press.

Shapiro, F. (1989). Eye movement desensitization procedure in the treatment of traumatic memories. *Journal of Behavior Therapy and Experimental Psychiatry*, **20**, 199–223.

Shapiro, F. (1995). *Eye Movement Desensitization and Reprocessing. Basic Principles, Protocols, and Procedures*. New York: Guilford Press.

Solomon, S.D., Keane, T.M., Newman, E. & Kaloupek, D.G. (1996). In E.B. Cadson (Ed.), *Trauma Research Methodology*. Lutherville, MD: Sidran Press.

Spitzer, R.L.& Williams, J.B. (1995). *Structured Clinical Interview for the DSM-IV*. Biomethics Research Department of New York State Psychiatric Institute. New York.

Weathers, F.W., Litz, B.T., Herman, D.S., Huska, J.A. & Keane, T.M. (1993). The PTSD Checklist (PCL): Reliability, validity, and diagnositic utility. International Society for Traumatic Stress Studies, 9th Annual Meeting, 24–27 Oct.

Wilson, S., Becker, L. & Tinker, R. (1995). Eye movement desensitization and reprocessing (EMDR) treatment for psychologically traumatized individuals. *Journal of Consulting and Clinical Psychology*, **63**, 928–937.

Yehuda, R. & McFarlane, A.C. (Eds). (1997). *Psychobiology of Post-traumatic Stress Disorder*. New York: New York Academy of Sciences.

Chapter 6

EATING DISORDERS, SELF-IMAGE DISTURBANCE AND MALTREATMENT

*Rachel Calam**

EATING DISORDERS AND SEXUAL ABUSE

The 1980s saw a tremendous amount of clinical and academic activity aimed at trying to understand the impact of sexual abuse on the development of disturbance. The coincidence of this research with a high level of interest in research into eating disorders led to a specific field of research, that of the search for links between sexual abuse and eating disorders, and considerable work went into attempts to establish whether there were links between the experience of abuse and the subsequent development of an eating disorder. There are a number of good reviews of the field (Connors & Morse, 1993; Pope & Hudson, 1992). While some authors report what appear to be clear links, including links between specific types of unwanted sexual experience and specific forms of eating disorder (Waller, 1992) others suggest that maltreatment in any form may lead to disturbance, the nature of which will depend upon the circumstances of the particular person (Welch & Fairburn, 1994). An important factor concerns the level of definition of sexual abuse. While some of these studies have considered any of a wide range of unwanted sexual experiences, others use far more stringent criteria, so that studies vary in the kinds of acts that might be considered abusive.

* Department of Clinical Psychology, University of Manchester, UK

Treating Complex Cases: The Cognitive Behavioural Therapy Approach.
Edited by Nicholas Tarrier, Adrian Wells and Gillian Haddock.

EATING DISORDERS AND MALTREATMENT

Some work has examined the extent to which maltreatment of any kind may be associated with the development of eating disorders. For example, Folsom et al. (1993) found comparably high rates of sexual abuse and physical abuse in eating disorder and general psychiatric patients. More general models of maltreatment that attempt to understand the pathways from maltreatment to disturbance require a complex and multifactorial model of causality. Mullen (1993) and Mullen et al. (1996) demonstrated that many of the associated factors usually coexisting with maltreatment, including poor living circumstances and family instability, will have an equally important, if not greater, influence on adjustment. In the case of eating disorders, Smolak, Levine and Sullins (1990) found some evidence that familial support was as important a factor as abuse in eating disorders, while a study of university students found that adverse family background, but not sexual abuse, was an aetiological factor in eating disturbance (Kinzl et al., 1994). In interpreting the findings in this field, therefore, it is important to bear in mind that while sexual abuse may not have a direct causal effect, it may combine with other adverse background factors in the clinical picture that is presented.

Developmental psychopathology emphasises chain effects, where earlier experiences or approaches contribute to later ones (Rutter & Rutter, 1992). Thus, family dysfunction may lead to vulnerability to sexual abuse. Further, the damaging effects of sexual abuse may be exacerbated by inappropriate response to disclosure. Everill and Waller (1995a) found that experience of disclosure of abuse contributed to the degree of eating disorder symptomatology shown; hence, not only the abuse itself, but the reactions of others to that abuse may have an important effect on the development of symptomatology. This may again reflect family support factors, as response to disclosure may be indicative of the nature of relationships within the family. A review of the area can be found in Waller, Everill and Calam (1994).

SEXUAL ABUSE, BODY IMAGE AND BODY SATISFACTION

Some research has looked specifically at the impact of sexual abuse on body image. It could be hypothesised that sexual abuse would lead to dislike of the body, which would then contribute to attempts to change body size, shape or appearance. There are some mixed findings in this area, although the majority, perhaps surprisingly, show little impact of abuse. Byram, Wagner and Waller (1994) found relationships between abuse and body image disturbance only in women with unhealthy eating attitudes, but not in women whose eating attitudes were normal. Schaaf and McCanne (1994), in a college population, found no association between body image disturbance, abuse and eating patterns, in contrast to Byram, Wagner and Waller's study. Calam, Griffiths and Slade (1997) looked at body image disturbance in two samples of women in therapy for eating disorders in the UK and Australia and found virtually no association between unwanted sexual experience and body dissatisfaction, so that there is only limited support for body dissatisfaction as a mediating factor in any association between abuse and eating attitudes.

ABUSE AND OTHER ASPECTS OF BODY IMAGE

Given a different combination of setting conditions, it may be some factor other than food which becomes the centre of the preoccupation. Bradbury (1993) described a woman who wanted to have her nose altered through plastic surgery because it reminded her of her abusing father. Women who request surgery may focus on some physical attribute rather than dealing directly with distress. This may again be a coping response which fulfils the same function, that of avoidance of other problems. A number of studies indicate rejection and lack of care within the family as being associated with body dysmorphic disorder (Phillips, 1991).

In a study of women seeking breast augmentation and reduction, Taylor (1996) found that women in both surgery groups were more likely to have experienced sexual contact with a male relative or rape than a comparison group. Unwanted sexual experience may have contributed to the desire to alter the body shape. This was consistent with case material collected in assessment prior to surgery (Calam, Bradbury & Taylor, 1996).

TREATMENT OF EATING DISORDERS

There are a number of established approaches to working with eating disorders; a full review is beyond the scope of this chapter, but some of these are summarised below. Even when working with complex cases, the same basic aims and approaches apply.

Anorexia nervosa

Goldner and Birmingham (1994) suggest that there are six major areas for intervention:

- Medical stabilisation
- Establishment of the therapeutic alliance
- Weight restoration
- Promotion of healthy eating attitudes, behaviours and activity levels
- Psychotherapeutic treatment
- Family and community interventions

These authors acknowledge that the best treatment approach to anorexia has not yet been determined, and the costs and benefits of different forms of programme to establish weight gain are still a matter for vigorous debate. For the cognitive behavioural therapist, a major task in therapy is the establishment of a strong alliance, as the patient will be required to undertake difficult tasks in order to change. Cognitive and behavioural approaches are used in helping the patient to redetermine their ideal weight, reward positive change and cope with their new size and shape. Goldner and Birmingham (1994) advocate discouraging frequent weighing and talking about weight, and encouraging alternative activities.

With respect to weight restoration, a number of tactics can be used. In working with severe anorexia, the therapist will be working as part of a multidisciplinary network. Behavioural approaches are often used in inpatient settings, with positive reinforcement being an effective tool (Toyuz et al., 1984).

The promotion of healthy eating attitudes, behaviour and activity levels requires a cognitive behavioural approach (Davis & de Groot, 1993; Fairburn & Cooper, 1989). Providing education about the condition is essential. Again, Goldner and Birmingham summarise the goals usefully as follows:

- Increasing calorific intake
- Expanding the range of meals
- Eating discrete meals and snacks
- Normalising the pace of eating
- Elimination of purging
- Elimination of binge eating
- Avoidance of diet foods
- Eating in the company of others.

In bringing about these changes, the use of diaries to keep a daily record of eating and any associated bingeing and purging is useful in monitoring change over time in what may be small changes and in increasing self-awareness.

Cognitive distortions have been recognised in women with anorexia. Garner and Bemis (1982) noted that common distortions include overgeneralisation, personalisation and self reference, magnification or overestimation, superstitious thinking, selective abstraction and dichotomous reasoning. Recognising and challenging these distortions is a further task of therapy. It therefore becomes important to be able to work flexibly at a number of different levels, providing basic education and behavioural guidance, while simultaneously recognising maladaptive cognitive patterns.

Bulimia nervosa

In working with bulimia, many of the same approaches apply, particularly as many women with bulimia will also have anorexic symptomatology. In helping to control bingeing, a number of controlled trials have suggested useful tactics which appear effective in both individual and group therapy (Fairburn et al., 1991). These include the following (Crow & Mitchell, 1994):

- Self-monitoring
- Advice on modifying eating patterns and meal planning
- Replacing bingeing with more stable eating patterns
- Exposure to feared foods
- Generating alternatives to bingeing
- Cue restriction
- Delaying vomiting

In the initial stages of therapy, the focus is the interruption of binge behaviour. Education on the relationships between food restriction and bingeing is valuable as part of an examination of cues to bingeing. Self-monitoring begins, and as the patient obtains a degree of control, the positive and negative consequences of bingeing can be considered. This enables cognitions associated with stages of the binge cycle to be identified and challenged. Later treatment focuses on relapse prevention, with high-risk situations and foods being revisited. A useful approach to work with bulimia is provided by Cooper (1995); this book has the advantage of being written for use by sufferers.

WORKING WITH WOMEN WITH EATING DISORDERS WITH A HISTORY OF MALTREATMENT

In clinical work, cases are encountered where the evidence for links between unwanted sexual experience or other forms of maltreatment and disturbance appears very clear in the formulation. When women have experienced maltreatment, their histories may lead to complexities in attempting to overcome the eating disorder. Gleaves and Eberenz (1994) described a group of women whose eating disorder symptoms were particularly difficult to treat, the majority of whom had experienced abuse of some form. In the clinical examples in this chapter, some of these complexities are highlighted, and the therapeutic steps taken considered. In considering the relationship between trauma and the development of symptomatology, it is helpful to see the patient's thoughts and behaviours in terms of adaptations to an abusive experience or environment; seen in this way, even extreme or apparently bizarre behavioural patterns begin to make sense as coping strategies. For example, a case to be described later, that of Tanya, shows how a severe eating disorder may serve to disrupt and block the emergence of overwhelmingly painful affect and cognitions. In order to make sense of these extreme adaptations, it is necessary to recognise the cognitive and behavioural adaptations that may be made by those who experience maltreatment.

The impact of trauma

Terr (1991) writing on childhood traumas, offers a distinction which is useful in considering the impact that adverse experiences may have on children. She distinguishes between unanticipated single events and longstanding or repeated exposure to extreme external events, both of which may have damaging effects. In the former case, where the child is exposed to a single event, the child may have a detailed memory of the event, and come to reappraise the event in ways that are associated with distress. Thus, the child attempts to cope with what has happened and find some meaning in the event. In the case of repeated or longstanding experiences, the child may respond by developing a range of coping strategies which include denial and numbing, self-hypnosis and dissociation, and may show rage and self-harm. Guilt may also be experienced. It should be emphasised that these responses are not specific to abuse, but to any of a wide range of negative experiences. This is important here, as women with eating disorders may show dissociation or self-harm in the absence of a history of sexual abuse.

The experience of a single abusive event may, depending upon pre-existing vulnerability, lead to disturbance. This is illustrated by the case described below of Sally, a deaf girl for whom the experience of unwanted touching probably acted as an important marker for the lifecycle tasks she was facing in growing up and planning for independence, of which she was highly fearful. The unwanted sexual approach, although apparently relatively minor and fleeting, acted as a catalyst for the development of disorder in the presence of clear, longstanding vulnerability.

Case Example: Sally

Sally, a profoundly deaf 15 year old, developed an eating disorder immediately after an unwanted sexual experience. She had been in residential schools for the deaf and had found separation from home difficult. Her school, educationally most appropriate, was a journey of several hours away. Her parents felt guilt over sending her to school, and over her disability. As she reached puberty, Sally experienced extreme sensitivity over her developing figure. At school, she was pushed over and kissed by another pupil. She began to diet, and her weight fell rapidly to a dangerous level. Her subsequent anorexia made her the focus of considerable attention at school and home, and each instance of weight loss led to a return home, which was in itself probably highly reinforcing, as her concerned parents worked hard to try to understand and help her. A diagrammatic formulation is shown in Figure 6.1.

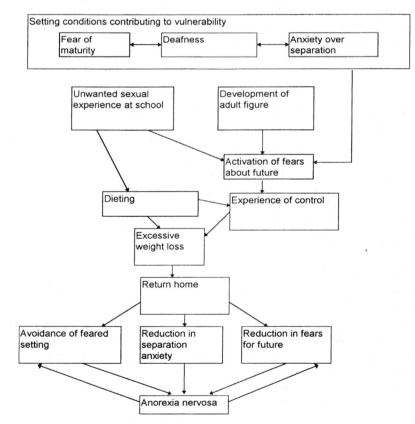

Figure 6.1   Formulation, Sally

The formulation of this case was relatively simple, the complexity lay in providing any kind of intervention given the gain of remaining at home when underweight. The likelihood of successful intervention was limited given the importance of the symptom in ensuring that she remained at home and was nurtured by her family. This example shows the way in which a single event can be a precipitant for major disorder.

Therapy for women who have been abused

Briere (1992) offers a useful discussion of the mechanisms involved in understanding the development of disturbance in women who have been abused which make clear the reasons why abuse may contribute directly to symptomatology. Establishing these links then makes clear the forms of therapy that should be employed; these are well described by Briere (1996). He describes cognitive and behavioural responses to abuse.

Cognitive responses

Women who have been abused may show cognitions that reflect their experiences. These include cognitive distortions, which would include feelings of guilt or responsibility for the abuse. The perception of the self may be distorted, with low self-esteem and a poor sense of self-worth (Jehu, 1988). Altered emotionality, in the form of depression or anxiety, is common in abused women. All these are also found in women with eating disorders. Impaired self reference has also been described. Briere (1992) describes the lack of access to a stable sense of self, which may be experienced in work with women with eating disorders. This probably reflects more pervasive negative influences of lack of secure relationships throughout development.

In the presence of repeated trauma in childhood, dissociative coping strategies may emerge, including detachment or numbing, disengagement from what is going on around them, perhaps observing others without interacting or perhaps showing amnesia (Vanderlinden, Vandereyken & Probst, 1995). Everill and Waller (1995b) provide a clear formulation of the relationship between bingeing, vomiting and dissociation. They suggest, as does Terr (1991) that trauma can lead to the development of dissociative schemata. When distress is experienced which is too strong to be blocked by cognitive strategies, however, bulimic or other impulsive behaviour may be employed as a coping strategy.

Behavioural adaptations following abuse

Briere (1992) describes behavioural adaptations to abuse which are highly relevant to the development of eating disorders. Abused women may show tension-reducing behaviours, where an activity is engaged in which functions to anaesthetise and reduce painful affect. Bingeing is a good example of this, as women report how absorbing it is, and its value in blocking out unwanted cognitions. Other tension-reducing behaviours, such as self-mutilation, may serve the same function. These behaviours serve to soothe or calm, through providing distraction, or perhaps the interruption of dissociative states. They may provide the sense of control that is central to descriptions of eating disorder, and provide temporary relief from guilt and self-hatred. These positive reinforcing qualities contribute to an avoidance learning paradigm, so that the behaviours are repeated whenever stress levels become too high.

Borderline personality disorder

Many of the women with difficult to treat eating disorders may also show characteristics associated with borderline personality disorder (Waller, 1994). Personality disorder and its treatment is discussed fully in Chapter 15 of this volume. An important source of complexity in work with eating disorders, however, is the changes in cognitive functioning and behaviour that may occur as a result of self-starvation. Goldner and Birmingham suggest that the label of borderline personality disorder may be wrongly applied to anorexics, as reduction in borderline symptoms following renutrition has been demonstrated (Kennedy, McVey & Katz, 1990).

In working with women with eating disorders who also have a history of unwanted sexual experiences or other forms of maltreatment, therefore, a wide range of factors need to be taken into consideration. A single unwanted sexual experience may have very different relevance to the disorder, compared to a longstanding history of maltreatment. The task, in assessing and formulating the case, is to decide on the relative importance of these factors, and how therapy will take account of these alongside the usual concerns over weight and dietary habits that will be of importance in therapy. Some of the issues of formulation raised above are illustrated with the following case which exemplifies a range of factors associated with a longstanding history of maltreatment.

Tanya (discussed below) exemplifies the vulnerability to disturbance described by Mullen et al. (1996); she was emotionally and physically neglected as a child, and then entered into relationships in her teens that were sexually or physically abusive. Both the abusive relationships and a severe eating disorder arose out of a history of emotional and physical neglect, which led to her vulnerability, with a poor sense of self-worth and a hopeless view of the future. Therapy was slow and characterised by uncertain engagement and periods of apparent chaos, signs of dissociative coping and of borderline personality disorder. Through working towards a shared formulation, making links between past experiences and current thoughts and beliefs, it was possible to produce some change in eating patterns, but work with this complex case was slow and only limited in success. It was only by formulating the therapeutic relationship itself, that progress could be understood. The case is described at some length as it exemplifies many of the complexities that may be encountered in working with women with a history of severe maltreatment and a serious, well established eating disorder.

Tanya

Referral and initial assessment

Tanya was referred at 19 with a long history of failing to engage in therapy and refusing treatment. She was maintaining a low body weight by dieting, bingeing and vomiting. She said that she was tired of being 'thin and gaunt'. She was bingeing 'to bury feelings inside', but could not describe these. Her eating disorder had begun with dieting when she joined a sports club at 13 and a boy had said she had fat legs. An important event for her had been a relationship with the sports coach, who had been 'like a father figure' and who had initiated a sexual relationship with her immediately following her 16th birthday, which she ended within a few weeks. She had moved in with her current partner at 16, following the exploitative relationship. She had begun to binge more recently, when her partner was at work, spending considerable amounts of time and money on this. She was at home, out of work, planning to go to college in the autumn, and found that the boredom made her more likely to binge.

Background

It was only after several months in therapy that Tanya began, painfully, to give full accounts of events from her early history. Prior to that, her accounts were incomplete, accompanied with intense, angry emotions, and hard to piece together. Once well engaged in therapy, Tanya was able to describe her childhood, but it was only 15 months into therapy that she was able to integrate the account and the accompanying emotions without resorting to dissociative cognitive and behavioural strategies. Her history was as follows.

As a child, Tanya had a father who was a heavy drinker, and physically abusive to all the family apart from her. She had vivid memories of her father attacking her mother and her mother covered in blood, having had her head beaten against the wall. She recalled physical abuse of her siblings, particularly her autistic brother, and that she slept on top of her bed, fully clothed, in case she had to run away, although she could not say from what.

Tanya described family mealtimes when she and her siblings were beaten by their father if they did not eat every morsel. She recalled, vividly, gagging as she ate. Her father left home when she was 10, and her mother became depressed and unable to provide for the children. Hunger was a usual state for Tanya, who survived on school lunches and any food that she could find in the house. She ran away at 13 to live with an aunt; it was round this time that her eating disorder began. She developed a close relationship with her older male cousin who subsequently committed suicide at 21.

Formulation

Figure 6.2 links together Tanya's history and her eating disorder. The foundations for her eating disorder were to be found in early physical and emotional neglect in an environment pervaded by the threat of violence and loss. The extent to which pathological interactions in the family centred around food was probably an important vulnerability factor. The trigger to sensitivity about weight, the comment about her legs, came at a time of intense vulnerability when she was leaving home. At the same time, her intensive sports training could also have been associated with considerable preoccupation with weight and shape. While dieting fulfilled a need for a sense of control, self-starvation led to hunger, and thus to binge eating, with vomiting as a strategy to prevent weight gain. A lack of parental care led to vulnerability to sexual exploitation, and the disgust at the exploitative relationship with the sports coach contributed to a sense of self-hatred. She believed herself to be a bad person, deserving blame, and she thought that she deserved violence from her partner. Also, as a result of her early history, Tanya had developed dissociative strategies to protect her from the intense fear that she experienced at home. These led to a range of dissociative strategies, both cognitive, blocking out memories, and behavioural, initially bingeing and vomiting. The range of these behaviours was to become wider as therapy progressed and the extent of her difficulties became clearer, to include parasuicide attempts, cutting and alcohol abuse.

Treatment of the eating disorder

When therapy commenced, little of Tanya's history was known and the extent of her difficulties was not clear. We agreed that Tanya should try to gain weight up to her desired weight of 8 stones and work to reduce the amount of bingeing during the day through the establishment of more regular eating patterns. She also agreed that she needed to seek out alternative activities with which to fill her time.

An important area that we discussed was the thoughts associated with the binge and vomit cycle. These followed the common pattern of self-starvation leading to a need to eat. This made her feel that she had lost control and was now fat;

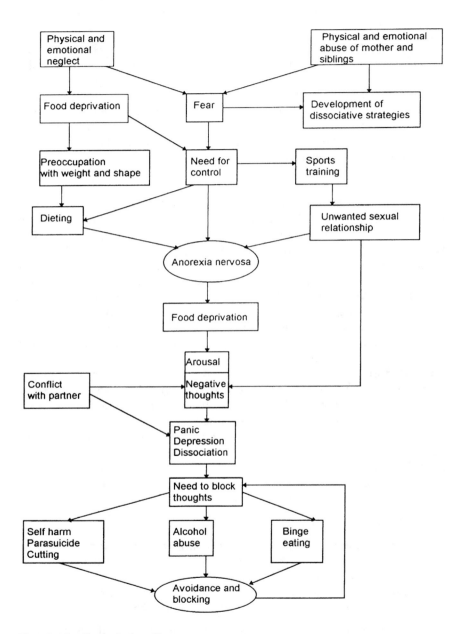

Figure 6.2   Formulation, Tanya.

bingeing suppressed these thoughts, but the returning fear of weight gain led to vomiting. After vomiting, the feelings of starvation would return, and she would need to eat again, thus triggering the cycle again.

Initially, therapy followed a standard approach and had the goal of attempting to establish more normal eating patterns. Components were as follows:

- Education about dieting, eating patterns and bingeing
- Agreeing a target weight
- Establishing more normative eating patterns, through introducing small quantities of food at regular times throughout the day, beginning with breakfast, which Tanya judged to be easiest
- Setting goals for reducing bingeing, for example, reducing the duration of binges
- Identifying and controlling cues for bingeing, for example, having less food available in the house, avoiding buying 'forbidden' foods such as crisps or sweets
- Avoiding boredom, a common trigger for bingeing, by seeking out alternative activities, such as walking the dog
- Setting realistic goals for exercise
- Planning for the future; finding a job
- Challenging beliefs about body size, weight and shape
- Discussion of the relationship with her partner and her views on domestic violence, as she was hit by her partner and believed that she deserved this

Challenges to these beliefs and the negotiation of ideas for different ways of proceeding led to an improvement. Tanya reduced the frequency and duration of bingeing, began to establish a more satisfactory eating pattern, and found a catering job. With this new routine, her bingeing reduced and then stopped completely. This process had taken around 4 months. She did not complete any of the written homework tasks, such as keeping diaries of food consumption, bingeing or vomiting, and had great difficulty in identifying associated thoughts.

Tanya trusted me sufficiently several months into therapy to describe the extent of her bingeing. She gave an account of a typical binge in the session, which is set out below:

A typical binge
20 slices of ham
1 loaf of bread
1 large pan homemade soup (several servings)
2 tins soup
1 large pan pasta, mushrooms and garlic (several servings)
1 tin of beans
2 sausages
5 packets of crisps

To accompany this, Tanya would have 5 litres of sugar-free soda to aid vomiting. She would eat a small quantity of a food and then vomit, repeating this 20 or 30 times in the course of the binge. The entire process took up to 6 hours.

We looked at the costs and benefits of this behaviour, which we summarised as follows:

Positive	Negative
keep busy	feel bad if stop eating
exercise going up and down stairs to bathroom	teeth are decaying and dental care is expensive
feel better for a while	
can look forward to it as a way of coping when left alone	

Tanya saw few disadvantages to her habit, but recognising this strengthened her resolve to seek alternative ways of filling the needs set out above. We looked at stimulus control or response prevention approaches, for example keeping little food in the house, but Tanya found this practically difficult to implement, as her boyfriend liked the house well stocked. The most effective strategy appeared to be to take the dog out for a walk when she felt tempted to binge, which would delay, but not entirely prevent the habit. Revealing the extent of her bingeing and identifying the positive aspects of binges for her, however, helped to reduce both the amount and frequency of her binges. Tanya did not believe that any cognitive control strategies would work, and refused to try them.

Self-harm

As our contact progressed, therapy was punctuated by parasuicide attempts, initially of increasing seriousness, and the extent of her disturbance at times meant that she was obliged to stay on the secure ward. The first attempt was around 4 months into therapy, when Tanya was found in the street having overdosed on alcohol and paracetamol. Her intention had been to die; she had tried to leave her partner, and found life alone too difficult to manage, which had challenged her beliefs in her self-efficacy, leading to depression. At such times of stress, she resumed bingeing and vomiting.

A second aspect of self-harm was a habit which she initially developed at home, and then became more skilled in under the tuition of another patient on the ward; cutting. Following sessions where she talked about her early history, she became conscious of a sense of 'wasted years of unacknowledged suffering'. She said that she could see the 'rejections going on for years and years into the future'. She first cut herself when, very distressed during an argument with her partner, she cut her forearm with a kitchen knife. Her boyfriend was immediately caring and helpful, and helped to reinforce a new tension-reducing behaviour which was to become a frequently used coping strategy for a time.

Tanya became increasingly preoccupied with what she saw as the abusive relationship with her coach and attempted, unsuccessfully, to force the club to take action against him. Angered by lack of success, she cut herself repeatedly. She also described using cutting to prevent 'panic attacks', where she experienced feelings of fear and being out of her body, which I hypothesised was a dissociative coping strategy. She was not, however, prepared to make these a focus of therapy. The cutting was formulated as a means of alleviating high levels of distress, initially externally triggered by anger with her boyfriend, but then used as a coping strategy to prevent internally generated emotional states.

The course of therapy

A significant aspect of the parasuicide attempts was the apparent improvements that followed these; in each case, there was an important gain of some sort. On the secure ward, following one serious attempt, she was able to discuss the simple formulation that self-harm was associated with anger against others and this enabled us to discuss more useful means of coping with anger. As a result, she told her mother her thoughts, rather than cutting or attempting to overdose. This emotional confrontation ended with them hugging as they had not done since she was a child. On discharge, keen to establish self-reliance, she began to keep a diary of instances of vomiting, and borrowed a self-help book on overcoming bulimia (Cooper, 1995), determined to be in control of her own recovery. This resulted in a substantial improvement in her eating disorder.

One striking feature of the therapeutic relationship was the extent to which we would have to cover the same ground repeatedly across sessions, returning constantly to the formulation and testing out aspects of it. Tanya would often disagree with the formulation, only to say some time later that she thought that it was correct. It was clearly essential to Tanya that she arrived at an understanding of some aspect of her life, or worked out a strategy for overcoming a problem, in her own time and in her own way, but the pacing was very slow indeed.

Later stages of therapy

Therapy in the later stages focused on identifying and challenging attitudes and beliefs and seeking alternative coping strategies. In addition, increasing awareness of the origins of schemas was important. These areas can be summarised as follows:

- Achieving openness with me over bingeing in order to bring about change
- Evaluating costs and benefits of bingeing
- Understanding the role of bingeing, cutting and overdosing as coping strategies

- Seeking alternative coping strategies, such as expressing emotions directly in order to bring about change in relationships and avoid dissociative strategies
- Making links between past and current relationships and understanding their role in the development and maintenance of the current difficulties
- Challenging negative beliefs about the past, present and future and reframing difficulties as attempts to cope

The final stage: damage limitation in the face of escalating difficulties

Tanya was brought to a session in a highly confused state, and eventually had to be restrained while being taken to the secure ward, where she had convulsions as a result of an overdose of prescribed haloperidol combined with large quantities of alcohol. The EEG was inconclusive, but Tanya described the fits in the same way as her panic attacks, where she would experience extreme fear and a sense of being outside her body. The sensations would build to a climax, at which point Tanya would think that she would go mad.

Once home, she attempted to divert these intolerable feelings by drinking. At this time she ranged between being uncontrolled and impulsive to vague and forgetful. We adopted a very simple strategy of pegging units of alcohol to the time at which bingeing would end each day. Hence, the first week, she stopped bingeing at 7 p.m., rather than 8 p.m., which was her habit, and reduced her alcohol intake from over 8 units, to 7. The next week the target was 6 p.m. and 6 units, and so on. This was negotiated and adjusted at each session. At this stage, however, her functioning was so impaired that the main tactics were very practically based and aimed at damage limitation. The main areas for intervention were then as follows:

- Understanding the role of drinking as a coping strategy to block out fears of the panic attacks
- Adopting a yet slower pace in setting limits to bingeing and alcohol consumption in order to give a sense of control
- Seeking alternative activities, e.g. voluntary work, college
- making realistic plans for the future, deciding what she wanted from life and how she could go about achieving this

Adopting these very simple tactics was beneficial, leading to clear, identifiable behavioural changes. She gave me a new copy of Cooper's book as her dog had eaten mine. She worked through the chewed pages of the copy she had kept and took more appropriate responsibility for change. She took the dog to obedience classes and signed up at college. She also showed evidence of cognitive change; she now had clear plans for her life through to her 30th birthday; previously she had expected to be dead by 21.

Unfortunately, it was not possible to bring therapy to a satisfactory termination.

Therapy ended with a serious fall as a result of a fit. An EEG suggested temporal lobe epilepsy. She was advised to rest, avoid stress, and postpone plans for college. Devastated by the diagnosis, she resumed bingeing and vomiting and drank excessively, and did not attend further appointments. Subsequent contact with her doctor confirmed that her difficulties remained.

Review

Contact with her left a number of mysteries. One concerned the nature of her 'panic attacks', which I had assumed to be dissociative. The eventual diagnosis of temporal lobe epilepsy is suggestive of organic difficulties, but it is not clear to what extent these attacks were related to the epilepsy, if at all. A second concerned the extent to which, through her repeated self-starvation, substance abuse and overdoses she might have contributed to organic impairment.

In reviewing the case, the pattern she maintained was clear. She would engage in therapy, on her own terms, and upon making some gain in controlling her symptoms, would return to the self-sufficient coping strategies that she had learned as a child, aiming to care for herself entirely so that she would not need to be reliant on anyone. Once out of contact with the therapeutic relationship, however, as alternative strategies were not well rehearsed, she would, under stress, return to other familiar coping responses, bingeing, using alcohol, and cutting. This was, however, a learning process, and, after a crisis, she would return to therapy better able to make connections between her early maladaptive coping responses and her current problems. This enabled her to consider new problem-solving approaches and construct new possible futures for herself, which she could then work towards. Unfortunately, these positive coping strategies were not sufficiently well established for her to withstand what she perceived as the devastating blow of her diagnosis of epilepsy.

PARTICULAR DIFFICULTIES IN WORKING WITH THIS CLIENT GROUP

Setting Realistic Goals

At times, Tanya and I appeared to move at a snail's pace. Textbook targets in establishing normal eating patterns and reducing bingeing were not appropriate, and Tanya would not keep any written records for much of the time. It was necessary to negotiate targets that were just within the limits of what could be tolerated. Even when the patient is unwilling to document this in diary form, within session records are helpful to review to see gradual improvement.

Dissociation and Borderline Personality Disorder

The relevance of dissociative processes and the likelihood of disturbance associated with borderline personality disorder have already been discussed. Tanya reported a number of experiences that were probably dissociative, and used bingeing, vomiting, alcohol and later cutting to block painful cognitions. Tobin (1995) provides some case-based examples of work with women with eating disorders who show dissociation, but stresses that this is a long-term and intensive undertaking, where the usual CBT approaches need to be counterbalanced with an appreciation of the extent of the dissociative strategies, the threat posed by the removal of symptoms and the likelihood of acting out and difficulties in the therapeutic alliance.

Optimising Emotional Processing

Where there is a history of maltreatment which is of clear relevance to the maintenance of current difficulties, enabling the client to be exposed to, and process, the difficult emotional material at a manageable level requires considerable skill (Foa & Riggs, 1993). Briere (1996) refers to this carefully controlled exposure as remaining within the therapeutic window. With too little exposure, the patient may dissociate or otherwise avoid to the extent that the emotion cannot be processed. With too much exposure, however, the patient may be overwhelmed by the experience. With Tanya, I probably both under- and overshot in therapy, so that she was able to avoid discussion of the panic attacks that were a core part of her difficulties, but also at times described memories that were so painful that she employed self-harming strategies. Clearly, to work in this way involves a degree of danger to the patient which must be carefully assessed.

Investigating Abuse Histories; the Risk of False Memories

The literature on abuse and eating disorders may have led therapists to seek for histories of abuse, or, where the patient provides no history of abuse, to assume that this has been forgotten or is being suppressed in some way. Aside from the risks of creating false memories, it is potentially an unhelpful approach, as it can prevent the therapist and patient from constructing a formulation of the problems based on what is currently known, and using this as a basis for effective problem solving. To pursue abuse as an explanation if this is not immediately apparent may be a risky strategy and there may be solutions which are far more readily apparent and accessible. With one patient, I pursued clues to a possible history of abuse which led to extensive and increasingly improbable disclosures. I grappled with these while ignoring important current factors contributing to disturbance which may well have been more relevant in therapy.

Boundary Violations in the Therapeutic Relationship and the Risk of Therapist Abuse

The relationship with Tanya was a long one, requiring a substantial period for her to come to trust me so that she could give a truthful account of her current and past experiences. As a female therapist, I found myself surprised, on occasion, by how apparently flirtatious and coquettish she was with me. In the course of therapy, she recounted several occasions when she had started brief relationships with other men and she was pleased at her ability to attract and exploit them. Clearly, one of her means of increasing her sense of power and control was to exploit her sexual attractiveness.

Her seductive manner put her at risk of sexual exploitation, and, were she to have seen a therapist whose needs or style permitted the formation of a more intimate relationship, she would, I believe, have been a likely target for victimisation within the therapeutic relationship. Another patient with a history of sexual abuse and of borderline personality disorder, who had recovered from a severe eating disorder, gave me a farewell gift of a pair of knickers, several sizes too large. Whatever the intention, and the difficulties in body size estimation which lay behind the choice, this was clearly a highly personal gift. An important question in work with complex cases is, I believe, whether there is a particular risk of boundary violation because of the nature of the patient's difficulties.

Jehu (1994) identified characteristics that may put the individual patient at risk, which can be related to early adverse relationships. Some of these are of general relevance, and some may be specifically risky for women who have concerns over their body image. For women who have been sexually abused previously, there is accumulating evidence on revictimisation in other relationships (Jehu, 1994) and this childhood experience has been associated with sexual abuse by therapists in a number of studies (Armsworth, 1989: Kluft, 1990; Pope & Vetter, 1991). The learned helplessness of the abused child, unassertiveness, low self-esteem, need for approval, excessive dependency, role reversal, oversexualisation, dissociation and borderline personality disorder all put the patient at risk of entering into an exploitative relationship with the therapist.

Some of Jehu's risk factors are highly relevant to this group; the very difficulties that increase the risk of the development of an eating disorder may also increase the risk of abuse by a therapist. For women with eating disorders, a central issue is one of power and control. A patient may enter into a sexual relationship as a means of controlling the other person, but in so doing, risks exploitation. Of course, the stakes are high, and the patient is ultimately able to bring about the therapist's professional ruin, but only if she is prepared to expose herself to scrutiny.

Dissociative reactions, so commonly associated with both abuse and eating disorders, also enable the patient to disengage from the abuse, or depersonalise the experience. Again, these may be well rehearsed forms of coping in women with a history of abuse. Borderline personality disorder, as exemplified by Tanya, may put patients and therapists at risk, through the combination of extreme neediness and dependence, confusion over boundaries and manipulation. This constellation of characteristics may be associated both with a history of abuse and with eating disorder.

It is important to recall, however, that the psychological risk factors associated with sexual abuse may well reflect other aspects of maltreatment, including neglect, and other adverse family factors, and so it may not be sexual abuse *per se*, but a combination of these other factors which contribute to risk. Tanya showed all the signs of disturbance associated with sexual abuse, but maintained that she had not been sexually abused until her relationship at 16.

A further risk factor associated with work with complex cases may lie in the long-term nature of the work, and the flexibility that may be required in renegotiating the timing, place and nature of sessions. Patient and therapist get to know each other very well, and this requires an increased level of vigilance on the part of the therapist for relaxation of normal codes of conduct and possible boundary violations.

Termination of therapy is a time at which boundary violations are again potentially important. Some therapists who enter into relationships with patients at the termination of therapy report that they believe that this is of continuing help to the patient (Jehu, 1994), but this is to misunderstand the entire basis of the relationship. There is also the risk to the therapist that the patient may, with increasing awareness, reappraise the relationship and report the unprofessional conduct. Scrupulous attention to boundaries is essential in work with complex cases in this area. Jehu (1994) offers suggestions on steps to be taken to prevent abuse by therapists, including awareness of dangers in the relationship.

Important risk factors are to be found in the results of what little empirical work there is to be found in this hard-to-research area. The most common pattern is that of older male therapists who become involved in relationships with female patients several years their junior (Gartrell et al., 1987;

Pope & Vetter, 1991). This is, of course, the age and gender balance of many eating disorder clinics, an important imbalance which could usefully be addressed in staff selection and training. Pairing this with the need to discuss issues of body shape, appearance and sexuality in the course of therapy is a potentially dangerous combination. Abusing therapists have often been found to be in some form of personal distress (Butler & Zelen, 1977), and isolated, dominating or antisocial.

Notably, abusing therapists have been described as having a grandiose sense of self-importance with respect to therapy, being uniquely able to fulfil the patient's needs. Such therapists may use unconventional or unorthodox approaches. The paradox with such therapists is that their confidence and perceived charisma may lead to their being afforded high status for their work if they are prepared to take on and treat cases with which other therapists have had little success. Unfortunately, women with severe eating disorders also fall into this group. The fact that these are difficult and complex cases leads to a dangerous circularity, as failure to improve will be seen as a factor of the patient, rather than the treatment, and their reputation will be preserved whatever the outcome. This indicates a clear need for supervision of work with such cases, and the value of auditing and peer scrutiny in work of this level of complexity, to ensure good practice and to protect both the patient and the therapist. As this chapter has shown, the degree of vulnerability of women who have experienced maltreatment, sexual victimisation and revictimisation, and their current high level of disturbance places them at particular risk of continuing exploitation.

REFERENCES

Armsworth, M.W. (1989). Therapy of incest survivors: abuse or support? *Child Abuse and Neglect*, **13**, 549–562.

Bradbury, E.T. (1993). *The interface between clinical psychology and cosmetic surgery.* Paper presented to the December Conference of the British Psychological Society, London.

Briere, J. (1992). *Child Abuse Trauma: Theory and Treatment of the Lasting Effects.* London: Sage.

Briere, J. (1996). A self-trauma model for treating adult survivors of severe child abuse. In J. Briere, L. Berliner, J.A. Bulkley, C. Jenny & T. Reid (Eds), *The APSAC Handbook on Child Maltreatment.* Thousand Oaks, CA: Sage.

Butler, S. & Zelen, S.L. (1977). Sexual intimacies between therapists and patients. *Psychotherapy, Research and Practice*, **14**, 139–145.

Byram, V., Wagner, H.L. & Waller, G. (1994). Sexual abuse and body image distortion. *Child Abuse and Neglect*, **19**, 507–510.

Calam, R.M., Griffiths, R. & Slade, P.D. (1997). Eating disorders, body satisfaction and unwanted sexual experience: UK, Australian and US data. *European Eating Disorders Review*, **5**, 158–170.

Calam, R., Taylor, S. & Bradbury, E. (1996). Body image in elective breast surgery patients. Abstract: *Proceedings of the British Association for Behavioural and Cognitive Psychotherapy Annual Conference, Southport*.

Connors, M.E. & Morse, W. (1993). Sexual abuse and eating disorders. *International Journal of Eating Disorders*, **13**, 1–11.

Cooper, P.J. (1995). *Bulimia Nervosa and Binge Eating: a Guide to Recovery* (revised edn). London: Robinson.

Crow, S.J. & Mitchell, J.E. (1994). Bulimia nervosa: methods of treatment. In L.A. Alexander Mott & D.B. Lumsden (Eds). *Understanding Eating Disorders*. Washington DC: Taylor & Francis.

Davis, R. & de Groot, J. (1993). Psychotherapy for the eating disorders. In SH. Kennedy (Ed.). *University of Toronto Handbook of Eating Disorders* (pp. 49–58). Toronto: University of Toronto Press.

Everill, J. & Waller, G. (1995a). Disclosure of sexual abuse and psychological adjustment in female undergraduates. *Child Abuse and Neglect*, **19**, 93–100.

Everill, J. & Waller, G. (1995b). Dissociation and bulimia: research and theory. *European Eating Disorders Review*, **3**, 127–128.

Fairburn, C.G. & Cooper, P.J. (1989). Eating disorders. In K. Hawton, P.M. Salkovskis, J. Kirk & D.M. Clark (Eds*). Cognitive Therapy for Psychiatric Problems: a Practical Guide* (pp. 277–314). Oxford: Oxford University Press.

Fairburn, C.G., Jones, R.T., Peveler, R.C., Carr, S.J., Solomon, R.A., O'Connor, M.E., Burton, J. & Hope, R.A. (1991). Three psychological treatments for bulimia nervosa. *Archives of General Psychiatry*, **48**, 463–469.

Foa, E.B. & Riggs, D.S. (1993). Post-traumatic stress disorder and rape. In R.S. Pynoos (Ed.), *Post-traumatic Stress Disorder: A Clinical Review* (pp. 133–163). Lutherville, MD, Sindran.

Folsom, V., Krahn, D., Nairn, K., Gold., L., Demitrack, M.A. & Silk, K.R. (1993). The impact of sexual and physical abuse on eating disordered and psychiatric symptoms: A comparison of eating disordered and psychiatric inpatients. *International Journal of Eating Disorders*, **13**, 249–257.

Fullerton, D.T., Wonderlich, S.A & Gosnell, B.A. (1995). Clinical characteristics of eating disorder patients who report sexual or physical abuse. *International Journal of Eating Disorders*, **17**, 243–249.

Garner, D.M. & Bemis, K. (1982). A cognitive behavioural approach to anorexia nervosa. *Cognitive Therapy and Research*, **6**, 123–150.

Gartrell, N., Herman, J.L, Olarte, S., Feldstein, M. & Localio, R. (1987). Psychiatrist-patient sexual contact: Results of a national survey, I:, Prevalence. *American Journal of Psychiatry*, **143**, 1126–1131.

Gleaves, D.H. & Eberenz, K.P. (1994). Sexual abuse histories among treatment resistant bulimia nervosa patients. *International Journal of Eating Disorders*, **15**, 227–231.

Goldner, E.M. & Birmingham, C.L. (1994). Anorexia nervosa: Methods of treatment. In L.A. Alexander Mott and D.B. Lumsden (Eds). *Understanding Eating Disorders*. Washington DC: Taylor & Francis.

Hastings, T. & Kern, J.M. (1994). Relationships between bulimia, childhood sexual abuse and family environment. *International Journal of Eating Disorders*, **15**, 103–111.

Jehu, D. (1988). *Beyond Sexual Abuse: Therapy with Women who were Childhood Victims*. Chichester: Wiley.

Jehu, D. (1994). *Patients as Victims: Sexual Abuse in Psychotherapy and Counselling*. Chichester: Wiley.

Kennedy, S.H., McVey, G. & Katz, R. (1990). Personaity disorders in anorexia nervosa and bulimia nervosa. *Journal of Psychiatric Research*, **24**, 259–269.

Kinzl, J.F., Traweger, C., Guenther, V. & Beibl, W. (1994). Family Background and Sexual Abuse Associated with Eating Disorders. *American Journal of Psychiatry*, **151**, 1127–1131.

Kluft, R.P. (1990). Incest and subsequent revictimisation: the case of therapist-patient sexual exploitation, with a description of the sitting duck syndrome. In *Incest Related Syndromes of Adult Psychopathology* R.P. Kluft (Ed). pp. 263–287. Washington, DC: American Psychiatric Press.

Mullen, P.E. (1993). Child sexual abuse and adult mental health: The development of disorder. *Journal of Interpersonal Violence*, **8**, 429–432.

Mullen, P.E., Martin, J.L., Anderson, J.C. & Romans, S.E. (1994). The effect of child sexual abuse on social, interpersonal and sexual function in adult life. *British Journal of Psychiatry*, **165**, 35–47.

Mullen, P.E., Martin, J.L., Anderson, J.C., Romans, S.E. & Herbison, G.P. (1996). The long term impact of the physical, emotional and sexual abuse of children: A community study. *Child Abuse and Neglect*, **20**, 7–22.

Phillips, K.A. (1991). Body dysmorphic disorder: The distress of imagined ugliness. *American Journal of Psychiatry*, **148**, 1138–1149.

Pope, H.G. & Hudson, J.I. (1992). Is childhood sexual abuse a risk factor for bulimia nervosa? *American Journal of Psychiatry*, **149**, 455–463.

Pope, K.S. & Vetter, V.A. (1991). Prior therapist-patient sexual involvement among patients seen by psychologists. *Psychotherapy*, **28**, 429–438.

Rutter, M. & Rutter, M. (1992). *Developing Minds: Challenge and Continuity Across the Lifespan*. Harmondsworth: Penguin Books.

Schaaf, K.K. & McCanne, T.R. (1994). Childhood abuse, body image disturbance and eating disorders. *Child Abuse and Neglect*, **18**, 607–615.

Sheldrick, C. (1991). Adult sequelae of child sexual abuse. *British Journal of Psychiatry*, **158**, 55–62.

Smolak, L., Levine, M.P., & Sullins, E. (1990). Are childhood experiences related to eating disordered attitudes and behaviours in a college sample? *International Journal of Eating Disorders*, **9**, 167–178.

Taylor, S. (1996). Links between the desire for cosmetic surgery, body perception and previous unwanted sexual experiences. Clin. Psy. D. doctoral thesis, University of Manchester.

Terr, L. (1991). Childhood traumas: An outline and overview. *American Journal of Psychiatry*, **148**, 10–20.

Tobin, D.L. (1995). Treatment of early trauma and dissociation in eating disorders of late onset. *European Eating Disorders Review*, **3**, 160–173.

Toyuz, S.W., Beumont, P.J.V., Glaun, D., Phillips, T. & Cowie, I. (1984). A comparison of lenient and strict operant conditioning programmes in refeeding patients with anorexia nervosa. *British Journal of Psychiatry*, **144**, 517–520.

Vanderlinden, J., Vandereyken, W. & Probst, M. (1995). Dissociative symptoms in eating disorders: A follow-up study. *European Eating Disorders Review*, **3**, 174–184.

Waller, G. (1991). Sexual abuse as a factor in eating disorders. *British Journal of Psychiatry*, **159**, 664–671.

Waller, G. (1992). Sexual abuse and the severity of bulimic symptoms. *British Journal of Psychiatry*, **161**, 90–93.

Waller, G. (1994). Childhood sexual abuse and borderline personality disorder in the eating disorders. *Child Abuse and Neglect*, **18**, 97–101.

Waller, G., Everill, J., & Calam, R. (1994). Sexual abuse and the eating disorders. In L.A. Alexander Mott & D.B. Lumsden (Eds). *Understanding Eating Disorders*. Washington DC: Taylor & Francis.

Welch, S.L. & Fairburn, C.G. (1994). Sexual abuse and bulimia nervosa: Three integrated case control comparisons. *American Journal of Psychiatry*, **151**, 402–407.

Chapter 7

ASSESSMENT AND FORMULATION IN THE COGNITIVE BEHAVIOURAL TREATMENT OF PSYCHOSIS

Gillian Haddock* and Nicholas Tarrier*

INTRODUCTION

The aim of this chapter is to examine issues relating to assessment and problem formulation that guides therapy with someone suffering from psychosis. Issues relating to therapy itself will be covered more fully in the next chapter. Although it is difficult to completely separate assessment from therapy, in this chapter we have attempted to focus on suggesting what type of information is helpful in assessment and how it can be obtained. Therapy is directed by the therapist's understanding of that individual's problems within the context of a general model of that specific disorder. Thus, the success of therapy will, in part, be determined by the quality of the therapist's assessment. Treating someone with a psychosis is especially complex because of the range of difficulties, disorders and handicaps associated with the disorder. Issues that are important in complex cases resulting from other diagnoses, such as engagement, maintenance in therapy, homework, speed and magnitude of recovery may be amplified by the specific nature of the psychosis and its ramifications. As a result of this complexity we have chosen to separate, probably somewhat artificially, assessment from treatment. First, however, we feel it will be helpful to cover some of the research evidence that indicates that consideration of a cognitive behavioural approach with psychotic patients is warranted.

* Department of Clinical Psychology, University of Manchester, UK

Treating Complex Cases: The Cognitive Behavioural Therapy Approach.
Edited by Nicholas Tarrier, Adrian Wells and Gillian Haddock.

TREATMENT EVALUATION RESEARCH

Cognitive behaviour therapy is a collective term for a range of techniques and methods that share common basic principles and are theoretically linked to learning and information processing theory. CBT approaches have been developed and successfully and consistently evaluated in the treatment of neurotic disorders. There is a strong argument that these types of disorder are acquired as a result of environmental stress. However, this is unlikely to be the case for schizophrenia for which at least some biological causation is probable. Nevertheless, there is evidence that the course of schizophrenia and the severity of its symptoms may be influenced by stress. A vulnerability–stress model (Nuechterlein & Dawson, 1984) is often used to explain the interaction between biological and environmental factors where the variance in symptomatology is influenced by environmental stressors and mediated by personal resources, such as coping strategies. In addition, people suffering from schizophrenia are also vulnerable to the acquisition of emotional disorders such as anxiety and depression. These emotions, with their attendant elevated arousal and cognitive distortions, may well exacerbate the psychotic process and increase symptomatology. Thus CBT, which focuses on the information processing architecture and the way this interacts with behaviour and physiological responses, could well act in tandem with medication and alleviate psychotic symptomatology.

For people experiencing psychotic symptoms the usual first line treatment is anti-psychotic medication. It is unusual for patients to be offered psychological treatment to aid in reducing the severity of the psychosis during the initial stages of a psychotic illness, although this may be more frequently provided to treat residual symptoms, such as treatment resistant hallucinations and delusions or associated anxiety and depression. It is with patients suffering from *chronic* psychotic illness that cognitive behavioural treatment has been able to demonstrate the most consistent benefits to patients. The majority of research has been in the form of case studies or case series (Haddock et al., 1996; Chadwick & Lowe, 1990; Kingdon & Turkington, 1991) which have demonstrated that psychological treatments can be effective with chronic psychotic patients. Recently, controlled studies have begun to confirm the positive results demonstrated by these case studies. For example, Tarrier's group in Manchester (Tarrier et al., 1993) compared two different cognitive behavioural approaches (coping strategy enhancement and problem solving) for treating persistent hallucinations and delusions in 27 patients experiencing persistent hallucinations and delusions. Coping strategy enhancement involved a systematic assessment of patients' naturalistic coping strategies for dealing with their hallucinations or delusions and treatment was designed to maximise and enhance these. The problem-solving approach was not aimed directly at psychotic symptoms but focused on a small number of key problems. Strategies designed to help patients to ameliorate these were employed. Both treatments significantly reduced anxiety and delusions compared to a waiting list control group with coping strategy enhancement showing some superiority over problem solving. However, the treatments were less effective for auditory hallucinations. These two treatments have recently been evaluated in combination by the Manchester group (Tarrier, 1997; Tarrier et al., 1998) in a larger randomised controlled trial. CSE was combined with problem solving and relapse prevention (CBT) and compared to a supportive counselling control and a treatment as usual control group in 79 chronic schizophrenic patients. Results showed that CBT was superior to supportive counselling which in turn was superior to treatment as usual. These results were significant in an intention-to-treat analysis for an aggregate of psychotic symptoms measured on the appropriate BPRS scale and for delusions. In a treatment-to-protocol analysis which included only treatment completers (n = 72) the results were significant for hallucinations, negative symptoms, overall psychopathology and a measure of individualised treatment goals.

In another recent study, Garety et al. (1994) compared a comprehensive cognitive behavioural treatment (n = 13) with a waiting list control (n = 7) in a group of chronic patients with persistent psychotic symptoms. The cognitive behavioural treatment produced significant benefits in terms of total Brief Psychiatric Rating Scale (BPRS: Overall & Gorham, 1962) scores compared with the control treatment. These authors have also carried out a larger controlled evaluation of their treatment (Kuipers et al., 1997) again confirming the superiority of CBT on total BPRS scores over a treatment as usual condition (case management and medication).

Despite the benefits demonstrated in these studies, treatment has generally been focused on patients with chronic schizophrenia and medication resistant psychotic symptoms, and there has been little research on patients experiencing recent onset or acute symptoms. An exception of this is an innovative study by Drury et al. (1996a, b) carried out with acute inpatients, some of whom were experiencing recent onset psychotic illnesses (patients had an average length of history of 6 years). Patients admitted to an acute psychiatric ward were randomly allocated to either a cognitive behavioural treatment consisting of individual sessions, group work and family sessions or a control treatment of activities matched for therapist time. Assessment of outcome was carried out on a number of symptom and service variables although the assessor was not blind to treatment group. The results were startling and showed that the cognitive behavioural treatment significantly speeded the time to recovery of symptoms by between 25 and 50% and reduced actual time spent in hospital by approximately 50% compared to the control group. The results also showed that these benefits were maintained in terms of lower relapse rates for the cognitive behavioural group. There were no significant differences on these variables between the treatment as usual control group and the activity control group. However, an attempt to partially replicate Drury et al.'s findings with blind and independent assessments found results in the predicted direction but failed to replicate the size of the treatment effect (Haddock et al., 1998a).

PSYCHOLOGICAL MODELS OF PSYCHOSIS

The cornerstone of any cognitive behavioural intervention is the individual formulation which serves to collate all relevant current and historical data provided by the patient during assessment, and produce a testable heuristic to explain that patient's problems and suggest a treatment strategy. Formulation with psychotic patients is especially crucial as their difficulties are generally extremely complex and multiple and spread across a number of domains as well as the psychological and behavioural. Problem formulation takes place within the context of a generalised explanatory psychological model of that particular disorder or problem category. In psychosis, however, this is hindered by the diverse and multiple models which have attempted to explain schizophrenia and its associated symptoms which have failed to reach any meaningful consensus of agreement. Indeed, it has been questioned whether models designed to understand and explain the occurrence of the syndrome of schizophrenia are helpful in terms of describing the aetiology, prognosis or treatment of the disorder (Bentall, Jackson & Pilgrim, 1988). As a result, many cognitive theorists have focused their attentions on the individual psychotic symptoms associated with schizophrenia such as hallucinations, delusions and negative symptoms. These models have been more useful in assisting in the development of cognitive behavioural treatment strategies, although they are in the very early stages of development.

Delusions

There is no consensus model to explain the occurrence and maintenance of delusional beliefs, although the similarity between delusional beliefs and ordinary belief processes in normal subjects has been noted. Maher (1988) hypothesised that delusions are the result of normal reasoning processes being applied to unusual or abnormal perceptual experiences (i.e. secondary to an abnormal perception), whereas Bentall and colleagues (Bentall, 1994) have suggested that although delusional beliefs may share important characteristics with 'normal' beliefs the deluded patient exhibits biases in their reasoning processes about the world which contribute to the formation of 'abnormal' beliefs which are not shared by the majority of the population. The implications of these models are not necessarily inconsistent as they both indicate that reasoning processes are crucial in the explanation and maintenance of the beliefs. This implies that therapeutic interventions designed to modify reasoning processes and strategies which enhance cognitive or other coping strategies will be effective at reducing the severity of delusional beliefs. These observations are supported by the literature on belief modification techniques which have been applied with deluded patients (see Chapter 8 this volume) which have shown that it is possible to significantly reduce the conviction and preoccupation with delusional beliefs (Chadwick & Lowe, 1990; Kuipers et al., 1997; Tarrier et al., 1998).

Hallucinations

The cognitive behavioural treatment of auditory hallucinations has developed from a number of different theoretical backgrounds and these are based partly on specific cognitive explanations of auditory hallucinations and partly on general psychological models as applied to emotional disorders. As with delusions, there is no consensus on a cognitive model for auditory hallucinations although most assume that auditory hallucinations are associated with speech processing in some way, for example that some sort of misattribution of inner speech is implicated. The accounts for which type of deficit or bias might bring about a misattribution of inner speech vary considerably. For example, Hoffman (1986) assumes that auditory hallucinations occur as a result of random firing of speech processing mechanisms which result in 'parasitic memories' being brought into consciousness. As these are unexpected and unplanned the experiencer perceives them as being alien and attributes them to an external source. David (1994) also accounts for auditory hallucinations in terms of a deficit in the speech processing mechanisms where a dysfunction in a particular part of the speech processing pathway results in different types of auditory experiences such as hallucinations, thought echo and so on. Frith (1992) proposes that the actual inner speech of hallucinators is normal but that an internal monitor of inner speech is faulty, resulting in unexpected alien speech which is perceived as originating from an external source. Finally, Bentall (1990) suggests that the speech processing pathways are performing normally in hallucinators but specific beliefs and attitudes produce biases which determine their interpretation of inner speech. He proposes that this would explain why cultural differences occur in the experience of hallucinations (Bourgignon, 1970) and why hallucinators are more susceptible to suggestions than non-hallucinators (Haddock, Bentall & Slade, 1996). Although there is not enough evidence to account satisfactorily for auditory hallucinations by any of these accounts alone, all attract some supportive evidence. It is possible that a combination of these accounts may be correct where there may be an underlying neuropsychological deficit (e.g. Hoffman, David, Frith) but that cognitive factors such as monitoring, beliefs and attributions (e.g. Frith, Bentall) determine their occurrence, interpretation and effect on the individual. Further research is required to elucidate the actual mechanisms involved and the relative contribution of each. Nevertheless, the models all have implications for cognitive behavioural treatment and there is considerable overlap between these accounts and the cognitive behavioural treatments which would remediate them. For example, the models of Hoffman, David and Frith suggest that some form of compensatory coping for dealing with the underlying deficits which produce the hallucination may be effective. The observation that hallucinations tend to worsen under conditions of increased arousal suggests that cognitive treatments which aim to reduce arousal may also be effective. Bentall's model and the observation that hallucinators may be more susceptible to the influence of suggestions indicated that an intervention designed to modify beliefs and attributions might also play an important part in modifying hallucinatory experience. Finally, as with delusions, all of the above models suggest that some form of coping skills enhancement would improve patient functioning.

The models related to the importance of environmental stress or emotional distress as a precursor to both hallucinations and delusions have been central to Tarrier and colleagues' ideas on their cognitive behavioural treatment of psychotic symptoms. They have observed that an instability in the level of arousal or its regulation is a common pathway to the exacerbation of psychotic symptoms (Tarrier & Turpin, 1992). From this conceptualisation, Tarrier and colleagues have inferred that reducing the emotional consequences of psychotic symptoms or alleviating environmental stress through enhanced coping strategies would reduce symptomatology (see Barrowclough & Tarrier, 1992, Ch.10). Figure 7.1 provides a clinical heuristic which attempts to integrate the factors which contribute to psychotic symptoms and provides a guide for directing therapy by describing the interaction between internal antecedents, such as biological factors or dysfunctional psychological beliefs and environmental influences.

All of the models described have some limitations but they have provided impetus for clinicians to successfully adapt cognitive behavioural therapies, originally developed for non-psychotic disorders, to hallucinations and

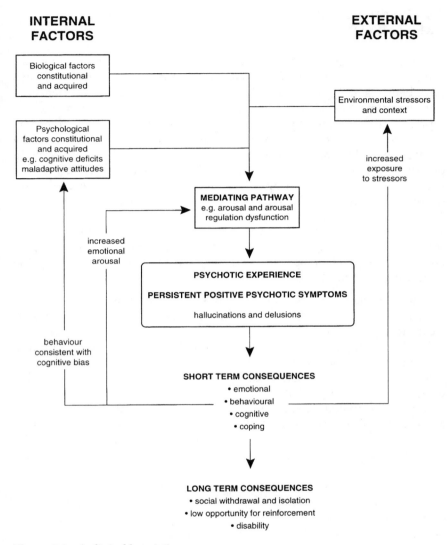

Figure 7.1   A clinical heuristic.

delusions. The specific elements of treatment which have influenced success in treating psychotic disorders are still being elucidated. Nevertheless, treatments are sufficiently evolved and evaluated to describe in detail for clinicians. The rest of this chapter will describe the assessment and formulation strategies useful in working with psychosis and specific interventions will be discussed in more detail in the following two chapters.

ASSESSMENT FOR COGNITIVE BEHAVIOURAL TREATMENT

The development of assessment tools for hallucinations and delusions has, until recently, been largely for diagnostic purposes, so that the symptoms have been elicited and measured in terms of their presence or absence, or different dimensions have been aggregated into a global unidimensional representation of 'severity'. This type of assessment has been driven by the degree of information which is necessary to prescribe treatment by medication rather than by psychological means. For example, prescribing of neuroleptic treatment for psychosis is directed by the psychiatric classificatory system which groups psychotic symptoms into discrete syndromes or diagnoses such as schizophrenia or manic depressive psychosis. Treatment is then directed towards the *syndrome* rather than individual symptoms. As a result of this, assessment has usually been used to assist solely with diagnosis, so that the majority of instruments for assessing psychosis have been developed to increase the reliability and validity of the diagnostic system.

Cognitive behavioural treatments may be directed towards individuals who have a similar diagnosis, but are not generally directed towards treating a 'syndrome'. Psychological treatment is usually directed towards eliciting the symptoms associated with a particular diagnosis and assessing the behavioural and cognitive determinants of these symptoms. It is then towards these causal and maintaining factors that treatment is directed. As a result of this, although diagnostic instruments can be invaluable in improving reliability in diagnosis and for eliciting symptoms, they are not primarily designed to provide sufficient information for therapists to arrive at a cognitive behavioural formulation of the patient's key problems. As a result, a number of other assessment tools have been developed which can assist in this process. Diagnostic instruments are useful as a starting point in assessment to identify specific symptoms which can then be explored in more detail, using more specialist and dedicated assessment instruments. More conventional methods of cognitive behavioural analysis can also be used to tease out the determinants of each symptom.

Instruments Which Elicit the Symptoms

Because of the multiple problems which are present in psychosis, a thorough assessment of a range of potential problem areas in addition to the key psychotic symptoms is necessary. This can help clinicians and patients to prioritise problems and to ensure that CBT is being applied to the psychotic symptoms appropriately. Eliciting information on non-psychotic symptoms is necessary as these may interact with and affect the occurrence of the psychotic symptoms. Thus, initially, all symptoms, non-psychotic and psychotic, should be elicited and an assessment or rating of their global severity can be made, for example, instruments such as the Schedule for Clinical Assessment in Neuropsychiatry (SCANS: WHO, 1992) can be used to elicit symptoms and rating scales such as the Positive and Negative Symptom Scale (PANSS: Kay, Opler & Lindenmayer, 1989), or the Brief Psychiatric Rating Scale (BPRS: Overall & Gorham, 1962) can be used to rate the severity of the symptoms. The latter two instruments provide a composite global rating based on a number of different dimensions of a symptom severity (e.g. duration, frequency, conviction in delusional beliefs, etc.) but do not quantify these different dimensions themselves.

Instruments Which Will Quantify the Dimensions of Psychotic Symptoms

The scales described above are not sufficiently specific to tell us anything about the nature of the individual dimensions of symptoms and how they co-vary. This is necessary in cognitive behavioural treatment to assess whether an improvement in overall severity is the result of a reduction in distress associated with a symptom or preoccupation, or other dimensions of a symptom. For example a patient who experiences a reduction in the loudness of their hallucinations as a result of treatment may not show a concurrent change in frequency or duration, therefore the improvement will not be picked up on measures of severity such as the BPRS. This is essential in psychological treatment which might be directed towards reducing the distress or other dimensions associated with a particular symptom. Scales are available which have been developed to measure the severity of a number of different dimensions of auditory hallucinations and delusions (e.g. Psychotic Symptom Rating Scales; PSYRATS: Haddock et al., 1998b). PSYRATS consists of 13 dimensions of auditory hallucinations (frequency, duration, amount of distress, intensity of distress, location, conviction of beliefs regarding origin, disruption, controllability, loudness, amount of negative content, degree of negative content, number, form), and 6 dimensions of delusions (amount of preoccupation, duration of preoccupation, amount of distress, intensity of distress, conviction, disruption) are elicited and rated by an interviewer on a five-point scale which has specified anchor points. This type of instrument can be used over treatment to track changes in dimensions over time and to assess specific changes in individual dimensions.

Instruments for Carrying Out a Cognitive Behavioural Analysis of Symptoms

Instruments as described above are important in allowing us to monitor changes in symptoms over time but they are not sufficient to help a therapist gain a detailed understanding of the variables which are contributing to the occurrence and maintenance of a symptom. This is essential in order to achieve a working formulation which will direct a psychological intervention. Structured interviews such as the Maudsley Assessment of Delusions Schedule (MADS: Buchanan et al., 1993) and the Antecedent and Coping Interview (ACI: Tarrier, 1992) have been designed to achieve this. For example the MADS is a structured interview which elicits information from the patient about their delusions in terms of a large number of different variables, such as the degree of conviction, the behaviours associated with the belief, the evidence which the patient holds which contributes to their conviction. The ACI is a semi-structured interview which is designed to elicit the behavioural and cognitive antecedents and consequences associated with a symptom. For example, a patient's delusional belief may be maintained by the types of behaviour which the patient engages in. A paranoid patient may engage in continual searching for evidence which will confirm his belief that the whole world is against him and ignore disconfirmatory evidence. A patient's high level of anxiety resulting from a delusional belief may produce elevated levels of arousal which increase the probability of hallucinations. A detailed analysis of these circumstances is essential to provide the basis for intervention, which might involve helping the patient to change their interpretation of behavioural evidence or reduce their anxiety. The aim of the ACI is to identify each psychotic symptom (hallucination and/or delusion) and to identify the conditions or situations under which it occurs. These may include external conditions such as location or place, and functional conditions such as periods of inactivity and disengagement, and also internal conditions such as subjective feelings of tension or over-stimulation. Having ascertained the nature of the symptoms and the context under which the patient has these experiences, the interviewer attempts to elucidate what happens subsequent to, or as a result of, these experiences. Included here is information concerning the emotional and behavioural reaction the patient has in response to their symptoms and their methods of coping. Coping signifies the active attempts the patient makes through cognitive and behavioural actions to reduce, overcome or master their symptoms. The majority of patients do actively attempt to cope with their symptoms and these attempts can be built upon to form the basis of a therapeutic strategy.

The above structure can contribute to an overall assessment with a patient, but this also must be carried out in the context of a general assessment of other important areas. Most patients who have a psychotic illness have multiple needs, and it is important to fully assess all areas before making a decision to intervene specifically with techniques aimed at reducing the occurrence and distress associated with the psychotic symptoms. For example, many patients with psychotic symptoms are depressed or anxious (Tarrier, 1997), or are suicidal (Falloon & Talbot, 1981), and these non-psychotic symptoms must be taken into account as a reduction of psychotic symptoms (especially if they are of a grandiose nature) may have an unanticipated but detrimental effect for a patient if the removal results in a further increase in depression or anxiety. Likewise, some patients have symptoms which form an important part of their life, for example supportive or comforting voices, for whom removal of their symptoms may have a negative impact. This does not mean to say that this person cannot be helped to improve their functioning, but that the focus for intervention may be to improve that person's access to other supportive and comforting supports before intervening directly with the symptoms. Thus, the potential functional value of a symptom should be assessed with a view to constructing other behaviours to replace that function. The issue of associated problems and specific factors that need to be considered will be taken into account later in this chapter.

Continued Assessment and Monitoring during Treatment

Instruments such as the PSYRATS can also be used throughout treatment to monitor the effect of treatment over time. In addition, more detailed ratings scales and monitoring tools can be used to explore hypotheses generated by a formulation. For example, it is possible that early assessment may reveal that one person's voices appear to be associated with certain types of interactions or events. It may be useful to get the patient to concurrently monitor these types of situations by recording the antecedent and consequential events surrounding a symptom occurring in terms of behavioural, physiological and cognitive factors. This may help the therapist and patient gain a clear idea of the types of thoughts and emotions which are contributing to symptoms' occurrence or worsening, and provide an ideal place for intervention. These types of ratings or diaries can be kept by the patient and can be made as simple or as complex as appropriate. They can also be an essential part of a treatment intervention, for example a patient who expresses paranoid beliefs may utilise this type of monitoring tool to keep a record of the types of evidence collected during times when the belief is held most strongly. This may help the patient to keep a more objective record of the evidence which is used in support of their belief and this may then be reviewed during therapy sessions.

Monitoring tools may not only play an important part in assessment but can also be used during an intervention with patients experiencing auditory hallucinations; for example, it has been noted that concurrent monitoring on these types of symptoms may reduce their severity (Reybee & Kinch, 1973). In addition, focusing on the nature of auditory hallucinations may reduce the distress associated with them (i.e. serve a desensitisation purpose for some patients) and help some patients to explore the content, their respondent thoughts and feelings, as well as to explore their underlying beliefs which can contribute to the distress associated with voices (Chadwick & Birchwood, 1994). Strategies which can aid this type of focusing approach have been described in detail by Haddock and colleagues (Haddock et al., 1994; Bentall, Haddock & Slade, 1994; Haddock et al., 1998c. For example, they describe a focusing approach which combines concurrent monitoring with a desensitisation programme in which the patients gradually expose themselves to increasingly emotive aspects of the hallucination. This is achieved by first asking the patient to monitor only the physical characteristics of their voices, such as number, gender, intensity, location and so on, but without attention to the actual content. When the patient feels comfortable with this they can describe the content of their hallucinations, and finally their resultant thoughts and beliefs which have been activated by the voices. Verbal and written shadowing (immediately repeating the content out loud or writing the content down) can aid focusing on voice content and thoughts and help the patient to discuss their voices without becoming aroused or distressed. These exercises can also be used to demonstrate that hallucinations can be experienced without distress and adverse consequences and may be controllable.

ASSOCIATED FEATURES

Psychotic disorders are frequently of long duration, sometimes lifelong, and often involve cognitive, psychological, social and vocational impairments and handicaps. These impairments require assessment and consideration when therapy is being considered. Furthermore, it is highly likely that the psychotic patient will have enduring contact with mental health services, and possibly social services, and be receiving a range of treatments (pharmacological and psychosocial), interventions and services. This needs to be considered both as a possible source of information and in how CBT may be integrated. A list of these associated features is presented in Table 7.1

It is important that during both assessment and therapy the therapist takes into acount any of these associated features that are present and may be impediments to therapy. Thus, it is important that a sound, trusting and

Table 7.1 Associated features: features which need to be assessed and possibly taken into consideration in CBT for psychotic patients

PSYCHOLOGICAL
- Interference, disrupted or slowed thought processes
- Difficulty discriminating signal from noise
- Restricted attention
- Hypersensitivity to social stressors and social interactions
- Difficulty processing social stimuli and acting appropriately
- Flat and restricted affect
- Elevated arousal or dysfunctional arousal regulation
- Hypersensitivity to stress and life events
- High risk of suicide
- Stigmatisation
- Risk of depression and hopelessness
- High risk of substance abuse
- Onset in late adolescence/early adulthood interfered with normal developmental processes

PSYCHOSOCIAL
- Hypersensitive to family environments and social relationships
- Risk of perpetrating, or being the victim of, violence
- Integration of CBT with other interventions, e.g. family interventions

SOCIAL
- Conditions of social deprivation
- Poor housing
- Downward social drift
- Unemployment and difficulty in competing in the job market
- Restricted social network
- Psychiatric career interferes with utilisation of other social resources

reinforcing relationship is built up so as to engage the patient, and sessions are geared in duration and content so as to be tolerable to the patient. The standard one hour outpatient appointment may not be the most suitable sessional structure and some time may be required while the patient accommodates to the stress of this type of social interaction. Interaction and communication should be clear and simple and avoid excessive complexity and ambiguity. Furthermore, individual therapy is probably most effective if integrated with family intervention should the patient be living or have close contact with relatives or a carer (see Barrowclough & Tarrier, 1992, for detailed instruction of family intervention). Lastly, people suffering from psychotic disorders appear especially sensitive to life events and stresses, therefore the therapist should be aware of times of predicted or unpredictable life changes when the patient may be especially vulnerable, and ensure that these periods are planned for if they can be anticipated and extra support given if they cannot. At all times it is important to keep in mind that psychotic patients do not necessarily present in the anticipated manner whilst under stress or suffering from distress.

Risk of Suicide

The risk of suicide in psychotic patients is high. One in ten patients diagnosed as suffering from schizophrenia will kill themselves and levels of depression, hopelessness, low self-worth and despondency are particularly prevalent. It is important that the therapist assesses and continues to monitor suicide risk in a psychotic patient. It is beyond the scope of this chapter to deal in detail with suicide risk assessment and prevention but a list of risk factors are presented in Table 7.2 and readers may find chapters 10 and 12 on self-esteem and suicide prevention useful.

Table 7.2 Risk factors for suicide in psychotic patients (Modified from Caldwell & Gottesman, 1990).

- Young and male
- Unmarried
- Unemployed
- Past history of suicide attempts
- Family history of suicide
- Family stress or instability
- Recent loss or rejection
- Limited external support
- Depression, depressed mood or sense of hopelessness
- Good pre-morbid functioning prior to a chronic illness with numerous exacerbations, and high levels of psychopathology and functional impairment
- Realistic awareness of deteriorative effects of illness and fear of further mental deterioration
- Excessive treatment dependence or loss of faith in treatment

INITIAL FORMULATION

There are a number of underlying assumptions which should be borne in mind when attempting to formulate the patient's key problems. For example, it is assumed that a person's mood or symptoms are influenced by cognition, that cognition is modifiable and that modification of cognition will result in some change in symptoms. These assumptions apply in psychosis as much as in other disorders. These assumptions should underpin all of the assessment work which leads towards a preliminary formulation to be shared with the patient.

The following information should provide a minimum basis for an initial formulation.

Summary of Initial Assessment

1. Basic demographic information.
2. Family circumstances.
3. Social problems, e.g. benefits, accommodation, legal problems.
4. Overview of the symptoms and mental state, e.g. anxiety, depression.
5. Detailed multidimensional assessment of symptoms (e.g. using PSYRATS), the frequency, duration, content, distress, etc., should be elicited for each symptom.
6. Cognitive behavioural assessment, the antecedents and context of each symptom with its affective, behavioural, physiological and cognitive consequences including how the patient copes with these experiences.
7. Further information gathering, including the additional information to be collected during the assessment and intervention phases to further elaborate the formulation and aid the therapeutic process. Techniques such as sampling, concurrent monitoring, shadowing, symptom simulation and diaries can be used.
8. The patient's view of his/her problems: it is important to elicit any positive aspects to the patient of their symptoms, and also to develop a shared understanding of the patient's experiences, which will be essential to the development of rapport.

Problem List

The above information should be sufficient to collaboratively generate a general problem list. This will include all of the patient's problems ideally described in his/her own words. The therapist may have identified some additional problems to add to the list but it is not necessary at this stage to identify these if the patient does not view them as problematic. This can be quite common for some types of delusional beliefs such as grandiose ideas, which are often not seen as delusional by the patient and indeed may be viewed quite positively. It may be possible, however, to work around these types of symptoms and prompt the patient to view the consequences of these types of belief as problematic. For example, such beliefs may lead to poor social interactions, socially inappropriate or challenging behaviour or to high levels of distress. Motivational interviewing strategies may be useful to increase patient engagement in treatment for some problems.

Prioritising Problems

Factors that need to be considered are: (i) safety, urgency and risk; (ii) issues relating to the facilitation of engagement; (iii) the level of distress created by the problem; (iv) patient's motivation; and (v) underlying themes. However, it is tactically wise to commence with a problem that is resolvable and likely to result in a successful outcome. This has a motivating effect for both patient and therapist and can be referred back to as an example at other times during therapy.

FORMULATION

An accurate and concise description of the patient's symptoms or main problems should be made in terms of their symptoms, key cognitions, affect, behaviour and beliefs. If possible this should be generated collaboratively with the patient in terms of a summary and reflection on the information obtained and should be presented as a possible working explanation rather than a definitive account. Patients with a psychotic illness frequently find the formulation useful as an explanation of their own experiences and a refreshing change to the 'you are suffering from an illness' account which is usually forthcoming from professionals. However, consideration needs to be given to the possible impact of the formulation on individual patients. For some, a simple summary of problem areas is sufficient but for others a more complex heuristic model can be provided. The formulation should be prepared in a way that the patient can understand and is usually presented in written or diagrammatic form as well as verbally. Audiotape recordings of the session are also useful and can be offered to the patient to listen to between sessions.

Case Example

Dave was in his early thirties and had a long history of psychiatric problems variously diagnosed as schizophrenia, schizoaffective disorder and personality disorder. He had experienced episodes during which he heard voices making derogatory comments about him, both directly to him and as commentary, and had had delusions of reference and persecution. These episodes were usually accompanied by low mood and suicidal thoughts, and social withdrawal and poor self-care. He had made a number of serious suicide attempts, the last about two years previously, when he had attempted to electrocute himself and suffered serious burns. He had spent some time in a specialist burns unit and had required extensive skin grafts and a temporary colostomy. He had recently experienced a relapse of his psychosis. He was hallucinating and deluded and had abandoned all of his activities and rarely went out of the house. His parents brought him to the appointment because he was talking about killing himself and they viewed this as a very serious concern. It appeared that he had begun to hallucinate while returning from a hospital follow-up appointment to monitor his skin grafts. He had heard two girls who were travelling on the bus making loud and abusive comments to him and talking about him. After he had alighted from the bus he noticed that people were looking at him in a strange way and shouting comments at him. He was convinced that they knew about his past colostomy and that they were actively ganging up on him because they thought him disgusting. He became very frightened and went home; he lived alone in a small flat. He stayed at home and did not visit his family as was usual and heard people come to his window and shout insulting and personal remarks. He became anxious, angry and very depressed. On further inquiry it became clear that initially he had been pleased with the outcome of his hospital appointment but he had began to ruminate over the injuries he had sustained and especially his embarrassment concerning his colostomy and fear that it would smell. He had been especially nervous when around female teenagers and young adults with whom he had great difficulties in relating at the best of times. In response to these thoughts his mood had become dramatically depressed and he had begun to hallucinate and assumed it was the two girl passengers who were talking about him. On further questioning it became apparent that he had not actually observed them make any remarks as they were sitting behind him on the bus. Furthermore, they had all got off at the same stop and they had not displayed any of the behaviour that might be expected from teenagers who were being insulting and intimidating. In fact Dave admitted that they had appeared to take no notice of him. It was possible through use of this type of information to suggest a tentative hypothesis formulation of Dave's relapse. The hospital appointment had focused his mind on his injuries and embarrassment concerning them, which had resulted in his becoming anxious and depressed so that he began to hallucinate. The content of the voices related to Dave smelling and being a 'farter'. Possibly these voices represented his own thoughts about the circumstances but for some reason he was unable to recognise them as such. Dave had attributed the source of the voices as external and to the only other passengers on that part of the bus, the two teenage girls, and had started to scan for evidence that would confirm his fear that everyone knew about him and that he was disgusting. By selectively attending to the behaviour of others he obtained confirmation of his fears, which resulted in his becoming more anxious and withdrawn, and disrupted his normal routines and ability to look after himself. Seeing no way out of his predicament and with everyone despising him, he again turned to suicide as the only solution. This formulation was presented to Dave and through sensitive questioning it was possible to put forward alternative explanations, based on the formulation or upon Dave's delusional and psychotic interpretation. This allowed the therapist and Dave to look for supportive evidence for each and begin to construct hypotheses to explain the actual evidence. Although the presentation of the formulation did not reduce Dave's hallucinations and delusions, which were by now quite entrenched, it provided a working explanation of events which was very reassuring to Dave, as it gave him an alternative explanation to the one he currently held, the inevitable conclusion of which was another suicide attempt. It also allowed a picture of Dave's problems to be constructed which would suggest intervention. This type of formulation would also possibly indicate Dave's schema that he was disgusting or disliked, which could be open to further assessment.

Refining Formulations

Formulations should be refined and modified with the patient as assessment and therapy progress. They act as an up-datable working explanation of the patient's problems, a blueprint for producing positive change, and as such should be referred back so as to reinforce their explanation. The intervention should help to generate information that supports the formulation, which may well motivate the patient, and also can help them explain other aspects of their problems that at present do not quite fit. The therapist and the patient can generate homework tasks designated to test out the formulation in the light of events that occur between sessions. This process helps the patient to fine tune the formulation and to increase motivation for change.

Intervention Strategies Based on the Formulation

Using the information recorded in the formulation, appropriate targets or goals should be prioritised for intervention. Thus, the formulation has a strategic function. These goals should be explicit although it is possible that there may be instances when the therapist may have different or additional goals to the patient. The potential outcome of implementing a particular intervention or strategy should be assessed in terms of positive and negative consequences with reference to the formulation. The interventions should be selected in terms of the degree of expected effectiveness with respect to the particular problem area targeted, but should also take into account the patient's motivation, ability, likelihood of success and the role of safety and risk factors.

In the absence of life-threatening difficulties, the initial goals are likely to be focused on symptom reduction or the modification of coping strategies. Core beliefs or schema may be addressed at a later stage in therapy, if appropriate, though there are instances when interventions might be concurrently targeted upon core beliefs. It should be kept in mind that therapeutic progress will probably be much slower than in patients from other diagnostic groups, and the influence of associated features that have been outlined previously may hinder the speed of progress. Therapists need to be aware of this and of possible frustrations that it may cause them.

Interventions

The formulation of the individual case should act as a blueprint for strategic intervention and intervention should follow logically to directly address the goals which have been identified, and which will most probably cover the following areas: delusions, hallucinations, anxiety, depression, suicide risk, relapse prevention/keeping well, schema, coping strategies, negative symptoms, medication compliance.

REFERENCES

Barrowclough, C. & Tarrier N. (1992). *Families of Schizophrenic Patients: Cognitive Behavioural Interventions*. London: Chapman & Hall.

Bentall, R.P. (1990). The illusion of reality: A review and integration of psychological research on hallucinations. *Psychological Bulletin*, **107**, 82–95.

Bentall, R.P. (1994). Cognitive bases and abnormal beliefs: towards a model of persecutory delusions. In A.S. David & J. Cutting (Eds), *The Neuropsychology of Schizophrenia*. London: Erlbaum.

Bentall, R.P., Haddock, G. & Slade, P.D. (1994). Cognitive behavior therapy for persistent auditory hallucinations: From theory to therapy. *Behavior Therapy*, **25**, 51–66.

Bentall, R.P., Jackson, H.F. & Pilgrim, D. (1988). Abandoning the concept of schizophrenia: Some implications of validity arguments for psychological research into psychotic phenomena. *British Journal of Clinical Psychology*, **27**, 156–169.

Bourgignon, E. (1970). Hallucinations and trance: An anthropologist's perspective. In W. Kemp (Ed.) *Origins and Mechanisms of Hallucinations*. New York: Plenum.

Buchanan, A., Reed, A., Wessely, S., Garety, P., Taylor, P., Grubin, & D. Dunn, G. (1993). Acting on delusions (2): The phenomenological correlates of acting on delusions. *British Journal of Psychiatry*, **163**, 77–81.

Caldwell, C.B. & Gottesman, I.I. (1990). Schizophrenics kill themselves too. *Schizophrenia Bulletin*, **16**, 571–590.

Chadwick, P.D.J. & Birchwood, M. (1994). The omnipotence of voices. A cognitive approach to auditory hallucinations. *British Journal of Psychiatry*, **164**, 190–201.

Chadwick, P. & Lowe, F. (1990). The measurement and modification of delusional beliefs. *Journal of Consulting and Clinical Psychology*, **58**, 225–232.

David, A. (1994). The neuropsychological origin of auditory hallucinations. In David, A. & Cutting, J. (Eds), *The Neuropsychology of Schizophrenia*. London: Erlbaum.

Drury, V., Birchwood, M., Cochrane, R. & Macmillan, F. (1996a). Cognitive therapy and recovery from acute psychosis. 1. Impact on psychotic symptoms. *British Journal of Psychiatry*, **169**, 593–601.

Drury, V., Birchwood, M., Cochrane, R. & Macmillan, F. (1996b). Cognitive therapy and recovery from acute psychosis. 2. Impact on recovery time. *British Journal of Psychiatry*, **169**, 602–607.

Frith, C.D. (1992). The Cognitive Neuropsychology of Schizophrenia. Hove, Sussex: Erlbaum.

Falloon, I.R.H. & Talbot, R.E. (1981). Persistent auditory hallucinations: Coping mechanisms and implications for management. *Psychological Medicine*, **11**, 329–339.

Garety, P.A., Kuipers, L., Fowler, D., Chamberlain, F. & Dunn, G. (1994). Cognitive behaviour therapy for drug resistant psychosis. *British Journal of Medical Psychology*, **67**, 259–271.

Haddock, G., Sellwood, W., Tarrier, N. & Yusupoff, L. (1994). Developments in cognitive behaviour therapy for persistent psychotic symptoms. *Behaviour Change*, **11**, 1–16.

Haddock, G., Bentall, R.P. & Slade, P.D. (1996). Focusing versus distraction in the psychological treatment of auditory hallucinations. In G. Haddock & P.D. Slade (Eds), *Cognitive Behavioural Interventions with Psychotic Disorders*. London: Routledge.

Haddock, G., Tarrier, N., Morrison, A., Hopkins, R., Drake, R. & Lewis, S. (1998a). A pilot study evaluating the effectiveness of individual cognitive-behavioural interventions in early psychosis. *Social Psychiatry and Psychiatric Epidemiology* (in press).

Haddock, G., McCarron, J., Tarrier, N. & Faragher, E.B. (1998b). Scales to measure dimensions of hallucinations and delusions: The psychotic symptom rating scales (PSYRATS). *Psychological Medicine* (in press).

Haddock, G., Slade, P.D., Bentall, R.P., Reid, D. & Faragher, E.B. (1996). A comparison of the long-term effectiveness of distraction and focusing in the treatment of auditory hallucinations. *British Journal of Medical Psychology*, **71**, 339–349.

Hoffman, R.E. (1986). Verbal hallucinations and language production processes in schizophrenia. *Behavioral and Brain Sciences*, **9**, 503–548.

Kay, S.R., Opler, L.A. & Lindenmayer, J.P. (1989). The positive and negative syndrome scale (PANSS): Rationale and standardisation. *British Journal of Psychiatry*, **155**, suppl. 7, 59–65.

Kingdon, D.G. & Turkington, D. (1991). Preliminary report. The use of cognitive behavior therapy and a normalizing rationale in schizophrenia. *Journal of Nervous & Mental Disease*, **179**, 207–211.

Kuipers, E., Garety, P., Fowler, D., Dunn, G., Bebbington, P., Freeman, D. & Hadley, C. (1997). London–East Anglia randomised controlled trial of cognitive behavioural therapy for psychosis. I: Effects of the treatment phase. *British Journal of Psychiatry*, **171**, 319–327.

Maher, B.A. (1988). Anomalous experience and delusional thinking: The logic of explanations. In T.F. Oltmans & B.A. Maher (Eds.), *Delusional Beliefs* (pp. 15–33). New York: Wiley.

Nuechterlein, K. H. & Dawson, M. E. (1984). A heuristic vulnerability/stress model of schizophrenic episodes. *Schizophrenia Bulletin*, **10**, 300–312.

Overall, J. & Gorham, D. (1962). The brief psychiatric rating scale. *Psychological Reports*, **10**, 799–812.

Reybee, J. & Kinch, B. (1973). Treatment of auditory hallucinations using focusing. Unpublished study.

Tarrier, N. (1992). Management and modification of residual positive psychotic symptoms. In, M. Birchwood & N. Tarrier (Eds), *Innovations in Psychological Management of Schizophrenia*. Chichester: Wiley.

Tarrier, N. (1997). Coping and Problem Solving in the Treatment of Persistent Psychotic Symptoms. Keynote address to the 2nd International Conference on Psychological Treatments for Schizophrenia, Oxford, UK, October 1997 (abstract published in the proceedings).

Tarrier, N. & Turpin, G. (1992). Psychosocial factors, arousal and schizophrenic relapse. The psychophysiological data. *British Journal of Psychiatry*, **161**, 3–11.

Tarrier, N., Beckett, R., Harwood, S., Baker, A., Yusupoff, L. & Ugarteburu, I. (1993). A trial of two cognitive behavioural methods of treating drug-resistant symptoms in schizophrenic outpatients : I. Outcome. *British Journal of Psychiatry*, **162**, 524–532.

Tarrier, N., Yusupoff, L., Kinney, C., McCarthy, E., Gledhill, A., Haddock, G. & Morris, J. (1998). A randomised controlled trial of intensive cognitive behaviour therapy for chronic schizophrenia. *British Medical Journal*, **317**, 303–307.

World Health Organisation (WHO) (1992). *SCAN—Schedules for Clinical Assessment in Neuropsychiatry*. Geneva: World Health Organisation.

Chapter 8

COGNITIVE BEHAVIOURAL THERAPY OF PSYCHOSIS: COMPLEXITIES IN ENGAGEMENT AND THERAPY

*David Kingdon**

AIM OF CHAPTER

It is not so long ago that psychosis, and certainly schizophrenia, was considered not just a complex problem but an absolute contraindication for cognitive behaviour therapy. Beck says that he talked about it as the one area where cognitive behaviour therapy could not be used, even though, 40 years ago, he wrote a case study demonstrating the potential of such work (Beck, 1952). This chapter will focus mainly on schizophrenia and particularly engagement and developing a shared understanding of how symptoms began and possible reasons why they developed. Many of the techniques described, here and in the other chapters on psychosis elsewhere in this book, are also being applied with other psychoses. Depressive psychosis needs separate consideration although the reality testing of paranoid and other delusions and hallucinations described here can probably be used in a similar way in depression (Chadwick, Birchwood & Trower, 1996).

THEORETICAL OVERVIEW

Cognitive behavioural therapy of psychosis has been developed from clinical practice and research (Kingdon, Turkington & Johns, 1993; Fowler,

* Dept. of Psychiatry, University of Southampton, UK.

Treating Complex Cases: The Cognitive Behavioural Therapy Approach.
Edited by Nicholas Tarrier, Adrian Wells and Gillian Haddock.
© 1998 John Wiley & Sons Ltd.

Garety & Kuipers, 1995; Haddock & Slade, 1996; Chadwick, Birchwood & Trower, 1996) that emphasises individual formulation with specific interventions for symptoms such as command hallucinations, delusions of reference or formal thought disorder. Vulnerability–stress interactions are used to understand the development of such symptoms and 'normalising' rationales (see later; Kingdon & Turkington, 1991) to explain them. Cognitive behavioural techniques used in psychosis are built upon those that have proved so useful in the treatment of depression and anxiety (see later).

Engagement is a rate-limiting step in therapy. Without face-to-face contact between therapist and patients, therapy is difficult, although not impossible, as will be elaborated later. Freud believed that such engagement with psychotic patients was not possible and that opinion has been highly influential although Sullivan and others have implicitly challenged it over time (for further discussion, see Mace & Margison, 1997). A collaborative relationship develops from exploring patients' beliefs based on their understanding of perceptual experiences that others do not share, for example, hallucinations, or do share but which are interpreted in idiosyncratic, including delusional, ways. If the patient's beliefs are explored and understood, although not necessarily accepted as accurate, they can be countered by alternative explanation. Bridging the gulf between the patient and those around him, including the therapist, is essential to forming a working partnership.

So there seem to be at least two essential components to engagement; understanding why the patient believes what he or she believes and providing credible alternative explanations. Psychiatric teaching currently tends to dismiss the circumstances leading up to a psychotic episode as basically irrelevant, or of marginal significance, to the illness and so such circumstances are given little importance. Certainly the way in which beliefs develop into delusions is not explored. Perhaps this is to do with a widespread concern that these beliefs will be reinforced by such exploration, although there is no research to support such a hypothesis. Explanations that are solely based on a biological model of schizophrenia lack credibility with many patients. Biological factors, such as for example, genetic predisposition, in vulnerability have been demonstrated but alone seem insufficient. When explored, stressful life events and circumstances often emerge which may be working in conjunction. Their effect on sleep, levels of anxiety and depression is apparent and understandable. 'Normalising' these symptoms reduces fear and confusion and, rightly or wrongly, patients feel 'understood'; this does not mean that the effect or importance of symptoms is minimised but collaboration has been developed and discussion of tactics to deal with the symptoms made possible.

This will usually include discussion of how medication may have a part to play (Kemp et al., 1996; Kemp, Hayward & David, 1997).

THERAPEUTIC PROCESS

Even in complex cases, the therapeutic process (see Table 8.1) involves the consideration of assessment, engagement, treating delusions and hallucinations, depression, negative symptoms and relapse prevention (Kingdon & Turkington, 1994). Further details of basic therapeutic techniques are given in the following chapter.

Selection of Patients for Cognitive Behaviour Therapy

Before commencing therapy, an initial assessment of symptomatology, circumstances and suitability is necessary (see chapter 7 this volume by Haddock & Tarrier). Before meeting a patient, an understanding of what is known of their personal history and mental state is invaluable for engagement and comprehensive assessment. However, it is also important that the information gathered does not lead to a prejudgement of the patient's psychotic symptoms and what they will have to say. Socratic questioning is an essential tool used early in assessment and engagement. This means inquiring about the patient's problems without making any assumptions that what they are saying is deluded; that is, taking their comments at face value. As described in the previous chapter, psychiatric assessment instruments may be valuable to therapists who have not been trained in psychiatric examination (for example, the Present State Examination: Wing et al., 1974). Rating instruments for psychiatric symptomatology may be useful for plotting progress, for example, Positive and Negative Symptom Scale and other psychotic symptom rating scales. Broader scales such as the Health of the Nation Outcome Scales (Wing et al., 1996) may also assist in reviewing wider aspects of health and social functioning.

Selection of patients for therapy needs careful consideration and some principles will be described. However, many mental health workers, including nurses and psychiatrists, have patients effectively selected for them: they are those who work on an acute admission ward or cover a sector of the population. In these circumstances, the use of cognitive behaviour therapy may be, or might become, their normal style of working although it may involve different components with individual patients. The components of cognitive behaviour therapy described in the Cognitive Therapy Scale (Young & Beck, 1980) are wide-ranging: the general therapeutic skills described include agenda setting, feedback, understanding, interpersonal

Table 8.1 The therapeutic process

Problem area	Action to be considered
Engagement	<ul><li>Obtain sufficient information before assessment</li><li>Don't jump to conclusions, take comments at face value</li><li>Persist but retreat if distress increases</li><li>use a conversational style, rather than staccato questioning</li><li>Don't try to do too much but keep the flow of discussion going</li><li>Aim for sessions to be positive, even enjoyable, experiences as far as it's reasonable to do so</li></ul>

Understanding experiences	<ul><li>Let the patient lead; explore their models of their mental health problems first</li><li>Normalise but don't minimise</li><li>Use vulnerability/stress model to explain illness</li><li>Explore alternative explanations for specific symptoms
	  anxiety symptoms:
	    giddiness = 'neighbour controlling my mind'
	  thought broadcasting:
	    beliefs about telepathy and evidence for and
	      against transmission of thoughts</li><li>Hallucinations
	  reattribute as 'thoughts': illicit drugs, deprivation
	    states, etc, can all produce 'voices'
	  discuss similarities to dreaming: 'living nightmare'</li><li>Explain automatic thoughts:
	  because you think something doesn't mean:
	    'it is true'
	    'you are evil'
	    'or that you have to act on it'</li></ul>

Tackling negative symptoms	<ul><li>Keep an open mind: patients will tell you of residual positive symptoms, when (if) they are ready</li><li>Reduce pressure to release motivation</li><li>Review personal stress management and coping strategies</li><li>Readjust expectations:
	  start with 'aim at feeling better/convalescing' then
	    very small, achievable, steps
	  five-year plans may be useful but need to be
	    modest in aspiration</li><li>Assess and work with reasons for isolation:
	  social phobia
	  delusions of reference
	  exacerbation or fear of onset of positive symptoms</li><li>Discuss appropriate avoidance:
	  staying up late may be relaxing and avoid conflict</li><li>Review family concerns and involve them in constructive support</li></ul>

effectiveness (that is, the use of warmth and genuineness with a professional manner), collaboration, pacing and efficient use of time. The specific techniques are guided discovery, focusing on key cognitions and behaviours, strategy for change, application of cognitive behavioural techniques and setting of homework. The former group of skills can and perhaps should be used with all psychotic patients. The latter are more specific to cognitive behaviour therapy and certain considerations will influence their use with psychotic patients.

Positive responders

Those who seem to respond best to cognitive behaviour therapy seem to be those who are anxious and distressed by their symptoms and have some, albeit fluctuating, insight into them (Garety et al., 1997). These are, of course, also the group who will respond best to medication so symptoms often remit rapidly with or without cognitive behaviour therapy. The added ingredient that cognitive behaviour therapy offers is a chance to understand and integrate the experience of psychosis. This may in itself reduce the likelihood of symptoms returning and also allow for early intervention to occur if they do. If patients recognise that they are becoming ill but deny this to themselves, early intervention is difficult. Recognition by others, for example, carers, of this occurring at an early stage can still allow debate with the patient. If, on the other hand, they are able to accept that they need to do something and feel positive and hopeful that intervention can be successful, this can occur early and intrude less on their life.

The duration of symptoms can be a factor in determining selection. Those with a longer history may be more resistant to change but paradoxically they may not be difficult to engage with. They may have despaired of other approaches and simply be very pleased to have someone who will listen to their concerns, that is, the content of their delusions and hallucinations. Medical and nursing teaching have generally counselled against discussing psychotic symptoms with patients because of the belief that this will reinforce them, but there is little evidence that discussion does reinforce such beliefs. Work on 'token economies' in the 1960s is sometimes cited in support of such views but this work focused on modifying particular behaviours, for example, self-care. It had some success, but transfer from the experimental situation to community settings has been more difficult (Birchwood, Hallett & Preston, 1988). Modification of specifically psychotic behaviour, for example, thought disorder, hallucinations and delusions, by the use of these methods has been even less successful. In other words, this research has not shown that restricting discussion of psychotic material reduces its frequency in normal social situations. Where delusional material has been explored and continues to be voiced in a way that causes the patient to be ostracised by others, there may be a place for discussion of these effects and for attempts to be made to modify the frequency of expression and where and to whom they are expressed. But this does not mean that they should not be discussed in the first place.

More difficult patients

Those who have been most difficult to work with have been those who are quite isolated and have become cut off from normal social interaction. They have often developed an equilibrium that is resistant to change. They project concerns outwards onto others and until the situation deteriorates to the extent that their actions require outside intervention, for example, compulsory admission to hospital, they can be very difficult to engage and maintain engagement with. There are some patients with whom it might be advisable to await the response to medication before attempting to gently engage; for example where they are hostile or considered suicidal. However, in these circumstances, if a patient wants to talk about their concerns, listening to what these are would seem to be an essential part of developing any relationship and, arguably, safer than trying to divert them from such discussion. The stance we generally take is one of a non-directive approach that allows them to express their views, and noncommittal responses when they want us to express ours. Sometimes the insistence on discussing emotionally charged topics or on seeking agreement to delusional ideas that the patient expresses is such that recourse to a repertoire of equivocal phrases is necessary. These might include 'I need to know more before I can agree', 'I can see you are quite sure about this', 'At the moment, I'm not sure but I'm quite prepared to listen', and so on. But in these circumstances, work as part of a team and availability of an experienced supervisor are important.

Selection therefore depends on situation; on an acute ward or working in a community setting with a caseload of patients, general therapeutic skills are probably relevant to all. Patients with specific symptoms who are distressed by them but not at significant risk of harm to themselves or others, are probably the group who will engage most effectively. But even patients with longstanding symptoms, if they have any desire to change how they feel or their situation, may benefit. However it is important to be prepared to work over a significant period of at least six months to a year with them, although often just using brief sessions (20–30 minutes) rather than longer interviews.

Having made an initial decision to select a patient to assess for therapy, that assessment becomes part of the engagement process and is interlocked with it. It is also difficult and probably counter-productive to try to disentangle assessment from therapy. The following descriptions will therefore describe how both are interweaved.

ENGAGING AND BUILDING RAPPORT

This should be a difficult area but, whether it is or is not does seem to differ depending on the nature of the professional relationship with the patient, as well as the individual's personality and psychopathology. It is very different and, I think, much more difficult to work with a psychotic patient as a 'therapist' who is simply engaging 'to offer cognitive behaviour therapy'. It is much easier to work using the techniques as part of a broader psychiatric, community mental health nursing, psychologist or social work relationship which means that it becomes incorporated into discussions about housing, finance, leave, medication and other supports. This became particularly apparent to us when we set up a pilot study and worked as 'therapists', in contrast to previous experience as 'psychiatrists'; 'rewards' previously available, such as assistance with housing or benefits, discussions about other supports, were no longer options. It was still possible to engage with all but one of the 19 we recruited but this might have been a complete sample if the therapist had been the patient's consultant. There are, however, disadvantages to being directly involved in management, for example, where a psychiatrist has had to detain under the Mental Health Act this can interfere, but doesn't inevitably do so. The patient can then believe we are agents of the government, which in a sense, we are. But in practice, it is usually possible to engage in discussion or involve an alternative team member to assist in overcoming that specific concern. This allows you to continue working, or to work through supervision of the therapist, or through the family or other carers, including staff of residential units. Sometimes it has then been possible to use what is almost a 'good guy/bad guy' routine: another team member may be able to work with the person using cognitive behaviour therapy or sometimes allow them a breathing space before the primary therapist can re-engage. There are ethical issues regarding the patient's rights to choose their therapist and whether there should be continued supervision of that therapist by someone they may have chosen not to engage with. Also there are issues which need consideration such as to whether discussions about home leave or medication can inappropriately become bargaining counters in the therapeutic relationship. The line between these being legitimate motivators to engage and illegitimate coercion is a fine one.

Persistence

Persistence is very important but this does not mean an insistent probing and cajoling; the time-scale involved in therapy needs to reflect the time-scale involved in the development of symptoms. The longer that they have been present, the longer they are likely to take to subside, although there may be substantial changes in levels of distress and disability within that period. An ability to avoid personalising is necessary when you are subject to critical comments. This probably occurs more often with this group than with those with neurotic disorders. 'You snivelling little wimp' is one of the more creative descriptions given to me by someone who, a few years on, has mellowed sufficiently to offer the object of her derision cups of tea when bringing visitors to look around the hospital hostel where she now lives. It may also sometimes be necessary to take a break for a few months before re-engaging, with assistance from a GP or others when an opportune moment arises.

'Non-specific factors' of therapy seem to be the key to progress in engagement. Warmth and humour can be very valuable and with some patients essential; the danger, of course, is that warmth and humour can be misinterpreted as laughing at them in contrast to the intention of letting them see the contradictions and incongruities in their beliefs and situation. In practice this means that beginning with a gentle, warm, relaxed conversational approach is important to engagement. Smiling gently may be perfectly appropriate at times during an interview, but watching for the patient's reaction is critical. If the response is positive, a spontaneous relationship can develop although this will need checking out as you go. A warm supportive framework to a relationship allows you to work more safely, but also quite rapidly and securely. Sitting and having a cup of tea, talking about football, a relaxed wander over to the shops may help (Fowler, Garety & Kuipers, 1995). Going to the patient, for example, to check out beliefs to do with their home, can be well worthwhile and cost-effective if it accelerates the development of the relationship. Engaging with family and staff members is also very important.

Where the patient's response to a smile or other non-verbal cue is guarded or suspicious, that needs exploration: 'Have I said or done something that has upset you?' 'Did my smiling at what you said concern you?' The balance needs to be struck between spontaneously reacting in a therapeutic relationship and being aware that certain responses can be more easily misinterpreted than others can. Laughter and silence both need to be carefully handled initially and probably avoided until a reasonably stable rapport is established. However, the blank unresponsive stance is also at least as likely to be misinterpreted and to lead to failure to engage.

There are characteristics of patients which are signals that extra care needs to be taken, especially with those who are isolated, suspicious and poorly socially skilled; engaging is an art which needs gentle pacing, an emphasis on building the relationship as if building a friendship. During the early stages of engagement, you may only briefly discuss delusions or hallucinations or they may be mentioned only in passing. Instead, you may spend time discussing personal circumstances, hobbies, and so on with some limited self-disclosure, for example discussion of music or sport, until they begin to find coming to see you or you going to see them a pleasant and a positive experience. You may chip away at the edges ('peripheral questioning') but one thing that is striking in reviewing tapes of sessions is how often working on specific symptoms and easing off—talking about less threatening topics, even casual social conversation—alternate.

Clear simple homework assignments which the patient can easily succeed at can assist in developing engagement, although the term 'homework' is one to use selectively because of its schoolday connotations which can often be quite negative. One of the key messages in relation to engagement is not to try to do too much in a session; counterbalance it with discussion of issues they want to discuss.

EXAMINING THE ANTECEDENTS OF PSYCHOTIC BREAKDOWN

Understanding of the circumstances surrounding the beginning of a psychotic illness is critical but too often overlooked. It may be difficult to do at the first time of meeting because the patient can't remember, is too ill and thought disorder interferes, or they are so full of delusional ideas or hallucinations that you don't get time to trace the relevant events. But if some understanding is to be gained and, more important, the patient can obtain an idea of where their symptoms have developed from, even years after the event, that first period preceding the episode is usually critical. Where the patient cannot or will not recall the details, the clinical notes, staff who know the patient, relatives and even GP records often have information that can be valuable. The details of the prodromal period can usually be found and recorded for future use. Using a conventional personal history approach can also allow the gradual build up to significant events to be plotted, and the patient can be allowed to make sense and often remember key details as they progress.

As the picture unfolds, the events described trigger the thoughts that were developing and can allow access to the way in which delusional ideas ('faulty cognitions') occurred by personalising, selective abstraction or arbitrary inference.

EXPLAINING PSYCHOSIS USING A NORMALISING RATIONALE

Patients vary in how much they want an explanation of what is happening to them. They may already be quite convinced by their own explanation, which may be delusional. However, where they are seeking explanations, these can be developed with them about their problems as a whole and about individual symptoms. Vulnerability/stress models of psychosis are intended to draw together the components recognised as contributing to predisposition, precipitation and perpetuation of disorders. They are relatively simple models to use with patients, essentially to explain that problems such as the ones they have can be brought on by stressful circumstances when they were vulnerable. It is then possible to individualise it for the person himself or herself.

These models are not, in themselves, contrary to biological theories of the origin of psychoses. But they are multidimensional and thus contrast with theories that suggest there is likely to be a single cause of, for example schizophrenia, which probably oversimplifies a complex disorder. In a sense this is not dissimilar to approaches to medical problems such as diabetes, in which insulin deficiency is the 'cause' but there are vulnerability factors, as for example, family history, and precipitating factors, for example, pancreatitis (inflammation of the pancreas) or viral infection. Management, in this example, involves a range of measures, including the use of insulin, but also modification to lifestyle, as perhaps through dietary measures.

The components predisposing an individual to psychosis may include biological factors, for example, genetic, which may be relevant in providing a specific vulnerability to psychosis or, possibly, through intermediary personality factors—determined by a combination of genetic and environmental factors. For example: people who are perfectionists may be more likely to respond to stress by becoming depressed. Those with more sensitive, schizoid or paranoid characteristics may be more likely to develop psychoses under similar stresses. The nature of the stress may also be a factor in determining the liability to become psychotic rather than depressed or anxious. Other biological vulnerability factors may include abnormalities to brain structure or function. These vulnerability factors do not cause psychosis from birth although they may cause abnormalities in childhood development, such as some developmental delay in reaching normal milestones (for example, toilet-training, walking) and also a tendency toward solitary play (Jones et al., 1994). There is some trigger or combination of triggers that precipitates psychosis. These triggers may be biological in nature but frequently stressful life events are cited by families and, after appropriate exploration (see later) by patients themselves (Bebbington et al., 1993). These events in themselves may be clearly and unambiguously significant, for example, a violent attack or rape, the sudden collapse of a business or marriage, but more frequently the occurrence is a 'life cycle event', such as leaving home or getting a job. This may not rate highly on life event schedules but may be of significance to the individual, either because of previous events or in combination with other circumstances. For example, one of our patients was a twin who had grown up in a very close and exclusive relationship with his twin. He found going away from home to college alone a more stressful event than it would have been for someone who had mixed regularly with others and had friends also going to the same college. The event, going away to college, is the same for the latter as the former but the significance is markedly different.

The significance may be even less obvious; for example, one patient described how the wind would bring on psychotic symptoms. This could only be understood when he explained that, before becoming ill, he decided to stop being a member of an evangelical Christian group. The elders of the group warned him against 'turning his back on God' in this way but he persisted. However, he had studied the book of Revelation, where the Judgement Day is described as being heralded by the blowing of strong winds. Storms one day led him to fear that that day had arrived and, although it hadn't, similar events subsequently brought on anxiety and psychotic symptoms. The significance of symptoms is a personal matter and tracing antecedents of symptoms can sometimes uncover matters which seem superficially insignificant, and often are dismissed as such by the patient and those around him but which, set in context, can be meaningful.

There is a danger that needs to be resisted, of attempting to interpret such significance to patients. Guided discovery of possibly significant events is much safer and through exploration the meaning of such events can be uncovered, where it exists. There is experimental evidence that lends support to the hypothesis that psychotic material can be significant (Harrow & Prosen, 1978) in addition to much anecdotal material.

Exploring Individual Symptoms

It is also important to take individual symptoms, find a common language or set of terms to discuss them and then find and debate relevant evidence. There is a very wide range of symptoms associated with psychosis but many seem to be related to anxiety. Delusions themselves may draw their strength of conviction from the extent to which they relieve feelings of tension and anxiety and conversely from the reactivation of these feelings when doubt about the delusion as an adequate explanation for their situation emerges. This means that when delusions are discussed, the development of dysphoric feelings needs to be carefully regulated—if alternative explanations are viewed as threatening and anxiety-provoking, they may be resisted for that reason.

Frequently, anxiety symptoms are misinterpreted, so it is necessary to ask the patient exactly what they are feeling, not what conclusion they have come to about the feeling. Then inquiry can proceed into how such feelings might be aroused, but avoiding saying, even implying, they are mistaken in their belief. If you are challenged, you can reflect the question back: 'well, what do you think about that feeling?'—focusing attention on the feeling rather than the consequent belief. The implication that the beliefs they have may not be quite as they describe them but could be illness- or stress-related may be seized upon negatively as confirming that you are 'like all the others' in disbelieving them. It is therefore essential that the pace at which disclosure/discovery occurs is carefully judged. It is much safer to move gradually towards the situation where they provide the evidence and draw the conclusions themselves. Until you are quite sure that they can accept the possibility that their symptoms are stress or illness-related, even direct questions such as 'do you think I am ill or that I'm wrong?' need reflecting back: 'well, what do you think?'

Thought Interference

Certain symptoms such as thought broadcasting and insertion are common and distressing to patients as they feel they have no privacy or freedom from interference. The common language used is 'telepathy' as most patients view such beliefs as analogous: it is then possible to discuss experimental evidence that fails to support such beliefs (see Kingdon & Turkington, 1994) and specifically that there is no evidence a complex chain of thoughts can be transmitted. Similarly the research about the effects of sleep deprivation can be useful with acute psychotic symptoms such as hallucinations. Association by strong emotional conditioning may be relevant, for example the sound of the crash in a road traffic accident can often be vivid and recurrent; the nature of very distressing thoughts or things said, for example, by an abuser can be conditioned, with resistance just making it worse. The difference between thoughts and actions can need stressing and an understanding of the nature of automatic thoughts need explaining. Thoughts, that is, voices, which are violent or sexual, can come automatically into a person's mind, but simply because they are so vivid does not mean that they have any power over the person.

Explaining the Cognitive Behavioural Model

In most areas of cognitive behaviour therapy, explaining the cognitive behavioural model is very important. This is also important with psychosis but needs to be simple and understood. Many of our patients would not identify the talking treatment they are involved with as cognitive behaviour therapy although we will usually use the term at some stage or other. They might recognise that they have been discussing what they've been thinking about, perhaps even how it affects the feelings they have and things they do. If asked what caused their problems, they'll probably speak about the trouble they had at work, or the hassle they were getting from their parents. Cognitive is a bit of a complicated concept for the 'normalising' models that we are using!

Treating any Co-existing Anxiety and Depression

Maintaining self-esteem is important with careful judgement about pacing and monitoring, and treatment of depression if it begins to emerge. This is balanced with supplementary supports, such as befriending, day care, social skill work, coping strategies for anxiety, and antidepressive therapies. Relaxation techniques and diversional conversation may help defuse tension and anxiety.

Reality Testing

Structured reasoning techniques with specific positive symptoms involve analysis of the symptoms, whether hallucinations or delusions, and the beliefs about them.

With hallucinations

Collaborative analysis of hallucinations is a relatively straightforward procedure but very important: essentially it is aiming at producing the shared conclusion that voices are your own thoughts misattributed; the 'voices' heard are the person's own thoughts, that is, 'your mind is playing tricks on you'. Sometimes complications can emerge, for example one patient said we couldn't hear her voices because our hearing wasn't good enough; another that the voices just come when no friend or ally is around, because 'they' know you are here with them. It's worth trying using tape recorders to 'record voices' in these circumstances but it is wise not to expect too much, although it can help to sow doubt. It may be worth going over and over the proposed reasons why others cannot hear the voices as this can be quite puzzling to the patient and open up fruitful alternative routes to explore.

With delusions

In tackling entrenched psychotic symptoms, a full collaborative assessment of the beliefs and supporting and disconfirming evidence for them is essential. Such reality testing assists in engagement, may begin to sow doubt on the belief, or sometimes brings out issues of relevance which have not been unearthed during the initial assessment. Frequently, however, a stalemate is reached where alternative explanations are not forthcoming or accepted. In these circumstances, inference chaining can be used to explore any underlying beliefs where they are not readily obvious. This involves agreeing to differ—'as you'll have gathered, I'm not really convinced that you are [for example, a Royal Princess] but if others did believe you, what would that mean to you?' The person usually will provide material that can then be explored further and may assist in identifying key problems in their life, which are amenable to intervention. Where these delusions are grandiose, issues related to self-esteem frequently emerge. This can mean that the delusion is effectively bypassed and may then recede in importance. For example, one of our patients was convinced she was related to royalty and had a convoluted explanation as to why this was the case. Straightforward discussion of evidence simply led to more delusional material emerging, supportive of the original belief. She was asked what it would mean to her if she were accepted as being related to royalty. Her response was that this would mean she would be 'regarded properly'. By whom? 'My husband and my daughter.' Further exploration established that there were problems in these relationships and it was agreed that these would become the focus of therapy. A marked improvement occurred, the delusional material receded and she was able to be more appropriately assertive in these relationships.

Emotional investment in the beliefs may need to be worked through or around, the patient may be prepared to change their actions despite clinging on to their delusional belief. Where progress is slow or absent, the use of lateral thinking and discussion with other colleagues working in this way can assist in revising approaches. Suspending normal judgement and assumptions can be difficult but treating the delusional ideas as if they were subjects of an academic debate may help. Patients themselves will often produce alternative arguments with time.

Tackle Negative Symptoms

Underestimation or failure to detect the existence of positive symptoms, including the ones that have not been disclosed, often occurs, so keeping an open mind about the completeness of any assessment is important. Paradoxically, even especially, when a patient seems lacking in drive and motivation, the aim should be to take the pressure off still further. It is probably not possible to push someone out of his or her negative symptoms. Frequently their expectations and even more important their understanding of other people's expectations (usually rightly) is that they are being required to make more effort and to pull themselves together. The opposite position is probably more appropriate—to let the patient slowly recover; this needs patience, and faith that it will happen. The analogy used is with convalescence; a process of healing from the effects of a serious illness is needed. If that healing keeps on getting disturbed, it simply prolongs the process. This means actively persuading family and other staff members to ease off the pressure: let him/her 'take their time'. Strauss and colleagues (1989) and Brenner, Hodel and Roper's (1990) work has proved valuable in devising these strategies for improving negative symptoms.

In reducing the pressure, setting realistic short-term goals seems particularly important. Teach the patients appropriate avoidance—if they feel tired or their concentration flags, they should stop or try something different. If they can't get up at, for example, 7 a.m., try just getting up half an hour or even ten minutes early each day, even though this may mean getting up at 3 p.m. instead to start with. It may even be that staying up at night is less stressful than getting up in the day and whilst other therapeutic work is proceeding, getting up in the morning may not be an appropriate immediate goal. Paradoxical intention can even be a useful strategy. With one patient who had difficulty getting to a day centre, it was suggested that she simply aimed to put in an appearance by late afternoon. She succeeded because she felt she was given permission to take her time to improve and felt under less pressure.

Some patients with 'negative' symptoms seem to be very fearful of positive symptoms recurring and of the probable consequences, that is, admission to hospital and increased medication, such that they avoid any source of stress as far as possible. This may therefore mean that they go out very rarely and avoid company, as these precipitate symptoms, especially delusions of reference or critical hallucinations. Essentially they may become agoraphobic and solitary but relatively free of positive symptoms. Explanation of this to the patient, and family, and then gradual desensitisation accompanied by structured work on the delusions of reference and development of coping strategies for hallucinations can sometimes allow progress to occur. This situation often occurs after acute episodes and the concept of 'convalescence' can be a very useful one (Strauss et al., 1989).

The following case study illustrates many of the problems of engagment and work with hallucinations.

Case Study

Gordon, aged 48, had a psychiatric history going back to teenage and had also spent lengthy periods in prison because of convictions for assault. His childhood had been disrupted by the separation of his parents when he was in his early teens. His relationship with his father, who had frequently been aggressive to his mother and Gordon, had always been poor. His relationship with his mother was good but she had died one year previously. He had some contact with a brother living in Scotland. He had made two serious suicide attempts and lacerated his arms on many occasions although this was not a current problem.

His diagnosis was paranoid schizophrenia in a paranoid personality. His symptoms were of auditory hallucinations of a critical and abusive nature and delusions of reference that had prompted assaults in the past. He had been an inpatient on an intensive care ward under a forensic psychiatrist for three years. He had been treated with high dose neuroleptics and Clozapine for 18 months. He remained on 250 mg b.d. of the latter. He was also being prescribed other medication including antidepressants and night sedation. He had recently been referred for psychosurgery at his request but had not been considered suitable. He was referred for a second opinion because of the severity of his symptoms and the distress that they caused him. However he wanted referral 'to London', as he thought there must be someone there who could help him.

The first interview was difficult. He asked for a nurse whom he knew to stay with him but was then convinced after the interview that we were 'talking about him'. This was of course true and the nature of those discussions and the necessity for them was explained at the second interview. A co-therapist was involved in the first interview but this probably did not help: a request to tape the interview certainly didn't. He reluctantly discussed his background and symptoms but repeatedly said that that it was pointless. He disclosed that the content of the voices was about violence. When there was further inquiry about this, he became agitated and angry, accusing the interviewer of saying that he was a criminal and should be locked up. The interview was quickly wound down and terminated— before he excited himself. He was told that the interviewer would come onto the ward at a specific time, the next week, to see if he was prepared to speak again.

Somewhat to the therapist's surprise, Gordon was waiting for him at the specified time. He remained suspicious and critical but did discuss the early development of his symptoms. These had started when he had begun work as an apprentice and had been bullied by older men—replicating his experience with his father. He was also prepared to begin to discuss whether what the 'voices' said was correct or not although the actual content was not explored. He also started to talk about his beliefs where the voices came from. As the interview progressed, it emerged that nurses on the ward had been encouraging him. In particular, one nurse who had known him for many years, had recently overcome his own scepticism through attendance at a workshop on CBT for acute ward nurses, to 'give the bloke a chance as nothing else seems to have worked'.

Subsequent weekly sessions have enabled exploration of the delusions of reference that have emerged as the most troublesome symptoms. He completed simple diary assignments for this and checked these beliefs with nursing staff and others. He has found a newsletter on 'Understanding Voices' helpful and has repeatedly referred to it. The voices have now receded. He currently remains on the ward but is spending time off it, shopping, and so on; he remains quite isolated but is more spontaneous and even humorous in conversation. He is now being seen monthly and beginning to contemplate where he will live in the future.

REDUCTION OF STIGMA

Finally, reducing stigma and assisting patients often needs to involve the acceptance that they have a mental health problem. Over the years, patients and friends with schizophrenia have expressed concern about the term. 'Isn't it time to get rid of it? Like we have done for idiocy, mental retardation, etc.' It is a confusing and inaccurate term semantically. Very few patients like the term with its association with violence—with many an agreement that they have had a 'nervous breakdown' or been stressed might be more acceptable and therapeutic. They may find it easier to agree to inpatient care, medication, and other treatment, when using such alternative terms. Many patients resist the term 'schizophrenia' because of its erroneous associations in most people's minds with deterioration and inevitable violence. Destigmatising the term is proving very difficult—just as destigmatising terms like 'idiocy' or 'mental retardation' has been; perhaps, as with them, a change is worth considering. Bleuler initially described 'the schizophrenias' as a group in 1911, not schizophrenia as a single entity and, in practice, there are clinical subgroups or themes. These divide into acute onset or anxiety-related psychoses, hallucinogenic drug-related psychoses, and what can sometimes helpfully be described as a sensitivity disorder where gradual onset and vulnerability to stress are prominent features (Kingdon & Turkington, 1998). These subgroups may overlap; as a mixture of depression and schizophrenia can occur, so sensitivity and drug-related psychosis may co-exist. But nevertheless such terms may be more useful and acceptable to patients, and attempts to describe more clearly the clinical groups we are working with may help both research developments and training.

REFERENCES

Bebbington, P., Wilkins, S., Jones, P., et al. (1993). Life events and psychosis. Initial results from the Camberwell Collaborative Psychosis Study. *British Journal of Psychiatry*, **162**, 72–79.

Beck, A.T. (1952). Successful outpatient psychotherapy of a chronic schizophrenic with a delusion based on borrowed guilt. *Psychiatry*, **15**, 305–312

Birchwood, M., Hallett, S. & Preston, M. (1988). *Schizophrenia: an Integrated Approach to Research and Treatment*. Harlow: Longman.

Birchwood, M., Smith, J., MacMillan, F. et al. (1989). Predicting relapse in schizophrenia: The development and implementation of an early signs monitoring system using patients and families as observers. *Psychological Medicine*, **19**, 649–656.

Brenner, H.D., Hodel, B. & Roper, V. (1990). Integrated cognitive and behavioural interventions in the treatment of schizophrenia. *Psychological Rehabilitation Journal*, **13**(3), 41–43.

Chadwick, P., Birchwood, M. & Trower, P. (1996). *Cognitive Therapy for Delusions, Voices and Paranoia*. Chichester: Wiley.

Drury, V., Birchwood, M. & MacMillan, F. (1996). Cognitive therapy and recovery from acute psychosis: A controlled trial. I. Impact on psychotic symptoms. II. Impact on recovery time. *British Journal of Psychiatry*, **169**, 593–607.

Fowler, D., Garety, P.A. & Kuipers, L. (1995). *Cognitive Behaviour Therapy for People with Psychosis: A Clinical Handbook*. Chichester: Wiley.

Garety, P.A., Kuipers, L., Fowler, D., Chamberlain, F. & Dunn, G. (1994). Cognitive behaviour therapy for drug resistant psychosis. *British Journal of Medical Psychology*, **67**, 259–271.

Garety, P.A., Fowler, D., Kuipers, L., et al. (1997). The London-East Anglia randomised controlled trial of cognitive behavioural therapy for psychosis. II: Predictors of outcome in CBT for psychosis. *British Journal of Psychiatry*, **171**, 420–426.

Haddock, G., Bentall, R.P. & Slade, P.D. (1996). Psychological treatment of auditory hallucinations: Focusing or distraction? In G. Haddock & P.D. Slade (Eds). *Cognitive Behavioural Interventions with Psychotic Disorders*. London: Routledge.

Haddock, G. & Slade, P.D. (Eds) (1996). *Cognitive Behavioural Interventions with Psychotic Disorders*. London: Routledge.

Harrow, M. & Prosen, M. (1978). Intermingling and disordered logic as influences on schizophrenic thought disorders. *Archives of General Psychiatry*, **35**, 1213–1218.

Jones, P., Rodgers, B., Murray, R. & Marmot, M. (1994). Child development risk factors for adult schizophrenia in the British 1946 birth cohort. *Lancet*, **344**, 1398–1402

Kemp, R., Heyward, P., Applewhaite, G., Everitt, B. & David, A. (1996). Compliance therapy in psychotic patients: A randomised controlled trial. *British Medical Journal*, **312**, 345–349.

Kemp, R., Heyward, P. & David, A. (1997). *Compliance Therapy Manual*. London: Jannsen-Cilag & Organon.

Kingdon, D.G. & Turkington, D. (1991). Preliminary report. The use of cognitive behavior therapy and a normalizing rationale in schizophrenia. *Journal of Nervous & Mental Disease*, **179**, 207–211.

Kingdon, D.G. & Turkington, D. (1994). *Cognitive Behavioral Therapy of Schizophrenia.* New York: Guilford, London: Psychology Press.

Kingdon, D.G. & Turkington, D. (1998). Cognitive behaviour therapy: styles, groups and outcomes. In Wykes, T., Tarrier, N. & Lewis, S. (Eds). *Outcome and Innovation in the Psychological Treatment of Schizophrenia.* Chichester: Wiley.

Kingdon, D.G., Turkington, D. & Johns, C.J. (1994). Cognitive behavioral therapy in schizophrenia. The amenability of delusions and hallucinations to reason. *British Journal of Psychiatry*, **164**, 581–587.

Lecompte, D. & Pelc, I. (1996). A cognitive-behavioral program to improve compliance with medication in patients with schizophrenia. *Int. J. Mental Health*, **25**, 51–56.

Mace, C. & Margison, F. (Eds) (1997). *Psychotherapy of Psychosis.* London: Gaskell. D.

Perry, A., Tarrier, N. & Morriss, R. (1995). Identification of prodromal signs and symptoms and early intervention in manic-depressive psychosis patients. *Behavioural and Cognitive Psychotherapy*, **23**, 399–409.

Strauss, J.S., Rakfeldt, J., Harding, C.M. & Lieberman, P. (1989). Psychological and social aspects of negative symptoms. *British Journal of Psychiatry*, **155** (Suppl 7), 128–132.

Tarrier, N., Beckett, R., Harwood, S. et al. (1993). A trial of two cognitive behavioural methods of treating drug-resistant psychotic symptoms in schizophrenic patients: I. Outcome. *British Journal of Psychiatry*, **162**, 524–532.

Wing, J.K., Cooper, J.E. & Sartorius, N. (1974). *The Measurement and Classification of Psychiatric Symptoms.* Cambridge: Cambridge University Press.

Wing, J.K., et al. (1996). Health of the Nation Outcome Scales. Research Unit: Royal College of Psychiatrists.

Young, J.E. & Beck, A.T. (1980). *The Cognitive Therapy Rating Scale.* Pennsylvania: Center for Cognitive Therapy.

Chapter 9

COGNITIVE BEHAVIOUR THERAPY FOR PSYCHOTIC SYMPTOMS IN SCHIZOPHRENIA

*Anthony P. Morrison**

This chapter aims to provide clinicians with an overview of cognitive behaviour therapy for psychotic symptoms in schizophrenic patients. The content and structure of therapy will be described, with particular attention being paid to the differences that exist between standard cognitive behaviour therapy and that applied to this client group. However, case examples illustrating some of the similarities and the use of familiar strategies with psychotic symptoms will also be provided. The importance of basing therapy on a cognitive model and using an idiosyncratic case formulation will also be discussed.

Cognitive behavioural interventions for schizophrenic symptoms are effective in reducing the distress and disability associated with this disorder, in addition to reducing the frequency and severity of psychotic symptoms (see Chapter 7 this volume by Haddock & Tarrier for a discussion of outcome studies); this is particularly the case where cognitive restructuring is employed as an intervention component (Bouchard et al., 1996). The following section will examine the practical application of cognitive therapy to schizophrenia.

COGNITIVE THERAPY

The general principles of cognitive therapy include being based on a cognitive model of the disorder in question, having a sound therapeutic

* Prestwich Hospital, Manchester, UK

Treating Complex Cases: The Cognitive Behavioural Therapy Approach.
Edited by Nicholas Tarrier, Adrian Wells and Gillian Haddock.
© 1998 John Wiley & Sons Ltd.

relationship as a necessary condition for change, and being problem-orientated, time-limited, structured and directive. It is often educational, employing the inductive method and a process of guided discovery and collaborative empiricism.

Content and Structure of Therapy

Overall therapy structure involves assessment, development of a problem list, socialisation (agreeing a shared understanding of the problem—usually based on a cognitive model and often involving normalisation), idiosyncratic case formulation, symptom-focused intervention (which often involves the testing of this formulation as an alternative explanation of a patient's problems using verbal and behavioural reattribution techniques), schema-focused intervention and relapse prevention. Each of these stages will be outlined in detail below, with the exception of assessment and developing a problem list which are comprehensively covered by Haddock and Tarrier in Chapter 7 and socialisation and engagement which is covered in depth by Kingdon in Chapter 8 of this volume (Haddock and Tarrier cover formulation in their chapter, but this will be briefly discussed as it is so central to treatment). The content of individual sessions will reflect the stage which therapy is at, but some general guidelines are also presented.

The structure of individual sessions

Overall, the structure of sessions is similar to cognitive therapy in general. Thus, they begin with a review of measures, then elicit feedback regarding the last session (paying particular attention to whether the patient understood what was discussed and why) and this is followed by agenda setting (with psychotic patients this becomes extremely important—one item, in addition to the feedback from the last homework and setting of new homework, will often be enough, and all agenda items should be related to the formulation). The additional agenda items will usually relate to the implementation of specific strategies targeted at identified problems, and should be collaboratively agreed between patient and therapist. The session concludes with the setting of new homework and feedback from the current session. It is important to spend adequate time discussing the new homework task (allocation of specific time for each agenda item can help this) to ensure that the patient understands exactly what the task is, and the rationale for completing it (this is easier if the patient chooses the homework task for him or herself, in relation to the content of the session). The patient should leave the session with a written summary of the session content, a concrete task for homework and a space to record their conclusions from the homework if it is a behavioural experiment; it is important to be flexible in the use of homework tasks (the ability to carry it out should be within the patient's repertoire), however, in order to ensure that it does not adversely affect the therapeutic relationship.

The pacing of sessions is often slower than for other client groups, with sessions frequently being between 25 to 35 minutes. Some patients can clearly tolerate longer, but given the cognitive deficits commonly found in schizophrenia, and the impairments that can be caused by medication, shorter, more frequent sessions with written summaries would seem to be indicated. It is also important that the first few sessions are particularly focused on developing a good therapeutic relationship and engaging the patient sufficiently to allow therapeutic progress to occur. This can be aided by ensuring that goals are achievable and initially unambitious, providing a success experience in therapy; ideally such goals should be realisable within a short time-limited period.

Case formulation

Intervention must be determined by formulation, rather than driven by the application of individual techniques (for a general discussion see Persons, 1989). Formulation should be based on a cognitive model, carried out in collaboration with the patient, and should incorporate the information gained from assessment. Initially, formulation should be done slowly in order to ensure that the patient understands and is in agreement with it; this is probably done most effectively using vicious circles incorporating recent specific incidents to illustrate the maintenance of particularly problematic symptoms or situations, as identified in the problem list. Such a formulation can be based on heuristic models of the links between cognitive, behavioural, emotional and physiological factors; these can either be generic (e.g. Greenberger & Padesky, 1995) or in relation to specific psychotic symptoms (Chadwick, Birchwood & Trower, 1996; Morrison, Haddock & Tarrier, 1995). For instance, the approach to auditory hallucinations outlined by Morrison, Haddock and Tarrier (see Figure 9.1) is easily modified to provide a maintenance formulation illustrating factors involved in a patient's idiosyncratic experience of hearing voices (as shown later in Figure 9.3).

The cognitive formulation of a patient's difficulties should be used as an alternative explanation of symptoms, along with all others that can be generated by the patient (in collaboration with the therapist) including that the symptoms are based on reality. This will help to engage and socialise a patient to a cognitive way of working, and will facilitate the

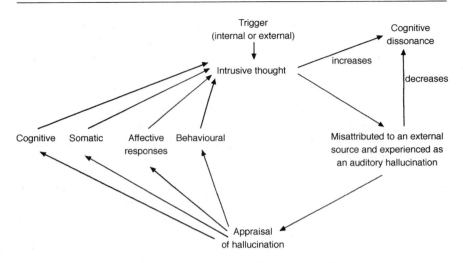

Figure 9.1 An heuristic model of auditory hallucinations. Source: Morrison, Haddock and Tarrier (1995). Reprinted with permission from *Behavioural and Cognitive Psychotherapy*, 23, 265–280.

choice of intervention strategies and homework tasks. Examples of such formulations will be given in the following section to help illustrate cognitive behavioural interventions for psychotic symptoms, and further information regarding formulation can be found in Haddock and Tarrier (Chapter 7). Once a formulation is obtained, verbal and behavioural reattribution methods can then be used to reach some conclusion about which explanation best accounts for the patient's experiences.

Implementation of specific intervention strategies

The choice of strategies used for intervention should be determined by the idiosyncratic formulation, and can often be negotiated through discussion with the patient. The aim of intervention is to reduce distress and disability and to increase quality of life. Keeping these aims in mind, the selection and prioritisation of the patient's goals from a problem list will also guide intervention (it is important to begin with the problem that is most amenable to change in order to provide a success experience in therapy). There are obviously many similarities between working with psychotic patients and any other type (for instance, if a patient's goals are to have a more active social life, to have a tidier flat or to feel less anxious when getting on a bus, these problems would be addressed in the same way as for a patient who is not psychotic, although the formulation could be used to predict certain difficulties that may occur when implementing such interventions). Therefore, this section will focus specifically on the psychological treatment of delusions and hallucinations.

Delusions

Delusions are a very common symptom of schizophrenia, with the International Pilot study of Schizophrenia (World Health Organisation, 1973) finding high incidence rates in schizophrenic patients for delusions of reference (67%), delusions of control (48%) and persecutory delusions (64%). There is considerable evidence that delusions are formed and maintained in a similar manner to normal beliefs (Garety & Hemsley, 1994), but that patients experiencing delusions exhibit overconfidence in their judgements and reach their judgements more rapidly than control groups (Huq, Garety & Hemsley, 1988; Garety, Hemsley & Wessely, 1991). These resemble Beck's (1976) thinking errors of all-or-nothing thinking or dichotomous reasoning and arbitrary inference or jumping to conclusions; therefore, it seems plausible that verbal reattribution techniques will be effective in altering delusional beliefs. An example of a cognitive formulation of a specific incident relating to a patient who believes that others are trying to harm him and that his thoughts are being broadcast is shown in Figure 9.2.

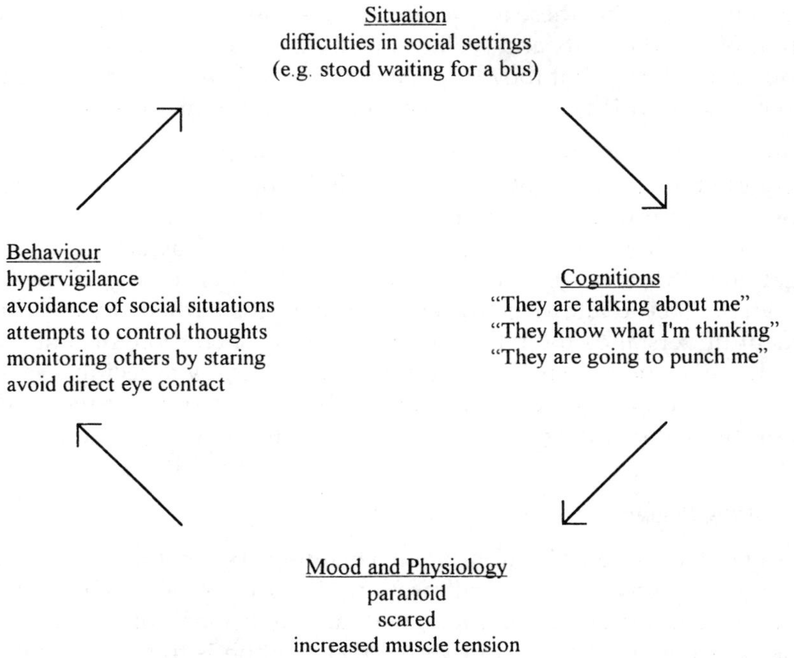

Situation
difficulties in social settings
(e.g. stood waiting for a bus)

Behaviour
hypervigilance
avoidance of social situations
attempts to control thoughts
monitoring others by staring
avoid direct eye contact

Cognitions
"They are talking about me"
"They know what I'm thinking"
"They are going to punch me"

Mood and Physiology
paranoid
scared
increased muscle tension

Figure 9.2   A formulation of a specific incident for delusional beliefs.

Verbal Reattribution

Identifying thoughts and feelings

Initially, it is important to demonstrate the links between thoughts, feelings and behaviour. This is best done using examples from the patient that arise during a session; however, there are also standard narratives that can be used for this purpose (Greenberger & Padesky, 1995; Salkovskis, 1996). Once this relationship has been demonstrated to a patient's satisfaction, it is easier to engage the patient in the process of monitoring their thoughts. This is often done using a dysfunctional thought record (DTR: for examples see Greenberger & Padesky, 1995; Fennell, 1989). This will initially consist of identifying and rating unpleasant emotions (such as fear or paranoia), recording the problematic situation in which these occur (e.g. watching television) and identifying the accompanying thoughts (e.g. 'It's talking about me'). It is also important to rate the degree to which the thoughts are believed using percentages. It can also be useful to encourage patients to identify how they behaved in such a situation, as this can provide valuable information regarding the maintenance of a problem (this will be discussed in more detail subsequently). Some patients find it difficult to fill in forms; this can be addressed by starting with only recording situations and using these as prompts for in-session collaborative identification of the thoughts and feelings, or by encouraging a patient to talk about a situation, what they thought and felt and what they did, onto an audiocassette which can then be listened to in a therapy session.

Common problems in the identification of thoughts and feelings that are encountered with psychotic patients include the subjective experience of thought withdrawal or thought blocking, cognitive avoidance and missing the emotive thoughts. These can often be addressed by asking a patient what goes through their mind before and after their thoughts are withdrawn or blocked and what the experience means to them, by ensuring a patient understands the rationale for recording such thoughts and limiting the time spent focusing on emotive thoughts, by agreeing a mechanism for changing the topic if a patient becomes too distressed, and by ensuring that the thoughts fit with the emotion experienced.

Evaluating thoughts using verbal reattribution

As suggested earlier, it is important to encourage patients to view the idiosyncratic cognitive behavioural case formulation as one possible explanation for their current experiences, with any delusional interpretations as other possibilities. The goal of verbal reattribution is to teach patients to view their thoughts as hypotheses and how to re-evaluate their thinking for themselves. This can be done using a variety of strategies including examining the evidence, considering alternative explanations, examining the advantages and disadvantages of holding such a belief, and education regarding normal psychological processes.

Consideration of alternative explanations. The purpose of encouraging the patient to generate as many alternative explanations as possible for situations or events is to facilitate their viewing thoughts as hypotheses; this is particularly important given the finding that people experiencing delusions form their opinions rapidly. Patients will often have a variety of explanations for their current circumstances and experiences which can range from the delusional to the mundane, and more can be generated simply by brainstorming. If someone is having difficulty generating alternatives for themselves, the following questions can be helpful:

- Have you ever thought there were any other explanations for this?
- What would you have thought about this before you became distressed?
- What might someone else think? This could be in relation to friends, family, a trusted or respected figure (teacher, social worker, priest) or even a character from a favourite television programme or novel.
- What would you suggest to a friend who came to you with this problem?

These explanations should include the idiosyncratic formulation, and all alternatives should be rated in terms of how much they are believed (0–100%). Any explanations that are generated should be related to the facts and the evidence for and against each can be considered, with belief ratings being taken regularly. An example of exploring alternative explanations, in combination with considering the evidence, is illustrated in the following dialogue (relating to the formulation in Figure 9.2):

Patient: When I was at the bus stop this man playing football in the park shouted 'It's crap' at me.

Therapist: How did you know that it was directed at you?

P: Well, they said it, and I was there … I just knew he meant me.

T: How much do you believe that he meant you sitting here now, and how much did you believe it at the time?

P: 100% at the time and about 80% now.

T: Was there anyone or anything else he could have been meaning?

P: No.

T: You said he was playing football. Were there any others playing?

P: Yes, it looked like eleven-a-side.

T: Is it possible that he could have shouting at one of the other players?

P: Yes, I suppose so. It might even have been at the referee.

T: If your friend was in this situation and asked you whether there was anyone else the man could have shouted at, what would you tell them?

P: That it could have been at the players or the referee.

T: Anything else?

P: I suppose it could have been directed at someone in the crowd, or even at the ball.

T: Were there any others waiting at the bus stop with you?

P: Yes, and it could have been aimed at one of them as well.

T: So, how many others could he have been talking to?

P: Including the players, the crowd and the others at the stop, probably about 50.

T: Have you ever said something similar?

P: Yes, often.

T: What sort of thing would you be saying it about if you were playing football?

P: I might say it about myself, having missed an open goal or given the ball away. Or maybe about a bad decision from the linesman or something.

T: OK. On the basis of what we have discussed, how much do you believe that he was talking about you at this moment?

P: About 20%.

T: And if you were in the situation again, how much would you believe that he was meaning you?

P: Probably about 50%.

Examining the evidence.   There is considerable empirical support for the notion that there are perceptual and interpretative biases in people experiencing delusions (Garety & Hemsley, 1994; Bentall, 1994). It is therefore important to uncover disconfirmatory evidence of which the patient is unaware, and to sensitively scrutinise the evidence on which a patient is basing their beliefs. The need for this can be illustrated to patients using Padesky's (1994) series of guiding questions to demonstrate schema as self-prejudice in order to provide a relevant example of perceptual and interpretative biases in operation. An example of how this can be done in practice is given in the subsequent section examining hallucinations.

Given the perceptual biases that schizophrenic patients exhibit, it is important to direct a patient's attention towards counter-evidence. This can be done using a positive or alternative data log in which a patient records specific occurrences that are inconsistent with a delusional belief. In addition to examining current evidence that a patient cites for a belief, it is useful to consider past evidence and see if it is open to reinterpretation (possibly by generating alternative explanations in the manner described above). It is also beneficial to encourage collaborative exploration of all possible alternative explanations for a piece of evidence, using pie charts. In this procedure, a circle is drawn and the patient is asked to list all possible causes and then allocate a section of the circle to each cause; when finished, there is often little room left for the patient's delusional explanation. It can also be useful to question the mechanism for a delusional idea and relate this to evidence for and against the belief, in addition to highlighting any inconsistencies in terms of modulating factors (for example, if someone finds that distraction helps them feel less persecuted, is that more consistent with their problem being that they are actually persecuted or that they believe they are being persecuted?). In addition, feelings (both physiological and emotional) are often used as evidence for a delusional belief; therefore, providing information regarding alternative explanations of such feelings can be useful, and can be investigated further using behavioural experiments.

Education regarding psychological processes. The provision of information and education regarding normal cognitive processes can be very useful in a number of ways. As mentioned earlier, the use of Padesky's prejudice example can illustrate how people operate confirmatory biases, selective attention and biases in memory. All of these processes are exaggerated in people with delusions (Garety & Hemsley, 1994; Kinderman, 1994; Kaney et al., 1992), which makes it more important to make patients aware of these biases so that attempts can be made to recognise them and possibly reverse them in order to facilitate disconfirmation. This can be done with reference to Wells and Matthews' (1994) Self-Regulatory Executive Function (S-REF) model of emotional dysfunction, which suggests identifying and challenging dysfunctional procedural beliefs (plans for processing), in order to accommodate disconfirmatory processing. They suggest that this be conducted using meta-cognitive profiling (gaining a detailed analysis of a patient's attentional, ideational and memory processes in problematic situations).

It is also useful to provide information regarding the prevalence of intrusive thoughts, impulses and imagery, as they are implicated in certain models of psychotic symptoms (Morrison, Haddock & Tarrier, 1995). This may help to challenge meta-cognitive beliefs (such as 'I must not have bad thoughts'; 'Thinking a bad thought makes me a bad person'; 'If I do not control my thoughts it is dangerous') that may be involved in the development or maintenance of psychotic symptoms (Bentall, 1990; Morrison, Haddock & Tarrier, 1995) and that are implicated in emotional dysfunction (Wells & Matthews, 1994). Such beliefs can also be challenged by examining the evidence for them, generating alternative explanations and using behavioural experiments.

As mentioned earlier, it is important to educate patients about the logical distortions that people make in thinking. These thinking errors include personalisation, selective abstraction, overgeneralisation, arbitrary inference or jumping to conclusions and dichotomous reasoning or all-or-nothing thinking (for a more exhaustive list and patient handouts see Burns, 1980, or Fennell, 1989). An understanding of these distortions facilitates a patient's identification and subsequent challenging of perceptual and interpretative biases.

Provision of information regarding normal anxiety sensations can also be useful, as some psychotic symptoms appear to be the result of misinterpreting anxiety in a culturally unacceptable manner. Thus, if someone misinterprets their racing thoughts or palpitations as a sign of alien control, they will be classified as delusional, whereas misinterpretation of the same sensation as a sign of impending madness or a heart attack, would be regarded as indicative of a panic attack. Similarly, a benign lump in one's skin may be misinterpreted as a sign of cancer by a hypochondriacal patient, but the misinterpretation of the same stimuli as being a transmitter installed by the secret police would be more likely to result in a patient being regarded as psychotic. However, education about the processes involved in anxiety, the sorts of sensations associated with anxiety, and provision of the cognitive models of anxiety disorders (e.g. Clark's, 1986, model of panic) as an alternative explanation for their experiences can be extremely beneficial in such cases; adapting the standard cognitive therapies for such disorders can also be of use. Similarly, employing a normalising rationale, and education regarding the incidence of psychotic symptoms following certain stressors can help reduce distress (see Kingdon, Chapter 8 this volume for further discussion of normalisation).

Consideration of the advantages and disadvantages

It is important to help the patient to examine the advantages and disadvantages of holding their particular beliefs. This can aid engagement, assist in motivating a patient to change when this is appropriate and to highlight any functional aspects of a particular symptom. If a delusional idea does have some advantages for a patient (this could be psychological, such as a grandiose delusion boosting self-esteem and sense of importance, or social, such as financial benefits or contact with carers) it is necessary to address these issues before challenging that belief. This may be conducted by working through any emotional investment in the idea or by providing an alternative method or source so that the advantage can be obtained in another way. Alternatively, it may be appropriate to modify the belief rather than challenge it directly (for instance, it may be less distressing to be able to predict the future than to be able to cause the future on the basis of one's dreams—in this way a patient can remain 'special' without necessarily having the associated responsibility and distress).

In considering such matters it is often useful to ascertain the personal meaning or significance of a delusional belief; this can be done using the downward arrow technique (Burns, 1980). Once the thoughts associated with a problematic situation are identified, this involves questioning the idiosyncratic meaning or significance of that thought were it to be true, and repeatedly questioning the subsequent responses in the same manner. Typical questions to aid this process include: 'What would that mean to you if it were true?'; 'What would that say about you as a person?'; 'What would be so bad about that?' (see Figure 9.3 for an example).

Behavioural Reattribution

Verbal reattribution should be routinely followed or accompanied by behavioural reattribution methods; indeed, Chadwick and Lowe (1990) found that behavioural testing following verbal challenging of delusions was a potent combination.

Behavioural experiments

As described previously, verbal reattribution techniques can be used to help patients evaluate their beliefs and the way they behave. Correspondingly, changes in behaviour can produce consequences that may contradict these beliefs and thus reduce their conviction further. The purpose of behavioural experiments is to allow a patient to test out the validity of a certain belief and to provide the possibility of obtaining disconfirmatory evidence. The stages involved in a behavioural experiment include making a prediction, reviewing the evidence for and against the prediction, devising a specific experiment to test the validity of the prediction, recording the results in detail and, finally, drawing a conclusion. For example, a patient who believed he was Jesus Christ was concerned that he was going to be crucified on Good Friday, so was planning to stay in for the whole week around Easter. After considering the evidence for and against this prediction, he was willing to go out on Good Friday, and

Situation: Stood at bus stop

Emotion: Scared, paranoid

Thoughts: They can read my mind

Supposing that was true, what would it mean to you?

They will know that I'm scared, and find out about what I've done in the past

If that were true, what would be so bad about that?

They would know that I've done bad things

And supposing they did, what would that mean to you?

They would learn that I am a bad person

And if that were true, what would that mean?

It would mean everyone wouldn't speak to me,
I would be alone forever and I couldn't live with the shame

Figure 9.3 An example of the downward arrow technique for a delusional belief.

decided that going to a local hardware shop where he would be in proximity to hammers and nails would be a good test of whether this would
occur; as expected, he was initially extremely anxious, but levels of anxiety declined and he was able to discover that he was not attacked in any
way, thereby weakening his persecutory beliefs. Such anxiety is not
uncommon when a patient attempts to test out a particularly threatening
belief; this can be minimised by using the formulation as a convincing
alternative to their fears, using verbal reattribution strategies to reduce

conviction in the delusional ideas and create ambivalence, predicting such anxiety and planning how to deal with it should it arise (challenging negative automatic thoughts, the use of applied relaxation or medication).

Safety behaviours

In the same way that people with anxiety disorders adopt certain behaviours in order to prevent some feared catastrophe (Salkovskis, 1991, 1996; Clark, 1996; Wells et al., 1994), it would appear that people with distressing delusions initiate attempts to avert any negative outcomes that are implied in the delusional belief. Thus, a patient who believes that they are being followed by the IRA may attempt to lose their trackers by taking varying routes to the shops, hiding behind cars and changing clothes regularly or going out in disguise. These strategies may inhibit cognitive change as they are preventing disconfirmation of the delusional belief by providing extenuating factors (in other words, a patient in the above situation could say that they would have been killed by the IRA by now if it was not for their vigilance). In the situation described in Figure 9.2, sitting near the door, avoiding eye contact and attempting to control their thoughts are all safety behaviours designed to prevent the patient from being attacked, but they may also prevent disconfirmation of this belief. If a patient is convinced by a cognitive formulation of their problems as a plausible account, it is possible to encourage them to provide a true test of their beliefs by dropping such behaviours and recording the results.

Coping strategy enhancement

Coping strategy enhancement, while not strictly a behavioural reattribution strategy, is a useful approach to promoting adjustment to psychotic symptoms. This approach involves building on a patient's existing coping repertoire following a detailed analysis of symptoms. Typically it incorporates demonstration of cognitive strategies, training in behavioural strategies using guided practice and *in vivo* practice of coping strategies. It is an extremely pragmatic approach, allowing for incorporation of any of the reattribution strategies already mentioned, with treatment initially targeting one symptom; if the strategy is successful, another symptom is selected, while if unsuccessful another coping strategy is adopted. Coping strategy enhancement is also the best evaluated psychological intervention for psychotic symptoms to date, with a case series and two randomised controlled trials showing it to be beneficial; for further details regarding this approach see Tarrier (1992) or Yusupoff and Tarrier (1996).

Auditory hallucinations

Auditory hallucinations are probably the most common psychotic symptom in patients with schizophrenia. All of the above strategies regarding delusions can be applied to a patient's beliefs about their voices, which are clearly implicated in the distress and disability associated with auditory hallucinations (Chadwick & Birchwood, 1994; Morrison, Haddock & Tarrier, 1995). In addition, there is general agreement that such hallucinations are the result of a misattribution of thoughts to an external source (Bentall, 1990; Morrison, Haddock & Tarrier, 1995), so many of the strategies developed for reducing distress associated with problematic thoughts (such as in obsessional intrusive thoughts) are also applicable. This is illustrated in the following case example (also see Morrison, 1994).

Case Example

Mr B has been hearing two abusive and persecutory male voices for the past year. He has associated delusions of persecution, believing that the voices are real people who are intent on causing him harm. Mr B avoids going out of the house as he fears being assaulted, but sometimes does escape from the house if he fears an imminent attack from the voices (usually based on what they are saying). When he does go out he is extremely wary (and often drinks in an attempt to remain calm). He also has panic attacks when he is concerned about being attacked—this is linked to his alternative belief regarding the voices, which is that he is 'losing his marbles'. This information is incorporated into a formulation for a specific incident in which he has popped into a pub to have a drink to calm his nerves and he hears the voices threaten to maim him (see Figure 9.4).

Intervention with this man was based upon such a cognitive formulation, and involved the majority of the change strategies mentioned in relation to delusions. Alternative explanations were generated for the appraisal of his voices; thus, in addition to them being real persecutors or a sign that he was going mad, the possibilities that they were stress related, related to a traumatic road traffic accident in which he was involved, or related to strong pain-relieving medication he had taken in the past were considered. The evidence for and against each of these possibilities was considered, as shown in Figure 9.5.

Clearly, when examining the evidence, it was important to provide education regarding the frequency of voice hearing, the fact that certain stressors can induce hallucinations and the fact that hearing voices is not always associated with mental illness. The content of the voices was monitored using shadowing in sessions and diaries between sessions, and this content was

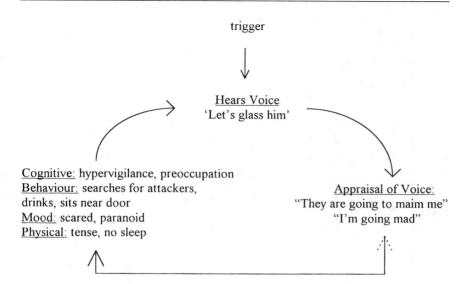

Figure 9.4 A formulation of a specific incident for auditory hallucinations.

examined with regard to its consistency with each of the explanations. It was agreed that it would be useful to provide a test of the most distressing appraisal which was that there were real people attempting to persecute him. He decided that an appropriate experiment would be to cease all of his safety behaviours that were designed to prevent him being attacked (such as sitting near the door, and checking in the attic or under floorboards for the potential assailants), and to sit still in his house and wait for one hour to see if they did come to attack him; it was particularly important to stop the safety behaviours as they appeared to have prevented cognitive change in the past. In other words, he attributed the fact that he had not yet been attacked to having performed these behaviours in the past. It was hoped that modifying the appraisal of the voices would reduce the distress associated with the experience (this was supported by the weekly ratings of distress, conviction and frequency, which all reduced in parallel). Another method that was employed to reduce distress and conviction was using a modified DTR to challenge the content of the voices on an ongoing basis; Mr B was encouraged to examine the evidence for and against what the voices said, and to record his associated mood (this appeared to be particularly effective in altering his emotional response when the voices were being abusive and insulting about him as a person). These rational responses to his voices were practised in session using roleplay (with the therapist modelling appropriate verbal challenges initially).

Reasons for hearing voices:

EXPLANATIONS	BELIEF RATING (0-100%)	EVIDENCE FOR	EVIDENCE AGAINST	RE-RATE BELIEF
Real Persecutors	90%	they sound real / what they say	my family cannot hear them / they have had many opportunities to harm me in the past / I've searched for them and not found anyone / alcohol helps - drinking would not stop them attacking (in fact it might make it easier)	50%
Madness	50%	feels like I'm going mad / get very panicky	panicking is a normal response to feeling scared / lots of people hear voices (probably about one million people in Britain alone) / voices are not always a sign of mental illness	30%
Stress	15%	I have been under a lot of stress recently / being in a car accident is traumatic / people who are stressed do hear voices sometimes	don't always feel stressed / had been stressed in past and never heard voices	50%
Road Traffic Accident	30%	a recent trauma is a common trigger for hearing voices / it coincided timewise with the voices	some people have accidents and don't hear voices	40%
Pain killers	0%	coincided timewise with the voices / strong medications can make people hallucinate	lots of people take strong medication without hearing voices	10%

Figure 9.5   An example of a worksheet regarding explanations for hearing voices.

Additional intervention strategies

There is evidence that a variety of distraction techniques are effective in reducing the frequency of auditory hallucinations; for instance listening to a Walkman or a radio, watching television, physical exercise and mental exercise such as reading or mental arithmetic (Haddock, Bentall & Slade, 1996; Margo et al., 1981; Morley, 1987; Nayani and David, 1996; Nelson, Thrasher & Barnes, 1991). However, the results are equivocal as to whether such interventions produce sustainable, lasting effects (Haddock, Bentall & Slade, 1996; Nelson, Thrasher & Barnes, 1991).

Another form of intervention specifically aimed at auditory hallucinations is focusing (Haddock, Bentall & Slade, 1996). This procedure encourages patients to examine the physical characteristics, location and content of their voices in this sequence. Then they are asked to examine the relation of their thoughts to their voices, and finally they are helped to attribute some personal meaning to the voices, in order to facilitate reattribution of the hallucinatory experience to an internal source if appropriate.

Co-morbid problems

Anxiety and depression are commonly observed in patients with a diagnosis of schizophrenia; studies have found rates of affective symptoms in between 25 and 40% of patients (Johnstone et al., 1991). Such patients also have a higher risk of suicide than other psychiatric populations (Caldwell & Gottesman, 1990). In addition, other disorders such as obsessive-compulsive disorder and post-traumatic stress disorder are frequently observed in schizophrenic patients. Indeed, there is some evidence that patients may develop post-traumatic stress as a response to their psychotic symptoms (McGorry et al., 1991). Therefore, the cognitive behavioural interventions that have been developed for such disorders (see Hawton et al., 1989; Wells, 1997; Chapters 3, 4, 5 in this book) are likely to be of benefit to psychotic patients who are experiencing co-morbid difficulties. In particular, cognitive behaviour therapy for anxiety or stress may be of use (as symptoms are often exacerbated by stress), and cognitive behaviour therapy for depression may help to improve social functioning and reduce hopelessness. The latter should also focus on decreasing stigmatisation, powerlessness and entrapment, which have been identified by Birchwood et al. (1993) as important factors in the levels of depression experienced by psychotic patients.

Negative symptoms

Negative symptoms (such as flat affect, poverty of speech, attentional impairment, underactivity and loss of interest or pleasure) are often confounding factors when attempting to intervene with positive symptoms, and usually adversely affect quality of life and social functioning. It is important to consider the possible causes of these symptoms before intervening, and to perform a thorough assessment using a cognitive behavioural interview or functional analysis. Commonly indicated contributory or confounding factors include depression, overmedication or side-effects of antipsychotic medication, avoidance of positive symptoms or a response to positive symptoms, contextual/environmental factors and behavioural contingencies that may be operating; these specific problems should be addressed prior to interventions targeted at negative symptoms. Typical interventions for negative symptoms include increasing activity levels using activity scheduling, social skills training and contingency management in the wider environment (see Hogg, 1996, for further details).

Relapse prevention

Relapse prevention should be incorporated within any cognitive behavioural intervention. This usually involves three components (schema-focused therapy, developing a blueprint summarising therapeutic progress and prodromal monitoring); each of these will be discussed in more detail.

Schema-focused intervention. The purpose of schema-focused work is to address core beliefs and dysfunctional assumptions that may act as vulnerability factors for future acute episodes (respective examples of such beliefs would include 'I am bad' or 'In order to be loved I must be perfect'). Effective relapse prevention will target these as they may be activated again in future by critical incidents or life events. Methods for modifying schemata include continuum work, historical test, examining evidence for these beliefs and searching for or constructing alternatives and the use of positive data logs (for further information see Padesky, 1994; Young, Chapter 15 this volume). In addition, the S-REF model of Wells and Matthews (1994) would suggest that dysfunctional procedural beliefs should also be modified. For instance, they suggest that style of processing can be a vulnerability factor and should be targeted in treatment (e.g. selective attention can be modified using attentional training; Wells, 1990).

Developing a blueprint. The therapeutic blueprint consists of a written summary detailing what the patient has learnt in treatment. This should include information regarding the development and maintenance of their psychotic symptoms, including a copy of the formulation(s), strategies for challenging beliefs and testing them out, detailed summaries of counter-evidence and the results of behavioural experiments. The patient should be encouraged to do as much of this as they can for homework, and even the gaps that are filled in with the therapist's help should be written by the patient if possible.

Prodromal monitoring.   The identification and monitoring of prodromes has been shown to be effective in reducing relapse in schizophrenia (Birchwood, 1996). This process involves identifying a patient's idiosyncratic prodromal symptoms or early warning signs that occur prior to a relapse, and designing an individualised method of monitoring these. A baseline measure is taken against which any changes can be compared, and action plans are negotiated with the patient and also services with the aim of acting quickly once the prodromal signs occur in order to prevent or ameliorate future episodes. There is similar work in being showing the benefits of such approaches in patients with bipolar disorder (Perry, Tarrier & Morriss, 1995).

SUMMARY

Recent developments in cognitive behavioural models and interventions for psychotic symptoms appear to offer significant benefits in addition to neuroleptic medication for patients with a diagnosis of schizophrenia. This chapter has outlined an approach to treatment that is based on idiosyncratic case formulation. Such conceptualisations can be used to determine the plan for intervention, in addition to offering an alternative explanation of a patient's difficulties and allowing the prediction of problems that may occur in therapy. The use of specific cognitive and behavioural reattribution strategies for psychotic symptoms and co-morbid problems can be guided by this formulation, and these have been discussed in detail. A variety of strategies for relapse prevention can also be used to maintain treatment gains and minimise the risk of future episodes.

REFERENCES

Beck, A.T. (1976). *Cognitive Therapy and the Emotional Disorders*. New York: International Universities Press.

Bentall, R.P. (1990). The syndromes and symptoms of psychosis: Or why you can't play twenty questions with the concept of schizophrenia and hope to win. In R.P. Bentall (Ed.), *Reconstructing Schizophrenia*. London: Routledge.

Bentall, R.P. (1994). Cognitive biases and abnormal beliefs: Towards a model of persecutory delusions. In A.S. David & J. Cutting (Eds), *The Neuropsychology of Schizophrenia*. London: LEA.

Birchwood, M. (1996). Early intervention in psychotic relapse: Cognitive approaches to detection and management. In G. Haddock & P. Slade (Eds), *Cognitive Behavioural Interventions with Psychotic Disorders*. London: Routledge.

Birchwood, M., Mason, R., McMillan, F. & Healy, J. (1993). Depression, demoralisation and control over illness: A comparison of depressed and non-depressed patients with a chronic psychosis. *Psychological Medicine*, **23**, 387–395.

Bouchard, S., Vallieres, A., Poy, M.A. & Maziade, M. (1996). Cognitive restructuring in the treatment of psychotic symptoms in schizophrenia: A critical analysis. *Behavior Therapy*, **27**, 257–278.

Burns, D. (1980). *Feeling Good*. New York: New American Library.

Caldwell, J. & Gottesman, I. (1990). Schizophrenics kill themselves too. *Schizophrenia Bulletin*, **16**, 571–590.

Chadwick, P. & Birchwood, M. (1994). The omnipotence of voices. A cognitive approach to auditory hallucinations. *British Journal of Psychiatry*, **164**, 190–201.

Chadwick, P., Birchwood, M. & Trower, P. (1996). *Cognitive Therapy for Delusions, Voices and Paranoia*. London: Wiley.

Chadwick, P. & Lowe, C.F. (1990). Measurement and modification of delusional beliefs. *Journal of Consulting and Clinical Psychology*, **58**, 225–232.

Clark, D.M. (1986). A cognitive approach to panic. *Behaviour Research and Therapy*, **24**, 461–470.

Clark, D.M (1996). Panic disorder: From theory to therapy. In P.M. Salkovskis (Ed.), *Frontiers of Cognitive Therapy*. New York: Guilford.

Fennell, M.J.V. (1989). Depression. In K. Hawton et al. (Eds), *Cognitive Behaviour Therapy for Psychiatric Problems*. Oxford: Oxford University Press.

Fowler, D. & Morley, S. (1989). The cognitive behavioural treatment of hallucinations and delusions: A preliminary study. *Behavioural Psychotherapy*, **17**, 267–282.

Garety, P.A. & Hemsley, D.R. (1994). *Delusions: Investigations into the Psychology of Delusional Reasoning*. Oxford: Oxford University Press.

Garety, P.A., Hemsley, D.R. & Wessely, S. (1991). Reasoning in deluded schizophrenic and paranoid patients: Biases in performance on a probabilistic inference task. *Journal of Nervous and Mental Disease*, **179**, 194–201.

Greenberger, D. & Padesky, C. (1995). *Mind Over Mood*. New York: Guilford.

Haddock, G., Bentall, R.P. & Slade, P. (1996). Psychological treatment of auditory hallucinations: Focusing or distraction?. In G. Haddock & P. Slade (Eds), *Cognitive-Behavioural Interventions with Psychotic Disorders*. London: Routledge.

Hawton, K., Salkovskis, P.M., Kirk, J. & Clark, D.M. (1989). *Cognitive Behaviour Therapy for Psychiatric Problems*. Oxford: Oxford University Press.

Hogg, L. (1996). Interventions for negative symptoms. In G. Haddock & P. Slade (Eds), *Cognitive Behavioural Interventions with Psychotic Disorders*. London: Routledge.

Huq, S.F., Garety, P.A. & Hemsley, D.R. (1988). Probabilistic judgements in deluded and non-deluded subjects. *Quarterly Journal of Experimental Psychology*, **40A**, 801–812.

Johnstone, E.C., Owens, D., Frith, C.D. & Leavy, J. (1991). Clinical findings: Abnormalities of mental state and their correlates. *British Journal of Psychiatry*, **159** (Supp. 13), 21–25.

Kaney, S., Wolfenden, M., Dewey, M.E. & Bentall, R.P. (1992). Persecutory delusions and recall of threatening propositions. *British Journal of Clinical Psychology*, **31**, 85–87.

Kinderman, P. (1994). Attentional bias, persecutory delusions and the self-concept. *Journal of Medical Psychology*, **67**, 53–66.

Margo, A., Hemsley, D.R. & Slade, P.D. (1981). The effects of varying auditory input on schizophrenic hallucinations. *British Journal of Psychiatry*, **139**, 122–127.

McGorry, P.D., Chanen, A., McCarthy, E., Van Riel, R., McKenzie, D. & Singh, B. (1991). Post-traumatic stress disorder following recent onset psychosis: An unrecognised postpsychotic syndrome. *Journal of Nervous and Mental Disease*, **179**, 253–258.

Morley, S. (1987). Modification of auditory hallucinations: Distraction vs attenuation. *Behavioural Psychotherapy*, **15**, 130–136.

Morrison, A.P. (1994). Cognitive behaviour therapy for auditory hallucinations without concurrent medication: A single case. *Behavioural and Cognitive Psychotherapy*, **22**, 259–264.

Morrison, A.P., Haddock, G. & Tarrier, N. (1995). Intrusive thoughts and auditory hallucinations: A cognitive approach. *Behavioural and Cognitive Psychotherapy*, **23**, 265–280.

Nayani, T.H. & David, A.S. (1996). The auditory hallucination: A phenomenological survey. *Psychological Medicine*, **26**, 177–189.

Nelson, H.E., Thrasher, S. & Barnes, T.R.E. (1991). Practical ways of alleviating auditory hallucinations. *British Medical Journal*, **302**, 307.

Padesky, C. (1994). Schema change processes in cognitive therapy. *Clinical Psychology and Psychotherapy*, **1**, 267–278.

Perry, A., Tarrier, N. & Morriss, R. (1995). Identification of prodromal signs and symptoms and early intervention in manic depressive psychosis patients: A case example. *Behavioural and Cognitive Psychotherapy*, **23**, 399- 409.

Persons, J.B. (1989). The advantages of studying psychological phenomena rather than psychiatric diagnoses. *American Psychologist*, **41**, 1252–1260.

Salkovskis, P.M. (1991). The importance of behaviour in the maintenance of anxiety and panic: A cognitive account. *Behavioural Psychotherapy*, **19**, 6–19.

Salkovskis, P.M. (1996). The cognitive approach to anxiety: Threat beliefs, safety-seeking behaviour, and the special case of health anxiety and obsessions. In P.M. Salkovskis (Ed.), *Frontiers of Cognitive Therapy*. New York: Guilford.

Tarrier, N. (1992). Management and modification of residual psychotic symptoms. In M. Birchwood & N. Tarrier (Eds), *Innovations in Psychological Management of Schizophrenia*. London: Wiley.

Tarrier, N., Beckett, R., Harwood, S., Baker, A., Yusupoff, L. & Ugarteburu, I. (1993). A trial of two cognitive behavioural methods of treating drug resistant residual psychotic symptoms in schizophrenic patients: I. Outcome. *British Journal of Psychiatry*, **162**, 524–532.

Wells, A. (1997). *Cognitive Therapy of Anxiety Disorders*. London: Wiley.

Wells, A. (1990). Panic disorder in association with relaxation-induced anxiety: An attentional training approach to treatment. *Behavior Therapy*, **21**, 273–280.

Wells, A., Clark, D.M., Salkovskis, P.M., Ludgate, J., Hackmann, A. & Gelder, M.G. (1994). Social phobia: The role of in-situation safety behaviours in maintaining anxiety and negative beliefs. *Behavior Therapy*, **24**, 163–171.

Wells, A. & Matthews, G. (1994). *Attention and Emotion*. London: LEA.

World Health Organisation (1973). *Report of the International Pilot Study of Schizophrenia (Vol. 1)*. Geneva: WHO.

Yusupoff, L. & Tarrier, N. (1996). Coping strategy enhancement for persistent hallucinations and delusions. In G. Haddock & P. Slade (Eds), *Cognitive Behavioural Interventions with Psychotic Disorders*. London: Routledge.

Chapter 10

LOW SELF-ESTEEM

Melanie J.V. Fennell

INTRODUCTION

Although low self-esteem has long been a focus of interest for psychological therapists, frequently encountered in clinical practice in association with a wide range of specific presenting problems, it is only recently that an explicit cognitive model of low self-esteem has been proposed, together with an associated programme of cognitive behavioural interventions (Fennell, 1997; Fennell, in preparation). Both model and treatment are intended for use within the framework of classical short-term cognitive therapy. However, they may also be modified in ways characteristic of long-term schema-focused work and helpfully applied with complex cases.

This chapter attempts to answer the question: What is complex about working cognitively with low self-esteem? Four main issues will be considered: (i) a cognitive model of low self-esteem will be briefly presented, and its links with cognitive models of emotional disorder and of personality disorder discussed; (ii) a cognitive behavioural treatment programme, deriving logically from the model, will be described and illustrated; (iii) variability in the role and expression of low self-esteem, and its impact on treatment, will be discussed; and (iv) adaptations to the delivery system, necessary for working with more complex, challenging cases, will be outlined with case examples.

DEFINING AND CONCEPTUALISING LOW SELF-ESTEEM

The first complexity, in attempting to work with low self-esteem within a cognitive framework, is the lack of an agreed definition or conceptualisation

* University of Oxford Department of Psychiatry, Oxford, UK

Treating Complex Cases: The Cognitive Behavioural Therapy Approach.
Edited by Nicholas Tarrier, Adrian Wells and Gillian Haddock.

of the problem. Recent developments in cognitive therapy may be considered as falling into two broad categories: investigations of the cognitive mechanisms central to specific disorders, and attempts to come to grips with the difficulties presented by patients meeting criteria for personality disorder.

Specific Axis I disorders

One line of research has consisted of highly specific clinical and experimental investigations of the precise cognitive mechanisms underlying particular diagnostic entities, and the development of standardised treatment programmes finely tuned to target those mechanisms in the most effective and efficient way. Examples include: Clark's model of panic (Clark, 1986) and Salkovskis's model of health anxiety (Salkovskis & Bass, 1997), both of which emphasise the central role of catastrophic misinterpretation of bodily sensations; Clark and Wells's model of social phobia (Clark & Wells, 1995), which highlights the role of self-focus and of safety behaviours designed to keep social behaviour within acceptable bounds; and Wells's model of generalised anxiety disorder (Wells, 1995), which suggests meta-cognitive processes (and in particular worry about worry) as prime targets for treatment.

Complex Long-term Cases and Personality Disorders

A second line of investigation has grown out of the clinical observation that short-term, classical cognitive therapy is not universally effective and indeed has little or no impact on a proportion of cases, including many patients who would meet formal diagnostic criteria for personality disorder, as defined for example by the Diagnostic and Statistical Manual (4th edition) of the American Psychiatric Association (DSM-IV, APA 1994). These observations have led to attempts to understand the nature of enduring cognitive structures and processes (e.g. Teasdale & Barnard, 1993), and to modify the cognitive therapy delivery system so as to work more effectively with chronic, treatment-resistant problems. Cognitive therapists working in this field, while sharing a fundamental cognitive conceptual framework together with common ideas about basic schema maintenance processes, have adopted somewhat different perspectives on these problems. A.T. Beck and his colleagues (Beck, Freeman & Associates, 1990) use the framework of DSM-IV as a basis for identifying developmental and maintaining processes specific to different personality disorders. Young (1990) in contrast, has developed his own system for categorising early maladaptive schemata and corresponding treatment interventions, based on extensive clinical observation. Padesky (1994) adopts a more idiographic view, emphasising the importance of identifying schemata in the language used by the client, focusing on maintenance processes common to a range of long-term, complex problems, and suggesting key interventions designed to target these (notably, continua). It is generally assumed that schema-focused interventions with complex long-term cases and personality disorders will require an extended timescale (18–24 months). It should be noted, however, that these new concepts and methods (unlike short-term classical cognitive therapy) remain, as yet, largely unevaluated by controlled outcome research.

Low self-esteem, unfortunately, does not quite fit into either of these categories, though work belonging to both is directly relevant to its understanding and treatment. On the one hand, it is not a specific Axis I diagnostic entity. In practice, we most commonly encounter it as a somewhat nebulous background difficulty, accompanying or underlying more precisely definable presenting problems. On the other hand, neither is it recognisable as a formal personality disorder, although I shall suggest that to a degree it fits comfortably within a schema framework. Equally, it does not necessarily require the extended 18–24 months of treatment often advocated for schema-focused cognitive therapy.

Definition

Granted these ambiguities, the essence of low self-esteem (what one might call the 'bottom line') may be understood as a schema in the sense that Bartlett originally defined them in his work on memory in the 1930s (Bartlett, 1932), that is, a generic cognitive representation of the self, which is derived from specific experiences, and which guides subsequent information processing and behaviour. Thus, the heart of low self-esteem may be seen as a learned, negative, global judgement about the self ('me as a person') which, once in place, shapes how the person thinks, feels and behaves on a day-to-day basis, and which in turn is maintained and indeed reinforced and strengthened by ongoing biases in cognitive processing and by maladaptive behaviour. The process of reciprocal feedback between high-level (schema) processing and immediate interpretation of events (negative automatic thoughts and meanings) produces a closed system, self-perpetuating and more or less resistant to change (c.f. Teasdale, Segal & Williams, 1994).

This definition of the 'bottom line' suggests a theoretical niche for low self-esteem, as a 'core belief' or 'unconditional assumption' which might act as a foundation for a range of other problems, some transitory, some long term. It has been suggested, for example, that low self-esteem may play a role in the development of depression (Andrews & Brown, 1995), eating disorders (Fairburn et al., 1987) and suicidal thinking and behaviour (Beck et al., 1990). Beck himself (cited in J.S. Beck, 1995, p.166) has suggested that negative self-concept lies at the heart of emotional disorders and has proposed that beliefs about the self, in conjunction with beliefs about other people, may be central to understanding some personality disorders (Beck, Freeman and Associates, 1990, pp.54–55). In Avoidant Personality Disorder, for example, the view of the self as socially inept and incompetent, in conjunction with a view of others as critical and demeaning, results in an understandable strategy of social anxiety, withdrawal and avoidance. Conversely, a view of the self as weak, helpless and incompetent, in conjunction with a view of others as nurturant and supportive, results in the strategy of care-seeking and social clinging characteristic of Dependent Personality Disorder. Similarly, a number of Young's (1990) Early Maladaptive Schemata directly express negative views of the self, for example, defectiveness/shame ('the feeling that one is defective, bad, unwanted, inferior or invalid in important respects; or that one would be unlovable to significant others if exposed'), dependence/incompetence ('belief that one is unable to handle one's *everyday responsibilities* in a competent manner') and failure ('the belief that one has failed, will inevitably fail, or is fundamentally inadequate stupid, inept, untalented, ignorant, lower in status, less successful than others, etc.'). Others, in contrast, may be viewed as strategies designed to compensate for perceived lack of worth, for example, subjugation ('excessive surrendering of control over one's behaviour, emotional expression and decisions'), unrelenting standards ('the underlying belief that one must strive to meet very high *internalised* standards of behaviour and competence'), and punitiveness ('the tendency to be angry, intolerant, harshly critical, punitive, and impatient with those people (including oneself) who do not meet one's expectations or standards'). The latter appear more akin to conditional dysfunctional assumptions than absolute beliefs about personal worth (see below).

Conceptualisation

The impact of the global negative view of the self at the heart of low self-esteem can be elaborated in a more detailed cognitive conceptualisation, which derives fairly straightforwardly from Beck's basic model of emotional disorder (Beck, 1979), and which suggests how the problem may develop and what cognitive and behavioural processes may maintain it. This model is illustrated in Figure 10.1. The model suggests that experience

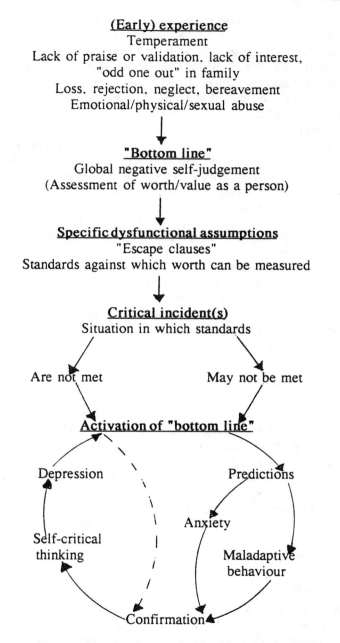

Figure 10.1   A cognitive model of low self-esteem. Reproduced with permission from Fennell, M.J.V. (1997). Low self-esteem: A cognitive perspective. *Behavioural and Cognitive Psychotherapy*, 25, 1–25.

(perhaps in interaction with temperament) leads to the formation of the 'bottom line', the global negative belief about the self. Since the 'bottom line' is perceived to be true, it leads in turn to the development of specific, conditional, dysfunctional assumptions or guidelines for living, standards of performance against which self-worth may be measured, and whose requirements must be met if self-esteem is to be maintained. Problems arise in situations where the person either fails, or might fail, to achieve the standards specified by the assumptions, thus placing self-esteem at risk. The model suggests that where in the perception of the patient the standards *might not be met* (i.e. there is a degree of uncertainty), anxiety results (the solid line in the diagram), characteristically followed by depression. Alternatively, where in the perception of the patient the standards *are not met* (i.e. there is no uncertainty), the result may be immediate depression (the dotted line in the diagram). In either case, a self-maintaining cycle is established which ensures continued activation of the 'bottom line'.

This model will now be elaborated in a case illustration (here and elsewhere, case details have been altered to protect the identity of the patient). Susan was referred by her General Practitioner for treatment of social anxiety at the age of 23. On assessment, she met formal diagnostic criteria (DSM-IV) for Social Phobia, Major Depressive Episode and Avoidant Personality Disorder.

Early Experience

Susan had always been the 'odd one out' in her family, and her sense of difference was exacerbated when her mother and chief advocate died when she was 10. She was not treated unkindly, but was a focus for affectionate teasing which continued into adulthood ('you're from a different planet, you are'). She began to experience difficulties in school in early adolescence after publicly 'making a complete fool of herself' when she was unable to complete a reading in the school assembly because sudden self-consciousness dried her mouth and made her mind go blank. She subsequently became increasingly nervous about speaking up or asking questions, with the result that she began to fall behind with her work. She eventually dropped out of school without obtaining any qualifications, which necessarily restricted the range of career opportunities available to her.

The 'Bottom Line'

Susan identified two core beliefs about herself: 'I'm weird' (apparently a product of her experiences in her family of origin) and 'I'm useless' (more a product of her school history). The first of these beliefs was primarily triggered in situations relating to social relationships, the second in situations where her performance might be evaluated.

Dysfunctional Assumptions

The assumptions associated with Susan's sense of weirdness were: 'If people find out what I am really like, they will not want anything to do with me' and 'I must be 100% OK all the time'. These dictated how Susan operated in social situations: her main objectives were to hide her true self, and to stick to a narrow range of social behaviours which she believed essential to continued acceptance by her friends. The main assumption related to her belief that she was useless was: 'Better not to try than to fail'. This meant that she had never felt able in adult life to make up for the deficits of her school education, or even to aim for more interesting (and thus more challenging) work. She was currently employed as cashier in a museum cafe, a position well below the promise of her early academic work.

Trigger Situations

Any social situation might trigger Susan's sense of being weird and unacceptable. In particular, situations where she did not know people well and where she felt an object of scrutiny were difficult for her. Her sense of being useless was relatively rarely triggered, since she deliberately avoided situations where her performance might be evaluated. However, she described inadvertent triggering by day-to-day events. For example, if the family washing machine broke down, she would automatically assume it must be her fault.

Predictions

In social situations, a sequence of negative predictions would run through Susan's mind. First, she believed that she would appear extremely nervous, and saw an image of herself in her mind's eye, noticeably shaking, sweating and panic-stricken. She assumed that people would notice how anxious she was, and that they would think there must be something wrong with her and want nothing further to do with her. In terms of performance, she predicted that she would make a mess of any job interview, and that if she attempted to return to education (which she would like to do) she would not be capable of carrying out the work successfully. Since changes in this area were something of a long-term project, addressed only in follow-up, the detail that follows will relate primarily to social anxiety, as this formed the main target for most treatment sessions.

Anxiety

Not surprisingly, given her predictions of what might happen, Susan felt extremely anxious in social situations. She felt shaky, her hands were clammy, her stomach churned, her heart raced, she felt lightheaded, tense and nervous, and found it hard to concentrate. As is often the case, her perception of these bodily symptoms, on which she tended to focus her attention, fuelled her conviction that she must be visibly anxious.

Maladaptive Behaviour

Some social situations Susan avoided outright, for example going anywhere unfamiliar, meeting new people, and going out if she was feeling less than '100% OK'. Other situations she would enter, albeit with difficulty, and would avoid specific aspects of interactions, such as for example talking openly about herself, initiating conversations, entering a room alone. In addition, she had developed a whole panoply of safety behaviours, designed to conceal her anxiety and make her look 'normal'. These included drinking alcohol in order to relax, holding her head with her hands in case it wobbled, gripping her glass tightly in case her hands shook, breathing deeply in order to relax, distracting herself, and making sure no silences were left in the conversation. Many of these strategies actually made things worse. For example, breathing deeply made her more lightheaded, distracting herself made it harder to concentrate, and holding her head did in fact look odd and had led people to ask on more than one occasion if she was alright.

Confirmation of the 'Bottom Line'

Avoidance and her extensive repertoire of safety behaviours prevented Susan from discovering whether anyone *did* actually notice her anxiety or react oddly to her natural self. Her assessment of the success of social occasions was based not on real observation of others' reactions to her, but on her own level of anxiety and impression of how she must be coming across. Since she was routinely anxious, this meant she saw most situations as confirmation of the truth of what she had always known, that is she was weird, and if other people realised this they would reject her. Even when things did go well, and she had direct evidence of her acceptability (for example, an invitation to a party or a request for a second date), she would discount the validity of these experiences on the basis that they were purely a product of the strict control she kept over herself, rather than of her own attractiveness. Thus no matter what the outcome of social situations, experience appeared to confirm the 'bottom line'.

Self-critical Thinking

Apparent failures in social situations would be followed for Susan by streams of self-critical thoughts: 'I'm really stupid', 'I'm a failure', 'I'm useless at everything', 'I'll never be able to get what I want out of life'. Not surprisingly, these thoughts had a major impact on her mood.

Depression

At the time of referral, and at one point during the course of treatment, Susan met formal criteria for Major Depression. She was sad and tearful, experienced a general loss of interest and pleasure, became low in energy despite much decreased levels of activity, lost her appetite, spent much of the day in bed, saw no one, and was preoccupied with thoughts of death and suicide. Once depressed, both negative predictions and self-critical thoughts became more frequent and more credible, thus producing a self-perpetuating vicious cycle which ensured continuing activation of the 'bottom line'.

AN OVERVIEW OF TREATMENT

The cognitive conceptualisation outlined above has immediate implications for treatment. Cognitive therapy potentially offers methods to target different elements of the developmental process and the maintaining cycle. Some of these derive from tried and tested cognitive therapies for depression and for anxiety disorders, while others derive from newer (and, as yet, less well validated) schema-focused cognitive therapy with complex long-term cases. Possible interventions are summarised in Figure 10.2, and are illustrated in relation to the treatment of Susan.

Classical short-term cognitive therapy normally begins with focused interventions designed to change thinking, behaviour and affect in the here and now, that is interventions designed to identify and change processes maintaining current problems. Given the nature of Susan's difficulties, treatment in early sessions contained elements from cognitive therapy for social anxiety (Clark & Wells, 1995), and elements from the cognitive treatment of depression (A.T. Beck et al., 1979). On the one hand, for example, she learned to test her predictions about social situations by dropping her safety behaviours while observing carefully how others responded. She discovered that people rarely showed any sign of being aware of how anxious she felt, and that when they did they were sympathetic and understanding rather than critical or rejecting. On the other hand, she learned depression-management skills including activity scheduling (in particular engagement in pleasurable activities), and how to question and answer negative automatic thoughts, including the hopeless thoughts that inclined her towards suicide. It became clear during the course of working in this way on immediate thoughts and behaviours that she routinely gave great weight to her weaknesses and failings while ignoring or screening out anything positive about herself. To correct this bias in perception, she made a list of positive qualities and began to monitor them in operation day by day. She obtained similar lists from a close friend and from her father and sisters, and was moved to discover how much they valued her. Changes in negative automatic thoughts and in behaviour began to break down Susan's conviction that she must at all costs hide her real self from

(Early) experience	
Historical test:	Are confirmatory data open to reinterpretation? Have disconfirmatory data been ignored or discounted?

'Bottom line'	
Meta-perspective:	Prejudice model
Correct perceptual bias:	Search for counter-evidence; positive data logs
Question interpretational bias:	Is supporting evidence open to reinterpretation?
Establish alternative self-representation:	Balanced view; realistic self-acceptance
Break down absolutes:	Continuum work

Dysfunctional assumptions	
Reformulation:	What standards/guidelines would be more realistic and helpful?

Negative automatic thoughts	
Correct perceptual bias:	Direct attention to assets/strengths
Correct interpretational bias:	Deal with specific examples of self-critical thinking, catastrophic predictions, etc., using Dysfunctional Thoughts Record

Symptoms	
Symptom management, behaviour change	Relaxation, distraction, increasing engagement in relaxing and pleasurable activities, time-management, graded task assignment, facing situations avoided, eliminating safety behaviours, etc.

Figure 10.2 Cognitive therapy for low self-esteem: An overview. Reproduced with permission from Fennell, M.J.V. (1997). Low self-esteem: A cognitive perspective. *Behavioural and Cognitive Psychotherapy*, 25, 1–25.

other people. Information gathered in the course of a series of experiments was used to question the validity of these standards and to formulate an alternative which then became a new guideline for living: 'I am OK the way I am. I won't get on with everyone, but that's normal'. Acting as if this was true (i.e. being her natural self, stripped of protective safety behaviours) and observing the outcome confirmed that the alternative was both more realistic and more helpful, and her belief in it rose from an initial 10% to 80%. The belief 'I am weird' decayed during this process without being specifically addressed. Later sessions began to focus more specifically on the 'bottom line' relating to performance: 'I'm useless'. The evidence for and against this belief was reviewed, with the result that Susan's belief in it fell from 100% to 10%. She formulated an alternative ('I have my faults like anyone else, I'm not perfect. But I'm no worse than anyone else either'), and with continued work her belief in this new perspective rose from 15% to 100%. To consolidate this change, she planned to write her new beliefs on flashcards, summarising the arguments in their favour on the other side. She would read these regularly (especially in situations which triggered the old system), continue to experiment with acting as if they were true, and deal with future negative predictions and self-critical thoughts using the Dysfunctional Thoughts Record. She was seen for a final follow-up session 9 months after completing treatment. She had left her job in order to re-enter full-time education and had found that, though initially extremely anxious, she had coped well with the work and with meeting new people. She reported an active social life, and was in a steady relationship with a new boyfriend. Her scores on standards measures indicated that she was no longer socially anxious or depressed.

TREATING LOW SELF-ESTEEM: A CONTINUUM OF DIFFICULTY

Susan stated that she had been 'unconfident' for as long as she could remember. She described a pattern of self-doubt and increasing social and occupational disability dating back to early adolescence and, as has already been mentioned, met formal diagnostic criteria for Avoidant Personality Disorder. That is, she had longstanding problems which significantly distressed her and had caused serious disruption in her life. Nonetheless, treatment was successfully completed within only 12 sessions spaced over four months. There were no major difficulties in establishing a friendly, collaborative therapeutic relationship. Susan was able to work in a systematic, focused way on her difficulties, readily took to the cognitive therapy rationale, and was assiduous and creative in carrying out between session self-help assignments. The sequence of interventions pursued was demonstrably effective (as evidenced by changes in belief ratings and in scores on standard measures of depression, anxiety and social phobia), and each built logically and helpfully on what had already been learned. Only a limited range of direct schema-change methods were required: review and reinterpretation of evidence consistent with the old belief, and an active search for counter-evidence (including a positive data log). These consolidated changes that had already occurred in the course of work on cognitive and behavioural processes maintaining Susan's current anxiety and depression and resulted in dramatic changes in her self-perspective and rules for living within a matter of weeks. Cognitive change (a more positive self-image) was directly reflected in observable changes in behaviour, both socially and in terms of career change, as well as in reported well-being. This case clearly illustrates that patients presenting with long-term problems, rooted in core beliefs about the self formed early in life (longstanding low self-esteem), do not *necessarily* require long-term treatment.

Self-esteem, however, is by no means a unitary phenomenon. On the contrary, it is highly variable in role, impact and severity. In some cases, it may operate primarily as an *aspect* of the presenting problem (for example, acute depression) and may resolve as the presenting problem is treated without requiring any direct interventions. In other cases, it may be primarily a *consequence* of the presenting problem (for example, a longstanding anxiety disorder or uncontrollable symptoms of post-traumatic stress). Here again, if the presenting problem is treated effectively, it may resolve without requiring any direct intervention (this may depend at least in part on the chronicity of the presenting problem, and the degree to which it has disrupted day-to-day functioning). Finally, low self-esteem may function as a *vulnerability factor* for a range of difficulties including depression, anxiety, relationship difficulties, problems with assertiveness, underachievement, eating disorders, substance misuse, and so on. In this case, dealing with the presenting problem on its own is unlikely to result in long-term change, and self-esteem is likely to require treatment in its own right.

Whatever the role of low self-esteem, its severity, its impact on the person's life, and the difficulty of treating it will vary, from relatively straightforward cases like Susan to cases where it may take some months for the patient even to *entertain the idea* that core beliefs about the self may not be entirely accurate. Low self-esteem may be viewed as falling on a continuum of difficulty (Fennell, in preparation). At one extreme lie people who experience occasional relatively mild self-doubt, often only in highly specific trigger situations (for example, an audition or job interview). The consequences are mainly affective (moments of uncertainty or apprehension), there is minimal interference with overt functioning, and negative predictions and self-critical thoughts are relatively easily dismissed in favour of a more realistic perspective on the self. The presence of such a perspective, even if it is not always immediately accessible, has been suggested as a key feature distinguishing between acute and chronic emotional disorders (e.g. Padesky, 1994). Because disability level is low, plentiful evidence is potentially available to support the more realistic perspective. At the other extreme lie people who experience constant self-flagellation, and whose self-hatred is triggered by even remote and trivial stimuli. These are characterised by intense affect (rage, despair, terror), considerable disability across many aspects of functioning (work, social relationships, intimate partnerships, self-care, leisure activities) and, often, self-harm and suicidal behaviour. The negative view of the self is perceived as a fact, not an opinion, and the extent of disability may provide plentiful 'evidence' to support it. More positive and realistic beliefs about the self may be not merely currently inaccessible, but non-existent.

Where on the continuum a particular patient falls may depend on a number of variables, including: the intensity of the negative view of the self (the degree to which the person believes it to be true); the intensity of affect aroused by activation of the belief; the degree of avoidance (cognitive, emotional and behavioural) associated with activation; the range of stimuli which lead to activation; the sensitivity (or threshold) for activation; the extent to which the belief leads to disability and disturbance in normal functioning; the system's chronicity; and, as already indicated, the presence or absence of an alternative more positive belief about the self. These in turn may be influenced, for example, by the aversiveness and consistency of formative experiences, the availability of rescue factors (such as one person in a generally hostile environment who valued the child), and the power and consistency of current maintaining factors (for example, abusive or highly critical close relationships, an absence of social support networks, or material difficulties such as poverty or unemployment).

ADAPTING THE COGNITIVE THERAPY DELIVERY SYSTEM FOR COMPLEX CASES

People who fall towards the more difficult extreme of the continuum are unlikely to fulfil the assumptions of classical short-term cognitive therapy, as outlined for example by Young (1990) and by Safran and his colleagues (Safran et al., 1990). Young suggests that in order to do well with short-term cognitive therapy, patients must: have access with minimal training to emotions, thoughts and images; have definable problems that can be worked on in a focused way; be motivated to carry out self-help assignments; be able to form a collaborative therapeutic relationship, so that problems in the relationship are not the main focus of treatment; and present with problems which are open to change through empirical analysis, experimentation and practice. Safran et al. (1990) propose similar factors and add: acceptance of personal responsibility for change; compatibility with the cognitive rationale (c.f. Fennell & Teasdale, 1987) on the extent to which initial acceptance of the rationale predicts response to cognitive therapy for depression); chronicity of presenting problems; degree of disruption produced in therapy by 'security operations' (processes designed to maintain the *status quo*); ability to remain task-oriented; and general optimism about therapy.

Patients at the extreme of difficulty are more likely to describe and demonstrate belief systems which, although similar in content to those of easier patients, have an intensity and comprehensiveness more characteristic of personality disorder when viewed from a cognitive therapy perspective. That is, they are 'overgeneralised, inflexible, imperative and resistant to change' (A.T. Beck et al., 1990, p.29), and 'part of normal, everyday processing of information' (ibid., p.32) rather than active only under special conditions. They may be recognisable because patients say they have 'always been this way' and view their problems as an integral part of themselves ('This is me' as opposed to 'This is an opinion I hold'). Alternatively, their effects may emerge in treatment, with or without the patient's awareness (for example, habitual non-compliance, widespread and tenacious avoidance, repeated and more or less insuperable blocks to progress, or major difficulties in the therapeutic relationship)

As a general principle, the relatively straightforward treatment programme outlined above may remain in essence similar in content no matter where on the continuum the patient falls. That is, it will include interventions designed to change the bottom line, to revise current guidelines for living and to change thinking, affect and behaviour on a day-to-day basis. Treatment interventions characteristic of short-term work have their equivalents within schema-focused cognitive therapy, as is illustrated in Figure 10.3. However, the order of interventions, the range of interventions used, and the time required for particular interventions to 'bite' will vary according to where on the continuum a particular patient falls. Some ways in which the cognitive therapy delivery system may have to be modified for effective work with more difficult patients will now be discussed and illustrated with comparisons between the treatment of Susan and the treatment of another patient who proved to be more challenging.

The Order of Events

In classical short-term cognitive therapy, work on specific processes maintaining current problems usually precedes dealing with more global issues (conditional dysfunctional assumptions and core beliefs). Susan's treatment illustrates the normal order of events. Her immediate difficulties clearly met DSM-IV diagnostic criteria for social phobia and depression. As described above, the processes maintaining both problem areas were straightforwardly and successfully treated with a combination of cognitive and behavioural methods. The work on social anxiety and on depression provided valuable information about Susan's beliefs about herself, and about the dysfunctional assumptions that guided her behaviour. It also began the process of chipping away at those beliefs and assumptions, in

Classical	Schema-focused
Cognitive model of emotional disorder Elucidate maintaining cycles Conceptualisation	Educate patient about schemata Prejudice model Conceptualisation
Identify and monitor negative automatic thoughts	Identify schemata, monitor their operation
Goal-setting Theory 1/2 Search for a balanced view	Identify alternative positive schema

Weekly Activity Schedule
List and monitor qualities, assets,
   skills and strengths
Search for evidence against negative
   automatic thoughts
	Positive data log
	Search for evidence consistent with
	   alternative positive schema

Re-evaluate evidence favouring negative
   automatic thoughts
	Re-evaluate evidence in favour of
	   schemata
	Historic test, life review

Identify thinking errors (process)	Identify ignoring, discounting, distorting, making exceptions (process)
Question black-and-white thinking Pie charts	Continuum work (adaptive continua, criteria continua, orthogonal continua)
Dysfunctional Thoughts Record	Core belief worksheet Schema flashcard Schema diary

Carry out and record behavioural
   experiments
	Carry out and record behavioural
	   experiments
	Predictions log, predictions diary
	Acting against the belief

Imagery work (current issues)	Imagery work (including reframing
	   painful memories and childhood
	   experiences)

Roleplay, reverse roleplay Reliving recent traumas Exposure	Psychodrama Reliving childhood experience Point-counter-point

Figure 10.3 Classical and schema-focused cognitive therapy: equivalent change procedures

that behavioural experiments designed to test specific predictions could subsequently be used to reconsider the validity of the broader issues. These became a focus in their own right towards the end of treatment at a point where more specific and concrete interventions had already produced substantial reductions in both anxiety and depression.

However, there are times when systematic, focused cognitive behavioural work on presenting problems proves impossible in the early stages because of the strength and rigidity of the patient's beliefs about the self, or because these beliefs are expressed through multiple (and thus confusing) presenting problems. In this case, from the outset 'schematic work is at the heart of the therapeutic endeavour' (A.T. Beck et al., 1990, p. 8). Lesley, a young woman of 25, came for treatment with a primary problem of health anxiety. Like Susan, she was both anxious and depressed. She stated that her goal was to become less preoccupied with worries about illness and disability. She began assiduously to monitor her concerns on a day-to-day basis, using the Dysfunctional Thoughts Record (DTR), and to carry out behavioural experiments designed to test her ideas that inexplicable body sensations were necessarily a sign of disease. Despite her diligence, however, her anxiety remained high. Broadening the focus of self-monitoring revealed that anxiety about her health was the tip of a substantial iceberg. A range of other problems emerged, including difficulties in her relationship with her boyfriend, conflict with her parents, extreme performance anxiety, obsessive-compulsive symptoms (especially relating to the preparation of food), lack of assertiveness, fears and phobias (for example of driving, and of being alone at night), and a pattern of sporadic overdrinking and binge eating. It now seemed unsurprising that change in one area had left her distress largely untouched.

When Lesley and her therapist examined her DTRs, recurrent themes emerged. They hypothesised that these might reflect global beliefs about herself, others and life which could be underpinning the full range of her difficulties. Examining the development of Lesley's problems revealed a global sense of vulnerability to harm which dated back to childhood. She felt that her parents had never adequately protected her or responded to her needs. Rather they had been distant, critical and unforgiving, and indeed remained so into young adulthood. She had many vivid memories of being distressed as a child, and of her parents ignoring her, sending her to her room or telling her to pull herself together. She had had a number of quite serious childhood illnesses, some of which had required lengthy and uncomfortable treatment, and felt that these had been minimised by her parents who had been reluctant to seek adequate medical help, and tended to expect her simply to put up with her symptoms and stop making a fuss. As a child, Lesley felt that her parents' lack of care and attention must reflect some inadequacy in herself and concluded: 'I am worthless' and 'No-one cares about me'. Since she saw herself as lacking adequate care and protection, she also believed 'I am vulnerable'. It seemed crucial that she be on her guard against possible danger at all times, and she had developed a set of dysfunctional assumptions around the need to look after herself and to take all possible steps to avert harm on all fronts, for example, 'I must always be top', 'I must always do what is expected of me, or I will be rejected', 'Any symptom could be a sign that something is seriously wrong', and (more generally) 'Unless I am extremely careful all the time, bad things will happen'.

Once this system of absolute and conditional beliefs had been elucidated, Lesley's many difficulties made perfect sense. This in itself was helpful to her because she had been feeling that to have difficulties in so many areas must be a sign of gross abnormality, and she was becoming increasingly hopeless about the possibility of change. Understanding the origins of her beliefs helped her to grasp that they were the understandable product of what had happened to her ('this is a result of my experience', rather than 'this is me'). Additionally, she began to feel more hopeful because she could now see that, rather than a mass of unconnected problems each of which would need to be worked on in turn (a discouraging prospect), she had a small number of core beliefs which expressed themselves in many ways, and that work on any one problem area could be generalised to others. That is, exploring the past not only led to insight about the development of her problems, but also illuminated the present, and had direct implications for action. In particular, the cognitive and behavioural work on her current anxieties became a means of examining the validity of her belief that she was vulnerable. At the same time, she began to question the evidence for her worthlessness and to collect data that were inconsistent with this belief.

In Susan's case, the work on central beliefs about herself grew naturally out of more specific work on cognitive and behavioural factors maintaining her current difficulties. With Lesley, in contrast, progress on presenting problems was not possible until her beliefs about her worthlessness and vulnerability had been elucidated, and some distance achieved by understanding their origins and mapping out their range of influence. Once this had been done, specific changes in everyday thinking, affect and behaviour began to occur.

Increasing Awareness of Positive Qualities

The speed and ease with which patients can acknowledge positive qualities and become routinely aware of them on a day-to-day basis varies considerably. As is characteristic of people with low self-esteem, Susan was extremely vigilant for evidence of her own weaknesses and flaws, while conversely screening out any information that did not fit with her prevailing view of herself. This *perceptual bias* meant that she tended to recall and dwell on negative aspects of any situation, while experiences that might otherwise have led her to revise her poor opinion of herself were either not perceived or quickly forgotten. For a homework assignment, Susan began a list of her qualities and strengths. Although the task felt awkward, a follow-up discussion with her therapist led to a solid workable list of 10 qualities. Further homework consisted of recording three specific examples of these qualities in action on a day-to-day basis, using the Weekly Activity Schedule which Susan was already familiar with from working on her depression. Additionally, she obtained similar lists from a close friend, her father and her sisters. Her family teased her a little about the assignment but nonetheless, when it came to the point, took it seriously and used it as an opportunity to express their affection for her and the value they placed on her. This helped to counter her idea that being different must also mean being unacceptable. Within 2–3 weeks Susan reported having a more balanced view of herself. She was now recording five examples of positive qualities daily. The written record was dropped on an experimental basis, to see how far Susan was able automatically to notice good things about herself, and indeed proved to be redundant. Susan could now appreciate her assets without a written prompt.

In contrast, Lesley was at first unable to list any positive qualities independently. Within session, even with considerable help from the therapist, she was able at first only to identify three qualities in all, and had significant doubts about all of them. It was suggested that she obtain a similar list from someone she loved and trusted. This proved to be a bad move. Lesley asked her mother, whose response was to say that she would not waste time on such a thing, as Lesley was already far too big headed. This experience graphically illustrated the roots of Lesley's negative beliefs about herself. However, it was also extremely painful and would have been better avoided. Subsequently, Lesley obtained a loving and respectful list from her boyfriend. However, she still had to work hard to believe that he meant what he said ('He just doesn't want to hurt me'). Over several weeks of careful record-keeping and discussion with the therapist, Lesley's own list grew and she became gradually able to notice and record examples of her qualities on a daily basis. However, although she persisted with the task and her records were regularly reviewed in session, very little change seemed to follow in her view of herself. It was only six months later, during the course of a discussion on another topic, that she announced casually that she thought she had faults and weaknesses like any other person, but was basically probably as good as anyone else. This statement, made in passing, was picked up by the therapist and contrasted with her original perception of herself as 'worthless'. Both therapist and patient then realised that a gradual process of change had been taking place. Her statement became the basis for a new, more positive belief: 'I am as good as anyone else', and the record of assets became the basis for a broader record of information supporting this new belief (positive data log).

Reviewing Evidence for and against the 'Bottom Line'

The impact of questioning and reinterpreting experiences ('evidence') that appear to support the negative view of the self will also vary from patient to patient. This may be true for the painfulness of the experience, the range of 'evidence' that needs to be considered (especially the extent to which past experiences must be taken into account), and the difficulty of accessing alternative interpretations. Often, change is relatively easy when the bulk of the 'evidence' is in the present, and relatively difficult when the bulk of the 'evidence' is in the distant past, a product of the child's view, and associated with vivid memories and intense distress.

Susan began the process of re-evaluating her central beliefs about herself as soon as change in cognitive and behavioural maintaining factors was solidly under way. The idea that she was 'weird' no longer had any power, but she still believed quite strongly that she was 'useless'. The evidence supporting this idea was identified and examined in the course of two sessions with the therapist, together with two homework assignments. Most of the evidence was in the recent past or the present day (for example, being anxious, having a dead end job, and having failed to pursue a college education). Much of this could be reinterpreted as a result of understandable anxiety, which she had worked hard to resolve, showing considerable courage and intelligence. She also became aware that she would be less critical of another person in her situation, and this helped her to see that encouragement and building on her strengths would be more useful strategies than labelling herself as useless. This understanding helped Susan to deal more effectively with specific self-critical thoughts occurring on a day-to-day basis, and became the basis for her blueprint for future action as the end of treatment approached. Because by this stage in treatment her anxiety and depression were low, the process of examining her beliefs aroused more curiosity and determination to get to grips with things than distress. As has already been described, her belief in the old perspective reduced radically in a matter of weeks, while her belief in the new perspective increased correspondingly.

Lesley on the other hand reported a lifetime of evidence consistent with her belief that she was worthless. Vivid and painful memories of being ignored, discounted and criticised were plentiful, from the earliest childhood up to the present day. The sheer weight of her past experience led the therapist to suggest a 'life review' or 'historical test' as an appropriate strategy. This would involve on the one hand identifying 'evidence' that appeared to support the belief and questioning its validity, and on the other hand actively seeking out experiences that might be inconsistent with the belief. This work ran in parallel with the work on identifying and monitoring positive qualities described above, and with cognitive and behavioural work on current anxieties and on relationship difficulties. Lesley's life was divided into five-year chunks. In each chunk, all the evidence apparently supporting the idea that she was worthless was listed. Each item was then explored, using guided discovery, to determine whether there might be any way of understanding it other than that it must reflect her lack of worth as a person. For example, the validity of blaming herself for her parents' behaviour was questioned. Lesley could see that if she were to observe another child being treated in the way that she had been, she would unhesitatingly have attributed responsibility to the parents. This idea assumed personal relevance when she recalled that her parents' behaviour towards her younger brother had in fact been similar, though as a physically healthy and temperamentally rumbustuous child he had attracted less disapproval than she had. The story of Cinderella became a metaphor for how she had been treated. Careful exploration unearthed memories of interactions with other people which were clearly not at all consistent with the idea that Lesley was worthless; for example, a doctor she had seen over some time who had always been kind and sensitive, a friend she had had at primary school, and an aunt with whom she had had two happy holidays. For each five-year period, the evidence favouring 'worthlessness' was summarised together with the new interpretations, and counter-evidence was listed. Finally, a new conclusion was formulated for each period, for example, 'My parents' behaviour cannot have been my fault. As a baby and a little girl, I deserved to be loved and cared for, and in fact other people *were* kind to me and loved me' (0–5). Lesley's final conclusion, arrived at only after a number of months of steady work, has already been mentioned above.

This rather dry account by no means reflects the emotional tone of this change procedure. Accessing numerous agonisingly painful memories of criticism, neglect and rejection aroused storms of rage and despair. This high level of emotion was also difficult for the therapist to manage comfortably. Sessions needed to be structured so as to allow time for 'grounding' before Lesley went home, and so as to ensure that work on current difficulties and on increasing awareness of positive qualities continued in parallel. Additionally, purely verbal and behavioural interventions were not always effective, especially in accessing and reframing early experiences. Experiential techniques (for example, imagery work and roleplay) were included in many sessions.

The Therapeutic Relationship

With patients falling towards the difficult end of the continuum, problems in the relationship between therapist and patient are more likely, and likely to be more persistent. This may repeatedly disrupt the flow of therapy, or may even prevent the formation of a workable therapeutic collaboration. In short-term classical cognitive therapy, establishing and maintaining a warm, collaborative therapeutic relationship is viewed as a crucial prerequisite for effective application of technical interventions. In cognitive therapy with long-term complex cases, the therapeutic relationship may be used in a more elaborated way. Firstly, responses to the therapist are valuable sources of information about the patient's belief systems and ways of operating interpersonally ('open windows into the patient's private world', A.T .Beck et al., 1990, p. 65). Secondly, the therapeutic relationship may also function as a major vehicle for change, a 'schema laboratory' where ideas about relationships may be tested out in relative safety, or an opportunity for the patient to experience (for example) warmth, consistency and caring that were missing in earlier relationships. With Susan the therapeutic relationship was never a problem and was never discussed. Lesley on the other hand, when giving feedback at the end of treatment, commented that the therapist's acceptance of her many problems, her 'violent' emotions, and her slow progress had been a crucial part of her experience of therapy which in itself had directly countered her beliefs that she was worthless and that no one cared.

It is important that patients' problematic responses to therapist and therapy are understood in terms of the overall conceptualisation of the case. Ideally, the conceptualisation should allow the therapist to predict difficulties that may arise (Persons, 1989). Another patient, for example, believed herself to be 'incapable'. The therapist had not thought carefully about how this might impact on treatment, and was astonished and somewhat wrong-footed when a casual mention of the number of sessions remaining was greeted by the patient bursting into tears. It is also important for therapists to be aware of their own thoughts and feelings, and the beliefs that underpin them, when working with more difficult patients. Lesley's therapist, for example, was horrorstruck initially by the intensity of her emotions, though managing to preserve a calm front. Reflection led to the realisation that intense emotion led to catastrophic predictions that Lesley would fall apart and it would be the therapist's fault. These thoughts were based on beliefs that extreme emotion was dangerous, and that the therapist was 100% responsible for patients' well-being. Dealing with these ideas was helpful and allowed the therapist to remain with Lesley's emotions and help her to work with them, rather than backing off. Finally, it should be emphasised that the purpose of a focus on the therapeutic relationship is to elucidate (and if appropriate change) how the patient operates in the world outside the therapy session, and not an end in itself (except in so far as relationship difficulties are preventing treatment from progressing).

CONCLUSION

The points elaborated above illustrate a number of shifts in emphasis advocated in the treatment of long-term complex cases and personality disorder, which are entirely relevant to work with longstanding low self-esteem, especially where this is accompanied by high levels of disability and by significant interpersonal difficulties. These are: an increased focus on central beliefs or schemata, even in the early stages of therapy; the importance of an individualised developmental conceptualisation in mapping complex problems and elucidating the links between past with present; the importance for the patient of achieving a meta-perspective on dysfunctional beliefs ('this is an opinion, not a fact'); the need for persistence when change is slow and variable; the importance of affect, and of experiential methods which target it directly; and the need to consider the therapeutic relationship, including the therapist's own thoughts and beliefs.

Despite these changes in emphasis, however, cognitive therapy for difficult patients with longstanding low self-esteem retains characteristics integral to classical short-term cognitive therapy. These include: a collaborative relationship in which the therapist is open and explicit about what he or she is doing and why, thus ensuring that the patient remains an informed consumer, actively engaged in the process of therapy; a focus on presenting problems and on producing changes not only in beliefs but also in thoughts, feelings and observable behaviours on a day-to-day basis; an empirical flavour, where cognitions are viewed as hypotheses open to question and to test through systematic change procedures, and where the interest in experimental and clinical research remains, though as yet in its infancy (studies of the impact of schema-focused interventions are urgently required); linked with this a requirement that change should be measurable and measured; and, finally, an emphasis on self-help assignments and on empowering patients to take charge of their own lives.

REFERENCES

American Psychiatric Association (APA) (1994). *Diagnostic and Statistical Manual of Mental Disorders* (4th edn). Washington, DC: Author.

Andrews, B. & Brown, G.W. (1995). Stability and change in low self-esteem: The role of psychosocial factors. *Psychological Medicine*, **25**, 23–31.

Bartlett, F.C. (1932). *Remembering*. Cambridge: Cambridge University Press.

Beck, A.T., Freeman, A. & Associates (1990). *Cognitive Therapy of Personality Disorders*. New York: Guilford.

Beck, A.T., Rush, A.J., Shaw, B.F. & Emery, G. (1979). *Cognitive Therapy of Depression*. New York: Guilford.

Beck, A.T., Steer, R.A., Epstein, N. & Brown, G. (1990). The Beck Self-Concept Test. *Psychological Assessment: A Journal of Consulting and Clinical Psychology*, **2**, 191–197.

Beck, J.S. (1995). *Cognitive Therapy: Basics and Beyond*. New York: Guilford.

Clark, D.M. (1986). A cognitive approach to panic. *Behaviour Research and Therapy*, **24**, 461–470.

Clark, D.M. & Wells, A. (1995). A cognitive model of social phobia. In R.Heimberg, M. Liebowitz, D.A.Hope and F.R. Schneier (Eds), *Social Phobia: Diagnosis, Assessment and Treatment*. New York: Guilford.

Fairburn, C.G., Kirk, J., O'Connor, M., Anastasiades, P. & Cooper, P.J. (1987). Prognostic factors in bulimia nervosa. *British Journal of Clinical Psychology*, **26**, 223–224.

Fennell, M.J.V. (1997). Low self-esteem: A cognitive perspective. *Behavioural and Cognitive Psychotherapy*, **25**, 1–25.

Fennell, M.J.V. (in preparation) Low self-esteem. In K. Hawton, P.M. Salkovskis, J. Kirk and D.M. Clark (Eds), *Cognitive Behaviour Therapy for Psychiatric Problems: A Practical Guide* (2nd edn). Oxford: Oxford University Press.

Fennell, M.J.V. & Teasdale, J.D. (1987). Cognitive therapy for depression: Individual differences and the process of change. *Cognitive Therapy and Research*, **11**, 253–271.

Padesky, C.A. (1994). Schema change processes in cognitive therapy. *Clinical Psychology and Psychotherapy*, **1**, 267–278.

Persons, J. (1989). *Cognitive Therapy in Practice: A Case Formulation Approach*. New York: Norton.

Safran, J.D., Segal, Z.V., Shaw, B.F. & Vallis, T.M. (1990). Patient selection for short term cognitive therapy. In J.D. Safran and Z.V. Segal, *Interpersonal Process in Cognitive Therapy*. Northdale, NJ: Jason Aronson.

Salkovskis, P.M. & Bass, C. (1997). Hypochondriasis. In D.M. Clark and C.G. Fairburn (Eds), *Science and Practice of Cognitive Therapy*. Oxford: Oxford University Press.

Teasdale, J.D. & Barnard, P. (1993). *Affect, Cognition and Change: Remodelling Depressive Thought*. Hove: Lawrence Erlbaum.

Teasdale, J.D., Segal, Z.V. & Williams, J.M.G. (1994). How does cognitive therapy prevent depressive relapse and why should attentional control (mindfulness) training help? *Behaviour Research and Therapy*, **33**, 25–39.

Wells, A. (1995). Meta-cognition and worry: A cognitive model of generalised anxiety disorder. *Behavioural and Cognitive Psychotherapy*, **23**, 301–320.

Young, J. (1990). *Cognitive Therapy for Personality Disorders: A Schema-focused Approach*. Sarasota, FL: Professional Resource Exchange.

Chapter 11

SHAME AND HUMILIATION IN THE TREATMENT OF COMPLEX CASES

Paul Gilbert*

Shame used to be considered the 'hidden emotion' in psychopathology and its destructive consequences were often missed in psychotherapy (Lewis, 1987a). In the last ten years, however, there has been an explosion of research and theory on shame with confirmation that shame can be highly pathogenic (e.g. Kaufman, 1989; Lewis, 1992; Nathanson, 1994a; Tangney & Fischer, 1995). This chapter explores some of this research, considers the value of therapeutic awareness of shame and ways of uncovering and working with shame.

THE COGNITIVE DOMAINS OF EXTERNAL AND INTERNAL SHAME

In the 1920s, Cooley coined the term the 'looking glass self'. This refers to the way we judge and feel about ourselves according to how we think others judge and feel about us. The looking glass self had three cognitive aspects: 'The imagination of our appearance to the other person; the imagination of his judgement of that appearance; and some sort of self feeling, such as pride or mortification' (as quoted by Scheff, 1988, p. 398). Theories of shame have a similar focus. These can be separated into internal and external domains.

Being Judged Negatively by Others

This concerns negative judgements that others have made (or will make)

* Mental Health Research Unit, Kingsway Hospital, Derby, UK

Treating Complex Cases: The Cognitive Behavioural Therapy Approach.
Edited by Nicholas Tarrier, Adrian Wells and Gillian Haddock.

about the self. One is an *object* of scorn, contempt or ridicule to others. One has been disgraced; judged and found wanting in some way. Gilbert (1997a) suggested the term *external shame* because the focus is on the outside world; of how one is seen by others or how one lives 'in the eyes of others' (Goss, Gilbert & Allan, 1994; Mollon, 1984; Retzinger, 1991; Scheff, 1988). Lewis (1992) has argued that it is in becoming 'an object' for others that our potential to feel shame begins in earnest. The experience of external shame depends on how important the views of others are to the self. For example, if one is judged as inadequate and useless by (say) a nazi-group, this may be less upsetting than being seen as useless and inadequate by other therapists. Thus, external shame is influenced by cognitions about the desirability of the judgements of others.

Generally, people try to present themselves in a positive light (Leary, 1995): that is to be seen as attractive to others. It matters little what type of relationship one considers, be it being chosen for the football team, as a lover, or to head up a therapy unit, people like to feel they have been chosen by others because others see them as good, able and talented. Shame is related to evaluations that one cannot create positive images in the eyes of others; one will not be chosen, will be found lacking in talent, ability, appearance, and so on; one will be passed over, ignored or actively rejected (Gilbert, 1998).

Negative Self-evaluations

This relates to the subjective sense of self (Lewis, 1992). Gilbert (1997a) referred to this as *internal shame*, derived from how the self judges the self. Thus, one sees oneself as bad, flawed, worthless, unattractive. When negative self-evaluation is the key focus of a measure of shame, factor analysis suggests that inferiority is a core factor of internal shame (e.g. Cook, 1993, 1996; Goss, Gilbert & Allan, 1994; see Harder, 1995; Tangney, 1995, for discussion of measurement issues). Internal shame often relates to an awareness of falling short of some internalised ideal or standard.

As is not uncommon in psychology, different research areas and theories have sprung up with no recognition of closely associated ones. Thus, the large shame literature (e.g. see Tangney & Fischer, 1995) has developed apace but with hardly any linkage with the cognitive literature on self-schema. Similarly in Segal and Blatt's (1993) important edition on self-schema related to various emotional disorders, the concept of shame (and guilt) barely gets a mention. It would, of course, be too great a task to try to knit these two literatures here (see Gilbert, 1992a,b) but it is important to note that the concept of negative self-evaluation is a central core concept to both. In the cognitive literature negative self-evaluation is linked to vulnerability for many disorders (Segal & Blatt, 1993) in particularly, depression (Beck et al., 1979; Segal & Muran, 1993). And depression has been strongly linked to shame (Gilbert, 1992a,b; Tangney, Burggraf & Wagner, 1995).

Attention

The idea that attention can be focused internally on the self (private self-consciousness), and/or externally, on what others might think of the self (public self-consciousness), is now well established in social psychology (e.g. see Gibbons, 1990, for a review). Many researchers see the attention of shame to be inwardly focused, involving a heightened self-consciousness as one becomes acutely aware of failings, flaws and deficits in the self. Tangney and Fischer (1995) see shame as essentially a self-conscious affect.

While internal and external shame are often highly correlated, they need not always be so. For example, a personal awareness of one's flaws may lead to little anxiety unless one believes that these will be exposed (Lewis, 1992). Another example is that a recognition that others find a person's behaviour shameful, but the person him/herself does not, can arise in anti-social behaviour. A paedophile acknowledged that others see the use of children as sexual objects as bad yet he had little internal shame for it but many justifications. Efforts to shame him in prison seemed to have done little except convince him to be more careful not to be caught (conceal his activities). He could acknowledge that his behaviour brought him severe social sanctions but not that he was internally shamed by the abusing itself. External shame requires an ability to anticipate how others might judge a behaviour or personal attribute. When behaviour is controlled purely by external shame, then if a person thinks they might 'avoid discovery', they may engage in a socially shamed behaviour (e.g. visiting prostitutes).

Partly because most shame research has been driven by affect theory (Tangney & Fischer, 1995) and not cognitive theory, to date most research measures do not clearly separate internal from external shame. Hence, Mascolo and Fischer (1995), in agreement with many other researchers, suggest that shame is generated by appraisals of having failed to live up to the standards of worth in the eyes of others and operates to 'highlight behaviours that threaten honour and self worth' (p. 68). Goss, Gilbert and Allan (1994) and Allan, Gilbert and Goss, (1994) attempted to measure separately 'negative self-judgements' from judgements of 'how one thinks others judge the self'. In students these judgements are commonly highly correlated ($p > 0.8$) indicating that if one judges oneself negatively one thinks others will too. However, it is possible to be aware of the possibility of (external) shame, and thus to conceal from others that which could be shameful, but not feel internally bad about such attributes (e.g. as in the examples given above, in some paranoid patients, and also in those who believe they must risk the scorn or even persecution of others to push forward a new idea, and so on).

Social Comparison

Because we often take our standards and ideals from other people (Suls & Wills, 1991) social comparison can also be a key cognition in shame. Two central dimensions are 'inferior–superior' and 'same–different' (Allan & Gilbert, 1995; Gilbert, 1992a). As noted above, evaluations of being inferior to others have long been associated with shame. Brewin and Furnham (1986) measured 'preattributional variables' in depression and found depressives often failed to reveal negative experiences to others because of a fear of being seen as different and scorned. In the well known experiments of Asch (1956) individuals could be made to change their (accurate) judgement of the relative length of a line in the face of others who gave a different judgement. Scheff (1988) argues that this is the result of fear of being seen as different and invoking scorn and being shamed. He notes:

> A reaction that occurred both in independent and yielding subjects was the fear that they were suffering from a defect and that the study would disclose this defect: 'I felt like a silly *fool*. ... A question of being a *misfit*...they'd think I was queer. It made me seem weak eyed or weak headed, like a black sheep. (p. 403, italics added)

Social comparison and the anticipation of how others will evaluate and respond to negative information about the self also plays a crucial role in acts of revelation. It is now known that keeping secrets (e.g. about previous abuse) can be psychologically costly, but revelation is not without its risks—especially if it results in rejection (Kelly & McKillop, 1996). One of the advantages of group therapy may be its providing opportunities for helpful social comparisons and sharing of negative information about the self (Yalom, 1985).

Focus of Shame

The precise focus of shame can vary greatly (Gilbert, 1997a,b; Kaufman, 1989). For example, shame can be focused on the body as in those who have been sexually abused (Andrews, 1995) or have diseases or disfigurements (Lazare, 1986). Certain types of medical examination (e.g. pelvic examinations) can be experienced as embarrassing and people may avoid them (Leary & Kowalski, 1995). Shame can be focused on feelings and emotions—we can be ashamed of (say) homosexual feelings or experiences of losing emotional control. Shame can be focused on achievement failures (e.g. failing an examination) or specific behaviours—such as being discovered to have had an affair. Shame can also be internalised from being a member of a discredited social group. Children of parents found guilty of war crimes have also suffered much shame (e.g. Serney, 1990). Hence, shame can be felt for other reasons apart from personal actions.

Emotions

The emotions and feelings that are associated with shame are complex (Gilbert, 1998). Shame has been called the affect of inferiority (Kaufman, 1989). Tangney (1995) points out that shame-proneness is essentially a proneness to experience certain types of *emotional states*. These emotions may be anxiety related but need not be. They can also be emotions of contempt, frustration, disgust and even hatred. For example, a person who feels shame because of previous sexual abuse may feel a number of emotions about the self and her/his body—including hatred and disgust. Indeed, some theorists suggest that 'disgust' is the primary affect underpinning shame (Power & Dalgleish, 1997). At the advent of shame (e.g. reaction to a harsh criticism or interpersonal rejection) a person may experience a sudden shift in affect, a flush or wave of anxiety or anger (Retzinger, 1991). The person may find their mind going blank with a loss of confidence and freedom of thought and behaviour, sometimes experienced as a sudden inhibition or paralysis (Lewis, 1986; Tangney, 1995).

Behaviour

In regard to specific behaviours there is general agreement that shame commonly motivates escape behaviour, hiding and concealment (Lindsay-Hartz, de Rivera & Mascolo, 1995; Tangney, 1995). Shame has been linked to psychobiological and behavioural mechanisms which underpin it (Gilbert, 1989, 1992a, 1997a; Gilbert & McGuire, 1998); an important one being submissive behaviour. Gilbert, Pehl and Allan (1994) found shame to be correlated with fear of negative evaluation and submissive behaviour (see also Allan, Gilbert & Goss, 1994; Goss, Gilbert & Allan, 1994). Keltner (1995) found shame to have distinctive facial expressions (different from embarrassment) typical of submissive displays (see also Dixon et al., submitted). At points of shame there can be various involuntary behavioural changes such as blushing, mind going blank, eye gaze avoidance, postural change, change in speech rhythm and so forth (Dixon et al., submitted; Keltner, 1995; Retzinger, 1991).

DISTINCTIONS BETWEEN GUILT, EMBARRASSMENT AND SOCIAL ANXIETY

There are a number of other social emotions with which shame is often confused or overlaps.

Guilt

Guilt is not related to global self-evaluations of badness or worthlessness but to more specific behaviours that may have harmed others (Baumeister, Stillwell & Heatherton, 1994; Wiess, 1993). Unlike shame (which motivates concealment and cover-ups), guilt is believed to motivate repair and making amends (Lindsay-Hartz, de Rivera & Mascolo, 1995; Wicker, Payne & Morgan, 1983). Guilt is focused on empathy for the (harmed) other. Whereas shame evolved from submissive behaviour, the psychological mechanisms for guilt evolved from altruism (Gilbert, 1989; Gilbert, Pehl & Allan, 1994; O'Connor et al., 1997). Guilt is associated with moral action in a way that shame is not, and has sometimes been seen as less pathogenic than shame (Tangney, Burggraf & Wagner, 1995; Tangney, Wagner & Gramzow, 1992). However, some caution should be exercised in regard to the latter point. Recent work suggests that much depends on how shame and guilt are measured as to which are pathogenic (Kugler & Jones, 1992). In a patient population O'Connor et al. (1997) found survivor guilt (beliefs that one should not have, or achieve, more than others, and feeling non-deserving) to be associated with depression. Pathological guilt can also involve delusional ideas of having harmed others or distorted views of personal responsibility for others' welfare. Delusional guilt is not uncommon in psychotic depression.

Embarrassment

Like shame, embarrassment refers to evaluations and affects that are self-focused. The embarrassed person is self-conscious and aware that he/she has acted in a way which breaks social rules and has courted others' negative evaluations. However, compared to shame, embarrassment is a mild(er) affect, focused on specific behaviours or attributes and may induce humorous or smiling responses (Miller, 1996). Miller and Tangney (1994) found that, 'whereas embarrassment resulted from surprising, relatively trivial accidents, shame occurs when foreseeable events revealed one's deep-seated flaws both to oneself and others'. Embarrassment may also have different though overlapping developmental pathways than shame (Lewis, 1995). Embarrassment has different non-verbal presentations than shame (Keltner, 1995).

Social Anxiety

From an evolutionary point of view it is clear that animals can be intensely fearful of their conspecifics without (presumably) much in the way of negative *self*-evaluation. All one needs to be socially anxious is an evaluation that 'the other' constitutes a threat in some way (Ohman, 1986). As noted elsewhere (Gilbert & Trower, 1990; Gilbert, Pehl & Allan, 1994) there is overlap between theories of shame and those of social anxiety. Both stress self-focused cognitions, fear of negative evaluation and defensive behaviours often exacerbate the problem. Beck, Emery and Greenberg (1985) placed shame-proneness centre ground in their theory of social anxiety. 'The experience of shame is important in discussions of social anxiety because the socially anxious person is fearful of being shamed in many situations' (p. 156). Recent cognitive models of social anxiety focus on context-specific cognitions, for example: 'others will think I am boring; others will see me shaking/sweating and think I'm odd' (Clark & Wells, 1995). Cognitive models also posit a role for emotional reasoning (Burns, 1980); for example, 'because I feel stupid I am stupid and others will see me as such' (Clark & Wells, 1995). Social anxiety theorists also note that although social phobics are exposed to many social situations, they are not desensitised to their phobia. The reasons for this are that socially anxious people engage in a multitude of 'in-situation safety behaviours' which are intended to avert social disasters. However, such behaviours also prevent disconfirmation of their negative beliefs. For example, someone who is frightened of being seen to shake while holding a drink, may decide never to accept a drink in public. This theory was tested in an experimental treatment study in which subjects were asked to expose themselves to a social fear, but not engage in safety behaviours. As predicted, reducing safety behaviour has a significant impact on social anxiety (Wells et al., 1995).

The cognitive model utilises general principles of cognitive behaviour theory (e.g. that certain types of cognitive distortion maintain disorders) and applies them to specific situations. Thus, for example, many patients use safety behaviours to avoid feared consequences (e.g. obsessional people may avoid contact with knives, prejudiced people avoid those who are the source of their prejudice) and are thus maintained in their negative beliefs. This useful approach opens important avenues for interventions (Wells et al., 1995). However, some theorists believe that the family of emotions underpinning embarrassment and shame are different from social anxiety (Leary & Kowalski, 1995; Lindsay-Hartz, de Rivera & Mascolo, 1995). For example, Miller (1996) points out that social anxiety is associated with sympathetic arousal whereas embarrassment (especially if it is passive) and shame are associated with parasympathetic arousal (Leary & Kowalski, 1995). Shame is associated with a sense of inadequacy and inferiority that one carries forward in time and is (often) located in actual memories of negative events (e.g. sexual abuse). Shame is what one feels one is, whereas social anxiety often focuses on what one might become (but which is preventable if one engages in safety behaviours). Beck, Emery and Greenberg (1985) also note that whereas social anxiety might decline after a person leaves an anxiety-provoking situation, in shame there is significant *rumination* on one's personal failings/inadequacies and what others will think. Indeed, such negative ruminations, although rarely studied in shame, may be one of its hallmarks.

ORIGINS OF SHAME

There are a variety of theories concerning the evolutionary (Gilbert, 1989) and developmental (Barrett, 1995) origins of shame, with increasing evidence that early shaming parent–child interactions can have serious long-term effects on development and vulnerability to psychopathology (Dutton, van Ginkel & Starzomski, 1995; Gilbert, Allan & Goss, 1996). In cognitive-based psychotherapies it is usual to see early experiences, such as shame, to be associated with basic self-other schemata (Beck, Emery & Greenberg, 1985). However, Gilbert (1992a) suggested that self–other schemata (especially shame-based ones) often arise from direct emotional experiences and function like *conditioned emotional responses* (Ferster, 1973). For example, misattunements between parent and the (preverbal) infant are powerful elicitors of negative affect. Research has shown that if the baby smiles and this is mirrored by the mother smiling, the interaction and shared affects stay positive. However, if the baby smiles but mother presents a blank face, the infant becomes automatically distressed and usually turns its gaze away. The blank face is aversive (Tronick & Cohen, 1989). Some have seen this early emotional response to negative social signals as the first prototypical form of a shame response (e.g. see Nathanson, 1994a;

Schore, 1994). The key aspect here is that the infant's distress is not a learned response but a biologically prepared, emotional one. The conditioning implications of affects that are automatically elicited in interactions can be seen by offering the following example.

Sue, a 3 year old, sits quietly doing a drawing. Then suddenly she jumps up, rushes to Mum and proudly holds up the drawing. Mum responds by kneeling down and saying, 'Wow – that's wonderful. Did you do that? (*Sue nods proudly.*) What a clever girl'. Now in this encounter Sue not only experiences her mother as proud of her, she also has emotions *in herself about herself*—she feels good about herself (psychoanalysts would call that a good self–object experience, Kohut, 1977). Positive affects become associated with display (in this case drawing). But suppose that when Sue goes to Mum with her drawing Mum responds with, 'Oh God, not another of those drawings. Look I'm busy right now. Can't you go off and play?' Clearly, the way Sue will experience both her mother, the interaction between them and the feelings in herself, about herself, will be quite different. In this case Sue is unlikely to have good feelings in herself and may have a sense of disappointment and probably shame. Her head goes down and she slinks away. Negative affects become associated with display of abilities. Thus, the lack of recognition (misattunement) and dismissal of the self, when the self tries to display something attractive to others, can elicit shame affect.

Shaming affective experiences may later become elaborated with cognitive descriptions of the self (as bad, useless, worthless, etc.), but their origins may not need (or have) much in the way of such complex cognitive elaborations. Rather they can occur before the cognitive capacity for self-cognitions develops, they are biologically prepared responses sensitive to associative learning.

As Schore (1994) points out, once a child becomes mobile, after the first year, the parent becomes a socialising agent. The parent will use rewards and punishments to control the child's behaviour as they enter the realm of 'dos and don'ts'. This is a time when the potential for shame is particularly acute. Typical shaming encounters may arise from rejections, harsh criticism for failure or doing what is forbidden, and direct labelling of the child as stupid, bad and/or inadequate. Such labels are paired with emotion elicited by the parent's anger at the child's behaviour and the child's emotions to the parental disproval. Thus, it is the affect associated with the label (of bad, stupid, etc.) that is crucial. One can anticipate that if a parent typically screams at the child when delivering a label, 'you are a stupid boy/girl' or withdraws affection from the child in such a way that produces strong affect, this will be more powerful than such labels given in a more neutral tone or against a background of love and affection. By the time people present for therapy these emotional experiences of self will be encoded with various descriptors or labels as bad, inadequate, and so on. But the 'strength of a belief' is related to affect-limbic processes.

CONCEPTUALISATION OF A CASE

Cognitive therapists conceptualise cases in terms of: (i) early formative experiences, (ii) development of basic beliefs about self and others, and (iii) development of dysfunctional beliefs about how life should be lived in order to maximise good things and minimise bad things (e.g. in order to be happy I should/must ...). It is believed that critical incidents (e.g. such as being rejected) trigger negative thoughts (e.g. it is my fault I was rejected), schemata of self (e.g. I am an unlovable person) and negative beliefs (e.g. I can never be happy). Negative beliefs can be global, affecting the whole self, or specific (e.g. I am bad *at* ... knitting, teaching, etc.). Gilbert (1992b, 1997b) pointed out that what is missing from some cognitive conceptualisations is a focus on social behaviour. It matters greatly how people actually behave in their social domains, because it is behaviour that often elicits rewards or punishments from the environment (Horowitz & Vitkus, 1986). A person with a basic belief of (say) inferiority may try to compensate for this by overachieving or may give up trying and withdraw. An example of a case conceptualisation is given in Figure 11.1.

Another major reason the analysis of social behaviour should be included in case formulation is because *cognitions do not always predict behaviour*. In therapy Betty spoke much of her social anxiety and beliefs of inferiority. She had felt constantly put down by her parents, and scored highly on the BDI. However, in the day hospital, observation of her behaviour was that she was aggressive, highly critical of others and self-pitying. This was in contrast to Joanne who had a similar background, expressed similar beliefs about the self, but behaved in very timid and withdrawn ways. (For further discussion see Segrin & Abramson, 1994.)

SHAME IN PSYCHOPATHOLOGY

The combination of negative views of self, and cognitions that one is judged negatively by others, is core to many shame problems and types of psychological difficulty. For reasons that may be related to how humans evolved (Gilbert, 1989, 1992a) and the salience of interpersonal relationships to well-being (Argyle, 1987, 1991; Brugha, 1995), the fears of rejection and being seen as bad, flawed, inadequate or weak are often associated with powerful affects. Shame has been linked to a variety of psy-

SOME TYPICAL EARLY EXPERIENCES

1. Parents critical and disapproving. Tend to label child (e.g. you are stupid, inadequate etc.).
2. Parents ignore, downplay or show envy of achievements.
3. Abusive experiences of various kinds.

SELF–OTHER SCHEMA

Self
Unlovable, rejectable, bad, stupid, disgusting

Other
Critical, aggressive, disgusted, dismissive

BASIC ATTITUDES AND RULES FOR LIVING

Concealment. I must not let others see or know about the real me. I can't cope with being criticised and therefore must avoid it.

Compensation. I must always try hard. I must avoid mistakes. I must never be seen to fail. I have to achieve things to maintain my sense of self-worth. If (but only if) I excel then others will accept, like and value me.

ROLES AND SOCIAL BEHAVIOUR

Concealment/withdrawal: Becomes anxious and avoidant if threatened with disapproval/discovery. Another style is obsessional control of feelings and behaviour.

Compensation. Behaves competitively with others. Constantly tries to impress others. Acts to elicit praise and admiration. Must have approval, e.g. from parents.

Projection. Constantly finds fault in others and feels good at putting others down.

Aggression. Flies into a rage or sulks if criticised. By-passed shame—lacks ability to allow shame affect.

CRITICAL INCIDENTS AND SITUATIONS

Lack of recognition, admiring attention.

Failures of various kinds at college, work, etc.

Being marginalised, criticised, rejected as not good enough. Shaming relationships.

NEGATIVE AUTOMATIC THOUGHTS

Depressive

It's my fault I am not successful.

I am not good enough. I am useless.

Others will not like or respect me now they know the real me.

I am a damaged, flawed, or bad person.

Aggressive

They had no right to criticise.

It is all so unfair.

I will make them show me respect

I will get my own back.

Figure 11.1   Conceptualisation of a case.

chopathologies (Kaufman, 1989; Lewis, 1987b, Tangney & Fischer, 1995) including: alcoholism (Bradshaw, 1988); depression (Andrews, 1995; Brown, Harris & Hepworth, 1995; Gilbert, Pehl & Allan, 1994; Allan, Gilbert & Goss, 1994; Tangney, Wagner & Gramzow, 1992); hostility (Retzinger, 1995; Scheff, 1994; Tangney et al., 1992); social anxiety (Beck, Emery & Greenberg, 1985; Gilbert & Trower, 1990); suicide (Mokros, 1995); eating disorders (Frank, 1991); personality disorders, including narcissism (Kinston, 1987; Lewis, 1987; Wurmser, 1987); obsessional (Miller, 1996) and borderline (Nathanson, 1994b; Linehan, 1993); interpersonal problems and recall of problematic early relationships (Gilbert, Allan & Goss, 1996); and dysfunctional family relationships (Fossum & Mason, 1986). Shaming interactions between parents and children have been found to play a role in brain maturation, especially in the development of the orbital frontal cortex, and may significantly disrupt the development of prosocial behaviour (Schore, 1994). In therapy, shame can exert a major impact on both patient and therapist, as each dances around the other in concealed efforts to avoid 'being shamed' and having inadequacies exposed (Kaufman, 1989). What may make the difference in some of these cases is not that they each may be rooted in shame injuries but that people employ very different ways of coping with them. In other words, cognitions about the acceptance or adequacy of coping behaviour are important. Two patients may have a fear of being seen as weak and criticised; one patient may believe that hiding is the best form of defence, the other that if you get your attacks in first others won't challenge you.

THERAPY

As a therapist encounters the sources of shame and/or begins to threaten exposure, it is the affects of shame that become powerfully present. A patient may talk about how useless or worthless they feel (i.e. can talk about the self in objective terms) but it is at the point of *emotional engagement* of these 'schemata' that the strongest affects are recruited. These may at times be overwhelming. In these contexts the patient may become intensely anxious, feel his/her mind going blank, fall silent, want to run from the room and hide, or may become angry in an effort to conceal possible exposure of badness or weakness. Like conditioned emotional responses these shame affects may be difficult to control via cognitions alone. As noted elsewhere (Gilbert, 1992a, 1994, 1995) the laws of associative learning hold good for many affective disorders and classical conditioning theory can be easily integrated with cognitive theory in this area.

Shame Spirals

What can make shame a particularly complex therapeutic problem is that the cognitions and affects aroused can spiral off in many different directions. Shame-anger spirals can be particularly common (Retzinger, 1991; Scheff, 1987). To illuminate this point consider the following example. Barry was a very depressed man with a long history of problematic interpersonal relationships. On the hospital ward he could interact with staff and patients on his good days but not on his bad days. We drew up a plan that when he felt particularly bad he would ask to talk to his key worker or me. However, he found this hard to do and insisted that he had to be able to 'hold himself together' before seeing me or the key worker. One day he had taken himself off the ward and had contemplated buying tablets to take an overdose. When we explored his thinking behind this behaviour his automatic thoughts were:

It is better to hide away when I feel bad.

I don't want others to see me or get close when I am like this.

I don't want others to be the worse for seeing me.

It is bad to cry or be angry/destructive—which is what I feel could happen.

Others would have nothing but contempt for me—even if they pretend to be nice.

I'm pathetic to get/be like this.

This kind of thinking and way of coping with his acute emotional pain acted as an *interpersonal distance regulator*. In other words, at the very times that he might have benefited from contact with others (e.g. his therapist) he actually withdrew. However, the problem did not stop there because withdrawal solved one problem but produced another. In distancing himself from others he felt alone and cut off. Whilst walking the streets, and thinking of taking an overdose, the shame spirals became overwhelming and started to feedback on themselves. His thoughts were then:

I'm now isolated, I feel alone, desperate, misunderstood, forgotten.

No one can help. It's pointless. I can't get back.

Angry with self and everyone and I hate these feelings. I hate myself.

Once Barry had removed himself from the ward and into an isolated position he had solved one problem (being seen as bad/weak and treated with contempt) only to create another problem of isolation and abandonment. This fuelled a new anger with the therapist and others for not being able to help him. Yet he also believed this anger was unreasonable and found it very difficult to talk about it to me. In such situations it is important to note the sequences: (i) cognitions that are associated with negative feeling in the first place; (ii) cognitions about how others would view this negative feeling in him; (iii) cognitions leading to specific behaviours (i.e. remove himself from the ward); (iv) cognitions about his own reactions and coping behaviours (e.g. anger at being isolated and not understood, feeling alone); (v) cognitions about his emotions (e.g. I have no right to be angry with others). In this kind of situation it can be useful to anticipate complex interacting sequences and attempt to separate each step. This may help patients who may feel overwhelmed and confused by the spirals of many different thoughts and emotions.

Dryden (1989) sees these kinds of processes as generating complex, multipath inference chains that might be difficult to pin down. The point about this is that in complex cases the withdrawal that often happens in shame can produce more problems as the myriad of feelings becomes overwhelming. Moreover, many of the affects of shame, for example, intense anxiety or anger, serve to disrupt further interpersonal relationships rather than heal them; they cause breakdowns in interpersonal bonds and relationships. Thus, in working with shame-based problems it is often useful to discuss with the person the complexities of shame and that there can be a variety of feelings: anxiety, fear of aloneness, fear of being seen as bad/worthless, cut-offness, and anger. Commonly, in strong shame experiences, people feel lost, overwhelmed and do not know how to get out of it, or back in contact with others. As in social anxiety (Wells et al., 1995) one seeks to reduce these 'defensive behaviours' such that the person can learn to dispute negative beliefs and have new emotional experiences.

Shaming Interactions in Therapy

Lazare (1986) notes that patients are often at high risk of experiencing shame in medical encounters and consultations. This is because they are presenting parts of themselves not normally shown to 'strangers' and because in illness these 'parts' can be abnormal, in smell, shape and texture or potential contagion. Some may actually avoid medical help (e.g. for bowel cancer) out of shame. Moreover, some illnesses are stigmatising (e.g. venereal disease) and as he says:

> As if the humiliation of disease, treatment and dying were not enough, there are medical and lay terms assigned to various conditions that may be intrinsically shaming: hyper*tension*, heart *failure*, coronary *insufficiency*, *failed* back, *lazy* eye, mongolian *idiocy*, and *incompetent* cervix. (p. 1645)

As for mental illness, nearly all forms are felt to be stigmatising and speak to a failure in character or personal weakness. Many patients dread the word 'neurotic' being ascribed to their conditions because it speaks (socially) of a dismissal of their suffering (it is *only* neurotic, or *just* in the mind) and shame. Even professionals dread themselves being found out as suffering from a mental illness because of shame (Williams & Rippere, 1985). Yet in order for therapy to unfold many patients have to be prepared to reveal their current problems and potential shaming events from the past (e.g. abuse). The process of seeking help and the process of revealing can be experienced as deeply shaming (Kelly & McKillop, 1996). Cognitive therapy's use of the language of 'cognitive distortions' or worse 'cognitive errors' can add to this shame (Gilbert, 1992b, 1997b).

Shame-prone patients rarely find interpersonal relationships easy, and some patients are very sensitive to non-verbal communication (Gilbert, 1992a). If signals of reassurance, and being valued, are not at the level needed or they are criticised and conflicts arise, behaviour can become defensive (as noted above: e.g. aggressive, self-attacking or withdrawn). These in turn tend to elicit dysfunctional behaviours from others and one can arrive at circles of shaming interactions (Retzinger, 1991). For example, an expression of a personal dissatisfaction in a relationship may provoke a counter-criticism from the other which provokes a gradually increasing escalation until one person backs down in resentment. These kinds of shaming interactions are not uncommon in some families (Fossum & Mason, 1986) and it can be useful to work with couples or families on their shaming interactions by clearly pointing out how shame works.

A therapist can be pulled into shaming interactions in various ways. For example, complaints by a patient of the behaviour of a third party invite collusion between the patient and therapist to gang up against the third party as when a patient reveals bad/uncaring behaviour of a spouse. The therapist and patient may develop tacit agreement that the spouse is indeed bad in some way. The therapist may feel angry with the spouse. The therapist gets caught up in cycles of victim, persecutor and rescuer, where the patient may look to the therapist to side with them against the other (e.g. spouse). The one not present is shamed.

A different example is when the therapist becomes the one shamed; that is, there is some tacit shared belief that: 'if you don't help me or are not nice to me then you are a bad uncaring therapist'. The patient's cognitions about, and behaviours in, therapy activate shame-based cognitions and defensive behaviour in the therapist. This is because cognitive affective processes are not static but highly responsive to social signals, even in moment-to-moment interactions. For example, if a patient becomes hopeless they may start to withdraw or express disappointment in the therapy.

The shame-based cognitions of the therapist might be: 'I'm lost with this patient. I don't know enough. If Beck or Ellis were here they'd do it much better. I'm not good enough. If the patient does not get better others will see me as a useless therapist. I can't cope with being stuck and lost.' Out of these cognitions might flow a renewed effort to offer more techniques to the patient in a desperate effort to avoid feelings of failure. The patient feels misunderstood, even more overwhelmed by the therapy and withdraws further.

Thus, in working with shame-based problems a therapist can keep an eye on their own counter-transference thoughts of being inadequate, not being good enough, and so forth. It can be helpful to 'slow down' rather than 'speed up' and reflect with the patient on the feelings of stuckness. One might check out if the patient is having thoughts that the therapist is expecting them to go faster than they can manage. Alternatively, there may be issues that are important to the patient but the focus on the techniques of therapy has not allowed these to emerge. Shame-based cognitions in the therapist can be a cue to seek supervision. Highly shame-prone therapists, or those early in training, however, may wish to talk more about their successes rather than about the patients they think they are failing with. The fear of criticisms and condemnation may (as it does for patients) stop therapists seeking help (Alonso & Rutan, 1988).

Shame-prone patients can easily induce shame in others. Labels such as 'this patient is resistant; this patient does not want to get better; or this patient is manipulative'—in other words labels and feelings that in some form devalue the patient, often have their roots in shame-based interactions. By blaming the patient the therapist can free him or herself of a possible sense of shame and inadequacy.

Therapeutic Issues of Shame

Cognitive behaviour therapists have become increasingly interested in the therapeutic relationship as a medium that facilitates change (Gilbert, Hughes & Dryden, 1989; Safran & Segal, 1990; Schaap et al., 1993; Spurling & Dryden, 1989), but have not yet considered shame directly. Given that shame is related to fear of exposure of inadequacy, motivates concealment and tends to be associated with rapid, affective shifts when elicited, there are key aspects to therapeutic engagement with the shame patient. The relationship becomes a central medium for healing shame—for it is via the relationship that shame is most likely to be activated. Even the act of attending (or needing) therapy in the first place can be seen as 'shameful'. Of special importance in working with the shame-prone patient is awareness of non-verbal communication (e.g. eye gaze and body postures, and speech patterns (Dixon et al, submitted; Retzinger, 1995). Other aspects of working with shame-prone patients include:

1. The patient will be monitoring not only their own internal world but also how they may appear to the therapist; how they 'exist' in the eyes/mind of the therapist (and others). Hence at times therapists will need to direct attention to transference issues and here-and-now feelings about the interaction. Some shame-prone patients may be distrustful and think that caring behaviour by the therapist is a pretence, simply because this is what they are paid for.

2. The general motto of the shame patient is *Hold Back—Test Out*. Shame motivates concealment and hiding. Thus, it has protective functions and one may expect various forms of camouflage. It is not uncommon to hear stories of patients having had contact with services but not having talked about their most distressing shame-related affects and experiences (e.g. sexual abuse). Hence, the therapist might ask: 'Are there things about yourself that you find difficult to talk about?' or 'Do you find it difficult to talk about things that bother you inside?' At times it may be preferable to avoid immediately jumping in with 'what are they?' as this could be seen as insensitive and put the person on the defensive. Note it for later. But sometimes themes simply do not emerge until the patient has built up enough trust to work on the issues. Trying to rush revelations can be experienced as harmful intrusions. One might ask, 'Do you think talking about them is something you would, at some point, see as important to do?' then 'What would help you explore these things?' As a therapist one can explore the feared consequences by saying: 'I appreciate that you are frightened to go into these things right now but I wonder if you could say a little about what you fear might happen if you did?'

3. Many shame affects happen involuntarily and are difficult to control. Thus, even if a person wishes to reveal something they might feel constrained from doing so (e.g. mind going blank, feeling paralysed and observed). Sometimes patients worry that 'it won't come out right' or 'sound right'. Sometimes there is a struggle for the language with which to talk about their feelings and experiences. This can be, in part, because they feel many different things about the same event and are confused by such complexity of affect. They may have no experience of talking about complex and intimate feelings, be unclear as to their meaning and fearful of what the therapist will make of them.

4. Therapists can bring attention to the pain and fear of revealing (related to various beliefs and expectancies) and respond empathically to the patient's feeling state. It is also useful to recognise possible rage as a shame-based affect. As noted above, a therapist can ask things like, 'What do you think might happen if you did talk about certain painful things?' If

the patient says 'You would laugh at me, think I was stupid, bad, evil or disgusting' or 'I might make a fool of myself', then one early response is to form an empathic bridge with something like, 'that must be a painful and lonely feeling'. From here it is sometimes possible to explore the feelings of being cut-off from others and not able to reveal, or a fear of losing control. The more empathically understood the patient, the more likely it is they will come to feel safe enough to explore. It is not necessarily the case that reassurance will help here as the patient may simply not believe it—hence the focus is on the pain/difficulty of it.

5. In general the therapist tries to open and facilitate a dialogue allowing the patient to explore shame experiences but at the patient's own pace. Sometimes patients will talk of having 'built up' to working on the shame problem. As a rule of thumb, if patients fall silent and this is experienced as awkward and not reflective it can be useful for the therapist to step in and say: 'Maybe there are just too many things going through your mind right now', or 'Maybe your mind has gone blank', or 'Maybe you are having trouble putting words to what you feel'. At times it is useful to talk about shame. Shame silences have been called the black hole of shame (Gilbert, 1992b) for as a patient starts to fall into it they have increasing difficulty getting out. At some point it might be useful to openly discuss shame experiences and explore whether the patient can monitor their inner experiences so that they can pick up on their shame signals early, or indicate to the therapist that they are falling into the black hole. How does it start? What are its typical triggers? How does it unfold?

Homework: Shame

It is well known that while some patients take to cognitive homework others do not, and some only do homework to please the therapist (not be shamed) with scant understanding of why they are doing it. So, for some patients, homework can be a very shame-prone time. Things that are understood in therapy may be forgotten outside or don't work. Consider this dialogue:

T: You have been trying to challenge your thoughts but it hasn't gone so well. I wonder what you've been thinking and feeling about that?

P: I just can't get the hang of it. It seems so sensible and logical yet when I get in one of my states it all goes out the window.

T: That must be a real disappointment for you.

P: Yeah. I just think I'm stupid or something.

T: I wonder if you have any other feelings about it not working well? Maybe you feel pretty fed-up with this therapy?

P: (*pauses and looks sheepish*) Well maybe I do say some bad things about it when it doesn't work right.

From here it was possible to reveal anger with herself; anger with the therapist because the therapy was not working; fear of talking about 'being given something' she couldn't make work; fear of her anger being seen as a sign of ingratitude, fear of being a useless patient; fear of seeming stupid or not trying; feeling that although angry and frustrated with the therapy's lack of impact she had no right to be feel angry or disappointed—and so forth in various spirals. Thus, even a seemingly simple task like homework can be filled with shame themes. Think back to your own days of homework, when you thought you understood it in class, but it would not work out right at home. There might have been anger with self, anger with the teacher for not teaching you right or making it easier, feelings that there was no point in trying and so forth. These kinds of reflections can help empathic bridging.

A therapist can get a lot out of exploring the disappointment of failed homework (e.g. attempts to control negative thoughts). He/she may address the points noted above and also offer the following: appreciation of the patient's efforts; point out that affects often follow their own logic; explore the distinction between affect control and affect acceptance (Linehan, 1993); note that affect control needs practice in a step-by-step way; note how difficult it must be with all these 'shame-thoughts' (Gilbert, 1997b) and feelings about doing homework; and that setbacks are understandable and useful because they help us get in touch with feelings and thoughts and so on.

Enabling patients to speak of their anger with the therapist/therapy and empathising with that (rather than being defensive) can be helpful for shame patients. Some shame patients have never been allowed to get angry with someone who is trying to help them and they may see such anger as 'shameful and unwarranted'.

HUMILIATION

Humiliation has many overlaps with shame, but there are also salient differences. If we think of torture we do not usually talk of it in terms of shame but of humiliation. Shame and humiliation depict different experiences. In humiliation-based problems there is a focus on the harm done by others. One is put in a powerless position (Gilbert, 1992a; 1997a; Miller, 1998; Silver et al., 1986). There is often a view that what was done (e.g. physical or sexual abuse) was unjust—or the person may alternate between both blaming others and blaming the self (e.g. 'they were bad to have done this and I was bad to have allowed it or not stopped it'). Key cognitions are that the self has been harmed, damaged and/or injured by the actions of others and this harm has in some way scarred them. It is now the (psychological) scars ('what they have turned me into') that are shameful. A view might be 'I wouldn't be like this if it wasn't for him/her doing what they did. I'd be a nice person but now I'm not.'

For example, a woman who was sexually abused in her marriage felt it to be a deep humiliation and placed the blame squarely on her husband. She did not feel shamed by her husband but did feel considerable anxiety and shame over revealing it or its becoming known. She was fearful that I would see her as a woman who had been raped (see Wilson & Daly, 1992, for a discussion of how rape can lead a person to feel they have lost status and been degraded). Her rage at him (she felt) had turned her nasty, distrustful and cynical (loss of the good self). She was clear that the feelings she had towards her husband were very different from those she had for me in disclosing it. To see the feelings about the abuse, feelings to the abuser, and feelings associated with the revelation, as all related to a single experience called shame would be to miss the very important affective differences between the experience of the abuse and its revelation to a potential supportive other (the therapist).

Another aspect that marks the humiliated person can be their feelings of hatred, desires to retaliate, and ease in becoming aggressive. Even quite small empathic failures on the part of the therapist can throw them into rages (Linehan, 1993). In regard to early life experiences there may also be differences. My own view is that the withdrawing, socially anxious patients tend to tell stories of emotional neglect, feeling unloved or 'in the way' or 'not good enough'. They have the idea that if only they can find out how to be good enough then love will come their way. Humiliated patients may have similar experiences but in addition have been subject to various forms of abuse, or come from families where violence or the threat of violence was more common. It leaves them with feelings that it's 'a dog eat dog world', that others will take advantage if you let them, and that they are bad and flawed. The overlapping and distinctive features of shame and humiliation are given in Figure 11.2.

Humiliation and Therapy

Although the distinction between shame and humiliation is difficult to be precise about there are some markers that can be used for therapeutic identification. The first, as noted, is the ease with which people feel anger and the extent to which they can easily experience burning hatred and

SHAME	HUMILIATION
COMMON TO BOTH	
Sensitivity to put down/injury	
Desire to protect self	
Increased arousal	
Complex affects	
Rumination	
DIFFERENT	
Internal attribution	External attribution
Self as bad/flawed	Other as bad
Internal sense of inferiority	Internal sense of inferiority not necessary
Heightened self-consciousness	Greater focus on the other
No obvious sense of injustice	Strong sense of injustice
No strong desire for revenge	Strong desire for revenge

Figure 11.2   Possible similarities and differences in shame and humiliation.

fear of being dominated. When anger and hatred for others over past humiliations dominate the clinical picture, therapy enters a new realm not seen in the purely socially anxious domain of shame and evaluation anxiety (Beck, Emery & Greenberg, 1985). When humiliation is present therapists can find themselves confronting the following difficult themes:

1. There is a greater focus on having been damaged, spoiled and/or scarred by others: 'What they have done to me or made me.' The person may wrestle with the degree to which they brought 'humiliation' on themselves but there remains a focus on the damage done by others. There can often be a sense of being beyond repair.

2. In serious cases there can be a history of early experiences of powerlessness—and of being victim to others (Harper & Hoopes, 1990). There may also be experiences of having suffered impotent rage and/or fear. Often the person felt powerless to escape or defend him or herself. These experiences form the basis for powerfully conditioned affects which can reappear in therapy. At times these feelings may show themselves in a desire to be powerful, dominate others and 'turn the tables'. Indeed, in many of us perhaps, the experience of others' aggressive or sadistic behaviours can activate sadistic desires for revenge (bomb the bastards; string 'em up, etc.).

3. A common experience is of being robbed of a 'good self'. Parts of self may no longer seem to belong to the person. Parts of the self may become a source of disgust, and are contaminated by the humiliator. Also living with fear and rage can seem as if one 'has been turned bad'.

4. The humiliated person may come to fear closeness and intimacy and may even fear being understood. This may be related to trust. As one patient said, 'If you understand me you will be able to manipulate me. You'll know my weak spots.'

5. Healing humiliation may involve grieving for what was lost, but the closeness necessary to contact grief and work with it may ignite fears of further shame–humiliations—weakness. Also a person may become terrified of their own (hidden) needs for love, protection, dependency and closeness (Harper & Hoopes, 1990).

6. Carrying feelings of disgust and rage/hatred is seen to make a person unattractive and unlovable. Inside they may feel 'nothing but hate'. This leads to feelings of being unattractive, isolated, and cut off from others.

7. A common experience can also be 'envy of the unshamed'. This envy may show itself in destructive behaviours to others who are envied, to shame them too, or bring them down in some way (Horner, 1989). At times therapists may need to recognise that patients may feel aggressive forms of envy for the therapist since they are seen as 'clean, able, talented, loved and unshamed.'

8. Humiliated fury can become a serious problem in the moment-to-moment process of therapy. Patients may blow up over small events. The counter-transference can be one of 'handling a volcano', and there can be a fear of igniting the patient's anger, and of what the patient may do to themselves or others if their anger is activated or not contained. Therapists who are vulnerable to shame themselves may find these emotionally tense encounters very difficult and try to avoid them. Alternatively, they may try to counter-shame (pull rank on) the patient to keep the patient's anger in check. A recent example was when a therapist, working with a difficult problem involving acting out, not doing homework, and the patient being highly critical of the therapist, exasperatedly said, 'Look Mr X, you come here for help but if you don't try to do what I tell you then how can you expect to get better?' In other words, the therapist knows what's good for the patient, acts like a parent, and is saying 'stop being a naughty boy and get to down to work'.

Therapeutic Tasks

The rage/hatred in humiliation confronts the therapist with major challenges, especially to their ability to maintain an empathic bridge with the person (Harper & Hoopes, 1990). Patients believe hatred to be an unattractive trait, and that therapists might dislike them for it. Thus, they can feel cut off and alone with it. Hate cuts them off from affection. If patients have cognitions about how bad they are to feel hatred—they see it as meaning they are nasty, horrible, unlovable, or evil people, then a focus on the reasons for hatred and how to move beyond it can be helpful. Hence a negative view might be, 'Hate/rage is bad and abnormal. I am bad to feel it. I should not feel like this'.

Possible interventions may include:

1. Possible relabelling of the affect: hate comes from feelings of hurt, fear, injury, being controlled, and so on. Hate has a focus on *something or some person(s)* usually seen as causing injury. Hate can be a source of the struggle to break free of something—it energises one to attack.

2. Distinguish feelings from global self-rating: for example, hate and destructive feelings may 'feel' bad but feelings do not make 'it' or oneself bad. Hence, the focus is on understanding sources of hatred rather than self-attacking or shaming. Here one counteracts emotional reasoning and self-labelling (Burns, 1980).

3. It can be noted that hate is a common human experience: that it is not abnormal. Evidence can be given by citing examples such as books and films. It may be undesirable but it is part of human nature.

4. It can also be useful to identify other feelings: for example, at the times when hate and anger are strongest there may also be fear, desire to escape, disappointment, a sense of betrayal, a need to be loved/valued or tension that felt/feels unbearable.

5. As in cognitive therapy for anxiety (Beck, Emery & Greenberg, 1985) the therapist can try to counteract globality. Exactly what is hated, when, under which contexts, and so on? The therapist may also note the degree of anger or hate: for example mild – strong, and hence what increases it and what decreases it.

6. Some patients suffering these kinds of problems may fear their destructive actions or loss of control. In these situations it can be useful to explore ways of gaining emotional control and make it clear that in working with humiliation this is not an encouragement to act out these feelings but to heal them. In this context it is useful to note that aggression can often be a response to feeling fearfully powerless. At the same time the validation of emotions is important (Linehan, 1993) as some patients may think they should not feel this way. Thus, a therapist may consider development of more assertive social skills. Some patients, for example, may have learnt only two ways of dealing with conflict: backing down and seething with resentment, or lashing out and then feeling ashamed, guilty and out of control (Gilbert, 1997b).

7. As therapy progresses, a therapist can explore: (i) advantages and disadvantages of maintaining the desire to retaliate; and (ii) what is needed to let go of hatred, perhaps asking, 'If you were to leave these feelings behind what would you need or need to do? For example, one patient who felt humiliated by his employers would oscillate between thoughts of fighting and taking them to court and then thinking he could never win, feeling defeated and suicidal. He would wake up at night angry and ruminating how he could 'get them.' But his anger was maintained by beliefs like: 'If I were a proper man I would get them. I can't let them get away with this. If I walk away now it will show I am weak.' In therapy we explored how his cognitions were activating his fight/flight system and maintaining him in a high state of arousal. We then explored issues of masculine identity and that it could be useful to try to win if one can but not to engage in hopeless battles that would lead to depression. Once he had accepted that he was not a 'weak man' for giving up the battle, his depression lifted and he began to see the benefits of being out of this particular job.

8. Sometimes a key process is grief. Feelings of humiliation can bypass grief. As Linehan (1993) notes, some patients can be paralysed by feelings of grief, and feeling out of control, weak or fearful of possible dependency. They may have very little experience of being comforted or of an empathic-sharing relationship with another person. In some shame and humiliated patients facilitating grieving for past injuries and losses may be helpful.

9. Working with the past is often essential for patients with early shame–humiliation experiences. This is in part because they need to be able to re-evaluate the past, work through a sense of injustice or be able to validate their own experiences. Moreover, at times there is work to do in 'undoing' the labels and self-definitions that were developed at this time (e.g. see Bergner, 1987).

10. In humiliation arising from the past, the need for revenge can be a source of painful rumination and at times the therapist may need to work on forgiveness (Fitzgibbons, 1986). Forgiveness like grief, however, is a complex process which involves a number of stages, including feeling understood, validated, a sense of justice, being in touch with the profound pain or hurt and desires to be free from one's anger (Enright, 1991). None of these things emerges quickly in therapy and so the therapist may need to be cautious of timing and the stage of therapy. Focusing on forgiveness too early in therapy may be read by the patient as crass insensitivity: 'Don't you know how bad it was? How the hell do you expect me to forgive them?'

CONCLUSION

Shame problems are common in many types of psychological difficulty. For reasons that may be related to how humans evolved (Gilbert, 1989,

1992a) and the salience of interpersonal relationship to well-being (Argyle, 1987, 1991; Brugha, 1995), the fear of rejection and being seen as bad, flawed, inadequate or weak is often associated with powerful affects. Coping with shame can also take many different routes (e.g. self or other attacking). As therapists become more focused on the role of possible shame sensitivity in complex cases they may choose to work more directly on shame issues, bearing in mind that the therapeutic relationship is crucial to their illumination and healing. Competency with the techniques of cognitive behaviour therapy will allow identification of a variety of cognitive processes such as emotional reasoning, all or nothing thinking and negative self-labelling (Gilbert, 1997b). Working with shame also requires a special focus on building empathic bridges to the patient's emotional state, and at times hidden fears. This can be especially true when anger and problems tolerating strong emotions dominate the clinical picture.

Special attention may be needed to look for shame spirals and shaming interpersonal interactions. Also, unaddressed shame activated in the therapist can throw a therapy off course. Patients who have additional problems of humiliation are easily shifted into anger or defensive withdrawal and may be especially difficult. Here the therapist may need to move through therapy in stages. The techniques of cognitive intervention remain salient but may need adapting in various ways (Linehan, 1993) to stay in tune with a patient's ability to cope with powerful, complex, difficult to acknowledge and at times overwhelming affects.

REFERENCES

Allan, S. & Gilbert, P. (1995). A social comparison scale: Psychometric properties and relationship to psychopathology. *Personality and Individual Differences*, **19**, 293–299.

Allan, S., Gilbert, P. & Goss, K. (1994). An exploration of shame measures: II: Psychopathology. *Personality and Individual Differences*, **17**, 719–722.

Alonso, A. & Rutan, J.S (1988). Shame and guilt in psychotherapy supervision. *Psychotherapy*, **25**, 576–584.

Andrews, B. (1995). Bodily shame as a mediator between abusive experiences and depression. *Journal of Abnormal Psychology*, **104**, 277–285.

Archer, J. (1994). Power and male violence. In J. Archer (Ed.), *Male Violence* (pp. 310–331). London: Routledge.

Argyle, M. (1987). *The Psychology of Happiness*. London: Methuen.

Argyle, M. (1991). *Cooperation: The Basis of Sociability*. London: Routledge.

Asch, S.E. (1956). Studies of independence and submission to group pressure: 1: A minority of one against a unanimous majority. *Psychological Monographs*, **70**, 8 (Whole No. 416).

Barrett, K.C. (1995). A functionalist approach to shame and guilt. In J.P. Tangney, & K.W. Fischer, (Eds), *Self-Conscious Emotions: The Psychology of Shame, Guilt, Embarrassment and Pride* (pp. 25–63). New York: Guilford.

Baumeister, R.F., Stillwell, A. & Heatherton, T.F. (1994). Guilt: An interpersonal approach. *Psychological Bulletin*, **115**, 243–267.

Beck, A.T., Emery, G. & Greenberg, R.L. (1985). *Anxiety Disorders and Phobias: A Cognitive Approach*. New York: Basic Books.

Beck, A.T., Rush, A.J., Shaw, B.F. & Emery, G. (1979). *Cognitive Therapy of Depression*. New York: Guilford.

Bergner, R.M. (1987). Undoing degradation. *Psychotherapy*, **24**, 25–30.

Bradshaw, J. (1988). *Healing the Shame that Binds You*. Deerfield Beach, FL: Health Communications.

Brewin, C.R. & Furnham, A. (1986). Attributional and pre-attributional variables in self-esteem and depression: A comparison and test of learned helplessness theory. *Journal of Personality and Social Psychology*, **50**, 1013–1020.

Brown, G.W., Harris, T.O. & Hepworth, C. (1995). Loss, humiliation and entrapment among women developing depression: A patient and non-patient comparison. *Psychological Medicine*, **25**, 7–21.

Brugha, T. (Ed.) (1995). *Social Support and Psychiatric Disorder*. Cambridge: Cambridge University Press.

Burns, D.D. (1980). *Feeling Good: The New Mood Therapy*. New York: Morrow.

Clark, D.M. & Wells, A. (1995). A cognitive model of social phobia. In R.G Heimberg., M.R Liebowitz., D.A Hope & R.R Schneier (Eds), *Social Phobia: Diagnosis, Assessment and Treatment* (pp. 69–93). New York: Guilford.

Cook, D.R. (1993). *The Internalized Shame Scale Manual*. Menomoniee, WI: Channel Press (available from Author: Rt. 7, Box 270a, Menomoniee, WI, 54751, USA).

Cook, D.R. (1996). Empirical studies of shame and guilt: The internalized shame scale. In D.L Nathanson (Ed.), *Knowing Feeling: Affect, Script and Psychotherapy* (pp 132–165). New York: Norton.

Crocker, J. & Major, B. (1989). Social stigma and self-esteem: The self-protective qualities of stigma. *Psychological Review*, **96**, 608–630.

Daly, M. & Wilson, M. (1994). Evolutionary psychology of male violence. In J. Archer (Ed.), *Male Violence* (pp. 253–288). London: Routledge.

Dixon, A.K., Gilbert, P., Huber, C., Gilbert, J. & Van der Hoek, G. (submitted). Changes in nonverbal behaviour in a neutral and 'shame' interview.

Driscoll, R. (1988). Self-condemnation: A conceptual framework for assessment and treatment. *Psychotherapy*, **26**, 104–111.

Dryden, W. (1989). The use of chaining in rational-emotive therapy. *Journal of Rational-Emotive Therapy*, **7**, 59–66.

Dutton, G.D., van Ginkel, C. & Starzomski, A. (1995). The role of shame and guilt in the intergeneration transmission of abusiveness. *Violence and Victims*, **10**, 121–131.

Enright, P.D. (1991). The moral development of forgiveness. In W.M. Kurtines & J.L. Gewirtz (Eds), *Handbook of Moral Behaviour and Development. Volume 1: Theory* (pp. 123–152). Hillsdale, NJ: Erlbaum.

Ferster, C.B. (1973). A functional analysis of depression. *American Psychologist*, **28**, 857–870.

Fitzgibbons, R.B. (1986). The cognitive and emotive uses of forgiveness in the treatment of anger. *Psychotherapy*, **23**, 629–633.

Fossum, M.A. & Mason, M.J. (1986). *Facing Shame: Families in Recovery*. New York: Norton Paperbacks.

Frank, E.S. (1991). Shame and guilt in eating disorders. *American Journal of Orthopsychiatry*, **61**, 303–306.

Gibbons, F.X. (1990). The impact of focus of attention and affect on social behaviour. In W.R. Cozier (Ed.), *Shyness and Embarrassment: Perspectives from Social Psychology* (pp. 119–143). Cambridge: Cambridge University Press.

Gilbert, P. (1989). *Human Nature and Suffering*. Hove: Erlbaum.

Gilbert, P. (1992a). *Depression: The Evolution of Powerlessness*. Hove: Erlbaum; New York: Guilford.

Gilbert, P. (1992b). *Counselling for Depression*. London: Sage.

Gilbert, P. (1994). Male violence: Towards an integration. In J. Archer (Ed.), *Male Violence* (pp. 352–389). London: Routledge & Kegan Paul.

Gilbert, P. (1995). Biopsychosocial approaches and evolutionary theory as aids to integration in clinical psychology and psychotherapy. *Clinical Psychology and Psychotherapy*, **2**, 135–156.

Gilbert, P. (1997a). The evolution of social attractiveness and its role in shame, humiliation, guilt and therapy. *British Journal of Medical Psychology*, **70**, 113–147.

Gilbert, P. (1997b). *Overcoming Depression: A Self-Help Guide using Cognitive Behavioral Techniques*. London: Robinson.

Gilbert, P. (1998) Shame: Some core issues and controversies. In P. Gilbert & B. Andrews (Eds), *Shame: Interpersonal Behavior, Psychopathology and Culture*. New York: Oxford University Press.

Gilbert, P., Allan, S. & Goss, K. (1996). Parental representations, shame interpersonal problems and vulnerability to psychopathology. *Clinical Psychology and Psychotherapy*, **3**, 23–34.

Gilbert, P., Hughes, W. & Dryden, W. (1989). The therapist as a crucial variable in psychotherapy. In W. Dryden & L. Spurling (Eds), *On Becoming a Therapist* (pp. 3–13). London: Routledge.

Gilbert, P. & McGuire, M. (1998). Shame, status and social roles: The psychobiological continuum from monkey to human. In P. Gilbert & B. Andrews (Eds), *Shame: Interpersonal Behaviour, Psychopathology and Culture*. New York: Oxford University Press.

Gilbert, P., Pehl, J. & Allan, S. (1994). The phenomenology of shame and guilt: An empirical investigation. *British Journal of Medical Psychology*, **67**, 23–36.

Gilbert, P., Price, J.S. & Allan, S. (1995). Social comparison, social attractiveness and evolution: How might they be related? *New Ideas In Psychology*, **13**, 149–165.

Gilbert, P, & Trower, P. (1990). The evolution and manifestation of social anxiety. In W.R. Crozier (Ed.), *Shyness and Embarrassment: Perspectives from Social Psychology* (pp.144–177). Cambridge: Cambridge University Press.

Goffman, E. (1968). *Stigma: Notes on the Management of a Spoiled Identity*. Harmondsworth: Penguin.

Goss, K., Gilbert, P. & Allan, S. (1994). An exploration of shame measures: I: The 'other as shamer scale'. *Personality and Individual Differences*, **17**, 713–717.

Harder, D.W. (1995). Shame and guilt assessment, and relationships of shame- and guilt-proneness to psychopathology. In J.P. Tangney, & K.W. Fischer (Eds), *Self-Conscious Emotions: The Psychology of Shame, Guilt, Embarrassment and Pride* (pp. 368–392). New York: Guilford.

Harper, J.C. & Hoopes, M.H. (1990). *Uncovering Shame: An Approach Integrating Individuals and their Family Systems.* New York: W.W. Norton.

Hewitt, P.L. & Flett, G.L. (1991a). Dimensions of perfectionism in unipolar depression. *Journal of Abnormal Psychology*, **100**, 98–101.

Hewitt, P.L. & Flett, G.L. (1991b). Perfectionism in the self and social contexts: Conceptualization, assessment, and association with psychopathology. *Journal of Personality and Social Psychology*, **60**, 456–470.

Hibbard, S. (1994). An empirical study of the differential roles of libidinous and aggressive shame components in normality and pathology. *Psychoanalytic Psychology*, **11**, 449–474.

Horner, A. (1989). *The Wish for Power and the Fear of Having It.* Northdale, NJ: Jason Aronson.

Horowitz, L.M. & Vitkus, J. (1986). The interpersonal basis of psychiatric symptoms. *Clinical Psychology Review*, **6**, 443–470.

Kaufman, G. (1989). *The Psychology of Shame.* New York: Springer.

Kelly, A.E. & McKillop, K.J. (1996). Consequences of revealing personal secrets. *Psychological Bulletin*, **120**, 450–465.

Keltner, D. (1995). Signs of appeasement: Evidence for the distinct displays of embarrassment, amusement and shame. *Journal of Personality and Social Psychology*, **68**, 441–454.

Kinston, W. (1987). The shame of narcissism. In D.L. Nathanson (Ed.), *The Many Faces of Shame* (pp. 214–245). New York: Guilford.

Kohut, H. (1977). *The Restoration of the Self.* New York: International Universities Press.

Kugler, K. & Jones, W.H. (1992). On conceptualizing and assessing guilt. *Journal of Personality and Social Psychology*, **62**, 318–327.

Lazare, A. (1986). Shame and humiliation in the medical encounter. *Archives of International Medicine*, **147**, 1653–1658.

Leary, M.R. (1995). *Self-Presentation: Impression Management and Interpersonal Behaviour,* Madison, WI: Brown & Benchmark.

Leary, M.R. & Kowalski, R.M. (1990). Impression management: A literature review and two-component model. *Psychological Bulletin*, **107**, 34–47.

Leary, M.R. & Kowalski, R.M. (1995). *Social Anxiety* New York: Guilford.

Lewis, H.B. (1986). The role of shame in depression. In M. Rutter, C.E. Izard & P.B. Read (Eds), *Depression in Young People: Developmental and Clinical Perspectives* (pp. 325–339). New York: Guilford.

Lewis, H.B. (1987a). Introduction: Shame—the 'sleeper' in psychopathology. In H.B. Lewis (Ed.), *The Role of Shame in Symptom Formation* (pp. 1–28). Hillsdale, NJ: Erlbaum.

Lewis, H.B. (1987b). Shame and the narcissistic personality. In D.L. Nathanson (Ed.), *The Many Faces of Shame* (pp. 93–132). New York: Guilford.

Lewis, M. (1992). *Shame: The Exposed Self:* New York: Free Press.

Lewis, M. (1995). Embarrassment: The emotion of self-exposure. In J.P. Tangney & K.W. Fischer (Eds), *Self-Conscious Emotions. The Psychology of Shame, Guilt, Embarrassment and Pride* (pp. 198–218). New York: Guilford.

Lindsay-Hartz, J., de Rivera, J. & Mascolo, M.F. (1995). Differentiating guilt and shame and their effects on motivations. In J.P. Tangney, & K.W. Fischer (Eds) *Self-Conscious Emotions. The Psychology of Shame, Guilt, Embarrassment and Pride* (pp. 274–300). New York: Guilford.

Linehan, M.M. (1993). *Cognitive Behavioral Therapy Treatment of Borderline Personality Disorder.* New York. Guilford.

Mascolo, M.F. & Fischer, K.W. (1995). Developmental transformations in appraisals of pride, shame and guilt. In J.P. Tangney & K.W. Fischer (Eds), *Self-Conscious Emotions: The Psychology of Shame, Guilt, Embarrassment and Pride* (pp. 64–113). New York: Guilford.

Miller, R.S. (1996). *Embarrassment: Poise and Peril in Everyday Life.* New York: Guilford.

Miller, R.S. & Tangney, J.P. (1994). Differentiating embarrassment and shame. *Journal of Social and Clinical Psychology,* **13,** 273–287.

Miller, S. (1998). Humiliation and shame: Comparing two affect states as indicators of narcissistic stress. *Bulletin of the Menninger Clinic,* **52,** 40–51.

Mokros, H.B. (1995). Suicide and shame. *American Behavioral Scientists,* **38,** 1091–1103.

Mollon, P. (1984). Shame in relation to narcissistic disturbance. *British Journal of Medical Psychology,* **57,** 207–214.

Nathanson, D.L. (Ed.) (1987). *The Many Faces of Shame.* New York: Guilford.

Nathanson, D.L. (1987). Shaming systems in couples, families and institutions. In D.L. Nathanson (Ed.), *The Many Faces of Shame* (pp. 246–270). New York: Guilford.

Nathanson, D.L. (1994a). *Shame and Pride: Affect, Sex and the Birth of the Self.* New York: Norton Paperbacks.

Nathanson, D.L. (1994b). Shame, compassion, and the 'borderline' personality. *Psychiatric Clinics of North America,* **17,** 785–810.

O'Connor, L., Berry, J., Weiss, J., Bush, M.H. & Sampson, H. (1997). Interpersonal guilt: The development of a new measure. *Journal of Clinical Psychology,* **53,** 73–89.

Ohman, A. (1986). Fear the beast and fear the face: Animal and social fears as prototypes for evolutionary analyses of emotion. *Psychophysiology,* **23,** 123–145.

Power, M. & Dalgleish, T. (1997). *Cognition and Emotions: From Order to Disorder:* Hove: Psychology Press.

Retzinger, S. (1991). *Violent Emotions: Shame and Rage in Marital Quarrels.* New York: Sage.

Retzinger, S.M. (1995). Identifying shame and anger in discourse. *American Behavioral Scientists,* **38,** 1104–1113.

Safran, J.D. & Segal, Z.V. (1990). *Interpersonal Process in Cognitive Therapy.* New York: Basic Books.

Schaap, C., Bennun, I., Schindler, L. & Hoogduin, K. (1993). *The Therapeutic Relationship in Behavioural Therapy.* Chichester: Wiley.

Scheff, T. (1987). The shame–rage spiral: A case study of an interminable quarrel. In H.B. Lewis (Ed.), *The Role of Shame in Symptom Formation* (pp. 109–149). Hillsdale, NJ: Erlbaum.

Scheff, T.J. (1988). Shame and conformity. The deference–emotion system. *American Review of Sociology*, **53**, 395–406.

Scheff, T.J. (1994). *Bloody Revenge: Emotions, Nationalism and War*. Boulder, Co: Westview Press.

Schore, A.N. (1994). *Affect Regulation and the Origin of the Self: The Neurobiology of Emotional Development*. Hillsdale, NJ: Erlbaum.

Segal, Z.V. & Blatt, S.J. (Eds) (1993). *The Self in Emotional Distress: Cognitive and Psychodynamic Perspectives*. New York: Guilford.

Segal, Z.V. & Muran, J.C. (1993). A cognitive perspective on self-representation in depression. In Z.V. Segal & S.J. Blatt (Eds), *The Self in Emotional Distress: Cognitive and Psychodynamic Perspectives* (pp.131–163). New York: Guilford.

Segrin, C. & Abramson, L.Y. (1994). Negative reactions to depressive behaviours: A communication theories analysis. *Journal of Abnormal Psychology*, **103**, 655–668.

Serney, G. (1990). The sins of the fathers. *Sunday Times Colour Magazine*, 23, September pp. 22–36.

Silver, M., Conte, R., Miceli, M. & Poggi, I. (1986). Humiliation: Feeling, social control and the construction of identity. *Journal for the Theory of Social Behaviour*, **16**, 269–283.

Spurling, L. & Dryden, W. (1989). The self and the therapeutic domain. In W. Dryden & L. Spurling (Eds), *On Becoming a Therapist* (pp. 191–214). London: Routledge.

Suls, J. & Wills, T.A. (Eds) (1991). *Social Comparison: Contemporary Theory and Research*. Hillsdale, NJ: Erlbaum.

Tangney, J.P. (1990). Assessing individual differences in shame proneness and guilt: The self-conscious affect and attribution inventory. *Journal of Personality and Social Psychology*, **59**, 102–111.

Tangney J.P. (1995). Shame and guilt in interpersonal relationships. In J.P. Tangney & K.W. Fischer (Eds), *Self-Conscious Emotions: The Psychology of Shame, Guilt, Embarrassment and Pride* (pp. 114–139). New York: Guilford.

Tangney, J.P., Burggraf, S.A. & Wagner, P.E. (1995). Shame-proneness, guilt-proneness, and psychological symptoms. In J.P. Tangney & K.W. Fischer (Eds), *Self-Conscious Emotions. The Psychology of Shame, Guilt, Embarrassment and Pride* (pp. 343–367). New York: Guilford.

Tangney, J.P. & Fischer, K.W. (Eds) (1995). *Self-Conscious Emotions: The Psychology of Shame, Guilt, Embarrassment and Pride*. New York: Guilford.

Tangney, J.P., Wagner, P. & Gramzow, R. (1992). Proneness to shame, proneness to guilt, and psychopathology. *Journal of Abnormal Psychology*, **101**, 469–478.

Tangney, J.P., Wagner, P., Fletcher, C. & Gramzow, R. (1992). Shamed into anger? The relation of shame and guilt to self-reported aggression. *Journal of Personality and Social Psychology*, **62**, 669–675.

Tangney, J.P., Wagner, P.E., Hill-Barlow, D., Marschall, D.E. & Gramzow, R. (1996). Relation of shame and guilt to constructive versus destructive responses to anger across the lifespan. *Journal of Personality and Social Psychology*, **70**, 797–809.

Tronick, E.Z. & Cohen, J.F. (1989). Infant–mother face-to-face interaction: Age and gender differences in coordination and the occurrence of miscoordination. *Child Development*, **60**, 85–92.

Weiss, J. (1993). *How Psychotherapy Works*. New York: Guilford.

Wells, A., Clark, D.M., Salkovskis, P., Ludgate, J., Hackman, A. & Gelder, M. (1995). Social phobia: The role of in-situation safety behaviours in maintaining anxiety and negative beliefs. *Behaviour Therapy*, **26**, 153–161.

Wicker, F.W., Payne, G.C. & Morgan, R.D. (1983). Participant descriptions of guilt and shame. *Motivation and Emotion*, **7**, 25–39.

Williams, R. & Rippere, V. (1985). *Wounded Healers*. Chichester: Wiley.

Wilson, M. & Daly, M. (1992). The man who mistook his wife for a chattel. In J.H. Barkow, L. Cosmides & J. Tooby (Eds), *The Adapted Mind: Evolutionary Psychology and the Generation of Culture* (pp. 289–322). New York: Oxford University Press.

Wurmser, L. (1987). Shame: The veiled companion of narcissism. In D.L. Nathanson (Ed.), *The Many Faces of Shame* (pp. 64–92). New York: Guilford.

Yalom, I. (1985). *The Theory and Practice of Group Psychotherapy* (3rd edn). New York: Basic Books.

Chapter 12

PARASUICIDE

*Gary L.Sidley**

INTRODUCTION

Parasuicide, defined as deliberate self-harm which is not lethal, constitutes a widespread problem for clinical services which, according to the Registrar-General's conservative figures for England and Wales, accounts for 70 000–80 000 admissions to hospital each year. In addition to presenting an important clinical phenomenon in its own right, it also represents a key risk factor for completed suicide, parasuicide patients being 100 times more likely to kill themselves in the following 12-month period when compared to the rate for the general population (Ovenstone & Kreitman, 1974; Kreitman & Foster, 1991).

Until relatively recently the outlook for effective clinical interventions to reduce parasuicide was bleak, with no demonstrable impact on repetition rates having been found for a wide range of medical, social and psychological interventions (see Hawton & Catalan, 1987, for a review). The last decade has seen an acceleration with respect to the empirical investigation of the psychological processes which underpin suicidal behaviour and these insights have been paralleled by the development of treatment interventions which have positively influenced rates of parasuicide in some high-risk groups. This chapter will start by reviewing this literature on the psychological disturbances which seem to characterise the final common pathway towards a suicidal act, together with outcome studies which suggest that parasuicide can be significantly reduced by outside intervention. Secondly, case examples will illustrate how these distinct psychological dysfunctions can variously present in routine clinical practice, thus emphasising the need for individual case formulations when

* Psychology Services, Mental Health Services of Salford NHS Trust, Manchester, UK

Treating Complex Cases: The Cognitive Behavioural Therapy Approach.
Edited by Nicholas Tarrier, Adrian Wells and Gillian Haddock.
© 1998 John Wiley & Sons Ltd.

working with this client group. Thirdly, it will be argued that the type of clinical intervention attempted can usefully be matched to the particular phase of the suicidal process, the imminence of self-destructive behaviour determining the appropriateness and timing of interventions which aim to promote either survival, problem solving, restructuring of beliefs, or schema change. Finally, the further complexities of working with suicidal patients will be outlined in so far as they require some modifications to the standard cognitive behaviour therapy package.

PSYCHOLOGICAL DYSFUNCTIONS IN PARASUICIDES

Sociodemographic characteristics of suicidal populations have been well established (Buglass & Horton, 1974; Kreitman & Foster, 1991). Identification of risk factors for parasuicide repetition (e.g. previous parasuicide, unemployed, not currently married and history of alcohol or drug abuse), can make a useful contribution to the overall assessment of a patient's vulnerability to future self-harm. However, when faced with an individual patient their value is limited by their low specificity in that they identify as at risk many patients who do not go on to further parasuicide (MacLeod, Williams & Linehan, 1992). A greater understanding of the psychological dysfunctions found in parasuicide patients offers the opportunity to enhance the specificity of risk assessment and, as importantly, develop more effective interventions for this large and vulnerable group. The three main psychological disturbances associated with parasuicide, namely poor interpersonal problem solving, a high level of hopelessness about the future, and a reduced ability to regulate mood, will now be discussed.

Interpersonal Problem Solving

Empirical studies have consistently demonstrated that parasuicide patients display some difficulties with interpersonal problem solving. McLeavey et al. (1987) found that a group of deliberate drug overdose patients were less effective at problem solving when compared to a mixed group of psychiatric patients who did not have a history of parasuicide. A similar dysfunction was measured by Schotte and Clum (1987) who found that psychiatric inpatients with high levels of suicide ideation were poorer problem solvers than a group of equally depressed but non-suicidal inpatient controls. Similar problem-solving dysfunctions have also been measured in adolescent female parasuicides (Rotherham-Borus et al., 1990).

To measure problem-solving ability, the above studies have mainly used the Means-End Problem Solving Test (MEPS: Platt, Spivack & Bloom, 1975) in which the patient is given the beginning of a story (e.g. 'a person moving into a new neighbourhood who wants to get to know his neighbours') and a successful ending (e.g. 'he has many good friends in the neighbourhood') and the patient is encouraged to generate ways by which the outcome could be achieved. The main dependent variable in these studies has been the *number* of relevant means produced. Other studies have detected deficits in the *quality* of solutions offered by parasuicide patients, finding them to be more passive, with an overreliance on others (Linehan et al., 1987; Orbach, Bar-Joseph & Dror, 1990).

The work of Mark Williams and his collaborators (Williams & Broadbent, 1986; Williams & Dritschel, 1988; Evans et al., 1992; Williams, 1996) has suggested that an enhanced degree of overgenerality in the recall of autobiographical memories may contribute to these problem-solving dysfunctions in parasuicide patients. The generality of autobiographical memory has been measured using the Autobiographical Memory Test (Williams & Broadbent, 1986) in which the patient is presented with emotional cue words (e.g. 'happy') and is asked to respond as quickly as possible with a *specific* memory, responses being deemed specific if they refer to a particular event or occurrence which did not span longer than 24 hours. Thus, a specific response to the cue word 'happy' might be 'a Christmas party I went to several years ago when Tom and I got rather drunk and spent most of the evening singing' whereas a general response might be 'when I go to parties'. Parasuicide individuals have been shown to be more overgeneral in their autobiographical memories than matched general medical ward patients (Williams & Broadbent, 1986 ; Evans et al., 1992) and than non-patient controls (Williams & Dritschel, 1988).

Although overgenerality of autobiographical memory is clearly not confined to parasuicide patients, having also been identified in groups of patients with primary depression (Williams & Scott, 1988), parents with relationship difficulties with their children (Wahler & Afton, 1980), sex abuse survivors (Kuyken & Brewin, 1995), and Vietnam veterans with post-traumatic stress disorder (McNally et al., 1994), it is plausibly argued that an overgeneral memory database is not conducive to creative problem solving as it provides fewer prompts for the generation of potential strategies to overcome life difficulties. The further findings of a significant correlation between the specificity of autobiographical memory and the effectiveness of problem solving (Evans et al., 1992; Sidley et al., 1997) strengthen this link, and highlight the clinical importance of repeatedly encouraging the patient to be more specific when detailing recent difficult situations, so as to facilitate the problem-solving process which often constitutes such an important part of the therapeutic intervention with parasuicide.

Hopelessness

It has been known for some time that hopelessness about the future is intimately associated with suicidal behaviour. The concept of hopelessness has typically been assessed using the Beck Hopelessness Scale (Beck et al., 1974) and scores on this self-rating questionnaire have been shown to be a powerful predictor of parasuicide repetition (Petrie, Chamberlain & Clarke, 1988) and completed suicide (Beck, Brown & Steer, 1989; Fawcett et al., 1990).

The relative contribution of positive and negative anticipation to the concept of hopelessness has been explored by MacLeod, Rose and Williams (1993). Using a 'future fluency' test in which subjects were asked to generate occurrences in the future they were either looking forward to or not looking forward to, it was found that parasuicide subjects were less able to think of future positive events when compared to controls, whereas there was no difference in their fluency for events they were not looking forward to. The associated finding that parasuicide patients show less impairment with positive anticipation when they are presented with further cues, suggests that these results cannot be wholly explained on the basis of parasuicide patients actually having less to look forward to due to harsh life circumstances. Furthermore, this lack of positive anticipation in parasuicide patients has recently been replicated by MacLeod et al. (1997), who also found it to be independent of depression. Thus it appears that the basis of hopelessness is reduced prediction of positive events, important or trivial, and this pessimism seems to apply for both the immediate and long-term future. It is plausible to suggest that the phenomenon of overgeneral retrieval of autobiographical memories (discussed above) might account for this lack of positive anticipation, since if a patient finds it very difficult to access specific memories of happier times it will be equally difficult to predict discrete positive events (Williams, MacLeod & Rose, 1992). Clearly, the challenging of beliefs regarding the absence of future positive events is an important component of the psychological intervention with parasuicide patients.

Affect Regulation

Many patients who engage in suicidal behaviour display difficulties in the management and tolerance of emotional experiences. Patients with borderline personality disorder, for whom deliberate self-harm is often a prominent feature, experience aversive and enduring affective states with parasuicidal acts appearing to be 'behavioural solutions to intolerably painful emotions' (Linehan, 1993). Anger and hostility are commonly heightened in parasuicidal populations (Crook, Raskin & Davis, 1975; Richman & Charles, 1976; Weissman, Fox & Klerman, 1973) and, in some individuals, self-harm might be negatively reinforced in the short term by achieving a reduction in the intensity of aversive emotion (clinical impression suggests that this feature is more prominent in self-cutting than in deliberate drug overdose). It is therefore important that the assessment of a patient who has recently engaged in parasuicide should include a detailed analysis of any emotional changes which occur in the period spanning before, during and after the self-harm.

INTERVENTIONS TO REDUCE PARASUICIDE

Demonstrably effective strategies to reduce suicidal behaviour have been rare. The potential primary preventive function of training General Practitioners to better recognise and treat depression has been suggested by the study of Rutz, von Knorring and Wolinder (1989) who reported a significant, albeit temporary, drop in the completed suicide rate for the small Swedish island of Gotland (compared to the Swedish mainland) in the year following two educational workshops. With regard to parasuicide, it has been demonstrated (Morgan, Jones & Owen, 1993) that the provision of a 'green card' to a patient in the aftermath of deliberate self-harm, which gives a name and number for the patient to contact a health professional, day or night, should a suicidal crisis return, can significantly reduce parasuicide repetition, although the benefits of this approach seem limited to those individuals without any prior history of self-harm behaviour.

Encouragingly, empirical evidence is emerging for the efficacy of cognitive behavioural interventions which target one or more of the psychological disturbances outlined above—namely, poor interpersonal problem solving, hopelessness about the future, and impaired affect regulation—in reducing the likelihood of future self-harm. Salkovskis, Ather and Storer (1990) used five 1-hour sessions of problem solving with a high-risk group of parasuicide patients and found a superior outcome to a 'treatment as usual' control group with regard to depression level, hopelessness, suicidal ideation and target problems. Furthermore, although at 18 months follow-up there was no significant difference between the two groups on parasuicide repetition, at 6 months there was a difference in favour of the problem solving intervention, suggesting that this brief period of problem solving had delayed post-treatment parasuicide. Consistent with the premise that problem solving dysfunction, and in particular overgeneral memory recall, may underpin some forms of suicidal behaviour, the emphasis on the specific (identifying discrete, personally relevant problems; 'brainstorming' potential solutions; generating further measurable targets in the light of results obtained) implicit in the brief treatment package of Salkovskis, Ather and Storer (1990) may account for the beneficial impact of such a brief intervention.

Dialectical Behaviour Therapy (DBT), Linehan, 1993) incorporates a range of therapeutic strategies which collectively address the psychological dysfunctions of parasuicide patients. Developed primarily for the treatment of female patients with borderline personality disorder, DBT targets suicidal behaviour as its first priority by teaching a combination of skills in problem solving, reducing aversive mood states, and cognitive restructuring. Treatment is intensive, involving weekly group and individual sessions spanning 12 months, and the dialectical focus throughout is on conveying a respectful acceptance of the way things are for the patient while also trying to facilitate change. An integral part of the individual sessions is to explore any recent incident of self-harm or suicidal ideation in minute detail, no matter how transient or trivial this behaviour might at first appear to be. Even if the patient is reluctant to do so, repeated encouragement is given to go beyond a general recollection of the incident and a fine-grained, chain analysis of the specific events leading up to the parasuicide is undertaken as a way of facilitating the identification of alternatives to self-harm. In addition, the DBT package incorporates instruction in several emotion-regulation skills, including contingency management, exposure to intense emotion without impulsive actions, and increasing mindfulness to current emotion.

The effectiveness of DBT in reducing parasuicide has been demonstrated by Linehan et al. (1991) who found that, in comparison to a 'treatment as usual' group, their group of female patients with borderline personality disorder were significantly less likely to engage in parasuicide during treatment, had less medically serious parasuicides, and had fewer inpatient psychiatric days per patient. These improvements with regard to suicidal behaviour were largely maintained at 12 months follow up (Linehan, 1993).

CASE ILLUSTRATIONS

A couple of real cases will now be described to illustrate how the psychological disturbances, reviewed above, can typically present in clinical practice (names and some details have been changed to ensure anonymity).

Frank was 35 years of age and was referred from the psychiatric department where initially he was an inpatient following a serious suicide attempt.

Presenting Problems

Frank identified phases of severe depression and habitual self-mutilation as being his priority problems. He also described clinical levels of anxiety, usually (but not exclusively) when in the company of other people, and for several years he had been using diazepam which he was now trying to reduce. In addition, he described periods of 'uncontrollable anger' during which he would typically smash objects or kick and punch walls and doors. As a means of coping with his powerful negative emotions, Frank had abused alcohol and illicit drugs intermittently in the past. Assessment shortly after referral showed Frank to meet DSM-IV criteria for Social Phobia, Major Depressive Episode, and Borderline Personality Disorder.

Early Experience

Frank originated from Ireland, where he was the youngest of the family, his two sisters being more than 10 years his senior. His childhood was unhappy since, largely as a result of their strong religious beliefs, his parents would not allow him to mix with other children in his neighbourhood. Frank described his mother as domineering, controlling and very critical towards him, and his father as cold, emotionless but manipulative and argumentative. Frank always felt he had little in common with his parents and siblings, maybe largely as a result of the age gap, and from his early teenage years he began to rebel by dressing outlandishly and dyeing his hair; these behaviours attracted further criticism from his family and probably resulted in a degree of exclusion from his peer group at school (thus strengthening his sense of alienation).

Core Beliefs and Assumptions

Frank identified two core beliefs about himself : 'I am different—don't fit in' and 'I am bad', both of which seemed to be the logical products of his background with its excessive criticism and isolation. Related assumptions were 'I deserve to be punished' and 'I don't deserve to be happy'.

Automatic Thoughts

Typical automatic thoughts which underpinned his feelings of depression and anxiety included: 'I'm letting people down again', 'I'm not good enough for her', 'She's making fun of me', 'There is no future—things will just get bleaker and bleaker', 'I hurt everyone who gets close' and 'It would be better for everyone if I ended it all'.

Parasuicide History

Frank started to deliberately self-harm in his early teenage years when he would scratch his arms with sharp metal implements or punch and head-butt walls. This form of self-injurious behaviour had persisted throughout his life, punctuated only by brief (no longer than 6 month) periods of abstinence. Over the last 12 months Frank had inflicted deeper, more severe cuts to his arms. In addition, during his adult life there had been five potentially life-threatening parasuicides (one attempt at carbon-monoxide poisoning from a car exhaust, an attempted hanging, and three major drug overdoses), an incidence of the latter having precipitated his current admission to psychiatric hospital. Further detailed assessment and conceptualisation revealed the presence of two distinct types of parasuicide, each with its own particular psychological mechanism and each with markedly different implications for treatment. Firstly, the self-cutting clearly served a *mood-regulatory* function. Analysis of emotional changes in the course of several recent self-mutilations demonstrated the following sequence: in the minutes immediately prior to self-cutting Frank felt tense and agitated ; during the cutting he reported experiencing excitement, a 'high'; immediately after the self-mutilation he stated he felt calm and relaxed ; and it was only some hours later that his mood would once again deteriorate with guilt being prominent, typically fuelled by self-condemnatory beliefs about him having cut again. Thus, the primary function of the self-cutting was short-term tension reduction. Indeed, Frank admitted he found it a comfort to carry some form of blade around with him as its presence reassured him in much the same way as a generally anxious or agoraphobic patient might carry a box of tranquillisers. Clearly, any effective clinical intervention for the self-mutilation would need to teach an alternative, less destructive means of tension reduction so as to enhance the patient's skills in regulating his own emotions. Secondly, and in complete contrast, the drug overdoses and other forms of suicidal behaviour occurred at times when Frank was extremely hopeless and could see no solution to his problems. This would typically be in response to something going wrong or not working out for him, such as a relationship ending or an unsuccessful attempt to change some aspect of his difficulties. This second strand of his parasuicide presentation appeared to be the product of *perceived hopelessness* and *ineffective problem solving*, and thereby required a different focus of treatment involving the cognitive restructuring of beliefs pertaining to the theme of 'no future' together with skills training in the area of problem solving. The presence of these two distinct strands of parasuicide within the same patient was neatly encapsulated in one of Frank's comments that he fully expected to kill himself at some point in the future and that the tension reduction of self-cutting helped him to 'get by' until this time.

The second illustrative case is that of Paul, a 43-year-old man, referred by his GP requesting help for his 'depression and inability to cope with life'.

Presenting Problems

During the initial assessment session, when asked to describe the difficulties for which he was seeking help, Paul responded with the comment ' I want to die because of everything' and when asked about his recent emotional state he said 'I don't feel anything' (these apparent difficulties with identifying specific problems and with describing emotional states are common occurrences in parasuicide patients and can frustrate the therapist's attempts to use standard cognitive behaviour therapy—this will be discussed further in the later sections). Further questioning revealed that intense and persistent anger was a major cause of Paul's distress, punctuated by phases of severe dysphoria. In addition, Paul identified an important behavioural problem in not being able to show affection to his two children, aged 6 and 11, and when the younger child was physically near to him Paul would experience a sharp increase in a range of somatic anxiety symptoms (sweats, palpitations, and muscle tension). At initial assessment, Paul met the formal DSM-IV criteria for Major Depressive Episode.

Early Experience

From the age of 7 years, Paul lived in children's homes with temporary carers. He was particularly distressed by a period in his childhood when he lived with an aunt and uncle who repeatedly abused him physically and who generally treated him poorly in comparison to their own son. At the age of 8 years Paul suffered an isolated incidence of sexual abuse from an adult male stranger he met in the street. The current phase of psychological difficulties had been precipitated three years ago when his longstanding relationship with his girlfriend, the mother of his children, started to break down.

Automatic Thoughts and Assumptions

Access to cognitive content was very difficult to achieve with Paul, particularly in the early stages of treatment. He found it hard to believe that his thought processes might be playing a contributory role to his distress and when directly questioned about thoughts he had at times of high levels of aversive emotion he would typically reply that he was 'not thinking anything' and that his 'mind just goes blank'. Early homework tasks to complete the standard 'situations–moods–thoughts' recording did not get beyond thought entries such as 'I want to die' and 'Thinking of taking all my tablets'. Further practice at accessing specific thoughts (see later discussion) revealed two recurring automatic thoughts, namely 'I'm not a proper father' and an image of his aunt /surrogate mother pushing him away as a child when he was seeking physical affection.

Important maintaining factors for his intense and pervasive anger were assumptions around the theme of fairness: 'Life must be fair and I can't tolerate it if it is not'; 'It is not right for my children to have fun in the light of how badly I was treated as a child'.

Parasuicide History

Paul's parasuicide history dated back to a period over 20 years ago when, between the ages of 20 to 22, he engaged in multiple impulsive drug overdoses. This phase in his life was a generally chaotic and stressful time during which he was involved in a range of criminal activities and served a brief prison sentence, and it was his inability 'to cope' with imprisonment which precipitated his first drug overdose. There was then a 15-year period without any instance of parasuicide while with his partner, but her decision to end the relationship three years ago had precipitated a further period of multiple, impulsive drug overdoses. In the 12-month period prior to referral Paul had overdosed on 20 occasions, many of these involving the ingestion of relatively small amounts (such as five sleeping tablets taken in the middle of the afternoon) with the expressed aim being 'to knock me out for a while'. Detailed assessment of recent mini-overdoses suggested they had a *mood-regulating* function, having the effect of achieving a temporary escape from phases of severe dysphoria. Interspersed within these relatively minor overdoses, had been four occasions when Paul had ingested much larger amounts which had resulted in hospitalisation, and these potentially life-threatening episodes were found to immediately follow periods of intense anger in addition to a depressed mood. Thus, these more severe drug overdoses also seemed to have a mood-regulatory function but, unlike the more frequent minor episodes, intolerable anger appeared to play a prominent, catalytic role. It followed from this conceptualisation that any effective intervention to reduce Paul's rate of suicidal behaviour would need to teach an alternative way of moderating his emotions of intense sadness and anger.

BROAD GUIDELINES FOR INTERVENTION

Parasuicide patients are a heterogeneous group of individuals for whom deliberate self-harm can serve different functions, and as such an individual conceptualisation of each case is essential for effective treatment. However, when working in the often highly stressful clinical circumstances of trying to reduce the likelihood of self-destruction, it may be helpful for the therapist to have a framework in mind for determining the appropriate timing for the different types of clinical intervention to counter suicidal behaviour. A useful heuristic is one that attempts to match potential interventions to the temporal proximity of suicidal behaviour, and such a framework is summarised in Figure 12.1.

Imminence of suicidal behaviour	Primary aim of intervention	Examples of strategies
IMPENDING—within hours	To increase chances of SURVIVAL	Observation/monitoring Reduce access to means Reasons for living/dying Use therapeutic relationship to buy time
VERY NEAR—within days	To resolve CRISIS	Problem solving Specificity training
NEAR—within weeks	To restructure BELIEFS which predispose to suicidal behaviour	Evidence for/against Pie charts Rectify thinking errors Behavioural experiments Emotional flooding
DISTAL—within months	To loosen SCHEMATA which confer vulnerability	Positive data log Continuum work Re-evaluate past evidence

Figure 12.1   A framework to guide clinical intervention based on the likely imminence of suicidal behaviour.

Survival

When the balance between the desire to live and the desire to die has swung markedly in the direction of self-destruction, the immediate and overriding aim becomes that of maximising the chances of survival. At the beginning of the third session with Frank, it was observed that he was notably quieter and more distant than he had been during previous contacts. He told me how, two days previously, he had argued with one of his few long-term friends during a visit to him on the ward (at this time Frank was an inpatient on an acute psychiatric ward) and this incident had confirmed to Frank his core belief about being a bad person and the corresponding assumption about not deserving to be happy. Since the argument he had been significantly more depressed and agitated. Further questioning revealed that about three hours ago he had made a decision to kill himself by hanging, planned for later that evening during the staff 'handover' period when he was less likely to be observed, and he had already managed to obtain a length of cord which he had removed from an old dressing gown and had chosen the location for his suicide (namely an exposed water pipe in the toilet on the ward). Worryingly, since making this decision, he reported feeling calmer as he was no longer agonising over whether he should or should not end his life. In this case, several strategies were used to try and promote survival. Firstly, after some discussion about my professional and ethical responsibilities to maintain life, Frank reluctantly agreed to my informing the ward staff of his intentions so that staff observation of him could be increased (even without Frank's consent, the staff would have been informed in circumstances such as this but it was felt to be preferable to obtain his agreement so as to maintain the therapeutic relationship). Secondly, access to means of self-harm was reduced by persuading Frank to hand over the cord to a nurse and by the ward staff trying to identify and where possible reduce opportunities for suicide in the short-term future. Thirdly, during this third session Frank was encouraged to generate reasons for living and dying. Reasons for dying were that it would end his psychological pain and that he would no longer keep hurting other people. Predictably, reasons for staying alive were more difficult to extract but, when Frank was asked to 'name any possible consequences of his suicide which he would not be 100% comfortable with', along with a lot of prompting, he was able to generate the following: 'Despite the problems we have in our relationship, my parents would be devastated'; 'My friend Tom would feel very guilty' (this was the friend with whom he had recently argued) ; 'If I survived I might suffer brain damage'; and 'Jack, my six-year-old son, would be very distressed to hear of my death and the stigma of a father who committed suicide would be with him for the rest of his life'. These negative consequences of dying were written on a card and Frank was asked to keep it near at all times, along with a picture of his son Jack, and to regularly look at and reflect upon the card and picture, particularly at times when he felt actively suicidal. Fourthly, an attempt was made to use the therapeutic relationship to at least delay any imminent suicidal behaviour (the urge to act on suicidal thoughts is often a transient one) by asking Frank to give some reassurance that he would not self-harm before our next session in seven days time, but he declined to do so; possibly, in part, a reflection of the infancy of our relationship. At the end of this session hopeful, but truthful, statements were made to Frank such as 'I have known several people who have felt similar to you who, at some point in the future, have felt much more positive about things'.

Upon leaving, Frank was notably more ambivalent about killing himself and, as a result, more agitated. To instil uncomfortable ambivalence about living or dying, and to maximise safety by reducing access to means and increasing awareness/observation of carers, are often appropriate, and perhaps the only realistic, short-term goals to look for with someone who has already decided to attempt suicide.

Crisis Resolution

Teaching traditional cognitive therapy skills to patients experiencing a suicidal crisis is, at best, very difficult. Demonstrating the links between thinking and emotions/behaviour, identification of 'hot' thoughts, and the challenging of them through the search for supportive and counter-evidence or via behavioural experiments (all important ingredients of the cognitive therapy package) often appear to have very little face validity for a patient in crisis who can only see an increasing number of situational problems which are deemed to be making life intolerable. Reframing a crisis as a range of problems that need to be solved is typically more acceptable to a patient who perceives escape through suicidal behaviour as his only option.

Paul arrived for his second outpatient appointment in just such a crisis. He was visibly agitated and told me he could no longer cope with the way he was feeling, and said he felt very near to taking a drug overdose as a way of ending his aversive emotional state. Questioning revealed that the current crisis had been precipitated by an incident the previous day when he was verbally abused by some youths who lived in the neighbourhood (a regular occurrence), soon followed by a letter from the housing department informing him that his application for relocation had been given 'low priority' status and that any house move would not be for at least 12 months. Paul was encouraged to view his current crisis as comprising a number of specific problems which potentially could be solved. Initially he described his difficulties in an overgeneral way ('I can't cope' and 'no happiness in my life') but with prompting he was able to list his current problems in terms of emotions and situations which he wanted to change (see Figure 12.2). Given the early stage of therapy, together with the desirability of quickly achieving some positive change to his crisis situation, Paul was asked to focus on the most recent problem ('harassment from his neighbours') but was reassured that his other, more enduring, problems

1. High levels of anger/agitation
2. Very low mood
3. Harassment from neighbours
4. Loneliness
5. Unable to show his children affection

Figure 12.2 Paul's problem list.

would certainly be addressed in subsequent sessions. In keeping with the traditional problem-solving approach (Hawton & Kirk, 1989), Paul was prompted to come up with possible alternative solutions, other than taking a drug overdose, to his neighbour harassment problem and to look at the pros and cons of each. However, rather than 'brainstorming' multiple alternatives, it was felt more manageable for a patient in crisis to examine just a couple of options in detail, in this case namely : 'to spend more time at his mother's house' or 'to make further applications to the housing department, supported by medical evidence regarding the stress he was experiencing'. By the end of this session, Paul opted to make further applications while in the meantime spending a greater proportion of the weekends (the time when most harassment occurred) at his mother's home, and as a result of this decision he felt a little more hopeful and less inclined to overdose.

The conceptualisation of Paul's parasuicides had indicated a prominent mood-regulatory function, and therefore problem-solving interventions were only likely to serve as a means of clearing away obstacles to the provision of further primary interventions aimed at modifying affect. In contrast, problem-solving dysfunctions appeared to contribute significantly to Frank's vulnerability to carrying out life-threatening parasuicides (see above) and therefore more treatment hours were devoted to training in this area. In addition to the teaching of basic problem-solving skills, a substantial part of treatment sessions 4–8 was aimed at increasing the specificity with which Frank viewed past events with the expressed aim of expanding his database of choices when wrestling with either situational problems or suicidal crises.

Thus, the sequence of events which preceded his recent, life-threatening drug overdose (the one which led to his admission to psychiatric hospital) was examined in excruciating detail with particular emphasis on 'choice points', defined as stages in the chain of occurrences where an alternative line of action was possible (see Figure 12.3). Frank's initial impression of this particular day was that a suicide attempt was inevitable from the moment he discovered his girlfriend was not at home. A closer analysis of events indicated that later in the chain there were several choice points, some options taking him nearer to parasuicide (for example, drinking heavily in the pub) whereas others would have most likely steered him away from self-harm (for example, ringing his friend Tom). Such an analysis, it was hoped, would make the constructive lines of action more salient and accessible the next time a crisis arose and thereby enrich the problem-solving process.

In addition to this detailed examination of recent parasuicides, Frank was also asked to attempt 'specificity training' as a homework exercise. This

Situation/choice point	Action taken	Alternative options
Felt depressed, walked to girlfriend's house but she wasn't at home	Walked aimlessly around the streets, thinking about the futility of it all	1. Return home 2. Ring Tom, a friend, and arrange to meet 3. Go to gym and do some exercise (sometimes makes me feel a bit better)
Came to telephone box, queued with initial intention of phoning CPN to tell him how bad I was feeling	Did not wait; walked away feeling angry and had first thoughts about taking a drug overdose	1. Wait in queue and phone CPN 2. Ask the person using the phone to please hurry up as I desperately need to contact someone 3. Walk to another phone box about half a mile away
Looking in the window of a chemist's shop	Went in and bought 200 paracetamol tablets	1. Walk past the chemist and go home 2. Once inside, buy something innocuous, like cough sweets 3. Tell the chemist how desperate I'm feeling and seek advice
About to enter an unfamiliar pub	Entered pub, sat at bar alone and drank 6 pints of beer and 4 large whiskies	1. Ring CPN or friend Tom from the phone in the pub 2. Walk to a more familiar pub where I am likely to meet someone I know 3. Enter unfamiliar pub but restrict myself to shandy and soft drinks
Leaving pub, very depressed and intoxicated	Returned home to empty flat and consumed 100 paracetamol tablets and a half bottle of vodka	1. Try girlfriend's house again 2. Go around to Tom's house 3. Take self to A&E department and seek help from liaison nurses

Figure 12.3 Choice points for the sequence of events preceding Frank's drug overdose

involved daily practice at generating (and writing down) the names of three people he had known at some point in his life, three places he had been to, and three activities in which he had engaged, and for each of these nine items he was asked to recall a specific memory. Although at first finding this exercise difficult and some of the negative memories it provoked distressing, Frank subsequently stated that often it was rewarding in so much as it rekindled events which were inconsistent with his perception of himself as a bad person.

Restructure Beliefs

When the patient is not experiencing an immediate suicidal crisis, and deliberate self-harm is unlikely to occur within hours or days, cognitive intervention to restructure beliefs which predispose to suicidal behaviour can be used to good effect. Such beliefs typically fall into two categories. Firstly, those which hold self-harm to be the preferred or only way out of one's difficulties, for example 'I cannot survive without Christine' and 'killing myself is the only way to get them to understand'. Secondly, beliefs which have a more indirect, but enduring role in maintaining the high levels of hopelessness or aversive affect which underpin suicidal behaviour.

As documented earlier, Paul at first had major difficulties in identifying 'hot' thoughts. However, asking him to vividly relive the situations which evoked recent suicidal crises revealed the reoccurrence of the thought 'I can't stand feeling this way' (depressed and agitated) and this belief was challenged in two ways. In the first instance the central cognitive method of marshalling evidence to support or refute this belief was used, and Paul was able to see that on several occasions he had successfully negotiated feeling really bad without resorting to parasuicide, although taking an overdose had typically been his main weapon for dealing with these emotions. A second way of challenging this belief involved a behavioural experiment, the aim of which was to recreate in the session an intense, aversive emotion and to explore what happened when he tried to tolerate it. This was achieved via a form of imaginal exposure in which a script was constructed of a recent episode which had been associated with powerful feelings of anger and dysphoria (which had resulted in overdose). This script was read repeatedly to Paul during the session, and he was asked to try and 'relive' it in imagination as vividly as possible but *without* picturing himself taking the overdose. The result of the experiment was that his discomfort level increased sharply in the session (up to 90% of maximum) but then declined to a manageable 50% after about 15 minutes. As a consequence Paul was able to consider an alternative belief that 'although these feelings are very unpleasant I can get through it, and it does start to get easier after a few minutes', but he still harboured doubts about being able to cope with these feelings when they were of 100% intensity away from the sessions.

A key belief of Paul's which was often responsible for his depressed mood, and which therefore made a significant (albeit indirect) contribution to his repeated parasuicides, was 'I'm not a proper father'. This conclusion was based almost entirely on his difficulty in showing his children physical affection. This was challenged by asking Paul to list the criteria he himself would use if he was to judge whether someone else was a capable or 'proper' father. He was able to generate 11 standards including 'to protect them from harm'; 'to praise them when they have done something good'; 'to often give them a kiss and cuddle'; and 'to show an interest in their school work'. Paul then went through each criterion in turn and gave himself a mark out of 10 for how well he fulfilled each one, and he was very pleasantly surprised to find that his overall score was 73%. Consequently, he was able to hold the alternative thought 'Although I have problems showing affection to my children, overall I am a reasonably good father' with a high level of conviction, and this discovery had an immediate and positive effect on his dysphoria (indeed Paul on several subsequent occasions would spontaneously comment on his finding that he was an "A" grade dad').

Schematic Change

Cognitive intervention at the belief level with Frank had limited scope with regard to modifying his recurrent parasuicidal behaviour. Although beliefs which might act as a direct precursor to self-harm (for example 'It would be better for everyone if I ended it all') were successfully challenged, it was reasoned that little sustainable improvement in this area could be achieved while he strongly held a self-schema 'I am bad' and the corresponding assumptions of 'I don't deserve to be happy' and 'I deserve to be punished'. This was particularly relevant to Frank's habitual self-mutilation which had a mood-regulatory function, as any hint of improvement in his affect would contravene assumptions about not deserving to feel happy, which in turn would trigger rebound dysphoria and agitation. Furthermore, the match between self-mutilation and the premise that he deserved censure could partly account for the tension reduction typically experienced by Frank during the process of cutting.

Therapeutic intervention to reduce Frank's vulnerability to self-harm targeted the core belief 'I am bad', largely drawing on the techniques of Greenberger and Padesky (1995). Initially, Frank agreed to collect each and every snippet of evidence in his daily life which suggested that his belief about being a bad person 'was not 100% true all of the time'. Consistent with the impression Frank gave of being a kind and thoughtful person, such evidence was in abundance and, after he had overcome his initial tendency to discount pieces of information on the basis of their triviality, he was typically able to document two occurrences per day which did not fit with his self-perception of badness (e.g. 'Sarah, an ex-work colleague, told me I was always thinking about other people's welfare'; 'I gave a cigarette to a fellow patient on the ward'). This positive data log was maintained over a period of 5 months (sessions 10–25) and as a result, for perhaps the first time in his life, he could actually recognise that his badness was not a fact but rather a belief. In parallel with this positive data collection, an attempt was made to re-evaluate historical information which, until now, Frank had taken as being testimony to his badness. Dividing his history into 5-year chunks, any evidence Frank took as being suggestive of his badness was listed. He found this task very difficult at first, his recollection even of this negative material being vague and patchy, but the ongoing specificity training (mentioned above) seemed to facilitate this endeavour and he was able to recall at least one piece of evidence for each time period which he had taken to be indicative of his badness. Once listed, an alternative interpretation of this evidence was constructed: for example at 8 years old his father calling him an 'evil bastard' in front of several family members (aunt, uncle, cousins) was reconstrued as being suggestive of his father's own inadequacy and lack of parenting skills rather than Frank's own badness. Also, counter-evidence to his badness was identified for each time period (for example, at 11 years old regularly helping an elderly grandmother with her shopping; in his late teenage years, working as a care assistant with adults with learning difficulties). By the end of this phase of schema-focused work his conviction in the belief 'I am bad' fell from 100% to 60% and the previous 4 months, during which his conviction had been less than 90%, had not witnessed any acts of parasuicide.

In contrast, little schema-focused work was done with Paul. The rules he held about it being imperative that life should treat him fairly were made explicit and their negative effects on his anger levels were discussed. Paul expressed a wish not to pursue these areas further as he already felt he had benefited sufficiently from the cognitive restructuring and also because he feared the pain of reliving traumatic/abusive experiences from his past.

Progress in Therapy

Regrettably, despite the parasuicide-free period described above, there was no successful, long-term outcome for Frank. Shortly after the weakening of his 'I am bad' belief had been achieved, his anxiolytic medication was reduced (against Frank's wishes) and the increase in general anxiety this evoked seemed to precipitate an increase in alcohol intake and subsequently the abuse of a range of psycho-active substances. Shortly after session 25, Frank dropped out of psychological treatment and two months later he entered an inpatient, drug treatment centre. He had also taken a large drug overdose around this time although it was uncertain as to whether this was deliberate or accidental. Interestingly, there had been no further incidents of self-mutilation.

For Paul there was a successful outcome in that there was no incidence of parasuicide during the 5 months he was in therapy, nor at 12-months follow-up. He remained lonely and rather isolated, although he did manage to get back into part-time work as a decorator. He was still prone to occasional angry outbursts but, at worst, these escalated into smashing objects in his home rather than self-harm.

To aid clarity, outlines of the treatment structures for Frank and Paul are given in Figures 12.4 and 12.5 respectively.

Intervention	Session number
Assessment	1 and 2
Survival strategies	3 and 4
Problem solving	4,5,6 and 7
Specificity training	5,6,7,8,9,10,11,12,13,14,15 and 16
Cognitive restructuring	8,9 and 10
Schema-focused work	10,11,12,13,14,15,16,17,18,19,20,21,22,23,24 and 25

Figure 12.4   Outline structure of Frank's treatment programme.

Intervention	Session number
Assessment	1,2 and 3
Problem solving	2,3 and 4
Cognitive restructuring	5,6,7,8,9 and 10
Imaginal flooding/behavioural experiments	8,9,10,11 and 12
Schema-focused work	13 and 14

Figure 12.5   Outline structure of Paul's treatment programme.

A SUMMARY OF THE EXTRA COMPLEXITIES OF WORKING WITH SUICIDAL PATIENTS

Difficulties with Accessing Thoughts

In many instances of deliberate self-harm, the decision to act is taken impulsively. Furthermore, patients who repeatedly engage in parasuicide over a long period of time (e.g. many patients with borderline personality disorder) typically experience intensely aversive emotions which they are inclined to short-circuit by self-injurious behaviour. Both these factors— impulsiveness and inability to tolerate strong negative emotions, some- times together with a fear about what introspection might reveal— collectively result in the identification and evaluation of thoughts often being an extremely difficult task for the suicidal patient, particularly dur- ing a crisis.

Therapeutic solutions to this difficulty involve either the use of the alter- native strategies of problem solving or emotional flooding (both described above) or the teaching of techniques to enhance thought identification. An example of the latter is 'cognitive self-observation' (Linehan, 1993) in which during sessions the patient is encouraged to repeatedly practise using his imagination to observe himself from the outside, and to tune in to what is going on at various points during the therapeutic discourse. Using this approach in-session in combination with the traditional thought recording as homework can facilitate the identification of the patient's thought processes and thinking style.

Greater Importance of the Therapeutic Relationship

Although a positive and trusting therapeutic relationship is an essential basis for any successful psychological intervention, it typically takes on greater sig- nificance when working with suicidal patients. In broad terms, there are two reasons for this. Firstly, in the case of chronically suicidal individuals, the core schemata which confer vulnerability are typically focused on interpersonal themes. For example, perceived needs for attachment or fears of abandon- ment are commonly seen in this group of patients. Similarly, self-beliefs about being 'defective' or 'unlovable' are often present along with percep- tions of others as being 'uncaring' or 'rejecting', and these core beliefs con- spire to make the interactions with the therapist the most immediate and accessible testing ground for these interpersonal constructs. Secondly, and in some ways a logical consequence of these core beliefs, during a suicidal crisis the relationship may at times be the only tool available to tip the balance away from self-destruction and to reinforce alternative ways of coping.

Linehan's 'Dialectical Behaviour Therapy' clearly emphasises the importance of the relationship when she advocates the need for the clinician to hit the balance between *acceptance* of the patient's behaviour as it currently is, while simultaneously believing that positive *change* can and will take place. She encapsulates the required attitude towards borderline parasuicide patients in several assumptions the therapist should hold, for example 'patients are doing the best they can' ; 'patients want to improve' ; 'their current lives are unbearable' ; and 'patients may not have caused all of their own problems, but they have to solve them anyway'.

Desirability of a Team Approach

Work with suicidal patients is characteristically very stressful, and therefore clinicians require access to regular support and supervision from colleagues. Also, given that parasuicide patients typically come into contact with a wide range of professionals (doctors and nurses in Accident and Emergency Departments, psychiatrists, community psychiatric nurses, psychologists) interdisciplinary liaison and cooperation are essential for good clinical practice. Such working relationships with colleagues can at times be difficult to maintain, partly as a result of the negative attitudes that chronically parasuicidal individuals can evoke in some professionals (the unilateral decision to reduce Frank's anxiolytic medication provides one example of less than optimal multidisciplinary teamwork). Furthermore, there can often be a tension between the demands to maximise the chances of a patient's survival and that of remaining therapeutic, and ongoing communication with medical colleagues is therefore essential. Although the central thrust of a cognitive-behavioural intervention for parasuicide can be provided via regular (at least weekly) outpatient sessions, close collaboration with other workers is essential if one is to achieve the consistency of approach, the supportive working milieu for therapists, and the provision of a safe environment, all of which are essential elements of a high-quality service for these vulnerable and often complex cases.

REFERENCES

Beck, A.T., Brown, G. & Steer, R.A. (1989). Prediction of eventual suicide in psychiatric inpatients by clinical ratings of hopelessness. *Journal of Consulting and Clinical Psychology*, **57**, 309–310.

Beck, A.T., Weissman, A., Lester, D. & Trexler, L. (1974). The measurement of pessimism: The hopelessness scale. *Journal of Consulting and Clinical Psychology*, **42**, 861–865.

Buglass, D. & Horton, J. (1974). A scale for predicting subsequent suicidal behaviour. *British Journal of Psychiatry*, **124**, 573–578.

Crook, T., Raskin, A. & Davis, D. (1975). Factors associated with attempted suicide among hospitalized depressed patients. *Psychological Medicine*, **5**, 381–388.

Evans, J.M., Williams, J.M.G., O'Loughlin, S. & Howells, K. (1992). Autobiographical memory and problem solving strategies of individuals who parasuicide. *Psychological Medicine*, **22**, 399–405.

Fawcett, J., Scheftner, W.A., Fogg, L., Clark, D.C., Young, M.A., Hedeker, D. & Gibbons, R. (1990). Time-related predictors of suicide in major affective disorder. *American Journal of Psychiatry*, **147**, 1189–1194.

Greenberger, D. & Padesky, C.A. (1995). *Mind over Mood: a Cognitive Therapy Treatment Manual for Clients*. New York: Guilford.

Hawton, K. & Catalan, J. (1987). *Attempted Suicide* (2nd edn). Oxford: Oxford University Press.

Hawton, K. & Kirk, J. (1989). Problem solving. In K. Hawton, P.M. Salkovskis, J. Kirk & D.M. Clark (Eds), *Cognitive Behaviour Therapy for Psychiatric Problems*. Oxford: Oxford Medical Publications.

Kreitman, N. & Foster, J. (1991). The construction and selection of predictive scales with particular reference to parasuicide. *British Journal of Psychiatry*, **159**, 185–192.

Kuyken, W. & Brewin, C.R. (1995). Autobiographical memory functioning in depression and reports of early abuse. *Journal of Abnormal Psychology*, **104**, 585–591.

Linehan, M.M. (1993). *Cognitive Behavioral Treatment of Borderline Personality Disorder*. New York: Guilford.

Linehan, M.M., Armstrong, H.E., Suarez, A., Allmon, D. & Heard, H.L. (1991). Cognitive behavioural treatment of chronically parasuicidal borderline patients. *Archives of General Psychiatry*, **48**, 1060–1064.

Linehan, M.M., Camper, P., Chiles, J.A., Strohsal, K. & Shearin, E.N. (1987). Inter-personal problem solving and parasuicide. *Cognitive Therapy and Research*, **11**, 1–12.

MacLeod, A.K., Pankhania, B., Lee, M. & Mitchell, D. (1997). Parasuicide, depression and the anticipation of positive and negative future experiences. *Psychological Medicine*, **27**, 973–977.

MacLeod, A.K., Rose, G.S. & Williams, J.M.G. (1993). Components of hopelessness about the future in parasuicide. *Cognitive Therapy and Research*, **17**(5), 441–455.

MacLeod, A.K., Williams, J.M.G., & Linehan, M.M. (1992). New developments in the understanding and treatment of suicidal behaviour. *Behavioural Psychotherapy*, **20**, 193–218.

McLeavey, B.C., Daly, R.J., Murray, C.M., O'Riordan, J. & Taylor, M. (1987). Interpersonal problem-solving deficits in self-poisoning patients. *Suicide and Life-threatening Behaviour*, **17**, 33–49.

McNally, R.J., Lasko, N.B., Macklin, M.L. & Pitman, R.K. (1995). Autobiographical memory disturbance in combat-related post-traumatic stress disorder. *Behaviour Research and Therapy*, **33**, 619–630.

McNally, R.J., Litz, B.T., Prassas, A., Shin, L.M. & Weathers, F.W. (1994). Emotional priming of autobiographical memory in post-traumatic stress disorder. *Cognition and Emotion*, **8**, 351–367.

Morgan, H.G., Jones, E.M. & Owen, J.H. (1993). Secondary prevention of non-fatal deliberate self-harm: The Green Card study. *British Journal of Psychiatry*, **163**, 111–112.

Orbach, I., Bar-Joseph, H. & Dror, N. (1990). Styles of problem solving in suicidal individuals. *Suicide and Life-threatening Behaviour*, **20**, 56–64.

Ovenstone, I.M.K. & Kreitman, N. (1974). Two syndromes of suicide. *British Journal of Psychiatry*, **124**, 336–345.

Petrie, K., Chamberlain, K. & Clarke, D. (1988). Psychological predictors of future suicidal behaviour in hospitalized suicide attempters. *British Journal of Clinical Psychology*, **27**, 247–258.

Platt, J.J., Spivack, G. & Bloom, W. (1975). *Manual for the Means-End Problem-Solving Procedure (MEPS): A Measure of Interpersonal Problem Solving Skill*. Philadelphia: Hahnemann Medical College and Hospital, Department of Mental Health Sciences, Hahnemann Community MH/MR.

Richman, J. & Charles, E. (1976). Patient dissatisfaction and attempted suicide. *Community Mental Health Journal*, **12**, 301–305.

Rotherham-Borus, M.J., Trautman, P.D., Dopkins, S.C. & Shrout, P.E. (1990). Cognitive style and pleasant activities among female adolescent suicide attempters. *Journal of Consulting and Clinical Psychology*, **58**, 554–561.

Rutz, W, von Knorring, L. & Wolinder, J. (1989). Frequency of suicide on Gotland after systematic postgraduate education of general practitiners. *Acta Psychiatrica Scandinavia*, **80**, 151–154.

Salkovskis, P.M., Ather, C. & Storer, D. (1990). Cognitive behavioural problem solving in the treatment of patients who repeatedly attempt suicide. *British Journal of Psychiatry*, **157**, 871–876.

Schotte, D.E. & Clum, G.A. (1987). Problem-solving skills in suicidal psychiatric patients. *Journal of Consulting and Clinical Psychology*, **55**, 49–54.

Sidley, G.L., Whitaker, K., Calam, R.M. & Wells, A. (1997). The relationship between problem-solving and autobiographical memory in parasuicide patients. *Behavioural and Cognitive Psychotherapy*, **25**, 195–202.

Wahler, R.G. & Afton, A.D. (1980). Attentional processes in insular and non-insular mothers: Some differences in their summary reports about child problem behaviours. *Child Behaviour Therapy*, **2**, 25–41.

Weissman, M., Fox, K. & Klerman, G.L. (1973). Hostility and depression associated with suicide attempts. *American Journal of Psychiatry*, **130**, 450–454.

Williams, J.M.G. (1996). Depression and the specificity of autobiographical memory. In D. Rubin (Ed.), *Remembering our Past: Studies in Autobiographical Memory*. Cambridge: Cambridge University Press.

Williams, J.M.G. & Broadbent, K. (1986). Autobiographical memory in attempted suicide patients. *Journal of Abnormal Psychology*, **95**, 144–149.

Williams, J.M.G. & Dritschel, B.H. (1988). Emotional disturbance and the specificity of autobiographical memory. *Cognition and Emotion*, **2**, 221–234.

Williams, J.M.G. & Scott, J. (1988). Autobiographical memory in depression. *Psychological Medicine*, **18**, 689–695.

Williams, J.M.G., Macleod, A.K. & Rose, G. (1992). Autobiographical memories and autobiographical futures in suicidal patients: The specificity heuristic. Unpublished manuscript.

Chapter 13

COGNITIVE BEHAVIOURAL INTERVENTIONS FOR ANGER, AGGRESSION AND VIOLENCE

*Kevin Howells**

INTRODUCTION

The emotion of anger and its links to behavioural problems of aggression and violence have been the subject of speculation and philosophical comment throughout history. This is unsurprising, given the commonness of anger as an experience in everyday life (Averill, 1982). It has only been in the latter half of the twentieth century, however, that anger has become the focus of more sustained scientific analysis, and the application of such analyses to therapeutic interventions has a short history indeed.

The pioneer of the clinical approach, and a major contemporary influence on theory and practice, has been the American psychologist Raymond Novaco (1975, 1978, 1997). In spite of such major contributions, we have not yet witnessed the extensive application of cognitive behavioural analysis and intervention for problems of anger that we have seen for problems of anxiety (Mathews, 1997; Clark, 1997) or depression (Teasdale, 1997; Williams, 1997). This is an undesirable state of affairs in that anger and the behaviours associated with it constitute a problem for individuals and society as a whole that is at least as great as that posed by the emotional disorders of anxiety and depression. Indeed, it would not be difficult to construct an argument that anger and aggression constitute the human problem most in need of remediation.

The many social problems for which anger may be a precursor include

* School of Psychology, University of South Australia

Treating Complex Cases: The Cognitive Behavioural Therapy Approach.
Edited by Nicholas Tarrier, Adrian Wells and Gillian Haddock.
© 1998 John Wiley & Sons Ltd.

violent offending (including homicide), family violence to children, marital violence, sexual offending, violence within psychiatric and penal institutions and cardiovascular disease (Levey & Howells, 1990; Novaco, 1994, 1997). The list of problems that can be linked to anger continues to grow. Recently, for example, the importance of anger problems in post-traumatic stress disorder has begun to be demonstrated (Chemtob et al., 1997b). While anger may be a factor contributing to these behaviours and conditions, it cannot, in general, be regarded as either a necessary or sufficient cause. Whilst many serious violent offences, for example, are anger-mediated, violence can occur in an instrumental fashion, with no affective arousal on the part of the perpetrator (e.g. the 'cold' use of a weapon to extort money in the course of an armed robbery). Some have expressed scepticism about the usefulness of the angry versus instrumental distinction in classifying violent acts (Indermaur, 1995) and it is clearly the case that many violent offences (e.g. violent property offending) typically construed as instrumental may have more complex affective antecedents.

Anger is also not a sufficient cause of violence, in that the majority of angry episodes do not result in a violent, or even aggressive, outcome (Averill, 1982). It follows, therefore, that anger should be viewed as only a contributing factor to the general phenomena of aggression and violence and that a broader range of variables need to be considered in planning treatment programmes.

THE ASSESSMENT AND FORMULATION OF ANGER/AGGRESSION PROBLEMS

The assessment and formulation of anger problems needs to be guided by current models of anger and aggression and by research findings relating to differences *between* aggressive people and non-aggressive controls, and differences *within* the population of aggressive individuals. This latter point follows from the recognized heterogeneity of perpetrators of aggression and violence (Blackburn, 1993).

In Table 13.1 classes of variables which would need to be covered in the clinical assessment and formulation of anger and aggression are summarised. Such variables form part of the functional analysis (Sturmey, 1996) of the problem behaviour that has been identified. In practice, the problem behaviour being addressed in the clinical setting is likely to be an act of overt aggression or violence. In a penal setting the problem behaviour may be a violent offence or series of offences. For the purposes of the table, therefore, anger is treated as an independent variable affecting the likelihood of a violent behaviour outcome, rather than as the dependent variable. Clearly, the

Table 13.1 Variables to include in functional analysis of aggression and violence

1. Frequency, intensity, duration and form of aggression
2. Environmental triggers (including background stressors)
3. Cognitive antecedents (including biases in appraisal of events, dysfunctional schemata, underlying beliefs and values supporting aggression)
4. Affective antecedents (emotions preceding aggressive acts, e.g. anger or fear)
5. Physiological antecedents
6. Coping problem-solving skills
7. Personality dispositions (e.g. anger-proneness, impulsivity, psychopathy, general criminality, overcontrol, undercontrol)
8. Mental disorder variables (mood, brain impairment, delusions, hallucinations, personality disorders)
9. Consequences/functions of aggressive acts (for perpetrator and others, short-term and long-term. Including emotional consequences such as remorse and peer group or institutional reinforcement)
10. Buffer factors (good relationships, family support, achievement in some area)
11. Opportunity factors (weapons, victim availability, restrictions)
12. Disinhibitors (alcohol, drugs).

emotion of anger itself can be subject to a functional analysis and some of the variables listed in the table (for example, cognitive and physiological antecedents) can be construed as antecedents for anger itself, in addition to any direct effect on aggressive behaviour.

Identifying the Problems and its Antecedents

The first task in cognitive behavioural work with anger is to describe the problem behaviour that needs to be addressed. It is rare for the experience of anger itself to constitute the presenting problem. More typically, anger has been the precursor of some act of aggression. It is not always easy to obtain clear and objective accounts of the nature and frequency of aggressive acts. In penal, and even in psychiatric or non-institutional settings, it may be perceived by the patient or client that it is in their interest to deny or minimise the details of their current or previous violent acts. Official records, criminal histories and medical casenotes are frequently insufficiently detailed as to the nature of what occurred.

The identification of triggering (usually environmental) events for anger and aggression is a core task, as it is for cognitive behavioural therapy in general. Direct structured observation and recording of incidents is desirable, but rarely possible outside of the institutional setting. Even in institutions designed for the custody of high-risk (see below) violent offenders, such as maximum security prisons or hospitals, violent incidents often have a very low frequency. This is a reassuring fact for the institution and its staff, but one that creates difficulties in establishing the pattern of triggering events for the client.

Case records, particularly when they cover an extended period of the client's life and when the client has perpetrated a large number of incidents, may be useful in identifying trigger patterns, but it will often be necessary for the cognitive behavioural therapist to devise a systematic method for extracting, summarising and classifying the relevant information.

Structured interviewing and client diaries (Kirk, 1989) have an important role in determining the environmental antecedents for angry and aggressive responses. The task of moving from the Cs (emotional or behavioural consequences) to the As (activating events) in cognitive behavioural assessment is a familiar one for the cognitive behavioural therapist. The methods described for this task in the general cognitive therapy literature (see, e.g. Trower, Casey & Dryden, 1988) and in texts for other difficult client groups (for example, Chadwick, Birchwood & Trower, 1996) are also relevant for the assessment of anger/aggression problems.

Assessing Contextual Factors

The assessment of triggering events needs to move beyond a description of the immediate (proximal) trigger to a consideration of the general temporal, social and environmental context in which the immediate trigger occurred (Novaco, 1993). The individual's threshold for angry and aggressive responding is lowered by prior exposure to aversive aspects of the physical and social environment. Aversive aspects of the physical environment include temperature variation, pain and high levels of noise (Berkowitz, 1982, 1993a,b).

Social stressors which may have similar effects include poor living conditions, financial problems and unemployment. Barefoot et al. (1991) found that hostility had strong statistical associations with sociological variables such as race, gender, income, education and occupation. Similarly, Catalano et al. (1993) found that being laid off from work was associated with large subsequent increases in violent behaviour.

Such effects would be predicted by a number of theories of anger and aggression, including Berkowitz's cognitive neo-associationist model (Berkowitz, 1990, 1993b), Zillmann's excitation transfer theory (Zillman, 1983) and Anderson, Anderson and Deuser's recent model, the 'affective aggression framework' (Anderson, Anderson & Deuser, 1996). The latter, for example, identify input variables such as frustration or discomfort through temperature variation as activators of three 'routes' to behavioural aggression: accessible hostile cognitions, accessible angry emotions and physiological arousal. All three of these routes lead to hostile immediate appraisal of the triggering event.

The implication of such work for assessment and formulation (and ultimately for treatment) is that a core task is to assess the contribution of such contextual factors to an episode of heightened anger or aggressive behaviour. It is not uncommon to observe such effects in the clinical setting where, for example, a parent's furious and violent response to his child's minor misdemeanour was clearly determined by his exposure to stressors occurring earlier that day (a financial crisis, medical worries).

A clinical example may help to illustrate the complexity of the triggering events for many forms of anger. Clear identification of the triggers often indicates what therapeutic strategies need to be used. Peter (aged 41 years) recently experienced an intense episode of anger (he called it 'blind rage') during which he was seriously physically violent to his elderly father. Although he had experienced mild resentment towards his father over the years, he had never before lost control of his temper, nor become violent towards him. His outburst of anger and aggression was 'ego dystonic', at variance with his view of himself, his previous behaviour and with his values.

The immediate triggering event was an argument with his father over why he (Peter) had failed to carry out a small chore for his father. His father began to criticise him and his failures, and then the explosion of anger and violence occurred. The context was that prior to visiting his father on the day of the incident, he had visited his (Peter's) former wife in an (unsuccessful) attempt to make a reconciliation. During the two preceding weeks he had been preoccupied with problems at work and his failure to achieve an expected promotion. These various events produced a lowering of his mood and a preoccupation with thoughts of his failure, and resentment of others for their inability to recognise and acknowledge how he might be feeling. Peter brought all this with him, in addition to two or three recent alcoholic drinks, to the argument with his father.

Assessing Angry Episodes

One of the clinical tasks, therefore, to be achieved through structured interviewing is analysis of the client's episodes of anger and aggression. Table 13.2 illustrates a format for collecting relevant information, and includes examples of material from a client with serious problems of anger and aggression.

Table 13.2   Categories for structured interview of angry episode

Triggering event	Inference	Emotion	Behaviour	Consequences
Immediate		Angry/nervous	*Verbal*	*Positive short term*
Another male made eye contact in a bar	He is staring at me	*Physiological*	Swore/insults	Felt better
Contextual	*Chain*	Tension in my arms	*Paralinguistic*	Stopped him
	He dislikes me	Heart thumping	High volume	*Negative short term*
	He will 'come at' me	*Intensity*	'Snarling'	Cut my lip
Already irritable because of argument earlier in the day	He may beat me in front of my friends	80 (scale 1–100)	*Non-verbal*	*Positive long term*
	My friends will think I am an idiot	*Duration*	Punched and pulled to floor	Kept my reputation
Aroused/stressed by long car journey in traffic	I would be a weak person	30 minutes: emotion decreased to 20 for remainder of evening		*Negative long term*
Expectations of 'trouble' in pubs through previous experience	*Evaluations*[a]	*Degree of control (0–100)*		Banned from pub
	That would be awful	20, "out of it"		'My Mum found out'
	I couldn't stand it			
	I must get him first			

[a] As defined by Trower, Casey and Dryden (1988)

Cognitive Antecedents

Cognitive analyses have increasingly dominated attempts to explain and model anger and aggression in recent years (Novaco & Welsh, 1989; Clore et al., 1993; Wyer & Srull, 1993). It is also the case that cognition has been the major focus for clinicians concerned with assessment and treatment (Howells, 1988, 1989; Levey & Howells, 1990; Novaco, 1994). The process of appraisal forms a major part of most contemporary theories of emotion in general and of anger in particular. A central premise of much of this work is that different emotions have specific patterns of appraisal associated with them (Roseman, Antoniou & Jose, 1996).

The evidence relating to the cognitive mediation (cognitive structures, propositions, operations and products) of anger has been extensively reviewed by Novaco and Welsh (1989). These workers identify five biases in information processing predisposing people towards anger: attentional cueing, perceptual matching, attribution error, false consensus and anchoring effects. They also suggest assessment procedures to detect and monitor such biases. In the present author's view, such innovative assessments are likely to be more productive that traditional psychometrics, but there is little indication, as yet that such methods have been widely taken up by clinicians, at least as far as can be judged from the published literature.

Peter (above) showed many of these cognitive biases. He paid considerable attention to cues of inattentiveness and lack of interest on the part of others (attentional cuing). His failed marriage facilitated future perceptions (at work) of failures (perceptual matching). He routinely attributed the causes of his distress to significant others letting him down (attribution error) and had difficulty in conceiving that others might view his apparent failures differently than he did (false consensus). Finally his judgements about himself and others were quite rigid and resistant to change (anchoring effects).

Cognitive scientists have been concerned to model the conditions giving rise to differing emotions and have attempted to describe the distinctive appraisals giving rise to anger. Ortony, Clore and Collins (1988) and Clore et al. (1993), for example stress the complexity of the emotion of anger, requiring as it does an appraisal of an *event* (the 'bad' thing that occurred) and of the *agent* of the event. This group of workers specify that a necessary condition for anger is that the person judges the agent of the aversive event to be *blameworthy*. The preconditions for judging them to be blameworthy are making the attribution that the agent's action was firstly undertaken out of free will and, secondly, that it was based on intention or negligence.

The second precondition is that the event being judged is *undesirable*. The intensity of anger experienced, according to this model, depends on the degree of blaming and on the level of undesirability of the event. Models such as these have not yet had the impact they should on cognitive behavioural assessment and therapy. They suggest, for example, that assessments should target the processes of social cognition involved in judging the blameworthiness or negligence of others. How do clients judge free-will on the part of others perceived as doing them harm? Do they take into account information indicating the other may not be acting out of free choice?

Ortony, Clore and Collins (1988) refer to the 'structure of standards' and 'structure of goals' within the mind which support appraisals of blameworthiness and undesirability. The implication is that there is a need to assess both these structures in the client. This would involve looking at the rules and moral imperatives that guide people's actions and assessing the rigidity with which moral rules are applied. Similarly, there is a clinical need to address the goal structure of the client. The fact that a client, for example, finds criticism profoundly undesirable and aversive (and hence potentially anger-eliciting) may alert the therapist to the importance of the goal of obtaining social approval.

The emphasis on blame and on moral imperatives as important variables for problematic anger is also found within Rational-Emotive Therapy (Ellis, 1977; Grieger, 1982; Howells, 1988). Within this framework, Grieger (1982) has made a useful distinction between *autistic anger* and *interpersonal anger*, the former depending on subjective (dysfunctional) 'must' and 'should' evaluations, the latter being based on the perceived violation of an explicit, consensual code of rules.

In assessing clients the present author uses a procedure for eliciting personal rules and evaluations in clinical assessments, based on repertory grid methods (Fransella & Bannister, 1977). The client is asked to generate (say) five recent situations in which they experienced anger. They are then asked to generate five similar situations where emotional arousal was experienced, but not of an angry sort (upset or depressed). Triads of these situations are presented on cards, each triad containing at least one angry and one non-angry situation. The client is then asked to compare and contrast the three situations and describe how they differ. Thus they might contrast an occasion when difficulties at work led to feelings of anger with two other similar situations in which they were upset but not angry. When pressed to articulate what the difference might be, the client discriminates the former situation from the latter two on the basis that 'someone was deliberately trying to screw things up' in the former, while in the latter 'things were bad but no one planned it'. Thus an important anger-related construct has been elicited, which may need to be explored further.

These biases in the attribution of blame need to be core targets for assessment and intervention. Equally, the client's framework of moral evaluations needs to be explored and modified, often in the direction of reducing the rigidity with which moral rules are applied. Changing the 'undesirability' of events is a task already addressed within cognitive behavioural therapy, under the rubric of challenging catastrophic and exaggerated evaluations (see Trower, Casey & Dryden, 1988).

The theories and research discussed above undoubtedly suggest that direct attempts need to be made to change anger-eliciting cognitions and schemata. However, it does not follow that cognitive change is always the primary goal in modifying angry aggression. Many theorists (for example, Berkowitz, 1993b; Izard, 1993) have argued against an over emphasis on cognition. Cognitive abnormalities may provide only one route to dysfunctional anger (Izard, 1993). Berkowitz has suggested: 'A growing body of laboratory experiments and field studies have now demonstrated that unpleasant occurrences can evoke aggressive reactions along with feelings of anger, irritation and annoyance, even though the events are not socially illegitimate and are unintended' (Berkowitz, 1993b, p.3).

It would seem that automatic and involuntary systems are sometimes involved in anger. Berkowitz's cognitive neo-associationist perspective suggests several different emphases for anger-management therapy, including greater attention to environmental features (for example weapon and temperature effects; Anderson, Anderson & Deuser, 1996) and to the effects of low mood on subsequent anger. This latter proposition has the implication that any intervention that has the effect of increasing the sense of subjective well-being, or reducing the frequency or intensity of aversive internal states, will tend to reduce the probability of angry aggression.

Personality, Anger and Aggression

The published literature is consistent with the notion that personality dispositions may predispose individuals to acts of aggression and violence. Firstly, some studies have indicated that people who are anger-prone are more likely to engage in violent behaviour (Novaco, 1993, 1994, 1997). Care needs to be taken in such studies to avoid tautological conclusions by ensuring that the dependent variable used is not itself an index of anger.

Blackburn (1993) has conducted extensive studies into personality in populations of violent offenders. Part of Blackburn's research effort has been directed at the question of whether violent offenders are homogeneous as a population or whether distinct sub-types exist. The answer to this question seems to be that violent offenders are markedly heterogeneous.

Blackburn's early work (1968, 1971) tested the hypothesis of Megargee (1966, 1971) that both *overcontrolled* and *undercontrolled* personality types can be found in the violent offender population. The former are typically seen as meek, unassertive people who are extremely inhibited about anger expression.

Under extreme provocation, or following a build-up of frustration over time, the overcontrolled person may finally display an extreme act of violence, such as a domestic homicide. The undercontrolled person, on the other hand, is easily aroused to anger and has few inhibitions about anger expression. Blackburn's work, and that of others, has broadly supported the undercontrol/overcontrol distinction, though it is apparent that the overcontrolled group can be further divided into *controlled* and *inhibited* subgroups.

The important lesson from this work for the cognitive behavioural therapist is that the functional analysis may be very different for the various types of aggressive people. It follows that the therapeutic requirements will also differ. Thus, within a cognitive behavioural therapeutic group for aggressive or violent people, may be found individuals with chronic dispositional problems of hostility, poor frustration tolerance and angry, impulsive acting out, but also individuals who are reluctant to make hostile inferences, report low levels of anger and who control their aggressive impulses until disinhibited by a crisis situation (see Peter above). In my own clinical experience, problems of excessively inhibited anger, leading to a later explosive outburst, are as common as the undercontrolled pattern.

Psychopathy

It is not difficult to distinguish overcontrolled and undercontrolled patterns in clinical assessments. The overcontrolled group would be expected to have low rather than high scores on measures of trait anger or anger expression (Novaco, 1994; Spielberger *et al.*, 1983). Additionally, the frequency of expressions of anger in the form of overt aggression would be expected to be low in the overcontrolled group, but high in the undercontrolled group.

The undercontrolled pattern described by Blackburn overlaps, to a degree, though not completely, with the classic psychopathic personality described by Hare and his co-workers (Hare, Strachan & Forth, 1993). Our understanding of psychopathy has been considerably advanced by the development of the Psychopathy Checklist (Revised), a reliable and valid instrument for assessing psychopathic characteristics in both the research and the clinical setting (Hare et al. 1990). Factor analysis of the PCL-R indicates that two factors underly the items: Factor 1 is defined by low empathy, callousness and egocentricity, and Factor 2 by impulsivity (Hare, Strachan & Forth, 1993).

It is not difficult to see how both factors might be relevant to anger expression and violence. It is likely that empathic reactions to others and reflecting on the consequences of our actions are both psychological processes that serve as inhibitors of anger expression. Indeed, Hare, Strachan and Forth (1993) have reported studies showing an association between psychopathy and violent crime (particularly assaults) and also violent institutional behaviour. The presence of psychopathic characteristics in a presenting client is likely to be a contraindication for anger-management therapy.

Violent offending, of course, is often part of a broader pattern of general criminality and antisocial behaviour (Farrington, 1996). Farrington's review of developmental risk factors reveals that childhood impulsivity and similar personality traits are associated with criminality in later years. The relevance of such findings for the cognitive behavioural clinician is that they alert us to the need to establish the generality or specificity of the problem behaviour presented by the client.

An individual may present with anger-control problems in the absence of other forms of antisocial behaviour or criminality, or, alternatively, they may occur in the context of antisocial behaviour, criminality and even significant personality disorder of a psychopathic type. Again, the functional analysis for these two individuals will be very different, as will their treatment requirements.

Anger, Violence and Disorder

The relationship between mental disorder and angry, aggressive and violent behaviour remains elusive. Psychiatric disorder is common in offender populations, though the prevalence varies markedly, depending on the characteristics and setting of the population under scrutiny (Monahan & Steadman, 1994; Shah, 1993). Equally, people suffering from a mental disorder can sometimes be shown to have a higher risk of violent offending than non-psychiatric controls, but the number of confounding factors is large. In recent years, however, the quality of studies has improved, allowing more reliable inferences to be drawn from the results (see reviews in Howells & Hollin, 1993; Monahan & Steadman, 1994; Hodgins, 1996).

Schizophrenia, in particular, now appears to have a significant association with violent behaviour, though the population of violent offenders with schizophrenia will comprise two groups: those with late-onset violent behaviour which is 'caused' by the development of a psychosis, and those whose criminality and violent behaviour preceded the development of the mental illness (Hodgins, 1996). Clearly, the psychiatric treatment of the mentally disordered perpetrator of violence can be expected to have an impact on that violence only for the first group. In the second group, causal influences (and, hence, therapeutic methods), will have to be identified elsewhere. It may be that specific symptoms of conditions such as schizophrenia (delusions and hallucinations) will prove to be better predictors of aggression and violence than the global disorder *per se* (McNiel, 1994; Taylor, 1994).

The possibility that similar cognitive abnormalities occur in delusional patients and in aggressive individuals is beginning to be explored in the literature and is a promising area for future research. Bentall's theorizing about paranoid delusions (Bentall, 1994; Bentall, Kinderman & Kaney, 1994) and Chadwick, Birchwood and Trower's (1996) hypotheses about 'poor me' paranoia involve similar processes (attribution biases) to those observed in anger and aggression (see above). Chadwick, Birchwood and Trower (1996) explicitly suggest that 'paranoid defence is like a form of the angry attributional style – individuals perceive interpersonal negative evaluation and construe it as being unjust, a form of persecution, and they reject the criticism and condemn the persecutor' (p. 137).

Amongst mentally abnormal violent offenders, some studies have reported brain abnormalities, particularly in the temporal lobe, in repetitive violent offenders (Wong et al., 1997a; Wong et al., 1997b). In formulating anger and violence problems, therefore, some attention needs to be paid to the possible role of organic impairment, particularly in mentally disordered violent offenders, a group beginning to be addressed in cognitive behavioural and anger-management therapy (Becker, 1997; Renwick et al., 1997).

Interventions

The content of cognitive behavioural therapeutic interventions for anger and aggression has been described in a substantial number of clinical accounts, research reports and reviews (Becker, 1997; Feindler & Ecton, 1986; Howells, 1988, 1989; Levey & Howells, 1990; Novaco, 1997; Towl, 1994). It is clear that anger-management training has a number of possible components, including relaxation training, social skills training and cognitive restructuring, and that these various components may have differential effects on the different dimensions of anger (Edmondson & Conger, 1996).

The Basic Strategies of Cognitive Behavioural Interventions

I have argued previously for a comprehensive approach to therapy for anger and violence problems, derived from theoretical models and empirical research (Howells, 1989; Howells et al., 1997). In Table 13.3 some examples of basic intervention methods are summarised. Which strategy should be adopted depends on the functional analysis of the presenting anger/violence problem.

Table 13.3 Some intervention strategies

1. IMPROVING CLIENT'S UNDERSTANDING OF THE NATURE AND COMPONENTS OF THE PROBLEM

As within CBT in general, a collaborative approach should be used, so that the CBT analysis is shared fully with the client. Novaco's model, for example (anger as a product of environmental events, cognitive processes, physiological arousal and behavioural reactions), could be used explicitly by and with the client. This strategy involves analysing previous episodes of anger, aggression and violence in CBT terms.

2. IDENTIFYING AND MODIFYING THE IMMEDIATE TRIGGERING EVENTS

Where the triggering events or situations are deemed by the therapist to be abnormal, the focus should be on modifying the triggering situation rather than the client's response to it. Stimulus control methods are also useful in this case, assisting the client to avoid situations that have been found to trigger the problem. A client, for example, might learn to avoid pubs or bars where conflict is likely to a rise.

3. IDENTIFYING AND MODIFYING CONTEXTUAL STRESSORS (SEE PREVIOUS DISCUSSION)

The client needs to learn the effects of previous stressors on how they deal with particular provocations. Reduction of these stressors should be a therapeutic target. Work or family problems, for example, may need to be dealt with because they adversely affect reactions to provocation in another context. Some structural contextual stressors (unemployment, poor living conditions) may be difficult to modify.

4. CHANGING COGNITIVE INFERENCES AND DYSFUNCTIONAL SCHEMATA

For the case summarised in Table 13.2, for example, many inferences in the inference chain are open to disconfirmation and change. Eye contact does not necessarily mean being stared at, nor does being stared at necessarily mean the other person has an aggressive intent. The evaluations that 'I must get him first' or, in another client, that 'If someone hurts me I must even the score' are powerful and dysfunctional beliefs.

continued overleaf

Table 13.3   *continued*

5. UNDERMINING DYSFUNCTIONAL INFERENCES AND SCHEMATA BY TRACING THEIR DEVELOPMENTAL ROOTS.

It may be helpful, for example, for a client to learn that the inference that 'this person is ridiculing me in front of others' has its roots in early experiences of this sort in a family or school environment.

6. IMPROVING CONTROL OF PHYSIOLOGICAL AROUSAL

Where arousal is an important part of the anger or violence problem then relaxation and similar techniques have a role. The relaxation response can be used to lower the baseline (pre-provocation) level of arousal, thus reducing the absolute level of arousal caused by the provocation. Alternatively, relaxation can be used as a self-control response in provoking situations, or as a response antagonistic to anger arousal in formal desensitisation to a provocation hierarchy.

7. BROADENING THE REPERTOIRE OF COPING RESPONSES

Problem solving, social skills training and related techniques can be used to generate new ways of coping with potential provocations. Standard social skills methods of role play, feedback, modelling, rehearsal and homework assignments have a role here.

8. PREVENTION OF ESCALATING SOCIAL BEHAVIOUR

Many incidents of aggression and explosive temper follow a behavioural escalation. A minor dispute, for example, 'gets out of hand' until serious aggression occurs. Clients need to understand the role of their own social behaviour in producing escalations and in preventing them. Social skills analysis and treatment methods have a role in changing this form of social behaviour.

9. STRENGTHENING COMMITMENT TO CHANGE

Motivational interviewing techniques, though developed mainly for problem drinking, have an important part to play in sensitising some clients to the negative consequences of their problematic behaviour. Such techniques are particularly likely to be needed with clients in forensic or similar settings, where they have not yet viewed themselves as having a problem requiring change.

The meta-analytic review of anger-management interventions conducted by Edmondson and Conger (1996) provides broad support for the effectiveness of such interventions with individuals who are high in trait anger. Such studies are of limited usefulness for the clinician, however, in that they are largely conducted with student populations, selected on the basis of high trait anger scores, rather than with people presenting to mental health or criminal justice services with significant problems of anger control (see reviews by Watt, 1996; Novaco, 1997).

Novaco's review (1997) of work conducted with offender or violent populations reveals that controlled intervention studies are few and far between, though, when conducted, these studies tend to offer a degree of support for the therapy (e.g. Chemtob et al., 1997a; Goldstein & Glick, 1996; Stermac, 1986).

Two controlled studies by Watt (1996), however, suggest a need for caution before applying anger management indiscriminately with violent prisoners. In two separate samples of violent prisoners undergoing anger-management therapy, Watt found no difference between the treatment groups and untreated controls on a range of dependent measures, including anger experience, anger expression, prison misconduct and observational measures of aggressive behaviour. Watt suggests several plausible reasons for these findings, including poor motivation of participants, the high complexity of the programme content and limited opportunities to practise the skills learned. It is also clear from Watt's account that the participants were not subjected to a pre-treatment assessment to establish whether their violent offending was actually anger-mediated.

Outcome research with 'real life' violence and offending behaviour is insufficiently developed to enable the clinician to identify which components of the content of anger management are most effective. Similarly we know little as yet about the optimum way to present and organise therapeutic interventions. Rather than sitting back to wait for the research to be done, there are two potential ways forward.

The first is to make interventions comprehensive in their content, rather than focusing on one component (whether it be cognitive restructuring or social skills training). Indeed, a comprehensive approach is entirely consistent with the underlying theoretical base for anger management, as originally elaborated by Raymond Novaco. Novaco (e.g. 1978) strongly emphasises the environmental, cognitive, physiological, affective and behavioural components of anger and the reciprocal relationships that exist between these components. The second way forward is to organise interventions in the light of principles which have been shown to be important for the treatment of offending behaviour *in general*. These will be briefly outlined towards the end of the chapter.

ISSUES AND PROBLEMS IN INTERVENTION

Problems arise in cognitive behavioural treatment of anger and aggression which are more acute than for other disorders, such as anxiety and depression. Anxiety and depression are distressing states for the person, who is, thereby, often motivated to change their affective state. Anger, and even aggression and violence, on the other hand, are not necessarily problematic for the person. I have suggested previously (Howells, 1989) that they may be either ego syntonic or ego dystonic. One person views their anger, for example, as legitimate, useful and even enjoyable (Hodge, 1997) while for another it is a scourge, a cause of unpleasant physical states and an instigator of behaviours they subsequently regret.

The location of anger within the goal structure of the person (Howells, 1989) needs to be taken into account in planning treatment. Anger and its expression may be: (i) congruent with short-and long-term goals (the person sees no short-term or long-term problems for themselves as a result of their expression of anger, even though it might be judged as inappropriate by others); (ii) congruent with short-term, but not long-term goals (the person acknowledges that anger 'works' for them, for example by inducing compliance in others, but dislikes the fact that they are unpopular because of their behaviour; (iii) incongruent with both short and long-term goals (the person, for example, immediately regrets losing their temper with their child, as they disapprove of such behaviour, and dislikes the long-term effects on their relationship with the child).

Individuals with goal structure (i) are not suited to straightforward training in anger-regulation skills (from their perspective they are already skilled) but require an intervention to change their evaluation of their goals. 'Is it really OK to use anger and violence to control others?' Structure (ii) requires an intervention to resolve the incompatibility of short- and long-term goals. The person needs to be made aware of the incompatibility and helped to generate alternative strategies to achieve long-term goals. 'How can you maintain the respect of others without using anger and violence?' Individuals with structure (iii) are less problematic, in that their behaviour is fully ego dystonic and a skills model is hence appropriate. 'How can you control your anger more effectively so you don't . . .?'

The implication of this analysis is that methods such as motivational interviewing (Miller & Rollnick, 1991) have an important part to play for some clients, particularly in a penal setting, where problems of low motivation and rejection of the skills model appear to be common.

As anger management and related methods begin to be implemented in forensic and psychiatric populations, with individuals who have serious, complex problems of violence, personality disorder and outright mental illness (Becker et al., 1997; Howells et al., 1997; Renwick et al., 1997), it is becoming apparent that many difficulties arise for the therapist. These difficulties are likely to be far less common in clients in the general community, who have generally been the focus of anger-management interventions (Edmondson & Conger, 1996).

Renwick et al. (1997) point to the therapeutic pessimism felt by both clients and therapists in such settings and to enduring problems of low motivation, treatment resistance and avoidance. These authors note the resentful, distrustful and even combative style of some participants in therapeutic groups. Additionally, the clients had realistic concerns about the effects of disclosure of their emotions and past behaviour on discharge plans. Novaco (1997), similarly, highlights the long histories of failure, institutionalisation and social rejection that characterise such clients and which entrench their anger and aggression.

Establishing a working alliance with the client, a prerequisite for cognitive behavioural therapy, is likely to be a challenging task in such settings. It may be that these difficulties in establishing engagement are a general feature of working with ego syntonic problems. It is striking, for example, that the 'threats to engagement' identified by Chadwick, Birchwood and Trower (1996) in working with schizophrenic symptoms parallel those discussed by Novaco (1997) and Renwick et al. (1997) working with forensic populations. Chadwick, Birchwood and Trower, for example, point to the therapist's difficulty in empathising with the client, the therapist's pessimism about therapeutic success, the client's expectation that the therapist will be punitive and controlling and the client's difficulty in forming a therapeutic relationship because of previous poor relationships.

The institutional settings in which anger-management programmes are sometimes based (for example, prisons and secure psychiatric hospitals) can themselves have anti-therapeutic effects. Different lessons may be learned about anger control in the therapeutic session than are learned in the course of everyday life in the institution. In our own work in a maximum security prison in Western Australia we are endeavouring to promote the systematic integration of an aggression control programme, and to facilitate behavioural generalisation, by involving prison officers as therapists (Howells et al., 1997). It is also important that staff looking after aggressive clients outside therapeutic sessions have been informed and educated about the goals of the therapy and the likely effects on participants' behaviour.

Tailoring Treatment to the Individual

The range of variables that may contribute to aggressive and violent behaviour is wide (see Table 13.1). It follows that aggressive behaviours that are topographically similar may be functionally dissimilar. Two men may each have committed a homicidal assault. For one it is the product of a broadly antisocial personality, poor impulse control and a hostile appraisal of the world in general. For the other the relevant antecedents are an intense crisis in a relationship, unexpressed anger, fantasised retaliation and disinhibition by alcohol. It is clear that the treatment needs of these two individuals are very different. My colleagues and I have argued elsewhere (Howells, 1996; Howells et al., 1997) that because of the varied functional analyses it is often inappropriate to offer a generic 'package' programme for perpetrators of violence. Group treatment is still viable, but it needs to be sufficiently intensive and extended to allow for individualised formulation and treatment. Given that anger is not a necessary condition for aggressive behaviour (above) not all aggression perpetrators should be offered anger management as the primary treatment method.

From Individuals to Systematic Programmes

One indication of the 'coming of age' and acceptance of a therapeutic method is that consideration starts to be given to how the treatment might be organised and delivered as a large-scale and routine service within the organisation. When this occurs it represents a shift from an exclusive focus on the clinical treatment of individual clients or groups of clients to broader questions of programme delivery.

It is timely for programme delivery issues to be addressed in relation to anger management and similar treatments for violent offenders. In recent years a renaissance of interest in offender rehabilitation has occurred in criminal justice systems around the world (McGuire, 1995). The era of 'Nothing Works' (Martinson, 1974) has begun to give way to a cautious optimism that some therapeutic programmes do have a modest but real impact. 'Some things work, sometimes' may be a more accurate catchphrase for the next century. As part of the rehabilitation of rehabilitation, attention has begun to be paid to defining the principles and elements of effective intervention programmes. Such definitions are likely to be as relevant for programmes of the anger-management type as they are for other rehabilitative interventions.

Three principles that have been influential in the literature have been those of risk, need and responsivity (Andrews & Bonta, 1994). The risk principle is that services should be directed at individuals of highest risk. In the criminal justice context, risk refers to the probability of reoffending and the level of harm that might be caused. In service planning for anger management and similar programmes, whether in a criminal justice or mental health setting, this would seem to be a sensible and important principle. Indeed, the way in which anger management has focused in the past on student populations (see discussion above) is, arguably, a vivid example of the risk principle not being applied by psychologists!

The need principle is that programmes should be based on an analysis of the functional needs of the individual. In effect, the needs principle can be equated with the notion (above) that treatment should address variables revealed as important by a functional analysis of the problem behaviour of individuals. The responsivity principle states that interventions should be matched to the learning styles and characteristics of the group. For example, in the context of our own work in Western Australia (Howells et al., 1997), the responsivity principle would require adapting anger management or violence programmes to the characteristics, attitudes and beliefs of Aboriginal people, who are dramatically over-represented in the offender population.

The task of defining other features of effective programmes is a crucial one and rapid progress is being made, using meta-analytic and other statistical methodologies. Such work tends to support the effectiveness of cognitive behavioural methods, multimodal interventions, maintaining treatment integrity, intensive as opposed to brief programmes, structured follow-ups, explicitly addressing poor motivation for change and using principles of effective organisational change in order to introduce programmes (Andrews, 1996; Losel, 1996; McGuire, 1995).

SUMMARY AND CONCLUSIONS

In this chapter I have argued that the interrelated problems of anger, aggression and violence are still neglected areas within cognitive behavioural therapy. Although anger-management and similar treatments have been developed, and evaluated to some degree, little of this work has focused on the major problems of aggression and violence which are of most concern in our society. One reason for this neglect is almost certainly that such problems, and the individual clients encountered, are indeed complex and a challenge to the practitioner.

I have suggested that anger is one of a broad range of variables that need to be assessed in the clinical formulation of aggressive and violent behaviour. The identification of environmental and cognitive antecedents is a particularly important task. However attention also need to be given to personality, mental disorder and other variables. We have a long way to go in understanding how interventions need to be adapted so that they will be successful with the truly complex individual, whose anger or violence problem forms part of a wide array of other difficulties and disorders.

I have described a number of difficulties which arise in cognitive behavioural work, including poor motivation, engagement problems, institutional effects and the failure to address individual differences in the functional analysis of anger, aggression and violence. More optimistically,

I suggest that anger management and similar interventions can benefit from developments in the broader field of offender rehabilitation and I have outlined some rehabilitation principles which are relevant.

Given the rich theoretical base which exists for this area of clinical practice, the encouraging results from an admittedly sparse outcome literature and the acute social need for well thought out and effective therapeutic interventions, this is an area of cognitive behavioural practice which warrants the attention and support of clinicians, researchers and society at large.

REFERENCES

Anderson, C.A., Anderson, K.B. & Deuser, W.E. (1996). Examining an affective aggression framework: Weapon and temperature effects on aggressive thoughts, affect and attitudes. *Personality and Social Psychology Bulletin*, **22**, 366–376.

Andrews, D.A. (1996). The psychology of criminal conduct and evidence-based assessment and intervention. In C.R. Hollin & K. Howells (Eds), *Clinical Approaches to Working with Young Offenders*. Chichester: Wiley.

Andrews, D.A. & Bonta, J. (1994). *The Psychology of Criminal Conduct*. Cincinnati: Anderson.

Averill, J.R. (1982). *Anger and Aggression: An Essay on Emotion*. New York: Springer-Verlag.

Barefoot, J.C., Peterson, B.L., Dahlstrom, W.C. & Siegler, I.C. (1991). Hostility patterns and health implications: correlates of Cook–Medley Hostility Scale scores in a national survey. *Health Psychology*. **10**, 10–84.

Becker, M., Love, C.C. & Hunter, M.E. (1997) Intractability is relative: behaviour therapy in the elimination of violence in psychotic forensic patients. *Legal and Criminological Psychology*, **2**, 89–101.

Bentall, R.P. (1994). Cognitive biases and abnormal beliefs. Towards a model of persecutory delusions. In A.S. David & J. Cutting (Eds), *The Neuropsychology of Schizophrenia*. London: Erlbaum.

Bentall, R.P., Kinderman, P. & Kaney, S. (1994). Cognitive processes and delusional beliefs: attributions and the self. *Behaviour Research and Therapy*. **32**, 331–341.

Beresford, S. & Omaji, P. (1995). *Aboriginal Juvenile Crime*. Freemantle: Freemantle Arts Press.

Berkowitz, L. (1982). Aversive conditions as stimuli to aggression. In L. Berkowitz (Ed), *Advances in Experimental Social Psychology*. vol. 15. New York: Academic Press.

Berkowitz, L. (1990). On the formation and regulation of anger and aggression. *American Psychologist*. **45**, 494–503.

Berkowitz, L. (1993a) *Aggression: Its Causes, Consequences and Control*. New York: McGraw-Hill.

Berkowitz, L. (1993b). Towards a general theory of anger and emotional aggression: Implications of the cognitive neo-associationistic perspective for the analysis of anger and other emotions. In R.S. Wyer & T.K. Srull (Eds), *Perspectives on Anger and Emotion: Advances in Social Cognition*, vol. VI. Hillsdale, NJ: Erlbaum.

Blackburn, R. (1968). Personality in relation to extreme aggression in psychiatric offenders. *British Journal of Psychiatry*, **114**, 821–828.

Blackburn, R. (1971). Personality types among abnormal homicides. *British Journal of Criminology*, **11**, 14–31.

Blackburn, R. (1993). *The Psychology of Criminal Conduct*. Chichester: Wiley.

Catalano, R., Dooley, D., Novaco, R.W. & Wilson, G. (1993). Using ECA survey data to examine the effect of job layoffs on violent behavior. *Hospital and Community Psychiatry*, **44**, 874–879.

Chadwick, P., Birchwood, M. & Trower, P. (1996). *Cognitive Therapy for Delusions, Voices and Paranoia*. Chichester: Wiley.

Chemtob, C.M., Novaco, R.W. Hamada, R.S. & Gross, D.M. (1997a). Cognitive behavioral treatment for severe anger in post-traumatic stress disorder. *Journal of Consulting and Clinical Psychology*, **65**, 184–189.

Chemtob, C.M., Novaco, R. W., Hamada, R.S., Gross, D.M. & Smith, G. (1997b). Anger regulation deficits in combat-related post-traumatic stress disorder. *Journal of Traumatic Stress*, **10**, 17–36.

Clark, D.M. (1997). Panic disorder and social phobia. In D.M. Clark & C.G. Fairburn (Eds), *Science and Practice of Cognitive Behaviour Therapy*. Oxford: Oxford University Press.

Clore, G.L., Ortony, A., Dienes, B. & Fujita, F. (1993). Where does anger dwell? In, R.S. Wyer & T.K. Srull (Eds), *Perspectives on Anger and Emotion*. Hillsdale, NJ: Lawrence Erlbaum.

Dodge, K.A. & Crick, N.R. (1990). Social information-processing bases of aggressive behaviour in children. *Personality and Social Psychology Bulletin*, **16**, 8–22.

Dodge, K.A. & Tomlin, A.M. (1987). Utilization of self-schemas as a mechanism of interpretational bias in aggressive children. *Social Cognition*. **5**, 280–300.

Edmondson, C.B. & Conger, J.C. (1996). A review of treatment efficacy for individuals with anger problems: Conceptual assessment and methodological issues. *Clinical Psychology Review*. **16**, 251–275.

Ellis, A. (1977). *How to Live With and Without Anger*. New York: Reader's Digest.

Farrington, D.P. (1996). Individual, family and peer factors in the development of delinquency. In C.R. Hollin & K. Howells (Eds), *Clinical Approaches to Working with Young Offenders*. Chichester: Wiley.

Feindler, E.L. & Ecton, R.B. (1986). *Adolescent Anger Control: Cognitive Behavioural Techniques*. New York: Pergamon.

Ferguson, T.J. & Rule, B.G. (1983). An attributional perspective on anger and aggression. In R.G. Geen & E.L. Donnerstein (Eds), *Aggression: Theoretical and Emperical Reviews*. Vol 1. New York: Academic Press.

Forgas, J.P. (1993). Affect, appraisal and action: Towards a multiprocess framework. In R.S. Wyer & T.K. Srull (Eds) *Perspectives on Anger and Emotion: Advances in Social Cognition*. vol. VI. Hillsdale, NJ: Erlbaum.

Fransella, F. & Bannister, D. (1977). *A Manual of Repertory Grid Technique*. London: Academic Press.

Goldstein, A.P. & Glick, B. (1996). Aggression replacement training: Methods and outcomes. In C.R. Hollin & K. Howells (Eds), *Clinical Approaches to Working with Young Offenders*. Chichester: Wiley.

Grieger, R. (1982) Anger problems. In R. Grieger & I.Z. Grieger (Eds), *Cognition and Emotional Disturbance*. New York: Human Sciences Press.

Hare, R.D., Harpur, T.J., Hakstian, A.R. Forth, A.E., Hart, S.D. & Newman, J.P. (1990). The revised Psychopathy Checklist: Reliability and factor structure. *Psychological Assessment: A Journal of Consulting and Clinical Psychology*, **2**, 338–341.

Hare, R.D., Strachan, C. & Forth, A.E. (1993). Psychopathy and crime: A review. In K. Howells & C.R. Hollin (Eds), *Clinical Approaches to the Mentally Disordered Offender*. Chichester: Wiley.

Hodge, J.E. (1997). Addiction to violence. In J.E. Hodge, M. McMurran & C.R. Hollin (Eds), *Addicted to Crime?* Chichester: Wiley.

Hodgins, S. (1996). The major mental disorders: New evidence requires new policy and practice. *Canadian Psychologist*, **37**, 95–111.

Howard, R. & Lumsden, J. (1996). A neurophysiological predictor of reoffending in special hospital patients. *Criminal Behaviour and Mental Health*, **6**, 147–156.

Howells, K. (1988). The management of angry aggression: A cognitive behavioural approach. In W. Dryden & P. Trower (Eds), *Developments in Cognitive Psychotherapy*. London: Sage.

Howells, K. (1989). Anger-management methods in relation to the prevention of violent behaviour. In J. Archer and K. Browne (Eds), *Human Aggression: Naturalistic Approaches*. London: Routledge.

Howells, K. (1996). The psychological management of violence in clinical and forensic settings: Pitfalls and remedies. *Psychiatry, Psychology and Law*, **3**, 71–76.

Howells, K. & Hollin, C.R. (Eds) (1993). *Clinical Approaches to the Mentally Disordered Offender*. Chichester: Wiley.

Howells, K., Watt, B., Hall, G. & Baldwin, S. (1997). Developing programs for violent offenders. *Legal and Criminological Psychology*, **2**, 117–128.

Indermaur, D. (1995). Violent Property Crime. Leichardt NSW: Federation Press.

Izard, C.E. (1993). Four systems for emotion activation: Cognitive and noncognitive processes. *Psychological Review*, **100**, 68–90.

Kirk, J. (1989). Cognitive behavioural assessment. In K. Hawton, P.M. Salkovskis, J. Kird & D.M. Clark (Eds), *Cognitive Behaviour Therapy for Psychiatric Problems: A Practical Guide*. Oxford: Oxford University Press.

Levey, S. & Howells, K. (1990). Anger and its management. *Journal of Forensic Psychiatry*, **1**, 305–327.

Losel, F. (1996). Working with young offenders: The impact of meta-analyses. In C.R. Hollin & K. Howells (Eds), *Clinical Approaches to Working with Young Offenders*. Chichester: Wiley.

Martinson, R. (1974). What works? Questions and answers about prison reform. *The Public Interest*, **35**, 22–54.

Mathews, A. (1997). Information-processing biases in emotional disorders. In D.M. Clark & C.G. Fairburn (Eds), *Science and Practice of Cognitive Behaviour Therapy*. Oxford: Oxford University Press.

McGuire, J. (Ed.) (1995). *What Works: Reducing Reoffending*. Chichester: Wiley.

McNiel, D.E. (1994). Hallucinations and violence. In J. Monahan & H.J. Steadman (Eds), *Violence and Mental Disorder*. Chicago: University of Chicago Press.

Megargee, E.I. (1966). Undercontrolled and overcontrolled personality types in extreme antisocial aggression. In J.E. Singer (Ed.). *The Control of Aggression and Violence: Cognitive and Physiological Factors*. London: Academic Press.

Megargee, E.I. (1971). The role of inhibition in the assessment and understanding of violence. In J.E. Singer (Ed.), *The Control of Aggression and Violence: Cognitive and Physiological Factors*. London: Academic Press.

Miller, W.R. & Rollnick, S. (1991). *Motivational Interviewing: Preparing People to Change*. New York: Guilford.

Monahan, J. & Steadman, H.J. (Eds) (1994). *Mental Disorder and Violence: Developments in Risk Assessment*. Chicago: University of Chicago Press.

Novaco, R.W. (1975). *Anger Control: The Development and Evaluation of an Experimental Treatment*. Lexington, DC: Heath Sand.

Novaco, R.W. (1978). Anger and coping with stress. In J.P. Foreyt & D.P. Rathjen (Eds), *Cognitive Behaviour Therapy*. New York: Plenum.

Novaco, R.W. (1993). Clinicians ought to view anger contextually. *Behaviour Change*, **10**, 208–218.

Novaco, R.W. (1994). Anger as a factor for violence among the mentally disordered. In J. Monahan & H.R. Steadmean (Eds), *Violence and Mental Disorder Developments in Risk Assessment*. Chicago: University of Chicago Press.

Novaco, R.W. (1997). Remediating anger and aggression with violent offenders. *Legal and Criminological Psychology*, **2**, 77–78.

Novaco, R.W. & Welsh, W.N. (1989). Anger disturbances: Cognitive mediation and clinical prescriptions. In K. Howells & C.R. Hollin (Eds), *Clinical Approaches to Violence*. Chichester: Wiley.

Ortony, A., Clore, G.L. & Collins, A. (1988). *The Cognitive Structure of Emotions*. Cambridge: Cambridge University Press.

Renwick, S.J., Black, L., Ramm, M. & Novaco, R.W. (1997). Anger treatment with forensic hospital patients. *Legal and Criminological Psychology*, **2**, 103–116.

Roseman, I.J., Antoniou, A.A. & Jose, P.E. (1996). Appraisal determinants of emotion: Constructing a more accurate and comprehensive theory. *Cognition and Emotion*, **10**, 241–277.

Shah, S.A. (1993). A clinical approach to the mentally disordered offender: An overview and some major issues. In K. Howells & C.R. Hollin (Eds), *Clinical Approaches to the Mentally Disordered Offender*. Chichester: Wiley.

Spielberger, C.D., Jacobs, G., Russell, S. & Crane, R.S. (1983). Assessment of anger: The State-Trait Anger Scale. In J.N. Butcher & C.D. Spielberger (Eds), *Advances in Personality Assessment*. Hillsdale, NJ: Erlbaum.

Stermac, L.E. (1986). Anger control treatment for forensic patients. *Journal of Interpersonal Violence*, **1**, 446–457.

Sturmey, P. (1996). *Functional Analysis in Clinical Psychology*. Chichester: Wiley.

Taylor, P.J. (1994). Delusions and violence. In J. Monahan & H.J. Steadman (Eds), *Violence and Mental Disorder: Developments in Risk Assessment*. Chicago: University of Chicago Press.

Teasdale, J.D. (1997). The relationship between cognition and emotion: The mind-in-place in mood disorders. In D.M. Clark & C.G. Fairburn (Eds), *Science and Practice of Cognitive Behaviour Therapy*. Oxford: Oxford University Press.

Towl, G. (1994). Anger-control groupwork in prison. In E.A. Stanko (Ed.), *Perspectives on Violence*. London: Quartet Books.

Trower, P., Casey, A. & Dryden, W. (1988). *Cognitive Behavioural Counselling in Action*. London: Sage.

Watt, B.D. (1996). Skills training for aggression control. Masters Thesis, Edith Cowan University, Perth, Western Australia.

Williams, J.M.G. (1997). Depression. In D.M. Clark & C.G. Fairburn (Eds), *Science and Practice of Cognitive Behaviour Therapy*. Oxford: Oxford University Press.

Wong, M., Fenwick, P., Fenton, G., Lumsden, J., Maisey, M. & Stevens, J. (1997a). Repetitive and non-repetitive violent offending behaviour in male patients in a maximum security mental hospital – clinical and neuroimaging findings. *Medicine, Science and Law*, **37**, 150–160.

Wong, M.T.H., Fenwick, P.B.C., Lumsden, J., Fenton, G.W., Maisey, M.N., Lewis, P. & Badawi, R. (1997b). Positron emission tomography in male violent offenders with schizophrenia. *Psychiatric Research*, **68**, 111–123.

Wong, M.T.H., Lumsden, J., Fenton, G.W. & Fenwick, P.B.C. (1994a). Electroencephalography, computed tomography and violence ratings of male patients in a maximum security mental hospital. *Acta Psychiatrica Scandanavica*, **90**, 97–101.

Wong, M.T.H., Lumsden, J., Fenton, G.W. & Fenwick, P.B.C. (1994b). Epilepsy and violence in mentally abnormal offenders in a maximum security hospital. *Journal of Epilepsy*, **7**, 253–258.

Wyer, R.S. & Srull, T.K. (Eds), (1993). *Perspectives on Anger and Emotion*: Advances in Social Cognition. Vol. VI. Hillsdale, NJ: Erlbaum.

Zillmann, D. (1983). Arousal and aggression. In R. Geen and E. Donnerstein (Eds)., *Aggression: Theoretical and Emperical Reviews*. Vol. 1. New York: Academic Press.

Chapter 14

COGNITIVE BEHAVIOURAL TREATMENT OF PERSONALITY DISORDERS

Arthur Freeman* and James T. Jackson*

Patients with personality disorders are encountered in various mental health settings and often provide therapists with some of the most challenging patients in their clinical caseload. The diagnosis of personality disorder is evocative and viewed frequently as prognostically negative, indicative of potential treatment difficulty, predictive of storminess both within and outside the therapy, having a potential for acting out, offering possibilities for displays of behaviour that may lead to danger to self and others, or, at its worst, all of the above. Most often presenting (as do most patients) for treatment of their Axis I problems (i.e. for treatment of anxiety or depression), Axis II patients frequently show poor response rates to standard treatment of anxiety or depression. Sometimes the Axis II behaviour is obvious and evident early in treatment. Other times it only surfaces as the therapy progresses from simpler to more complex issues. The therapist may find that therapy becomes more difficult and stormy, and therapeutic issues become increasingly more complex, convoluted, 'messy', and crisis laden.

At this point, the clinician may rightly, or wrongly, attribute these treatment dynamics to motivational deficits such as patient resistances, rather than the more likely characterological problems inherent in the personality disorder. Frequent occurrence of such experiences in clinical practice points to the need for treatment approaches yielding more useful understanding and effective treatment of these common problems.

* Philadelphia College of Osteopathic Medicine, Philadelphia, PA, USA

Treating Complex Cases: The Cognitive Behavioural Therapy Approach.
Edited by Nicholas Tarrier, Adrian Wells and Gillian Haddock.
© 1998 John Wiley & Sons Ltd.

Given the long-term nature of the patients' characterological problems, their general avoidance of psychotherapy, their frequent referral through family pressure or legal remand, and their seeming reluctance or inability to change, they are often the most difficult patients in a clinician's caseload. They generally require more work within the session, a longer time for therapy, and more therapist energy than do other patients. All of this expenditure occurs without the same rate of change and satisfaction (for therapist or patient) as is gained with other patients.

In recent years, cognitive and cognitive behavioural therapists (Beck, Freeman & Associates, 1990; Freeman, 1988a,b; Freeman & Leaf, 1989; Layden et al., 1993; Linehan, 1988, 1993; Young, 1990; Young & Swift, 1988) have offered comprehensive cognitive behavioural treatment protocols for treating the Axis II behaviours. In so doing, these authors generally acknowledge the need to modify standard short-term cognitive behavioural approaches to better serve the patient with an Axis II disorder (cf. Fleming & Pretzer, 1990). Suggested modifications include: placing an emphasis on individual case conceptualisation when designing intervention strategies; collaborative development of clearly identified, shared goals; use of efficacy-enhancing and anxiety-reducing interventions; and a focus on identifying and modifying core beliefs or schemata. To these goals we would add the following:

1. Stability of the framework for treatment.
2. Increased activity of the therapist.
3. The therapist's ability to tolerate negative transference.
4. Establishing a connection between the patient's actions and feelings in the present.
5. Making self-destructive behaviours ungratifying.
6. Blocking acting-out behaviours.
7. Focusing clarifications and interpretations on the here and now.
8. Paying careful attention to counter-transference feelings (Waldinger & Gunderson, 1987, pp. 8–9).

This discussion will focus on an elaboration and integration of suggested modifications to the treatment of the patient with an Axis

II disorder within the framework of a cognitive behavioural approach. Cognitive theorists maintain that it is usually more productive to identify and modify 'core problems' in treating personality disorders. This is in contrast to the treatment of more common Axis I problems wherein the problems may be dealt with without necessarily addressing and/or changing the personality. This Axis I focus or 'symptom therapy' approach is useful in working with many patients. A clinician may not be aware initially of the characterological nature, chronicity, and severity of the patient's problems when they first present for therapy. (Koenigsberg et al., 1985; Fabrega et al., 1985; Karno et al., 1986). Often, these are the very patients whose social functioning is worst (Casey, Tryer & Platt, 1985). When Axis II problems are a focus at intake the patient may not be willing, al treatment onset, to work on the personality disorders, but rather may choose to work on the symptoms for which he or she was referred. For example, a patient may present for therapy as unassertive, socially anxious or 'shy.' The patient may also meet criteria for being diagnosed with an Avoidant Personality Disorder. With some number of patients with this symptom configuration, we might treat the social anxiety with a combination of assertiveness training, a challenging of anxiogenic thinking, progressive relaxation, imaginal and *in vivo* exposure, role playing and stress inoculation.

For another group of patients with the same anxiety/avoidant configuration, the treatment will be confounded because the Axis II disorder (Avoidant Personality Disorder) fuels and exacerbates the Axis I social anxiety. With this group it becomes essential to deal with the Axis II problems to reduce the manifest social anxiety.

For yet another group, the Axis I anxiety problems excite and stimulate the Axis II Avoidant Personality Disorder, making it difficult to deal with the social anxiety.

For the patient group that likely comprises the majority of those with a personality disorder, there is a bi-directional influence. The Axis I problems excite the Axis II disorder and the Axis II disorder fuels the Axis I social anxiety. For the combination of Axis I and Axis II diagnoses, the course of treatment is far more complicated than for the typical non-Axis II patient with the same complaints of social anxiety. The duration of treatment, the frequency of the treatment sessions, the goals and expectations for both therapist and patient and the available techniques and strategies need to be altered in the CT treatment of personality disorders.

It is important to remember that the patient's goals, and not those of others (including the therapist), are the initial focus of treatment. The patient's schemata are the agent, as well as the target of therapeutic change. If an externally referred patient is not willing to work on 'core' issues, the therapist may attempt to persuade the patient to be trusting, and to follow the therapist's agenda. This kind of agenda-setting can be set up as an experiment, and as one of life's challenges.

The personality disorder is one of the most striking representations of Beck's concept of schemata (Beck, 1964, 1967; Beck, Freeman & Associates, 1990; Freeman, 1988a,b; Freeman et al., 1990). These schemata may be personal, cultural, family, religious, gender, and age-related (Freeman, 1988;

Freeman & Leaf, 1989). In point of fact, the schemata of individuals with a personality disorder are so vivid and obvious that they may appear to be a caricature of what one would expect in 'normal' individuals. Generically, the schemata serve to organise information, structure categorical judgement and assist in making classifications. Schemata also provide the instructions to guide the directions and qualities of one's daily life. While the schemata may not typically be in awareness, the products of this process are largely conscious and with special training can become more accessible to consciousness. Dysfunctional feelings and conduct are largely due to the function of certain schemata that tend to produce consistently biased judgements and a concomitant tendency to make cognitive errors in certain types of situations.

The personality disordered patient will often see the difficulties that they encounter in dealing with other people or coping with life tasks as externally generated and independent of their behaviour. Much of what they experience is, in their view, 'done to them' or generally coming from the ill-will or negative actions of those around them. This 'other-blaming' position often places them in conflict with peers, and often puts them in conflict with larger agencies and institutions. Such patients often have little idea about how they got to be the way they are, how they contribute to their life problems, or how to change. They are often referred by family members or friends who recognise a dysfunctional pattern, or who have reached their personal limit in attempting to cope with this individual. Their style of behaving and responding seems normal and reasonable to them. Other personality disordered patients are very much aware of the self-defeating nature of their personality problems (e.g. overdependence, inhibition, excessive avoidance) but are at a total loss as to how to change these patterns. Still other patients may have the motivation to change but lack the basic skills necessary to modify their behaviour or to alter their relationships and interactions with co-workers and significant others.

ASSESSMENT AND DIAGNOSIS

In some cases, the behaviour that is now part of the Axis II disorder has been functional in life. Witness the hard-driving executive who was up at 5:00a.m. each morning and worked until 8:00p.m. in the evening and then took work home with him. He may have worked his way up in the company over the years, and may have been a harsh boss and taskmaster. He may have demanded high levels of performance from himself and others. He may have been a 'by-the-book' executive who followed policy and procedures to the letter. In his work life many appellations might have been appropriate, some pejorative, for example 'workaholic,' or 'type-A,' or some quite positive, for example 'hard worker,' or 'dedicated.'

Having worked so hard, having been successful, having become financially secure, and having been a good provider for his family, he is at a loss to explain his difficulty at the point of his retirement. He is depressed and feels himself to be a failure, based on his lack of productivity. The same schemata ('You are what you produce,' 'What you do is who you are,' 'Rules must be followed without variance') that have driven him to be successful now drive him to despair. He may now carry the diagnoses of Depression (Axis I) and Obsessive-Compulsive Personality Disorder (Axis II). For many individuals appropriate (or fortuitous) life choices serve to structure their lives so that they are adaptive. When the structure offered by a job, a relationship, an organisation, a behavioural regimen, or hobby is removed, what has always been in place may become (or be viewed as) pathological. For example, an individual with a dependent personality may be a perfect fit for service in the military, in government bureaucracies, or in large corporations because they are compliant with orders and procedures. For instance, a 66-year-old man, diagnosed as having Obsessive-Compulsive, Dependent, and Avoidant Personality Disorders stated: 'The best time in my life was when I was in the army. I didn't have to worry about what to wear, what to do, or what to eat. I went where they told me and didn't have to search out guys to be with. We were all together in our squad.'

Axis II problems arc not always diagnosed at intake, though early diagnosis and treatment planning are likely to be more effective (Morrison & Shapiro, 1987). Many Axis II patients are silent about their personality problems, or deny them, as a reflection of the disorders themselves. Whether or not they are diagnosed as having personality disorders, many patients believe that their personalities and changing the way that they do things are an appropriate focus of treatment. Other patients fear such a focus. The collaborative nature of goal setting is one of the most important features of cognitive therapy inasmuch as power struggles over conflicting goals usually impede progress (Foon, 1985).

A summary of heuristic diagnostic signs that *may* point to the possibility of Axis II problems includes the following scenarios:

1. A patient or significant other reports, 'Oh, he/she has always done that, since he's a little boy/girl,' or the patient may report, 'I've always been this way.'
2. The patient is not compliant with the therapeutic regimen. While non-compliance or resistance is a common element in psychotherapy for many reasons, ongoing non-compliance should be used as a signal for further exploration of Axis II issues.

3. Therapy seems to have come to a sudden inexplicable stop. The clinician working with these patients can often help the patient to reduce the problems of anxiety or depression only to be blocked in further therapeutic work by the personality disorder.

4. The patient seems entirely unaware of the effect of their behaviour on others. They report the responses of others, but fail to address any provocation or dysfunctional behaviour that they might exhibit that might, in any way, elicit the response from others.

5. There is a question of the motivation of the patient to come for therapy and/or to change. This problem is especially true for those patients who have 'been sent' to therapy by family members or the courts.

6. The patient's personality problems appear to be acceptable and natural to them. For example, a depressed patient without an Axis II diagnosis may say. 'I just want to get rid of this depression. I know what it is like to feel good. and I want to feel that way again.' The Axis II patient may see the problems as them: 'This is how I am', 'This is who I am.

Thus a therapist might begin to understand the content, style, and impact of the personality disorder by focusing on clinically relevant schemata. The schemata can be inferred from behaviour or assessed through interview and history. The degree to which particular schemata are on the continuum from active to inactive, as well as the degree to which they are on the continuum from unchangeable to changeable, are essential dimensions in conceptualising the patient's problems (Beck, 1964, 1967; Beck, Freeman & Associates, 1990; Freeman, 1988a,b; Freeman et. al., 1990). The *active schemata* govern our usual integration of information and our everyday behaviour. These schemata have to do with how we monitor and integrate our understanding of other people' S behaviour, and how we generally relate to people and tasks. This activity is particularly prominent in the neuroses (Axis I disorders) where every situation may be interpreted in terms of personal loss or defeat (depression) or danger (anxiety).

Inactive schemata are generally out of awareness and only become active and serve to govern behaviour when the individual is under stress. When the stressful stimulus/situation is no longer present, the inactive schemata recede to their previous state of dormancy. For example, a person may generally believe, 'It's silly to be worried about what strangers think of you.' However, if we were to put this person in the role of giving a speech to a room full of strangers he or she might feel very anxious. In this instance the latent schema related to fear of disapproval or disgrace has been activated and governs mood and behaviour. When the stressor is removed and the speech is over, the person may report a sense of relief and that, 'it really wasn't *too* bad.' In the personality disorders, the schemata are often highly charged and global.

Schemata may also be classified and placed on a continuum from non-compelling to compelling. A non-compelling schema is one that the individual believes in but can relatively easily challenge and/or surrender. Compelling beliefs are not easily challenged and are modified only with great difficulty (or not at all). Historical examples would be the religious or political martyrs who chose to die rather than surrender their compelling views of God, or a political belief.

Since Axis II patients are generally governed by longlasting habitual schemata these deeply ingrained rules and beliefs are not easily changed, even when the patient is highly motivated to do so. The chronicity of the personality disorder results from the development of these dysfunctional schemata relatively early in life.

From birth through middle childhood, schemata are, ideally, in a constant stage of evolution. According to a Piagetian model, there is a continuous adaptation to the requirements of life. Through the interactive processes of assimilation and accommodation, these schemata facilitate the organisation and understanding of the phenomenological world. For many reasons, some of the schemata do not mature and are maintained at an earlier level of development. This is the beginning of an Axis II problem. The schemata that are basically functional in this earlier part of life are being applied during later, more demanding times. While most of these early schemata were at one time functional they have long since lost their functional value by dint of never having been modified by the individual to meet changing life/world experiences. For example, if a one-year-old child would like to be picked up, it conveys that message to a caretaker by lifting its arms and grunting or crying. The caretaker responds by picking the child up. We might infer that the child has a belief, 'I am weak and helpless and need a large person to meet my needs.' As the child matures, the schema, 'I can do things for myself' develops, and the child no longer has the schematic world view that, 'I need others to take care of me and meet my basic needs.' When a child at age one is demanding of attention and help, it is often thought of as cute. When that same schema is manifested at age 31, it is not cute, but may be dysfunctional and given the diagnosis of 'Dependent Personality Disorder.' Given the chronic nature of the problems, one must question as to why these behaviours are maintained. They may cause difficulty at work, in school, or in one's personal life. In some cases they are reinforced by the society, that is, a child who is 'a real hard worker', 'a kid that doesn't fool around', 'a kid who hasn't messed around while other kids are messing around', 'a kid who really works hard and gets all perfect grades' may, in later life, get labelled as Obsessive-Compulsive. At later points, these compelling schemata which a patient may often 'know' are erroneous, are hard to change. They are rationalised by questioning, 'What is wrong with wanting to do one's best?'

One of the most important treatment considerations in working with personality disordered individuals is to be aware that when the therapy approaches the active and compelling schema we will evoke anxiety. The individual is being asked to *give* up 'who they are' and to step out of their safety zone. It may be uncomfortable, limiting, and lonely in the safety zone, but to go out means, 'I may get hurt, and feel anxious.'

Before a patient would accept an appropriate therapeutic strategy, the therapist would probably have to try to reshape the patient's initial expectations about the goals, time course, and procedures of therapy. It would be important to help the patient achieve some relatively immediate and practical gains, and develop a trusting and supportive collaborative relationship, thus attempting to limit the anxiety.

Beck and Emery (1985) in discussing the treatment of agoraphobia, state: 'It is crucial that the patient experience anxiety in order to ensure that the primitive cognitive levels have been activated, since these levels are directly connected to the affects. The repeated, direct, on-the-spot recognition that the danger signals do not lead to catastrophe enhance(s) the response of the primitive level to more realistic inputs from above' (p. 129). In discussing plans for therapy with a patient diagnosed at intake as having depression and a Borderline Personality Disorder the therapist discussed the possibility of the patient becoming increasingly anxious as the therapy progressed. She asked, 'Why are you trying to control my anxiety? I'm depressed, I'm not anxious at all.' At that point the therapist explained to her that as the therapy work challenged her strongly held beliefs, anxiety would be increased. He also explained about the need to master anxiety-reduction skills. These skills, it was pointed out, would be an essential factor in successful therapy.

In the same circumstance, another patient responded that, 'it's good to have that safety signal. It says that when people get too close to me I can respond, so I don't understand why I should ever give it up.' Unless the therapist starts to help the patient to cope with the increased anxiety they may leave therapy. (Space limitations preclude a detailed discussion of anxiety treatment: cf. Wells, 1997).

Given the importance of the schematic changes, the therapist must recognise that they are difficult to alter. The schemata are held firmly in place by behavioural, cognitive and affective elements. Changing only one factor will probably not be effective at changing the schemata. The therapist must take a tripartite approach. Using behavioural approaches alone is not going to be successful in isolation. Taking a cognitive approach and trying to argue the patient out of their distortions and schemata will not work. Having the patient abreact within the session to fantasies or recollections will not be successful by itself. A therapeutic program that addresses all three areas is essential.

The therapist has several broad options for what might be done to work with the schemata. The first option is schematic restructuring. This may be likened to urban renewal. Having decided that a structure is unsound, the decision is made to tear down the old structure and build a new one in its place. (This has been a goal of therapy for many years, particularly in psychoanalysis). Whether this restructuring is reasonable or possible is very questionable. An example of schematic restructuring is to have a paranoid personality become a fully trusting individual.

A second possibility is schematic modification. This involves smaller changes in the basic manner of responding to the world. An example would be to have the person with a paranoid personality disorder modify the idea that 'people cannot be trusted,' to 'in many cases people cannot be totally trusted.' This gives them greater adaptability and flexibility in their reactions and interactions with others.

The third possibility is schematic reinterpretation. This involves helping the patient to understand and reinterpret their schemata in more functional ways. The individual with a Paranoid Personality Disorder may gravitate, without therapeutic input, to careers, jobs, lifestyles, or living arrangements that are more solitary and bring them out of contact with others. Their lifestyle might be termed independent rather than isolated. By schematic reinterpretation the therapist can find ways for the patient to deal with their schemata/rules in a more adaptive and functional manner. Given that the rules are not necessarily good or bad, it would depend on how they are interpreted. For example, if someone had a great need to be loved or admired they might choose to teach pre-school children, who kiss and hug the teacher. If one wants to be looked up to and respected, earning or buying a title, such as Professor, Doctor, or Colonel, can meet the need for status. Many choices are made because the career or occupation offers an opportunity to meet the schematic press. They can also work on restructuring schemata—if that is possible. The most reasonable goal when working with an Axis II patient, is to either modify or reinterpret the schemata.

A final treatment focus is what we would term schematic camouflage. This involves direct changes that are more cosmetic. For example, a schizoid individual was told to try a certain prosocial behaviour with a co-worker. While the patient did not fully understand the meaning and subtleties of the behaviours, he was willing to carry them out, thereby making himself much more acceptable in the office.

COGNITIVE BEHAVIOURAL TREATMENT

The initial goal of therapy is an assessment of the problems and the development of a conceptualisation of the patient problems with an appropriate treatment plan. When therapists recognise that cases involve personality disorders, they view them as especially difficult (Merbaum & Butcher, 1982; Rosenbaum, Horowitz & Wilner, 1986). Anticipated patient 'resistance' is probably the main source of such perceptions. In fact, these expectations are often accurate. When treating personality disorders, it may be difficult to agree about goals and to maintain good therapeutic collaboration. For example, a prominent wealthy businessman whose principal problem, in the view of the therapist, was a narcissistic personality disorder, entered therapy, in response to his wife's entreaties. His goal was to deal with problems of anger, anxiety and guilt arising from marital conflict. Like most patients who were not self-referred, he was not interested in schema-therapy, but only in symptom-therapy (Chamberlain et al., 1984).

An excellent technique for assessment and for structuring the treatment is the use of the Diagnostic Profile System using the diagnostic criteria of DSM-IV or ICD-10. (Figure 14.1).

By profiling all of the relevant diagnoses on a separate profile, the therapist can assess overlapping criteria. The following profile of a patient diagnosed as Borderline Personality will then focus the therapy of those areas that are critical for that patient, at that time (Figure 14.2).

Following the assessment, the therapist must make sure that the patient is socialised or educated to the CT model. To make sure that there is appropriate informed consent for therapy, the therapist must explain what the therapy involves, the goals and plans of the therapy, the importance of therapeutic collaboration, the particular areas of difficulty that will be emphasised, and the likely techniques that will be used in therapy.

The initial therapeutic focus may be on relieving the presenting symptoms, such as anxiety or depression. In helping the patient to deal with their anxiety or depression, the therapist can teach the patient the basic cognitive therapy skills that are going to be necessary in working with the more difficult personality disorder. If the therapist can help the patient become less depressed or less anxious the patient may accept that this therapy could have some value after all, and it may be worthwhile continuing to work in therapy.

The essential nature of the therapeutic collaboration and the building of a strong working alliance is nowhere more important than with the patient with an Axis II disorder. The therapeutic relationship will be a microcosm of

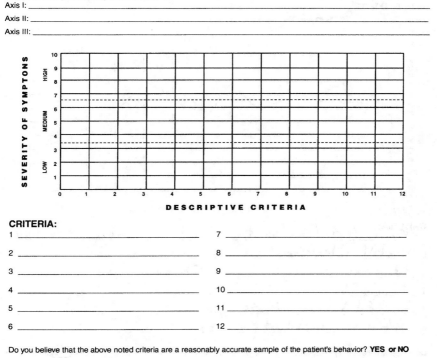

DIAGNOSTIC PROFILING SYSTEM
(© FREEMAN, 1998) REVISED EDITION

Date of Assessment:_____

Session#:_____Evaluator:_____

Patient Name:_____ Patient#: _____Location:_____

Birthdate: _____Age: _____Race: _____ Gender: _____ Birthorder: _____Marital/Children:_____

Employment: _____Education: _____Disability: _____Medication:_____

Physician: _____Referral Question:_____

Instructions: Record the diagnosis including the code number. Briefly identify the criteria for the selected diagnosis. Working with the patient either directly or as part of the data gathering of the clinical interview, SCALE the SEVERITY of EACH CRITERION for the patient at the PRESENT TIME. Indicate the level of severity on the grid.

DIAGNOSIS (DSM/ICD) with Code:
Axis I: _____
Axis II: _____
Axis III: _____

CRITERIA:

1 _____   7 _____

2 _____   8 _____

3 _____   9 _____

4 _____   10 _____

5 _____   11 _____

6 _____   12 _____

Do you believe that the above noted criteria are a reasonably accurate sample of the patient's behavior? **YES or NO**

If **NO**, please indicate why:_____

Are there any reasons to believe that this individual is an imminent danger to himself/herself or others? **YES or NO**

If **YES**, please indicate the danger._____

Figure 14.1   Diagnostic profile system.

DIAGNOSTIC PROFILING SYSTEM
(© FREEMAN, 1998) REVISED EDITION

Date of Assessment:_____

Session#:_____ Evaluator:_____

Patient Name: Ellen Smythe Patient#: 00273 Location:_____

Birthdate: 8-20-60 Age: 38 Race: Cau. Gender: F Birthorder: 1 Marital/Children: 0/0

Employment: Unemployed Education: 12 yrs Disability: — Medication: refused

Physician: Dr. Freeman Referral Question:_____

Instructions: Record the diagnosis including the code number. Briefly identify the criteria for the selected diagnosis. Working with the patient either directly or as part of the data gathering of the clinical interview, SCALE the SEVERITY of EACH CRITERION for the patient at the PRESENT TIME. Indicate the level of severity on the grid.

DIAGNOSIS (DSM/CD) with Code:

Axis I: GAD

Axis II: Bdline Personality Dis

Axis III: _____

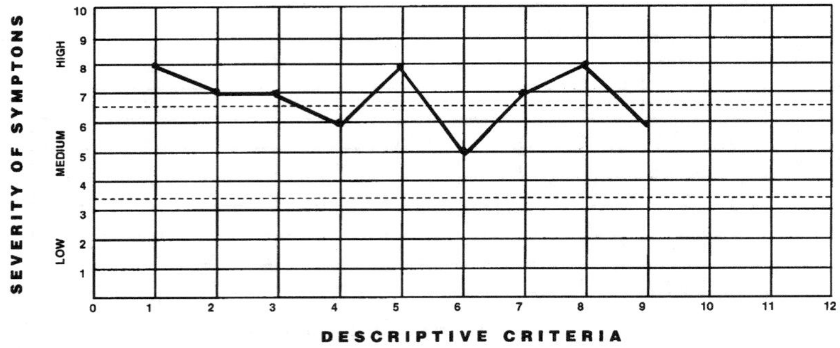

CRITERIA:
1. Frantic efforts / abandonment
2. Unstable interpersonal rel.
3. Identity dist.
4. Impulsivity
5. Suicidal behavior / thrts
6. Affective instability
7. Chronic feelings of emptiness
8. Intense anger
9. Stress rel. para. idea.
10. _____
11. _____
12. _____

Do you believe that the above noted criteria are a reasonably accurate sample of the patient's behavior? YES or NO

If **NO**, please indicate why:_____

Are there any reasons to believe that this individual is an imminent danger to himself/herself or others? YES or NO

If **YES**, please indicate the danger._____

Figure 14.2 Profile of a patient with a borderline personality.

the patient's responses to others in their environment. The sensitive nature of the relationship means that the therapist must exercise great care in working with individuals in this patient group. Being even two minutes late for a session with the dependent personality may evoke anxiety about abandonment. The same two minutes will raise the spectre of being taken advantage of by the paranoid personality. Building and maintaining trust, essential to good therapy generally, is essential. Given the imperative nature of trust and a relationship, few patients test the patience and mettle of a therapist more than those in the Axis II group. Issues of the therapist's counter-transference must be acknowledged and addressed directly by the therapist.

The collaborative nature of the therapy must be constantly stressed. The therapy of the personality disorder must include a strong supportive/expressive component. Without the therapist's active support, the patient may quickly become frightened and disillusioned and leave therapy. The collaborative set involves setting mutually acceptable, reasonable and proximal goals for therapy. The patient who expects to become a totally different person as a result of therapy will, invariably, be disappointed. Similarly, the therapist who expects that the result of the therapy will be a totally different person will be disappointed. By making small steps towards the desired goals, therapy can move ahead slowly but effectively. Therapists must keep in mind that a collaboration is not always 50:50. With patients with Axis II disorders, the collaboration may be 80:20, or 90:10.

The rate of treatment and frame of treatment must also be discussed. The patient who expects that they will be 'cured' in the same 12–20 sessions that they have read about in the Cognitive Therapy treatment of depression must be apprised of the greater severity and chronicity of their problems and that these problems will take a longer time for treatment. A period of 12–20 months (or more) may be a far more reasonable time frame for the treatment of personality disorders.

The patient's significant others can be invaluable allies in the therapeutic endeavour by helping the patient to do homework and reality testing, and by offering support in making changes. The significant others can also be important sources of data about the patient's past behaviours. On the other hand, meeting with the significant others may enable the therapist to piece together a family history of problems, and to understand the family system dynamics that keep the patient behaving in the same dysfunctional way. Finally, the significant others might be involved in marital or family therapy with the patient.

Non-compliance or resistance by the patient is often interpreted as a sign of treatment failure. The notion of resistance has always carried the connotation that somehow, the patient doesn't want to 'get well.' We would prefer to examine treatment non-compliance in terms of four areas of impediments to therapy. These are first, patient factors, that is factors that are specific to a particular individual. Second are the impediments to therapy that are characteristic of a particular diagnosis. Third are the impediments that are specific to the patient's environment. Finally, there are those impediments that are contributed by the therapist. We can list these as:

Patient Factors

1. Lack of patient skill to comply with the requests and demands of therapy—given the chronic nature of the personality disorder, the patient may be skill-deficient.
2. The patient may have negative cognitions regarding previous therapy failure. The patient has a negative cognitive set having often been in therapy for many years with many different therapists. They are not therefore optimistic about the therapy process or the present therapist helping them.
3. The patient may have negative cognitions regarding the consequences to others of the patient changing. The patient may believe that their change will alienate others from them or may damage the others in their life.
4. The patient may be getting some secondary gain by maintaining symptoms—special care and attention come from being 'sick,' or 'impaired.'
5. The patient has a fear of changing—essentially the patient believes that the devil that they know is better than the devil that they do not know.
6. There is a lack of motivation to change—the patient does not anticipate benefits great enough to compensate for the required effort and risk.
7. The patient may have a perception of lowered status by being in therapy—being in therapy means that one is sick, disturbed, or crazy.
8. The patient may have limited or poor self-monitoring of thoughts, feelings and actions—this leads to situational problems in their life.
9. The patient may have limited or poor monitoring of others—they miss what may, to others, be obvious cues.
10. The patient has a narcissistic and other-blaming style—they see their problems as 'out there.'

Problem or Pathology Factors

1. Patient rigidity foils compliance—the need to maintain the familiar and the *status quo* may mitigate against change.
2. Existence of medical/physiological problems—changes could be limited because of medical factors.

3. Difficulty in establishing trust—problems in establishing and maintaining the relationship with the therapist may hinder therapy.
4. The patient experiences autonomy press—seen especially in Clusters A and B, the need for independence and autonomy prevents or injures the therapeutic alliance.
5. There is significant impulsivity—the planned, incremental, deliberate nature of therapy is foiled by the patient's impulsive actions.
6. The patient experiences confusion—seen typically in schizotypal patients, but may also be present in borderline patients.
7. Limited cognitive ability—this is common as a consequence of depression, head injuries, schizophrenia, developmental issues.
8. Symptom profusion—the patient has multiple diagnoses on Axes I-V.
9. Excessive dependence—the patient might avoid the loss of the therapist by maintaining symptoms.
10. Self-devaluation—this negative view is common in depression and many of the Cluster C patients.
11. The patient has limited energy—typically seen when depression is present, but also common in the Cluster A group.
12. There is dissociative behaviour—this is common in patients with Cluster B disorders, especially Borderline Personality Disorder.

Environmental Factors

1. Environmental stressors preclude changing—individuals who play a particular role in a work, family, or social environment may find that individuals within that environment (or the conditions of the situation) may mitigate against change.
2. Significant others may sabotage or foil therapy—through either overt or covert interventions, family and other significant individuals in the patient's life may sabotage the therapy, dismiss the therapist, or actively work against the therapeutic goals.
3. There is agency reinforcement of pathology through compensation or benefits for maintaining the pathology—patients who are funded through government agencies for their mental emotional disabilities may lose their funding by 'getting better.'
4. Cultural issues may preclude compliance—some cultural groups may be against therapy as being exploitative or intrusive of family or individual privacy.
5. The family system is in a state of homeostasis that will be disrupted by the patient's changing—the identified patient serves as a convenient target for others in the family system. If the patient changes, the systemic balance is upset.

6. There is significant family pathology—related to symptom profusion, if there is significant family or system pathology, change becomes harder, or impossible.

Therapist Factors

1. Lack of therapist skill—patients with Axis II disorders are among the hardest to treat. They are often assigned to younger, front-line therapists in community agencies.
2. Patient and therapist distortions are congruent—the patient might voice hopelessness about ever being able to change. The therapist may implicitly agree, thus negatively impacting on therapy
3. The therapist has not socialised the patient to the therapy model—the patient not educated or attuned to the therapy model cannot be expected to collaborate.
4. There is a lack of collaboration and working alliance—the therapist has not established a working alliance and established a collaborative set.
5. The therapist is working from a point of minimal or total lack of data—drawing conclusions and establishing a treatment plan without adequate data may lead to impaired therapy.
6. Therapeutic narcissism—therapists might be so taken with their illusion of power that they could set goals that are impossible for the patient to reach, thereby setting up the potential for treatment failure that may then be attributed to the patient.
7. Poor timing of interventions—it has been said that timing is everything in life. Nowhere is this more true than in therapy. An excellent intervention that is poorly timed may even be counter-productive in the therapy.
8. Lack of experience—therapy with patients with Axis II disorders takes a great deal of experience. The more the therapist does it the better they get at doing it. Self-, peer-, or other supervision is crucial.
9. The therapy goals are unstated, unrealistic, or vague—the patient must be invited into the therapeutic process by the therapist offering clear, realistic, and specific goals for the therapy.
10. Lack of agreement with therapy goals—the patient must agree to the therapy, both generally (be part of the process), and specifically (agreeing to particular strategies and interventions).

In addition to the above, the nature of Axis II problems makes the treatment different from Axis I therapy. One may skip steps when dealing with symptomatic problems (Axis I) where therapy proceeds rapidly, but in working with personality disordered patients it *is* best to make sure they have a clear understanding of why schemata are the major focus of cognitive therapy, of the pace at which *they* can expect progress with *their* problems, and the kind of support they can and cannot expect from their therapist. If schemata were all visual, a clear picture of our schema for therapy might show a therapist pointing at maps and pictures of existing and more accurate schemata, with the patient looking at the scenes pointed to and trying to practice, with eyes closed, reconstructing eidetic images of the more accurate scenes. A more skillful or experienced therapist might have more maps and pictures than a less skillful one, but the patient's vigilance about the details of the figures and the patient's willingness and ability to recall the images when under stress are more important than the therapist's armamentarium. In addition, in order to maintain trust, it is important for these patients to understand in advance that they are on their own when they try to effect changes in their lives, but can expect encouragement to proceed and moral support from their therapist whatever their performance and whatever its outcome.

Treatment Planning

In treatment planning the therapist must differentiate between therapeutic strategies and therapeutic techniques. Strategies are overall goals of therapy while the interventions or techniques are the means of effecting the strategy and reaching the goal. For example, if the target problem is overdependence, and the patient wishes to modify that behaviour, the strategy or goal of the therapy would be decreased dependence. The therapist would not set *independence* as a goal inasmuch as it may be too great a distance between where the patient is and where they may want to be. The step-wise and more proximal goal setting allows for growth over time. Given the goal of decreased dependence, the therapist can then choose from the menu of available cognitive and behavioural techniques that can be used to help the patient to decrease their dependence.

The dichotomy often used is that there are 'pure' cognitive and ' pure' behavioural interventions. For example, one might argue that the use of imagery is a behavioural intervention while it would be seen by others as a cognitive technique. For the purposes of instruction, we can arbitrarily divide the techniques into two menus: one that is *primarily* cognitive and one that is *primarily* behavioural, with the understanding that there is debate and overlap. The therapist can then plan which interventions have the greatest likelihood of success given the patient's goals, the patient's motivation and investment in therapy, the therapist's skills, the available time, and so on. The behavioural menu would include, but not be limited to:

- Activity planning and scheduling
- Mastery and pleasure activities

- Graded task assignments
- Social skills training
- Assertiveness training
- Fixed role therapy
- Shame attack exercises
- Bibliography
- Role playing
- Behavioural rehearsal
- Progressive relaxation
- Imaginal techniques, meditation and yoga
- *In vivo* exposure
- Biofeedback
- Eye movement desensitization and reprocessing
- Aversive techniques

Cognitive techniques would include, but not be limited to:

- Understanding idiosyncratic meaning
- Questioning the evidence
- Reattribution
- Decatastrophising
- Finding alternatives of thought/feeling action
- Eliciting fantasised consequences
- Advantages vs disadvantages
- Labelling of distortions
- Guided association
- The use of exaggeration
- Scaling
- Turning adversity to advantage
- Developing replacement imagery
- Cognitive rehearsal
- Externalization of voices + role reversal
- Self-instruction
- Distraction
- Direct challenge or disputation
- Developing and then resolving cognitive dissonance

The relative mix of the cognitive and the behavioural can be estimated using the following heuristic tool (Figure 14.3).

The more severe the disorder or the greater the level of dysfunction, the more behavioural work is needed. The less severe the dysfunction the more the techniques might be chosen from the cognitive menu. By estimating the level of dysfunction and drawing a vertical line at that point, one can estimate the rough percentage of each type of intervention in the therapy.

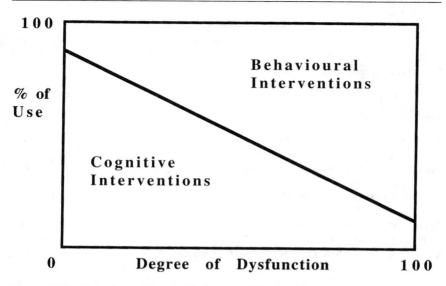

Figure 14.3   Use of cognitive and behavioural interventions.

SUMMARY

Given the chronic nature of personality disorders, the therapist can effect significant change in the thinking, actions, and feelings of individuals with these disorders. Much depends on the severity of the disorder. The more mild the disorder, the better the prognosis. The more severe and debilitating, the less positive we can be about change.

By evaluating vulnerability factors that may exacerbate the disorder and the four areas of impediments to treatment, the therapist can plan for the best possible outcome. By using the Diagnostic Profiling System the therapist can identify those areas that are the best targets for change.

Using the standard cognitive therapy techniques, the therapist can choose from the cognitive and behavioural menus. The more severe the target behaviour, the more likely the therapist should choose a behavioural technique. The less dysfunctional the behaviour, the more likely the therapist would choose from the cognitive menu.

The case illustration (Figure 14.2) demonstrates that the high level of structure, use of homework, and the challenging of the internal negative dialogue can have a significant effect in a single session.

Finally, the individual with a personality disorder is treatable, but only after the therapist accepts the patient's behaviour as the result of significant developmental deficits, The therapist must initiate active, directed, problem-focused, solution-oriented, collaborative, structured, dynamic, and psychoeducational therapy work that is the hallmark of cognitive behavioural therapy.

REFERENCES

Beck, A.T. (1964). Thinking and depression: II. Theory and therapy *Archives of General Psychiatry,* **10**, 561–571

Beck, A.T. (1967). *Depression: Clinical Experimental, and Theoretical Aspects.* New York: Harper & Row.

Beck, A.T. & Emery, G. (with Greenberg, R.L.) (1985). Anxiety *Disorders and Phobias. A Cognitive Perspective.* New York: Basic Books.

Beck, A.T., Freeman, A. & Associates (1990). *Cognitive Therapy of Personality Disorders* New York: Guilford.

Casey, P.R., Tryer, P.J. & Platt, S. (1985). The relationship between social functioning and social functioning in primary care. *Social Psychiatry,* **20**(1), 5–9.

Chamberlain, P., Patterson, G., Reid, J., Kavanaugh, K. & Forgatch, M. (1984). Observation of client resistance. *Behavior Therapy,* **15**, 144–155.

Fabrega, H., Mezzich, J.E., Mezzich, A.C. & Coffinan, GA. (1985). Descriptive validity of DSM-III depressions. *Journal of Nervous and Mental Disease,* **174**(10), 573–584.

Fleming, B. & Pretzer, J. (1990). Cognitive behavioural approaches to personality disorders. In M. Hersen (Ed.), *Advances in Behavior Therapy.* Newbury Park, CA: Sage.

Foon, A.E. (1985). The effect of social class and cognitive orientation on clinical expectations. *British Journal of Medical Psychology,* **58**(4) 357–364.

Freeman, A. (1988a). Cognitive therapy of personality disorders, In C. Perris, I. Blackburn & H. Perris (Eds), *Cognitive Psychotherapy: Theory and Practice.* New York: Springer-Verlag.

Freeman, A. (1988b). Cognitive therapy of personality disorders. In C. Peruris & M. Eismann (Eds) *Cognitive Psychotherapy: An Update.* Umea, Sweden: DOPUU Press.

Freeman, A. & Leaf, R.C. (1989). Cognitive therapy applied to personality disorders. In A. Freeman, K.M. Simon, L.E. Beutler & H. Arkowitz (Eds), *Comprehensive Handbook of Cognitive Therapy.* New York: Plenum Press.

Freeman, A., Pretzer, J., Fleming, B. & Simon, K.M. (1990). *Clinical Applications of Cognitive Therapy.* New York: Plenum Press.

Freeman, A. & Simon, K.M. (1989). Cognitive therapy of anxiety. In A. Freeman, K. Simon, L. Beutler & H. Arkowitz (Eds), *Comprehensive Casebook of Cognitive Therapy.* New York: Plenum Press.

Karno, M., Hough, R.L., Burnam, M. A., Escobar, J. I., Timbers, D. M., Santana, F. & Boyd, J.H. (1986). Lifetime prevalence of specific psychiatric disorders among Mexican Americans and non-Hispanic whites in Los Angeles. *Archives of General Psychiatry,* **44**(8), 695–701.

Koeningsberg, H., Kaplan, R., Gilmore, M. & Cooper, A. (1985). The relationship between syndrome and personality disorder in DSM-III: Experience with 2462 patients. *American Journal of Psychiatry,* **142**, 207–212.

Layden, M.A., Newman, C.F., Freeman, A. & Byers-Morse, S. (1993). *Cognitive Therapy of Borderline Personality Disorder*. Needham Heights, MA: Allyn & Bacon.

Linehan, M.M. (1988). Perspectives on the interpersonal relationship in behavior therapy. *Journal of Integrative and Eclectic Psychotherapy*, **7**, 278–290.

Linehan, M.M. (1993). *Cognitive Behavioural Treatment of Borderline Personality Disorder*. New York: Guilford.

Merbaum, M. & Butcher, J.N. (1982).Therapists' liking of their psychotherapy patients: Some issues related to severity of disorder and treatability. *Psychotherapy: Theory, Research and Practice*, **19**(1), 6–76.

Morrison, L. A. & Shapiro, D.A. (1987). Expectancy and outcome in prescriptive vs exploratory psychotherapy. *British Journal of Clinical Psychology*, **26**(1), 59–60.

Rosenbaum, R.L., Horowitz, M.J. & Wilner, N. (1986). Clinician assessments of patient difficulty. *Psychotherapy*, **23**(3), 417–422.

Turner, S.M. (1987). The effects of personality disorder diagnosis on the outcome of social anxiety symptom reduction. *Journal of Personality Disorders*, **1**, 136–143.

Waldingeur, R.J. & Gunderson, J.G. (1987). *Effective Psychotherapy with Borderline Patients: Case Studies*. New York: Macmillan.

Wells, A. (1997). *Cognitive Therapy of Anxiety Disorders: A Practice Manual and Conceptual Guide*. Chichester: Wiley.

Young, J.E. (1990). *Cognitive Therapy for Personality Disorders: A Schema Focused Approach*. Sarasota, FL: Professional Resource Exchange.

Young, J.E. & Swift, W. (1988), Schema focused cognitive therapy for personality disorders: Part I. *International Cognitive Therapy Newsletter*, **4**(5), 13–14.

Chapter 15

SCHEMA-FOCUSED THERAPY FOR PERSONALITY DISORDERS

Jeffrey Young* and Wendy T. Behary†

INTRODUCTION

One of the most recent challenges in cognitive therapy has been to develop an effective treatment approach for clinicians working with patients with personality disorders. These patients present with the most complex and resistant problems within the therapist's caseload. Growing interest in examining the core structures and processes that facilitate or inhibit personal growth and change (Mahoney, 1993) has led to the development of new models for treating such patients. As cognitive therapists began to move into treating more chronic characterological disorders, some of the limitations of Beck's earlier model of cognitive therapy (Beck et al., 1979) became evident. Influenced by the constructivist movement (Mahoney, 1993), Young (1994a) has designed an integrative model called *Schema-Focused Therapy* (SFT), to expand upon Beck's original model and to deliberately address the needs of patients with longstanding characterological and other chronic disorders. This chapter addresses both the theoretical tenets and clinical applications of Schema-Focused Therapy.

ORIGINS OF SCHEMA-FOCUSED THERAPY

Beck's Model

Beck's model of cognitive therapy examines distorted thought patterns. The cognitive therapist attempts to understand how patients with disturbing

* Cognitive Therapy Centers of New York & Connecticut and Department of Psychiatry, Colombia University, USA and † Cognitive Therapy Center of New Jersey

Treating Complex Cases: The Cognitive Behavioural Therapy Approach.
Edited by Nicholas Tarrier, Adrian Wells and Gillian Haddock.
© 1998 John Wiley & Sons Ltd.

emotional states interpret events in their lives. Therapists enlist their patients in altering these distorted thoughts and images so that the accompanying distress will improve.

Beck's cognitive therapy followed his efforts to test Freud's theory that anger turned inward leads to depression. His examination of thoughts and dreams of depressed patients led to repeated observations of patients' feelings of defeat, and a consistent bias toward negative interpretations of the self, the environment, and the future, rather than Freud's theme of internalised anger. On the basis of his continuing studies, Beck developed his general cognitive theory of emotional disorders, which stated that shifts in information processing are central to psychopathology. Therefore, negative emotions and the biased appraisals from which they resulted became the major focus of cognitive theory and practice.

Challenging the psychoanalytic notion of active repression, Beck proposed that core assumptions about the self and the world, formed in early childhood, remain unconscious due to the normal mechanisms by which other habits of thinking and behaving become automatic.

Beck began to train patients to heighten their awareness of their 'stream of consciousness', so as to expose the rigid, automatic thoughts influencing their emotional responses. He then taught patients specific procedures for combating their erroneous 'automatic thoughts,' such as 'dysfunctional thought records,' that would utilise empirical methods to reality test the distortions and replace them with more accurate thoughts.

As patients learned to gain distance from their depressive feelings, symptoms improved over time, as they learned to process information with more accuracy. 'Collaborative empiricism' became the working style of cognitive therapy: the therapist and patient work together actively and systematically, testing the validity of the patient's cognitions in a present-oriented, time-limited, structured, and problem-focused manner.

Through scientific outcome studies to test its efficacy, Beck's cognitive therapy became one of the most widely researched psychotherapies.

The Constructivist Movement

The constructivist movement began within the cognitive sciences as core assumptions and clinical strategies in general cognitive therapy were being challenged by several developments in psychology (Mahoney, 1993). These included: new findings on the nature of emotions; the study of unconscious processes in cognitive psychology; an acknowledgment of social, biological and embodiment processes in therapy; the use of experiential techniques in psychotherapy; and a growing interest in self-organising and self-protective processes in personality development.

Constructivists propose that human systems are composed of self-organising dynamics and that these systems evolve in such a way as to protect their internal coherence. The human condition is seen as anticipatory and operative as opposed to passive and determined. Based on cumulative experiences over time, individuals rely upon their capacity to make predictions about current and future experiences even when biased or distorted.

As a result, constructivist therapists focus on changes in broader systems of personal constructs, rather than challenging narrow thought units (Neimeyer, 1993). Much attention is paid to the developmental dimensions of the patients' psychopathology and their primary attachment relationships. Interventions are likely to be creative, elaborative, reflective, and personally distinctive, whereas the goal of the highly structured, mainstream cognitive model would emphasise more corrective, analytical, and technically instructive target interventions.

Constructivists look at personal interpretations that embody the subtext of the patient's statements. The use of imagery and metaphor is widely utilised in this process. Resistance is viewed as a means for protecting the self at times when the therapist may be experienced as threatening the patient's core ordering processes. Emotions become information to the therapist, in that they mirror patients' efforts to construct meaning out of their experiences.

Cognitive Therapy and Personality Disorders

The limitations of Beck's original model became more apparent as cognitive therapists began to focus on personality and other chronic disorders. Young (1994a) proposed that several conditions had to be met for patients with these disorders to succeed with Beck's model: that patients can engage in a collaborative relationship with the therapist; can identify specific life problems; have access to thoughts and feelings; have the capacity for, and motivation to do, homework assignments; and have cognitions that are malleable enough to respond to cognitive behavioural processes.

Unfortunately, patients with personality disorders often cannot meet these conditions. Young proposed that Beck's original model would often fail unless significant changes were made to address these limitations. Rothstein and Vallis (1991) explain that, 'Given the nature of personality disorders, the impact of existing treatment interventions is often limited.'

One of the hallmarks of character pathology is the difficulty such individuals encounter in their interpersonal experiences. Another primary criterion is the severely rigid and inflexible coping styles that perpetuate tenacious beliefs and expectations. Freeman and Leaf (1989) state that: 'Given the long-term nature of patients' characterological problems, their general avoidance of psychotherapy, their frequent referral through family pressure ... their seeming reluctance or inability to change ... they can and often do require more work within the session ... and more energy than other patients.'

Young (1994a) elaborated on the psychological characteristics that distinguish patients with personality disorders from straightforward Axis I cases, and thus make them much less suitable for standard cognitive therapy. These characteristics include diffuse presentation, interpersonal problems, rigidity, and avoidance.

Diffuse presentation

Patients with personality disorders often cannot specify identifiable problems to focus on. Despite their often chronic, high levels of dysfunction, these patients often present with ambiguous, vaguely defined complaints, and with non-specific triggers. Given the absence of a specific target, typical cognitive therapy techniques require modification.

Interpersonal problems

DSM-IV (American Psychiatric Association, 1994) emphasises interpersonal difficulties as central problems for patients with Axis II diagnoses. Some patients may find it difficult to engage in a therapeutic relationship, while others may become excessively dependent upon their therapist. The traditional model of cognitive therapy expects patients to engage in a collaborative relationship with the therapist in a brief period. This often leads to a significant challenge for this patient population; and, unfortunately, the early model does not offer an adequate protocol for addressing this challenge.

Rigidity

In the original model of cognitive therapy, patients are assumed to have a degree of flexibility that enables them to challenge and modify their thoughts and behaviours through empirical examination, experimentation, rational dialogue, graded steps, and consistent repetition. However, patients with personality disorders usually exhibit deeply cemented patterns of thinking and behaving that may not be relinquished for a significant period.

Rigid, longstanding, impenetrable characteristics dilute the potential for successful outcomes in traditional cognitive treatment settings.

Avoidance

Young (1994a) hypothesised that the chronic affective, cognitive, and behavioural avoidance that characterises patients with personality disorders develops as a result of aversive conditioning. Anxiety, depression, and other unpleasant affective states become conditioned to memories, situations, and cognitions, leading to avoidance. These avoidance processes are not addressed in traditional cognitive therapy.

Schema-Focused Therapy versus Cognitive Therapy

Schema-Focused Therapy integrates cognitive, behavioural, experiential (e.g. gestalt), and interpersonal (e.g. object relations) techniques, utilising the concept of a *schema* as the unifying element. It assimilates and adapts strategies that are utilised in standard cognitive therapy, but goes beyond the short-term approach by combining interpersonal and experiential techniques within a cognitive behavioural framework.

Schema-Focused Therapy includes greater use of the therapeutic relationship as a means for change. It also involves a more elaborate discussion of early life experiences and the childhood aetiology of problems. More attention is paid to affective experiences through the use of imagery and role-playing, which promotes higher levels of affect in sessions. The model also advocates more direct and active confrontation of cognitive and behavioural patterns. In addition, because these patterns are often tightly entrenched and more resistant to change, the course of treatment is often longer when treating personality disorders using the schema-focused model.

SCHEMA-FOCUSED CONCEPTUAL MODEL

The schema-focused model is intended as a working theory, integrating and guiding the clinical interventions of practitioners treating patients with character disorders. The model was not designed as a comprehensive theory of psychopathology.

The four main constructs that Young proposed and that we discuss in this chapter are Early Maladaptive Schemata, Schema Domains, Schema Processes, and Schema Modes. Practical application of the model will be illustrated with case examples illustrating work with two of the most

challenging areas of character pathology: borderline and narcissistic personality disorders.

Definition of an Early Maladaptive Schema

Segal (1988) defines schemata as 'organised elements of past reactions and
experience that form a relatively cohesive and persistent body of knowledge
capable of guiding subsequent perception and appraisals.' Furthermore,
Freeman and Leaf (1989) describe that, 'These schemata are evolutionary
and develop as the individual moves through life. They are the basic rules
that people live by ... The schemata that are basically functional in this earlier part of life are being applied during later, more demanding times. These
schemata become fixed when they are reinforced and/or modelled by parents.' The importance of schemata was noted by Beck (1967) in some of his
earliest studies on depression: 'a schema is a (cognitive) structure for screening, coding, and evaluating the stimuli that impinge on the organism ...'

Young (1994a) proposes a subset of schemata called Early Maladaptive
Schemata (EMSs). Whereas traditional cognitive therapy focuses primarily
on automatic thoughts and underlying assumptions, SFT proposes a
major emphasis on the Early Maladaptive Schema (the deepest level of
cognition and affect).

Young's model (1994a) defines schemata as 'broad, pervasive themes
regarding oneself and one's relationship with others, developed during
childhood and elaborated throughout one's lifetime, and dysfunctional to
a significant degree.' Young (1994a) has identified 18 EMSs thus far; definitions of these 18 schemata, along with their associated developmental
domains, are presented in Appendix A. (Note: the use of the term 'schema'
throughout the chapter will refer to an Early Maladaptive Schema.)

For example, children who have received too little emotional nurturance,
understanding, guidance or protection from parents usually develop the
Emotional Deprivation schema. The same children, as adults, often experience feelings of emptiness and loneliness, accompanied by an exaggerated
belief that they are misunderstood, unloved, and not cared for adequately
by others. They may attempt to adapt to these beliefs and feelings by
becoming overly self-reliant in relation to others.

Characteristics of Early Maladaptive Schemata

In contrast to Beck's underlying assumptions, schemata are typically
unconditional and implicit themes held by individuals. They are

perceived to be irrefutable and, therefore, are far more inflexible to change efforts.

Schemata develop out of an interplay between the child's innate temperament and ongoing noxious experiences of the child with parents, siblings, or peers (such as abuse, instability, neglect, excessive criticism, abandonment, or overprotection). Schemata are essentially valid representations of early childhood experiences, and serve as templates for processing and defining later behaviours, thoughts, feelings, and relationships with others. Schemata include entrenched patterns of distorted thinking, disruptive affect, and dysfunctional behaviours.

Because they begin early in life, schemata become familiar and thus comfortable. They are often centrally linked to the individual's self-concept and that of the environment. Even when presented with evidence that disproves the schema, individuals tenaciously distort data to maintain its validity.

For example, a woman with a Defectiveness schema may continue to feel flawed and worthless, despite being told repeatedly by others that she is lovable and valuable. Schematic change feels too threatening to her with regard to the organisation of core cognitions; hence, a variety of cognitive, emotive, and behavioural coping actions reinforce the schema.

Schemata are perpetuated throughout one's lifetime and become activated under conditions relevant to that particular schema. They have the potential to generate high levels of affect, and they serve as filters for an individual's experience. In an attempt to cope with the distress associated with schemata, individuals often develop self-defeating cycles that lead to negative consequences. These may include, for example, addictions, work performance problems, psychosomatic disorders like ulcers or insomnia, depression or panic, and (in severe cases such as borderline patients), dissociation and suicidality.

Let us consider the example of a borderline patient whose Abandonment and Defectiveness schemata are triggered when her husband travels on business. She describes enormous terror and a profound sense of loss, as if he would never return to her. She believes that he will find someone else more desirable and reject her, as she had always anticipated. She overeats and contemplates self-mutilation in order to cope with her painful feelings.

This vignette illustrates the characteristics of the borderline patient who, in schema-focused terms, views herself as defective and unlovable, and expects to be rejected or abandoned by others. The engulfing negative affect generated by the activation of her schema leads to dysfunctional coping behaviours (which represent schema processes to be discussed later). Most attempts to recast the interpretation or to combat the 'truths' of the schemata will be initially too threatening. The patient will describe the shame she feels for having binged or cut, which may further reinforce the schematic beliefs that she is worthless and defective, and that people will want to reject and abandon her.

Schema Domains and Developmental Origins

Young proposes five broad categories of schemata that he refers to as Schema Domains. Each of the five domains represents an important component of a child's core needs. Specific EMSs interfere with the child's attempts to get the core needs met within each domain. The following section will provide a description of each Schema Domain with its associated schemata.

Disconnection and rejection.

This domain is characterised by the expectation that one's needs for safety, security, acceptance, nurturance, stability, protection, empathy, and guidance will not be met in a constant or predictable manner. Schemata within this domain are: *Abandonment/Instability, Mistrust/Abuse, Emotional Deprivation, Defectiveness/Shame,* and *Social Isolation/ Alienation.* They arise from explosive, critical, rejecting, detached, withholding, unpredictable, or abusive families of origin.

Impaired autonomy and performance

Patients with schemata in this domain *(Dependence/Incompetence, Vulnerability to Danger, Enmeshment/Undeveloped Self,* and *Failure)* have certain expectations about themselves and their environment that interfere with their perceived ability to separate, survive, function independently, or perform successfully. This is typically the result of an enmeshed, overprotective, or undermining family of origin that has failed to reinforce the child for performing competently outside the family, or has neglected to foster skills for independent functioning.

Impaired limits.

Schemata within this domain *(Entitlement/Grandiosity* and *Insufficient Self-Control/Self-Discipline)* pertain to a deficiency in internal limits, responsibility to others, or long-term goal orientation. These schemata lead to difficulty in respecting the rights of others, cooperating with others, making commitments, or setting and meeting realistic personal goals. Patients with these schemata typically have families characterised by permissiveness, indulgence, or a sense of superiority, rather than appropriate confrontation, discipline, and limits in relation to taking responsibility, cooperating in a reciprocal manner, treating others as equals, and setting goals. In some cases the child may not have been pushed to tolerate normal levels of discomfort.

Other-directedness

This domain involves an excessive focus on the feelings, wishes, and desires of others, at the expense of one's own needs—in order to gain approval, acceptance, love and connection, or to avoid retaliation, rejection, blame or loss. This usually involves the suppression of one's natural inclinations and one's awareness of anger. The child typically comes from an environment where acceptance was conditional: the child learns to suppress normal needs and emotions in order to gain attention, approval, and love. In many cases, the parents' emotional needs and desires are valued more than the unique needs and feelings of the child. The schemata within this domain are *Self-Sacrifice, Subjugation,* and *Approval-Seeking.*

Overvigilance and inhibition

Schemata within this domain include *Negativity/Vulnerability to Error, Overcontrol/Emotional Inhibition, Unrelenting Standards/ Hypercriticalness,* and *Punitiveness.* Within this domain, there is often excessive emphasis on controlling one's spontaneous feelings, impulses, and choices in order to avoid making mistakes. Parents usually stress meeting rigid, internalised rules and expectations about performance and ethical behaviour, often at the expense of happiness, self-expression, relaxation, close relationships, or health. The typical family origin is grim and sometimes punitive: performance, duty, perfectionism, following rules and avoiding mistakes predominate over pleasure, joy, and relaxation. There is usually an undercurrent of pessimism and worry that things could fall apart if one fails to be vigilant and careful at all times.

Schema Processes

As the schema-focused therapist examines and helps challenge these core schemata, the patient simultaneously engages in a variety of cognitive, affective, and behavioural manoeuvres, called *schema processes.* These schema processes, or coping styles, serve both to maintain the validity of the schema and to avoid experiencing the painful affect associated with schema activation. *Schema Maintenance, Schema Avoidance,* and *Schema Compensation* are the three broad forms of schema processes that are initially activated by, and ultimately reinforce, the schemata. These processes overlap with the psychoanalytic concepts of resistance and defense mechanisms.

Schema maintenance

This process refers to the individual's use (usually unconscious) of cognitive distortions and dysfunctional behaviour patterns to perpetuate schemata. This can also be viewed as the patient's surrendering to the schema. For example, an individual with the Defectiveness schema may select a romantic partner who is critical and demeaning, thus maintaining her schematic view that she is defective and unlovable. Additionally, she may misinterpret minor suggestions for change from others as further evidence of her unlovability and worthlessness.

Schema avoidance

This schema process refers to the individual's attempt to avoid triggering a schema and the accompanying intense affect through cognitive, behavioural, and emotional avoidance strategies. For example, a patient with a Failure schema may avoid working on his project because he believes that he will receive a poor evaluation, which in turn would trigger the shame associated with failure. By avoiding the assignment, he contributes to the outcome he fears—a negative evaluation further reinforcing the Failure schema.

Schema compensation

This process refers to behaviours that overcompensate for a schema; they present as the opposite of what one would expect based on the knowledge of the patient's Early Maladaptive Schemata. Schema compensation represents early functional attempts by the child to adapt to the pain of mistreatment or neglect by parents, siblings, or peers. It is illustrative of the child's efforts to 'fight back' against that mistreatment. However, when schema compensation carries over into adulthood, the behaviours designed to fight back against the schema are often too extreme for the healthier environment and thus overshoot the mark. Therefore, the over-compensation ultimately backfires and serves to reinforce the schema.

Let us return to the example of a borderline patient. In her attempts to compensate for her Emotional Deprivation schema, she often demands inordinate amounts of attention. Moreover, in an effort to fight against her Abandonment schema, she often becomes clingy and overly attached to others. In both scenarios, she is likely to alienate the people close to her, and thus feel further deprived and abandoned. Another example is the narcissistic patient who, in his attempts to compensate for his Defectiveness schema, becomes overly critical and demeaning of others in anticipation of their negative appraisals of him. This compensatory behaviour leads others to find him arrogant and insensitive, and to reject him. This rejection in turn reinforces his Defectiveness schema.

Schema Modes

Although several schemata may underlie an individual's thoughts, feelings, behaviours, and relationships with others, some may remain dormant while others are triggered. A *schema mode* represents a group of schemata or processes that are *currently* active for an individual; the schemata or processes have erupted into strong affect or rigid coping styles that take over and predominate an individual's functioning. An individual may shift from one schema mode into another; as that shift occurs, a different group of schemata or processes, previously dormant, become active. Young defines a schema mode as 'a facet of the self, involving a natural grouping of schemata and schema processes, that has not been fully integrated with other facets.'

Schema modes are viewed along a spectrum of dissociative states, with Multiple Personality Disorder at the extreme end and normal shifts in mood on the other end of the dissociative spectrum. Along that continuum, the individual in a schema mode is somewhere above the middle of the spectrum; how far above the middle depends on how powerful the mode is for the particular person. A mode, therefore, is a part of the self that is cut off, to some degree, from other aspects of the self.

Young proposes four general categories of modes (elaborated in Appendix B): the *child modes*, the *maladaptive coping modes*, the *maladaptive parent modes*, and the *healthy adult mode*. Child modes refer to states that we presume to be innately present in everyone from birth. Child modes include the 'normal' experiences and presentations of the child, including feelings and cognitions of sadness, anger, terror, happiness, and other basic affects; and behavioural inclinations such as crying, temper tantrums, and demandingness. For example, a borderline patient tearfully describes the sense of terror and sadness she feels as she experiences the potential loss of her romantic partner. While grieving is a reasonable response to anticipated loss, the patient presents with disproportionate affect and exaggerated feelings of vulnerability, aloneness, isolation, emptiness, and unlovability. This is the borderline patient in the Abandoned Child mode. The schemata triggered in this example are Emotional Deprivation, Abandonment, and Defectiveness. Borderline patients in the Abandoned Child mode usually feel overwhelmed by fear of harm or abandonment, and typically experience intense depression, hopelessness, fear, worthlessness, unlovability, victimisation, loneliness, and neediness. Consequently, they may engage in frenetic efforts to avoid abandonment, and may even attempt suicide.

Once a Borderline patient is in the Abandoned Child mode, she often 'flips' into the Detached Protector mode as she attempts to recoup her functioning. In this mode, she blankly stares, explaining that she is numb and no longer feels the pain of the Abandoned Child, and states that the loss of her partner does not really matter after all. The Detached Protector is the maladaptive coping mode characterised by avoidance; this is the 'default' mode for most borderline patients, by which we mean that most borderlines seem to spend the greatest portion of their time in this mode. The Detached Protector mode serves to detach patients from other people and from experiencing emotions. The borderline patient in the Detached Protector mode will usually experience a sense of depersonalisation, emptiness, or boredom and may appear excessively compliant. The borderline patient periodically dissociates while in the Detached Protector mode. Substance abuse, bingeing, self-mutilation, and psychosomatic complaints are sometimes characteristic of this mode: all efforts to avoid or detach from the distress associated with the core child schemata.

A third mode common in borderline patients is the Punitive Parent mode (part of the general category of modes we refer to as maladaptive parent modes). In this mode, the patient generally believes that she has done something wrong (such as feeling 'too much' anger), and that she is evil, bad, or dirty. The Punitive Parent mode generally involves intense feelings of self-hatred, self-condemnation, and self-directed anger. The patient may punish herself harshly for having made a mistake, often through self-mutilating behaviours.

The Abandoned Child and Detached Protector modes create immense anger in patients with Borderline Personality Disorder, because they both involve the suppression of intense feelings and needs. As the anger accumulates and builds up, it can no longer be contained. Often one event is perceived as the last straw, and the patient flips into another child mode, the Angry Child. In this mode the suppressed emotions and needs become released, and the patient may adopt an enraged, demanding, demeaning, manipulative, controlling, or abusive position both with the therapist and with others. While her underlying desire is to stand up for her legitimate rights, she expresses these rights and needs in destructive ways. She may, for example, become impulsive, make suicide attempts, verbally assault others, or engage in promiscuity.

To summarise, the four basic modes that Young proposes for patients with Borderline Personality Disorder are: the Abandoned Child (a child mode), the Angry Child (a child mode), the Detached Protector (a maladaptive coping mode), and the Punitive Parent (a maladaptive parent mode). Through the therapy relationship, the schema-focused therapist becomes a model for the Healthy Adult mode, which the patient gradually internalises. The Healthy Adult mode learns adaptive strategies for healing, rechannelling, integrating, or fighting the other modes, so that the patient ultimately becomes a unified, well-functioning, contented individual.

Patients with a Narcissistic Personality Disorder flip among three modes, the *Self-Aggrandiser*, the *Lonely Child*, and the *Detached Self-Soother*. The Self-Aggrandiser mode (a subtype of the overcompensator mode) is the default mode for most narcissists. This mode usually includes one or more of four schemata: Entitlement, Approval-Seeking, Unrelenting Standards, and Mistrust. In the Self-Aggrandiser mode, narcissists act superior, status-oriented, entitled, and critical of others, showing little or no regard for others' feelings or rights. In this mode, the narcissistic patient makes efforts to overcompensate for the underlying schemata of Defectiveness, Emotional Deprivation, or Subjugation. Paradoxically, however, the narcissist in the Self-Aggrandiser mode ultimately perpetuates these core schemata rather than healing them by alienating others through his arrogant, grandiose, superior, demeaning and devaluing style.

Narcissistic patients often flip into the Lonely Child mode when they are cut off from sources of approval and validation; for example, when they receive negative feedback or criticism. The Lonely Child is a subtype of the Vulnerable Child Mode, comprising the schemata of Defectiveness and Emotional Deprivation, as well as other EMSs. In the Lonely Child mode, the narcissist acutely experiences a loss of specialness and feels devalued and alone.

In order to escape the pain associated with being ordinary, devalued, and isolated, the narcissist will either flip back into the Self-Aggrandiser mode or will switch to the third mode, the Detached Self-Soother (one of the maladaptive coping modes). The function of the Detached Self-Soother is to distract from, and numb the pain of, the Emotional Deprivation and Defectiveness schemata. Compulsive stimulation-seeking behaviours (e.g. gambling, investing, workaholism, sexual addiction), drug and alcohol abuse, and overeating are a few of the many forms that the Detached Self-Soother mode may take.

Tim is a 42-year old, married attorney who came into treatment with a Narcissistic Personality Disorder. He reported that he was feeling lonely and 'disenchanted with his life.' Tim said that his wife was simply not a very stimulating partner—that she was a 'bore.' He went on to describe that it was very difficult for him to achieve a sense of pleasure from his interactions with other people, because he was 'an esoteric type' and was, therefore, often misunderstood by others. Tim felt that his thought style was far too 'avante garde' for his peers. He was quick to point out his achievement as a professional in terms of both recognition and monetary compensation. Tim said that he worked long hours and felt 'excited' by it.

Tim's early presentation illustrates some classic features of narcissism in the Self-Aggrandiser mode: devaluing (wife, others), approval-seeking (achievement, money), and self-aggrandising (self compared to others) behaviours. By staying in this mode, Tim could avoid the underlying pain of the Lonely Child mode.

Since schema modes are relatively cut off from each other, and patients exhibit different cognitions, behaviours, and emotions in each mode, the therapist must utilise different treatment strategies in response to each mode. The overall therapeutic goal with narcissistic patients, as with Borderlines, is to create a Healthy Adult mode capable of gradually healing; modifying, and integrating the more adaptive modes, while eliminating dysfunctional modes.

CLINICAL APPLICATIONS OF SCHEMA-FOCUSED THERAPY: ASSESSMENT

Schema-focused treatment is composed of two phases: assessment and change. The assessment phase of treatment focuses on the identification and activation of schemata that are most pertinent to each patient. The change phase of treatment attempts to modify the relevant schemata and maladaptive behaviour patterns.

The assessment phase includes four components:

- *schema identification*
- *schema activation*
- *schema conceptualisation*
- *schema education*

Schema Identification

During this stage, relevant schemata are identified through clinical probing and elaboration of the presenting problem and life history. The clinician pays close attention to early and ongoing patterns in the therapy relationship. The schema-focused therapist also utilises inventories, including the Young Schema Questionnaire (Young & Brown, 1990/1994), a 205-item self-report inventory which consists of self-statements related to each schema; the Multimodal Life History Inventory (Lazarus & Lazarus, 1991), a record of important current historical features of the patient's life, which enables the clinician to generate hypotheses about relevant schemata; schema diaries and journals; and the Young Parenting Inventory (YPI: Young, 1994b), an instrument targeting the origins of schemata through patient ratings of their mothers and fathers during childhood.

Having identified the relevant schemata, the therapist must explore how patients characteristically maintain, avoid, and compensate for them. For example, a patient with an Abandonment/Instability schema may select a partner who is rarely available, thereby perpetuating a sense of abandonment. Two instruments are utilised to identify patterns of avoidance and compensation. The Young–Rygh Avoidance Inventory (YRAI: Young & Rygh, 1994) looks at the degree and types of schema avoidance, while the Young Compensation Inventory (YCI; Young, 1994c) taps the degree and type of schema compensation.

Schema modes are also identified during this stage. Clinicians must not only differentiate the modes, they must also be aware of the environmental triggers that activate each mode, and note the cognitive, emotional, and behavioural manifestations within each mode. As mentioned earlier, patients with characterological disorders, such as the borderline and the narcissist, may experience the activation of a clustering of schemata simultaneously, thereby creating a prime focus on the presenting modes as representative of the many core schemata.

Schema Activation

Schema activation involves triggering the affect associated with a particular schema. This is most commonly accomplished with experiential techniques, especially imagery. A patient is asked to imagine upsetting childhood and adult scenes that come to mind; through dialogues among the characters in the dreams, the affect associated with the core schema is usually triggered.

The goal of the schema activation component of assessment is a dual one. First, we hypothesise that schemata that elicit the highest levels of affect during activation exercises are more primary, while those that do not elicit such strong emotion are considered more secondary for the patient. The therapist utilises this information to decide which schemata to target first in the change phase of treatment; primary schemata are usually addressed before secondary ones for a particular patient.

Secondly, schema activation is used to overcome schema avoidance. We have observed that schemata change more easily when they are activated than when they are dormant. However, as we mentioned earlier, most characterological patients exhibit significant affective and cognitive avoidance. So long as the patient avoids thoughts and memories that trigger painful emotions, the therapist and patient cannot work effectively. Through the use of imagery, the therapist first helps patients tolerate low levels of schema-related affect, and then gradually intensifies the experience until patients are able to tolerate more emotionally laden imagery exercises without withdrawing from the image. Activating schemata through experiential exercises thus allows the schema-avoidant patient to tolerate painful feelings without escaping. Through this process, the therapist and patient gain access to previously blocked thoughts and emotions; this facilitates the change phase of treatment, because the therapist can utilise change techniques while the schemata are triggered.

Schema Conceptualisation

Material gathered throughout the assessment stage is integrated into an overall diagram of the patient's problems using the Schema Conceptualisation Form (Young, 1992). Dependent upon how fragile, self-protective, avoidant, compensated, or wounded the patient is, and the duration and complexity of the issues, it may require several sessions to complete the preliminary case conceptualisation.

Schema conceptualisation is customised for each patient, in that the patterning of schemata and the specific ways in which they interact are always unique. A narcissistic patient and a borderline patient may come across very differently, although they both have a primary Defectiveness schema. The narcissist comes across as self-absorbed, self-aggrandising, and eager to talk about superficial aspects of himself, whereas the borderline might be extremely self-punitive and focused on connecting to the therapist.

Schema Education

Finally, before the change phase begins, it is essential to explain to patients the nature of their schemata. This cultivates a collaborative understanding of the problems and the core issues. Therefore, the therapist translates the assessment data into 'schema terms' for the patient and asks for feedback to confirm the schema conceptualisation and to agree on a broad treatment plan.

To further assist in patients' understanding of schemata, we routinely recommend that they read *Reinventing Your Life* (Young & Klosko, 1993), a self-help book based on the schema-focused approach. We also give most new patients the *Client's Guide to Schema-Focused Therapy* (Bricker & Young, 1991). This six-page handout explains the schema-focused approach in everyday language and provides relevant examples of how schemata operate.

THE CHANGE PHASE OF TREATMENT

As previously mentioned, Schema-Focused Therapy is an integrative approach, combining cognitive, behavioural, experiential, and interpersonal techniques in one model for treating patients with chronic and difficult disorders. While standard cognitive and behavioural strategies are incorporated, and will be summarised in the following section, the chapter will place more emphasis on techniques that are more specific to the schema-focused approach.

Cognitive Techniques

The basic objective of cognitive strategies is to reconstruct the distorted view held by the patient regarding the self and others, as manifested in their Early Maladaptive Schemata, by generating evidence to refute them and thereby creating more accurate perceptions. The goal is to improve the patient's internal information processing system as it relates to their schemata.

The 'life review' is a cognitive exercise that examines evidence that supports and contradicts the schema, by asking the patient for relevant data. The goals are: (i) to help patients appreciate how their schemata distort their perceptions and feelings, thus keeping the schemata intact; and (ii) to begin a process of distancing from, rather than identifying with, their schemata.

For example, when a borderline patient is asked about her sense of unlovability (Defectiveness schema), she can usually provide ample data drawn from a lifetime of experiences and memories to support her schemata: 'My mother ignored me because I was a bad child ... I had few friends because I was shy and ugly ... My stepfather abused me because I was too provocative ... Boyfriends abandoned me because I was either boring, not good enough, or too jealous … Therapists cannot tolerate me because I am too needy.'

When asked to provide data to contradict the schema, the therapist may ask: 'Is there any evidence at all that anyone can love you or value you?' The patient is likely to struggle to find contradictory information to prove that she is lovable because the Defectiveness schema negates any examples. She may only be able to describe very few experiences where she felt good about herself or where others viewed her as good and lovable. The clinician may need to coach her gently towards supportive statements based upon other information gathered in the earlier life history review, or based on the clinician's own view of the patient.

Young's philosophy of the borderline patient includes a view of the patient as 'genuinely needy, not greedy.' The therapist, therefore, attempts to alter the basic belief of the borderline patient that her neediness is evidence of defectiveness; instead, we explain her neediness as the 'abandoned child' part of herself whose early needs were never met and who deserves now to be loved and protected, guided and nurtured.

Flashcards (see Young & Klosko, 1994) are also utilised as part of the cognitive work, so that patients may continue the distancing process outside therapy. A flashcard is written on a piece of paper or an index card, and is usually developed by the therapist, in collaboration with the patient. The flashcard lists the most powerful evidence and counter-arguments against the schemata. Patients are encouraged to carry the flashcards with them wherever they go and are asked to read them repeatedly, particularly when a schema is triggered (that is, when they have a 'schema attack'). The continuous repetition of rational responses based on empirical evidence contradictory to the schema, at the time of schema activation, helps patients to gain distance from the schema and the related feelings, and ultimately prevents dysfunctional coping behaviours. Patients are guided toward identifying with a newer, healthier, and more objectively accurate voice. Flashcards may also be audiotaped. Some clinicians find that with more fragile patients, such as borderlines, the therapist's voice on tape keeps them anchored to the therapist in a supportive, nurturing manner, thereby enhancing the credibility of the positive response. Conceptually, the flashcard is asking the patient to pause during distress to perform a reality check on the emotions, beliefs, and impulses being experienced, as cues to question the schemata or schema modes being triggered.

The flashcard strengthens the healthy voice to provide distance from the schemata. It also provides the individual with more adaptive behavioural responses. Thoughtful, accurate, and empathic language is utilised in constructing an effective flashcard, whether written or spoken. Linehan (1993) writes that a: 'key function of emotional suffering and maladaptive behaviours for borderline patients is self-validation. Thus, therapeutic changes cannot be made unless another source of self-validation is developed.'

The following is an example of a flashcard developed for a borderline patient to read when she felt she was a bad mother. For example, she reported that, in phoning her daughter one night, she quickly perceived that her daughter was not interested in talking because the daughter ended the call in a seemingly 'abrupt' manner. The patient reported that she felt cut off (Abandonment schema), unlovable (Defectiveness schema), and that this was her punishment (Punitive Parent mode) for being a 'bad' mother. She recalled wanting to just 'numb out' (Detached Protector mode) in order to block the painful feelings. She looked into her bathroom and reported thoughts of cutting herself. At this point she picked up her flashcard and read it:

> Right now I feel rejected, undesirable, and lonely. I feel that I am a bad mother and a bad person who deserves to be punished. I also feel a certain numbness trying to come over me as I realise these feelings about myself. I know that I am likely to detach and potentially harm myself when I feel this way.
>
> I know that these are my schemata of Abandonment and Defectiveness, which lead me directly to my Detached Protector and Punitive Parent modes.
>
> The truth is that the relationship with Norma [her daughter] is a very challenging one and has been for years since my recovery from alcohol. She is not ready to trust me yet but has made some strides to be closer. I am a good, loving, and worthy person. Some people have tried to tell me this, like Rabbi Michael, my supervisor, my therapist, and others. It's just so hard for me to believe and accept this when my schemata are triggered. I learned these schemata in my childhood both directly from my family and indirectly as an explanation that I created to make sense out of the chaos.
>
> The truth is that sometimes I am simply looking to be loved and affirmed for being good and worthy, but I make choices that may disappoint me and bring me back to my original beliefs about myself, like calling Norma at 11: 00 at night when I know that she is very tired late in the evening and not much of a phone person. It's my schema's way of defeating my goal for closeness by blurring my vision when making certain choices. I also know that, because I believe that I will always be rejected and judged harshly, I am likely to cling to people or make demands that may be unrealistic.
>
> That is why it is important for me to keep reading this and repeating the truths to myself—that I am good, loving, worthy, and capable—so that I can come to believe it more automatically and make more consistently healthy choices for myself.
>
> It is important that I act in ways that are consistent with these truths by taking care of myself and being loving and patient. I can take a warm bath, which I enjoy. I can listen to music, call my best friend Carole who cares deeply for me, etc.

Ultimately, she was able, with the help of her flashcard, to fight the schemata, then turn on her favorite music and take a warm bath before going to bed.

The flashcard is essentially a constructive weapon, reminding the patient that there are two possible views of an upsetting experience—the schema side and the healthy side. Building up the healthy side means continuing to refute the schema with solid counter-evidence and counter-movement. We observe that flashcards keep the patient more effectively anchored to the therapy process and therapy goals outside sessions.

Experiential Techniques

Experiential techniques have been increasingly added to cognitive therapy regimens in recent years (e.g. Daldrup et al., 1988; Safran & Segal, 1990; Vallis, Howes & Miller, 1991; Layden et al., 1993) and are used to bring patients' emotions in sync with cognitive changes. These techniques appear to be among the most useful of all strategies in Schema-Focused Therapy and seem to change underlying schemata in a fundamental way that is often more powerful than with cognitive techniques alone. Patients experience affective arousal associated with the schema through experiential techniques, which facilitates modification of the schema. The following are two of the most commonly used techniques: imagery exercises and schema dialogues.

Imagery

Imagery techniques are among the most dramatic approaches to changing schemata. In the assessment phase, imagery is used for recalling and tolerating the pain associated with the schema; in the change phase, patients are now guided and encouraged to modify the image and, consequently, the schema.

For example, patients with the Emotional Deprivation schema would be asked to close their eyes and capture an image of themselves feeling deprived, or not understood, as children by a parent. They are then asked to describe details of the situation as vividly as possible, including their appearance at that age and that of their parents; details of the environment; and exactly what is happening in the childhood image. Patients are asked to describe their feelings and thoughts in the imagined scene, and to communicate them to the depriving parent in the image. (With borderline patients, this part of the exercise often requires significant coaching and protection by the therapist, in the image, as the patient often experiences terror in facing their often abusive 'perpetrator' even in an image.) The patient is encouraged, with the help and advocacy of the therapist, to state her rights as a child to be loved, nurtured, and protected.

Confronting the depriving parent in imagery enables the patient to understand the parent's role in forming her schema, instead of attributing the rejection to herself. The imagery exercise reinforces a healthier, reconstructed information processing system begun through cognitive exercises: 'a primary goal of the exercise is to modify the schema by empowering the 'child' patient with the knowledge, rationality, and compassion of the adult patient' (Layden et al., 1993).

Schema dialogues

The schema dialogue is an essential technique in the change phase for modifying schemata and schema modes. Patients learn to battle the feelings elicited by the schema and to strengthen the healthy aspects of themselves. They strengthen the 'healthy voice' that can accurately interpret the meaning of their experiences. For example, patients with the Defectiveness schema can be taught that, while they *feel* they are bad at a core level (the schema side), some part of themselves, however small initially, can see themselves as worthwhile and can experience relief from shame and other associated emotions (the healthy side).

In the schema dialogue, patients are asked to refute the schema by providing contradictory evidence. In the first phase of the dialogue, patients are asked to role-play the 'voice' of the schema (i.e. thoughts consistent with their schema). Patients are usually able to do this with ease because their schema-driven thoughts form the core of their self-concept. In the next phase, patients are encouraged to respond to the schema from their 'healthy side.' Here the patient experiences more difficulty, since refuting the schema requires acknowledging the validity of contradictory evidence, which is usually not within their immediate grasp. Clinicians 'coach' the patient by pointing out the evidence gathered already from the patient's life history.

The following is a case example of a therapist utilising the schema dialogue technique with Tim, the narcissistic patient described earlier. The therapist aims to engage the patient in a dialogue that includes his Self-Aggrandiser mode (or Special Tim), his Lonely Child mode (Devalued Tim), and his Detached Self-Soother mode.

T: Tim, be the part of yourself that we call Special Tim—the part of you that feels he is superior to others and intolerant of them. Let me hear that voice.

Tim: I'm tired of the nonsense I have to put up with being married to a woman who is just not up to my standards of intelligence; she's such a zero.

T: Okay, now be Devalued Tim, the side of yourself that believes that it is really you who is bad and therefore unworthy of getting your needs met.

Tim: Oh, I should talk about standards, when I *picked* this woman. I keep making mistakes and complaining about them. I'm nothing but a loser.

T: Okay, now, let's hear what Special Tim says about that.

Tim: I'm no loser, she is. I've done better at my firm this year than any of my sorry partners. Women are just deceitful and tricky. She graduated from a prestigious law school. How could I know that she would be a manipulative bore?

T: Be Devalued Tim now.

Tim: Yeah, you think you're such a winner at work, but where are your friends and your family? No one wants to be in your company, they know the truth about you—you're shallow and empty'

Tim (*pauses and flips into his Detached Self-Soother mode*): Oh, who cares anyway, I don't need anyone. Just a few beers, a cigarette, some TV, my computer, I'll be raring to go on that big project that I'm working on at the firm.

The strength of Devalued Tim was about equal to the Special Tim mode. Devalued Tim created sufficient discomfort for the patient to flip into his Detached Self-Soother mode ('I don't need anyone'; images of soothing the pain through beers and cigarettes). The therapist, in this early phase of the exercise, is merely a facilitator, guiding the schema modes to communicate with each other.

The therapist next works to help the patient access the early feelings of the Lonely Child mode, and then to develop a Healthy Adult mode to validate the painful feelings and to promote the healthy needs that are part of Tim's vulnerable side. Linehan (1993) states that: 'Both validation and problem-solving strategies are used in every interaction with the patient. Many treatment impasses result from an imbalance of one strategy over the other.'

Tim (*Lonely Child*): I'm lonely and scared that it will always be this way— no one who understands and no one who really wants me.

Tim (*Healthy Side, with coaching from therapist*): Of course I'm frightened when I feel this way. I deserve to be loved, respected, and accepted by my mother and father for being the lovable little boy that I am. I need to learn skills to allow people to get close to me now, ways of relating to people more caringly, with regard for their feelings and rights. This is hard for me because no one taught me, treated me that way, or modelled this for me. But I'm working at it now, so maybe I can change it.

Tim (*Devalued feelings of the Lonely Child*): You're hopeless and insatiable. You know that there is no one out there who will adequately meet your needs; they never have and never will.

Tim (*Healthy Side*): It's true that I do slip back to that belief so easily because it's been a part of me for a long time. But I have, in fact, made some progress already: through my son's basketball league, I've made some nice friends who care about me just for being part of the parents' group; spending more time outdoors has helped me to meet some nice people in the neighbourhood who seem to like me.

In addition to providing distance from the schema, the schema dialogue also enables patients to appreciate that the *voice* of the schema is just one aspect of the self, and thus these feelings are not inherently valid. With sufficient practice, patients gradually learn to assume the role of the Healthy Adult. They feel emancipated as they arrive at the stage where they can more easily express angry and vulnerable feelings, and also can reject the schema that has caused such problems. Newer, healthier ways of thinking and feeling become more natural.

Interpersonal Techniques within the Therapy Relationship

Since one of the hallmarks of character pathology is difficulty in establishing therapeutic relationships, and since interpersonal problems are often core issues for these patients, the therapeutic relationship is a vital medium for schema modification.

One aspect of the therapist's role is described by Young as 'limited reparenting.' The therapist attempts to provide a therapeutic relationship that directly counteracts the child's early childhood experiences with the parents. Limited reparenting is most valuable for patients with schemata in the Disconnection and Rejection domain. This is especially important for patients with personality disorders, who have often experienced extreme criticism, abuse, instability, deprivation, or rejection as children. For example, if the patient's parents were withholding, the therapist endeavors to be as nurturing as possible. The therapist, however, only offers an approximation of the missed emotional nurturance, while maintaining the ethical and professional boundaries of the relationship. There is no attempt by the therapist to re-enact becoming the parent, nor to regress the patient to a child-like state of dependency.

For example, Young (1994a) proposes 'limited reparenting' strategies for treating each of the four schema modes that characterise the borderline patient:

- *Detached Protector*. Patients are reassured that the therapist will help them to deal with overwhelming affect. Increased frequency of contact with the patient and encouragement to express feelings towards the therapist are promoted. The therapist works to validate, rather than correct, feelings in this mode.
- *Abandoned Child*. The therapist becomes the stable, nurturing transitional base, and guides the patient towards gradual autonomy. The therapist gratifies the patient's child-like needs whenever possible and appropriate.
- *Punitive Parent*. The therapist praises and forgives the patient, while encouraging the patient to express emotions and needs in the session without rejection. The therapist actually fights against the internalised voice of the abusive or punitive parent.
- *Angry Child*. The therapist sets limits based on personal rights and patient safety, while encouraging ventilation of feelings. The therapist offers empathy for the underlying needs of the child, and a framework to reality test the experiences. Finally, the clinician helps patients practice more appropriate ways of getting needs met.

Schemata triggered in the therapy relationship

Since many of the patient's schemata (e.g. Emotional Deprivation, Subjugation, Dependence, Defectiveness) emerge in relation to the therapist, addressing the patient's thoughts and feelings about the therapist is an important strategy for identifying and modifying schemata.

When a patient's schema is believed to be activated in relation to the therapist, the schema-focused therapist works directly and collaboratively with the patient in identifying and modifying any schema-driven thoughts and feelings. This may involve self-disclosure on the therapist's part to correct the distorted beliefs and expectations. The therapist invites the patient to express highly charged feelings directly in the session. For example, when therapists go on vacation, many patients' Abandonment schemata are triggered. The patient and therapist spend time in the session discussing sympathetically any feelings that are triggered, such as loss or anger, because the vacation is experienced by the patient as abandonment. The therapist may gently point out that a vacation is a time for the therapist to get rest and pleasure, and to replenish resources for continued work together.

Schema-focused therapists utilise what Young terms *empathic confrontation* as their primary working style or stance toward the patient. Empathic confrontation involves a careful balancing of validation and reality testing. The therapist fully acknowledges and validates distressing feelings and schema-driven beliefs, while tactfully pointing out another, more accurate, view. This process repeatedly demonstrates to patients how their schemata operate to keep dysfunctional thoughts rigidly intact, and also serves to challenge and modify these negative cognitions as they arise during sessions. According to Linehan (1993), 'crucial to the balance of acceptance and change is the therapist's ability to express warmth and control simultaneously in therapy settings. Much of the control in changing patient behaviour is achieved through the use of the relationship ... without a significant level of concurrent warmth and acceptance, the therapist will probably be experienced as hostile and demanding rather than as caring and helpful.'

For example, to foster tolerance and empathy when borderline patients direct their anger at the therapist in a devaluing way, Young suggests that therapists superimpose the face of a young child over that of the adult who sits across from them. This enables therapists to override their own schemata that are often triggered in these difficult interactions, and thus avoid becoming defensive or counter-attacking. Therapists learn to calmly express their rights to be respected so that the patient may learn skills for more effective communication of their vulnerable feelings. Through the therapy relationship, the therapist furnishes the patient with a model of a healthy adult, based on the therapist's responses to the patient.

Interpersonal techniques outside the therapy relationship

Schemata are maintained by the patient's current interpersonal environment outside the therapy, including friends, family, and intimate partners. Patterns observed within the therapeutic relationship are generalised to interpersonal relationships outside.

The schema-focused therapist may (when desirable and with the patient's permission) invite friends or spouses, when possible, to sessions to assist patients in assessing the validity of their schemata and to modify any dysfunctional relationships. The results of such meetings can be dramatic, as the therapist not only assesses the potential for a healthy outcome, given the relative health of significant others, but also enables participants to see how their own schemata interact to produce conflict and disappointment, and may sabotage the patient's progress. Such sessions also allow patients to express previously suppressed feelings to others in a safe environment.

Behavioural Pattern-breaking Techniques

Behavioural techniques are utilised in the schema-focused approach to alter self-defeating patterns of behavioural avoidance, compensation, and maintenance that have been perpetuating the patient's schemata. Behavioural exercises are used in combination with cognitive and experiential work to further challenge schema-driven thoughts and behaviours under discrete conditions. For example, patients with an avoidant coping style may have lifelong patterns of overeating, oversleeping, or abusing substances, as a way of numbing the painful feelings that arise with schema activation. Therapy aims to enlist patients in developing a better tolerance for their discomfort through identification of feelings, validation, and alternative methods for 'healthy' distraction, such as relaxation techniques, exercise, calling a friend, writing in a journal, or taking a walk. Essentially the schema-focused therapist, when appropriate, employs many of the well-established techniques of behavioural treatment, such as assertiveness training, graduated exposure, social skills exercises, and behavioural reconditioning to change behaviours that reinforce the schema.

The use of role-plays and guided visualisation enables the patient to experience new behaviours not previously in their repertoire, before *in vivo* exposure takes place. New behaviours are primed in the image, thus increasing the likelihood of success outside therapy, as patients work through the anxiety and discomfort generated by schemata in the image. Once the patients successfully complete each step within the hierarchy of behaviours through imaginal exposure, they are asked to perform it outside the therapy session (*in vivo* exposure).

Often flashcards are useful to help patients battle with their schemata while making behavioural changes. If the patient is unsuccessful outside the therapy, the situation is discussed at length to target the reasons for failure. Having done this, the same exercise is rehearsed again during session before the patient experiments outside therapy. As patients perform successfully outside, they are reinforced in the session and then guided through the next, more difficult behavioural exercise in the hierarchy.

CLINICAL AND EMPIRICAL VALIDATION OF SCHEMA-FOCUSED THERAPY

In our clinical experience, we have successfully applied Young's schema-focused model to patients with a range of DSM-IV disorders including: prevention of relapse in depression (Young, Beck & Weinberger, 1993) and anxiety disorders; avoidant, dependent, compulsive, passive-aggressive, histrionic, borderline, and narcissistic personality disorders; substance abuse disorders during the recovery phase; and to patients with a history of eating disorders, chronic pain, or childhood abuse with related PTSD

(McGinn, Young & Sanderson, 1995). A number of studies have been completed that evaluate the validity of Young's schema constructs through analysis of the Young Schema Questionnaire. Early results are extremely promising, both in terms of the instrument itself and of the validity of Young's schema construct. Controlled clinical outcome trials assessing the clinical efficacy of Schema-Focused Therapy are in progress, but data are not yet available.

CONCLUSION

Schema-Focused Therapy proposes an integrative model of treatment for a wide spectrum of chronic, difficult, and characterological problems. It was developed to meet the needs of patients who did not benefit fully from Beck's original model of cognitive therapy. The concept of an Early Maladaptive Schema is the unifying element in a treatment that adapts, synthesises, and goes beyond traditional cognitive behavioural approaches. Young's innovative model combines interpersonal and experiential approaches within a cognitive behavioural framework, thus encouraging greater treatment flexibility with difficult patients.

REFERENCES

American Psychiatric Association (1994). *Diagnostic and Statistical Manual of Mental Disorders (4th edn.)*. Washington, DC: Author.

Beck, A. T. (1967). *Depression: Clinical, Experimental and Theoretical Aspects*. New York: Harper & Row.

Beck, A. T. (1976). *Cognitive Therapy and the Emotional Disorders*. New York: International Universities Press.

Beck, A. T., Emery, G. & Greenberg, R. L. (1985). *Anxiety Disorders and Phobias: A Cognitive Perspective*. New York: Basic Books.

Beck, A.T., Freeman, A. & Associates (1990). *Cognitive Therapy of Personality Disorders*. New York: Guilford.

Beck, A. T., Rush, A. J., Shaw, B. F, & Emery, G. (1979). *Cognitive Therapy of Depression*. New York: Guilford.

Beckham, E. E. & Watkins, J. T. (1989). Process and outcome in cognitive therapy. In A. Freeman, K. Simon, L. Beutler & H. Arkowitz (Eds), *Comprehensive Handbook of Cognitive Therapy* (pp. 61–81). New York: Plenum Press.

Bricker, D. C. & Young, J. E (1991). *A Client's Guide to Schema-focused Therapy*. New York: Cognitive Therapy Center of New York.

Bricker, D. C., Young, J. E. & Flanagan, C. M. (1993). Schema-focused cognitive therapy: A comprehensive framework for characterological problems. In K. T. Kuehlwein & H. Rosen (Eds), *Cognitive Therapies in Action* (pp. 88–125). San Francisco: Jossey-Bass.

Daldrup, R. J., Beutler, L. E., Engle, D, & Greenberg, L. S. (1988). *Focused expressive psychotherapy: Freeing the overcontrolled patient. Journal of Consulting and Clinical Psychology*, **57**, 414–419.

Dobson, K. S. (1988). *Handbook of Cognitive Behavioral Therapies.* New York: Guilford.

Ellis, A. (1962). *Reason and Emotion in Psychotherapy.* New York: Lyle Stuart.

Freeman, A.& Leaf, R.C. (1989). Cognitive therapy applied to personality disorders. In A. Freeman, K.M. Simon, L.E. Beutler & H. Arkowitz (Eds), *Comprehensive Handbook of Cognitive Therapy.* New York: Plenum Press.

Freeman, A., Simon, K., Beutler, L.E. & Arkowitz, H. (Eds) (1989). *Comprehensive Handbook of Cognitive Therapy.* New York: Plenum Press.

Haaga, D.A. & Davison, G.C. (1991). Disappearing differences do not always reflect healthy integration: An analysis of cognitive therapy and rational-emotive therapy. *Journal of Psychotherapy Integration,* **1**, 287–303.

Layden, M., Newman, C., Freeman, A. & Morse, S.B. (1993). *Cognitive Therapy of Borderline Personality Disorder.* Boston: Allyn & Bacon.

Lazarus A. A. & Lazarus, C. N. (1991). *Multimodal Life History Inventory* (2nd edn). Champaign, IL: Research Press.

Linehan, M. M. (1993). *Cognitive Behavioral Treatment of Borderline Personality Disorder.* New York: Guilford.

Mahoney, M.J. (1993). Introduction to special section: Theoretical developments in the cognitive psychotherapies. *Journal of Consulting and Clinical Psychology,* **2**, 187–193.

McGinn, L. K., Young, J. E. & Sanderson, W. C. (1995). When and how to do longer-term therapy without feeling guilty. *Cognitive and Behavioral Practice,* **2**(1), 187–212.

McGinn, L.K., Young, J.E. & Sanderson, W.C. (in press).

Neimeyer, R.A. (1993). An appraisal of constructivist psychotherapies. *Journal of Consulting and Clinical Psychology,* **2**, 221–234.

Robins, C. J. & Hayes, A. M. (1993). An appraisal of cognitive therapy. *Journal of Consulting and Clinical Psychology,* **2**, 205–214.

Rothstein, M.M. & Vallis T.M. (1991). The application of cognitive therapy to patients with personality disorders. In T.M. Vallis & J.L. Howes (Eds), *The Challenge of Cognitive Therapy: Applications to Non-traditional Populations.* New York: Plenum Press.

Safran, J. D. & Segal, Z. V. (1990). *Interpersonal Processes in Cognitive Therapy.* New York: Basic Books.

Schmidt, N. B. (1994). The schema questionnaire and the schema avoidance questionnaire. *Behavior Therapist,* **17**(4), 90–92.

Schmidt, N. B., Joiner, T. E., Young, J. E. & Telch, M. J. (1995). The schema questionnaire: Investigation of psychometric properties and the hierarchical structure of a measure of maladaptive schemata. *Cognitive Therapy and Research,* **19**(3), 295–321.

Segal, Z. V. (1988). Appraisal of the self-schema construct in cognitive models of depression. *Psychological Bulletin,* **103**(2), 147–162.

Vallis, T.M., Howes, J.L. & Miller, P.C. (Eds) (1991). *The Challenge of Cognitive Therapy.* New York: Plenum Press.

Young, J. E. (1992). *Schema Conceptualization Form.* New York: Cognitive Therapy Center of New York.

Young, J. E. (1994a). *Cognitive Therapy for Personality Disorders: A Schema-focused Approach* (rev. edn). Sarasota, FL: Professional Resource Press.

Young, J. E. (1994b). *Young Parenting Inventory*. New York: Cognitive Therapy Center of New York.

Young, J. E. (1994c). *Young Compensation Inventory*. New York: Cognitive Therapy Center of New York.

Young, J. E., Beck, A. T. & Weinberger, A. (1993). Depression. In D. H. Barlow (Ed.), *Clinical Handbook of Psychological Disorders* (2nd edn) (pp. 240–277). New York: Guilford.

Young, J. E. & Brown, G. (1990/1994). Young schema questionnaire (2nd edn). In. J.E. Young, *Cognitive Therapy for Personality Disorders: A Schema-focused Approach* (rev. edn, pp. 63–76). Sarasota, Florida: Professional Resource Press.

Young, J. E. & Klosko, J. (1993). *Reinventing your Life*. New York: Plume.

Young, J. E. & Flanagan, C. (1998). Schema-focused therapy for narcissistic patients. In E. Ronningstam (Ed.), *Disorders of Narcissism—Theoretical, Empirical, and Clinical Implications*. Washington, DC: American Psychiatric Press.

Young, J. E. & Rygh, J. (1994). *Young–Rygh Avoidance Inventory*. New York: Cognitive Therapy Center of New York.

APPENDIX A. EARLY MALADAPTIVE SCHEMATA WITH DOMAINS

(Revised January, 1995)

DISCONNECTION AND REJECTION
(Expectation that one's needs for security, safety, stability, nurturance, empathy, sharing of feelings, acceptance, and respect will not be met in a predictable manner. Typical family of origin is detached, cold, rejecting, withholding, lonely, explosive, unpredictable, or abusive.)

1. ABANDONMENT / INSTABILITY
The perceived *instability* or *unreliability* of those available for support and connection.

Involves the sense that significant others will not be able to continue providing emotional support, connection, strength, or practical protection because they are emotionally unstable and unpredictable (e.g. angry outbursts), unreliable, or erratically present; because they will die imminently; or because they will abandon the patient in favor of someone better.

2. MISTRUST / ABUSE
The expectation that others will hurt, abuse, humiliate, cheat, lie, manipulate, or take advantage. Usually involves the perception that the harm is intentional or the result of unjustified and extreme negligence. May include the sense that one always ends up being cheated relative to others or 'getting the short end of the stick.'

3. EMOTIONAL DEPRIVATION
Expectation that one's desire for a normal degree of emotional support will not be adequately met by others. The three major forms of deprivation are:

  A. *Deprivation of Nurturance*: Absence of attention, affection, warmth, or companionship.
  B. *Deprivation of Empathy*: Absence of understanding, listening, self-disclosure, or mutual sharing of feelings from others.
  C. *Deprivation of Protection*: Absence of strength, direction, or guidance from others.

4. DEFECTIVENESS / SHAME
The feeling that one is defective, bad, unwanted, inferior, or invalid in important respects; or that one would be unlovable to significant others if exposed. May involve hypersensitivity to criticism, rejection, and blame; self-consciousness, comparisons, and insecurity around others; or a sense

of shame regarding one's perceived flaws. These flaws may be private (e.g. selfishness, angry impulses, unacceptable sexual desires) or public (e.g. undesirable physical appearance, social awkwardness).

5. SOCIAL ISOLATION / ALIENATION
The feeling that one is isolated from the rest of the world, different from other people, and/or not part of any group or community

IMPAIRED AUTONOMY AND PERFORMANCE
(Expectations about oneself and the environment that interfere with one's perceived ability to separate, survive, function independently, or perform successfully. Typical family of origin is enmeshed, undermining of child's confidence, overprotective, or failing to reinforce child for performing competently outside the family.)

6. DEPENDENCE / INCOMPETENCE
Belief that one is unable to handle one's *everyday responsibilities* in a competent manner, without considerable help from others (e.g. take care of oneself, solve daily problems, exercise good judgement, tackle new tasks, make good decisions). Often presents as helplessness.

7. VULNERABILITY TO HARM OR ILLNESS
Exaggerated fear that 'random' catastrophe could strike at any time and that one will be unable to prevent it. Fears focus on one or more of the following:

    A. *Medical*: e.g. heart attack, AIDS;
    B. *Emotional*: e.g. go crazy;
    C. *Natural / Phobic*: e.g. elevators, crime, airplanes, earthquakes.

8. ENMESHMENT / UNDEVELOPED SELF
Excessive emotional involvement and closeness with one or more significant others (often parents), at the expense of full individuation or normal social development. Often involves the belief that at least one of the enmeshed individuals cannot survive or be happy without the constant support of the other. May also include feelings of being smothered by, or fused with, others OR insufficient individual identity. Often experienced as a feeling of emptiness and floundering, having no direction, or in extreme cases questioning one's existence.

9. FAILURE
The belief that one has failed, will inevitably fail, or is fundamentally inadequate relative to one's peers, in areas of *achievement* (school, career, sports,

etc.). Often involves beliefs that one is stupid, inept, untalented, ignorant, lower in status, less successful than others, etc.

IMPAIRED LIMITS

(Deficiency in internal limits, responsibility to others, or long-term goal-orientation. Leads to difficulty respecting the rights of others, cooperating with others, making commitments, or setting and meeting realistic personal goals. Typical family of origin is characterised by permissiveness, overindulgence, lack of direction, or a sense of superiority — rather than appropriate confrontation, discipline, and limits in relation to taking responsibility, cooperating in a reciprocal manner, and setting goals. In some cases, child may not have been pushed to tolerate normal levels of discomfort, or may not have been given adequate supervision, direction, or guidance.)

10. ENTITLEMENT / GRANDIOSITY

The belief that one is superior to other people; entitled to special rights and privileges; or not bound by the rules of reciprocity that guide normal social interaction. Often involves insistence that one should be able to do or have whatever one wants, regardless of what is realistic, what others consider reasonable, or the cost to others; OR an exaggerated focus on superiority (e.g. being among the most successful, famous, wealthy) — in order to achieve *power* or *control* (not primarily for attention or approval). Sometimes includes excessive competitiveness toward, or domination of, others: asserting one's power, forcing one's point of view, or controlling the behaviour of others in line with one's own desires—without empathy or concern for others' needs or feelings.

11. INSUFFICIENT SELF-CONTROL / SELF-DISCIPLINE

Pervasive difficulty or refusal to exercise sufficient self-control and frustration tolerance to achieve one's personal goals, or to restrain the excessive expression of one's emotions and impulses. In its milder form, patient presents with an exaggerated emphasis on *discomfort-avoidance*: avoiding pain, conflict, confrontation, responsibility, or overexertion—at the expense of personal fulfilment, commitment, or integrity.

OTHER-DIRECTEDNESS

(An excessive focus on the desires, feelings, and responses of others, at the expense of one's own needs — in order to gain love and approval, maintain one's sense of connection, or avoid retaliation. Usually involves suppression and lack of awareness regarding one's own anger and natural inclinations. Typical family of origin is based on conditional acceptance: children must suppress important aspects of themselves in order to gain love, attention, and approval. In many such families, the parents' emotional needs and desires — or social acceptance and status — are valued more than the unique needs and feelings of each child.)

12. SUBJUGATION

Excessive surrendering of control to others because one feels *coerced* —
usually to avoid anger, retaliation, or abandonment. The two major forms
of subjugation are:

   A. *Subjugation of Needs*: Suppression of one's preferences, decisions, and
      desires.
   B. *Subjugation of Emotions*: Suppression of emotional expression, espe-
      cially anger.

Usually involves the perception that one's own desires, opinions, and feelings are not valid or important to others. Frequently presents as excessive
compliance, combined with hypersensitivity to feeling trapped. Generally
leads to a build up of anger, manifested in maladaptive symptoms (e.g.
passive-aggressive behaviour, uncontrolled outbursts of temper, psychosomatic symptoms, withdrawal of affection, 'acting out', substance abuse).

13. SELF-SACRIFICE

Excessive focus on *voluntarily* meeting the needs of others in daily situations, at the expense of one's own gratification. The most common reasons
are: to prevent causing pain to others; to avoid guilt from feeling selfish; or
to maintain the connection with others perceived as needy. Often results
from an acute sensitivity to the pain of others. Sometimes leads to a sense
that one's own needs are not being adequately met and to resentment of
those who are taken care of. (Overlaps with concept of co-dependency.)

14. APPROVAL-SEEKING / RECOGNITION-SEEKING

Excessive emphasis on gaining approval, recognition, or attention from
other people, or fitting in, at the expense of developing a secure and true
sense of self. One's sense of esteem is dependent primarily on the reactions of others rather than on one's own natural inclinations. Sometimes
includes an overemphasis on status, appearance, social acceptance,
money, or achievement — as means of gaining *approval, admiration,* or
attention (not primarily for power or control). Frequently results in major
life decisions that are inauthentic or unsatisfying; or in hypersensitivity to
rejection.

OVERVIGILANCE AND INHIBITION

*(Excessive emphasis on controlling one's spontaneous feelings, impulses, and
choices in order to avoid making mistakes OR on meeting rigid, internalised rules
and expectations about performance and ethical behaviour — often at the expense of
happiness, self-expression, relaxation, close relationships, or health. Typical family
of origin is grim (and sometimes punitive): performance, duty, perfectionism, following rules, and avoiding mistakes predominate over pleasure, joy, and relaxation.*

There is usually an undercurrent of pessimism and worry—that things could fall apart if one fails to be vigilant and careful at all times.)

15. NEGATIVITY / VULNERABILITY TO ERROR
A pervasive, lifelong focus on the negative aspects of life (pain, death, loss, disappointment, conflict, guilt, resentment, unsolved problems, potential mistakes, betrayal, things that could go wrong, etc.) while minimising or neglecting the positive or optimistic aspects OR an exaggerated expectation— in a wide range of work, financial, or interpersonal situations that are typically viewed as 'controllable'— that things will go seriously wrong, or that aspects of one's life that seem to be going well will fall apart at any time. Usually involves an inordinate fear of making mistakes that might lead to: financial collapse, loss, humiliation, being trapped in a bad situation, or loss of control. Because potential negative outcomes are exaggerated, these patients are frequently characterised by chronic worry, vigilance, pessimism, complaining, or indecision.

16. OVERCONTROL / EMOTIONAL INHIBITION
The excessive inhibition of spontaneous action, feeling, or communication — usually to create a sense of security and predictability; or to avoid making mistakes, disapproval by others, catastrophe and chaos, or losing control of one's impulses. The most common areas of excessive control involve: (a) inhibition of *anger* & aggression; (b) compulsive *order* & planning; (c) inhibition of *positive impulses* (e.g. joy, affection, sexual excitement, play); (d) excessive adherence to routine or ritual; (e) difficulty expressing *vulnerability* or *communicating* freely about one's feelings, needs, etc.; or (f)excessive emphasis on *rationality* while disregarding emotional needs. Often the overcontrol is extended to others in the patient's environment.

17. UNRELENTING STANDARDS / HYPERCRITICALNESS
The underlying belief that one must strive to meet very high *internalised standards* of behaviour and performance, usually to avoid criticism. Typically results in feelings of pressure or difficulty slowing down; and in hypercriticalness toward oneself and others. Must involve significant impairment in: pleasure, relaxation, health, self-esteem, sense of accomplishment, or satisfying relationships.

Unrelenting standards typically present as: (a) *perfectionism*, inordinate attention to detail, or an underestimate of how good one's own performance is relative to the norm; (b) *rigid rules* and 'shoulds' in many areas of life, including unrealistically high moral, ethical, cultural, or religious precepts; or (c) preoccupation with *time and efficiency*, so that more can be accomplished.

18. PUNITIVENESS
The belief that people should be harshly punished for making mistakes. Involves the tendency to be angry, intolerant, punitive, and impatient with those people (including oneself) who do not meet one's expectations or standards. Usually includes difficulty forgiving mistakes in oneself or others, because of a reluctance to consider extenuating circumstances, allow for human imperfection, or empathise with feelings.

APPENDIX B. SCHEMA MODE LISTING

Revised August, 1996

CHILD MODES

1. *Vulnerable Child:*   feels lonely, isolated, sad, misunderstood, unsupported, defective, deprived, overwhelmed, incompetent, doubts self, needy, helpless, hopeless, frightened, anxious, worried, victimised, worthless, unloved, unlovable, lost, directionless, fragile, weak, defeated, oppressed, powerless, left out, excluded, pessimistic.

2. *Angry Child:* feels intensely angry, enraged, infuriated, frustrated, impatient because the *core emotional* (or physical) *needs* of the vulnerable child are not being met.

3. *Impulsive/Undisciplined Child:* acts on *non-core desires or impulses* in a selfish or uncontrolled manner to get his or her own way and often has difficulty delaying short-term gratification; often feels intensely angry, enraged, infuriated, frustrated, impatient when these non-core desires or impulses cannot be met; may appear 'spoiled'.

4. *Happy Child:*   feels loved, contented, connected, satisfied, fulfilled, protected, accepted, praised, worthwhile, nurtured, guided, understood, validated, self-confident, competent, appropriately autonomous or self-reliant, safe, resilient, strong, in control, adaptable, included, optimistic, spontaneous.

MALADAPTIVE COPING MODES

5. *Compliant Surrenderer:*   acts in a passive, subservient, submissive, approval-seeking, or self-deprecating way around others out of fear of conflict or rejection; tolerates abuse and/or bad treatment; does not express healthy needs or desires to others; selects people or engages in other behaviour that directly maintains the self-defeating schema-driven pattern.

6. *Detached Protector:* cuts off needs and feelings; detaches emotionally from people and rejects their help; feels withdrawn, spacey, distracted, disconnected, depersonalised, empty or bored; pursues distracting, self-soothing, or self-stimulating activities in a compulsive way or to excess; may adopt a cynical, aloof or pessimistic stance to avoid investing in people or activities.

7. *Overcompensator:*   feels and behaves in an inordinately grandiose, aggressive, dominant, competitive, arrogant, haughty, condescending,

devaluing, overcontrolled, controlling, rebellious, manipulative, exploitative, attention-seeking, or status-seeking way. These feelings or behaviours must originally have developed to compensate for or gratify unmet core needs.

MALADAPTIVE PARENT MODES

8. Punitive Parent: feels that oneself or others deserves punishment or blame and often acts on these feelings by being blaming, punishing, or abusive towards self (e.g. self-mutilation) or others. This mode refers to the *style* with which rules are enforced rather than the *nature* of the rules.

9. Demanding Parent: feels that the 'right' way to be is to be perfect or achieve at a very high level, to keep everything in order, to strive for high status, to be humble, to put others' needs before one's own or to be efficient or avoid wasting time; or the person feels that it is *wrong* to express feelings or to act spontaneously. This mode refers to the *nature* of the internalised high standards and strict rules, rather than the *style* with which these rules are enforced; these rules are not compensatory in their function.

HEALTHY ADULT MODE

10. *Healthy Adult:* nurtures, validates and affirms the vulnerable child mode; sets limits for the angry and impulsive child modes; promotes and supports the healthy child mode; combats and eventually replaces the maladaptive coping modes; neutralises or moderates the maladaptive parent modes. This mode also performs appropriate adult functions such as working, parenting, taking responsibility, and committing; pursues pleasurable adult activities such as sex; intellectual, aesthetic, and cultural interests; health maintenance; and athletic activities.

Chapter 16

ISSUES IN TREATING RAPE AND SEXUAL ASSAULT

Terri L. Weaver,* Kathleen M. Chard[†] and Patricia A. Resick*

INTRODUCTION

Implementing trauma-focused therapy with victims of rape and sexual assault presents many challenges to the treating therapist. Victims often present with multiple co-morbid psychological complaints secondary to the assault, including post-traumatic stress disorder (PTSD), fears, substance abuse and/or dependence, panic disorder, and depression (Frank & Stewart, 1984; Kramer & Green, 1991; Lurigio & Resick, 1990; Norris & Feldman-Summers, 1981; Resnick et al., 1993; Santiago, et al., 1984; Steketee & Foa, 1987; Veronen & Kilpatrick, 1980). Additionally, victims often report experiencing difficulties in their interpersonal relationships, compromised functioning within their work and/or family environment, and pronounced changes in their views of themselves and other people (APA, 1994; Frazier, 1990; McCann, Sakheim & Abrahamson, 1988; Meyer & Taylor, 1986; Resick & Schnicke, 1993).

Victims may also present with histories of multiple victimisation experiences (Kilpatrick, Edmunds & Seymour, 1992; Ruch et al., 1991; Wyatt & Newcomb, 1990; Wyatt, Guthrie & Notgrass, 1992). These added experiences may further complicate the recovery process by occasioning symptomatology which is more entrenched. Given the array of difficulties which may emanate from the victimisation experience(s), therapists who embark on trauma-focused therapy are frequently thwarted by many complicating factors. Therapists may also have their own reactions to

---

* Center for Trauma Recovery, University of Missouri-St. Louis, USA and [†] Department of Education and Counseling Psychology, University of Kentucky, USA

Treating Complex Cases: The Cognitive Behavioural Therapy Approach.
Edited by Nicholas Tarrier, Adrian Wells and Gillian Haddock.
© 1998 John Wiley & Sons Ltd.

trauma-focused treatment, which may further complicate movement toward recovery.

This chapter will present a detailed examination of strategies for dealing with some of the most common difficulties which arise when the therapist is conducting trauma-focused therapy for rape and sexual assault. Toward this end, the chapter will briefly review the research describing the available treatments for rape and sexual assault and will describe the theoretical underpinnings of victims' responses and associated treatment approaches. The majority of the chapter will then focus on specific strategies for dealing with complex cases and difficulties which arise during treatment, first with regard to client factors, and then with regard to therapist issues. Throughout the chapter the term client and victim will be used interchangeably. Also, because most of our work is with female victims, the female pronoun will be used.

THEORETICAL FRAMEWORK FOR RAPE AND SEXUAL ASSAULT TREATMENT

Cognitive Behavioural Treatments for Post-traumatic Stress Disorder (PTSD)

There are a number of different standardised treatments for rape-related PTSD. These treatment protocols and their efficacy data are summarised in this section. Interested readers are referred to the referenced citations for a more expanded explanation of treatment implementation.

The first treatment developed to target the symptoms of PTSD and other functional difficulties experienced by rape victims was stress inoculation training (SIT: Meichenbaum, 1974). This intervention was developed to help the rape victim *cope* with the resulting fear and anxiety, rather than *avoid* these symptoms (Veronen & Kilpatrick, 1983). This approach includes a collection of anxiety-management skills, including deep muscle relaxation, controlled breathing, thought stopping, cognitive restructuring, and guided self-dialogue. This approach has received some empirical support for producing significantly more improvement on PTSD symptoms immediately following treatment compared with supportive counseling (SC), and a wait-list comparison group (WL) (Foa et al, 1991).

Subsequently, treatment development began to draw from the theoretical framework of emotional processing theory. In emotional processing theory, Foa, Steketee and Rothbaum (1989) utilise the information processing work of Lang (1977) and posit that information is stored in fear networks that consist of stimuli, responses, and the meaning of the stimulus and response elements. The network can then be thought of as a program to stimulate avoidance behaviour. With time, any stimulus associated with the assault can become a part of the fear network. Therefore persons, places, objects, thoughts, and physical sensations can become fear-producing. Based on emotional processing theory, Foa (Foa et al., 1991) developed prolonged exposure (PE) therapy which combines flooding and systematic desensitisation techniques. The goal is to expose clients to the conditioned fear stimuli utilising imaginal and *in vivo* techniques, thus reducing the avoidant behaviours and altering the fear network with corrective information (Foa & Kozak, 1986). In PE, clients attend between 9 and 12 sessions of 90 minutes during which they recount the details of the assault repeatedly in the present tense, describing their full sensory experience. Clients are asked to monitor their fear/anxiety level throughout this imaginal exposure, using a subjective unit of distress (SUDS) rating. Outside the session clients systematically conduct *in vivo* exposures to cues in the environment that they have been avoiding. The client is asked to stay in the safe, but fear-producing, situation for at least 45 minutes, or until her anxiety level is reduced by 50% on the SUDS rating scale. Often the client will enlist a 'coach', someone who stays with her, initially, and then, successively, plays a smaller and smaller role. Foe et al. (1991) have found dramatic results when they use PE with rape victims in comparison to a wait-list control, with gains maintained in 3-month follow-up assessments. In addition, Dancu, Foa and Smucker (1993) completed a pilot study using PE techniques with adult survivors of incest with great initial success.

Resick and Schnicke (1993) utilised an expanded information processing model in their development of cognitive processing therapy (CPT). They suggest that assault victims suffer from a variety of emotions in addition to fear. These reactions often prevent women from integrating the rape experience because they are inconsistent with a preexisting positive schema or appear to confirm negative schemata. Instead of accommodating schemata appropriately, the event is either distorted to fit prior beliefs (assimilation) or prior beliefs are altered too much (over-accommodation). After an assault has occurred, women often assimilate the event instead of accommodating to it, causing symptoms of intrusion and avoidance to occur. The CPT treatment protocol is specifically designed to address these cognitive distortions and to aid the client in moving toward a healthy accommodation of the experience.

Cognitive Processing Therapy (CPT) is a 12-session structured treatment program that can be used in either an individual or a group setting. Individual therapy is conducted once or twice a week in 60-minute sessions, and group treatment is conducted in weekly 90-minute sessions preferably with co-leaders. Chard (Chard, Weaver & Resick, 1997) has altered CPT to create Cognitive Processing Therapy for Sexual Abuse (CPT-SA) for the treatment of adult survivors of incest. Pilot data show that this treatment offered in either a group/individual or individual alone format is effective in reducing PTSD and related symptomatology.

CLIENT FACTORS INTERFERING WITH TRAUMA-FOCUSED TREATMENT

Client factors refer to aspects about the clients themselves, such as motivation or readiness for therapy, prior trauma history, or dissociation as well as aspects of the client's larger environment, including their family and support network, status of their legal or civil case, and other external stressors. Aspects of each of these variables can arise and interfere with the implementation of a structured, short-term, trauma-focused treatment approach.

CLIENT NONCOMPLIANCE AND PROBLEMATIC STYLES OF AVOIDANCE

Getting the Therapeutic Commitment

The treatment contract in psychotherapy involves a fairly explicit agreement between therapist and client regarding the collaborative work designed to alleviate the client's presenting difficulties. Establishing a therapeutic commitment is an essential part of therapy; so important, in fact, that a lack of such a commitment on the therapist's part, the client's part, or both, may be one of the chief reasons for therapy 'failures' (Linehan, 1993). Therapists may also misattribute clients as having a lack of motivation when clients actually have a different agenda for treatment. For example, one of the authors was working with one client who appeared to be 'dancing around the relevant issues'. When this process was noted, the client responded by saying she felt she had a different agenda than the therapist. She said that she thought the therapist's agenda was to alleviate her PTSD symptoms and her agenda was to 'just see what we [our research group] were doing in this type of therapy.' Only when a mutual agenda was clarified and a commitment was established did the client being making progress. The steps to getting the therapeutic agreement include: (i) agreeing that therapeutic treatment is needed; (ii) agreeing on the objectives of treatment; and (iii) agreeing on specific treatment arrangements such as time, place, frequency, fee for sessions, and accessibility of the therapist for between sessions interactions (Weiner, 1975).

For victims of rape and sexual assault, there may be great ambivalence about targeting the assault and assault-related sequelae in treatment. There may be a long history of avoidance of the very things the therapist is now asking the client to focus on. Additionally, clients may have been urged by family and friends to 'just forget about' what happened or to keep the 'past in the past'. In getting the client's commitment that treatment is needed, this ambivalence is discussed in a very open manner. Additionally, examples are elicited from the client about ways in which avoidance has not been successful. The client is also provided with information regarding the effectiveness of the particular treatment approach chosen and the minimal length of time expected before the client will begin to experience symptomatic relief.

Once the client has agreed to participate in the trauma-focused treatment, the procedures involved in the treatment intervention are discussed. Additionally, the treatment is framed as a collaborative approach with the therapist cast as a facilitator/educator. As practical aspects of the treatment are being presented, the inclusion of homework is emphasised and the importance of committing to this particular aspect of treatment is discussed.

Along these lines, the client is engaged in predicting barriers which they might experience in completing the expected tasks. Barriers may include having chaotic lifestyles with little organisation and little discretionary time, or living with family members or intimate partners who are not supportive of the treatment. Each of these barriers is conceptualised as a challenge to be overcome and the therapist and client engage in problem solving to generate coping strategies for limiting the intrusion of these barriers. For example, one therapy case involved the husband of a rape victim who was repeatedly reading her homework accounts and 'quizzing her' on her responsibility for the rape. These inquisitions resulted in the woman becoming very defensive and prevented her from being able to challenge some of her own beliefs about (her responsibility for) the rape. In this case, a session was scheduled with the woman's husband. The therapist addressed some of the husband's concerns about his wife's rape and challenged some of the stereotypes which he held regarding rape. Emphasis was also placed on his playing an integral role in his wife's recovery, highlighting that he could facilitate her getting better by respecting her privacy, 'being there' if she wanted to talk, and not pushing her to talk if she wasn't ready. Her husband was able to give his wife more space and she was increasingly able to challenge her own beliefs, which focused on her self-blame. She then was able to talk more with her husband about the rape. Interestingly, her willingness to talk with him about the rape led to his feeling less 'shut out' and less like she 'had something to hide', resulting in an overall improvement in their relationship.

After getting the agreement that the rape or sexual assault will be the focus for treatment, the objectives for sexual assault recovery are targeted. Often these objectives include alleviating presenting diagnostic complaints, such as PTSD, depression, anxiety, or fear that has become over-generalised. However, objectives also may include having relationships which are more satisfying, feeling better about oneself, and having a greater sense of confidence in one's ability to accomplish goals in life. It is very important for the objectives to be specific and explicit, rather than general, such as 'I'm here to get over the rape.' In meeting these objectives, clients will often experience an initial increase in symptoms, primarily due to the fact that they have been historically engaging in avoidance. This increase in symptoms is framed as normal and a positive sign that the individual is beginning to deal with, rather than avoiding, the sexual assault.

Finally, the specific treatment arrangements are specified. In doing trauma-focused therapy, an important aspect of the arrangements includes specifying how the therapist can be reached between sessions. Therapists should be available between sessions for discussion/clarification of homework assignments or crisis stabilisation. Toward this end, opportunities to reach the therapist include ways in which the therapist can be reached directly during business hours and ways that the therapist may be reached after hours via other modalities (e.g. pagers, answering services, voice mail). Similarly, a distinction is made between routine contacts with the therapist and emergency situations, defined as situations in which the client is imminently suicidal. Emergency procedures include a number of 24-hour back-up services which the clients may utilise if the therapist is not immediately available, usually defined as reachable within 30 minutes. (However, it should be pointed out that exposure work does not begin with someone who is suicidal or parasuicidal or recently suicidal. In fact, suicidal ideation emerging during therapy has been rare.)

Having established that the client will be focusing on the sexual assault or rape, obtaining agreement on the stated objectives, and determining the specific arrangements for therapist contact, the therapist is now in an ideal position to refer back to the 'contract' when the agreement is not being honoured. For example, when the client continually brings in topics for discussion, other than the rape, the therapist can remind the client that the rape and sexual assault are the focus of treatment. It is also expected that getting the client's commitment to treatment is a layered process and that the therapist may have to work with the client at different points in therapy to get a recommitment to treatment (Lineham, 1993).

Homework Compliance

Regardless of the treatment approach chosen, the completion of home-work assignments between sessions plays an integral role in clients' progress towards recovery. Completion of homework is also important in maintaining successful gains after the termination of therapy (Beck et al., 1979). Additionally, clients' efforts on homework assignments constitute a rich source of information about issues/cognitions which need further attention, issues which may be resolved, and subtleties which may not be readily apparent within the confines of the one hour treatment session.

In order to maximise compliance with homework, a very cogent rationale is offered for homework before the assignment of the first homework task. One part of this rationale includes the observation that clients who com-plete their homework tend to have better treatment recovery (Resick & Schnicke, 1993). Time is also spent predicting that the clients may have dif-ficulty with the homework, so if clients do have difficulty, they will not make personal attributions for it. Sometimes, clients will attempt the home-work but find that while they initially understood the assignment in the session, they are confused by the work once they get home. Rather than giving up entirely on the assignment, clients are encouraged to call between sessions for clarification on the assignment. In addition, all home-work assignments are written out and given to the clients along with an ample supply of whatever forms are being used at that juncture in therapy.

Clients have said that their motivation to do homework is poor because in previous therapies no one ever asked about the assignment in the next week's session. Therefore, homework is reviewed very early in the follow-ing session and the client is given lots of positive feedback for completing the assignment. The client's completion of homework is also shaped by praising any attempts, no matter how small. If the client did not complete the homework at all, part of the session is spent focusing on the reasons for not completing the task. During this exploration, the therapist attempts to determine whether (i) the client is engaging in avoidance; (ii) the client did not understand the assignment, or (iii) the client did not feel that the assignment would be helpful.

Regardless of the reason the client did not complete the homework assignment, the issue of noncompliance is addressed in a nonjudgmental and nonpunitive fashion. The rationale for the homework is given and the session proceeds somewhat differently depending on the reason for the noncompliance.

When clients fail to do the homework because of avoidance secondary to evoked or anticipated emotional distress, therapists sometimes mistakenly think the client isn't motivated to be in treatment for the rape or sexual assault. This noncompliance is reframed as simply another type of PTSD avoidance and clients are asked to complete the homework in session. At the end of the session homework is reassigned. After completing the homework in session, clients are praised for being able to do the assignment and an assessment is made as to whether the client has had some decrease in their level of affective distress via the completion of the assignment. Often, clients do experience this decrease in emotional distress and the power of not giving in to the avoidance is reemphasised.

When clients fail to do the homework because they didn't understand the assignment, part of the session is used to complete at least one part of homework and the client is given ample latitude for asking questions and getting clarification on the assignment. This process is framed as normative and the analogy of needing repeated lessons and clarifications to learn any new skill is made. The 'lack of understanding' is also framed as a therapist problem in that the therapist was not clear enough in the initial explanation. In cases where a client's cognitive functioning may be somewhat limited or extremely concrete, the tasks at hand are modified to be commensurate with the client's level of cognitive functioning.

A slight variation of the 'do not understand' problem arises with clients who understand the homework but turn in half-hearted efforts. When clients do not appear to be performing to the full extent of their capabilities, the reasons for these incomplete attempts are addressed. Often, clients are avoiding doing their homework until the last minute and are not giving themselves enough time to do a thorough job. This issue is addressed by helping the client to schedule their homework time so that they can get the full benefit from the assignment. Often this approach also includes getting the client to reinvest their commitment to the therapy and reiterating the problem with avoidance.

When clients fail to do the homework because they think the assignment would not be helpful, time in the session is devoted to exploring the automatic thoughts associated with the homework assignment. Sometimes these thoughts are related to a sense of hopelessness that things can ever get better, thoughts that their problems are too complex to be addressed with simple assignments, or fears that the therapist will be evaluating them on their spelling, grammar, or logic. These concerns are addressed by reiterating the rationale for the homework. The complexity of their problems is acknowledged and the importance of breaking down their complex problems into 'workable', more manageable, pieces, vis-à-vis the homework is discussed. Finally, therapists emphasise that they are not 'evaluating' their client's homework but rather working collaboratively on the trauma-related issues. The therapist also emphasises that the essence of the homework is what matters, not each of the individual pieces or parts.

In summary, homework compliance is an invaluable part of cognitive behavioural treatment for rape or sexual assault. Our research group tends to have very high rates of homework compliance with the clients who are seen in treatment. Ensuring compliance to homework assignments rests on providing a cogent and convincing rationale for its inclusion, using the completed homework as the cornerstone of the therapy work, addressing avoidance which arises in treatment, and addressing any number of cognitive 'road blocks' for completing homework which may develop during the course of therapy.

Prior Trauma History

An issue that is frequently asked is how to treat clients with prior trauma histories. Studies (Russell, 1983; Wyatt, Guthrie & Notgrass, 1992) have shown that around 50–65% of adult rape victims also report a history of childhood sexual abuse. This trend is consistent with rates in our clinic, with women commonly reporting more than one incident of assault, (often) by different perpetrators. Some of these women are childhood sexual abuse survivors (40%) who were subsequently raped as adults, while others indicate that they were raped more than once as adults (20%). In spite of the multiplicity of their trauma history, clients are usually able to identify one or two incidents that they deem to be the most traumatic. These are often the events that cause the most intrusive symptomatology and are linked to the most avoidant behaviours. If these incidents are rape-related, the therapist could offer the client one of the two time-limited cognitive behavioural intervention programs, Prolonged Exposure (PE) or Cognitive Processing Therapy (CPT), that focus directly on the memories of the rape(s). If the client states that she is more distressed by her history of chronic childhood incest she could receive an adaptation of CPT, Cognitive Processing Therapy for Sexual Abuse (CPT-SA: Chard, Weaver & Resick, 1997), that includes five additional sessions to address issues specific to child abuse survivors. This may include more of a focus on the loss of trust and safety within the family.

There has been no difference in our laboratory success rates between clients who have been assaulted once and clients who have experienced repeated victimisation. Clients with multiple traumas report that most of the other incidents become less relevant as treatment progresses, or they may describe ways in which they are working on the events outside the therapy session (e.g. writing about the assault, conducting an *in vivo* exposure to an avoided stimulus). Within the context of information and emotional processing this practice is viewed as an opportunity to generalise the habituation of negative affect from one incident to another. A critical issue for therapists is not to get side-tracked by multiple incidents. The client's jumping from one trauma to the next may serve as an avoidance strategy.

While on the topic of prior trauma history, clients may also present to therapy while experiencing concurrent traumatic events. That is, there can be clients who present for trauma-focused therapy who are currently in relationships which are violent, who are continuing to be stalked by their perpetrators, or who have to see their perpetrators repeatedly. It is very important for individuals to be living in relative safety while they are participating in trauma-focused therapy. Specifically, it is important for the victim to be truly experiencing *post*-traumatic symptoms rather than to be responding to real danger. Therefore, if a client is currently in a situation which is dangerous, work initially focuses on helping the client to achieve relative safety, via safety planning and problem solving before delving into the trauma-related material. Often, this approach includes many of the same cognitive techniques used to deal with the trauma-related material, but may focus more on enhancing the recognition that they are in danger rather than challenging the veracity of such thoughts.

Dissociation

Dissociation refers to a compartmentalisation of the trauma experience (van der Kolk, McFarlane & Weisaeth, 1996). Rape and sexual assault victims may dissociate during the assault (peritraumatic dissociation), and/or may dissociate after the assault experience. While dissociation is a form of avoidance in terms of its function, it is distinct in that dissociation is a non-effortful and spontaneous process. Clinically, dissociation is associated with the victim having amnesia for parts of the assault experience, having difficulty 'staying with' assault-related negative emotions, and difficulty in staying 'connected' with the rape or sexual assault-related memory. Instead, the victim may report that she is feeling nothing or feeling numb while talking about the sexual assault experience, or report that she is 'spacing out' or daydreaming when the topic is broached.

Clients can present for treatment wondering whether they can be treated because they do not have all of their memories. These memory fragments can be because the victim was dissociating at the time of the assault. However, victims may also have amnesia secondary to ingesting drugs or alcohol prior to the sexual assault, being struck on the head and losing consciousness for part (or all) of the assault, or having extreme sensory experiences, such as high levels of pain, which conflict with the encoding of the event.

This issue is addressed by first saying that trauma memories are often encoded as memory fragments. It is possible to work with the client on the memory fragments which they *do* have rather than worrying about trying to recover memories which may not be there. Trauma-focused treatments emphasise that the victim has PTSD and other symptomatology to material which is remembered and our focus is on treating these symptoms, not on treating 'memories'. At the extreme end, there are rape victims who have absolutely no memory of the rape. For example, recently within the United States, a new 'date rape' drug, Rohypnol, has been used in the commission of rapes. This drug, when ingested by the recipient, results in the failure to encode information. Thus, rape victims will wake up and have no memory of the sexual assault. Several victims of this type of rape, who have no memory of any part of the sexual assault, have been treated by our research group. These rape victims will evidence PTSD symptomatology linked to the 'information' that they were raped or have evidenced PTSD symptoms to the response of friends or family members who may minimise this experience (e.g. 'Well you were raped but it's not so bad because at least you can't remember it'). Trauma-focused work with victims with little or (no) memory focuses on their thoughts and fears about the experience. For example, there can be a profound impact on the individual's sense of personal control, thoughts about the malevolence of others, and imagined 'worst case scenarios.'

In terms of dissociative responses which inhibit the victim from connecting with the affect associated with the experience, this type of dissociation is conceptualised as another, albeit spontaneous, form of avoidance. Often in the process of writing the account of the incident in CPT or in the exposure in PE, the client remembers parts of the event that had been missing previously. Fears related to connecting with trauma-related feelings will also be explored. For example, many victims fear that they will lose control and hurt themselves, hurt the perpetrator, or go crazy. Cognitive behavioural strategies are then used to address each of these concerns.

External Barriers to Recovery

Rape and sexual assault, like any life experience, occur within the broader context of an individual's life. At times, external situations or life experiences arise which may complicate attempts to conduct trauma-focused therapy. External situations may include logistical complications, such as difficulty in getting transportation to treatment, trauma-related stressful life events, such as court proceedings, depositions, and probation hearings, and nontrauma-related stressful life events, such as family illnesses, deaths, or divorces.

Once clients have started treatment, it is not uncommon for logistical issues to arise which make it difficult or inconvenient for the client to come to the scheduled session. When clients begin missing scheduled appointments due to logistical issues, clinical work focuses on helping the client to evaluate whether these issues are the reason why the client is missing therapy or whether these logistical difficulties are being used to contribute to the client's avoidance of treatment. The timing of the problems may provide an invaluable source of information as to whether the difficulties are, at least in part, due to client avoidance. For example, 'car problems' may arise when clients are beginning to deal with the details of the rape or sexual assault or have confronted material in a previous session which is particularly painful or shameful.

Typically, the first time that logistical difficulties arise, these problems are taken at face value and the client's session is rescheduled. When difficulties arise on a repeated basis or when the therapist has information suggesting that the logistical difficulties are *only* impacting on the client's ability to attend treatment (but not impacting on the client's ability to do other things), the discussion focuses on the process of avoidance and hypotheses are shared about what factors may be contributing to the avoidance (e.g. recent disclosure of shameful material, anticipation of strong affect). In order to have this discussion, vigorous and active attempts are used to contact the client directly. While some forms of therapy tend to eschew therapist attempts to contact the client and view these attempts as a violation of the client's sense of self-determination or a sign that the client isn't motivated to be in treatment, therapist attempts to contact a client during times of avoidance are viewed as a critical component of doing trauma-focused therapy. Clearly, the client's participation in therapy is still viewed as her choice and her choice only. However, the therapy focuses on creating the opportunity to talk directly with the client about the importance of not avoiding, to help her to problem-solve the logistical issue at hand, and to reinitiate the client's commitment to the therapy. If the client then wants to terminate treatment, this therapeutic approach advocates making an active and informed choice to discontinue, rather than fading contact indefinitely.

External barriers to continuing with trauma-focused treatment may also arise, via client participation within the civil or criminal justice system. Sexual assault victims may have initial or ongoing interactions with the criminal justice systems via the preparation of their cases for trial, attendance at the trial, or attendance at probation and parole hearings. While participation in criminal justice proceedings can have a beneficial impact on victims (Cluss et al., 1983; Resick et al., 1988), the process can be very stressful, particularly when the process is protracted (Sales, Baum & Shore, 1984). These interactions can be very traumatic because the victim may have to see her perpetrator, to reexperience and recount the details of the sexual assault in a public forum, to face the possibility of having her perpetrator released, or may be questioned by defense attorneys in such a way that she feels blamed for the rape.

Trauma-focused treatment needs to accommodate the criminal justice proceedings by making the criminal justice process the focus of treatment when the legal case or probation hearing is imminent. This work may include court preparation, which might involve assisting the client with relaxation procedures for court, assisting the client with visits to the courtroom to desensitise her to the surroundings, educating the client on the expected process during the court hearing, and working with the prosecuting attorney to educate the client on the range of possible outcomes. We also use the same cognitive therapy skills to challenge her automatic thoughts about court.

A final note regarding legal cases which are going forward for prosecution. Before the case goes forward, work with the victim focuses on helping her examine her expectations for the outcome of the court process. Often she will think that a conviction in her case will mean that 'justice has been served and that now society is endorsing the fact that the rape was wrong and was not her fault.' This way of thinking has frequently been a set-up for victims to feel very demoralised and hopeless if the legal case does not proceed in that direction. Rather, this preparatory work with the client helps her to define the 'rules' within the legal arena by saying that the job of the criminal justice system is to evaluate the relative strength of the evidence and make a ruling beyond a reasonable doubt (for criminal cases) or based on the weight of the evidence (for civil cases). Along these lines, a distinction is made between the 'truth,' which is based on the victim's experience, and the verdict within the courts, which is based on the weight of the evidence. This discussion frequently helps sexual assault victims to contextualise the findings from the legal case. Ongoing civil cases for damages or disability provide another impediment to treatment. The goals of such litigation may be in opposition with treatment progress and clients may experience conflict ('If I get better, the jury won't understand how terrible this event was.') The therapist and attorney need to work together to give congruent messages to the client: that her recovery and effective life functioning are paramount.

Sometimes, cases go to trial and/or probation hearings will continue after the client has terminated treatment. Therefore, it is not uncommon for victims of sexual assault to have completed an effective course of treatment and to recontact the treating therapist because of an interaction with the criminal justice system. In these cases, we see the client for a few 'booster' sessions to process the experience and reinforce the work which was originally done.

Finally, life experiences may arise which are overwhelming to the client and not trauma-related. Each of these experiences is evaluated on a case-by-case basis. Sometimes it is possible to continue to focus on the sexual assault by using the issues which arose secondary to the sexual assault as the lens through which the current experience is being viewed. For example, one of the authors worked with an adolescent with a sexual assault history who was also going through a number of extensive medical procedures for a life-threatening illness. While she was going through the medical procedures, the client's parents frequently avoided being in the same room because it was so difficult to see their child in pain. This avoidance led to the client's experiencing a catastrophic depression as she felt that her parents were abandoning her during the medical procedure in the same way that they 'abandoned' her to experience her sexual assault. Making these connections helped the client to place her current experiences (the medical procedures) in context. If the life experiences are not catastrophic, 'the problem of the day' is viewed as, potentially, another type of avoidance and therapy works to keep the focus on the rape or sexual assault.

THERAPIST FACTORS INTERFERING WITH TRAUMA-FOCUSED TREATMENT

Therapist factors refer to aspects of therapists, themselves, including therapist misconceptions about the treatment approach and inadvertent collusion with the client's press to avoid the traumatic event. Therapist factors will also refer to vicarious traumatisation which can arise as the therapist repeatedly encounters horrific details of traumatic events.

Misconceptions about Trauma-focused Treatment

We have often heard therapists lament the fact that they are unable to do cognitive interventions, such as challenging their clients' automatic thoughts, because their clients are limited in their intellectual functioning. In fact, for these reasons some theorists have argued that rape victims with lower intellectual functioning may respond better to prolonged exposure (PE) rather than cognitive processing therapy (CPT) (Foa, 1996). On the contrary, there is existing research finding no differences in the level of intelligence across either CPT or PE on post-treatment PTSD intensity scores or depression scores (Astin & Resick, 1996). In fact, our laboratory has treated victims with IQs ranging from 70 to 120. However, if clients do have lower intellectual functioning, it can be very helpful to distill the questions used to challenge the automatic thoughts down to some of the most basic questions. Some of these basic questions include 'What is the evidence for this thought?' and 'What is the evidence against this thought?' and 'Can you think of any exception to this thought?' It also may be helpful to hone the challenging questions to just a few core stuck points. For example, it may be most helpful with clients who have lower intellectual functioning to challenge the victim's self-blame and leave some of the finer distinctions untouched. Often, clients with more limited intelligence may have a very limited number of core cognitions which may be serving as the hub of their symptomatology. Of course, choosing prolonged exposure or a combination of cognitive therapy plus prolonged exposure is also an option with the client with lower intellectual functioning.

When therapists are beginning to do cognitive behavioural treatment for rape and sexual assault, there may be times in which the therapist gets drawn into the victim's way of conceptualising the rape or sexual assault. This issue might arise because therapists hold shared stereotypes about rape or sexual assault, or the particular automatic thought might overlap with a therapist issue. Typically, the therapist will identify that this is happening when they are trying to assist the victim with challenging the particular thought. While trying to challenge the thought, they may reach an impasse and say to themselves, 'the reason that we can't challenge this thought is that the thought is true; it's not a distortion.' At the same time, there is, typically, still a part of the therapist's way of thinking in which they *know* that the thought is a distortion, but they just can't see another way of looking at the issue.

For example, when one of the authors was initially learning CPT she had an experience with a client who was engaging in checking behaviours when she approached her car at night. She would check underneath the car, check the back seat, and would scan the surrounding areas. Initially, it *felt* like there was something excessive about this behaviour. However, the therapist felt stuck when trying to identify the nature of the problem. After all, isn't it wise to check the car at night before getting in? Discussion with a colleague helped to clarify that it wasn't the checking behaviour, *per se*, that was problematic, but her level of fear while engaging in the behaviour that was the problem. The entire time that she was checking the car, the client's heart was racing and she was terrified. This change in perspective helped the therapist to see that it was the client's stated perception that 'having fear will give me control and keep me safe (i.e. keep me on guard, alert to my surroundings),' was the stuck point which needed challenging and not her specific checking behaviour.

If therapists find that they are beginning to share the client's distortions, it is important to recognise that this is happening. Next, it is important for the therapist to say to the client, 'It seems like something is being distorted here. Even if we can't identify the source right now, it will be important for us to continue to explore the core cognition underlying this stuck point.' The therapist can use Socratic questioning approaches to identify this thought. Socratic questions may include, 'What does it mean to you that you are feeling so much fear while checking the car? What role does your fear play in determining your safety?' Often, just stepping back from the situation can also help in identification of the stuck point, because working closely with distorted thoughts can result in shared misperceptions.

The most common therapist error is to confuse blame for the rape with engaging in high-risk behaviour. Engaging in certain behaviours may render someone less able to gauge the relative safety of a situation (e.g. alcohol, drugs) or reduce the likelihood of resistance, but they do not *cause* rape. Blame implies intentionality. Girls or women may do things that may expose them to greater risk, but their intention is not to be viciously attacked.

Inadvertent Collusion with Client Avoidance

This section will focus on ways in which the therapist may inadvertently collude with client avoidance strategies. This process can be very subtle. One signal that the therapist may be colluding with the avoidance is if the therapist finds that the session is nearing the end and very little trauma-related work has been done. Rather, therapists may avoid talking about the sexual assault because they fear that they will be making their clients more upset and possibly be retraumatising them. Therapists may also collude with the client's avoidance as they try to 'fix everything in the client's life,' or focus every session on 'the crisis of the week.' This next section addresses ways of countering each type of therapist pitfall.

Avoidance of exposure work

The most commonly encountered collusion comes from well-meaning therapists who do not want their clients to experience any distress. The term that was bandied about for several years was 'retraumatisation' and therapists came away with the idea that if clients experienced their genuine affect about a traumatic event, then the therapist had somehow been abusive. When the client says in explicit or subtle ways that she doesn't want to deal directly with the trauma, the therapist agrees and they talk around the event, sometimes for years. In this case, the therapist does not understand the maintaining role that avoidance plays in symptoms. The therapist may also not be acknowledging that the client is already distressed and both client and therapist may be anticipating a flood of affect that neither the client nor therapist can handle. This concern emerges regularly in training. However, the more common problem is actually getting numbed PTSD clients to experience some affect, not the converse. For trauma-focused treatment, the most fragile clients are typically excluded from exposure work (i.e. the suicidal, parasuicidal, psychotic, substance-addicted). This screening practice deceases the likelihood of clients experiencing problems with overwhelming affect and simulatenously prevents an inordinate problem with dropout. Cognitive work on fear of affect may precede exposure, and information about the decreasing intensity of affect over time may be helpful in getting the client (and therapist) over the avoidance of exposure work. Otherwise a good therapeutic alliance and support are all that are needed.

Working on the trauma vs fixing everything

Often our clients present to treatment years after the assault has occurred and they report generalised symptom disturbances that can affect all aspects of their lives, for example work, family, marriage, friendships, sexuality. Short-term therapy treatments do not propose to 'fix' all of the areas that need attention. Instead we focus our attention on the presenting symptoms of PTSD, depression, and cognitive distortions. In lieu of the amount of work that must be covered in the protocols, therapists then must resist the temptation to try and do too much.

Toward this end, the client is informed that treatment is teaching her tools that she can utilise when dealing with other current impediments, or to address future problems that may develop. The client may bring up issues regarding other areas of her interpersonal functioning. If possible, attempts are made to tie these problems into the homework assignments (e.g. complete an antecedent, thought, feeling sheet on her communications with her husband). At times these issues are too extensive to be covered in the brief therapy and the client is directed to stay on topics related to the assault. This may feel uncomfortable to the therapist who would like to address all areas of current distress with the client, but this tendency can lead to client avoidance of homework and processing related directly to the rape. Exceptions can be made if the client is in such a state of crisis that she is in danger of hurting herself or if therapeutic progress is being impaired by the crisis. At this point problems are addressed with cognitive behavioural interventions in an attempt to stabilise or remediate the crisis before reentering the trauma-focused treatment.

After a brief trauma-focused program has been completed, the client is asked to take a couple of months to process what she has learned and to apply it to other aspects of her life. At this point referrals can be made to appropriate therapists if she is still interested in seeking other services. We often make referrals for such things as marital therapy or career counseling.

Getting stuck in the crisis of the week

As clients begin therapy they may have a tendency to downplay the impact that the assault has had on their lives, for example PTSD and related symptomatology. In fact, they may even become resistant to focusing the treatment session on the assault, stating that the rest of their life is 'falling apart and they cannot begin/continue to work on the incident.' This resistance may also materialise with the client bringing a new 'crisis' into each session. These crises will often revolve around interpersonal relationships or work situations. The client may insist that she is immobilised or overwhelmed by the situation, thus she is prevented from focusing on the rape or sexual assault. The therapist may be unintentionally drawn into addressing the crisis, believing that the client will not be able to successfully continue with the trauma-focused treatment unless the other issue is resolved. It is here that we use our judgement to reach a balance. If the client is at risk of decompensation, their crisis should be addressed immediately. On the other hand, if the crisis appears to be anxiety related to internal or external variables, cognitive behavioural exercises can be used to challenge the client's self-defeating thoughts and give support to the client's strengths. When the therapist is uncertain if the client is avoiding or is truly in need of crisis intervention, the client should be given the benefit of the doubt by addressing the crisis briefly within the session. If a new crisis each session becomes a pattern, without the client showing signs of decompensation, this behaviour is now labeled as avoidance. This identification will often help the client to clarify why this part of treatment is so difficult that they are feeling a need to avoid the work. The therapist and client can then collaborate by identifying future avoidance, with the client often using the cognitive behavioural tools to address it on her own before she even comes into the next session.

Vicarious Traumatisation

One of the largest concerns therapists face in treating assault victims is vicarious traumatisation. The sequelae to trauma work can affect therapists in a number of different ways including increased sadness, anger, anxiety, vulnerability, guilt, loss of control, or on the extreme end, emotional numbing. Therapists may also report that they have noncontextualised, traumatic memory fragments that return as flashbacks, nightmares, or intrusive thoughts. These disruptions can be short term or may result in chronic changes in the therapists' schemata and expectations regarding self and others. While these shifts may become permanent they are only detrimental if the information is not properly addressed. Vicarious traumatisation occurs when the therapist is unable to process information that is too discrepant to be integrated emotionally or cognitively (McCann & Pearlman, 1990).

In their study with trauma therapists, Schauben and Frazier (1995) found that therapists who work with large numbers of assault clients showed increases in disruptions of cognitive schemata, PTSD symptoms, burnout, and self-reports of vicarious traumatisation. The therapists who engaged in active coping strategies were able to decrease the likelihood of these symptoms and interestingly there was no correlation between a therapist's prior victimisation and their likelihood of experiencing vicarious traumatisation. If a therapist recognises that s/he is colluding with the client's avoidance because of their own anticipated reaction, the therapist should seek out immediate supervision. On a final note, not all therapists can be expected to excel at all kinds of therapy. If trauma therapy is too distressing or disruptive for the therapist, he or she should consider referring these clients on. Understanding the limits of one's expertise may be a good therapeutic decision for both client and therapist.

REFERENCES

American Psychiatric Association (1994). *Diagnostic and Statistical Manual of Mental Disorders* (4th edn). Washington, DC: Author.

Astin, M. C. & Resick, P. A. (1996, November). *The role of intelligence in cognitive behavioral treatments for rape victims.* Paper presented at the International Society for Traumatic Stress Studies, San Francisco, CA.

Beck, A. T., Rush, A. J., Shaw, B. F. & Emery, G. (1979). *Cognitive Therapy of Depression.* New York: Guilford.

Becker, J. V., Skinner, L. J., Abel, G. G., Axelrod, R. & Cichon, J. (1982). Incidence and types of sexual dynsfunctions in rape and incest victims. *Journal of Sex and Marital Therapy,* **8,** 65–74.

Chard, K. M., Weaver, T. L. & Resick, P. A. (1997). Adapting cognitive processing therapy for work with survivors of child sexual abuse. *Cognitive and Behavioral Practice,* **4,** 31–52.

Cluss, P. A., Boughton, J., Frank, L. E., Stewart, B. D. & West, D. G. (1983). The rape victim: Psychological correlates of participation in the legal process. *Criminal Justice and Behavior,* **10,** 342–357.

Dancu, C. V., Foa, E. B. & Smucker, M. R. (1993). *Treatment of chronic post-traumatic stress disorder in adult survivors of incest: Cognitive/behavioral interventions.* Paper presented at the annual meeting of the Association for Advancement of Behavior Therapy, Atlanta, Georgia.

Foa, E. B. (1996, August). *Failure of emotional processing: Post-trauma psychopathology and its treatment.* Invited address presented at the annual meeting of the American Psychological Association, Toronto, Canada.

Foa, E. B. & Kozak, M. J. (1986). Emotional processing of fear: Exposure to corrective information. *Psychological Bulletin*, **99**(1), 20–35.

Foa, E. B., Rothbaum, B. O., Riggs, D. S. & Murdock, T. B. (1991). Treatment of post-traumatic stress disorder in rape victims: A comparison between cognitive behavioral procedures and counseling. *Journal of Consulting and Clinical Psychology*, **59**(5), 715–723.

Foa, E. B., Steketee, G. & Rothbaum, B. O. (1989). Behavioral/cognitive conceptualization of post-traumatic stress disorder. *Behavior Therapy*, **20**, 155–176.

Frank, E. & Stewart, B. (1984). Depressive symptoms in rape victims: A revisit. *Journal of Affective Disorders*, **7**, 77–85.

Frazier, P. (1990). Victim attributions and post-rape trauma. *Journal of Personality and Social Psychology*, **59**, 298–304.

Holmes, M. R. & St. Lawrence, J. S. (1983). Treatment of rape-induced trauma: Proposed behavioral conceptualization and review of the literature. *Clinical Psychology Review*, **3**, 417–433.

Kilpatrick, D. G., Edmunds, C. & Seymour, A. (1992). *Rape in America: A Report to the Nation.* Arlington, VA: National Victim Center.

Kilpatrick, D. G., Veronen, L. J. & Resick, P. A. (1982). Psychological sequelae to rape: Assessment and treatment strategies. In D. Doleys, R. L. Meredith & A. R. Ciminero (Eds). *Behavioral Medicine: Assessment and Treatment Strategies* (pp. 473–481). New York: Plenum.

Kramer, T. & Green, B. (1991). Post-traumatic stress disorder as an early response to sexual assault. *Journal of Interpersonal Violence*, **6**(2), 160–173.

Lang, P. J. (1977). An information processing analysis of fear. *Behavior Therapy*, **8**, 862–886.

Linehan, M. M. (1993). *Cognitive Behavioral Treatment of Borderline Personality Disorder.* New York: Guilford.

Loftus, E. F., Polensky, S. & Fullilove, M. T. (1994). Memories of childhood sexual abuse: Remembering and repressing. *Psychology of Women Quarterly*, **18**, 67–84.

Lurigio, A. & Resick, P. A. (1990). Healing the psychological wounds of criminal victimization: Predicting postcrime distress and recovery. In A. Lurigio, W. Skogam & R. Davis (Eds), *Victims of Crime: Problems, Policies, and Programs* (pp. 50–86). Beverly Hills, CA: Sage.

McCann I. L. & Pearlman, L. A. (1990). Vicarious traumatization: A framework for understanding the psychological effects of working with victims. *Journal of Traumatic Stress*, **3**(1), 131–149.

McCann, I., Sakheim, D. & Abrahamson, D. (1988). Trauma and victimization: A model of psychological adaptation. *The Counseling Psychologist*, **16**, 531–594.

Meichenbaum, D. (1974). *Cognitive Behavior Modification: An Integrative Approach.* Morristown, NJ: General Learning Press.

Meichenbaum, D. (1994). A clinical handbook/practical therapist manual for assessing and treating adults with Post-Traumatic Stress Disorder (PTSD), Waterloo, Ontario, Canada: Institute Press.

Meyer, C. & Taylor, S. (1986). Adjustment to rape. *Journal of Personality and Social Psychology*, **50**(6), 1226–1234.

Mowrer, O. H. (1960). *Learning Theory and Behavior*. New York: Wiley.

Norris, J. & Feldman-Summers, S. (1981). Factors related to the psychological impacts of rape on the victim. *Journal of Abnormal Psychology*, **90**(6), 562–567.

Resick, P. A. (1993). The psychological impact of rape. *Journal of Interpersonal Violence*, **8**, 223–255.

Resick, P. A., Jordan, C., Girelli, S., Hutter, C. & Marhoefer-Dvorak, S. (1988). A comparative outcome study of behavioral group therapy for sexual assault victims. *Behavior Therapy*, **19**, 385–401.

Resick, P. A. & Schnicke, M. K. (1993). *Cognitive Processing Therapy for Rape Victims*. Newbury Park, CA: Sage.

Resnick, H. S., Kilpatrick, D. G., Dansky, B. S., Saunders, B. E. & Best, C. L. (1993). Prevalence of civilian trauma and post-traumatic stress disorder in a representative national sample of women. *Journal of Consulting and Clinical Psychology*, **61**(6), 984–991.

Ruch, L. O., Amedeo, S. R., Leon, J. J. & Gartrell, J. W. (1991). Repeated sexual victimization and trauma change during the acute phase of the sexual assault trauma syndrome. *Women and Health*, **17**(1), 1–19.

Russell, D. E. H. (1983). The incidence and prevalence of intrafamilial and extrafamilial sexual abuse of female children. *Child Abuse and Neglect*, **7**, 133–146.

Sales, E., Baum, M. & Shore, B. (1984). Victim readjustment following assault. *Journal of Social Issues*, **40**, 117–136.

Santiago, J., McCall-Perez, F., Gorcey, M. & Beigel, A. (1984). Long-term psychological effects of rape in 35 rape victims. *American Journal of Psychiatry*, **142**(11), 1338–1340.

Schauben, L. J. & Frazier, P. A. (1995) Vicarious trauma: The effects on female counselors of working with sexual violence survivors. *Psychology of Women Quarterly*, **19**, 49–64.

Steketee, G. & Foa, E. (1987). Rape victims: Post-traumatic stress responses and their treatment. *Journal of Anxiety Disorders*, **1**, 69–86.

van der Kolk, B. A., McFarlane, A. C. & Weisaeth, L. (1996). *Traumatic Stress: The Effects of Overwhelming Experience on Mind, Body, and Society*. New York: Guilford.

Veronen, L. & Kilpatrick, D. G. (1980). Self-reported fears of rape victims: A preliminary investigation. *Behavior Modification*, **4**(3), 383–396.

Veronen, L. J. & Kilpatrick, D. G. (1983). Stress management for rape victims. In D. Meichenbaum & M. E. Jaremko (Eds), *Stress Reduction and Prevention* (pp. 341–374). New York: Plenum Press.

Weiner, I. B. (1975). *Principles of Psychotherapy*. New York: Wiley.

Williams, L. (1994). Adult memories of childhood abuse. *Journal of Consulting and Clinical Psychology*, **62**(6), 1167–1176.

Wyatt, G. E., Guthrie, D. & Notgrass, C. M. (1992). Differential effects of women's child sexual abuse and subsequent sexual revictimization. *Journal of Consulting and Clinical Psychology*, **60**(2), 167–173.

Wyatt, G. E. & Newcomb, M. (1990). Internal and external mediators of women's sexual abuse in childhood. *Journal of Consulting and Clinical Psychology*, **58**(6), 758–767.

Chapter 17

COMPLEX RELATIONSHIP CASES: CONCEPTUALISATION, ASSESSMENT AND TREATMENT

W. Kim Halford* and Ruth Bouma*

Marriage is one of the most nearly universal of human institutions. No other touches so intimately the lives of practically every member of the earth's population. (Terman, 1939, p.1)

Terman's 60-year-old assertion is still largely true in the last few years of the twentieth century. In most western countries more than 90% of adults get married before age 45 (de Guibert-Lantoine & Monnier, 1996; McDonald, 1995). Whilst there has been a decline in rates of marriage in many western countries, amongst those people who choose not to marry, the overwhelming majority still enter committed relationships which share many of the characteristics of marriage (de Guibert-Lantoine & Monnier, 1996; McDonald, 1995). Regardless of whether couples are formally married or not, expectations of couple relationships are high. In western cultures the vast majority of adults perceive the relationship with their partner as their primary source of support and affection (Levinger & Huston, 1990). Most young unmarried adults expect to marry at some point in their lives, expect that marriage to be lifelong, and expect their partners to show sexual monogamy, honesty, expressions of affection, intimacy and support (Millward, 1990).

Good couple relationships greatly enhance the partners' quality of life. People in mutually satisfying relationships are, on average, better off than people not in such relationships on a wide variety of indices of health, happiness and well-being (Halford, Markman & Kelly, 1997). A strong satisfying

* School of Applied Psychology, Griffith University, Australia

Treating Complex Cases: The Cognitive Behavioural Therapy Approach.
Edited by Nicholas Tarrier, Adrian Wells and Gillian Haddock.
© 1998 John Wiley & Sons Ltd.

relationship provides a centre of belonging to the partners' lives, and a buffer against life's hardships. However, when relationships are distressed, this can produce severe misery. Second only to a death in the immediate family, marital distress and divorce are rated as the most severe of commonly occurring stresses experienced by adults (Bloom, Asher & White, 1978). Relationship distress is associated with increased risk for development of a range of individual psychological disorders including depression, particularly in women (Bebbington, 1987; Coyne, Kahn & Gotlib, 1987; Hooley, Orley & Teasdale, 1986), alcohol abuse, particularly in men (O'Farrell, 1989), and anxiety disorders (Craske & Zoellner, 1995) and sexual dysfunction in both sexes (Zimmer, 1983). Marital conflict is also associated with increased behaviour problems and poorer psychological adjustment in the couple's children (Emery, 1982; Emery, Joyce & Fincham, 1987; Grych & Fincham, 1990).

Couple relationship problems are common. The most statistically reliable index of marital distress is divorce rates, and divorce has reached epidemic proportions in most western societies. About 45% of Australian marriages, 55% of American couples, 42% of English couples, and 37% of German couples end in divorce (de Guibert-Lantoine & Monnier, 1996; McDonald, 1995). Painful as the experience of divorce is for many people, most divorcees still aspire to be in a committed relationship. In the United States about 75% of divorced people remarry within five years of the end of their first marriage (Glick, 1989; Martin & Bumpass, 1989). However, the divorce rates of second marriages are even higher than for first marriages (Glick, 1989).

Divorce rates represent only a portion of couples experiencing relationship problems. Many couples have significant relationship distress, but opt to stay together for various reasons such as the financial implications of divorce, and personal and cultural expectations about marriage (Gottman, 1994). Surveys of representative samples of married adults show that between 80 and 85% report they are very satisfied with their current relationship (Beach, Arias & O'Leary, 1986; Eddy, Heyman & Weiss, 1991, Gallup Poll, 1989; Reynolds et al., 1979). However, satisfied partners tend to make unrealistically positive comments and predictions about their relationship functioning (Fowers, Lyons & Montel, 1996). For example, the majority of maritally satisfied partners believe there is zero probability that they will ever divorce, despite the well publicised evidence of how common divorce is (Fowers, Lyons & Montel, 1996). Furthermore, of the married people who report high relationship satisfaction, 40% also report having seriously considered leaving their current partners at some point (Gallup Poll, 1989). Thus it seems that problems occur, even within those couples who report high satisfaction in their relationship. All these figures converge on the point that significant relationship distress is a common problem in most western societies.

Given the prevalence of relationship problems, it is not surprising that relationship distress is one of the most common presenting problems of adults seeking psychological assistance (Veroff, Kulka & Douvan, 1981). There is now a well established research literature demonstrating the efficacy of couples therapy in reducing relationship problems (see Halford, Markman & Fraenkel, in press; Lebow & Gurman, 1995, for reviews of this literature). There also are a number of detailed descriptions of how to conduct effective couples therapy (e.g. Baucom & Epstein, 1990; Jacobson & Christensen, 1996; Weiss & Halford, 1996).

Many couples delay seeking assistance when their relationship is distressed, and longlasting relationship problems often result in additional problems for the partners. For example, the stress of ongoing relationship problems often affects people's performance at work, which in turn becomes a problem in its own right (Thompson, 1997). Infidelity often occurs during sustained periods of relationship distress, and the sense of betrayal often associated with discovery of an affair further undermines the relationship (Glass & Wright, 1997). Aggression and spouse abuse are common when couples experience sustained distress, and this aggression can often result in the female partner becoming fearful of her spouse (Cascardi, Langhinrichsen & Vivian, 1992). Prolonged relationship conflict can also produce behaviour problems in the couple's children (Sanders, Nicholson & Floyd, 1997). Hence, sustained relationship problems often are associated with a variety of other problems that develop secondary to the relationship problems themselves.

Relationship problems develop as a result of the interaction of a complex set of risk factors (Halford & Markman, 1997; Karney & Bradbury, 1995). For example, relationship problems are more common when one or both partners has a psychological disorder (Halford et al, in press), or in the presence of personal vulnerabilities such as low tolerance for stress (Karney & Bradbury, 1995). Relationship problems are also more likely to occur when individual partners or the couple are confronted by major life stresses such as ill health (Burman & Margolin, 1992; Schmaling & Sher, 1997), severe parenting difficulties with children (Sanders, Nicholson & Floyd, 1997), or work stress (Thompson, 1997).

Despite the strength of evidence showing an association between a variety of individual and environmental factors and relationship problems, the overwhelming majority of the published research and clinical descriptions of couples therapy does not include descriptions of how to respond to these complexities when treating relationship problems. In this chapter we examine the conceptualisation, assessment and treatment of complex cases of relationship problems. We begin by analysing the multiple influences on relationship problems, and offering a conceptual framework for integrating that information. We then describe how to assess the interaction of relationship problems with other problems and life circumstances. We then review the key components of cognitive behavioural couples therapy, and suggest how these components need to be modified for the management of complex cases. Finally, we present a detailed case example to illustrate the clinical application of the ideas presented.

CONCEPTUALISATION OF COMPLEX RELATIONSHIP PROBLEMS

Consider this presentation for couples therapy. Rob (35) is a business executive and Jodie (36) is a former teacher now attending to home duties. Rob and Jodie have been married 8 years, and have three children ranging in ages from 5 years to 18 months. Six months ago Rob and Jodie emigrated from New Zealand to Australia, seeking better work opportunities. They presented reporting severe relationship distress. Their major concern was high levels of conflict. They each reported that they had always argued quite heatedly, but that these arguments were getting much worse over the last three to four months. They were prompted to seek help when, during a recent argument, their 5-year-old child burst into tears and begged them not to keep fighting. The partners also reported a gradual loss in positive feelings for each other. Jodie is depressed, and Rob is drinking alcohol at hazardous levels.

In the first couple of sessions I (WKH) talked with each of them to identify some of the factors affecting their relationship. Jodie described the pressure of the constant demands in caring for their three young children, she reported having difficulty managing the behaviour of two of their children, and she felt cut off from her family and friends since moving to Australia. She also described a loss of self-confidence since ceasing paid employment some years ago. Jodie reported that she found it hard to enjoy things she used to enjoy, and was often teary and weepy. She had a history of depression in her adolescence, but had not been depressed in adulthood till now. Rob related the pressure he felt in trying to advance his career to ensure he could provide for his young family, and the stress he felt from working long hours. He reported that he had felt pressured when in New Zealand, and often used drinking with workmates as a means to relieve stress. His drinking at lunch times and after work since arriving in Australia had been a source of heated arguments with Jodie, in part because he had lost a previous job in New Zealand as a result of drinking during work hours.

How should we understand the relationship problems of Rob and Jodie? Therapy could focus on their individual problems, such as Jodie's depression or Rob's alcohol consumption. Alternatively, the parenting problems could be the primary focus of therapy. Or, should the therapy focus upon the relationship? If all these factors need to be attended to, then the therapist is posed with the dilemma of which issues to address first and in what order. In order to make decisions about the nature of the key presenting concerns, and how therapy can respond to the complex of problems, it is useful to have a conceptual model to integrate the variables that often impact upon relationship functioning.

The Variables that Impact Upon Relationships

There are over 100 published studies assessing the longitudinal course of couple relationship satisfaction and stability (Karney & Bradbury, 1995). This comprehensive literature can be summarised by a model of the determinants of relationship problems suggested by Bradbury (1995). We present this model as a useful way to integrate the complex information included in cases such as that of Rob and Jodie. In the model it is proposed that there are three broad classes of variables which impact upon the aetiology of relationship problems: adaptive processes within the couple system, stressful events impinging upon the couple system, and enduring individual vulnerabilities of the partners (Bradbury, 1995).

Adaptive processes

Adaptive processes refer to the cognitive, behavioural and affective processes that occur during couple interaction. Certain dysfunctions in these adaptive processes seem to predispose couples to relationship problems. More specifically, dysfunctions in communication and conflict management behaviours observed in engaged couples prospectively predict divorce and relationship dissatisfaction over the first ten years of marriage (Markman & Hahlweg, 1993). Interestingly, this has no relationship with their reported relationship satisfaction or commitment at the time of engagement (Markman & Hahlweg, 1993; Sanders, Halford & Behrens, 1997). In couples who have been married for some time, these same communication difficulties predict deterioration in relationship satisfaction, and decreased relationship stability (Gottman, 1993, 1994). Dysfunctional communication in engaged couples also predicts the development of verbal and physical aggression in the first few years of marriage (Murphy & O'Leary, 1989; O'Leary et al, 1989), at least for mild to moderate severity aggression. Relationship aggression is often established early in the relationship, and usually continues and escalates once established (Murphy & O'Leary, 1989; O'Leary et al., 1989).

The beliefs and expectations individuals have when entering into relationships predict the risk of divorce in the first few years of marriage (Olson & Fowers, 1986; Olson & Larsen, 1989). Couples characterised by unrealistic expectations and beliefs in areas such as importance of communication, appropriate methods of conflict resolution, and the importance of family and friends, and gender roles, are at higher risk for relationship distress than couples not so characterised. Negative attributional patterns, in which partners attribute blame for relationship problems to stable, negative characteristics of their spouse, also prospectively predict deterioration in relationship satisfaction (Fincham & Bradbury, 1990). Thus, certain communication and cognitive characteristics of the couple's adaptive processes predate, and prospectively predict, relationship problems.

Stressful events

Stressful events refer to the developmental transitions, and acute and chronic circumstances, which impinge upon the couple or individual partners. Relationship problems are more likely to develop during periods of high rates of change and stressful events (Karney & Bradbury, 1995). For example, the transition to parenthood is often associated with decline in couple relationship satisfaction (Cowen & Cowen, 1992), as is an increase in work demands (Thompson, 1997). Retirement is another major transition for couples which can be associated with relationship distress (Dickson, 1997). One partner developing a major health problem also puts couples at increased risk for relationship and sexual problems (Schmaling & Sher, 1997).

A common stressful transition worthy of special mention is entering a second marriage. Second marriages in which there are dependent children from an earlier relationship break down at very high rates (Booth & Edwards, 1992; Martin & Bumpass, 1989). Negotiating parenting roles in stepfamilies is a common source of interpartner conflict, and unresolved differences in this area are the most common stated reason for relationship breakdown in stepfamilies (Lawton & Sanders, 1994).

Couples with less robust adaptive processes are believed to be particularly vulnerable to the negative effects of a range of stressful events (Markman, Halford & Cordova, 1997). In particular, couples who lack communication skills, or who have inflexible or unrealistic expectations of relationships, find it hard to negotiate the changes required to adapt to major life transitions. For example, one of us (WKH) is studying couples in which the woman was recently diagnosed with breast or gynaecological cancer. In couples with good communication and effective mutual support the adversity of cancer diagnosis and treatment seems to bring the couples closer together, and to reinforce the relationship bonds. In contrast, couples with poor adaptive processes show deterioration in their relationships, and poor individual coping with the cancer.

Enduring individual vulnerabilities

Enduring vulnerabilities refer to the stable historical, personal, and experiential factors which each partner brings to a relationship (Bradbury, 1995). Family of origin experiences have been widely studied as historical factors which correlate with the risk of relationship problems. For example, the adult offspring of divorcees are more likely than the rest of the population to divorce (Glenn & Kramer, 1987), and interparental aggression is associated with increased risk for being in an aggressive relationship as an adult (Widom, 1989). The mechanisms by which exposure to parental divorce or aggression may impact upon subsequent adult relationships are becoming clearer. Exposure to parental divorce is associated with more negative expectations of marriage (Black & Sprenkle, 1991; Gibardi & Rosen, 1991), and with observable dysfunctions in communication and conflict management in couples prior to marriage (Halford, Sanders & Behrens, 1994). Adult offspring of parents who were aggressive also show dysfunctions in communication and conflict management skills in dating and marital relationships (Halford et al, 1997; Sanders Nicholson & Floyd, 1997). Negative expectations and communication dysfunctions may well be learned from the parents' relationship and subsequently these learned behaviours impact negatively upon the adult relationships of the offspring. The argument that communication difficulties may be acquired through observation and interaction with parents is supported by the finding that couple communication style assessed premaritally predicts subsequent communication style when the partners become parents and are interacting with their children (Howes & Markman, 1989).

The association between personality variables and relationship problems has been widely studied. Normal personality variations do not seem to contribute much variance to relationship satisfaction (Gottman, 1994; Karney & Bradbury, 1995). One exception is that low ability to regulate negative affect (high neuroticism) consistently has been found to predict higher risk for relationship problems and divorce (Karney & Bradbury, 1995). How this personality characteristic may impact upon relationship problems is not yet understood.

Another major risk indicator for relationship distress and divorce is a past or present history of psychological disorder. Individuals with severe psychiatric disorder are much less likely than the rest of the population to develop a satisfactory and committed relationship in the first place (Mulder, 1991). Those who do, are reported to experience higher rates of relationship problems and divorce (Halford, 1995), as are people with depression, alcohol abuse and some anxiety disorders (Emmelkamp, De Haan & Hoogduin, 1990; Halford, et al., in press; Halford & Osgarby, 1993; O'Farrell & Birchler, 1987; Reich & Thompson, 1985; Ruscher & Gotlib, 1988; Weissman, 1987). As described earlier in this chapter, relationship problems and individual problems can both exacerbate each other (Halford et al., in press). In addition, certain personal vulnerabilties may predispose people to both psychological disorders and relationship problems. For example, dysfunctions in interpersonal communication and negative affect regulation are risk factors that predict the onset of both alcohol abuse (Block, Block & Keyes, 1988), and relationship problems (Markman & Hahlweg, 1993). This common risk factor might be part of the explanation for the common co-occurrence of relationship and alcohol problems.

A Model for Integrating Information on Relationship Problems

Figure 17.1 presents a schematic representation of Karney and Bradbury's (1995) model depicting the influences on relationship outcomes. In summary, relationship problems can usefully be conceptualised as the interaction of couple-adaptive processes, individual vulnerabilities, and stressful events. If we return to the case of Jodie and Rob, the social

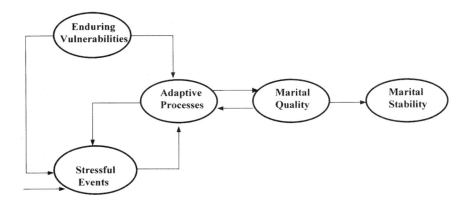

Figure 17.1 A vulnerability–stress–adaptation model of marriage. From Karney and Bradbury (1995).

isolation resulting from the transition between countries, the stresses of child rearing, and the work pressures, might all be seen as stressful environmental factors. The histories of depression in Jodie and drinking in Rob probably reflect individual vulnerabilities to these problems. The history of poor conflict management is an example of inadequate couple-adaptive processes. Each of these factors probably exacerbates the effects of each of the others. For example, it is well established that high levels of interparental conflict are associated with poorer child adjustment, and increased child behaviour problems (Grych & Fincham, 1990). At the same time increased stress from managing the behaviour of a severely misbehaving child can exacerbate relationship problems (Sanders Nicholson & Floyd, 1997).

ASSESSMENT OF RELATIONSHIP PROBLEMS

Given the strong association between couple and individual problems, it is important that clients be screened for both individual and couple problems when either is the presenting complaint (Halford et al., in press). Thus, couples who nominate relationship problems as the presenting concern should also be screened for individual psychological disorder. Conversely, individuals in committed relationships who present with problems such as alcohol abuse, anxiety, or depression, should also be screened for relationship problems. Furthermore, all couples need to be assessed for the impact of stressful life events on their relationship functioning.

Table 17.1 provides a summary of some useful measures for assessing relationship aspects of the presentation. The measures provide indices of relationship outcomes, such as relationship satisfaction and stability, and couple-adaptive processes. Couple-adaptive processes include areas such as communication, problem solving, relationship cognitions, and relationship behaviour exchange. Assessing relationship aggression is also important, as such aggression often goes underdetected by those providing couple therapy (O'Leary & Vivian, 1990). Up to 70% of couples presenting with relationship problems have experienced at least one act of physical aggression from their partner in the last year, and for 10% or more of couples there has been repeated and severe aggression (O'Leary & Vivian, 1990). Ensuring that steps are taken to protect the victim(s) of violence is critical when severe violence is detected.

Table 17.2 lists some useful measures for screening common individual problems. Even when the primary presenting problem is relationship distress, there are a variety of individual problems which may be influencing the partners' behaviour and functioning. While it is unrealistic to assess for

Table 17.1   Key areas of assessment for couples therapy

Area	Example measure	Explanation
Relationship satisfaction	Dyadic Adjustment Scale (Spanier, 1976); 31-item self-report inventory	Level of distress, global evaluations of relationship
Divorce potential	Marital Status Inventory (Weiss & Cerreto, 1980); a 14-item rating scale	Steps toward separation, high steps predict poor prognosis
Behaviour exchange	Areas of Change Questionnaire (Weiss & Perry, 1983); 34 items rating extent of requested behaviour change by partner	Current patterns of daily interaction, identify behaviour change preferences of each client
Communication and conflict management		The most common presenting concern, and a key area requiring attention in much couples therapy
Aggression and violence	Conflict Tactics Scale (Strauss, 1979)	Verbal, psychological and physical aggression between partners

Table 17.2   Measures for screening for individual psychopathology often co-existing with presenting relationship problems

Measure	Authors	Brief description
Beck Depression Inventory (BDI)	Beck et al., (1961)	28-item self-report measure of depression, with emphasis on cognitive symptoms
Canterbury Alcohol Screening Test (CAST)	Elvy & Wells (1984)	Self-report measure of alcohol abuse and alcohol-related problems
Depression, Anxiety, Stress Scale (DASS)	Lovibond & Lovibond (1995)	Self-report measure of depression, anxiety, and stress
Khavari Alcohol Test (KAT)	Khavari & Faber (1978)	14 items self- or partner-report measure of frequency, mean and maximum alcohol consumption
Symptom Checklist (SCL-90)	Derogatis, Lipman & Copui (1973)	90-item self-report measure of occurrence of psychiatric symptoms

all the possible disorders in detail, it is suggested that alcohol abuse, anxiety, and depression be routinely assessed for given their high prevalence and association with relationship distress. Furthermore, it is recommended that all couple therapists ask each partner individually if they have ever received past psychological or psychiatric care, either as an inpatient or outpatient. Given the potentially extreme impact of severe psychiatric disorder in relationships, a positive history will prompt attention to necessary issues such as medication management as part of the therapy process.

If the couple have children living with them, then asking about the parenting relationships and adjustment of the children is important. Even for couples who decide to separate, the issue of parenting is important. High levels of interparental conflict after separation are associated with poorer child adjustment (Grych & Fincham, 1990). Therapists can often assist the partners to negotiate a low conflict separation, and if combined with a mutually acceptable co-parenting agreement, this can promote well-being in both the parents and the children (Baris & Garrity, 1997).

Given the potential impact of additional stressful life events on relationship functioning, it is also important that these be assessed in couples. It is useful in the context of the intake interview simply to ask partners to recount the development of their relationship, and to identify key changes that have occurred in their lives together. Often, couples do not recognise the potential importance of major life events on relationship interaction, and simply identifying such events, and posing the question about their impact, can lead couples to recognise the impact of external events upon their relationship. This shift to an external attribution can be associated with significant reductions in anger and hostility toward the partner even in the absence of further change (Jacobson & Christensen, 1996).

Developing a Collaborative Set with Couples

The assessment process in couples therapy is more than the therapist gathering information. Partners often enter therapy with disparate views of the nature and causes of their relationship problems, and these views often do not promote positive change in the relationship. Clinical descriptions of cognitive behavioural couples therapy emphasise the importance of developing therapeutic alliances with each partner, developing a shared understanding of relationship problems and goals which promotes adaptive change, and explicit negotiation with couples about their roles in therapy (e.g. Beach, Sandeen & O'Leary, 1990; Christensen, Jacobson & Babcock, 1995; Baucom & Epstein, 1990; Weiss & Halford, 1996). Assessment is crucial in achievement of these process outcomes in couples therapy. In essence, the therapist seeks through assessment both to establish an empathic understanding of each partner's experience of the relationship, and to promote a shared conceptualisation of problems in terms of relationship interactions. The shared conceptualisation is the basis for participants to negotiate goals of therapy, and to determine how those goals are to be achieved.

Establishing a shared conceptualisation of relationship problems is sometimes a difficult therapeutic task. Therapists tend to see relationship problems in terms of the adaptive processes occurring between the partners. In contrast, couples often enter therapy conceptualising their relationship problems as being due to stable, global negative characteristics of their partners (Fincham & Bradbury, 1990), and believe there is little they can do individually to improve their relationship.

To achieve a shared, productive relationship focus in couples therapy the therapist initially assesses the presenting concerns from the perspective of each partner. Often these initial descriptions by clients are critical and blaming of the partner (e.g. 'he does not communicate', 'she is too demanding'). The therapist then uses a variety of strategies to promote a relationship focus. For example, strategic use of questioning can promote attention to relationship interaction (e.g. 'How do you two resolve conflict?' 'As a couple, how do you ensure you have quality time together?'). Particular assessment tasks also prompt attention to relationship interaction. For example, undertaking certain communication tasks can be used to identify strengths and weaknesses in communication. Reframing summaries also can foster a relationship focus. For example, suppose a couple argue about parenting. One partner may present this issue as: 'he is too soft on the children when they misbehave'. The spouse might describe the issue as: 'she is too harsh in her discipline of the children'. The therapist may summarise this as: 'as a couple you struggle to agree on the best ways to manage your children's behaviour'. The therapist's summary reframes the issue as a relationship challenge the couple can work on together.

In cases of co-existing individual and couple problems a number of unhelpful beliefs may exist which can interfere with the development of a shared understanding. These unhelpful beliefs may include: (i) one partner attributing all relationship problems to their partner's psychological disorder; (ii) the partner with the disorder attributing all blame for their disorder to the relationship or other partner; and (iii) the partner with the disorder blaming themselves for all relationship problems (Halford & Bouma, 1997). Assessment is central to helping partners to relinquish such unhelpful beliefs, and to develop a shared understanding of how both the individual disorder and the relationship problems interact. During the interview the therapist initially assesses key concerns from the perspective of each partner. This is followed by the use of strategic questioning to promote a dyadic focus. Through questions such as 'How do you know when he is depressed?' or 'What changes do you notice when she drinks?' each partner can be prompted to consider how the disorder is expressed within the relationship. How this expression is then responded to within the relationship context can be prompted by asking 'What do you think and do when he is depressed?' or 'How do you react to her when she has been drinking?' These questions help to develop the understanding of how individual and couple problems interact, and how co-existing individual and relationship problems can rarely be explained adequately by simple unidirectional causes.

More extensive assessments can be used to help clients who are having difficulties with this concept. Monitoring the specific circumstances in which the partner displays the problems, and monitoring the immediate consequences of that behaviour, can assist the couple further in identifying which relationship processes may be part of the problem (Halford & Bouma, 1997). Through this process, problems are reframed to a dyadic focus and the couple and therapist are able to define a shared understanding of how individual and couple problems interact, and may then proceed to developing agreed-upon goals for therapy (Halford & Bouma, 1997).

Couples with relationship problems also tend to pay little attention to the role of stressful events on their relationship. Relationship problems tend to be attributed much more to stable, internal characteristics of the partner (Bradbury & Fincham, 1990). For example, Roger and Frances presented to one of us with a history of frequent conflict and little or no interest in each other sexually. In individual interviews each partner attributed the relationship problems primarily to personality character flaws of the other person. Roger described Frances as cold and unemotional, whilst Frances described Roger as untrustworthy and a liar. Frances reported that their history of sexual difficulties had its initial onset about two years earlier, when Frances discovered that Roger was having an affair. She believed the affair showed he could not ever be trusted. Roger thought their sexual relationship had never been particularly good, and felt that Frances was emotionally distant from him, apart from the first few months of their relationship.

In an individual interview Frances reported that she had been the victim of a particularly vicious rape as a teenager. After the rape she had felt anxious in the company of men, and had not had sex with anyone till she met Roger. When she and Roger first got together as a couple she had enjoyed sex, and felt overwhelmed by the passion she felt for Roger. As the relationship developed, she had felt less interest in sex, but still felt the relationship was satisfactory. She had never disclosed the rape to Roger. The couple reported that they had never had great communication together.

In BCT there is a strategic separation of assessment and therapy. At the completion of assessment the therapist provides the couple with structured feedback on the results of the assessment. This feedback summarises and integrates the assessment information, and focuses the results on how the problems can be conceptualised within a relationship framework. In the case of Roger and Frances, Roger finding out about the rape made a huge difference to the couple. Roger cried as he heard Frances describe her struggle to trust enough to enter the relationship with him, and how she struggled to overcome her trauma and be his sexual partner. Frances heard from Roger how he had felt she was somehow distant, uninterested in him for a long time, and how much that hurt him as he loved her deeply.

The process of feedback of assessment typically involves the therapist presenting the results of the assessment to the couple, one assessment instrument at a time. The therapist continually checks that the descriptions and conclusions being reached are accurate according to each partner. After presenting all the key findings the therapist summarises the results, and discusses with the couple possible goals for therapy. The most commonly identified goals are improving communication, controlling conflict, enhancing quality time together, and renegotiating key relationship responsibilities. Other common goals include working together to improve parenting difficulties, enhancing support for each other, and enhancing the expression of intimacy and closeness. For Roger and Frances, the goals they developed included improving their communication, spending more time together, and for Frances to reduce the trauma symptoms still remaining from the rape experience.

After developing a shared relationship focus, the next step in couples therapy is to have each partner define what she or he can do to change problematic interactions. This emphasis on self-change (also known as self-regulation), focuses therapy on that which each client has the most direct control over: namely their own behaviour (Halford, Sanders & Behrens, 1994). This is not to say that changes in the partner are unimportant, but rather that the most productive method of achieving change is for each partner to focus on their own opportunities to change.

In summary, assessment needs to focus on stressful life events, individual vulnerabilities, and couple-adaptive processes. The therapist works with the couple to develop a shared understanding of the presenting problems, using this broad framework. The process of assessment culminates in the integration of the assessment findings into an agreed-on set of goals for the relationship, and definition of individual goals for achieving those relationship outcomes.

COGNITIVE BEHAVIOURAL COUPLES THERAPY

Intervention with relationship problems potentially can target couples' adaptive processes, stressful events, or enduring vulnerabilities, as each of these classes of variables influences relationship problems. The focus of all interventions evaluated in research has been on modifying couples' adaptive processes, either through conjoint therapy for couples with existing relationship problems (e.g. Baucom & Epstein, 1990; Halford, in press), or through brief programmes to prevent the development of relationship problems (Halford & Behrens, 1996; Markman & Hahlweg, 1993). In complex cases interventions are adapted to take account of the enduring vulnerabilities of the partners, and stressful life events impinging on the couple. For example, there has been considerable research on therapy with couples in which one partner has depression (Beach, Sandeen & O'Leary, 1990), or alcohol abuse (O'Farrell & Rotunda, 1997). Some recent work has focused on developing couples' adaptive processes to manage particular stressful life events, such as entering a stepfamily (Lawton & Sanders, 1994), or responding to the effects of an affair on the relationship (Glass & Wright, 1997).

A number of different approaches to couples therapy, including behavioural, cognitive, cognitive behavioural, emotion-focused, and insight-oriented couples therapy, have been demonstrated to improve the relationship satisfaction of the majority of couples who present for therapy (Baucom & Epstein, 1990; Greenberg & Johnson, 1988; Hahlweg & Markman, 1988; Halford, Sanders & Behrens, 1993; Shadish et al, 1993; Snyder, Wills & Grady-Fletcher, 1991). Of all these styles of couples therapy the cognitive behavioural approach has been most widely researched, and we focus the rest of the chapter on this approach and how it is adapted for complex cases.

The Content of Cognitive Behavioural Couples Therapy

Behaviour exchange

Based upon the premise that a relationship is defined by the exchange of behaviours between partners, cognitive behavioural couples therapy (CBCT) began as the application of behavioural contracting to the treatment of relationship problems. Couples were trained to monitor their partners' behaviour and, based on such assessments, contingency contracts were developed to reduce displeasing, and increase pleasing behaviours within the relationship (e.g. Azrin, Naster & Jones, 1973; Stuart, 1969; Weiss, Hops & Patterson, 1973). Such contracting initially stressed tightly structured 'quid pro quo' agreements, in which spouses were taught systematically and immediately to reward desired behaviour from the partner (Azrin, Naster & Jones, 1973; Stuart, 1969). This was later replaced by unilateral 'good faith' contracts in which partners were asked to undertake positive change for the good of the relationship (e.g. Weiss, Birchler & Vincent, 1974). Subsequently emphasis has been placed on each partner actively seeking out information in order to self-select and implement self-change goals to enhance the relationship (Halford, Sanders & Behrens, 1994; Weiss & Halford, 1996). Although the details of the procedures have been refined, an emphasis on changing relationship behaviours remains an important element of CBCT.

In Table 17.3 some of the key behaviours identified as promoting long-term satisfying relationships are identified. In couples therapy partners are helped to self-identify behaviours that they wish to change within these different domains to enhance their intimacy with their partner. There are several ways of doing this. For example, partners can be asked to self-monitor behaviours within a given class and then to identify behaviours they wish to increase in that domain. A second example is the Caring Days Exercise (Weiss & Halford, 1996). In this procedure each person is encouraged to identify some small specific behaviours which they can follow which demonstrate caring for their partner. To enhance their ability to

Table 17.3 Classes of behaviour most strongly related to marital satisfaction

Class of behaviour	Examples
Affection	Saying 'I love you' Giving a hug or kiss Enjoying a shared laugh or joke Saying they enjoy partner's company
Respect	Listening to the partner's opinion Telling partner of admiration/respect Showing confidence in partner's abilities Introducing partner to others with pride
Support	Doing errands for partner Making self available to do work for partner Asking partner about their day Doing something to save partner time/energy
Communication of ideas	Telling partner about their day Discussing topical events Giving an opinion Talking about mutual interest(s)
Shared quality time	Spending an hour or more just talking Work together on a project Take a drive or walk Go out together, just the two of you Discuss personal feelings

self-select appropriate caring behaviours, we make suggestions to people about how to be more creative in generating ideas for themselves. For example, people can just sit down and try and think of things, or they can ask their partner about things that would demonstrate caring effectively to them, they can ask friends about caring behaviours that they engage in within their relationships, they can observe others demonstrating caring in their normal day-to-day lives, or they can read through some of the checklists of ideas and suggestions that we can provide as leaders. The self-regulatory focus that we adopt is asking each person to take individual responsibility for being creative in identifying behaviours that they will engage in. We then ask them to set themselves a homework task of trying to implement the behavioural changes that they have identified.

Communication and problem-solving skills

A second element of CBCT is communication and problem-solving skills training. These process skills are conceptualised as providing couples with the means to enhance intimate communication, and resolve their current and future sources of conflict (Jacobson & Margolin, 1979). In most applications of CBCT the communication skills targeted in training were identified by the therapist, based upon contrasting the couple's current communication with a model of adaptive marital communication. The models of adaptive marital communication were derived, in large part, from research contrasting the communication behaviours of maritally distressed and non-distressed couples in problem-solving interactions within research laboratories (see Weiss & Heyman, 1990, 1997, for reviews of this literature). Often CBCT would teach couples a relatively fixed curriculum of skills (e.g. paraphrasing, asking open-ended questions, behavioural pinpointing), based on the assumption that all of these skills were adaptive as communication skills.

Recent research shows that there is no clear relationship between the use of particular, specific communication behaviours (e.g. paraphrasing, minimal encouragers) and relationship problems (Halford, Hahlweg & Dunne, 1990). Rather, it seems that there are a few broad classes of adaptive relationship communication behaviours, such as validation (active, positive listening to partner) and positive engagement, and adoption of any of a wide variety of behaviours within these broad classes is associated with improvements in relationship problems (Sayers et al., 1991). The specific behaviours within the broad classes which are functional vary across relationships, time and settings (Halford et al., 1992). In other words, different communication styles suit different relationships and circumstances, but we can be reasonably confident that an adaptive communication style will need to involve validation and positive engagement.

Our approach to communication skills training is to apply a self-regulation model in which each partner is assisted to self-select goals for changing his or her own communication, and to self-evaluate his or her own, rather than the partner's, communication. For example, we routinely have clients review their own discussions (e.g. an audiotape of a conversation at home on a difficult topic) with the therapist in sessions, with partners each focusing on their own communication. This maintains the therapeutic focus on what the client can change (i.e. his or her own behaviour). Based on the assumption that adaptive marital communication is defined by its functional impact within the relationship, self-directed attempts at changes in communication are seen as behavioural experiments. Consequently when a partner makes a change in communication that produces a negative outcome (e.g. making an assertive rather than aggressive request for change by the partner when discussing a particular issue elicits verbal abuse from the spouse), this shows that assertion was not adaptive in this context, and a different approach is needed.

Cognitive strategies

A third element of CBCT is altering the subjective experience of relationship interaction. Although CBCT always included recognition of the importance of internal mediators of external experience (Weiss, 1984), more recent developments have placed greater emphasis on cognitive and affective change strategies. Many of these strategies apply standard cognitive therapy procedures to relationship problems. For example, self-instructional strategies are used to modify negative attributions (Baucom & Lester, 1986) or control anger (Schindler & Vollmer, 1984), and guided discovery, Socratic dialogue and behavioural experiments are used to challenge irrational relationship beliefs (Baucom & Epstein, 1990; Halford, in press).

The greater emphasis on changing subjective experience in CBCT is particularly evident in recent changes in managing destructive conflict within distressed couples. Earlier versions of CBCT emphasised teaching communication and problem-solving skills to reduce conflict. More recently emphasis has been placed on exploring with each partner the attributions, meaning and significance attached to the issues which are sources of conflict (e.g. Christensen, Jacobson & Babcock, 1995; Weiss & Halford, 1996). Whilst there are variations in the details of the therapeutic process used by different authors, the common emphasis is on altering how partners respond to behaviours of their spouses which they dislike. Christensen, Jacobson & Babcock, (1995) describe the goal of this process as promoting acceptance, which they define behaviourally as the reduction of attempts to get the other person to change. In essence there is an attempt to balance a combination of behaviour change to alter relationship interaction, and change in the subjective experience of existing relationship interactions.

The CBCT approach to relationship dissatisfaction can usefully be summarised within an extension of the self-regulation framework proposed by Halford, Sanders and Behrens (1994). Subjective dissatisfaction with your relationship can be responded to in one of five ways. First, you can alter the ways in which you attempt to persuade your partner to change, so that you get change. Second, you can alter your own behaviour to enhance relationship functioning. These first two options were the focus of traditional behavioural couples therapy, producing behaviour change through procedures such as behavioural contracting and negotiation. Third, you can alter your own subjective response to negative aspects of relationship interactions, so that those aspects are less stressful and you feel no pressing need for change. This is what Christensen, Jacobson and Babcock (1995) call acceptance. Fourth, you can decide that particular existing behaviours are unacceptable, intolerable, and unchangeable, and that you will therefore leave the relationship. Finally, you can do nothing, and maintain the *status quo*. In our experience few clients have explored all of these options for individual actions which are open to them.

Adapting Couples Therapy for Complex Cases

Sequencing therapy

If there are multiple presenting problems, including relationship difficulties, then it is necessary to determine the sequence in which various elements of therapy are to be attempted. For example, in instances where couple and individual therapy are both necessary, it is possible to do individual therapy first, couple therapy first, or to run individual and couple therapy conjointly. In some instances the decision about sequencing may be relatively straightforward. There are some basic entry skills that people need if they are to benefit from couple therapy, and individuals with significant psychopathology may lack these entry skills. More specifically, it seems unlikely that people will benefit from couple therapy if an individual's mental state is severely disturbed by an acute psychotic episode, or if their abuse of alcohol inhibits their ability to engage effectively in therapy. Similarly, if someone is so severely depressed that they have very low levels of activity, and are minimally affectively responsive, then individual treatment probably needs to precede couple therapy.

Assuming that both individuals do have the entry skills to engage in couple therapy, then there are several other criteria by which the clients and therapist may negotiate the sequencing of therapy. First, attention should be paid to the salience of individual versus couple problems to both partners. Second, the functional analysis suggesting the interrelationship of the variables should be taken into account. Third, those aspects of the complex problems which are most likely to be changed easily should be targeted first, as success initially will help to maintain engagement and commitment to therapy.

Duration of therapy

Traditionally couple therapy, as it is described in the research literature, lasts anything from 15 to 20 conjoint sessions. If individual therapy of a similar length is added to the conjoint therapy, then therapy becomes a very substantial expense and commitment for clients. For that reason, we advocate trying to deliver therapy at the minimum necessary therapeutic dose to achieve the desired result. Brief couples interventions may well be effective in helping people with individual psychological disorders. For example, Dadds, Schwartz and Sanders (1987) found that just three sessions of intensive couples therapy, focusing on supporting partners to be better parents, improved marital satisfaction and enhanced the effectiveness of behavioural parent training with children with conduct disorders. This effect was only evident for parents who were maritally distressed. In other words, the combination of traditional parent training and a very brief marital intervention was significantly helpful for these couples.

Brief relationship interventions may be particularly effective if therapy is provided in the context of early detection of individual and relationship problems (Halford & Behrens, 1996). Recent work that we have undertaken (Halford, Osgarby, & Kelly, 1996) showed that brief interventions of just three sessions can be effective for couples with mild to moderate marital distress. The lengthy courses of therapy more typical of programmes reported in the literature may discourage many people from seeking therapy until problems become severe. At the same time, there are couples who require very extensive intervention. Individuals with severe psychotic disorders are unlikely to benefit from brief one or two session interventions. In fact, the available data suggest that family interventions with people with schizophrenia need to run for a substantial period of time in order to produce sustained effects (Halford, 1994, 1995).

Engaging the reluctant partner

A challenging common problem in couples therapy is when only one partner is presenting, and the other partner is believed to be reluctant to enter therapy (Halford & Osgarby, 1993). The published literature on marital therapy focuses almost exclusively on working with couples when both partners are in therapy. There is some evidence that you can improve a distressed relationship by seeing only one partner, though the results seem to be much better if both partners are engaged (Bennun, 1997; Halford et al., in press).

The presenting client needs to be assisted to reach an informed decision on whether he or she wants the reluctant partner involved with therapy. To assist the client to make that decision the therapist can help to clarify the options, and provide information. Often we find the presenting client reports that the absent partner would not attend. It is important to explore with the client the evidence for that assertion. Often the topic of attending therapy has not explicitly been raised, and an inference is made that therapy would not be attended. We routinely ask where, when, and under what circumstances the presenting client has said exactly what to the absent spouse about attending therapy. Rarely, in our experience, has the presenting client calmly and clearly asked their partner to come to therapy in a collaborative way. It is common for the issue of therapy only to be raised in the context of a heated argument. (Rarely, in our experience, do spouses respond well to a message such as: 'You're crazy, you need to see a shrink' shouted in the middle of an argument.) It can be helpful to work with the client to identify where, when and under what circumstances the spouse might be most responsive to an invitation to attend therapy. Also helping the client to practise a form of words which extends a collaborative, positively framed invitation is important.

It is often helpful for the therapist to extend an invitation to the absent partner to attend therapy. Routinely we would, with the permission of the presenting spouse, ring the non-presenting partner. There is a risk that the non-presenting partner may feel blamed for the presenting client's concerns. Consequently, we usually frame this initial contact as an invitation to provide information which would help with the therapy of the presenting client (Halford & Bouma, 1997). Such an invitation is less threatening than a request to be part of therapy.

Sometimes it is better not to attempt to engage the absent spouse. For example, in a study we recently conducted assisting women who reported excessive drinking by their partners, we had a number of presentations by women who reported significant fear of assault if their partners knew they were seeking assistance (Halford et al., in press). In most instances the absent partner had a history of severe violence toward the presenting client, suggesting such fears were quite realistic.

Case Illustration

A number of the issues about complex cases are illustrated by the case of Lech (52), who was on a disability pension, and Carole (47) who was on extended sick leave from a job as an office manager. The couple had been married for five years at the time of presentation. Carole had two adult children from an earlier relationship, Trevor (22) and Rosine (24), both of whom lived with Lech and Carole. Lech had a 20-year history of bipolar disorder, and also had been abusing alcohol for many years. In the last two months Lech had been taking Lithium, but prior to that had been non-adherent to that medication. Carole had a history of depression. She had been diagnosed with bone cancer in the arm six months earlier, and had undergone surgery and radiotherapy. Her arm was healing very slowly, she was in persistent pain, and three months ago had been severely depressed. She was on tricyclic antidepressants at the time of presentation, and was still moderately depressed.

Lech was referred to the first author (WKH) by his case manager at the local mental health centre. At initial presentation he was very upset, saying that his wife was going to leave him. Lech stated Carole would never come and see a psychologist, that she always said he was the crazy one in their relationship. The therapist explored with Lech why he believed Carole would not agree to attend; Lech reported that he had not specifically raised the possibility of couple therapy. After some rehearsal of when and how he could issue a positive invitation to attend therapy, Lech went home to raise this with Carole. The therapist followed up with a telephone call to Carole the next day and she agreed to attend an initial assessment session.

At the initial session the therapist spent some time with Carole alone. She reported significant desperation about the relationship with Lech, and was actively considering ending the marriage, but she decided to complete an assessment process and determine whether to continue the relationship. Assessment continued for three sessions, with a mix of conjoint sessions with the couple and individual interviews with both Carole and Lech. Carole reported that Lech was gentle and caring most of the time, but that when he became depressed his drinking was a major problem. When he drank he was verbally abusive, and she became very depressed when he was abusive toward her. Furthermore, he gambled and lost their money when he was drinking. Given that Carole was on sick leave at half pay, Lech was on a disability pension, and that Carole's two children were unemployed, the loss of money was a real problem for them at the moment. She also stated that Lech had not been to see her in hospital during her surgery, had not been supportive during her recuperation, and had been drinking particularly heavily over the last three weeks.

Lech described how he felt inadequate as a husband, how he had not held down a job for nearly six years. He described the five years with Carole as the best of his life. Lech also reported that he felt overwhelmed by Carole's cancer. He was terrified she would die, and was sleeping very poorly. Lech reported he was drinking three or four days per week, and drinking 12 to 15 standard drinks on those days. The drinking episodes were often preceded by an argument with Carole. Lech described feeling guilty about his drinking, but especially feeling guilty because he lost money gambling and got verbally abusive toward Carole when drinking.

A feedback session was held with the couple, summarising the range of problems that had been assessed. A series of potential goals were identified collaboratively with the couple. The key individual goals agreed to for Lech were: to moderate his drinking to a limit of drinking only two days per week, with a limit of five drinks on any given occasion; to give up any form of gambling; and to learn more about his bipolar illness and how to manage the medication necessary to control his mood swings. Carole set the following goals for herself: to learn to control her depression more effectively, and to learn to control her anger outbursts. As a couple they identified learning to manage conflict more effectively, and finding inexpensive ways to have enjoyable couple activities as their key goals.

Conjoint couple therapy continued on a weekly basis over a seven-month period. The first three sessions were spent exploring the history of the couple's relationship in some detail. In this process the therapist drew out descriptions of the positive features each partner saw in the other to build motivation to produce positive change in the relationship. Emphasis was also placed on identifying the various stresses that impinged on the couple, such as lack of money, living in a blended family with the challenges of four adults sharing one home, and Carole's cancer and treatment. We also explored the vulnerabilities of each partner, focusing first on Lech's bipolar disorder and his drinking, and then discussing Carole's depression.

The purpose of the exploration of relationship history and individual vulnerabilities was to develop helpful cognitions which enhanced the couple's engagement in couples therapy. The therapist used guided exploration questions to highlight the relationship issues needing to be addressed in therapy. For example, Lech disclosed how he used drinking to block out his sense of inadequacy as a partner, and how he felt ashamed of drinking when Carole disliked it so much, so this made him avoid contact with Carole. Carole stated how much she loved Lech, and that when he drank it made her feel he did not love her. The couple at this point identified Lech controlling his drinking as a priority goal, and also Carole identified the need to show her feelings for Lech more obviously so he would know he was loved.

At this point in therapy the therapist and couple agreed to focus on control of Lech's drinking, since that had severe negative consequences for the couple.

The approach taken was a standard brief cognitive behavioural intervention combining motivational interviewing, goal setting, identification of high-risk settings, and application of coping skills to manage those high-risk settings. In addition Lech contracted with Carole to adhere to his Lithium medication for three more months. Lech also commenced twice weekly attendance at a Psychiatric Rehabilitation Unit to learn more about his bipolar disorder. Carole went to the unit on three occasions to attend a relative education group. After five weeks Lech's drinking was substantially reduced and the therapy focus changed to promoting shared couple activities. The couple expanded their shared activities greatly, for example they took up painting as a shared hobby. The focus then moved to couple communication and conflict management. Fifteen sessions were spent predominantly with this couple focus. Integrated within the communication training was work on anger management for both partners. Cognitive restructuring was an important element of the couple work. Three additional individual sessions were held with Carole at this point, focusing on the use of cognitive procedures to control depression.

In week 23 there was a major setback in therapy. Carole's daughter was engaged to be married and wanted a large wedding. Lech wanted to spend Carole's and his savings to give Rosine her desired wedding, but Carole felt they had to arrange a more modest wedding, and keep their savings. An argument ensued, Lech became very upset and went on a drinking binge with an old friend. Lech stayed away from home for three days, and he finished up having a psychotic relapse and being admitted to hospital. The therapist saw Carole individually when Lech was in hospital, and she was very upset, reporting that she was depressed, and that 'we are back to where we started'. In a joint session the next week the therapist explored with Lech and Carole the circumstances of the argument, how the conflict became destructive. Examination was conducted of how the couple and each person had relapsed, the couple had gone back to destructive conflict, Lech returned to heavy drinking and medication non-adherence, and Carole relapsed to negative cognitions and depression. Extensive cognitive challenging was done to relabel the episode as a lapse, rather than as a failure. Detailed relapse prevention plans were developed. Over the next six weeks Lech and Carole recovered, negotiated a compromise with Rosine about the size of the wedding, and made steady progress.

At a three- and then seven-month follow-up the couple reported continuing positive feelings about their relationship. Scores on the Dyadic Adjustment Scale administered before and after therapy, and at the follow-up confirmed both partners had moved from distressed to satisfied in their relationship. Carole was no longer taking antidepressants, and Lech had not experienced any further relapses in his bipolar disorder. He had had one further episode of binge drinking during follow-up, but the couple had recovered from that. Overall, the range of goals for therapy had largely had been achieved.

SUMMARY

This chapter began by outlining how relationship problems develop as a result of the interaction of a complex set of risk factors (Halford & Markman, 1997; Karney & Bradbury, 1995). In that sense *all* couples present sufficient complexity to warrant our taking the time to develop a comprehensive understanding of these factors. Responding appropriately to more complex couple cases relies heavily on a systematic and comprehensive assessment. However, assessment needs to be efficient so it can be conducted in a reasonable length of time.

Many complex couple cases can be managed effectively within the general framework of traditional cognitive behavioural couples therapy (CBT). We described how to adapt the process and content of CBCT with complex cases involving high levels of individual vulnerability in partners, or where particularly stressful life events are relevant.

Each complex presentation of a couple for therapy has its own unique set of adaptive processes, enduring vulnerabilities, and stressful environmental events impacting on the relationship. Yet numerous similarities exist across distressed couples in terms of risk factors, relationship characteristics, and long-term consequences. We hope this chapter provides readers with useful guidelines for meeting the challenge of helping couples with complex problems.

AUTHOR NOTES

Preparation of this chapter was supported by an Australian Research Council grant entitled 'Prevention of relationship problems' to W. Kim Halford, Matthew R. Sanders & Brett C. Behrens, and a Research in Drug Abuse Grant from the Australian Health Department entitled 'Prevention of alcohol and relationship problems' to W. Kim Halford, Ruth Bouma, and Ross Young. Please address correspondence to Professor Kim Halford, School of Applied Psychology, Griffith University, Nathan, Queensland 4111, Australia; email: K.Halford@Griffith.edu.au

REFERENCES

Azrin, N. H., Naster, B. J. & Jones, R. (1973). A rapid learning-based procedure for marital counselling. *Behaviour Research and Therapy*, **11**, 365–382.

Baris, M. A. & Garrity, C. B. (1997). Co-parenting post-divorce: Helping parents negotiate and maintain low-conflict separations. In W.K. Halford & H.J. Markman (Eds), *Clinical Handbook of Marriage and Couples Interventions* (pp. 619–650). Chichester, UK: Wiley.

Baucom, D. H. & Epstein, N. (1990). *Cognitive Behavioral Marital Therapy*. New York: Brunner-Mazel.

Baucom, D. H. & Lester, G. W. (1986). The usefulness of cognitive-restructuring as an adjunct to behavioral marital therapy. *Behavior Therapy*, **17**, 385–403.

Beach, S. R. H., Arias, I. & O'Leary, K. D. (1986). The relationship of marital satisfaction and social support to depressive symptomatology. *Journal of Psychopathology and Behavioral Assessment*, **8**, 305–316.

Beach, S. R. H., Sandeen, E. E. & O'Leary, K. D. (1990). *Depression in Marriage: a Model for Etiology and Treatment*. New York: Guilford.

Bebbington, P. E. (1987). Marital status and depression: A study of English national admission statistics. *Acta Psychiatrica Scandinavica*, **75**, 640–650.

Beck, A. T., Ward, C. H., Mendelson, M., Mock, J. E. & Erbaugh, J. K. (1961). An inventory for measuring depression. *Archives of General Psychiatry*, **4**, 451–471

Bennun, I. (1997). Relationship interventions with one partner. In W. K. Halford & H. J. Markman (Eds) *Clinical Handbook of Marriage and Couples Interventions* (pp. 451–470). Chichester, UK: Wiley.

Black, L. E. & Sprenkle, D. H. (1991). Gender differences in college students: Towards divorces and their willingness to marry. *Journal of Divorce and Remarriage*, **1**, 47–69.

Block, J., Block, J. H. & Keyes, S. (1988). Longitudinally foretelling drug usage in adolescence. Early childhood personality and environmental precursors. *Child Development*, **59**, 336–355.

Bloom, B. L., Asher, S. J. & White, S. W. (1978). Marital disruption as a stressor: A review and analysis. *Psychological Bulletin*, **85**, 867–894.

Booth, A. & Edwards, J. N. (1992). Starting over: Why remarriages are more unstable. *Journal of Family Issues*, **13**, 179–194.

Bradbury, T. N. (1995). Assessing the four fundamental domains of marriage. *Family Relations*, **44**, 459–468.

Bradbury, T. N. & Fincham, F. D. (1990). Attribution in marriage: Review and critique. *Psychological Bulletin*, **107**, 3–33.

Burman, B. & Margolin, G. (1992). Analysis of the association between marital relationships and health problems: An interactional perspective. *Psychological Bulletin*, **112**, 39–63.

Cascardi, M., Langhinrichsen, J. & Vivian, D. (1992). Marital aggression: Impact, injury and health correlates for husbands and wives. *Archives of Internal Medicine*, **152**, 1178–1184.

Christensen, A., Jacobson, N. S. & Babcock, J. (1995). Integrative behavioral couple therapy. In N. S. Jacobson & A. S. Gurman (Eds), *Clinical Handbook of Couple Therapy* (pp. 31–64). New York: Guilford.

Cowen, C. P. & Cowen, P. A. (1992). *When Partners Become Parents*. New York: Basic Books.

Coyne, J. C., Kahn, J. & Gotlib, I. H. (1987). Depression: In T. Jacob (Ed.), *Family Interaction and Psychopathology* (pp. 509–534). New York: Plenum.

Craske, M. G. & Zoellner, L. A. (1995). Anxiety disorders: The role of marital therapy. In N. S. Jacobson & A. S. Gurman (Eds), *Clinical Handbook of Couple Therapy* (pp. 394–410). New York: Guilford.

Dadds, M. R., Schwartz, S. & Sanders, M. R. (1987). Marital discord and treatment outcome in the treatment of child conduct disorders. *Journal of Consulting and Clinical Psychology*, **55**, 396–403.

De Guibert-Lantoine, C. & Monnier, A. (1996). La conjoncture démographique: L'Europe et les pays développés d'Outre-Mer. *Population*, July-August.

Derogatis, L., Lipman, R. & Copui, L. (1973). The SCL-90: An outpatient rating scale. *Psychopharmacology Bulletin*, **9**, 13–28.

Dickson, F. C. (1997). Aging and marriage: Understanding the long-term, later-life marriage. In W. K. Halford & H. J. Markman (Eds), *Clinical Handbook of Marriage and Couples Interventions* (pp. 255–272). Chichester, UK: Wiley.

Eddy, J. M., Heyman, R. E. & Weiss, R. L. (1991). An empirical evaluation of the Dyadic Adjustment Scale: Exploring the differences between marital 'satisfaction' and 'adjustment'. *Behavioural Assessment*, **13**, 199–220.

Elvy, G. A. & Wells, J. E. (1984). The Canterbury Alcoholism Screening Test (CAST): A detection instrument for use with hospitalised patients. *New Zealand Medical Journal*, **97**, 111–115.

Emery, R. E. (1982). Interparental conflict and the children of discord and divorce. *Psychological Bulletin*, **92**, 310–330.

Emery, R. E., Joyce, S. A. & Fincham, F. D. (1987). The assessment of child and marital problems. In K. D. O'Leary (Ed.), *Assessment of Marital Discord* (pp. 223–262). Hillsdale, NJ: Erlbaum.

Emmelkamp, P. M. G., DeHaan, E. & Hoogduin, C. A. I. (1990). Marital adjustment and obsessive-compulsive disorder. *British Journal of Psychiatry*, **156**, 55–60.

Fincham, F. D. & Bradbury, T. D. (1990). *The Psychology of Marriage*. New York: Guilford.

Fowers, B. J., Lyons, E. M. & Montel, K. H. (1996). Positive marital illusions: Self-enhancement or relationship enhancement? *Journal of Family Psychology*, **10**, 192–208.

Gallup Poll (1989). *Marriage Satisfaction*. Los Angeles, CA: Los Angeles Times Syndicate.

Gibardi, L. & Rosen, L. A.(1991). Differences between college students from divorced and intact families. *Journal of Divorce and Remarriage*, **15**, 175–191.

Glass, S. P, & Wright, T. L. (1997). Reconstructing marriage after the trauma of infidelity. In W. K. Halford & H. J. Markman (Eds), *Clinical Handbook of Marriage and Couples Interventions* (pp. 471–507). Chichester, UK: Wiley.

Glenn, N. D. & Kramer, K. B. (1987). The marriages and divorces of the children of divorce. *Journal of Marriage and the Family*, **49**, 811–825.

Glick, P. C. (1989). Remarried families, stepfamilies and stepchildren: A brief demographic profile. *Family Relations*, **38**, 24–27.

Gottman, J. M. (1993). The role of conflict engagement, escalation, and avoidance in marital interaction: A longitudinal view of five types of couples. *Journal of Consulting and Clinical Psychology*, **61**, 6–15.

Gottman, J. M. (1994). *What Predicts Divorce? The Relationship between Marital Processes and Marital Outcomes*. Hillsdale, NJ: Erlbaum.

Greenberg, L. S. & Johnson, S. M. (1988). *Emotionally Focused Therapy for Couples*. New York: Guilford.

Grych, J. H. & Fincham, F. D. (1990). Marital conflict and children's adjustment: A cognitive-contextual framework. *Psychological Bulletin*, **108**, 267–290.

Hahlweg, K. & Markman, H. J. (1988). Effectiveness of behavioral marital therapy: Empirical status of behavioral techniques in preventing and alleviating marital distress. *Journal of Consulting and Clinical Psychology*, **56**, 440–447.

Halford, W.K. (1994). Familial factors in psychiatry. *Current Opinion in Psychiatry,* **7,** 186–191.

Halford, W. K. (1995). Behavior therapy and schizophrenia in context: Challenges and opportunities provided within the changing mental health system. *Behaviour Change,* **12,** 41–50.

Halford, W. K. (in press). *Couples Therapy: Helping Partners Manage Change.* New York: Guilford.

Halford, W. K. & Behrens, B. C. (1996). Prevention of marital difficulties. In P. Cotton & H. J. Jackson (Eds), *Early Intervention and Preventive Mental Health Applications of Clinical Psychology.* Melbourne: Australian Psychological Society.

Halford, W. K. & Bouma, R. O. (1997). Individual psychopathology and marital distress. In W. K. Halford & H. J. Markman (Eds), *Clinical Handbook of Marriage and Couples Interventions* (pp. 291–322). Chichester, UK: Wiley.

Halford, W. K., Bouma, R. O., Kelly, A. & Young, R. McD. (in press). Individual psychopathology and marital distress: Analysing the association and implications for therapy. *Behavior Modification.*

Halford, W. K., Gravestock, F., Lowe, R., & Scheldt, S. (1992). Towards a behavioral ecology of stressful marital interactions. *Behavioural Assessment,* **14,** 199–217.

Halford, W. K., Hahlweg, K. & Dunne, M. (1990). The cross-cultural consistency of marital communication associated with marital distress. *Journal of Marriage and the Family,* **52,** 109–122.

Halford, W. K. & Markman, H. J. (Eds) (1997). *Clinical Handbook of Marriage and Couples Interventions.* Chichester, UK: Wiley.

Halford, W. K., Markman, H. J. & Fraenkel, P. (in press). Relationship problems. In P. Salkovskis (Ed.), *Comprehensive Clinical Psychology Vol. 7. Adult Disorders: Clinical Formulation and Treatment.* New York: Elsevier.

Halford, W. K., Markman, H. J. & Kelly, A. B. (1997). The concept of a healthy marriage. In W. K. Halford & H. J. Markman (Eds), *Clinical Handbook of Marriage and Couples Interventions* (pp. 3–12). Chichester, UK: Wiley.

Halford, W. K. & Osgarby, S. M. (1993). Alcohol abuse in clients presenting with marital problems. *Journal of Family Psychology,* **6,** 1–11.

Halford, W. K., Osgarby, S. M. & Kelly, A. B. (1996). Brief behavioral couples therapy: A preliminary evaluation. *Behavioural and Cognitive Psychotherapy,* **24,** 263–273.

Halford, W. K., Sanders, M. R., & Behrens, B. C. (1993). A comparison of the generalisation of behavioral marital therapy and enhanced behavioral marital therapy. *Journal of Consulting and Clinical Psychology,* **61,** 51–60.

Halford, W. K., Sanders, M. R. & Behrens, B. C. (1994). Self-regulation in behavioral couples therapy. *Behavior Therapy,* **25,** 431–452.

Halford, W. K., Skuja, K., Sanders, M. R. & Behrens, B. C. (1997). Repeating the errors of our parents? Behavioral correlates of exposure to paternal violence in the problem solving of engaged and dating couples. Paper under review.

Hooley, J. M., Orley, J. & Teasdale, J. D. (1986). Levels of expressed emotion and relapse in depressed patients. *British Journal of Psychiatry,* **148,** 642–647.

Howes, D. & Markman, H. J. (1989). Marital quality and child functioning: A longitudinal study. *Child Development,* **60,** 1044–1051.

Jacobson, N. S. & Christensen, A. (1996). *Integrative Behavioral Couple Therapy.* New York: Norton.

Jacobson, N. S. & Margolin, G. (1979). *Marital Therapy: Strategies Based on Social Learning and Behaviour Exchange Principles*. New York: Guilford.

Karney, B. R. & Bradbury, T. N. (1995). The longitudinal course of marital quality and stability: A review of theory, method, and research. *Psychological Bulletin, 118*, 3–34.

Khavari, K. A. & Farber, P. D. (1978). A profile instrument for the quantification and assessment of alcohol consumption. *Journal of Studies on Alcohol, 39*, 1525–1539.

Lawton, J. M. & Sanders, M. R. (1994). Designing effective behavioral family interventions for stepfamilies. *Clinical Psychology Review, 14*, 463–496.

Lebow, J. L. & Gurman, A. S. (1995). Research assessing couple and family therapy research. *Annual Review of Psychology, 46*, 27–57.

Levinger, G. & Huston, T. L. (1990). The social psychology of marriage. In F. D. Fincham & T. N. Bradbury (Eds), *The Psychology of Marriage* (pp. 19–58). New York: Guilford.

Lovibond, S. H. & Lovibond, P. F. (1995). *Manual for the Depression Anxiety Stress Scale*. Sydney: The Psychology Foundation of Australia.

Markman, H. J. & Hahlweg, K. (1993). Prediction and prevention of marital distress: A cross-cultural perspective. *Clinical Psychology Review, 13*, 29–43.

Markman, H. J., Halford, W. K. & Cordova, A. D. (1997). A grand tour of future directions in the study and promotion of healthy relationships. In W. K. Halford & H. J. Markman (Eds), *Clinical Handbook of Marriage and Couples Interventions* (pp. 695–714). Chichester, UK: Wiley.

Martin, T. C. & Bumpass, L. (1989). Recent trends in marital disruption. *Demography, 26*, 37–51.

McDonald, P. (1995). *Families in Australia: A Socio-demographic Perspective*. Melbourne, Australia: Australian Institute of Family Studies.

Miller, W. R. & Rollnick, S. (1991). *Motivational Interviewing: Preparing People to Change Addictive Behaviour*. New York: Guilford.

Millward, C. (1990). What marriage means to young adults. *Family Matters, 29*, 26–28.

Mulder, R. T. (1991). Personality disorders in New Zealand. *Acta Psychiatrica Scandiniavica, 84*, 197–202.

Murphy, C. M. & O'Leary, K. A. (1989). Psychological aggression predicts physical aggression in early marriage. *Journal of Consulting and Clinical Psychology, 57*, 579–582.

O'Farrell, T. J. (1989). Marital and family therapy in alcoholism treatment. *Journal of Substance Abuse Treatment, 6*, 23–29.

O'Farrell, T. J. & Birchler, G. R. (1987). Marital relationships of alcoholic, conflicted, and nonconflicted couples. *Journal of Marital and Family Therapy, 13*, 259–274.

O'Farrell, T. J. & Rotunda, R. J. (1997). Couples interventions and alcohol abuse. In W. K. Halford & H. J. Markman (Eds), *Clinical Handbook of Marriage and Couples Interventions* (pp. 555–588). Chichester, UK: Wiley.

O'Leary, K. D., Barling, J., Arias, I., Rosenbaum, A., Malone, J. & Tyree, A. (1989). Prevalence and stability of physical aggression between spouses: A longitudinal analysis. *Journal of Consulting and Clinical Psychology, 57*, 263–268.

O'Leary, K. D. & Vivian, D. (1990). Physical aggression in marriage. In F. D. Fincham & T. N. Bradbury (Eds), *The Psychology of Marriage* (pp. 323–348). New York: Guilford.

Olson, D. H. & Fowers, B. J. (1986). Predicting marital satisfaction using PREPARE: A replication study. *Journal of Marital and Family Therapy*, **12**, 403–413.

Olson, D. H. & Larsen, A. S. (1989). Predicting marital satisfaction using PREPARE: A replication study. *Journal of Marital and Family Therapy*, **15**, 311–322.

Reich, J. & Thompson, W. D. (1985). Marital status of schizophrenic and alcoholic patients. *Journal of Nervous and Mental Disease*, **173**, 499–502.

Reynolds, I., Rizzo, D., Gallagher, H. & Speedy, B. (1979). *Psychosocial Problems of Sydney Adults*. Sydney: Health Commission of New South Wales.

Ruscher, S. M. & Gotlib, I. H. (1988). Marital interaction patterns of couples with and without a depressed partner. *Behavior Therapy*, **19**, 455–470

Sanders, M. R., Halford, W. K. & Behrens, B. C. (1997). Behavioral correlates of parental divorce in conflict management in engaged couples: An observational study. Manuscript under review.

Sanders, M. R., Nicholson, J. M. & Floyd, F. J. (1997). Couples' relationships and children. In W. K. Halford & H. J. Markman (Eds), *Clinical Handbook of Marriage and Couples Interventions* (pp. 225–254). Chichester, UK: Wiley.

Sayers, S. L., Baucom, D. H., Sher, T. G., Weiss, R. L. & Heyman, R. E. (1991). Constructive engagement, behavioral marital therapy and changes in marital satisfaction. *Behavioral Assessment*, **13**, 25–49.

Schindler, L. & Vollmer, M. (1984). Cognitive perspectives in behavioral marital therapy: Some proposals for bridging theory, research, and practice. In K. Hahlweg & N. S. Jacobson (Eds), *Marital Interaction: Analysis and Modification* (pp. 309–324). New York: Guilford.

Schmaling, K. B. & Sher, T. G. (1997). Physical health and relationships. In W. K. Halford & H. J. Markman (Eds), *Clinical Handbook of Marriage and Couples Interventions* (pp. 323–348). Chichester, UK: Wiley.

Shadish, W. R., Montgomery, L. M., Wilson, P., Wilson, M. R., Bright, I., & Okwumabua, T. (1993). Effects of family and marital psychotherapies: A meta-analysis. *Journal of Consulting and Clinical Psychology*, **61**, 992–1002.

Snyder, D. K., Wills, R. M. & Grady-Fletcher, A. (1991). Long-term effectiveness of behavioral versus insight-oriented marital therapy. *Journal of Consulting and Clinical Psychology*, **59**, 138–141.

Sobell, M. B. & Sobell, L. C. (1993). *Problem Drinkers: Guided Self-change Treatment*. New York: Guilford.

Spanier, G. B. (1976). Measuring dyadic adjustment: New scales for assessing the quality of marriage and similar dyads. *Journal of Marriage and the Family*, **38**, 15–28.

Strauss, M. A. (1979). Measuring intrafamily conflict and violence: The conflict tactics scale. *Journal of Marriage and the Family*, **41**, 75–78.

Stuart, R. B. (1969). Operant-interpersonal treatment of marital discord. *Journal of Consulting and Clinical Psychology*, **33**, 675–682.

Terman, L. M. (1939). *Psychological Factors in Marital Happiness*. New York: McGraw-Hill.

Thompson, B. (1997). Couples and the work–family interface. In W. K. Halford & H. J. Markman (Eds), *Clinical Handbook of Marriage and Couples Interventions* (pp. 273–290). Chichester, UK: Wiley.

Veroff, J., Kulka, R. A. & Douvan, E. (1981). *Mental Health in America: Patterns of Helpseeking from 1957 to 1976*. New York: Basic Books.

Weiss, R. L. (1984). Cognitive and strategic interventions in behavioral marital therapy. In K. Hahlweg & N. S. Jacobson (Eds), *Marital Interaction: Analysis and Modification* (pp. 337–355). New York: Guilford.

Weiss, R. L., Birchler, G. R. & Vincent, J. P. (1974). Contractual models for negotiation training in marital dyads. *Journal of Marriage and the Family,* **36**, 321–330.

Weiss, R. L. & Cerreto, M. S. (1980). The Marital Status Inventory: Development of a measure of dissolution potential. *American Journal of Family Therapy,* **8**, 80–85.

Weiss, R. L. & Halford, W. K. (1996). Managing marital therapy: Helping partners change. In V. Van Hasselt & M. Hersen (Eds), *Sourcebook of Psychological Treatment Manuals for Adult Disorders* (pp. 489–537). New York: Plenum.

Weiss, R. L. & Heyman, R. E. (1990). Marital distress and therapy. In A. S. Bellack, M. Hersen & A. Kazdin (Eds), *International Handbook of Behavior Modification* (2nd edn) (pp. 475–502). New York: Plenum.

Weiss, R. L. & Heyman, R. E. (1997). A clinical-research overview of couples interactions. In W. K. Halford & H. J. Markman (Eds), *Clinical Handbook of Marriage and Couples Interventions* (pp. 13–35). Chichester, UK: Wiley.

Weiss, R. L., Hops, H. & Patterson, G. R. (1973). A framework for conceptualizing marital conflict: A technology for altering it. Some data for evaluating it. In L. D. Handy & E. L. Mash (Eds), *Behavior Change: Methodology Concepts and Practice* (pp. 309–342). Champaign, IL: Research Press.

Weiss, R. L. & Perry, B. A. (1983). The Spouse Observation Checklist: Developments and clinical applications. In E. E. Filsinger (Ed.), *Marriage and Family Assessment: A Sourcebook for Family Therapy* (pp. 65–84). Beverly Hills, CA: Sage.

Weissman, M. M. (1987). Advances in psychiatric epidemiology: Rates and risk for major depression. *American Journal of Public Health,* **77**, 445–451.

Widom, C. S. (1989). Does violence beget violence? A critical examination of the literature. *Psychological Bulletin,* **106**, 3–28.

Zimmer, D. (1983). Interaction patterns and communication skills in sexually distressed, maritally distressed, and normal couples: Two experimental studies. *Journal of Sex and Marital Therapy,* **9**, 251–266.

INDEX

Index compiled by Mary Kirkness

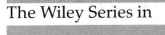

The Wiley Series in

CLINICAL PSYCHOLOGY